CLASSICS OF WESTERN THOUGHT

VOLUME III

The Modern World

THIRD EDITION

CLASSICS OF WESTERN THOUGHT

Under the General Editorship of
Thomas H. Greer
Michigan State University

I **The Ancient World** THIRD EDITION
Edited by
Stebelton H. Nulle
Michigan State University

II **Middle Ages, Renaissance,
and Reformation** THIRD EDITION
Edited by
Karl F. Thompson
Michigan State University

III **The Modern World** THIRD EDITION
Edited by
Charles Hirschfeld
Late of Richmond College,
The City University of New York
and
Edgar E. Knoebel
Michigan State University

IV **The Twentieth Century**
Edited by
Donald S. Gochberg
Michigan State University

CLASSICS OF
WESTERN
THOUGHT

The
Modern
World

VOLUME III   THIRD EDITION

Edited by   **Charles Hirschfeld**
Late of Richmond College,
The City University of New York

and

Edgar E. Knoebel
Michigan State University

 HARCOURT BRACE JOVANOVICH, INC.
New York   San Diego   Chicago   San Francisco   Atlanta

ISBN: 0-15-507680-9

Library of Congress Catalog Card Number: 79-90091

Printed in the United States of America

IN MEMORIAM

Charles Hirschfeld
1913–1975

Introduction to the Classics Series

Writings by the great minds of the Western tradition offer contemporary Westerners the best possible introduction to their humanistic heritage. To provide such an introduction, the editors of this series have brought together works that we consider classics of the Western tradition—of Western *thought,* in the broad sense. For the most part, these volumes of primary documents are intended for use in college-level courses in humanities or the history of civilization, normally in the company of a brief narrative text. One such text, designed especially for use with this series, is my *Brief History of Western Man,* Third Edition (Harcourt Brace Jovanovich, 1977).

The number and range of documents in Western civilization are, of course, enormous, and good reasons can always be advanced for choosing one work over another. We have sought works that are truly *classic,* that is to say, valuable both for their intrinsic merit and for having exerted a paramount influence on their own and later times—works that display judgment applied to observation as well as creative thought and literary skill. In deciding upon the length and quantity of selections, we have aimed to keep in balance two considerations: having each selection long enough to give a clear view of the author's ideas and, at the same time, offering selections from a substantial number of the foremost writers.

In previous years the Classics of Western Thought series has consisted of three volumes: *The Ancient World; Middle Ages, Renaissance, and Reformation;* and *The Modern World*—this third volume including documents of the last four centuries. Now a fourth volume, *The Twentieth Century,* has been added to the series. Containing writings from this century alone, it is suited especially for courses in contemporary history or humanities. As in the other volumes, each document of this collection is introduced by a brief account of the author's life, the author's role in shaping the Western tradition, and the significance of the particular work.

In preparing the present volumes, the editors have given careful attention to the suggestions of students and teachers who have read and taught from the series over the years. Our addition of a fourth volume is a response to these comments. Also in accordance with readers' suggestions, we have added to the first three volumes a number of selections that enrich and enliven their content, while deleting a few selections that were used infrequently. Most of the selections in the prior edition have been kept, however; and some of these works have been enhanced by means of new and improved translations. Finally, footnotes have been introduced throughout the volumes to explain parts of documents that might otherwise be obscure to some readers. As a result of these measures, we believe that both old and new readers of the series will find it an enjoyable aid in understanding and savoring the Western intellectual heritage.

Thomas H. Greer

Preface to the Third Edition

This volume, the third in the Classics of Western Thought series, offers classic and representative expressions of the main currents of Western thought during the last four hundred years. Arranged in chronological order, the volume's selections reflect the modern mind in its variety and complexity—its history, literature, philosophy, science, and social and religious thought.

The origins of the modern mind are to be found in the great advances of the seventeenth and eighteenth centuries. These advances, mainly in mathematics and the natural sciences, effected an intellectual revolution that rejected medieval scholasticism and recast the perceptions of human beings regarding the universe and their place in it. The emergence of the modern European state system, composed of absolute, sovereign nation-states, further weakened the traditional political and economic order. Political absolutism was, in turn, challenged by the great liberal revolutions in England, America, and France. Liberalism in its many aspects found intellectual expression in the reforming gospel of the eighteenth-century Enlightenment, or Age of Reason. Based on scientific discoveries and new methods of inquiry, it embodied a confident faith in the orderliness of nature and in the ability of humans to be the masters of their own fate. Reason and order were also the shaping concepts of the neoclassical drama and poetry of the period.

In the nineteenth century, the development of the Industrial Revolution was accompanied by the triumph of political and economic liberalism and its impact upon democratic thought and practice. Conservatism and socialism challenged this new order from the right and left respectively. Nationalism, as an emotional and social force, came to dominate the European scene. The tenets of the Age of Reason gave way before the gospel of romanticism in the fields of intellectual and artistic endeavor. The biological theory of organic evolution gave a new direction to science, and its implications were worked out in social and philosophical thought as well.

Since 1880, the Western world has undergone catastrophic change and social and intellectual ferment and dislocation. World wars, economic crises, the rise and fall of empires, the appearance of collectivist and totalitarian societies and ideologies, the amazing developments of science and technology, the emergence of a mass society—all have transformed the character of Western thought. The new age has wrought havoc with traditional modes of society and thought. Social and political thinkers, artists, and intellectuals have rebelled against all received tradition and have sought through free experiment to give people a new sense of purpose and direction. Optimism and certainty have given way to growing doubts and pessimism. The rational tradition of centuries has been displaced by emphasis on the irrational and the indeterminate. The ensuing moral crisis has brought forth efforts to give individuals a new faith and a new reality by an active exercise of the will.

Following the untimely and lamented death of Charles Hirschfeld, in July 1975, I was asked to succeed him as editor of this third volume in the Classics of Western Thought series. In preparing this edition, I have made it a principle to retain those selections that have proven their value over the years; and in my choice of new documents, I have endeavored to honor the concept and spirit that Professor Hirschfeld gave this work in its earlier versions.

The new selections in this edition of *The Modern World* include excerpts from the writings of Michael Bakunin, Pope Leo XIII, Friedrich Nietzsche, Sigmund Freud, and Carl Jung. Also added is the complete text of the play *The Firebugs,* by Max Frisch. Racine's play *Phaedra* remains in the anthology, but it is now presented in a superb translation by the American poet Robert Lowell. The other retained works appearing in versions more accessible than the previous ones are Bacon's *New Organon* and Descartes' *Discourse on Method.* Finally, the selections from Voltaire and Goethe have been lengthened somewhat in this edition in order that their meanings may be conveyed more thoroughly. It is hoped that these carefully considered revisions will make the volume even more valuable to the reader than it has been in previous editions.

Edgar E. Knoebel

Contents

CLASSICS OF WESTERN THOUGHT

VOLUME III

The Modern World

THIRD EDITION

1

Francis Bacon

The New Organon

Francis Bacon (1561–1626), a contemporary of Shakespeare and Queen Elizabeth, was a true "man of the Renaissance." Versatile, ambitious, and unscrupulous, he was a man of affairs as well as a man of letters and a philosopher. Bacon attained the high office of Lord Chancellor under James I, but was impeached and found guilty of taking bribes, and died in disgrace. His Essays won him literary fame; however, his reputation rests largely on his work as the philosopher of scientific method who rejected the views of the Middle Ages and looked forward to the general acceptance of the new science, which would give human beings power over nature. A prophet of the scientific revolution of the seventeenth century, he thus helped to usher in a new age. In his philosophical works, Bacon attacked the deductive methods of scholasticism and formulated new principles of acquiring true and useful knowledge of the world through empiricism. He insisted on the necessity of direct observation of nature as the only way to know truth. The purpose of such knowledge was power, power to control nature and thereby advance the welfare of humanity. Bacon thus anticipated the eighteenth-century faith that human beings could master their own destiny.

Bacon's New Organon (1620), or method of scientific inquiry, was intended to replace the old Organon of Aristotle. In this work, which consists of a series of aphorisms, or short statements, Bacon analyzes the shortcomings of deductive, a priori methods of inquiry and proposes the inductive method, based on the direct observation of nature. While his formulation lacked precision and underrated the value of hypotheses, it was a significant attempt to

Francis Bacon, *The New Organon,* in *The New Organon and Related Writings,* edited by Fulton H. Anderson, copyright © 1960 by The Bobbs-Merrill Company, 39–49, 53, 66, 78, 80, 87–89, 93–94, 96–99, 107, 113–14. Reprinted with permission.

free people from their barren prejudices, faulty thinking, loose use of language, and vain fictions, and to encourage them to go directly to nature to discover its secrets. The following selection features a number of Bacon's most significant aphorisms.

1

Man, being the servant and interpreter of Nature, can do and understand so much and so much only as he has observed in fact or in thought of the course of nature. Beyond this he neither knows anything nor can do anything.

3

Human knowledge and human power meet in one; for where the cause is not known the effect cannot be produced. Nature to be commanded must be obeyed; and that which in contemplation is as the cause is in operation as the rule.

8

Moreover, the works already known are due to chance and experiment rather than to sciences; for the sciences we now possess are merely systems for the nice ordering and setting forth of things already invented, not methods of invention or directions for new works.

9

The cause and root of nearly all evils in the sciences is this—that while we falsely admire and extol the powers of the human mind we neglect to seek for its true helps.

10

The subtlety of nature is greater many times over than the subtlety of the senses and understanding; so that all those specious meditations, speculations, and glosses in which men indulge are quite from the purpose, only there is no one by to observe it.

11

As the sciences which we now have do not help us in finding out new works, so neither does the logic which we now have help us in finding out new sciences.

12

The logic now in use serves rather to fix and give stability to the errors which have their foundation in commonly received notions than to help the search after truth. So it does more harm than good.

18

The discoveries which have hitherto been made in the sciences are such as lie close to vulgar notions,[1] scarcely beneath the surface. In order to penetrate into the inner and further recesses of nature, it is necessary that both notions and axioms[2] be derived from things by a more sure and guarded way, and that a method of intellectual operation be introduced altogether better and more certain.

19

There are and can be only two ways of searching into and discovering truth. The one flies from the senses and particulars to the most general axioms, and from these principles, the truth of which it takes for settled and immovable, proceeds to judgment and to the discovery of middle axioms. And this way is now in fashion. The other derives axioms from the senses and particulars, rising by a gradual and unbroken ascent, so that it arrives at the most general axioms last of all. This is the true way, but as yet untried.

24

It cannot be that axioms established by argumentation should avail for the discovery of new works, since the subtlety of nature is greater many times over than the subtlety of argument. But axioms duly and orderly formed from particulars easily discover the way to new particulars, and thus render sciences active.

[1] Popular ideas unsupported by evidence or reason.
[2] Established principles universally recognized as true.

25

The axioms now in use, having been suggested by a scanty and manipular experience and a few particulars of most general occurrence, are made for the most part just large enough to fit and take these in; and therefore it is no wonder if they do not lead to new particulars. And if some opposite instance, not observed or not known before, chance to come in the way, the axiom is rescued and preserved by some frivolous distinction; whereas the truer course would be to correct the axiom itself.

26

The conclusions of human reason as ordinarily applied in matters of nature, I call for the sake of distinction *Anticipations of Nature* (as a thing rash or premature). That reason which is elicited from facts by a just and methodical process, I call *Interpretation of Nature*.

28

For the winning of assent, indeed, anticipations are far more powerful than interpretations, because being collected from a few instances, and those for the most part of familiar occurrence, they straightway touch the understanding and fill the imagination; whereas interpretations, on the other hand, being gathered here and there from very various and widely dispersed facts, cannot suddenly strike the understanding; and therefore they must needs, in respect of the opinions of the time, seem harsh and out of tune, much as the mysteries of faith do.

29

In sciences founded on opinions and dogmas,[3] the use of anticipations and logic is good; for in them the object is to command assent to the proposition, not to master the thing.

31

It is idle to expect any great advancement in science from the superinducing and engrafting of new things upon old. We must begin anew from the very foundations, unless we would revolve forever in a circle with mean and contemptible progress.

---

[3] Statements (of faith) that are accepted as true by believers.

32

The honor of the ancient authors, and indeed of all, remains untouched, since the comparison I challenge is not of wits or faculties, but of ways and methods, and the part I take upon myself is not that of a judge, but of a guide.

36

One method of delivery alone remains to us which is simply this: we must lead men to the particulars themselves, and their series and order; while men on their side must force themselves for a while to lay their notions by and begin to familiarize themselves with facts.

37

The doctrine of those who have denied that certainty could be attained at all has some agreement with my way of proceeding at the first setting out; but they end in being infinitely separated and opposed. For the holders of that doctrine assert simply that nothing can be known. I also assert that not much can be known in nature by the way which is now in use. But then they go on to destroy the authority of the senses and understanding; whereas I proceed to devise and supply helps for the same.

38

The idols and false notions which are now in possession of the human understanding, and have taken deep root therein, not only so beset men's minds that truth can hardly find entrance, but even after entrance is obtained, they will again in the very instauration[4] of the sciences meet and trouble us, unless men being forewarned of the danger fortify themselves as far as may be against their assaults.

39

There are four classes of Idols which beset men's minds. To these for distinction's sake I have assigned names, calling the first class *Idols of the Tribe;* the second, *Idols of the Cave;* the third, *Idols of the Market Place;* the fourth, *Idols of the Theater.*

---

[4] Reconstruction.

40

The formation of ideas and axioms by true induction[5] is no doubt the proper remedy to be applied for the keeping off and clearing away of idols. To point them out, however, is of great use; for the doctrine of Idols is to the interpretation of nature what the doctrine of the refutation of sophisms[6] is to common logic.

41

The Idols of the Tribe have their foundation in human nature itself, and in the tribe or race of men. For it is a false assertion that the sense of man is the measure of things. On the contrary, all perceptions as well of the sense as of the mind are according to the measure of the individual and not according to the measure of the universe. And the human understanding is like a false mirror, which, receiving rays irregularly, distorts and discolors the nature of things by mingling its own nature with it.

42

The Idols of the Cave are the idols of the individual man. For everyone (besides the errors common to human nature in general) has a cave or den of his own, which refracts and discolors the light of nature, owing either to his own proper and peculiar nature; or to his education and conversation with others; or to the reading of books, and the authority of those whom he esteems and admires; or to the differences of impressions, accordingly as they take place in a mind preoccupied and predisposed or in a mind indifferent and settled; or the like. So that the spirit of man (according as it is meted out to different individuals) is in fact a thing variable and full of perturbation, and governed as it were by chance. Whence it was well observed by Heraclitus[7] that men look for sciences in their own lesser worlds, and not in the greater or common world.

43

There are also Idols formed by the intercourse and association of men with each other, which I call Idols of the Market Place, on ac-

[5] In logic, the process of reasoning from particulars to the general, or from the individual to the universal.
[6] Arguments that sound plausible, but are defective.
[7] Greek philosopher (fifth century B.C.).

count of the commerce and consort of men there. For it is by discourse that men associate, and words are imposed according to the apprehension of the vulgar. And therefore the ill and unfit choice of words wonderfully obstructs the understanding. Nor do the definitions or explanations wherewith in some things learned men are wont to guard and defend themselves, by any means set the matter right. But words plainly force and overrule the understanding, and throw all into confusion, and lead men away into numberless empty controversies and idle fancies.

44

Lastly, there are Idols which have immigrated into men's minds from the various dogmas of philosophies, and also from wrong laws of demonstration. These I call Idols of the Theater, because in my judgment all the received systems are but so many stage plays, representing worlds of their own creation after an unreal and scenic fashion. Nor is it only of the systems now in vogue, or only of the ancient sects and philosophies, that I speak; for many more plays of the same kind may yet be composed and in like artificial manner set forth; seeing that errors the most widely different have nevertheless causes for the most part alike. Neither again do I mean this only of entire systems, but also of many principles and axioms in science, which by tradition, credulity, and negligence have come to be received.

51

The human understanding is of its own nature prone to abstractions and gives a substance and reality to things which are fleeting. But to resolve nature into abstractions is less to our purpose than to dissect her into parts; as did the school of Democritus,[8] which went further into nature than the rest. Matter rather than forms should be the object of our attention, its configurations and changes of configuration, and simple action, and law of action or motion; for forms are figments of the human mind, unless you will call those laws of action forms.

[8]Greek philosopher (*ca.* 460–*ca.* 362 B.C.) who developed an atomic theory of matter.

68

So much concerning the several classes of Idols and their equipage,[9] all of which must be renounced and put away with a fixed and solemn determination, and the understanding thoroughly freed and cleansed; the entrance into the kingdom of man, founded on the sciences, being not much other than the entrance into the kingdom of heaven, whereinto none may enter except as a little child.

81

Again there is another great and powerful cause why the sciences have made but little progress, which is this. It is not possible to run a course aright when the goal itself has not been rightly placed. Now the true and lawful goal of the sciences is none other than this: that human life be endowed with new discoveries and powers. But of this the great majority have no feeling, but are merely hireling and professorial; except when it occasionally happens that some workman of acuter wit and covetous of honor applies himself to a new invention, which he mostly does at the expense of his fortunes. But in general, so far are men from proposing to themselves to augment the mass of arts and sciences, that from the mass already at hand they neither take nor look for anything more than what they may turn to use in their lectures, or to gain, or to reputation, or to some similar advantage. And if any one out of all the multitude court science with honest affection and for her own sake, yet even with him the object will be found to be rather the variety of contemplations and doctrines than the severe and rigid search after truth. And if by chance there be one who seeks after truth in earnest, yet even he will propose to himself such a kind of truth as shall yield satisfaction to the mind and understanding in rendering causes for things long since discovered, and not the truth which shall lead to new assurance of works and new light of axioms. If then the end of the sciences has not as yet been well placed, it is not strange that men have erred as to the means.

83

This evil, however, has been strangely increased by an opinion or conceit, which though of long standing is vain and hurtful, namely, that the dignity of the human mind is impaired by long and close in-

---

[9] Accompanying "baggage."

tercourse with experiments and particulars, subject to sense and bound in matter; especially as they are laborious to search, ignoble to meditate, harsh to deliver, illiberal to practice, infinite in number, and minute in subtlety. So that it has come at length to this, that the true way is not merely deserted, but shut out and stopped up; experience being, I do not say abandoned or badly managed, but rejected with disdain.

89

Neither is it to be forgotten that in every age natural philosophy has had a troublesome and hard to deal with adversary—namely, superstition, and the blind and immoderate zeal of religion. For we see among the Greeks that those who first proposed to men's then uninitiated ears the natural causes for thunder and for storms were thereupon found guilty of impiety. Nor was much more forbearance shown by some of the ancient fathers of the Christian church to those who on most convincing grounds (such as no one in his senses would now think of contradicting) maintained that the earth was round, and of consequence asserted the existence of the antipodes.[10]

Moreover, as things now are, to discourse of nature is made harder and more perilous by the summaries and systems of the schoolmen[11] who, having reduced theology into regular order as well as they were able, and fashioned it into the shape of an art, ended in incorporating the contentious and thorny philosophy of Aristotle,[12] more than was fit, with the body of religion.

To the same result, though in a different way, tend the speculations of those who have taken upon them to deduce the truth of the Christian religion from the principles of philosophers, and to confirm it by their authority, pompously solemnizing this union of the sense and faith as a lawful marriage, and entertaining men's minds with a pleasing variety of matter, but all the while disparaging things divine by mingling them with things human. Now in such mixtures of theology with philosophy only the received doctrines of philosophy are included; while new ones, albeit changes for the better, are all but expelled and exterminated.

Lastly, you will find that by the simpleness of certain divines,[13]

---

[10] Any two places on the globe that are diametrically opposite.
[11] Medieval "scholastic" philosophers.
[12] Greek philosopher (384–322 B.C.) regarded as "The Philosopher" of antiquity.
[13] Clergy, theologians.

access to any philosophy, however pure, is well-nigh closed. Some are weakly afraid lest a deeper search into nature should transgress the permitted limits of sober-mindedness, wrongfully wresting and transferring what is said in Holy Writ [14] against those who pry into sacred mysteries, [15] to the hidden things of nature, which are barred by no prohibition. Others with more subtlety surmise and reflect that if second causes are unknown everything can more readily be referred to the divine hand and rod, a point in which they think religion greatly concerned—which is in fact nothing else but to seek to gratify God with a lie. Others fear from past example that movements and changes in philosophy will end in assaults on religion. And others again appear apprehensive that in the investigation of nature something may be found to subvert or at least shake the authority of religion, especially with the unlearned. But these two last fears seem to me to savor utterly of carnal wisdom; as if men in the recesses and secret thought of their hearts doubted and distrusted the strength of religion and the empire of faith over the sense, and therefore feared that the investigation of truth in nature might be dangerous to them. But if the matter be truly considered, natural philosophy is, after the word of God, at once the surest medicine against superstition and the most approved nourishment for faith, and therefore she is rightly given to religion as her most faithful handmaid, since the one displays the will of God, the other his power. For he did not err who said, "Ye err in that ye know not the Scriptures and the power of God," thus coupling and blending in an indissoluble bond information concerning his will and meditation concerning his power. Meanwhile it is not surprising if the growth of natural philosophy is checked when religion, the thing which has most power over men's minds, has by the simpleness and incautious zeal of certain persons been drawn to take part against her.

90

Again, in the customs and institutions of schools, academies, colleges, and similar bodies destined for the abode of learned men and the cultivation of learning, everything is found adverse to the progress of science. For the lectures and exercises there are so ordered that to think or speculate on anything out of the common way can hardly

---

[14] Sacred Scriptures: the Bible.
[15] Profound secrets, claimed to be beyond human comprehension.

occur to any man. And if one or two have the boldness to use any liberty of judgment, they must undertake the task all by themselves; they can have no advantage from the company of others. And if they can endure this also, they will find their industry and largeness of mind no slight hindrance to their fortune. For the studies of men in these places are confined and as it were imprisoned in the writings of certain authors, from whom if any man dissent he is straightway arraigned as a turbulent person and an innovator. But surely there is a great distinction between matters of state and the arts; for the danger from new motion and from new light is not the same. In matters of state a change even for the better is distrusted, because it unsettles what is established; these things resting on authority, consent, fame and opinion, not on demonstration. But arts and sciences should be like mines, where the noise of new works and further advances is heard on every side. But though the matter be so according to right reason, it is not so acted on in practice; and the points above mentioned in the administration and government of learning put a severe restraint upon the advancement of the sciences.

95

Those who have handled sciences have been either men of experiment or men of dogmas. The men of experiment are like the ant, they only collect and use; the reasoners resemble spiders, who make cobwebs out of their own substance. But the bee takes a middle course: it gathers its material from the flowers of the garden and of the field, but transforms and digests it by a power of its own. Not unlike this is the true business of philosophy; for it neither relies solely or chiefly on the powers of the mind, nor does it take the matter which it gathers from natural history and mechanical experiments and lay it up in the memory whole, as it finds it, but lays it up in the understanding altered and digested. Therefore from a closer and purer league between these two faculties, the experimental and the rational (such as has never yet been made), much may be hoped.

97

No one has yet been found so firm of mind and purpose as resolutely to compel himself to sweep away all theories and common notions, and to apply the understanding, thus made fair and even, to a fresh examination of particulars. Thus it happens that human knowledge, as we have it, is a mere medley and ill-digested mass, made up of much credulity and much accident, and also of the childish notions which we at first imbibed. . . .

100

But not only is a greater abundance of experiments to be sought for and procured, and that too of a different kind from those hitherto tried; an entirely different method, order, and process for carrying on and advancing experience must also be introduced. For experience, when it wanders in its own track, is, as I have already remarked, mere groping in the dark, and confounds men rather than instructs them. But when it shall proceed in accordance with a fixed law, in regular order, and without interruption, then may better things be hoped of knowledge.

102

Moreover, since there is so great a number and army of particulars, and that army so scattered and dispersed as to distract and confound the understanding, little is to be hoped for from the skirmishings and slight attacks and desultory movements of the intellect, unless all the particulars which pertain to the subject of inquiry shall, by means of Tables of Discovery, apt, well arranged, and, as it were, animate, be drawn up and marshaled; and the mind be set to work upon the helps duly prepared and digested which these tables supply.

104

The understanding must not, however, be allowed to jump and fly from particulars to axioms remote and of almost the highest generality (such as the first principles, as they are called, of arts and things), and taking stand upon them as truths that cannot be shaken, proceed to prove and frame the middle axioms by reference to them; which has been the practice hitherto, the understanding being not only carried that way by a natural impulse, but also by the use of syllogistic[16] demonstration trained and inured[17] to it. But then, and then

---

[16] Characterized by a set form of reasoning (logic) consisting of a major premise and a minor premise and a necessary conclusion drawn from them.
[17] Accustomed to.

only, may we hope well of the sciences when in a just scale of ascent, and by successive steps not interrupted or broken, we rise from particulars to lesser axioms; and then to middle axioms, one above the other; and last of all to the most general. For the lowest axioms differ but slightly from bare experience, while the highest and most general (which we now have) are notional and abstract and without solidity. But the middle are the true and solid and living axioms, on which depend the affairs and fortunes of men; and above them again, last of all, those which are indeed the most general; such, I mean, as are not abstract, but of which those intermediate axioms are really limitations.

The understanding must not therefore be supplied with wings, but rather hung with weights, to keep it from leaping and flying. Now this has never yet been done; when it is done, we may entertain better hopes of the sciences.

106

But in establishing axioms by this kind of induction, we must also examine and try whether the axiom so established be framed to the measure of those particulars only from which it is derived, or whether it be larger and wider. And if it be larger and wider, we must observe whether by indicating to us new particulars it confirm that wideness and largeness as by a collateral [18] security, that we may not either stick fast in things already known, or loosely grasp at shadows and abstract forms, not at things solid and realized in matter. And when this process shall have come into use, then at last shall we see the dawn of a solid hope.

117

And as I do not seek to found a school, so neither do I hold out offers or promises of particular works. It may be thought, indeed, that I who make such frequent mention of works and refer everything to that end, should produce some myself by way of earnest. But my course and method, as I have often clearly stated and would wish to state again, is this—not to extract works from works or experiments from experiments (as an empiric), [19] but from works and

---

[18] Accompanying; parallel.
[19] A person who relies solely on practical experience.

experiments to extract causes and axioms, and again from those causes and axioms new works and experiments, as a legitimate interpreter of nature. And although in my tables of discovery, and also in the examples of particulars, and moreover in my observations on the history, any reader of even moderate sagacity and intelligence will everywhere observe indications and outlines of many noble works; still I candidly confess that the natural history which I now have, whether collected from books or from my own investigations, is neither sufficiently copious nor verified with sufficient accuracy to serve the purposes of legitimate interpretation. . . .

124

Again, it will be thought, no doubt, that the goal and mark of knowledge which I myself set up (the very point which I object to in others) is not the true or the best, for that the contemplation of truth is a thing worthier and loftier than all utility[20] and magnitude of works; and that this long and anxious dwelling with experience and matter and the fluctuations of individual things, drags down the mind to earth, or rather sinks it to a very Tartarus[21] of turmoil and confusion, removing and withdrawing it from the serene tranquility of abstract wisdom, a condition far more heavenly. Now to this I readily assent, and indeed this which they point at as so much to be preferred is the very thing of all others which I am about. For I am building in the human understanding a true model of the world, such as it is in fact, not such as a man's own reason would have it to be; a thing which cannot be done without a very diligent dissection and anatomy of the world. But I say that those foolish and apish images of worlds which the fancies of men have created in philosophical systems must be utterly scattered to the winds. Be it known then how vast a difference there is (as I said above) between the idols of the human mind and the ideas of the divine. The former are nothing more than arbitrary abstractions; the latter are the Creator's own stamp upon creation, impressed and defined in matter by true and exquisite lines. Truth, therefore, and utility are here the very same things; and works themselves are of greater value as pledges of truth than as contributing to the comforts of life.

[20] Practical usefulness or advantage.
[21] In Greek mythology, the part of the afterworld for souls receiving severe punishment.

2

René Descartes

Discourse on Method

If Bacon stressed the empirical element in scientific inquiry, René Descartes (1596–1650), a French mathematician and philosopher, established the necessity for a rigorous, rational analysis and explanation of natural phenomena. A more profound and precise thinker than Bacon, Descartes was the mathematical genius who worked out the new discipline of analytic geometry. Descartes' philosophical work ranged, with typical French clarity, over the fields of metaphysics, ethics, and psychology, and he is generally considered the founder of modern philosophy. His emphasis on mathematical methods of reasoning, on one hand, gave contemporary scientists a means of guaranteeing the certainty of their knowledge of the physical universe. On the other hand, his metaphysical thought was to establish a rational basis for religious belief. In fact, he attributed his insights, scientific and metaphysical alike, to divine revelations made to him in a series of dreams. But the Christian churches thought otherwise and condemned his work. What most inspired ecclesiastical displeasure was Descartes' dualism—his belief that mind and matter are essentially different substances subject to different laws. It was this philosophical dualism that enabled him to separate scientific inquiry from religious thought and to treat the world of nature as a mechanical one, operating strictly according to mathematical law.

The following selection from the Discourse on Method (1637), the most important of Descartes' philosophical writings, provides a superb demonstration of Cartesian dualism. Descartes began his inquiry into the phenomena tangible to human existence with the deliberate rejection of all

René Descartes, *Discourse on Method*, trans. Laurence J. Laufleur, copyright © 1950, 1956 by The Liberal Arts Press, a division of The Bobbs-Merrill Company, Inc., 1–2, 7, 10–14, 20–25, 41–42. Reprinted with permission.

previous knowledge, opinions, and customs. In addition, before accepting re-
placements, he worked out four steps of inquiry considered to be the true
method; these were to be an unfailing safeguard against any and all errors
that might otherwise impede his discovery of truth. For Descartes, assurance
that he was not deceived in this process resided in his ability to doubt. And
he concluded that since he doubted, he must exist—or, even more
pointedly, that since he was capable of thinking, he existed.

At a certain point in his work, Descartes must have realized that his
method was not an adequate tool for an inquiry into whether or not God ex-
ists. The strict application of the method in this specific instance might have
resulted in the denial of a divine existence. Since Descartes rejected atheism,
for reasons of upbringing as well as inclination, he saw himself compelled to
find a way in which to prove that God exists. Thus developed the following
line of thought: Descartes reasoned that it was impossible that he could have
received the notion of God from nothing; nor could he accept that he had de-
veloped this notion within himself. Much rather, his ability to think of some-
thing more perfect than himself reassured him that some more perfect being
existed. In addition, the feeling that he was dependent upon this being and
that he had received from it all he possessed added to his certainty about
God's existence. Having investigated this topic at length, Descartes con-
cluded that God's existence is at least as certain as any demonstration of
geometry.

The dualism in his philosophy caused Descartes to be attacked and de-
famed by scientists as well as by religious leaders. The former accused him of
having propped up religion, while the latter, Roman Catholics and Protes-
tants alike, charged him with having laid an ax to the very roots of Christian
religion. No wonder that Descartes, who above everything else cherished a
quiet existence, felt forced to spend a significant portion of his lifetime corres-
ponding with his detractors, trying to convince them that they had either
misread or misunderstood his works.

If this discourse seems too long to be read at one sitting, it may be
divided into six parts. In the first will be found various thoughts on
the sciences; in the second, the principal rules of the method the author has used; in the third, some moral rules derived from this
method; in the fourth, his proofs of the existence of God and of the
human soul which form the basis of his philosophy; in the fifth are

treated some questions of physics, especially the explanation of the heartbeat and of some other difficulties in medicine, as well as the difference between the souls of men and animals; and in the last, some prerequisites for further advances in the study of nature, as well as the author's reasons for writing this work.

PART ONE

Some Thoughts on the Sciences

Good sense is mankind's most equitably divided endowment, for everyone thinks that he is so abundantly provided with it that even those most difficult to please in other ways do not usually want more than they have of this. As it is not likely that everyone is mistaken, this evidence shows that the ability to judge correctly, and to distinguish the true from the false—which is really what is meant by good sense or reason—is the same by nature in all men; and that differences of opinion are not due to differences in intelligence, but merely to the fact that we use different approaches and consider different things. For it is not enough to have a good mind: one must use it well. The greatest souls are capable of the greatest vices as well as of the greatest virtues; and those who walk slowly can, if they follow the right path, go much farther than those who run rapidly in the wrong direction. . . .

It is true that while I did nothing but observe the customs of other men, I found nothing there to satisfy me, and I noted just about as much difference of opinion as I had previously remarked among philosophers. The greatest profit to me was, therefore, that I became acquainted with customs generally approved and accepted by other great peoples that would appear extravagant and ridiculous among ourselves, and so I learned not to believe too firmly what I learned only from example and custom. Also I gradually freed myself from many errors which could obscure the light of nature and make us less capable of correct reasoning. But after spending several years in thus studying the book of nature and acquiring experience, I eventually reached the decision to study my own self, and to employ all my abilities to try to choose the right path. This produced much better results in my case, I think, than would have been produced if I had never left my books and my country.

PART TWO

The Principal Rules of the Method

I had discovered in college that one cannot imagine anything so strange and unbelievable but that it has been upheld by some philosopher; and in my travels I had found that those who held opinions contrary to ours were neither barbarians nor savages, but that many of them were at least as reasonable as ourselves. I had considered how the same man, with the same capacity for reason, becomes different as a result of being brought up among Frenchmen or Germans than he would be if he had been brought up among Chinese or cannibals; and how, in our fashions, the thing which pleased us ten years ago and perhaps will please us again ten years in the future, now seems extravagant and ridiculous; and I felt that in all these ways we are much more greatly influenced by custom and example than by any certain knowledge. Faced with this divergence of opinion, I could not accept the testimony of the majority, for I thought it worthless as a proof of anything somewhat difficult to discover, since it is much more likely that a single man will have discovered it than a whole people. Nor, on the other hand, could I select anyone whose opinions seemed to me to be preferable to those of others, and I was thus constrained to embark on the investigation for myself.

Nevertheless, like a man who walks alone in the darkness, I resolved to go so slowly and circumspectly that if I did not get ahead very rapidly I was at least safe from falling. Also, I did not want to reject all the opinions which had slipped irrationally into my consciousness since birth, until I had first spent enough time planning how to accomplish the task which I was then undertaking, and seeking the true method of obtaining knowledge of everything which my mind was capable of understanding.

Among the branches of philosophy, I had, when younger, studied logic, and among those of mathematics, geometrical analysis and algebra; three arts or sciences which should be able to contribute something to my design. But in examining them I noticed that as far as logic was concerned its syllogisms [1] and most of its other methods

---

[1] Set forms of reasoning consisting of a major premise and a minor premise and a necessary conclusion drawn from the two.

serve rather to explain to another what one already knows, or . . . to speak without judgment of what one does not know, than to learn new things. Although it does contain many true and good precepts, they are interspersed among so many others that are harmful or superfluous that it is almost as difficult to separate them as to bring forth a Diana or a Minerva[2] from a block of virgin marble. Then, as far as the analysis of the Greeks and the algebra of the moderns is concerned, besides the fact that they deal with abstractions and appear to have no utility, the first is always so limited to the consideration of figures that it cannot exercise the understanding without greatly fatiguing the imagination, and the last is so limited to certain rules and certain numbers that it has become a confused and obscure art which perplexes the mind instead of a science which educates it. In consequence I thought that some other method must be found to combine the advantages of these three and to escape their faults. Finally, just as the multitude of laws frequently furnishes an excuse for vice, and a state is much better governed with a few laws which are strictly adhered to, so I thought that instead of the great number of precepts of which logic is composed, I would have enough with the four following ones, provided that I made a firm and unalterable resolution not to violate them even in a single instance.

The first rule was never to accept anything as true unless I recognized it to be evidently such: that is, carefully to avoid precipitation and prejudgment, and to include nothing in my conclusions unless it presented itself so clearly and distinctly to my mind that there was no occasion to doubt it.

The second was to divide each of the difficulties which I encountered into as many parts as possible, and as might be required for an easier solution.

The third was to think in an orderly fashion, beginning with the things which were simplest and easiest to understand, and gradually and by degrees reaching toward more complex knowledge, even treating as though ordered materials which were not necessarily so.

The last was always to make enumerations so complete, and reviews so general, that I would be certain that nothing was omitted.

Those long chains of reasoning, so simple and easy, which enabled the geometricians to reach the most difficult demonstrations, had made me wonder whether all things knowable to men might not fall

---

[2] Roman goddesses, often the objects of sculpture.

into a similar logical sequence. If so, we need only refrain from accepting as true that which is not true, and carefully follow the order necessary to deduce each one from the others, and there cannot be any propositions so abstruse that we cannot prove them, or so recondite that we cannot discover them. It was not very difficult, either, to decide where we should look for a beginning, for I knew already that one begins with the simplest and easiest to know. Considering that among all those who have previously sought truth in the sciences, mathematicians alone have been able to find some demonstrations, some certain and evident reasons, I had no doubt that I should begin where they did, although I expected no advantage except to accustom my mind to work with truths and not to be satisfied with bad reasoning. I do not mean that I intended to learn all the particular branches of mathematics; for I saw that although the objects they discuss are different, all these branches are in agreement in limiting their consideration to the relationships or proportions between their various objects. I judged therefore that it would be better to examine these proportions in general, and use particular objects as illustrations only in order to make their principles easier to comprehend, and to be able the more easily to apply them afterwards, without any forcing, to anything for which they would be suitable. I realized that in order to understand the principles of relationships I would sometimes have to consider them singly, and sometimes in groups. I thought I could consider them better singly as relationships between lines, because I could find nothing more simple or more easily pictured to my imagination and my senses. But in order to remember and understand them better when taken in groups, I had to express them in numbers, and in the smallest numbers possible. Thus I took the best traits of geometrical analysis and algebra, and corrected the faults of one by the other.

The exact observation of the few precepts which I had chosen gave me such facility in clarifying all the issues in these two sciences that it took only two or three months to examine them. I began with the most simple and general, and each truth that I found was a rule which helped me to find others, so that I not only solved many problems which I had previously judged very difficult, but also it seemed to me that toward the end I could determine to what extent a still-unsolved problem could be solved, and what procedures should be used in solving it. In this I trust that I shall not appear too vain, considering that there is only one true solution to a given problem, and whoever finds it knows all that anyone can know about it. Thus, for example, a child who has learned arithmetic and had performed an addition according to the rules may feel certain that as far as that particular sum is concerned, he has found everything that a human mind can discover. For, after all, the method of following the correct order and stating precisely all the circumstances of what we are investigating is the whole of what gives certainty to the rules of arithmetic.

What pleased me most about this method was that it enabled me to reason in all things, if not perfectly, at least as well as was in my power. In addition, I felt that in practicing it my mind was gradually becoming accustomed to conceive its objects more clearly and distinctly, and since I had not directed this method to any particular subject matter, I was in hopes of applying it just as usefully to the difficulties of other sciences as I had already to those of algebra. Not that I would dare to undertake to examine at once all the difficulties that presented themselves, for that would have been contrary to the principle of order. But I had observed that all the basic principles of the sciences were taken from philosophy, which itself had no certain ones. It therefore seemed that I should first attempt to establish philosophic principles, and that since this was the most important thing in the world and the place where precipitation and prejudgment were most to be feared, I should not attempt to reach conclusions until I had attained a much more mature age than my then twenty-three years, and had spent much time in preparing for it. This preparation would consist partly in freeing my mind from the false opinions which I had previously acquired, partly in building up a fund of experiences which should serve afterwards as the raw material of my reasoning, and partly in training myself in the method which I had determined upon, so that I should become more and more adept in its use.

• • •

PART FOUR

Proofs of the Existence of God and of the Human Soul

I do not know whether I ought to touch upon my first meditations here, for they are so metaphysical and out of the ordinary that they might not be interesting to most people. Nevertheless, in order to show whether my fundamental notions are sufficiently sound, I find myself more or less constrained to speak of them. I had noticed for a long time that in practice it is sometimes necessary to follow opinions which we know to be very uncertain, just as though they were indubitable, as I stated before; but inasmuch as I desired to devote myself wholly to the search for truth, I thought that I should take a course precisely contrary, and reject as absolutely false anything of which I could have the least doubt, in order to see whether anything would be left after this procedure which could be called wholly certain. Thus, as our senses deceive us at times, I was ready to suppose that nothing was at all the way our senses represented them to be. As there are men who make mistakes in reasoning even on the simplest topics in geometry, I judged that I was as liable to error as any other, and rejected as false all the reasoning which I had previously accepted as valid demonstration. Finally, as the same precepts which we have when awake may come to us when asleep without their being true, I decided to suppose that nothing that had ever entered my mind was more real than the illusions of my dreams. But I soon noticed that while I thus wished to think everything false, it was necessarily true that I who thought so was something. Since this truth, *I think, therefore I am,* was so firm and assured that all the most extravagant suppositions of the sceptics were unable to shake it, I judged that I could safely accept it as the first principle of the philosophy I was seeking.

I then examined closely what I was, and saw that I could imagine that I had no body, and that there was no world nor any place that I occupied, but that I could not imagine for a moment that I did not exist. On the contrary, from the very fact that I doubted the truth of other things, it followed very evidently and very certainly that I existed. On the other hand, if I had ceased to think while all the rest of what I had ever imagined remained true, I would have had no reason to believe that I existed; therefore I concluded that I was a substance whose whole essence or nature was only to think, and which, to exist, has no need of space nor of any material thing. Thus it follows that this ego, this soul, by which I am what I am, is entirely distinct from the body and is easier to know than the latter, and that even if the body were not, the soul would not cease to be all that it now is.

Next I considered in general what is required of a proposition for it to be true and certain, for since I had just discovered one to be such, I thought I ought also to know of what that certitude consisted. I saw that there was nothing at all in this statement, "I think, therefore I am," to assure me that I was saying the truth, unless it was that I saw very clearly that to think one must exist. So I judged that I could accept as a general rule that the things which we conceive very clearly and very distinctly are always true, but that there may well be some difficulty in deciding which are those which we conceive distinctly.

After that I reflected upon the fact that I doubted, and that, in consequence, my spirit was not wholly perfect, for I saw clearly that it was a greater perfection to know than to doubt. I decided to ascertain from what source I had learned to think of something more perfect than myself, and it appeared evident that it must have been from some nature which was in fact more perfect. As for my ideas about many other things outside of me, as the sky, earth, light, heat, and thousands of other things, I was not so much troubled to discover where they came from, because I found nothing in them superior to my own nature. If they really existed, I could believe that whatever perfection they possessed might be derived from my own nature; if they did not exist, I could believe that they were derived from nothingness, that is, that they were derived from my own defects. But this could not be the explanation of my idea of a being more perfect than my own. To derive it from nothingness was manifestly impossible, and it is no less repugnant to good sense to assume what is more perfect comes from and depends on the less perfect than it is to assume that something comes from nothing, so that I could not assume that it came from myself. Thus the only hypothesis left was that this idea was put in my mind by a nature that was really more perfect than I was, which had all the perfections that I could imagine, and which was, in a word, God. To this I added that since I knew some perfections which I did not possess, I was not the only being in existence (I will here use freely, if you will pardon me, the terms of the schools),[3] and that it followed of necessity that there was some-one else more perfect upon whom I depended and from whom I had acquired all that I possessed. For if I had been alone and independent of anything else, so that I had bestowed upon myself all that limited quantity of value which I shared with the perfect Being, I would have been able to get from myself, in the same way, all the surplus

---

[3] That is, medieval scholastic philosophy.

which I recognize as lacking in me, and so would have been myself infinite, eternal, immutable, omniscient, omnipotent, and, in sum, I would possess all the perfections that I could discover in God.

For, following the reasoning which I have just explained, to know the nature of God as far as I was capable of such knowledge, I had only to consider each quality of which I had an idea, and decide whether it was or was not a perfection to possess it. I would then be certain that none of those which had some imperfection was in him, but that all the others were. I saw that doubt, inconstancy, sorrow and similar things could not be part of God's nature, since I would be happy to be without them myself. In addition, I had ideas of many sensible and corporeal entities, for although I might suppose that I was dreaming and that all that I saw or imagined was false, I could not at any rate deny that the ideas were truly in my consciousness. Since I had already recognized very clearly that intelligent nature is distinct from corporeal nature, I considered that composition is an evidence of dependency and that dependency is manifestly a defect. From this I judged that it could not be a perfection in God to be composed of these two natures, and that consequently he was not so composed. But if there were in the world bodies, or even intelligences or other natures that were not wholly perfect, their being must depend on God's power in such a way that they could not subsist without him for a single moment.

At this point I wished to seek for other truths, and proposed for consideration the object of the geometricians. This I conceived as a continuous body, or a space infinitely extended in length, breadth, and height or depth; divisible into various parts which can have different shapes and sizes and can be moved or transposed in any way: all of which is presumed by geometricians to be true of their object. I went through some of their simplest demonstrations and noticed that the great certainty which everyone attributes to them is only based on the fact that they are evidently conceived, following the rule previously established. I noticed also that there was nothing at all in them to assure me of the existence of their object; it was clear, for example, that if we posit a triangle, its three angles must be equal to two right angles, but there was nothing in that to assure me that there was a single triangle in the world. When I turned back to my idea of a perfect Being, on the other hand, I discovered that existence was included in that idea in the same way that the idea of a triangle contains the equality of its angles to two right angles, or that the idea of a sphere includes the equidistance of all its parts from its center. Perhaps, in fact, the existence of the perfect Being is even more evident. Consequently, it is at least as certain that God, who is this perfect Being, exists, as any theorem[4] of geometry could possibly be.

What makes many people feel that it is difficult to know of the existence of God, or even of the nature of their own souls, is that they never consider things higher than corporeal objects. They are so accustomed never to think of anything without picturing it—a method of thinking suitable only for material objects—that everything which is not picturable seems to them unintelligible. This is also manifest in the fact that even philosophers hold it as a maxim in the schools that there is nothing in the understanding which was not first in the senses, a location where it is clearly evident that the ideas of God and of the soul have never been. It seems to me that those who wish to use imagery to understand these matters are doing precisely the same thing that they would be doing if they tried to use their eyes to hear sounds or smell odors. There is even this difference: that the sense of sight gives us no less certainty of the truth of objects than do those of smell and hearing, while neither our imagery nor our senses could assure us of anything without the co-operation of our understanding.

Finally, if there are still some men who are not sufficiently persuaded of the existence of God and of their souls by the reasons which I have given, I want them to understand that all the other things of which they might think themselves more certain, such as their having a body, or the existence of stars and of an earth, and other such things, are less certain. For even though we have a moral assurance of these things, such that it seems we cannot doubt them without extravagance, yet without being unreasonable we cannot deny that, as far as metaphysical certainty goes, there is sufficient room for doubt. For we can imagine, when asleep, that we have another body and see other stars and another earth without there being any such. How could one know that the thoughts which come to us in dreams are false rather than the others, since they are often no less vivid and detailed? Let the best minds study this question as long as they wish, I do not believe they can find any reason good enough to remove this doubt unless they presuppose the existence of God. The very principle which I took as a rule to start with, namely, that all those things which we conceived very clearly and very dis-

----

[4] A general statement that has been proven.

tinctly are true, is known to be true only because God exists, and because he is a perfect Being, and because everything in us comes from him. From this it follows that our ideas or notions, being real things which come from God insofar as they are clear and distinct, cannot to that extent fail to be true. Consequently, though we often have ideas which contain falsity, they can only be those ideas which contain some confusion and obscurity, in which respect they participate in nothingness. That is to say, they are confused in us only because we are not wholly perfect. It is evident that it is no less repugnant to good sense to assume that falsity or imperfection as such is derived from God, as that truth or perfection is derived from nothingness. But if we did not know that all reality and truth within us came from a perfect and infinite Being, however clear and distinct our ideas might be, we would have no reason to be certain that they were endowed with the perfection of being true.

• • •

PART SIX

Some Prerequisites for Further Advances in the Study of Nature

I noticed that experimentation becomes more necessary in proportion as we advance in knowledge. In beginning an investigation it is better to restrict ourselves to our usual experiences, which we cannot ignore if we pay any attention to them at all, than to seek rarer and more abstruse experiences. The reason for this is that these latter are often deceiving when the causes of the more common phenomena are still unknown, as the circumstances on which they depend are almost always so particular and so minute that it is very difficult to discover them. My own procedure has been the following: I first tried to discover the general principles or first causes of all that exists or could exist in the world, without taking any causes into consideration but God as creator, and without using any evidence save certain indications of the truth which we find in our own minds. After that I examined what were the first and commonest effects which could be deduced from these causes; and it seems to me that by this procedure I discovered skies, stars, an earth, and even, on the earth, water, air, fire, minerals, and several other things which are the commonest of all and the most simple, and in consequence the easiest to understand. Then, when I wanted to descend to particulars, it seemed to me that there were so many different kinds that I believed it impossible for the human mind to distinguish the forms or species of objects found on earth from an infinity of others which might have been there if God had so willed. It thus appeared impossible to proceed further deductively, and if we were to understand and make use of things, we would have to discover causes by their effects, and make use of many experiments. In consequence, reviewing in my mind all the objects which had ever been presented to my senses, I believe I can say that I have never noticed anything which I could not explain easily enough by the principles I had found. But I must also admit that the powers of nature are so ample and vast, and that these principles are so simple and so general, that I hardly ever observed a particular effect without immediately recognizing several ways in which it could be deduced. My greatest difficulty usually is to find which of these is the true explanation, and to do this I know no other way than to seek several experiments such that their outcomes would be different according to the choice of hypotheses.

For the rest, I have now reached the point, it seems to me, where I see clearly enough the direction in which we should go in this research; but I also see that the character and the number of experiments required is such that neither my time nor my resources, were they a thousand times greater than they are, would suffice to do them all. In proportion, therefore, to the opportunity I shall have in the future to do more or fewer of them, I will advance more or less in the understanding of nature. This I expected to convey in my treatise, and I hoped to show so clearly how useful my project might be that I would oblige all those who desire human benefit, all those who are truly virtuous and not merely so in affectation or reputation, both to communicate to me the experiments that they have already made and to assist me in the prosecution of what remained to be done.

. . .

3

Thomas Hobbes
Leviathan

The new seventeenth-century science found philosophical expression in the work of Thomas Hobbes (1588–1679). The patronage of the Cavendishes, a powerful, noble English family, to whom he owed his social position and his livelihood, enabled Hobbes to carry on his scientific and philosophical studies and to travel and meet the leading intellectual figures of his day. He knew the work of such scientists as Bacon, Descartes, and Galileo, and incorporated their methods and findings into his own philosophy. He completely rejected medieval scholasticism and evolved a system that was materialist and determinist. For Hobbes, human beings and their ideas were simply forms of matter in motion. Such unorthodox views brought upon him charges of impiety and atheism and earned him such epithets as the "Bugbear of the Nation" and the "Monster of Malmesbury."

The political views held by Hobbes, which are expressed systematically in the masterpiece Leviathan (1651), were shaped as much by his own assumptions of philosophical materialism as by the personal and political circumstances of his troubled times. Living through the bloody conflicts of the English civil wars, Hobbes was stirred by "grief for the present calamities of my country," and his primary concern was the restoration of peace and order to England. His association with royalist circles inclined him to accept a strong monarchy as the instrument of such peace.

The Leviathan is a vigorous and realistic exposition of the case for political absolutism. Its title, taken from the name of a terrifying sea monster referred to in the Old Testament, is meant to suggest the frightening authority Hobbes considers necessary to compel obedience and order in human society.

Thomas Hobbes, *Leviathan*, in *The Ethics of Hobbes*, edited by E. Hershey Sneath (Boston: Ginn and Company, 1898), 177–82, 319–20, 330–33, 335–36, adapted.

Absolute sovereignty, Hobbes argues, is indispensable for the maintenance of order. His theories, however, pleased neither his royalist friends nor his anti-royalist enemies. For, though he favored an absolute monarchy, he was ready to accept any government powerful enough to maintain civil peace. Hobbes also rejected the traditional concepts of the divine rights of kings and the "organic" community. In his view, the origins of society were wholly secular and atomistic: society resulted from a social contract among selfish, warring individuals moved by necessity and fear. Sovereignty, once delegated, was irrevocable and indivisible. Since the seventeenth century, the influence of Hobbes and his reputation as a realistic political scientist have steadily grown: his ideas have increasingly served as a rationale for the exercise of absolute power and the glorification of the state.

OF THE CAUSES, GENERATION, AND DEFINITION OF A COMMONWEALTH

The final cause, end, or design of men, who naturally love liberty and dominion over others, in the introduction of that restraint upon themselves in which we see them live in commonwealths is the foresight of their own preservation, and of a more contented life thereby; that is to say, of getting themselves out from that miserable condition of war which is necessarily consequent . . . to the natural passions of men when there is no visible power to keep them in awe and tie them by fear of punishment to the performance of their covenants, and observation of the laws of nature. . . .

For the laws of nature, as "justice," "equity," "modesty," "mercy," and, in sum, "doing to others as we would be done to," of themselves, without the terror of some power to cause them to be observed, are contrary to our natural passions, that carry us to partiality, pride, revenge, and the like. And covenants without the sword are but words, and of no strength to secure a man at all. Therefore, notwithstanding the laws of nature, which every one has then kept when he has the will to keep them, when he can do it safely, if there be no power erected, or not great enough for our security; every man will, and may lawfully rely on his own strength and art, for protection against all other men. And in all places where men have lived by small families, to rob and spoil one another has been a trade, and so far from being reputed against the law of nature that the greater spoils they gained, the greater was their honor; and men observed no other laws therein but the laws of honor; that is, to abstain from cruelty, leaving to men their lives and instruments of livelihood. And as small families did then, so now do cities and kingdoms, which are but greater families, for their own security enlarge their dominions upon all pretenses of danger and fear of invasion or assistance that may be given to invaders, and endeavor as much as they can to subdue or weaken their neighbors by open force and secret arts, for lack of other protection, justly; and are remembered for it in later ages with honor.

Nor is it the joining together of a small number of men that gives them this security, because in small numbers small additions on the one side or the other make the advantage of strength so great as is sufficient to carry the victory; and therefore gives encouragement to an invasion. The multitude sufficient to confide in for our security is not determined by any certain number but by comparison with the enemy we fear; and is then sufficient when the advantage of the enemy is not so visible and conspicuous to determine the event of war as to move him to attempt it.

And should there not be so great a multitude, even if their actions be directed according to their particular judgments and particular appetites, they can expect thereby no defense nor protection, neither against a common enemy nor against the injuries of one another. For being distracted in opinions concerning the best use and application of their strength, they do not help but hinder one another, and reduce their strength by mutual opposition to nothing; whereby they are easily not only subdued by a very few that agree together, but also, when there is no common enemy, they make war upon each other for their particular interests. For if we could suppose a great multitude of men to consent in the observation of justice and other laws of nature without a common power to keep them all in awe, we might as well suppose all mankind to do the same; and then there neither would be, nor need to be, any civil government or commonwealth at all, because there would be peace without subjection.

Nor is it enough for the security which men desire should last all the time of their life that they be governed and directed by one judgment for a limited time, as in one battle or one war. For though they obtain a victory by their unanimous endeavor against a foreign enemy, yet afterwards, when either they have no common enemy or he that by one group is held for an enemy is by another group held for a friend, they must needs, by the difference of their interests, dissolve, and fall again into a war among themselves.

It is true that certain living creatures, as bees and ants, live sociably one with another, which are therefore by Aristotle[1] numbered among political creatures, and yet have no other direction, than their particular judgments and appetites; nor speech whereby one of them can signify to another what he thinks expedient for the common benefit; and therefore some man may perhaps desire to know why mankind cannot do the same. To which I answer:

First, that men are continually in competition for honor and dignity, which these creatures are not; and consequently among men there arises on the ground envy and hatred and finally war, but among these not so.

Secondly, that among these creatures the common good differ not from the private; and being by nature inclined to their private, they procure thereby the common benefit. But man, whose joy consists in comparing himself with other men, can relish nothing but what is eminent.

Thirdly, that these creatures, having not, as man, the use of reason, do not see nor think they see any fault, in the administration of their common business; whereas among men, there are very many that think themselves wiser and abler to govern the public better than the rest; and these strive to reform and innovate, one this way, another that way, and thereby bring it into distraction and civil war.

Fourthly, that these creatures, though they have some use of voice in making known to one another their desires and other affections, yet they lack that art of words by which some men can represent to others that which is good in the likeness of evil; and evil in the likeness of good; and augment or diminish the apparent greatness of good and evil, making men discontented and troubling their peace at their pleasure.

Fifthly, irrational creatures cannot distinguish between "injury" and "damage"; and, therefore, as long as they be at ease they are not offended with their fellows; whereas man is then most troublesome when he is most at ease; for then it is that he loves to show his wisdom and control the actions of them that govern the commonwealth.

---

[1] Greek philosopher (384–322 B.C.)

Lastly, the agreement of these creatures is natural, that of men is by covenant only, which is artificial; and therefore, it is no wonder if there be somewhat else required besides covenant to make their agreement constant and lasting, which is a common power to keep them in awe and to direct their actions to the common benefit.

The only way to erect such a common power which may be able to defend them from the invasion of foreigners and the injuries of one another, and thereby to secure them in such sort so that by their own industry and by the fruits of the earth they may nourish themselves and live contentedly, is to confer all their power and strength upon one man, or upon one assembly of men that may reduce all their wills, by plurality of voices, unto one will; which is as much as to say, to appoint one man or assembly of men to bear their person; and every one to accept and acknowledge himself to be author of whatsoever he that so bears their person shall act or cause to be acted in those things which concern the common peace and safety, and therein to submit their wills every one to his will, and their judgments to his judgment. This is more than consent or concord; it is a real unity of them all in one and the same person, made by covenant of every man with every man, in such manner as if every man should say to every man, "I authorize and give up my right of governing myself to this man, or to this assembly of men, on this condition, that you give up your right to him and authorize all his actions in like manner." This done, the multitude so united in one person is called a "commonwealth," in Latin *civitas*. This is the generation[2] of that great "leviathan," or rather, to speak more reverently, of that "mortal god," to which we owe, under the "immortal God," our peace and defense. For by this authority, given him by every particular man in the commonwealth, he has the use of so much power and strength conferred on him that, by terror thereof, he is enabled to form the wills of them all to peace at home and mutual aid against their enemies abroad. And in him consists the essence of the commonwealth, which, to define it, is "one person, of whose acts a great multitude, by mutual covenants one with another, have made themselves the author, to the end he may use the strength and means of them all as he shall think expedient for their peace and common defense."

---

[2] Origination, process of creation.

And he that carries this person is called "sovereign" and said to have "sovereign power"; and every one besides, his "subject."

The attaining to this sovereign power is by two ways. One, by natural force, as when a man makes his children to submit themselves and their children to his government, as being able to destroy them if they refuse; or by war subdues his enemies to his will, giving them their lives on that condition. The other is when men agree among themselves to submit to some man or assembly of men voluntarily, on confidence that they will be protected by him against all others. This latter, may be called a political commonwealth, or commonwealth by "institution," and the former, a commonwealth by "acquisition." . . .

OF THE OFFICE[3] OF THE SOVEREIGN REPRESENTATIVE

The office of the sovereign, be it a monarch or an assembly, consists in the end for which he was trusted with the sovereign power, namely, the securing of "the safety of the people"; to which he is obliged by the law of nature, and to render an account thereof to God, the author of that law, and to none but him. But by safety here is not meant a bare preservation but also all other contentments of life which every man by lawful industry, without danger or hurt to the commonwealth, shall acquire to himself.

And this is to be done, not by care applied to individuals further than their protection from injuries when they shall complain, but by a general provision contained in public instruction, both of doctrine and example, and in the making and executing of good laws to which individual persons may apply their own cases.

And because, if the essential rights of sovereignty . . . be taken away, the commonwealth is thereby dissolved and every man returns into the condition and calamity of a war with every other man, which is the greatest evil that can happen in this life; it is the office of the sovereign, to maintain those rights entire, and consequently against his duty, first, to transfer to another or to lay from himself any of them. For he that deserts the means deserts the ends; and he deserts the means when, being the sovereign, he acknowledges him-

---

[3] Duty, function.

self subject to the civil laws and renounces the power of supreme judicature,[4] or of making war or peace by his own authority; or of judging of the necessities of the commonwealth; or of levying money and soldiers when and as much as in his own conscience he shall judge necessary; or of making officers and ministers both of war and peace; or of appointing teachers and examining what doctrines are conformable or contrary to the defense, peace, and good of the people. Secondly, it is against his duty to let the people be ignorant or misinformed of the grounds and reasons of those his essential rights, because thereby men are easy to be seduced and drawn to resist him when the commonwealth shall require their use and exercise.

And the grounds of these rights have the need to be diligently and truly taught, because they cannot be maintained by any civil law or terror of legal punishment. For a civil law that shall forbid rebellion (and such is all resistance to the essential rights of the sovereignty), is not, as a civil law, any obligation, but by virtue only of the law of nature that forbids the violation of faith; which natural obligation if men know not, they cannot know the right of any law the sovereign makes. And for the punishment, they take it but for an act of hostility which when they think they have strength enough, they will endeavor by acts of hostility, to avoid. . . .

To the care of the sovereign belongs the making of good laws. But what is a good law? By a good law I mean not a just law; for no law can be unjust. The law is made by the sovereign power, and all that is done by such power is warranted and owned by every one of the people; and that which every man will have so, no man can say is unjust. It is in the laws of a commonwealth as in the laws of gaming; whatsoever the gamesters all agree on is injustice to none of them. A good law is that which is "needed" for the "good of the people" and "perspicuous."[5]

For the use of laws, which are but rules authorized, is not to bind the people from all voluntary actions but to direct and keep them in such a motion as not to hurt themselves by their own impetuous desires, rashness, or indiscretion; as hedges are set not to stop travellers, but to keep them in their way. And, therefore, a law that is not needed, having not the true end of a law, is not good. A law may be

[4] Judicial authority.
[5] Clear, easily understood.

conceived to be good when it is for the benefit of the sovereign, though it be not necessary for the people, but it is not so. For the good of the sovereign and people cannot be separated. It is a weak sovereign, that has weak subjects, and a weak people, whose sovereign lacks power to rule them at his will. Unnecessary laws are not good laws but traps for money; which, where the right of sovereign power is acknowledged, are superfluous, and where it is not acknowledged, insufficient to defend the people. . . .

It belongs also to the office of the sovereign to make a right application of punishments and rewards. And seeing the end of punishing is not revenge and discharge of anger, but correction, either of the offender, or of others by his example; the severest punishments are to be inflicted for those crimes that are of most danger to the public; such as are those which proceed from malice to the government established; those that spring from contempt of justice; those that provoke indignation in the multitude; and those which, unpunished, seem authorized, as when they are committed by sons, servants, or favorites of men in authority. For indignation carries men not only against the actors and authors of injustice, but against all power that is likely to protect them; as in the case of Tarquin,[6] when for the insolent act of one of his sons he was driven out of Rome and the monarchy itself dissolved.[7] But crimes of infirmity, such as are those which proceed from great provocation, from great fear, great need, or from ignorance, whether the fact be a great crime or not, there is place many times for leniency without prejudice to the commonwealth; and leniency, when there is such place for it, is required by the law of nature. The punishment of the leaders and teachers in a commotion, not the poor seduced people, when they are punished, can profit the commonwealth by their example. To be severe to the people is to punish that ignorance which may in great part be imputed to the sovereign, whose fault it was that they were no better instructed.

In like manner it belongs to the office and duty of the sovereign,

[6] Lucius Tarquinius Superbus (that is, the "Proud," 534–510 b.c.), last of the Roman kings; said to have been a cruel despot, though a capable ruler.

[7] The offending son was Tarquinius Sextus (died *ca.* 496 b.c.). According to legend, the Romans drove his father from the throne because Sextus had raped Lucretia, the virtuous wife of his cousin, Lucius Tarquinius Collatinus. Following the successful rebellion, the Romans transformed their state into a *republic* (509 b.c.), with Lucius Tarquinius Collatinus, the wronged husband, serving as one of the first two consuls (chief executives).

to apply his rewards so that there may arise from them benefit to the commonwealth, wherein consists their use, and end; and is then done when they that have well served the commonwealth are, with as little expense of the common treasure as is possible, so well recompensed as others thereby may be encouraged both to serve the same as faithfully as they can and to study the arts by which they may be enabled to do it better. To buy with money or preferment from a popular ambitious subject to be quiet and desist from making ill impressions in the minds of the people has nothing of the nature of reward (which is ordained not for disservice, but for service past), nor a sign of gratitude, but of fear; nor does it tend to the benefit but to the damage of the public. It is a contention with ambition like that of Hercules with the monster Hydra which, having many heads, for every one that was vanquished there grew up three. For in like manner, when the stubbornness of one popular man is overcome with reward there arise many more, by the example, that do the same mischief in hope of like benefit; and as all sorts of manufacture, so also malice increases by being salable. And though sometimes a civil war may be deferred by such ways as that, yet the danger grows still the greater and the public ruin more assured. It is therefore against the duty of the sovereign, to whom the public safety is committed, to reward those that aspire to greatness by disturbing the peace of their country, and not rather to oppose the beginnings of such men with a little danger than after a longer time with greater. . . .

When the sovereign himself is popular, that is, revered and beloved of his people, there is no danger at all from the popularity of a subject. For soldiers are never so generally unjust as to side with their captain though they love him, against their sovereign, when they love not only his person but also his cause. And therefore those who by violence have at any time suppressed the power of their lawful sovereign, before they could settle themselves in his place have been always put to the trouble of contriving their titles to save the people from the shame of receiving them. To have a known right to sovereign power is so popular a quality as he that has it needs no more, for his own part, to turn the hearts of his subjects to him but that they see him able absolutely to govern his own family; nor, on the part of his enemies, but a disbanding of their armies. For the greatest and most active part of mankind has never hitherto been well contented with the present.

Concerning the offices[8] of one sovereign to another, which are comprehended in that law which is commonly called the "law of nations," I need not say anything in this place because the law of nations and the law of nature is the same thing. And every sovereign has the same right, in securing the safety of his people that any particular man can have in securing the safety of his own body. And the same law that dictates to men that have no civil government what they ought to do and what to avoid in regard of one another dictates the same to commonwealths, that is, to the consciences of sovereign princes and sovereign assemblies, there being no court of natural justice but in the conscience only; where not man but God reigns whose laws, such of them as oblige all mankind, in respect of God as he is the author of nature are "natural," and in respect of the same God as he is King of kings are "laws."

[8] Relationships.

4

Blaise Pascal

Thoughts

Blaise Pascal (1623–1662) is famous both as a scientist-mathematician and as a Christian thinker and defender. In his youth he was a mathematical prodigy, having written a book on conic sections by age sixteen. Later, he went on to become a colleague of Descartes and other French scientists, to formulate "Pascal's principle" in physics, to invent one of the first computers, and to make important contributions to probability theory. At age twenty-three, he underwent a mystical experience that converted him to Jansenism, that austere, almost predestinationist version of Roman Catholicism. Some years later, after the death of his father, a worsening of his own physical condition, and another conversion experience in 1654, Pascal gave up his scientific work, rejected the world in order to participate in the life of the Jansenist religious community at Port Royal, and spent the rest of his life elaborating and defending his religious views. In recent years his reputation has rested more on his role as a precursor of modern religious existentialism than on his role as a scientist. After his final conversion, Pascal was torn between his love of science and his new religious views; his Thoughts *(Pensées) are essentially an attempt to reconcile the method of science with the content of religion. He accepts Descartes' method of reaching certainty through total doubt, but differs with Descartes' conclusions. Reason, according to Pascal, is indeed the key to understanding nature; but it is useless as a means of understanding and satisfying spiritual needs or of resolving the bewildering paradoxes of life. Reason cannot know God or prove his existence. The real test for such religious truths, according to Pascal, is not their*

Blaise Pascal, *Thoughts and Minor Works,* trans. W. F. Trotter *et al.,* in *Harvard Classics* (New York: Collier, 1910), vol. 48, 25–31, 42–43, 45, 58, 62–63, 71–72, 77–79, 82–83, 88, 98–99, 120, 124, 127, 131, 134, 136–37, 145–47, 150, 157, 174–75. Adapted.

rational consistency but their moral value. Moral certainty—the faith that life has some purpose and value—can come only from an act of will. Only such self-conscious choice distinguishes human beings from the rest of nature and raises them above the predicament of miserable, blundering animals.

Thoughts is based on fragmentary notes for a defense of Christianity. Written by Pascal in his last years, the notes were first published, in imperfect and incomplete form, in 1670 (eight years after his death); a complete, scholarly edition appeared in 1844. Full of brilliant paradoxes and acute insights into human nature and behavior, the following excerpts embody Pascal's anguished struggle to find certainty, and his alternation between despair, mystical hope, and pious resignation. The selected excerpts include the section titles under which they appear in the original collection.

MISERY OF MAN WITHOUT GOD

Let man then contemplate the whole of nature in her full and grand majesty, and turn his vision from the low objects which surround him. Let him gaze on that brilliant light, set like an eternal lamp to illumine the universe; let the earth appear to him a point in comparison with the vast circle described by the sun; and let him wonder at the fact that this vast circle is itself but a very fine point in comparison with that described by the stars in their revolution round the firmament. But if our view be arrested there, let our imagination pass beyond; it will sooner exhaust the power of conception than nature that of supplying material for conception. The whole visible world is only an imperceptible atom in the ample bosom of nature. No idea approaches it. We may enlarge our conceptions beyond all imaginable space; we only produce atoms in comparison with the reality of things. It is an infinite sphere, the center of which is everywhere, the circumference nowhere. In short, it is the greatest sensible mark of the almighty power of God that imagination loses itself in that thought.

Returning to himself, let man consider what he is in comparison with all existence; let him regard himself as lost in this remote corner of nature; and from the little cell in which he finds himself lodged, I mean the universe, let him estimate at their true value the earth, kingdoms, cities, and himself. What is a man in the Infinite?

But to show him another prodigy equally astonishing, let him examine the most delicate things he knows. Let a mite [1] be given him, with its minute body and parts incomparably more minute, limbs with their joints, veins in the limbs, blood in the veins, humors [2] in the blood, drops in the humors, vapors in the drops. Dividing these last things again, let him exhaust his powers of conception, and let the last object at which he can arrive be now that of our discourse. Perhaps he will think that here is the smallest point in nature. I will let him see therein a new abyss. I will paint for him not only the visible universe, but all that he can conceive of nature's immensity in the womb of this abridged atom. Let him see therein an infinity of universes, each of which has its firmament, its planets, its earth, in the same proportion as in the visible world; in each earth, animals, and in the last mites, in which he will find again all that the first had, finding still in these others the same thing without end and without cessation. Let him lose himself in wonders as amazing in their littleness as the others in their vastness. For who will not be astounded at the fact that our body, which a little while ago was imperceptible in the universe, itself imperceptible in the bosom of the whole, is now a colossus, a world, or rather a whole, in respect of the nothingness which we cannot reach? He who regards himself in this light will be afraid of himself, and observing himself sustained in the body given by nature between those two abysses of the Infinite [3] and Nothing, will tremble at the sight of these marvels; and I think that, as his curiosity changes into admiration, he will be more disposed to contemplate them in silence than to examine them with presumption.

For, in fact, what is man in nature? A Nothing in comparison with the Infinite, an All in comparison with the Nothing, a mean between nothing and everything. Since he is infinitely removed from comprehending the extremes, the end of things and their beginning are hopelessly hidden from him in an impenetrable secret; he is equally incapable of seeing the Nothing from which he was made, and the Infinite in which he is swallowed up.

What will he do then, but perceive the appearance of the middle of things, in an eternal despair of knowing either their beginning or their end. All things proceed from the Nothing, and are borne to-

---

[1] A tiny, parasitic insect.
[2] In seventeenth-century physiology, one of four fluids believed to be in the blood.
[3] That having no boundaries or limits.

ward the Infinite. Who will follow these marvellous processes? The Author of these wonders understands them. None other can do so.

Through failure to contemplate these Infinites, men have rashly rushed into the examination of nature, as though they bore some proportion to her. It is strange that they have wished to understand the beginnings of things, and thence to arrive at the knowledge of the whole, with a presumption as infinite as their object. For surely this design cannot be formed without presumption or without a capacity infinite like nature. . . .

We naturally believe ourselves far more capable of reaching the centre of things than of embracing their circumference. The visible extent of the world visibly exceeds us; but as we exceed little things, we think ourselves more capable of knowing them. And yet we need no less capacity for attaining the Nothing than the All. Infinite capacity is required for both, and it seems to me that whoever shall have understood the ultimate principles of being might also attain to the knowledge of the Infinite. The one depends on the other, and one leads to the other. These extremes meet and reunite by force of distance and find each other in God, and in God alone.

Let us, then, take our compass; we are something, and we are not everything. The nature of our existence hides from us the knowledge of first beginnings which are born of the Nothing; and the littleness of our being conceals from us the sight of the Infinite.

Our intellect holds the same position in the world of thought as our body occupies in the expanse of nature.

Limited as we are in every way, this state which holds the mean between two extremes is present in all our impotence. Our senses perceive no extreme. Too much sound deafens us; too much light dazzles us; too great distance or proximity hinders our view. Too great length and too great brevity of discourse tend to obscurity; too much truth is paralyzing. . . . First principles are too self-evident for us; too much pleasure disagrees with us. Too many concords are annoying in music; too many benefits irritate us; we wish to have the means to overpay our debts. "Benefits are pleasant while it is possible to repay them; when they become much greater, they produce hatred rather than gratitude."[4] We feel neither extreme heat nor extreme cold. Excessive qualities are prejudicial to us and not percepti-

---

[4] Quotation from Publius Cornelius Tacitus (*ca*. A.D. 55–117), Roman politician and historian.

ble by the senses; we do not feel but suffer them. Extreme youth and extreme age hinder the mind, as also too much and too little education. In short, extremes are for us as though they were not, and we are not within their notice. They escape us, or we them.

This is our true state; this is what makes us incapable of certain knowledge and of absolute ignorance. We sail within a vast sphere, ever drifting in uncertainty, driven from end to end. When we think to attach ourselves to any point and to fasten to it, it wavers and leaves us; and if we follow it, it eludes our grasp, slips past us, and vanishes forever. Nothing stays for us. This is our natural condition and yet most contrary to our inclination; we burn with desire to find solid ground and an ultimate sure foundation whereon to build a tower reaching to the Infinite. But our whole groundwork cracks, and the earth opens to abysses.

Let us, therefore, not look for certainty and stability. Our reason is always deceived by fickle shadows; nothing can fix the finite between the two Infinites, which both enclose and fly from it.

If this be well understood, I think that we shall remain at rest, each in the state wherein nature has placed him. As this sphere which has fallen to us as our lot is always distant from either extreme, what matters it that man should have a little more knowledge of the universe? If he has it, he but gets a little higher. Is he not always infinitely removed from the end, and is not the duration of our life equally removed from eternity, even if it lasts ten years longer?

In comparison with these Infinites, all finites are equal, and I see no reason for fixing our imagination on one more than on another. The only comparison which we make of ourselves to the finite is painful to us.

If man made himself the first object of study, he would see how incapable he is of going further. How can a part know the whole? But he may perhaps aspire to know at least the parts to which he bears some proportion. But the parts of the world are all so related and linked to one another that I believe it impossible to know one without the other and without the whole.

Man, for instance, is related to all he knows. He needs a place wherein to abide, time through which to live, motion in order to live, elements to compose him, warmth and food to nourish him, air to breathe. He sees light; he feels bodies; in short, he is in a dependent alliance with everything. To know man, then, it is necessary to know how it happens that he needs air to live, and, to know the air, we must know how it is thus related to the life of man, and so on. Flame cannot exist without air; therefore, to understand the one, we must understand the other.

Since everything, then, is cause and effect, dependent and supporting, mediate and immediate, and all is held together by a natural though imperceptible chain which binds together things most distant and most different, I hold it equally impossible to know the parts without knowing the whole and to know the whole without knowing the parts in detail. . . .

And what completes our incapability of knowing things is the fact that they are simple and that we are composed of two opposite natures, different in kind, soul and body. For it is impossible that our rational part should be other than spiritual; and if any one maintain that we are simply corporeal, this would far more exclude us from the knowledge of things, there being nothing so inconceivable as to say that matter knows itself. It is impossible to imagine how it should know itself.

So, if we are simply material, we can know nothing at all; and if we are composed of mind and matter, we cannot know perfectly things which are simple, whether spiritual or corporeal. Hence it comes that almost all philosophers have confused ideas of things, and speak of material things in spiritual terms, and of spiritual things in material terms. For they say boldly that bodies have a tendency to fall, that they seek after their centre, that they fly from destruction, that they fear the void, that they have inclinations, sympathies, antipathies, all of which attributes pertain only to mind. And in speaking of minds, they consider them as in a place, and attribute to them movement from one place to another; and these are qualities which belong only to bodies.

Instead of receiving the ideas of these things in their purity, we color them with our own qualities, and stamp with our composite being all the simple things which we contemplate.

Who would not think, seeing us compose all things of mind and body, but that this mixture would be quite intelligible to us? Yet it is the very thing we least understand. Man is to himself the most wonderful object in nature; for he cannot conceive what the body is, still less what the mind is, and least of all how a body should be united to a mind. This is the consummation of his difficulties, and yet it is his very being. "The manner in which spirits are united to bodies cannot be understood by men, yet such is man. . . ."[5]

• • •

There is an universal and essential difference between the actions of the will and all other actions.

The will is one of the chief factors in belief, not that it creates belief, but because things are true or false according to the aspect in which we look at them. The will, which prefers one aspect to another, turns away the mind from considering the qualities of all that it does not like to see; and thus the mind, moving in accord with the will, stops to consider the aspect which it likes and so judges by what it sees.

• • •

The nature of self-love and of this human Ego[6] is to love self only and consider self only. But what will man do? He cannot prevent this object that he loves from being full of faults and wants. He wants to be great, and he sees himself small. He wants to be happy, and he sees himself miserable. He wants to be perfect, and he sees himself full of imperfections. He wants to be the object of love and esteem among men, and he sees that his faults merit only their hatred and contempt. This embarrassment in which he finds himself produces in him the most unrighteous and criminal passion that can be imagined; for he conceives a mortal enmity against that truth which reproves him and which convinces him of his faults. He would annihilate it, but, unable to destroy it in its essence,[7] he destroys it as far as possible in his own knowledge and in that of others; that is to say, he devotes all his attention to hiding his faults both from others and from himself, and he cannot endure either that others should point them out to him, or that they should see them.

Truly it is an evil to be full of faults; but it is a still greater evil to be full of them and to be unwilling to recognize them, since that is to add the further fault of a voluntary illusion. We do not like others to deceive us; we do not think it fair that they should be held in higher esteem by us than they deserve; it is not, then, fair that we should

---

[5] Quotation from St. Augustine (354–430), philosopher, bishop, and Church Father.
[6] The conscious self.
[7] True substance.

deceive them and should wish them to esteem us more highly than we deserve.

Thus, when they discover only the imperfections and vices which we really have, it is plain they do us no wrong, since it is not they who cause them; they rather do us good, since they help us to free ourselves from an evil, namely, the ignorance of these imperfections. We ought not to be angry at their knowing our faults and despising us; it is but right that they should know us for what we are and should despise us, if we are contemptible. . . . Man is, then, only disguise, falsehood, and hypocrisy, both in himself and in regard to others. He does not wish anyone to tell him the truth; he avoids telling it to others, and all these dispositions, so removed from justice and reason, have a natural root in his heart.

· · ·

Men are intrusted from infancy with the care of their honor, their property, their friends, and even with the property and the honor of their friends. They are overwhelmed with business, with the study of languages, and with physical exercise; and they are made to understand that they cannot be happy unless their health, their honor, their fortune and that of their friends be in good condition, and that a single thing wanting will make them unhappy. Thus they are given cares and business which make them bustle about from break of day. It is, you will exclaim, a strange way to make them happy! What more could be done to make them miserable? Indeed! What could be done? We should only have to relieve them from all these cares; for then they would see themselves; they would reflect on what they are, whence they came, where they go, and thus we cannot employ and divert them too much. And this is why, after having given them so much business, we advise them, if they have some time for relaxation, to employ it in amusement, in play, and to be always fully occupied.

How hollow and full of ribaldry is the heart of man!

· · ·

He who will know fully the vanity of man has only to consider the causes and effects of love. The cause is *I know not what* [8] and the effects are dreadful. This *I know not what,* so small an object that we

---

[8] That is, an indescribable something.

cannot recognize it, agitates a whole country, princes, armies, the entire world.

Cleopatra's nose: had it been shorter, the whole aspect of the world would have been altered.

*   *   *

THE NECESSITY OF HOPE

We do not require great education of the mind to understand that here is no real and lasting satisfaction; that our pleasures are only vanity; that our evils are infinite; and, lastly, that death, which threatens us every moment, must infallibly place us within a few years under the dreadful necessity of being forever either annihilated or unhappy.

There is nothing more real than this, nothing more terrible. Be as heroic as we like, that is the end which awaits the noblest life in the world. Let us reflect on this and then say whether it is not beyond doubt that there is no good in this life but in the hope of another; that we are happy only in proportion as we draw near it; and that, as there are no more woes for those who have complete assurance of eternity, so there is no more happiness for those who have no insight into it.

Surely then it is a great evil thus to be in doubt, but it is at least an indispensable duty to seek when we are in such doubt; and thus the doubter who does not seek is altogether completely unhappy and completely wrong. And if besides this he is easy and content, professes to be so, and indeed boasts of it; if it is this state itself which is the subject of his joy and vanity, I have no words to describe so silly a creature.

How can people hold these opinions? What joy can we find in the expectation of nothing but hopeless misery? What reason for boasting that we are in impenetrable darkness? . . .

*   *   *

Let us imagine a number of men in chains and all condemned to death, where some are killed each day in the sight of the others, and those who remain see their own fate in that of their fellows and wait their turn, looking at each other sorrowfully and without hope. It is an image of the condition of men.

•   •   •

When I consider the short duration of my life, swallowed up in the eternity before and after, the little space which I fill and even can see, engulfed in the infinite immensity of spaces of which I am ignorant and which know me not, I am frightened and am astonished at being here rather than there; for there is no reason why here rather than there, why now rather than then. Who has put me here? By whose order and direction have this place and time been allotted to me?

•   •   •

The eternal silence of these infinite spaces frightens me.

•   •   •

Why is my knowledge limited? Why my stature? Why my life to one hundred years rather than to a thousand? What reason has nature had for giving me such, and for choosing this number rather than another in the infinity of those from which there is no more reason to choose one than another, trying nothing else?

•   •   •

The last act is tragic, however happy all the rest of the play is; at the last a little earth is thrown upon our head, and that is the end forever.

•   •   •

We are fools to depend upon the society of our fellowmen. Wretched as we are, powerless as we are, they will not aid us; we shall die alone. We should therefore act as if we were alone, and in that case [why] should we build fine houses, and so on? We should seek the truth without hesitation; and, if we refuse it, we show that we value the esteem of men more than the search for truth.

•   •   •

Between us and heaven or hell there is only life, which is the frailest thing in the world.

•   •   •

This is what I see and what troubles me. I look on all sides, and I see only darkness everywhere. Nature presents to me nothing which is not matter of doubt and concern. If I saw nothing there which revealed a Divinity, I would come to a negative conclusion; if I saw everywhere the signs of a Creator, I would remain peacefully in faith. But, seeing too much to deny and too little to be sure, I am in a state to be pitied; wherefore I have a hundred times wished that if a God maintains nature, she should testify to Him unequivocally, and that, if the signs she gives are deceptive, she should suppress them altogether; that she should say everything or nothing, that I might see which cause I ought to follow. Whereas in my present state, ignorant of what I am or of what I ought to do, I know neither my condition nor my duty. My heart inclines wholly to know where is the true good, in order to follow it; nothing would be too dear to me for eternity.

I envy those whom I see living in the faith with such carelessness and who make such a bad use of a gift of which it seems to me I would make such a different use.

• • •

It is incomprehensible that God should exist, and it is incomprehensible that He should not exist, that the soul should be joined to the body, and that we should have no soul; that the world should be created, and that it should not be created, and so on; that original sin should be, and that it should not be.

• • •

We must live differently in the world, according to these different assumptions: (1) that we could always remain in it; (2) that it is certain that we shall not remain here long, and uncertain if we shall remain here one hour. This last assumption is our condition.

• • •

OF THE MEANS OF BELIEF

Reason would never submit, if it did not judge that there are some occasions on which it ought to submit. It is then right for it to submit, when it judges that it ought to submit.

• • •

If we submit everything to reason, our religion will have no mysterious and supernatural element. If we offend the principles of reason, our religion will be absurd and ridiculous.

• • •

All our reasoning reduces itself to yielding to feeling.

But fancy is like, though contrary to, feeling, so that we cannot distinguish between these contraries. One person says that my feeling is fancy, another that his fancy is feeling. We should have a rule. Reason offers itself; but it is pliable in every sense; and thus there is no rule.

• • •

The heart has its reasons, which reason does not know. We feel it in a thousand things. I say that the heart naturally loves the Universal Being, and also itself naturally, according as it gives itself to them; and it hardens itself against one or the other at its will. You have rejected the one and kept the other. Is it by reason that you love yourself?

• • •

It is the heart which experiences God, and not the reason. This, then, is faith: God felt by the heart, not by the reason.

• • •

THE PHILOSOPHERS

Thought constitutes the greatness of man.

• • •

Man is but a reed, the most feeble thing in nature, but he is a thinking reed. The entire universe need not arm itself to crush him. A vapor, a drop of water suffices to kill him. But, if the universe were to crush him, man would still be more noble than that which killed him, because he knows that he dies and the advantage which the universe has over him; the universe knows nothing of this.

• • •

It is not from space that I must seek my dignity, but from the government of my thought. I shall have no more if I possess worlds. By space the universe encompasses and swallows me up like an atom; by thought I comprehend the world.

.   .   .

All the dignity of man consists in thought. Thought is, therefore, by its nature a wonderful and incomparable thing. It must have strange defects to be contemptible. But it has such, so that nothing is more ridiculous. How great it is in its nature! How vile it is in its defects!

.   .   .

Discourses on humility are a source of pride in the vain, and of humility in the humble. So those on scepticism[9] cause believers to affirm. Few men speak humbly of humility, chastely of chastity, few doubtingly of scepticism. We are only falsehood, duplicity, contradiction; we both conceal and disguise ourselves from ourselves.

.   .   .

We have an incapacity of proof, insurmountable by all dogmatism.[10] We have an idea of truth, invincible to all scepticism.

.   .   .

Notwithstanding the sight of all our miseries, which press upon us and take us by the throat, we have an instinct which we cannot repress and which lifts us up.

.   .   .

There is internal war in man between reason and the passions.
If he had only reason without passions . . .
If he had only passions without reason . . .
But having both, he cannot be without strife, being unable to be at peace with the one without being at war with the other. Thus he is always divided against and opposed to himself.

.   .   .

[9]Perpetual doubting.
[10]Positive, authoritative assertion of opinion.

It is dangerous to make man see too clearly his equality with beasts without showing him his greatness. It is also dangerous to make him see his greatness too clearly, apart from his vileness. It is still more dangerous to leave him in ignorance of both. But it is very advantageous to show him both. Man must not think that he is on a level either with beasts or with the angels, nor must he be ignorant of both sides of his nature; but he must know both.

*   *   *

Let man now know his value. Let him love himself, for there is in him a nature capable of good; let him not for this reason love the vileness which is in him. Let him despise himself, for this capacity is barren; but let him not therefore despise this natural capacity. Let him hate himself, let him love himself; he has within him the capacity of knowing the truth and of being happy, but he possesses no truth, either constant or satisfactory.

I would then lead man to the desire of finding truth; to be free from passions, and ready to follow it where he may find it, knowing how much his knowledge is obscured by the passions. I would, indeed, that he should hate in himself the lust which determined his will by itself so that it may not blind him in making his choice, and may not hinder him when he has chosen.

*   *   *

All these contradictions, which seem most to keep me from the knowledge of religion, have led me most quickly to the true one.

*   *   *

MORALITY AND DOCTRINE

The chief arguments of the sceptics [11]—I pass over the lesser ones—are that we have no certainty of the truth of these principles apart from faith and revelation, except insofar as we naturally perceive them in ourselves. Now this natural intuition [12] is not a convincing proof of their truth; since, having no certainty, apart from faith, whether man was created by a good God, or by a wicked

[11] Persons who habitually doubt.
[12] Knowledge without resort to reason.

demon, or by chance, it is doubtful whether these principles given to us are true, or false, or uncertain, according to our origin. Again, no person is certain, apart from faith, whether he is awake or sleeps, seeing that during sleep we believe that we are awake as firmly as we do when we *are* awake; we believe that we see space, figure, and motion; we are aware of the passage of time, we measure it; and in fact we act as if we were awake. So that half of our life being passed in sleep, we have on our own admission no idea of truth, whatever we may imagine. As all our intuitions are, then, illusions, who knows whether the other half of our life, in which we think we are awake, is not another sleep a little different from the former, from which we awake when we suppose ourselves asleep? . . .

These are the chief arguments on one side and the other.

I omit minor ones, such as the sceptical talk against the impressions of custom, education, manners, country and the like. Though these influence the majority of common folk, who dogmatize only on shallow foundations, they are upset by the least breath of the sceptics. We have only to see their books if we are not sufficiently convinced of this, and we shall very quickly become so, perhaps too much.

I notice the only strong point of the dogmatists,[13] namely, that, speaking in good faith and sincerely, we cannot doubt natural principles. Against this the sceptics set up in one word the uncertainty of our origin, which includes that of our nature. The dogmatists have been trying to answer this objection ever since the world began.

So there is open war among men, in which each must take a part and side either with dogmatism or scepticism. For he who thinks to remain neutral is above all a sceptic. This neutrality is the essence of the sect; he who is not against them is essentially for them. [In this appears their advantage.] They are not for themselves; they are neutral, indifferent, in suspense as to all things, even themselves being no exception.

What, then, shall man do in this state? Shall he doubt everything? Shall he doubt whether he is awake, whether he is being pinched, or whether he is being burned? Shall he doubt whether he doubts? Shall he doubt whether he exists? We cannot go so far as that; and I lay it down as a fact that there never has been a real complete sceptic. Nature sustains our feeble reason and prevents it raving to this extent.

---

[13] Persons who positively assert their opinions.

Shall he, then, say, on the contrary, that he certainly possesses truth—he who, when pressed ever so little, can show no title to it and is forced to let go his hold?

What a chimera,[14] then, is man! What a novelty! What a monster, what a chaos, what a contradiction, what a prodigy! Judge of all things, imbecile worm of the earth; depositary of truth, a sink of uncertainty and error; the pride and refuse of the universe!

Who will unravel this tangle? Nature confutes the sceptics, and reason confutes the dogmatists. What, then, will you become, O men! who try to find out by your natural reason what is your true condition? You cannot avoid one of these sects, nor adhere to one of them.

Know then, proud man, what a paradox you are to yourself. Humble yourself, weak reason; be silent, foolish nature; learn that man infinitely transcends man, and learn from your Master your true condition, of which you are ignorant. Hear God.

For in fact, if man had never been corrupt, he would enjoy in his innocence both truth and happiness with assurance; and if man had always been corrupt, he would have no idea of truth or bliss. But, wretched as we are, and more so than if there were no greatness in our condition, we have an idea of happiness and cannot reach it. We perceive an image of truth and possess only a lie. Incapable of absolute ignorance and of certain knowlege, we have thus been manifestly in a degree of perfection from which we have unhappily fallen.

· · ·

We desire truth, and find within ourselves only uncertainty.

We seek happiness, and find only misery and death.

We cannot but desire truth and happiness, and are incapable of certainty or happiness. This desire is left to us, partly to punish us, partly to make us perceive where from we are fallen.

· · ·

We are full of things which take us out of ourselves.

Our instinct makes us feel that we must seek our happiness outside ourselves. Our passions impel us outside, even when no objects present themselves to excite them. External objects tempt us of themselves, and call to us, even when we are not thinking of them.

---

[14] An imaginary animal.

And thus philosophers have said in vain, "Retire within yourselves, you will find your good there." [15] We do not believe them, and those who believe them are the most empty and the most foolish.

• • •

There are only two kinds of men: the righteous, who believe themselves sinners; the rest, sinners, who believe themselves righteous.

• • •

Christianity is strange. It bids man recognize that he is vile, even abominable, and bids him desire to be like God. Without such a counterpoise, this dignity would make him horribly vain, or this humiliation would make him terribly abject.

• • •

With how little pride does a Christian believe himself united to God! With how little humiliation does he place himself on a level with the worms of earth!

A glorious manner to welcome life and death, good and evil!

• • •

[15] Quotation from the ancient Stoic philosophers.

5

Jean Racine

Phaedra

Jean Racine (1639–1699), the greatest tragic dramatist of the French neoclassical theater, is also, in the opinion of many, the world's greatest dramatist since Shakespeare. In his youth Racine studied for a career in the Church, and his dramatic writing would always show the impress of a severe doctrinal training. When Racine turned to literature, he achieved quick success and became a member of the company of literary lights that adorned the court of Louis XIV. His tragedies were written in a manner that conformed admirably to the highly stylized, cultivated court life of the Sun King. However, at the height of his success, Racine retired from the theater and its easy morals to a life of quiet, domestic piety.

The tragedies written by Racine were modeled on those of the Greeks; they merge the Greek sense of fate with a Christian emphasis on original sin. In contrast to the precious and complex subtleties of the baroque manner, Racine's plays embody the classical ideals of order, symmetry, and clarity. They may be seen as expressions of Cartesian rationalism in drama, portraying in disciplined form and elevated language the universal, tragic aspects of the conflict of human passion with rational duty. Their controlled form serves to accentuate the violence of the passions portrayed. Dramatically, the characters determine the action: the protagonists are all persons of strong emotions who became the victims of their feelings.

Phaedra (1677) is based on the Hippolytus of Euripides but differs from its model in that it makes the legendary queen the heroic figure. Shunning the framework of workaday reality and physical details, the play concentrates on the timeless and the universal. Despite this abstract quality, it is rooted in

Jean Racine, *Phaedra,* trans. Robert Lowell, in *Phaedra and Figaro* (New York: Farrar, Straus and Cudahy, 1961), 11–90. Reprinted by permission.

the real truths of human feelings. Its story concerns the overwhelming passion of Phaedra for Hippolytus, her stepson. The queen is torn between her desire and her sense of sin and, after suffering remorse and horror over the consequences of this passion, is driven to a tragic doom.

Characters

THESEUS, *son of Aegeus and King of Athens*
PHAEDRA, *wife of Theseus and daughter of Minos and Pasiphae*
HIPPOLYTUS, *son of Theseus and Antiope, Queen of the Amazons*
ARICIA, *princess of the royal blood of Athens*
OENONE, *nurse of Phaedra*
THERAMENES, *tutor of Hippolytus*
ISMENE, *friend of Aricia*
PANOPE, *waiting-woman of Phaedra*
Guards

The scene is laid at Troezen, a town of the Peloponnesus in Southern Greece

PRONUNCIATION:

Theseus—Theésoos	Hippolytus—Hipoleétes
Phaedra—Pheédra	Aricia—Arísha
Oenone—Eenónee	Theramenes—Therámeneés
Ismene—Ismeénee	Panope—Pánopeé

ACT 1

SCENE I. *Hippolytus, Theramenes*

HIPPOLYTUS.   No, no, my friend, we're off! Six months have passed
   since Father heard the ocean howl and cast
   his galley on the Aegean's skull-white froth.
   Listen! The blank sea calls us—off, off, off!
   I'll follow Father to the fountainhead
   and marsh of hell. We're off. Alive or dead,
   I'll find him.
THERAMENES.   Where, my lord? I've sent a host
   of veteran seamen up and down the coast;

each village, creek and cove from here to Crete [1]
has been ransacked and questioned by my fleet;
my flagship skirted Hades' rapids, [2] furled
sail there a day, and scoured the underworld.
Have you fresh news? New hopes? One even doubts
if noble Theseus wants his whereabouts
discovered. Does he need helpers to share
the plunder of his latest love affair;
a shipload of spectators and his son
to watch him ruin his last Amazon— [3]
some creature, taller than a man, whose tanned
and single bosom slithers from his hand,
when he leaps to crush her like a waterfall
of honeysuckle?

HIPPOLYTUS.   You are cynical,
    my friend. Your insinuations wrong a king,
    sick as myself of his philandering.
    His heart is Phaedra's and no rivals dare
    to challenge Phaedra's sole possession there.
    I sail to find my father. The command
    of duty calls me from this stifling land. [4]

THERAMENES.   This stifling land? Is that how you deride
    this gentle province where you used to ride
    the bridle-paths, pursuing happiness?
    You cured your orphaned childhood's loneliness
    and found a peace here you preferred to all
    the blaze of Athens' brawling protocol.
    A rage for exploits blinds you. Your disease
    is boredom.

[1] Greek island forming the southern border of the Aegean Sea.
[2] The Greeks believed that the souls of the dead went to an underworld called Hades. Through and around Hades flowed five rivers, the best known being Styx and Acheron. The river Acheron, after cutting through northwestern Greece, flowed into the Ionian Sea; the entrance to Hades was thought to be located somewhere upriver.
[3] A member of a mythical tribe of female warriors believed to live to the east of the Greeks. Each Amazon supposedly had her right breast cut (or burnt) off, so that it would not interfere with her use of a bow. Amazons came in contact with men for only two reasons: war and procreation. Sons born to them were returned to the boys' fathers—although captured male warriors were enslaved. The Amazons kept and raised their daughters.
[4] Troezen, in Argolis, in the Peloponnesus, south of Athens and about thirty-five miles across the sea.

HIPPOLYTUS.   Friend, this kingdom lost its peace,
    when Father left my mother for defiled
    bull-serviced Pasiphae's child. The child
    of homicidal Minos is our queen![5]
THERAMENES.   Yes, Phaedra reigns and rules here. I have seen
    you crouch before her outbursts like a cur.
    When she first met you, she refused to stir
    until your father drove you out of court.
    The news is better now; our friends report
    the queen is dying. Will you cross the seas,
    desert your party and abandon Greece?
    Why flee from Phaedra? Phaedra fears the night
    less than she fears the day that strives to light
    the universal ennui of her eye—
    this dying woman, who desires to die!
HIPPOLYTUS.   No, I despise her Cretan vanity,
    hysteria and idle cruelty.
    I fear Aricia; she alone survives
    the blood-feud that destroyed her brothers' lives.[6]
THERAMENES.   Prince, Prince, forgive my laughter. Must you fly
    beyond the limits of the world and die,
    floating in flotsam, friendless, far from help,
    and clubbed to death by Tartars[7] in the kelp?
    Why arm the shrinking violet with a knife?
    Do you hate Aricia, and fear for your life,
    Prince?
HIPPOLYTUS.   If I hated her, I'd trust myself
    and stay.
THERAMENES.   Shall I explain you to yourself?
    Prince, you have ceased to be that hard-mouthed, proud
    and pure Hippolytus, who scorned the crowd
    of common lovers once and rose above

[5] The queen, Phaedra, was one of the children of Minos, king of Crete, and his wife Pasiphae. Pasiphae also was seduced by a white bull (which had been sent by Poseidon, god of the sea). She then gave birth to the Minotaur, a monster with the head of a bull and the body of a man. According to the myth, the Minotaur each year devoured seven boys and seven girls—all sent as tribute from Athens. The minotaur, who was Phaedra's half-brother, was later slain by Theseus.

[6] Aricia and her fifty brothers were cousins of Theseus. Theseus killed all fifty men when they attempted to prevent him from taking the royal throne.

[7] Violent, unruly men.

your wayward father by despising love.
Now you justify your father, and you feel
love's poison running through you, now you kneel
and breathe the heavy incense, and a god
possesses you and revels in your blood!
Are you in love?

HIPPOLYTUS.   Theramenes, when I call
and cry for help, you push me to the wall.
Why do you plague me, and try to make me fear
the qualities you taught me to revere?
I sucked in prudence with my mother's milk.
Antiope,[8] no harlot draped in silk,
first hardened me. I was my mother's son
and not my father's. When the Amazon,
my mother, was dethroned, my mind approved
her lessons more than ever. I still loved
her bristling chastity. Later, you told
stories about my father's deeds that made me hold
back judgment—how he stood for Hercules,[9]
a second Hercules who cleared the Cretan seas
of pirates, throttled Scirron, Cercyon,
Procrustes, Sinnis, and the giant man
of Epidaurus writhing in his gore.
He pierced the maze and killed the Minotaur.[10]
Other things turned my stomach: that long list
of women, all refusing to resist.
Helen,[11] caught up with all her honeyed flesh
from Sparta; Periboea,[12] young and fresh,
already tired of Salinis.[13] A hundred more,

---

[8] A princess of the Amazons whom Theseus brought to his home after waging a campaign against them. To free her, the Amazons attacked Athens; Antiope died in the struggle, fighting on the side of Theseus.

[9] A great hero and lover who had many wives and many mistresses and fathered many children.

[10] Theseus grew up at the court of his grandfather Pittheus in Troezen. While on his way to his father in Athens, he performed many famous deeds, killing brigands and strong men. In another exploit he killed the Minotaur.

[11] This very beautiful woman was the daughter of the god Zeus and Leda. When a mere child, Helen was kidnapped by Theseus and his friend Pirithous, king of the legendary Lapiths. Theseus took her from Sparta to Attica.

[12] Second wife of Telamon of Salamis and mother of the hero Ajax (or Aias).

[13] Salamis, an island about three miles west of the Athenian harbor (at Piraeus).

their names forgotten by my father—whore
and virgin, child and mother, all deceived,
if their protestations can be believed!
Ariadne [14] declaiming to the rocks,
her sister, Phaedra, kidnapped. Phaedra locks
the gate at last! You know how often I
would weary, fall to nodding and deny
the possibility of hearing the whole
ignoble, dull, insipid boast unroll.
And now I too must fall. The gods have made me creep.
How can I be in love? I have no specious heap
of honors, friend. No mastered monsters drape
my shoulders—Theseus' excuse to rape
at will. Suppose I chose a woman. Why
choose an orphan? Aricia is eternally
cut off from marriage, lest she breed
successors to her fierce brothers, and seed
the land with treason. Father only grants
her life on one condition. This—he wants
no bridal torch to burn for her. Unwooed
and childless, she must answer for the blood
her brothers shed. How can I marry her,
gaily subvert our kingdom's character,
and sail on the high seas of love?

THERAMENES.   You'll prove
nothing by reason, for you are in love.
Theseus' injustice to Aricia throws
her in the light; your eyes he wished to close
are open. She dazzles you. Her pitiful
seclusion makes her doubly terrible.
Does this innocent passion freeze your blood?
There's sweetness in it. Is your only good
the dismal famine of your chastity?
You shun your father's path? Where would you be,
Prince, if Antiope had never burned
chastely for Theseus? Love, my lord, has turned

---

[14] Another daughter of King Minos of Crete and his wife Pasiphae—and thus
Phaedra's sister. Unraveling a ball of thread, Ariadne helped Theseus escape from
the labyrinth maze of the (devouring) Minotaur. Ariadne and Theseus married
thereafter, but Theseus deserted her at the island (rocks) of Naxos.

the head of Hercules, and thousands—fired
the forge of Vulcan![15] All your uninspired,
cold moralizing is nothing, Prince. You have changed!
Now no one sees you riding, half-deranged
along the sandbars, where you drove your horse
and foaming chariot with all your force,
tilting and staggering upright through the surf—
far from their usual course across the turf.
The woods are quiet . . . How your eyes hang down!
You often murmur and forget to frown.
All's out, Prince. You're in love; you burn. Flames, flames,
Prince! A dissimulated sickness maims
the youthful quickness of your daring. Does
lovely Aricia haunt you?

HIPPOLYTUS.   Friend, spare us.
I sail to find my father.

THERAMENES.   Will you see
Phaedra before you go?

HIPPOLYTUS.   I mean to be
here when she comes. Go, tell her. I will do
my duty. Wait, I see her nurse. What new
troubles torment her?

SCENE II. *Hippolytus, Theramenes, Oenone*

OENONE.   Who has griefs like mine,
my lord? I cannot help the queen in her decline.
Although I sit beside her day and night,
she shuts her eyes and withers in my sight.
An eternal tumult roisters through her head,
panics her sleep, and drags her from her bed.
Just now she fled me at the prime
of day to see the sun for the last time.
She's coming.

HIPPOLYTUS.   So! I'll steal away. My flight
removes a hateful object from her sight.

---

[15] Roman name of the crippled god of fire and metalworkers who had his mighty
forge in Mount Aetna under the island of Sicily. He was married to beautiful Venus
(Aphrodite), but she was frequently unfaithful to him.

SCENE III. *Phaedra, Oenone*

PHAEDRA.   Dearest, we'll go no further. I must rest.
  I'll sit here. My emotions shake my breast,
  the sunlight throws black bars across my eyes.
  My knees give. If I fall, why should I rise,
  Nurse?
OENONE.   Heaven help us! Let me comfort you.
PHAEDRA.   Tear off these gross, official rings, undo
  these royal veils. They drag me to the ground.
  Why have you frilled me, laced me, crowned me, and wound
  my hair in turrets? All your skill torments
  and chokes me. I am crushed by ornaments.
  Everything hurts me, and drags me to my knees!
OENONE.   Now this, now that, Madam. You never cease
  commanding us, then cancelling your commands.
  You feel your strength return, summon all hands
  to dress you like a bride, then say you choke!
  We open all the windows, fetch a cloak,
  rush you outdoors. It's no use, you decide
  that sunlight kills you, and only want to hide.
PHAEDRA.   I feel the heavens' royal radiance cool
  and fail, as if it feared my terrible
  shame has destroyed its right to shine on men.
  I'll never look upon the sun [16] again.
OENONE.   Renunciation o'er renunciation!
  Now you slander the source of your creation.
  Why do you run to death and tear your hair?
PHAEDRA.   Oh God, take me to some sunless forest lair . . .
  There hoof-beats raise a dust-cloud, and my eye
  follows a horseman [17] outlined on the sky!
OENONE.   What's this, my lady?
PHAEDRA.   I have lost my mind.
  Where am I? Oh forget my words! I find
  I've lost the habit now of talking sense.
  My face is red and guilty—evidence

---

[16] The Greek word for sun is *helios*. Helios was the sun-god who, with Perseis, begot Pasiphae, the mother of Phaedra.
[17] Hippolytus, whose name means "the one who unhitches the horses," was on her mind.

of treason! I've betrayed my darkest fears,
Nurse, and my eyes, despite me, fill with tears.
OENONE.   Lady, if you must weep, weep for your silence
that filled your days and mine with violence.
Ah deaf to argument and numb to care,
you have no mercy. Spare me, spare
yourself. Your blood is like polluted water,
fouling a mind desiring its own slaughter.
The sun has died and shadows filled the skies
thrice now, since you have closed your eyes;
the day has broken through the night's content
thrice now, since you have tasted nourishment.
Is your salvation from your terrified
conscience this passive, servile suicide?
Lady, your madness harms the gods who gave
you life, betrays your husband. Who will save
your children? [18] Your downfall will orphan them,
deprive them of their kingdom, and condemn
their lives and future to the discipline
of one who abhors you and all your kin,
a tyrant suckled by an amazon,
Hippolytus . . .
PHAEDRA.   Oh God!
OENONE.   You still hate someone;
thank heaven for that, Madam!
PHAEDRA.   You spoke his name!
OENONE.   Hippolytus, Hippolytus! There's hope
in hatred, Lady. Give your anger rope.
I love your anger. If the winds of love
and fury stir you, you will live. Above
your children towers this foreigner, this child
of Scythian [19] cannibals, now wild
to ruin the kingdom, master Greece, and choke
the children of the gods beneath his yoke.
Why dawdle? Why deliberate at length?
Oh, gather up your dissipated strength.
PHAEDRA.   I've lived too long.

---

[18] Phaedra had two sons with Theseus, Acamas and Demophon, both of whom partic-
ipated in the Trojan War.
[19] Later on it was held that the Amazons were from Scythia, near the Black Sea.

OENONE.   Always, always agonized!
  Is your conscience still stunned and paralyzed?
  Do you think you have washed your hands in blood?
PHAEDRA.   Thank God, my hands are clean still. Would to God
  my heart were innocent!
OENONE.   Your heart, your heart!
  What have you done that tears your soul apart?
PHAEDRA.   I've said too much. Oenone, let me die;
  by dying I shall escape blasphemy.
OENONE.   Search for another hand to close your eyes.
  Oh cruel Queen, I see that you despise
  my sorrow and devotion. I'll die first,
  and end the anguish of this service cursed
  by your perversity. A thousand roads
  always lie open to the killing gods.
  I'll choose the nearest. Lady, tell me how
  Oenone's love has failed you. Will you allow
  your nurse to die, your nurse, who gave up all—
  nation, parents, children, to serve in thrall.
  I saved you from your mother, King Minos' wife! [20]
  Will your death pay me for giving up my life?
PHAEDRA.   What I could tell you, I have told you. Nurse,
  only my silence saves me from the curse
  of heaven.
OENONE.   How could you tell me anything
  worse than watching you dying?
PHAEDRA.   I would bring
  my life and rank dishonor. What can I say
  to save myself, or put off death a day.
OENONE.   Ah Lady, I implore you by my tears,
  and by your suffering body. Heaven hears,
  and knows the truth already. Let me see.
PHAEDRA.   Stand up.
OENONE.   Your hesitation's killing me!
PHAEDRA.   What can I tell you? How the gods reprove
  me!
OENONE.   Speak!

[20] Pasiphae.

PHAEDRA.   Oh Venus,[21] murdering Venus! love
   gored Pasiphae with the bull.[22]

OENONE.   Forget
   your mother! When she died, she paid her debt.

PHAEDRA.   Oh Ariadne, oh my Sister, lost
   for love of Theseus on that rocky coast.[23]

OENONE.   Lady, what nervous languor makes you rave
   against your family; they are in the grave.

PHAEDRA.   Remorseless Aphrodite drives me. I,
   my race's last and worst love-victim, die.

OENONE.   Are you in love?

PHAEDRA.   I am insane with love!

OENONE.   Who
   is he?

PHAEDRA.   I'll tell you. Nothing love can do
   could equal . . . Nurse, I am in love. The shame
   kills me. I love the . . . Do not ask his name.

OENONE.   Who?

PHAEDRA.   Nurse, you know my old loathing for the son
   of Theseus and the barbarous amazon?

OENONE.   Hippolytus! My God, oh my God!

PHAEDRA.   You,
   not I, have named him.

OENONE.   What can you do,
   but die? Your words have turned my blood to ice.
   Oh righteous heavens, must the blasphemies
   of Pasiphae fall upon her daughter?
   Her Furies[24] strike us down across the water.
   Why did we come here?

PHAEDRA.   My evil comes from farther off. In May,
   in brilliant Athens, on my marriage day,
   I turned aside for shelter from the smile
   of Theseus. Death was frowning in an aisle—
   Hippolytus! I saw his face, turned white!

---

[21] The goddess of love; the Greeks called her Aphrodite.
[22] A reference to Pasiphae's infatuation with the white bull sent by Poseidon.
[23] See footnote 14.
[24] In Greek and Roman mythology, the three avenging female spirits who pursued evildoers and sometimes inflicted madness upon them.

My lost and dazzled eyes saw only night,
capricious burnings flickered through my bleak
abandoned flesh. I could not breathe or speak.
I faced my flaming executioner,
Aphrodite, my mother's murderer!
I tried to calm her wrath by flowers and praise,
I built her a temple, fretted months and days
on decoration. I even hoped to find
symbols and stays for my distracted mind,
searching the guts of sacrificial steers.
Yet when my erring passions, mutineers
to virtue, offered incense at the shrine
of love, I failed to silence the malign
Goddess. Alas, my hungry open mouth,
thirsting with adoration, tasted drouth—
Venus resigned her altar to my new lord—
and even while I was praying, I adored
Hippolytus above the sacred flame,
now offered to his name I could not name.
I fled him, yet he stormed me in disguise,
and seemed to watch me from his father's eyes.
I even turned against myself, screwed up
my slack courage to fury, and would not stop
shrieking and raging, till half-dead with love
and the hatred of a stepmother, I drove
Hippolytus in exile from the rest
and strenuous wardship of his father's breast.
Then I could breathe, Oenone; he was gone;
my lazy, nerveless days meandered on
through dreams and daydreams, like a stately carriage
touring the level landscape of my marriage.
Yet nothing worked. My husband sent me here
to Troezen, far from Athens; once again the dear
face shattered me; I saw Hippolytus
each day, and felt my ancient, venomous
passion tear my body limb from limb;
naked Venus was clawing down her victim.
What could I do? Each moment, terrified
by loose diseased emotions, now I cried
for death to save my glory and expel

my gloomy frenzy from this world, my hell.
And yet your tears and words bewildered me,
and so endangered my tranquility,
at last I spoke. Nurse, I shall not repent,
if you will leave me the passive content
of dry silence and solitude.

SCENE IV. *Phaedra, Oenone, Panope*

PANOPE.   My heart breaks. Would to God, I could refuse
to tell your majesty my evil news.
The King is dead! Listen, the heavens ring
with shouts and lamentations for the King.
PHAEDRA.   The King is dead? What's this?
PANOPE.   In vain
you beg the gods to send him back again.
Hippolytus has heard the true report,
he is already heading for the port.
PHAEDRA.   Oh God!
PANOPE.   They've heard in Athens. Everyone
is joining factions—some salute your son,
others are calling for Hippolytus;
they want him to reform and harden us—
even Aricia claims the loyalty
of a fanatical minority.
The Prince's captains have recalled their men.
His flag is up and now he[25] sails again
for Athens. Queen, if he appear there now,
he'll drag the people with him!
OENONE.   Stop, allow
the Queen a little respite for her grief.
She hears you, and will act for our relief.

SCENE V. *Phaedra, Oenone*

OENONE.   I'd given up persuading you to live;
death was your refuge, only death could give

[25] Hippolytus.

you peace and save your troubled glory. I
myself desired to follow you, and die.
But this catastrophe prescribes new laws:
the king is dead, and for the king who was,
fate offers you his kingdom. You have a son;
he should be king! If you abandon
him, he'll be a slave. The gods, his ancestors,
will curse and drive you on your fatal course.
Live! Who'll condemn you if you love and woo
the Prince? Your stepson is no kin to you,
now that your royal husband's death has cut
and freed you from the throttling marriage-knot.
Do not torment the Prince with persecution,
and give a leader to the revolution;
no, win his friendship, bind him to your side.
Give him this city and its countryside.
He will renounce the walls of Athens, piled
stone on stone by Minerva [26] for your child.
Stand with Hippolytus, annihilate
Aricia's faction, and possess the state!
PHAEDRA.   So be it! Your superior force has won.
I will live if compassion for my son,
devotion to the Prince, and love of power
can give me courage in this fearful hour.

ACT 2

SCENE I. *Aricia, Ismene*

ARICIA.   What's this? The Prince has sent a messenger?
The Prince begs me to wait and meet him here?
The Prince begs! Goose, you've lost your feeble wits!
ISMENE.   Lady, be calm. These are the benefits
of Theseus' death: first Prince Hippolytus
comes courting favors; soon the populous
cities of Greece will follow—they will eat
out of your hand, Princess, and kiss your feet.

---

[26] Roman name for the goddess Athena, the chief deity of the Athenians.

ARICIA.   This felon's hand, this slave's! My dear, your news
    is only frivolous gossip, I refuse
    to hope.
ISMEME.   Ah Princess, the just powers of hell
    have struck. Theseus has joined your brothers!
ARICIA.   Tell
    me how he died.
ISMENE.   Princess, fearful tales
    are circulating. Sailors saw his sails,
    his infamous black sails, spin round and round
    in Charybdis'[27] whirlpool; all hands were drowned.
    Yet others say on better evidence
    that Theseus and Pirithous[28] passed the dense
    darkness of hell to rape Persephone.[29]
    Pirithous was murdered by the hound;
    Theseus, still living, was buried in the ground.
ARICIA.   This is an old wives' tale. Only the dead
    enter the underworld, and see the bed
    of Queen Persephone. What brought him there?
ISMENE.   Princess, the King is dead—dead! Everywhere
    men know and mourn. Already our worshipping
    townsmen acclaim Hippolytus for their king;
    in her great palace, Phaedra, the self-styled
    regent, rages and trembles for her child.
ARICIA.   What makes you think the puritanical
    son of Theseus is human. Will he recall
    my sentence and relent?
ISMENE.   I know he will.
ARICIA.   You know nothing about him. He would kill
    a woman, rather than be kind to one.
    That wolf-cub of a fighting amazon
    hates me above all women. He would walk
    from here to hell, rather than hear me talk.

---

[27] Charybdis, daughter of the sea god Poseidon and the earth goddess Gaea, was a
    monster associated with a dangerous whirlpool off the coast of Sicily.
[28] King of the Lapiths, a legendary people living in northern Greece. Pirithous was
    Theseus' closest friend.
[29] According to the legend, Theseus and Pirithous attempted to abduct Persephone,
    the queen of Hades. Both were caught; Pirithous perished, but Theseus later es-
    caped.

ISMENE.   Do you know Hippolytus? Listen to me.
  His famous, blasphemous frigidity,
  what is it, when you've seen him close at hand?
  I've watched him like a hawk, and seen him stand
  shaking beside you—all his reputation
  for hating womenkind bears no relation
  to what I saw. He couldn't take his eyes
  off you! His eyes speak what his tongue denies.
ARICIA.   I can't believe you. Your story's absurd!
  How greedily I listen to each word!
  Ismene, you know me, you know how my heart
  was reared on death, and always set apart
  from what it cherished—can this plaything of
  the gods and furies feel the peace of love?
  What sights I've seen, Ismene! "Heads will roll,"
  my brothers told me, "we will rule." I, the sole
  survivor of those fabulous kings, who tilled
  the soil of Greece, have seen my brothers killed,
  six brothers murdered! In a single hour,
  the tyrant, Theseus, lopped them in their flower.
  The monster spared my life, and yet decreed
  the torments of this childless life I lead
  in exile, where no Greek can look at me;
  my forced, perpetual virginity
  preserves his crown; no son shall bear my name
  or blow my brothers' ashes into flame.
  Ismene, you know how well his tyranny
  favors my temperament and strengthens me
  to guard the honor of my reputation;
  his rigor fortified my inclination.
  How could I test his son's civilities?
  I'd never even seen him with my eyes!
  I'd never seen him. I'd restrained my eye,
  that giddy nerve, from dwelling thoughtlessly
  upon his outward grace and beauty—on mere
  embellishments of nature, a veneer
  the Prince himself despises and ignores.
  My heart loves nobler virtues, and adores
  in him his father's hard intelligence.
  He has his father's daring and a sense

of honor his father lacks. Let me confess,
I love him for his lofty haughtiness
never submitted to a woman's yoke.
How could Phaedra's splendid marriage provoke
my jealousy? Have I so little pride,
I'd snatch at a rake's heart, a heart denied
to none—all riddled, opened up to let
thousands pass in like water through a net?
To carry sorrows to a heart, alone
untouched by passion, inflexible as stone,
to fasten my dominion on a force
as nervous as a never-harnessed horse—
this stirs me, this enflames me. Devilish Zeus[30]
is easier mastered than Hippolytus;
heaven's love-infatuated emperor
confers less glory on his conqueror!
Ismene, I'm afraid. Why should I boast?
His very virtues I admire most
threaten to rise and throw me from the brink
of hope. What girlish folly made me think
Hippolytus could love Aricia?

ISMENE.   Here
he is. He loves you, Princess. Have no fear.

SCENE II. *Aricia, Ismene, Hippolytus*

HIPPOLYTUS.   Princess, before
I leave here, I must tell you what's in store
for you in Greece. Alas, my father's dead.
The fierce forebodings that disquieted
my peace are true. Death, only death, could hide
his valor from this world he pacified.
The homicidal Fates[31] will not release
the comrade, friend and peer of Hercules.
Princess, I trust your hate will not resent
honors whose justice is self-evident.

---

[30] The chief Greek god. Besides being married a number of times, Zeus was always ready for an extramarital adventure. His queen, Hera, was always enraged when she discovered one of her husband's clandestine romances.
[31] Three goddesses (Atropos, Clotho, and Lachesis) who determine human destiny.

A single hope alleviates my grief,
Princess, I hope to offer you relief.
I now revoke a law whose cruelty
has pained my conscience. Princess, you are free
to marry. Oh enjoy this province, whose
honest, unhesitating subjects choose
Hippolytus for king. Live free as air,
here, free as I am, much more free!

ARICIA.   I dare
   not hope. You are too gracious. Can you free
   Aricia from your father's stern decree?

HIPPOLYTUS.   Princess, the Athenian people, torn in two
   between myself and Phaedra's son, want you.

ARICIA.   Want me, my Lord!

HIPPOLYTUS.   I've no illusions. Lame
   Athenian precedents condemn my claim,
   because my mother was a foreigner.
   But what is that? If my only rival were
   my younger brother, his minority
   would clear my legal disability.
   However, a better claim than his or mine
   now favors you, ennobled by the line
   of great Erectheus.[32] Your direct descent
   sets you before my father; he was only lent
   this kingdom by adoption. Once the common
   Athenian, dazed by Theseus' superhuman
   energies, had no longing to exhume
   the rights that rushed your brothers to their doom.
   Now Athens calls you home; the ancient feud
   too long has stained the sacred olive wood;
   blood festers in the furrows of our soil
   to blight its fruits and scorch the farmer's toil.
   This province suits me; let the vines of Crete
   offer my brother a secure retreat.
   The rest is yours. All Attica[33] is yours;
   I go to win you what your right assures.

---

[32] One of the legendary kings of Athens, an ancestor of Aricia.
[33] The territory of the ancient Greek city-state of Athens.

ARICIA.   Am I awake, my lord? Your sayings seem
    like weird phantasmagoria [34] in a dream.
    How can your sparkling promises be true?
    Some god, my lord, some god, has entered you!
    How justly you are worshiped in this town;
    oh how the truth surpasses your renown!
    You wish to endow me with your heritage!
    I only hoped you would not hate me. This rage
    your father felt, how can you put it by
    and treat me kindly?
HIPPOLYTUS.   Princess, is my eye
    blind to beauty? Am I a bear, a bull, a boar,
    some abortion fathered by the Minotaur?
    Some one-eyed Cyclops,[35] able to resist
    Aricia's loveliness and still exist?
    How can a man stand up against your grace?
ARICIA.   My lord, my lord!
HIPPOLYTUS.   I cannot hide my face,
    Princess! I'm driven. Why does my violence
    so silence reason and intelligence?
    Must I be still, and let my adoration
    simmer away in silent resignation?
    Princess, I've lost all power to restrain
    myself. You see a madman, whose insane
    pride hated love, and hoped to sit ashore,
    watching the galleys founder in the war;
    I was Diana's [36] liegeman,[37] dressed in steel.
    I hoped to trample love beneath my heel—
    alas, the flaming Venus burns me down,
    I am the last dependent on her crown.
    What left me charred and writhing in her clutch?
    A single moment and a single touch.
    Six months now, bounding like a wounded stag,
    I've tried to shake this poisoned dart, and drag

[34] A series of fantastic images.
[35] One of the legendary giants with only one eye, in the middle of the forehead; they supposedly lived on the island of Sicily.
[36] Diana (to the Greeks, Artemis) was the twin sister of Apollo, and among her duties was the protection of hunting.
[37] A loyal follower (of Diana); a hunter, or warrior.

myself to safety from your eyes that blind
when present, and when absent leave behind
volleys of burning arrows in my mind.
Ah Princess, shall I dive into the sea,
or steal the wings of Icarus [38] to flee
love's Midas' [39] touch that turns my world to gold?
Your image drives me stumbling through the cold,
floods my deserted forest caves with light,
darkens the day and dazzles through my night.
I'm grafted to your side by all I see;
all things unite us and imprison me.
I have no courage for the Spartan [40] exercise
that trained my hand and steeled my energies.
Where are my horses? I forget their names.
My triumphs with my chariot at the games
no longer give me strength to mount a horse.
The ocean drives me shuddering from its shores.
Does such a savage conquest make you blush?
My boorish gestures, headlong cries that rush
at you like formless monsters from the sea?
Ah, Princess, hear me! Your serenity
must pardon the distortions of a weak
and new-born lover, forced by you to speak
love's foreign language, words that snarl and yelp . . .
I never could have spoken without your help.

SCENE III. *Aricia, Ismene, Hippolytus, Theramenes*

THERAMENES.   I announce the Queen. She comes hurriedly,
    looking for you.
HIPPOLYTUS.   For me!
THERAMENES.   Don't ask me why;
    she insisted. I promised I'd prevail
    on you to speak with her before you sail.

---

[38] Wings (of feathers and wax) fashioned by the great inventor Daedalus for his son Icarus.

[39] Midas was king of Phrygia in Asia Minor, to whom the gods granted his wish that everything he touched would turn to gold. When he touched his daughters, they, too, turned to gold.

[40] Refers to the citizens of Sparta, a city-state located in the southern part of the Peloponnesus. They were noted for physical toughness and courage.

HIPPOLYTUS.   What can she want to hear? What can I say?
ARICIA.   Wait for her, here! You cannot turn away.
Forget her malice. Hating her will serve
no purpose. Wait for her! Her tears deserve
your pity.
HIPPOLYTUS.   You're going, Princess? And I must go
to Athens, far from you. How shall I know
if you accept my love.
ARICIA.   My lord, pursue
your gracious promise. Do what you must do,
make Athens tributary to my rule.
Nothing you offer is unacceptable;
yet this empire, so great, so glorious,
is the least precious of your gifts to us.

SCENE IV. *Hippolytus, Theramenes*

HIPPOLYTUS.   We're ready. Wait, the Queen's here. I need you.
You must interrupt this tedious interview.
Hurry down to the ship, then rush back, pale
and breathless. Say the wind's up and we must sail.

SCENE V. *Hippolytus, Oenone, Phaedra*

PHAEDRA.   He's here! Why does he scowl and look away
from me? What shall I do? What shall I say?
OENONE.   Speak for your son, he has no other patron.
PHAEDRA.   Why are you so impatient to be gone
from us, my lord? Stay! we will weep together.
Pity my son; he too has lost his father.
My own death's near. Rebellion, sick with wrongs,
now like a sea-beast, lifts its slimey prongs,
its muck, its jelly. You alone now stand
to save the state. Who else can understand
a mother? I forget. You will not hear
me! An enemy deserves no pity. I fear
your anger. Must my son, your brother, Prince,
be punished for his cruel mother's sins?
HIPPOLYTUS.   I've no such thoughts.

PHAEDRA.   I persecuted you
    blindly, and now you have good reason to
    return my impudence. How could you find
    the motivation of this heart and mind
    that scourged and tortured you, till you began
    to lose the calm composure of a man,
    and dwindle to a harsh and sullen boy,
    a thing of ice, unable to enjoy
    the charms of any civilized resource
    except the heavy friendship of your horse,
    that whirled you far from women, court and throne,
    to course the savage woods for wolves alone?
    You have good reason, yet if pain's a measure,
    no one has less deserved your stern displeasure.
    My lord, no one has more deserved compassion.
HIPPOLYTUS.   Lady, I understand a mother's passion,
    a mother jealous for her children's rights.
    How can she spare a first wife's son? Long nights
    of plotting, devious ways of quarrelling—
    a madhouse! What else can remarriage bring?
    Another would have shown equal hostility,
    pushed her advantage more outrageously.
PHAEDRA.   My lord, if you had known how far my love
    and yearning have exalted me above
    this usual weakness . . . Our afflicting kinship
    is ending . . .
HIPPOLYTUS.   Madam, the precious minutes slip
    by, I fatigue you. Fight against your fears.
    Perhaps Poseidon has listened to our tears,
    perhaps your husband's still alive. He hears
    us, he is surging home—only a short
    day's cruise conceals him, as he scuds for port.
PHAEDRA.   That's folly, my lord. Who has twice visited
    black Hades and the river of the dead
    and returned? No, the poisonous Acheron
    never lets go. Theseus drifts on and on,
    a gutted galley on that clotted waste—
    he woos, he wins Persephone, the chaste . . .
    What am I saying? Theseus is not dead.

He lives in you. He speaks, he's taller by a head,
I see him, touch him, and my heart—a reef . . .
Ah Prince, I wander. Love betrays my grief . . .
HIPPOLYTUS.   No, no, my father lives. Lady, the blind
   furies release him; in your loyal mind,
   love's fullness holds him, and he cannot die.
PHAEDRA.   I hunger for Theseus. Always in my eye
   he wanders, not as he appeared in hell,
   lascivious eulogist of any belle
   he found there, from the lowest to the Queen;[41]
   no, faithful, airy, just a little mean
   through virtue, charming all, yet young and new,
   as we would paint a god—as I now see you!
   Your valiant shyness would have graced his speech,
   he would have had your stature, eyes, and reach,
   Prince, when he flashed across our Cretan waters,
   the loved enslaver of King Minos' daughters.
   Where were you? How could he conscript the flower
   of Athens' youth against my father's power,
   and ignore you? You were too young, they say;
   you should have voyaged as a stowaway.
   No dawdling bypath would have saved our bull,
   when your just vengeance thundered through its skull.
   There, light of foot, and certain of your goal,
   you would have struck my brother's monstrous soul,
   and pierced our maze's slow meanders, led
   by Ariadne and her subtle thread.
   By Ariadne? Prince, I would have fought
   for precedence; my every flaming thought,
   love-quickened, would have shot you through the dark,
   straight as an arrow to your quaking mark.
   Could I have waited, panting, perishing,
   entrusting your survival to a string,
   like Ariadne, when she skulked behind,
   there at the portal, to bemuse her mind
   among the solemn cloisters of the porch?
   No, Phaedra would have snatched your burning torch,

---

[41] Persephone.

and lunged before you, reeling like a priest
of Dionysus[42] to distract the beast.
I would have reached the final corridor
a lap before you, and killed the Minotaur!
Lost in the labyrinth, and at your side,
would it have mattered, if I lived or died?

HIPPOLYTUS.   What are you saying, Madam? You forget
my father is your husband!

PHAEDRA.   I have let
you see my grief for Theseus! How could I
forget my honor and my majesty,
Prince?

HIPPOLYTUS.   Madam, forgive me! My foolish youth
conjectured hideous untruths from your truth.
I cannot face my insolence. Farewell . . .

PHAEDRA.   You monster! You understood me too well!
Why do you hang there, speechless, petrified,
polite! My mind whirls. What have I to hide?
Phaedra in all her madness stands before you.
I love you! Fool, I love you, I adore you!
Do not imagine that my mind approved
my first defection, Prince, or that I loved
your youth light-heartedly, and fed my treason
with cowardly compliance, till I lost my reason.
I wished to hate you, but the gods corrupt
us; though I never suffered their abrupt
seductions, shattering advances, I
too bear their sensual lightnings in my thigh.
I too am dying. I have felt the heat
that drove my mother through the fields of Crete,
the bride of Minos, dying for the full
magnetic April thunders of the bull.
I struggled with my sickness, but I found
no grace or magic to preserve my sound
intelligence and honor from this lust,
plowing my body with its horny thrust.
At first I fled you, and when this fell short
of safety, Prince, I exiled you from court.

---

[42] The god of wine and re-birth. His priestesses often indulged in mad dances and revels.

Alas, my violence to resist you made
my face inhuman, hateful. I was afraid
to kiss my husband lest I love his son.
I made you fear me (this was easily done);
you loathed me more, I ached for you no less.
Misfortune magnified your loveliness.
I grew so wrung and wasted, men mistook
me for the Sibyl.[43] If you could bear to look
your eyes would tell you. Do you believe my passion
is voluntary? That my obscene confession
is some dark trick, some oily artifice?
I came to beg you not to sacrifice
my son, already uncertain of his life.
Ridiculous, mad embassy, for a wife
who loves her stepson! Prince, I only spoke
about myself! Avenge yourself, invoke
your father; a worse monster threatens you
than any Theseus ever fought and slew.
The wife of Theseus loves Hippolytus!
See, Prince! Look, this monster, ravenous
for her execution will not flinch.
I want your sword's spasmodic final inch.

OENONE.   Madam, put down this weapon. Your distress
attracts the people. Fly these witnesses.
Hurry! Stop kneeling! What a time to pray!

SCENE VI. *Theramenes, Hippolytus*

THERAMENES.   Is this Phaedra, fleeing, or rather dragged away
sobbing? Where is your sword? Who tore
this empty scabbard from your belt?

HIPPOLYTUS.   No more!
Oh let me get away! I face disaster.
Horrors unnerve me. Help! I cannot master
my terror. Phaedra . . . No, I won't expose
her. No! Something I do not dare disclose . . .

---

[43] A prophetess who lived in a cave at Cumae, near Naples. Apollo had granted her a life of one thousand years, but not lasting youth (since she had forgotten to ask for it).

THERAMENES.   Our ship is ready, but before you leave,
  listen! Prince, what we never would believe
  has happened: Athens has voted for your brother.
  The citizens have made him king. His mother
  is regent.
HIPPOLYTUS.   Phaedra is in power!
THERAMENES.   An envoy sent from Athens came this hour
  to place the scepter in her hands. Her son
  is king.
HIPPOLYTUS.   Almighty gods, you know this woman!
  Is it her spotless virtue you reward?
THERAMENES.   I've heard a rumor. Someone swam aboard
  a ship off Epirus. He claims the King
  is still alive. I've searched. I know the thing
  is nonsense.
HIPPOLYTUS.   Search! Nothing must be neglected.
  If the king's dead, I'll rouse the disaffected
  people, crown Aricia, and place our lands,
  our people, and our lives in worthy hands.

ACT 3

SCENE I. *Phaedra, Oenone*

PHAEDRA.   Why do my people rush to crown me queen?
  Who can even want to see me? They have seen
  my downfall. Will their praise deliver me?
  Oh bury me at the bottom of the sea!
  Nurse, I have said too much! Led on by you,
  I've said what no one should have listened to.
  He listened. How could he pretend my drift
  was hidden? Something held him, and made him shift
  his ground . . . He only wanted to depart
  and hide, while I was pouring out my heart.
  Oh how his blushing multiplied my shame!
  Why did you hold me back! You are to blame,
  Oenone. But for you, I would have killed
  myself. Would he have stood there, iron-willed
  and merciless, while I fell upon his sword?

He would have snatched it, held me, and restored
my life. No! No!

OENONE.   Control yourself! No peace
comes from surrendering to your disease,
Madam. Oh daughter of the kings of Crete,
why are you weeping and fawning at the feet
of this barbarian, less afraid of fate
than of a woman? You must rule the state.

PHAEDRA.   Can I, who have no courage to restrain
the insurrection of my passions, reign?
Will the Athenians trust their sovereignty
to me? Love's despotism is crushing me,
I am ruined.

OENONE.   Fly!

PHAEDRA.   How can I leave him?

OENONE.   Lady, you have already banished him.
Can't you take flight?

PHAEDRA.   The time for flight has passed.
He knows me now. I rushed beyond the last
limits of modesty, when I confessed.
Hope was no longer blasting through my breast;
I was resigned to hopelessness and death,
and gasping out my last innocent breath,
Oenone, when you forced me back to life.
You thought I was no longer Theseus' wife,
and let me feel that I was free to love.

OENONE.   I would have done anything to remove
your danger. Whether I'm guilty or innocent
is all the same to me. Your punishment
should fall on one who tried to kill you, not
on poor Oenone. Lady, you must plot
and sacrifice this monster, whose unjust
abhorrence left you dying in the dust.
Oh humble him, undo him, oh despise
him! Lady, you must see him with my eyes.

PHAEDRA.   Oenone, he was nourished in the woods;
he is all shyness and ungracious moods
because the forests left him half-inhuman.
He's never heard love spoken by a woman!
We've gone too far. Oenone, we're unwise;

perhaps the young man's silence was surprise.
OENONE.   His mother, the amazon, was never moved
by men.
PHAEDRA.   The boy exists. She must have loved!
OENONE.   He has a sullen hatred for our sex.
PHAEDRA.   Oh, all the better; rivals will not vex
my chances. Your advice is out of season;
now you must serve my frenzy, not my reason!
You tell me love has never touched his heart;
we'll look, we'll find an undefended part.
He's turned his bronze prows seaward; look, the wind
already blows like a trumpeter behind
his bulging canvas! The Acropolis [44]
of Athens and its empire shall be his!
Hurry, Oenone, hunt the young man down,
blind him with dazzling visions of the crown.
Go tell him I relinquish my command,
I only want the guidance of his hand.
Let him assume these powers that weary me,
he will instruct my son in sovereignty.
Perhaps he will adopt my son, and be
the son and mother's one divinity!
Oenone, rush to him, use every means
to bend and win him; if he fears the Queen's
too proud, he'll listen to her slave. Plead, groan,
insist, say I am giving him my throne . . .
No, say I'm dying!

SCENE II. *Phaedra*

PHAEDRA.   Implacable Aphrodite, now you see
the depths to which your tireless cruelty
has driven Phaedra—here is my bosom;
every thrust and arrow has struck home!
Oh Goddess, if you hunger for renown,
rise now, and shoot a worthier victim down!

---

[44] The "high city," or hill, on which the Athenians built their defenses and sacred temples.

Conquer the barbarous Hippolytus,
who mocks the graces and the power of Venus,
and gazes on your godhead with disgust.
Avenge me, Venus! See, my cause is just,
my cause is yours. Oh bend him to my will! . . .
You're back, Oenone? Does he hate me still?

SCENE III. *Phaedra, Oenone*

OENONE.   Your love is folly, dash it from your soul,
gather your scattered pride and self-control,
Madam! I've seen the royal ship arrive.
Theseus is back, Theseus is still alive!
Thousands of voices thunder from the docks.
People are waving flags and climbing rocks.
While I was looking for Hippolytus . . .
PHAEDRA.   My husband's living! Must you trouble us
by talking? What am I living for?
He lives, Oenone, let me hear no more
about it.
OENONE.   Why?
PHAEDRA.   I told you, but my fears
were stilled, alas, and smothered by your tears.
Had I died this morning, I might have faced
the gods. I heeded you and die disgraced!
OENONE.   You are disgraced!
PHAEDRA.   Oh Gods of wrath,
how far I've travelled on my dangerous path!
I go to meet my husband; at his side
will stand Hippolytus. How shall I hide
my thick adulterous passion for this youth,
who has rejected me, and knows the truth?
Will the stern Prince stand smiling and approve
the labored histrionics of my love
for Theseus, see my lips, still languishing
for his, betray his father and his King?
Will he not draw his sword and strike me dead?
Suppose he spares me? What if nothing's said?

Am I a gorgon,[45] or Circe,[46] or the infidel
Medea,[47] stifled by the flames of hell,
yet rising like Aphrodite from the sea,[48]
refreshed and radiant with indecency?
Can I kiss Theseus with dissembled poise?
I think each stone and pillar has a voice.
The very dust rises to disabuse
my husband—to defame me and accuse!
Oenone, I want to die. Death will give
me freedom; oh it's nothing not to live;
death to the unhappy's no catastrophe!
I fear the name that must live after me,
and crush my son until the end of time.
Is his inheritance his mother's crime,
his right to curse me, when my pollution stains
the blood of heaven bubbling in his veins?
The day will come, alas, the day will come,
when nothing will be left to save him from
the voices of despair. If he should live
he'll flee his subjects like a fugitive.

OENONE.   He has my pity. Who has ever built
firmer foundations to expose her guilt?
But why expose your son? Is your contribution
for his defense to serve the prosecution?
Suppose you kill yourself? The world will say
you fled your outraged husband in dismay.
Could there be stronger evidence and proof
than Phaedra crushed beneath the horse's hoof
of blasphemous self-destruction to convince
the crowds who'll dance attendance on the Prince?
The crowds will mob your children when they hear
their defamation by a foreigner!
Wouldn't you rather see earth bury us?

[45] One of three sisters who were so ugly that anyone who looked at them turned to stone.

[46] Circe, the sister of Phaedra's mother Pasiphae, was a cruel and evil enchantress who turned Odysseus' companions into swine.

[47] A sorceress who helped the hero Jason and his companions to steal the Golden Fleece. When Jason left her, she vengefully killed the two children she had borne to him.

[48] The newborn Aphrodite emerged from the foam of the sea.

Tell me, do you still love Hippolytus?

PHAEDRA.   I see him as a beast, who'd murder us.

OENONE.   Madam, let the positions be reversed!
You fear the Prince; you must accuse him first.
Who'll dare assert your story is untrue,
if all the evidence shall speak for you:
your present grief, your past despair of mind,
the Prince's sword so luckily left behind?
Do you think Theseus will oppose his son's
second exile? He has consented once!

PHAEDRA.   How dare I take this murderous, plunging course?

OENONE.   I tremble, Lady, I too feel remorse.
If death could rescue you from infamy,
Madam, I too would follow you and die.
Help me by being silent. I will speak
in such a way the King will only seek
a bloodless exile to assert his rights.
A father is still a father when he smites,
You shudder at this evil sacrifice,
but nothing's evil or too high a price
to save your menaced honor from defeat.
Ah Minos, Minos, you defended Crete
by killing young men? Help us! If the cost
for saving Phaedra is a holocaust
of virtue, Minos, you must sanctify
our undertaking, or watch your daughter die.
I see the King.

PHAEDRA.   I see Hippolytus!

SCENE IV. *Phaedra, Theseus, Hippolytus, Oenone*

THESEUS.   Fate's heard me, Phaedra, and removed the bar
that kept me from your arms.

PHAEDRA.   Theseus, stop where you are!
Your raptures and endearments are profane.
Your arm must never comfort me again.
You have been wronged, the gods who spared your life
have used your absence to disgrace your wife,
unworthy now to please you or come near.
My only refuge is to disappear.

SCENE V. *Theseus, Hippolytus*

THESEUS.   What a strange welcome! This bewilders me.
   My son, what's happened?
HIPPOLYTUS.   Phaedra holds the key.
   Ask Phaedra. If you love me, let me leave
   this kingdom. I'm determined to achieve
   some action that will show my strength. I fear
   Phaedra. I am afraid of living here.
THESEUS.   My son, you want to leave me?
HIPPOLYTUS.   I never sought
   her grace or favor. Your decision brought
   her here from Athens. Your desires prevailed
   against my judgment, Father, when you sailed
   leaving Phaedra and Aricia in my care.
   I've done my duty, now I must prepare
   for sterner actions, I must test my skill
   on monsters far more dangerous to kill
   than any wolf or eagle in this wood.
   Release me, I too must prove my manhood.
   Oh Father, you were hardly half my age,
   when herds of giants writhed before your rage—
   you were already famous as the scourge
   of insolence. Our people saw you purge
   the pirates from the shores of Greece and Thrace,
   the harmless merchantman was free to race
   the winds, and weary Hercules could pause
   from slaughter, knowing you upheld his cause.
   The world revered you. I am still unknown;
   even my mother's deeds surpass my own.
   Some tyrants have escaped you; let me meet
   with them and throw their bodies at your feet.
   I'll drag them from their wolf-holes; if I die,
   my death will show I struggled worthily.
   Oh, Father, raise me from oblivion;
   my deeds shall tell the universe I am your son.
THESEUS.   What do I see? Oh gods, what horror drives
   my queen and children fleeing for their lives
   before me? If so little warmth remains,
   oh why did you release me from my chains?

Why am I hated, and so little loved?
I had a friend, just one.[49] His folly moved
me till I aided his conspiracy
to ravish Queen Persephone.
The gods, tormented by our blasphemous
designs, befogged our minds and blinded us—
we invaded Epirus instead of hell.
There a diseased and subtle tyrant fell
upon us as we slept, and while I stood
by, helpless, monsters crazed for human blood
consumed Pirithous. I myself was chained
fast in a death-deep dungeon. I remained
six months there, then the gods had pity,
and put me in possession of the city.
I killed the tyrant; now his body feasts
the famished, pampered bellies of his beasts.
At last, I voyaged home, cast anchor, furled
my sails. When I was rushing to my world—
what am I saying? When my heart and soul
were mine again, unable to control
themselves for longing—who receives me? All run
and shun me, as if I were a skeleton.
Now I myself begin to feel the fear
I inspire. I wish I were a prisoner
again or dead. Speak! Phaedra says my home
was outraged. Who betrayed me? Someone come
and tell me. I have fought for Greece. Will Greece,
sustained by Theseus, give my enemies
asylum in my household? Tell me why
I've no avenger? Is my son a spy?
You will not answer. I must know my fate.
Suspicion chokes me, while I hesitate
and stand here pleading. Wait, let no one stir.
Phaedra shall tell me what has troubled her.

SCENE VI. *Hippolytus*

HIPPOLYTUS.   What now? His anger turns my blood to ice.
    Will Phaedra, always uncertain, sacrifice

[49] Pirithous.

herself? What will she tell the King? How hot
the air's becoming here! I feel the rot
of love seeping like poison through this house.
I feel the pollution. I cannot rouse
my former loyalties. When I try to gather
the necessary strength to face my father,
my mind spins with some dark presentiment . . .
How can such terror touch the innocent?
I LOVE ARICIA! Father, I confess
my treason to you is my happiness!
I LOVE ARICIA! Will this bring you joy,
our love you have no power to destroy?

ACT 4

SCENE I. *Theseus, Oenone*

THESEUS.   What's this, you tell me he dishonors me,
and has assaulted Phaedra's chastity?
Oh heavy fortune, I no longer know
who loves me, who I am, or where I go.
Who has ever seen such disloyalty
after such love? Such sly audacity!
His youth made no impression on her soul,
so he fell back on force to reach his goal!
I recognize this perjured sword; I gave
him this myself to teach him to be brave!
Oh Zeus, are blood-ties no impediment?
Phaedra tried to save him from punishment!
Why did her silence spare this parricide?
OENONE.   She hoped to spare a trusting father's pride.
She felt so sickened by your son's attempt,
his hot eyes leering at her with contempt,
she had no wish to live. She read out her will
to me, then lifted up her arm to kill
herself. I struck the sword out of her hand.
Fainting, she babbled the secret she had planned
to bury with her in the grave. My ears
unwillingly interpreted her tears.

THESEUS.   Oh traitor! I know why he seemed to blanch
      and toss with terror like an aspen branch
      when Phaedra saw him. Now I know why he stood
      back, then embraced me so coldly he froze my blood.
      Was Athens the first stage for his obscene
      attentions? Did he dare attack the Queen
      before our marriage?
OENONE.   Remember her disgust
      and hate then? She already feared his lust.
THESEUS.   And when I sailed, this started up again?
OENONE.   I've hidden nothing. Do you want your pain
      redoubled? Phaedra calls me. Let me go,
      and save her. I have told you what I know.

SCENE II. *Theseus, Hippolytus*

THESEUS.   My son returns! Oh God, reserved and cool,
      dressed in a casual freedom that could fool
      the sharpest. Is it right his brows should blaze
      and dazzle me with virtue's sacred rays?
      Are there not signs? Should not ADULTERER
      in looping scarlet script be branded there?
HIPPOLYTUS.   What cares becloud your kingly countenance,
      Father! What is this irritated glance?
      Tell me! Are you afraid to trust your son?
THESEUS.   How dare you stand here? May the great Zeus stone
      me, if I let my fondness and your birth
      protect you! Is my strength which rid the earth
      of brigands paralyzed? Am I so sick
      and senile, any coward with a stick
      can strike me? Am I a schoolboy's target? Oh God,
      am I food for vultures? Some carrion [50] you must prod
      and poke to see if it's alive or dead?
      Your hands are moist and itching for my bed,
      Coward! Wasn't begetting you enough
      dishonor to destroy me? Must I snuff
      your perjured life, my own son's life, and stain
      a thousand glories? Let the gods restrain

[50] Decaying flesh.

my fury! Fly! Live hated and alone—
there are places where my name may be unknown.
Go, find them, follow your disastrous star
through filth; if I discover where you are,
I'll add another body to the hill
of vermin I've extinguished by my skill.
Fly from me, let the grieving storm-winds bear
your contagion from me. You corrupt the air.
I call upon Poseidon. Help me, Lord
of Ocean, help your servant! Once my sword
heaped crucified assassins on your shore
and let them burn like beacons. God, you swore
my first request would be fulfilled. My first!
I never made it. Even through the worst
torments of Epirus I held my peace;
no threat or torture brought me to my knees
beseeching favors; even then I knew
some greater project was reserved for you!
Poseidon, now I kneel. Avenge me, dash
my incestuous son against your rocks, and wash
his dishonor from my household; wave on wave
of roaring nothingness shall be his grave.

HIPPOLYTUS.   Phaedra accuses me of lawless love!
Phaedra! My heart stops, I can hardly move
my lips and answer. I have no defense,
if you condemn me without evidence.

THESEUS.   Oh coward, you were counting on the Queen
to hide your brutal insolence and screen
your outrage with her weakness! You forgot
something. You dropped your sword and spoiled your plot.
You should have kept it. Surely you had time
to kill the only witness to your crime!

HIPPOLYTUS.   Why do I stand this, and forbear to clear
away these lies, and let the truth appear?
I could so easily. Where would you be,
if I spoke out? Respect my loyalty,
Father, respect your own intelligence.
Examine me. What am I? My defense
is my whole life. When have I wavered, when

have I pursued the vices of young men?
Father, you have no scaffolding to rig
your charges on. Small crimes precede the big.
Phaedra accused me of attempting rape!
Am I some Proteus,[51] who can change his shape?
Nature despises such disparities.
Vice, like virtue, advances by degrees.
Bred by Antiope to manly arms,
I hate the fever of this lust that warms
the loins and rots the spirit. I was taught
uprightness by Theramenes. I fought
with wolves, tamed horses, gave my soul to sport,
and shunned the joys of women and the court.
I dislike praise, but those who know me best
grant me one virtue—it's that I detest
the very crimes of which I am accused.
How often you yourself have been amused
and puzzled by my love of purity,
pushed to the point of crudeness. By the sea
and in the forests, I have filled my heart
with freedom, far from women.

THESEUS.   When this part
was dropped, could only Phaedra violate
the cold abyss of your immaculate
reptilian soul. How could this funeral urn
contain a heart, a living heart, or burn
for any woman but my wife?

HIPPOLYTUS.   Ah no!
Father, I too have seen my passions blow
into a tempest. Why should I conceal
my true offense? I feel, Father, I feel
what other young men feel. I love, I love
Aricia. Father, I love the sister of
your worst enemies. I worship her!
I only feel and breathe and live for her!

THESEUS.   You love Aricia? God! No, this is meant
to blind my eyes and throw me off the scent.

[51] A sea divinity; Poseidon had given him the power to change his own shape at will.

HIPPOLYTUS.   Father, for six months I have done my worst
    to kill this passion. You shall be the first
    to know . . . You frown still. Nothing can remove
    your dark obsession. Father, what will prove
    my innocence? I swear by earth and sky,
    and nature's solemn, shining majesty. . . .

THESEUS.   Oaths and religion are the common cant
    of all betrayers. If you wish to taunt
    me, find a better prop than blasphemy.

HIPPOLYTUS.   All's blasphemy to eyes that cannot see.
    Could even Phaedra bear me such ill will?

THESEUS.   Phaedra, Phaedra! Name her again, I'll kill
    you! My hand's already on my sword.

HIPPOLYTUS.   Explain
    my terms of exile. What do you ordain?

THESEUS.   Sail out across the ocean. Everywhere
    on earth and under heaven is too near.

HIPPOLYTUS.   Who'll take me in? Oh who will pity me,
    and give me bread, if you abandon me?

THESEUS.   You'll find fitting companions. Look for friends
    who honor everything that most offends.
    Pimps and jackals who praise adultery
    and incest will protect your purity!

HIPPOLYTUS.   Adultery! Is it your privilege
    to fling this word in my teeth? I've reached the edge
    of madness . . . No, I'll say no more. Compare
    my breeding with Phaedra's. Think and beware . . .
    She had a mother . . . No, I must not speak.

THESEUS.   You devil, you'll attack the queen still weak
    from your assault. How can you stand and face
    your father? Must I drive you from this place
    with my own hand. Run off, or I will flog
    you with the flat of my sword like a dog!

SCENE III.   *Theseus*

THESEUS.   You go to your inevitable fate,
    Child—by the river immortals venerate.[52]

---

[52] The river Styx, which supposedly flowed around Hades. It had great meaning even
    for the gods; they swore their most sacred oaths by the river.

Poseidon gave his word. You cannot fly:
death and the gods march on invisibly.
I loved you once; despite your perfidy,
my bowels writhe inside me. Must you die?
Yes; I am in too deep now to draw back.
What son has placed his father on such a rack?
What father groans for such a monstrous birth?
Oh gods, your thunder throws me to the earth.

SCENE IV. *Theseus, Phaedra*

PHAEDRA.   Theseus, I heard the deluge of your voice,
and stand here trembling. If there's time for choice,
hold back your hand, still bloodless; spare your race!
I supplicate you, I kneel here for grace.
Oh, Theseus, Theseus, will you drench the earth
with your own blood? His virtue, youth and birth
cry out for him. Is he already slain
by you for me—spare me this incestuous pain!
THESEUS.   Phaedra, my son's blood has not touched my hand;
and yet I'll be avenged. On sea and land,
spirits, the swift of foot, shall track him down.
Poseidon owes me this.[53] Why do you frown?
PHAEDRA.   Poseidon owes you this? What have you done
in anger?
THESEUS.   What! You wish to help my son?
No, stir my anger, back me to the hilt,
call for blacker colors to paint his guilt.
Lash, strike and drive me on! You cannot guess
the nerve and fury of his wickedness.
Phaedra, he slandered your sincerity,
he told me your accusation was a lie.
He swore he loved Aricia, he wants to wed
Aricia. . . .
PHAEDRA.   What, my lord!
THESEUS.   That's what he said.
Of course, I scorn his shallow artifice.

---

[53] Theseus had called down on Hippolytus one of the three curses Poseidon had
granted him.

Help me, Poseidon, hear me, sacrifice
my son. I seek the altar. Come! Let us both
kneel down and beg the gods to keep their oath.

SCENE V. *Phaedra*

PHAEDRA.   My husband's gone, still rumbling his own name
and fame. He has no inkling of the flame
his words have started. If he hadn't spoken,
I might have . . . I was on my feet, I'd broken
loose from Oenone, and had just begun
to say I know not what to save his son.
Who knows how far I would have gone? Remorse,
longing and anguish shook me with such force,
I might have told the truth and suffered death,
before this revelation stopped my breath:
Hippolytus is not insensible,
only insensible to me! His dull
heart chases shadows. He is glad to rest
upon Aricia's adolescent breast!
Oh thin abstraction! When I saw his firm
repugnance spurn my passion like a worm,
I thought he had some magic to withstand
the lure of any woman in the land,
and now I see a schoolgirl leads the boy,
as simply as her puppy or a toy.
Was I about to perish for this sham,
this panting hypocrite? Perhaps I am
the only woman that he could refuse!

SCENE VI. *Phaedra, Oenone*

PHAEDRA.   Oenone, dearest, have you heard the news?
OENONE.   No, I know nothing, but I am afraid.
How can I follow you? You have betrayed
your life and children. What have you revealed,
Madam?
PHAEDRA.   I have a rival in the field,
Oenone.

OENONE.　　What?

PHAEDRA.　　　　Oenone, he's in love—
　　this howling monster, able to disprove
　　my beauty, mock my passion, scorn each prayer,
　　and face me like a tiger in its lair—
　　he's tamed, the beast is harnessed to a cart;
　　Aricia's found an entrance to his heart.

OENONE.　　　　　　　　　　Aricia?

PHAEDRA.　　Nurse, my last calamity
　　has come. This is the bottom of the sea.
　　All that preceded this had little force—
　　the flames of lust, the horrors of remorse,
　　the prim refusal by my grim young master,
　　were only feeble hints of this disaster.
　　They love each other! Passion blinded me.
　　I let them blind me, let them meet and see
　　each other freely! Was such bounty wrong?
　　Oenone, you have known this all along,
　　you must have seen their meetings, watched them sneak
　　off to their forest, playing hide-and-seek!
　　Alas, such rendezvous are no offense:
　　innocent nature smiles of innocence,
　　for them each natural impulse was allowed,
　　each day was summer and without a cloud.
　　Oenone, nature hated me. I fled
　　its light, as if a price were on my head.
　　I shut my eyes and hungered for my end.
　　Death was the only God my vows could bend.
　　And even while my desolation served
　　me gall and tears, I knew I was observed;
　　I never had security or leisure
　　for honest weeping, but must steal this pleasure.
　　Oh hideous pomp; a monarch only wears
　　the robes of majesty to hide her tears!

OENONE.　　How can their folly help them? They will never
　　enjoy its fruit.

PHAEDRA.　　　　Ugh, they will love forever—
　　even while I am talking, they embrace,
　　they scorn me, they are laughing in my face!
　　In the teeth of exile, I hear them swear

they will be true forever, everywhere.
Oenone, have pity on my jealous rage;
I'll kill this happiness that jeers at age.
I'll summon Theseus; hate shall answer hate!
I'll drive my husband to annihilate
Aricia—let no trivial punishment,
her instant death, or bloodless banishment . . .
What am I saying? Have I lost my mind?
I am jealous, and call my husband! Bind
me, gag me; I am frothing with desire.
My husband is alive, and I'm on fire!
For whom? Hippolytus. When I have said
his name, blood fills my eyes, my heart stops dead.
Imposture, incest, murder! I have passed
the limits of damnation; now at last,
my lover's lifeblood is my single good.
Nothing else cools my murderous thirst for blood.
Yet I live on! I live, looked down upon
by my progenitor, the sacred sun,
by Zeus, by Europa,[54] by the universe
of gods and stars, my ancestors. They curse
their daughter. Let me die. In the great night
of Hades, I'll find shelter from their sight.
What am I saying? I've no place to turn:
Minos, my father, holds the judge's urn.[55]
The gods have placed damnation in his hands,
the shades[56] in Hades follow his commands.
Will he not shake and curse his fatal star
that brings his daughter trembling to his bar?
His child by Pasiphae forced to tell
a thousand sins unclassified in hell?
Father, when you interpret what I speak,
I fear your fortitude will be too weak

[54] A lovely princess whom the philanderer Zeus approached in the guise of a white
bull. Riding on his back, she was taken to Crete, where she bore him three sons,
Minos, Rhadamantus, and Sarpedon.
[55] Upon their deaths the brothers Minos and Rhadamantus were appointed judges in
Hades. The lots in Minos' urn determined the part of Hades a soul would be sent to
for punishment.
[56] Souls of the dead.

to hold the urn. I see you fumbling for
new punishments for crimes unknown before.
You'll be your own child's executioner!
You cannot kill me; look, my murderer
is Venus, who destroyed our family;
Father, she has already murdered me.
I killed myself—and what is worse I wasted
my life for pleasures I have never tasted.
My lover flees me still, and my last gasp
is for the fleeting flesh I failed to clasp.

OENONE.   Madam, Madam, cast off this groundless terror!
Is love now an unprecedented error?
You love! What then? You love! Accept your fate.
You're not the first to sail into this strait.
Will chaos overturn the earth and Jove,[57]
because a mortal woman is in love?
Such accidents are easy, all too common.
A woman must submit to being woman.
You curse a failure in the source of things.
Venus has feasted on the hearts of kings;
even the gods, man's judges, feel desire,
Zeus learned to live with his adulterous fire.

PHAEDRA.   Must I still listen and drink your poisoned breath?
My death's redoubled on the edge of death.
I'd fled Hippolytus and I was free
till your entreaties stabbed and blinded me,
and dragged me howling to the pit of lust.
Oenone, I was learning to be just.
You fed my malice. Attacking the young Prince
was not enough; you clothed him with my sins.
You wished to kill him; he is dying now,
because of you, and Theseus' brutal vow.
You watch my torture; I'm the last ungorged
scrap rotting in this trap your plots have forged.
What binds you to me? Leave me, go, and die,
may your punishment be to terrify
all those who ruin princes by their lies,
hints, acquiescence, filth, and blasphemies—

---

[57] Jove and Jupiter are Roman names for Zeus.

panders who grease the grooves of inclination,
and lure our willing bodies from salvation.
Go die, go frighten false flatterers, the worst
friends the gods can give to kings they've cursed!
OENONE.   I have given all and left all for her service,
almighty gods! I have been paid my price!

ACT 5

SCENE I. *Hippolytus, Aricia*

ARICIA.   Take a stand, speak the truth, if you respect
your father's glory and your life. Protect
yourself! I'm nothing to you. You consent
without a struggle to your banishment.
If you are weary of Aricia, go;
at least do something to prevent the blow
that dooms your honor and existence—both
at a stroke! Your father must recall his oath;
there is time still, but if the truth's concealed,
you offer your accuser a free field.
Speak to your father!
HIPPOLYTUS.   I've already said
what's lawful. Shall I point to his soiled bed,
tell Athens how his marriage was foresworn,
make Theseus curse the day that he was born?
My aching heart recoils. I only want
God and Aricia for my confidants.
See how I love you; love makes me confide
in you this horror I have tried to hide
from my own heart. My faith must not be broken;
forget, if possible, what I have spoken.
Ah Princess, if even a whisper slips
past you, it will perjure your pure lips.
God's justice is committed to the cause
of those who love him, and uphold his laws;
sooner or later, heaven itself will rise
in wrath and punish Phaedra's blasphemies.
I must not. If I rip away her mask,

I'll kill my father. Give me what I ask.
Do this! Then throw away your chains; it's right
for you to follow me, and share my flight.
Fly from this prison; here the vices seethe
and simmer, virtue has no air to breathe.
In the confusion of my exile, none
will even notice that Aricia's gone.
Banished and broken, Princess, I am still
a force in Greece. Your guards obey my will,
powerful intercessors wish us well:
our neighbors, Argos [58] citadel
is armed, and in Mycenae [59] our allies
will shelter us, if lying Phaedra tries
to hurry us from our paternal throne,
and steal our sacred titles for her son.
The gods are ours, they urge us to attack.
Why do you tremble, falter and hold back?
Your interests drive me to this sacrifice.
While I'm on fire, your blood has changed to ice.
Princess, is exile more than you can face?

ARICIA.   Exile with you, my lord? What sweeter place
is under heaven? Standing at your side,
I'd let the universe and heaven slide.
You're my one love, my king, but can I hope
for peace and honor, Prince, if I elope
unmarried? This . . . I wasn't questioning
the decency of flying from the King.
Is he my father? Only an abject
spirit honors tyrants with respect.
You say you love me. Prince, I am afraid.

HIPPOLYTUS.   Aricia, you shall never be betrayed;
accept me! Let our love be sanctified,
then flee from your oppressor as my bride.
Bear witness, oh you gods, our love released
by danger, needs no temple or a priest.
It's faith, not ceremonial, that saves.
Here at the city gates, among these graves

---

[58] The principal city of Argolis, in the northeastern part of the Peloponnesus.
[59] The town and citadel located on a hill at the edge of the valley of Argos.

the resting places of my ancient line,
there stands a sacred temple and a shrine.
Here, where no mortal ever swore in vain,
here in these shadows, where eternal pain
is ready to engulf the perjurer;
here heaven's scepter quivers to confer
its final sanction; here, my Love, we'll kneel,
and pray the gods to consecrate and seal
our love. Zeus, the father of the world will stand
here as your father and bestow your hand.
Only the pure shall be our witnesses:
Hera, the guarantor of marriages,
Demeter[60] and the virgin Artemis.[61]

ARICIA.   The King is coming. Fly. I'll stay and meet
his anger here and cover your retreat.
Hurry. Be off, send me some friend to guide
my timid footsteps, husband, to your side.

SCENE II. *Theseus, Ismene, Aricia*

THESEUS.   Oh God, illuminate my troubled mind.
Show me the answer I have failed to find.

ARICIA.   Go, Ismene, be ready to escape.

SCENE III. *Theseus, Aricia*

THESEUS.   Princess, you are disturbed. You twist your cape
and blush. The Prince was talking to you. Why
is he running?

ARICIA.   We've said our last goodbye,
my lord.

THESEUS.   I see the beauty of your eyes
moves even my son, and you have gained a prize
no woman hoped for.

ARICIA.   He hasn't taken on
your hatred for me, though he is your son.

---

[60] The goddess of fertility and human fruitfulness.
[61] Artemis (or Diana) was also the protector of unmarried girls and chastity.

THESEUS.   I follow. I can hear the oaths he swore.
  He knelt, he wept. He has done this before
  and worse. You are deceived.

ARICIA.   Deceived, my lord?

THESEUS.   Princess, are you so rich? Can you afford
  to hunger for this lover that my queen
  rejected? Your betrayer loves my wife.

ARICIA.   How can you bear to blacken his pure life?
  Is kingship only for the blind and strong,
  unable to distinguish right from wrong?
  What insolent prerogative obscures
  a light that shines in every eye but yours?
  You have betrayed him to his enemies.
  What more, my lord? Repent your blasphemies.
  Are you not fearful lest the gods so loathe
  and hate you they will gratify your oath?
  Fear God, my lord, fear God. How many times
  he grants men's wishes to expose their crimes.

THESEUS.   Love blinds you, Princess, and beclouds your reason.
  Your outburst cannot cover up his treason.
  My trust's in witnesses that cannot lie.
  I have seen Phaedra's tears. She tried to die.

ARICIA.   Take care, your Highness. While your killing hand
  drove all the thieves and reptiles from the land,
  you missed one monster, one was left alive,
  one . . . No, I must not name her, Sire, or strive
  to save your helpless son; he wants to spare
  your reputation. Let me go. I dare
  not stay here. If I stayed I'd be too weak
  to keep my promise. I'd be forced to speak.

SCENE IV. *Theseus*

THESEUS.   What was she saying? I must try to reach
  the meaning of her interrupted speech.
  Is it a pitfall? A conspiracy?
  Are they plotting together to torture me?
  Why did I let the rash, wild girl depart?
  What is this whisper crying in my heart?

A secret pity fills my soul with pain.
I must question Oenone once again.
My guards, summon Oenone to the throne.
Quick, bring her. I must talk with her alone.

SCENE V. *Theseus, Panope*

PANOPE.   The Queen's deranged, your Highness. Some accursed
madness is driving her; some fury stalks
behind her back, possesses her, and talks
its evil through her, and blasphemes the world.
She cursed Oenone. Now Oenone's hurled
herself into the ocean, Sire, and drowned.
Why did she do it. No reason can be found.
THESEUS.   Oenone's drowned?
PANOPE.   Her death has brought no peace.
The cries of Phaedra's troubled soul increase.
Now driven by some sinister unrest,
she snatches up her children to her breast,
pets them and weeps, till something makes her scoff
at her affection, and she drives them off.
Her glance is drunken and irregular,
she looks through us and wonders who we are;
thrice she has started letters to you, Sire,
thrice tossed the shredded fragments in the fire.
Oh call her to you. Help her!
THESEUS.   The nurse is drowned? Phaedra wishes to die?
Oh gods! Summon my son. Let him defend
himself, tell him I'm ready to attend.
I want him!
Exit Panope
                  Neptune,[62] hear me, spare my son!
My vengeance was too hastily begun.
Oh why was I so eager to believe
Oenone's accusation? The gods deceive
the victims they are ready to destroy!

---

[62] The Roman name for Poseidon, god of the sea.

SCENE VI. *Theseus, Theramenes*

THESEUS.   Here is Theramenes. Where is my boy,
    my first-born? He was yours to guard and keep.
    Where is he? Answer me. What's this? You weep?
THERAMENES.   Oh, tardy, futile grief, his blood is shed.
    My lord, your son, Hippolytus, is dead.
THESEUS.   Oh gods, have mercy!
THERAMENES.   I saw him die. The most
    lovely and innocent of men is lost.
THESEUS.   He's dead? The gods have hurried him away
    and killed him? . . . just as I began to pray . . .
    What sudden thunderbolt has struck him down?
THERAMENES.   We'd started out, and hardly left the town.
    He held the reins; a few feet to his rear,
    a single, silent guard held up a spear.
    He followed the Mycenae highroad, deep
    in thought, reins dangling, as if half asleep;
    his famous horses, only he could hold,
    trudged on with lowered heads, and sometimes rolled
    their dull eyes slowly—they seemed to have caught
    their master's melancholy, and aped his thought.
    Then all at once winds struck us like a fist,
    we heard a sudden roaring through the mist;
    from underground a voice in agony
    answered the prolonged groaning of the sea.
    We shook, the horses' manes rose on their heads,
    and now against a sky of blacks and reds,
    we saw the flat waves hump into a mountain
    of green-white water rising like a fountain,
    as it reached land and crashed with a last roar
    to shatter like a galley on the shore.
    Out of its fragments rose a monster, half
    dragon, half bull;[63] a mouth that seemed to laugh
    drooled venom on its dirty yellow scales
    and python belly, forking to three tails.
    The shore was shaken like a tuning fork,

[63] This monstrous creature sent from the sea by Poseidon caused Hippolytus' horses to shy and drag their master to his death.

ships bounced on the stung sea like bits of cork,
the earth moved, and the sun spun round and round,
a sulphur-colored venom swept the ground.
We fled; each felt his useless courage falter,
and sought asylum at a nearby altar.
Only the Prince remained; he wheeled about,
and hurled a javelin through the monster's snout.
Each kept advancing. Flung from the Prince's arm,
dart after dart struck where the blood was warm.
The monster in its death-throes felt defeat,
and bounded howling to the horses' feet.
There its stretched gullet and its armor broke,
and drenched the chariot with blood and smoke,
and then the horses, terror-struck, stampeded.
Their master's whip and shouting went unheeded,
they dragged his breathless body to the spray.
Their red mouths bit the bloody surf, men say
Poseidon stood beside them, that the god
was stabbing at their bellies with a goad.
Their terror drove them crashing on a cliff,
the chariot crashed in two, they ran as if
the Furies screamed and crackled in their manes, their fallen hero
    tangled in the reins,
jounced on the rocks behind them. The sweet light
of heaven never will expunge this sight:
the horses that Hippolytus had tamed,
now dragged him headlong, and their mad hooves maimed
his face past recognition. When he tried
to call them, calling only terrified;
faster and ever faster moved their feet,
his body was a piece of bloody meat.
The cliffs and ocean trembled to our shout,
at last their panic failed, they turned about,
and stopped not far from where those hallowed graves,
the Prince's fathers, overlook the waves.
I ran on breathless, guards were at my back,
my master's blood had left a generous track.
The stones were red, each thistle in the mud
was stuck with bits of hair and skin and blood.
I came upon him, called; he stretched his right

hand to me, blinked his eyes, then closed them tight.
"I die," he whispered, "it's the gods' desire.
Friend, stand between Aricia and my sire—
some day enlightened, softened, disabused,
he will lament his son, falsely accused;
then when at last he wishes to appease
my soul, he'll treat my lover well, release
and honor Aricia. . . ." On this word, he died.
Only a broken body testified
he'd lived and loved once. On the sand now lies
something his father will not recognize.

THESEUS.   My son, my son! Alas, I stand alone
before the gods. I never can atone.

THERAMENES.   Meanwhile Aricia, rushing down the path,
approached us. She was fleeing from your wrath,
my lord, and wished to make Hippolytus
her husband in God's eyes. Then nearing us,
she saw the signs of struggle in the waste,
she saw (oh what a sight) her love defaced,
her young love lying lifeless on the sand.
At first she hardly seemed to understand;
while staring at the body in the grass,
she kept on asking where her lover was.
At last the black and fearful truth broke through
her desolation! She seemed to curse the blue
and murdering ocean, as she caught his head
up in her lap; then fainting lay half dead,
until Ismene somehow summoned back her breath,
restored the child to life—or rather death.
I come, great King, to urge my final task,
your dying son's last outcry was to ask
mercy for poor Aricia, for his bride.
Now Phaedra comes. She killed him. She has lied.

SCENE VII. *Theseus, Phaedra, Panope*

THESEUS.   Ah Phaedra, you have won. He's dead. A man
was killed. Were you watching? His horses ran
him down, and tore his body limb from limb.

Poseidon struck him, Theseus murdered him.
I served you! Tell me why Oenone died?
Was it to save you? Is her suicide
A proof of your truth? No, since he's dead, I must
accept your evidence, just or unjust.
I must believe my faith has been abused;
you have accused him; he shall stand accused.
He's friendless even in the world below.
There the shades fear him! Am I forced to know
the truth? Truth cannot bring my son to life.
If fathers murder, shall I kill my wife
too? Leave me, Phaedra. Far from you, exiled
from Greece, I will lament my murdered child.
I am a murdered gladiator, whirled
in black circles. I want to leave the world;
my whole life rises to increase my guilt—
all those dazzled, dazzling eyes, my glory built
on killing killers. Less known, less magnified,
I might escape, and find a place to hide.
Stand back, Poseidon. I know the gods are hard
to please. I pleased you. This is my reward:
I killed my son. I killed him! Only a god
spares enemies, and wants his servants' blood!

PHAEDRA.   No, Theseus, I must disobey your prayer.
Listen to me. I'm dying. I declare
Hippolytus was innocent.

THESEUS.   Ah Phaedra, on your evidence, I sent
him to his death. Do you ask me to forgive
my son's assassin? Can I let you live?

PHAEDRA.   My time's too short, your highness. It was I,
who lusted for your son with my hot eye.
The flames of Aphrodite maddened me;
I loathed myself, and yearned outrageously
like a starved wolf to fall upon the sheep.
I wished to hold him to me in my sleep
and dreamt I had him. Then Oenone's tears,
troubled my mind; she played upon my fears,
until her pleading forced me to declare
I loved your son. He scorned me. In despair,
I plotted with my nurse, and our conspiracy

made you believe your son assaulted me.
Oenone's punished; fleeing from my wrath,
she drowned herself, and found a too easy path
to death and hell. Perhaps you wonder why
I still survive her, and refuse to die?
Theseus, I stand before you to absolve
your noble son. Sire, only this resolve
upheld me, and made me throw down my knife.
I've chosen a slower way to end my life—
Medea's poison,[64] chills already dart
along my boiling veins and squeeze my heart.
A cold composure I have never known
gives me a moment's poise. I stand alone
and seem to see my outraged husband fade
and waver into death's dissolving shade.
My eyes at last give up their light, and see
the day they've soiled resume its purity.

PANOPE.   She's dead, my lord.

THESEUS.   Would God, all memory
of her and me had died with her! Now I
must live. This knowledge that has come too late
must give me strength and help me expiate
my sacrilegious vow. Let's go, I'll pay
my son the honors he has earned today.
His father's tears shall mingle with his blood.
My love that did my son so little good
asks mercy from his spirit. I declare
Aricia is my daughter and my heir.

---

[64] The sorceress Medea put poison in a robe that she sent as a gift to a rival princess; the princess, wearing the robe, perished in agony.

6

John Locke

An Essay Concerning Human Understanding

John Locke (1632–1704), the great English philosopher, was also a student of science, a practicing physician, and one of the founders of the Royal Society, the oldest scientific organization in Great Britain. As a philosopher, he carried on the empirical tradition that was so important for the development of scientific method. Through his writings he did for human nature what his contemporary Newton did for the cosmos, and thereby became the official philosopher of his age. He was, however, no "closet thinker." Living through the English revolutions of the seventeenth century, Locke had strong political preferences and acted on them. He opposed royal absolutism and supported the Whigs in their bid for parliamentary supremacy; for these activities, he suffered exile and the loss of his fortune. Philosophically, Locke was an empiricist, although he was not thoroughly consistent in his views. He said he was driven to study the process of knowing because of the fruitlessness of metaphysical discussions of absolute truth and reality. For Locke, there were no absolute principles of knowledge. All knowledge was partial and tentative, formed progressively by the use of what was given in sense perception. By his common-sense arguments, Locke freed the psychological process of knowing from the doctrine of "innate" ideas and brought it down to earth. He thus discredited abstract rationalism, which hampered scientific investigation, and disallowed original sin and heredity as the chief sources of human behavior. This environmental psychology gave society an instrument with which to refashion the world; for, if people are the products of their

John Locke, *An Essay Concerning Human Understanding,* in The *Philosophical Works of John Locke,* ed. J. A. St. John (London: George Bell and Sons, 1892), I, 134–37, 142–47, 205–08, 210–11, 221–27, 279–80. Adapted.

environment, then by changing the environment society could remake humankind—a basic article of faith of the Enlightenment.

In An Essay Concerning Human Understanding *(1690), Locke explores introspectively the operations of the mind and tells us what knowledge is, how it is acquired, and how valid it is. He denies the existence of innate logical or moral principles, picturing the mind at birth as a blank tablet* (tabula rasa) *on which experience and reasoning write the script. His theory, which may seem commonplace and incomplete today, was quite revolutionary in its time.*

NO INNATE PRINCIPLES IN THE MIND

The way shown how we come by any Knowledge, sufficient to prove it not innate.—It is an established opinion among some men, that there are in the understanding certain innate[1] principles; some primary notions,[2] characters, as it were stamped upon the mind of man; which the soul receives in its very first being, and brings into the world with it. It would be sufficient to convince unprejudiced readers of the falseness of this supposition, if I should only show (as I hope I shall in the following parts of this discourse) how men, barely by the use of their natural faculties, may attain to all the knowledge they have, without the help of any innate impressions; and may arrive at certainty, without any such original notions or principles. For I imagine any one will easily grant that it would be impertinent to suppose the ideas of colors innate in a creature to whom God has given sight, and a power to receive them by the eyes from external objects: and no less unreasonable would it be to attribute several truths to the impressions of nature, and innate characters, when we may observe in ourselves faculties fit to attain as easy and certain knowledge of them, as if they were originally imprinted on the mind.

But because a man is not permitted without censure to follow his own thoughts in the search of truth, when they lead him ever so little out of the common road, I shall set down the reasons that made me doubt of the truth of that opinion, as an excuse for my mistake,

[1] Inborn; not acquired.
[2] Ideas unsupported by evidence or reason.

if I be in one; which I leave to be considered by those who, with me, dispose themselves to embrace truth wherever they find it.

General Assent the great Argument.—There is nothing more commonly taken for granted than that there are certain principles, both speculative and practical (for they speak of both), universally agreed upon by all mankind, which therefore, they argue, must needs be constant impressions, which the souls of men receive in their first beings, and which they bring into the world with them, as necessarily and really as they do any of their inherent faculties.

Universal Consent proves nothing innate.—This argument, drawn from universal consent, has this misfortune in it, that if it were true in matter of fact, that there were certain truths wherein all mankind agreed, it would not prove them innate, if there can be any other way shown how men may come to that universal agreement, in the things they do consent in, which I presume may be done.

"What is, is," and "it is impossible for the same Thing to be and not to be," not universally assented to.—But, which is worse, this argument of universal consent, which is made use of to prove innate principles, seems to me a demonstration that there are none such; because there are none to which all mankind give an universal assent. I shall begin with the speculative, and instance in those magnified principles of demonstration, "whatsoever is, is," and "it is impossible for the same thing to be and not to be"; which, of all others, I think have the most allowed title to innate. These have so settled a reputation of maxims[3] universally received, that it will no doubt be thought strange if any one should seem to question it. But yet I take liberty to say, that these propositions are so far from having an universal assent, that there are a great part of mankind to whom they are not so much as known.

Not on the Mind naturally imprinted, because not known to Children, Idiots, and so forth.—For, first, it is evident that all children and idiots have not the least apprehension or thought of them. And the want of that is enough to destroy that universal assent which must be the necessary concomitant[4] of all innate truths: it seems to me near a contradiction to say that there are truths imprinted on the soul, which it perceives or understands not: imprinting, if it signify anything, being nothing else but the making certain truths to be perceived. For to imprint anything on the mind without the mind's

[3] Statements generally accepted as true.
[4] Accompanying condition.

perceiving it, seems to me hardly intelligible. If therefore children and idiots have souls, have minds, with those impressions upon them, they must unavoidably perceive them, and necessarily know and assent to these truths; which since they do not, it is evident that there are no such impressions. For if they are not notions naturally imprinted, how can they be innate? And if they are notions imprinted, how can they be unknown? To say a notion is imprinted on the mind, and yet at the same time to say that the mind is ignorant of it, and never yet took notice of it, is to make this impression nothing. No proposition can be said to be in the mind which it never yet knew, which it was never yet conscious of. . . .

The Steps by which the Mind attains several Truths.—The senses at first let in particular ideas, and furnish the yet empty cabinet, and the mind by degrees growing familiar with some of them, they are lodged in the memory, and names got to them. Afterwards, the mind proceeding further, abstracts them, and by degrees learns the use of general names. In this manner the mind comes to be furnished with ideas and language, the materials about which to exercise its discursive faculty. And the use of reason becomes daily more visible, as these materials that give it employment increase. But though the having of general ideas and the use of general words and reason usually grow together, yet I see not how this any way proves them innate. The knowledge of some truths, I confess, is very early in the mind; but in a way that shows them not to be innate. For, if we will observe, we shall find it still to be about ideas, not innate, but acquired; it being about those first which are imprinted by external things, with which infants have earliest to do, which make the most frequent impressions on their senses. In ideas thus got, the mind discovers that some agree and others differ, probably as soon as it has any use of memory; as soon as it is able to retain and perceive distinct ideas. But whether it be then or no, this is certain, it does so long before it has the use of words; or comes to that which we commonly call "the use of reason." For a child knows as certainly before it can speak the difference between the ideas of sweet and bitter (that is, that sweet is not bitter), as it knows afterwards (when it comes to speak) that wormwood and sugarplums are not the same thing.

Assent to supposed innate truths depends on having clear and distinct ideas of what their terms mean, and not on their innateness.—A child knows not that three and four are equal to seven, till he comes to be able to count seven, and has got the name and idea of equality; and then, upon explaining those words, he presently assents to, or rather perceives the truth of that proposition. But neither does he then readily assent because it is an innate truth, nor was his assent wanting till then because he wanted the use of reason; but the truth of it appears to him as soon as he has settled in his mind the clear and distinct ideas that these names stand for. And then he knows the truth of that proposition upon the same grounds and by the same means that he knew before that a rod and a cherry are not the same thing; and upon the same grounds also that he may come to know afterwards "that it is impossible for the same thing to be and not to be," as shall be more fully shown hereafter. So that the later it is before any one comes to have those general ideas about which those maxims are; or to know the signification of those general terms that stand for them; or to put together in his mind the ideas they stand for; the later also will it be before he comes to assent to those maxims;—whose terms, with the ideas they stand for, being no more innate than those of a cat or a weasel, he must stay till time and observation have acquainted him with them; and then he will be in a capacity to know the truth of these maxims, upon the first occasion that shall make him put together those ideas in his mind, and observe whether they agree or disagree, according as is expressed in those propositions.[5] And therefore it is that a man knows that eighteen and nineteen are equal to thirty-seven, by the same self-evidence that he knows one and two to be equal to three: yet a child knows this not so soon as the other; not for want of the use of reason, but because the ideas the words eighteen, nineteen, and thirty-seven stand for, are not so soon got as those which are signified by one, two, and three.

Assenting as soon as proposed and understood, proves them not innate.— This evasion therefore of general assent when men come to the use of reason, failing as it does, and leaving no difference between those supposed innate and other truths that are afterwards acquired and learned, men have endeavored to secure an universal assent to those they call maxims, by saying they are generally assented to as soon as proposed, and the terms they are proposed in understood: seeing all men, even children, as soon as they hear and understand the terms, assent to these propositions, they think it is sufficient to prove them innate. For, since men never fail after they have once understood the words, to acknowledge them for undoubted truths, they would infer

---

[5] Statements that are either true or false.

that certainly these propositions were first lodged in the understanding, which, without any teaching, the mind, at the very first proposal immediately closes with and assents to, and after that never doubts again.

If such an Assent be a Mark of Innate, then "that one and two are equal to three, that Sweetness is not Bitterness," and a thousand the like, must be innate.—In answer to this, I demand whether ready assent given to a proposition, upon first hearing and understanding the terms, be a certain mark of an innate principle? If it be not, such a general assent is in vain urged as a proof of them: if it be said that it is a mark of innate, they must then allow all such propositions to be innate which are generally assented to as soon as heard, whereby they will find themselves plentifully stored with innate principles. For upon the same ground, that is, of assent at first hearing and understanding the terms, that men would have those maxims pass for innate, they must also admit several propositions about numbers to be innate; and thus, that one and two are equal to three, that two and two are equal to four, and a multitude of other the like propositions in numbers, that everybody assents to at first hearing and understanding the terms, must have a place among these innate axioms.[6] Nor is this the prerogative of numbers alone, and propositions made about several of them; but even natural philosophy, and all the other sciences, afford propositions which are sure to meet with assent as soon as they are understood. That "two bodies cannot be in the same place" is a truth that nobody any more sticks at than at these maxims, that "it is impossible for the same thing to be and not to be," that "white is not black," that "a square is not a circle," that "bitterness is not sweetness." These and a million of such other propositions, as many at least as we have distinct ideas of, every man in his wits, at first hearing, and knowing what the names stand for, must necessarily assent to. If these men will be true to their own rule, and have assent at first hearing and understanding the terms to be a mark of innate, they must allow not only as many innate propositions as men have distinct ideas, but as many as men can make propositions wherein different ideas are denied one of another. Since every proposition wherein one different idea is denied of another, will as certainly find assent at first hearing and understanding the terms as this general one, "it is impossible for the same thing to be and not to be," or that

---

[6] Established principles universally recognized as true.

which is the foundation of it, and is the easier understood of the two, "the same is not different"; by which account they will have legions of innate propositions of this one sort, without mentioning any other. But, since no proposition can be innate unless the ideas about which it is be innate, this will be to suppose all our ideas of color, sounds, tastes, figure, and so forth, innate, than which there cannot be anything more opposite to reason and experience. Universal and ready assent upon hearing and understanding the terms is, I grant, a mark of self-evidence; but self-evidence, depending not on innate impressions, but on something else (as we shall show hereafter), belongs to several propositions which nobody was yet so extravagant as to pretend to be innate.

• • •

OF IDEAS IN GENERAL AND THEIR ORIGIN

Idea is the Object of Thinking.—Every man being conscious to himself that he thinks, and that which his mind is applied about while thinking being the ideas that are there, it is past doubt that men have in their minds several ideas,—such as are those expressed by the words whiteness, hardness, sweetness, thinking, motion, man, elephant, army, drunkenness, and others. It is in the first place then to be inquired, how he comes by them? I know it is a received doctrine that men have native ideas, and original characters, stamped upon their minds in their very first being. This opinion I have at large examined already; and, I suppose what I have [already] said . . . will be much more easily admitted, when I have shown where the understanding may get all the ideas it has; and by what ways and degrees they may come into the mind;—for which I shall appeal to every one's own observation and experience.

All Ideas come from Sensation or Reflection.—Let us then suppose the mind to be, as we say, white paper, void of all characters, without any ideas.—How comes it to be furnished? From where comes that vast store which the busy and boundless fancy of man has painted on it with an almost endless variety? From where has it all the materials of reason and knowledge? To this I answer, in one word, from experience. In that all our knowledge is founded; and from that it ultimately derives itself. Our observation employed either, about external sensible objects, or about the internal operations of our minds perceived and reflected on by ourselves, is that which supplies our understandings with all the materials of thinking. These two are the fountains of knowledge, from where all the ideas we have, or can naturally have, do spring.

The Objects of Sensation one Source of Ideas.—First, our senses, conversant about particular sensible objects, do convey into the mind several distinct perceptions of things, according to those various ways wherein those objects do affect them. And thus we come by those ideas we have of yellow, white, heat, cold, soft, hard, bitter, sweet, and all those which we call sensible qualities; which when I say the senses convey into the mind, I mean, they from external objects convey into the mind what produces there those perceptions. This great source of most of the ideas we have, depending wholly upon our senses, and derived by them to the understanding, I call sensation.

The Operations of our Minds, the other Source of them.—Secondly, the other fountain from which experience furnishes the understanding with ideas is, the perception of the operations of our own mind within us, as it is employed about the ideas it has got; which operations, when the soul comes to reflect on and consider, do furnish the understanding with another set of ideas, which could not be had from things without. And such are perception, thinking, doubting, believing, reasoning, knowing, willing, and all the different actings of our own minds;—which we being conscious of, and observing in ourselves, do from these receive into our understandings as distinct ideas as we do from bodies affecting our senses. This source of ideas every man has wholly in himself; and though it be not sense, as having nothing to do with external objects, yet it is very like it, and might properly enough be called internal sense. But as I call the other sensation, so I call this reflection, the ideas it affords being such only as the mind gets by reflecting on its own operations within itself. By reflection then, in the following part of this discourse, I would be understood to mean that notice which the mind takes of its own operations, and the manner of them, by reason whereof there come to be ideas of these operations in the understanding. These two, I say, namely, external material things, as the objects of sensation, and the operations of our own minds within, as the objects of reflection are to me the only origin from where all our ideas take their beginnings. The term operations here I use in a large sense, as comprehending not barely the actions of the mind about its ideas, but some sort of passions arising sometimes from them, such as is the satisfaction or uneasiness arising from any thought.

All our Ideas are of the one or the other of these.—The understanding seems to me not to have the least glimmering of any ideas which it does not receive from one of these two. External objects furnish the mind with the ideas of sensible qualities, which are all those different perceptions they produce in us; and the mind furnishes the understanding with ideas of its own operations.

These, when we have taken a full survey of them, and their several modes, combinations, and relations, we shall find to contain all our whole stock of ideas; and that we have nothing in our minds which did not come in one of these two ways. Let any one examine his own thoughts, and thoroughly search into his understanding; and then let him tell me, whether all the original ideas he has there, are any other than of the objects of his senses, or of the operations of his mind, considered as objects of his reflection. And how great a mass of knowledge soever he imagines to be lodged there, he will, upon taking a strict view, see that he has not any idea in his mind but what one of these two have imprinted;—though perhaps, with infinite variety compounded and enlarged by the understanding, as we shall see hereafter. . . .

The Soul begins to have Ideas when it begins to perceive.—To ask, at what time a man has first any ideas, is to ask, when he begins to perceive;—having ideas, and perception, being the same thing. I know it is an opinion, that the soul always thinks, and that it has the actual perception of ideas in itself constantly, as long as it exists; and that actual thinking is as inseparable from the soul as actual extension is from the body; which if true, to inquire after the beginning of a man's ideas is the same as to inquire after the beginning of his soul. For, by this account, soul and its ideas, as body and its extension, will begin to exist both at the same time. . . .

No Ideas but from Sensation and Reflection, evident, if we observe Children.—I see no reason, therefore, to believe that the soul thinks before the senses have furnished it with ideas to think on; and as those are increased and retained, so it comes, by exercise, to improve its faculty of thinking in the several parts of it; as well as, afterwards, by compounding those ideas, and reflecting on its own operations, it increases its stock, as well as facility in remembering, imagining, reasoning, and other modes of thinking.

State of a child in the mother's womb.—He that will suffer himself to be informed by observation and experience, and not make his own hypothesis the rule of nature, will find few signs of a soul accustomed to much thinking in a newborn child, and much fewer of any reasoning at all. And yet it is hard to imagine that the rational soul should think so much, and not reason at all. And he that will consider that infants newly come into the world spend the greatest part of their time in sleep, and are seldom awake but when either hunger calls for the teat, or some pain (the most importunate of all sensations), or some other violent impression on the body forces the mind to perceive and attend to it;—he, I say, who considers this, will perhaps find reason to imagine that a foetus in the mother's womb differs not much from the state of a vegetable, but passes the greatest part of its time without perception or thought; doing very little but sleep in a place where it needs not seek for food, and is surrounded with liquor,[7] always equally soft, and near of the same temper; where the eyes have no light, and the ears so shut up are not very susceptible of sounds; and where there is little or no variety, or change of objects to move the senses.

The mind thinks in proportion to the matter it gets from experience to think about.—Follow a child from its birth, and observe the alterations that time makes, and you shall find, as the mind by the senses comes more and more to be furnished with ideas, it comes to be more and more awake; thinks more, the more it has matter to think on. After some time it begins to know the objects which, being most familiar with it, have made lasting impressions. Thus it comes by degrees to know the persons it daily converses with, and distinguishes them from strangers; which are instances and effects of its coming to retain and distinguish the ideas the senses convey to it. And so we may observe how the mind, by degrees, improves in these; and advances to the exercise of those other faculties of enlarging, compounding, and abstracting its ideas, and of reasoning about them, and reflecting upon all these; of which I shall have occasion to speak more hereafter.

A man begins to have ideas when he first has sensation. What sensation is.—If it shall be demanded then, when a man begins to have any ideas, I think the true answer is,—when he first has any sensation. For, since there appear not to be any ideas in the mind before the senses have conveyed any in, I conceive that ideas in the under-

---

[7] Liquid (amniotic fluid).

standing are coeval[8] with sensation; which is such an impression or motion made in some part of the body, as produces some perception in the understanding. It is about these impressions made on our senses by outward objects that the mind seems first to employ itself, in such operations as we call perception, remembering, consideration, reasoning, and so forth.

The Origin of all our Knowledge.—In time the mind comes to reflect on its own operations about the ideas got by sensation, and thereby stores itself with a new set of ideas, which I call ideas of reflection. These are the impressions that are made on our senses by outward objects that are extrinsical[9] to the mind; and its own operations, proceeding from powers intrinsical and proper to[10] itself, which, when reflected on by itself, become also objects of its contemplation—are, as I have said, the origin of all knowledge. Thus the first capacity of human intellect is—that the mind is fitted to receive the impressions made on it; either through the senses by outward objects, or by its own operations when it reflects on them. This is the first step a man makes toward the discovery of anything, and the groundwork whereon to build all those notions which ever he shall have naturally in this world. All those sublime thoughts which tower above the clouds, and reach as high as heaven itself, take their rise and footing here: in all that great extent wherein the mind wanders, in those remote speculations it may seem to be elevated with, it stirs not one jot beyond those ideas which sense or reflection have offered for its contemplation.

In the Reception of simple Ideas, the Understanding is for the most part passive.—In this part the understanding is merely passive; and whether or not it will have these beginnings and, as it were, materials of knowledge, is not in its own power. For the objects of our senses do, many of them, obtrude[11] their particular ideas upon our minds whether we will or not; and the operations of our minds will not let us be without, at least, some obscure notions of them. No man can be wholly ignorant of what he does when he thinks. These simple ideas, when offered to the mind, the understanding can no more refuse to have, nor alter when they are imprinted, nor blot them out

[8] Concurrent.
[9] External.
[10] Internal and belonging to.
[11] Thrust forward; to force (upon).

and make new ones itself, than a mirror can refuse, alter, or obliterate the images or ideas which the objects set before it do therein produce. As the bodies that surround us do diversely affect our organs, the mind is forced to receive the impressions; and cannot avoid the perception of those ideas that are annexed to them.

OF SIMPLE IDEAS

Uncompounded Appearances.—The better to understand the nature, manner, and extent of our knowledge, one thing is carefully to be observed concerning the ideas we have; and that is, that some of them are simple and some complex.

Though the qualities that affect our senses are, in the things themselves, so united and blended, that there is no separation, no distance between them; yet it is plain, the ideas they produce in the mind enter by the senses simple and unmixed. For, though the sight and touch often take in from the same object, at the same time, different ideas;—as a man sees at once motion and color; the hand feels softness and warmth in the same piece of wax; yet the simple ideas thus united in the same subject are as perfectly distinct as those that come in by different senses. The coldness and hardness which a man feels in a piece of ice being as distinct ideas in the mind as the smell and whiteness of a lily; or as the taste of sugar, and smell of a rose. And there is nothing can be plainer to a man than the clear and distinct perception he has of those simple ideas; which, being each in itself uncompounded, contains in it nothing but one uniform appearance, or conception in the mind, and is not distinguishable into different ideas.

The Mind can neither make nor destroy them.—These simple ideas, the materials of all our knowledge, are suggested and furnished to the mind only by those two ways above mentioned, which are sensation and reflection. When the understanding is once stored with these simple ideas, it has the power to repeat, compare, and unite them, even to an almost infinite variety, and so can make at pleasure new complex ideas. But it is not in the power of the most exalted wit, or enlarged understanding, by any quickness or variety of thought, to invent or frame one new simple idea in the mind, not taken in by the ways before mentioned: nor can any force of the understanding destroy those that are there. The dominion of man, in this little world of his own understanding being much the same as it is in the great world of visible things: wherein his power, however managed by art and skill, reaches no farther than to compound and divide the materials that are made to his hand; but can do nothing toward the making the least particle of new matter, or destroying one atom of what is already in being. The same inability will every one find in himself, who shall go about to fashion in his understanding one simple idea, not received in by his senses from external objects, or by reflection from the operations of his own mind about them. I would have any one try to fancy any taste which had never affected his palate; or frame the idea of a scent he had never smelled: and when he can do this, I will also conclude that a blind man has ideas of colors, and a deaf man true distinct notions of sounds.

Only the qualities that affect the senses are imaginable.—This is the reason why—though we cannot believe it impossible to God to make a creature with other organs, and more ways to convey into the understanding the notice of corporeal things than those five, as they are usually counted, which he has given to men—yet I think it is not possible for any one to imagine any other qualities in bodies, howsoever constituted, whereby they can be taken notice of, besides sounds, tastes, smells, visible and tangible qualities. And had mankind been made but with four senses, the qualities then which are the objects of the fifth sense had been as far from our notice, imagination, and conception, as now any belonging to a sixth, seventh, or eighth sense can possibly be;—which, whether yet some other creatures, in some other parts of this vast and stupendous universe, may not have, will be a great presumption to deny. He that will not set himself proudly at the top of all things, but will consider the immensity of this fabric, and the great variety that is to be found in this little and inconsiderable part of it which he has to do with, may be apt to think that, in other mansions of it, there may be other and different intelligent beings, of whose faculties he has as little knowledge or apprehension as a worm shut up in one drawer of a cabinet has of the senses or understanding of a man; such variety and excellency being suitable to the wisdom and power of the Maker. I have here followed the common opinion of man's having but five senses; though, perhaps there may be justly counted more;—but either supposition serves equally to my present purpose.

OF SIMPLE IDEAS OF SENSE

Division of simple Ideas.—The better to conceive the ideas we receive from sensation, it may not be amiss for us to consider them, in reference to the different ways whereby they make their approaches to our minds, and make themselves perceivable by us.

First, then, There are some which come into our minds by one sense only.

Secondly, There are others that convey themselves into the mind by more senses than one.

Thirdly, Others that are had from reflection only.

Fourthly, There are some that make themselves known, and are suggested to the mind, by all the ways of sensation and reflection.

We shall consider them apart under their several heads.

Ideas of one Sense.—There are some ideas which have admittance only through one sense, which is peculiarly adapted to receive them. Thus light and colors, as white, red, yellow, blue; with their several degrees or shades and mixtures, as green, scarlet, purple, sea-green, and the rest, come in only by the eyes. All kinds of noises, sounds, and tones, only by the ears. The several tastes and smells, by the nose and palate. And if these organs, or the nerves which are the conduits to convey them from without to their audience in the brain,—the mind's presence-room (as I may so call it)—are any of them so disordered as not to perform their functions, they have no postern [12] to be admitted by; no other way to bring themselves into view, and be perceived by the understanding.

The most considerable of those belonging to the touch, are heat and cold, and solidity: all the rest, consisting almost wholly in the sensible configuration, as smooth and rough; or else, more or less firm adhesion of the parts, as hard and soft, tough and brittle, are obvious enough.

• • •

OF COMPLEX IDEAS

Made by the Mind out of simple Ones.—We have hitherto considered those ideas, in the reception whereof the mind is only passive, which

[12] Entrance.

are those simple ones received from sensation and reflection before mentioned, whereof the mind cannot make one to itself, nor have any idea which does not wholly consist of them. But as the mind is wholly passive in the reception of all its simple ideas, so it exerts several acts of its own, whereby out of its simple ideas, as the materials and foundations of the rest, the others are framed. The acts of the mind, wherein it exerts its power over its simple ideas, are chiefly these three: (1) Combining several simple ideas into one compound one; and thus all complex ideas are made. (2) The second is bringing two ideas, whether simple or complex, together, and setting them by one another, so as to take a view of them at once, without uniting them into one; by which way it gets all its ideas of relations. (3) The third is separating them from all other ideas that accompany them in their real existence: this is called abstraction, and thus all its general ideas are made. This shows man's power, and its ways of operation, to be much the same in the material and intellectual world. For the materials in both being such as he has no power over, either to make or destroy, all that man can do is either to unite them together, or to set them by one another, or wholly separate them. I shall here begin with the first of these in the consideration of complex ideas, and come to the other two in their due places. As simple ideas are observed to exist in several combinations united together, so the mind has a power to consider several of them united together as one idea; and that not only as they are united in external objects, but as itself has joined them together. Ideas thus made up of several simple ones put together, I call complex;—such as are beauty, gratitude, a man, an army, the universe; which, though complicated of various simple ideas, or complex ideas made up of simple ones, yet are, when the mind pleases, considered each by itself, as one entire thing, and signified by one name.

Made voluntarily.—In this faculty of repeating and joining together its ideas, the mind has great power in varying and multiplying the objects of its thoughts, infinitely beyond what sensation or reflection furnished it with; but all this still confined to those simple ideas which it received from those two sources, and which are the ultimate materials of all its compositions. For simple ideas are all from things themselves, and of these the mind can have no more, nor other than what are suggested to it. It can have no other ideas of sensible qualities than what come from without by the senses; nor any ideas of other kind of operations of a thinking substance, than what it finds in itself. But when it has once got these simple ideas, it is not confined barely to observation, and what offers itself from without; it can, by its own power, put together those ideas it has, and make new complex ones, which it never received so united.

• • •

7

John Locke

Of Civil Government

Locke opposed dogmatism not only in philosophy but also in religion and politics. He favored a greater degree of freedom in religion and education; in political thought, he provided the philosophical basis of classical liberalism— the theory and practice of limited, representative government. He wished to liberate society from the unnatural restrictions imposed by royal absolutism and to free the individual for maximum development according to the laws of nature. Locke's political ideas, set down in Two Treatises of Government *(1690), served as a justification of the English "Glorious Revolution" of 1688 and strongly influenced the eighteenth-century revolutions in America and France and, subsequently, the development of constitutional democracy. The first treatise attacked the theory of absolute monarchy; the second treatise,* Of Civil Government—*from which the following selection is taken—was written, as Locke says in the preface, "to establish the throne of our great restorer, our present King William; to make good his title in the consent of the people . . ., and to justify to the world the people of England whose love of their just and natural rights, with their resolution to preserve them, saved the nation. . . ." Although the second treatise sounds like a response to events of 1688 and 1689, it was actually written some years before, probably in 1681. In this work, Locke based all government on the natural rights of the individual and on the social contract. Specifically, this meant that government should rest on the consent of the governed and be limited in its powers. It is important to note the secular origin of government in Locke's theory as well as its fundamental individualism, which held that*

John Locke, *Two Treatises of Government,* in *The Works of John Locke* (London: Thomas Tegg, 1823), V, 339–42, 353–54, 357, 387–89, 394–96, 411–13, 416–17, 423–24, 457, 459, 469–73, 483–85. Adapted.

human beings were free moral agents who existed prior to the establishment of government and that they were the very basis of it. Locke thus denied the intrinsic authority of the state; he lodged sovereignty in the individuals who make up the state and held that no government might intrude into their private affairs.

OF THE STATE OF NATURE

To understand political power right, and derive it from its original, we must consider what state all men are naturally in, and that is a state of perfect freedom to order their actions and dispose of their possessions and persons as they think fit, within the bounds of the law of nature, without asking leave or depending upon the will of any other man.

A state also of equality, wherein all the power and jurisdiction is reciprocal,[1] no one having more than another; there being nothing more evident than that creatures of the same species and rank, promiscuously[2] born to all the same advantages of nature and the use of the same faculties, should also be equal one amongst another without subordination or subjection; unless the Lord and Master of them all should, by any manifest declaration of his will, set one above another, and confer on him by an evident and clear appointment an undoubted right to dominion and sovereignty. . . .

But though this be a state of liberty, yet it is not a state of license; though man in that state have an uncontrollable liberty to dispose of his person or possessions, yet he has not liberty to destroy himself, or so much as any creature in his possession, but where some nobler use than its bare preservation calls for it. The state of nature has a law of nature to govern it which obliges every one; and reason, which is that law, teaches all mankind who will but consult it that, being all equal and independent, no one ought to harm another in his life, health, liberty, or possessions; for men being all the workmanship of one omnipotent and infinitely wise Maker-all the servants of one sovereign master, sent into the world by his order, and

[1] Mutual.
[2] Indiscriminately.

about his business they are his property whose workmanship they are, made to last during his, not one another's, pleasure; and being furnished with like faculties, sharing all in one community of nature, there cannot be supposed any such subordination among us that may authorize us to destroy another, as if we were made for one another's uses as the inferior ranks of creatures are for ours. Every one, as he is bound to preserve himself and not to quit his station wilfully, so by the like reason, when his own preservation comes not in competition, ought he, as much as he can, to preserve the rest of mankind, and may not, unless it be to do justice to an offender, take away or impair the life, or what tends to the preservation of life: the liberty, health, limb, or goods of another.

And that all men may be restrained from invading others' rights and from doing hurt to one another, and the law of nature be observed which wills the peace and preservation of all mankind, the execution of the law of nature is, in that state, put into every man's hands, whereby every one has a right to punish the transgressors of that law to such a degree as may hinder its violation; for the law of nature would, as all other laws that concern men in this world, be in vain, if there were nobody that in the state of nature had a power to execute that law and thereby preserve the innocent and restrain offenders. And if any one in the state of nature may punish another for any evil he has done, every one may do so; for in that state of perfect equality, where naturally there is no superiority or jurisdiction of one over another, what any may do in prosecution of that law, every one must needs have a right to do.

And thus in the state of nature one man comes by a power over another; but yet no absolute or arbitrary power to use a criminal, when he has got him in his hands, according to the passionate heats or boundless extravagancy of his own will; but only to retribute to him, so far as calm reason and conscience dictate, what is proportionate to his transgression, which is so much as may serve for reparation and restraint. For these two are the only reasons why one man may lawfully do harm to another, which is what we call punishment. In transgressing the law of nature, the offender declares himself to live by another rule than that of reason and common equity, which is that measure God has set to the actions of men for their mutual security; and so he becomes dangerous to mankind, the tie which is to secure them from injury and violence being slighted and broken by him. Which being a trespass against the whole species and the peace and safety of it provided for by the law of nature, every man upon this score, by the right he has to preserve mankind in general, may restrain, or, where it is necessary, destroy things noxious to them, and so may bring such evil on any one who has transgressed that law, as may make him repent the doing of it and thereby deter him, and by his example others, from doing the like mischief. And in this case, and upon this ground, every man has a right to punish the offender and be executioner of the law of nature. . . .

OF PROPERTY

God, who has given the world to men in common, has also given them reason to make use of it to the best advantage of life and convenience. The earth and all that is therein, is given to men for the support and comfort of their being. And though all the fruits it naturally produces and beasts it feeds belong to mankind in common, as they are produced by the spontaneous hand of nature; and nobody has originally a private dominion exclusive of the rest of mankind, in any of them, as they are thus in their natural state; yet, being given for the use of men, there must of necessity be a means to appropriate them some way or other before they can be of any use or at all beneficial to any particular man. The fruit or venison which nourishes the wild Indian, who knows no enclosure[3] and is still a tenant in common, must be his, and so his, that is, a part of him, that another can no longer have any right to it before it can do him any good for the support of his life.

Though the earth and all inferior creatures be common to all men, yet every man has a property in his own person; this nobody has any right to but himself. The labor of his body and the work of his hands, we may say, are properly his. Whatsoever then he removes out of the state that nature has provided and left it in, he has mixed his labor with, and joined to it something that is his own, and thereby makes it his property. It being by him removed from the common state nature has placed it in, it has by this labor something annexed to it that excludes the common right of other men. For this

[3] Boundary enclosing private property.

labor being the unquestionable property of the laborer, no man but he can have a right to what that is once joined to, at least where there is enough and as good left in common for others. . . .

God gave the world to men in common; but since he gave it them for their benefit and the greatest conveniences of life they were capable to draw from it, it cannot be supposed he meant it should always remain common and uncultivated. He gave it to the use of the industrious and rational—and labor was to be his title to it—not to the fancy or covetousness of the quarrelsome and contentious. He that had as good left for his improvement as was already taken up needed not complain, ought not to meddle with what was already improved by another's labor; if he did, it is plain he desired the benefit of another's pains which he had no right to, and not the ground which God had given him in common with others to labor on, and whereof there was as good left as that already possessed, and more than he knew what to do with, or his industry could reach to. . . .

OF POLITICAL OR CIVIL SOCIETY

Man, being born, as has been proved, with a title to perfect freedom and an uncontrolled enjoyment of all the rights and privileges of the law of nature equally with any other man or number of men in the world, has by nature a power not only to preserve his property[4]—that is, his life, liberty, and estate[5]—against the injuries and attempts of other men, but to judge of and punish the breaches of that law in others as he is persuaded the offense deserves, even with death itself in crimes where the heinousness of the fact in his opinion requires it. But because no political society can be, nor subsist, without having in itself the power to preserve the property and, in order thereunto, punish the offenses of all those of that society, there and there only is political society where every one of the members has quitted[6] his natural power, resigned it up into the hands of the community in all cases that exclude him not from appealing for protection to the law established by it. And thus, all private judgment of every particular member being excluded, the community comes to be umpire by settled standing rules, indifferent and the same to all

[4] Whatever belongs to an individual.
[5] Material possessions.
[6] Given up.

parties, and by men having authority from the community for the execution of those rules, decides all the differences that may happen between any members of that society concerning any matter of right, and punishes those offenses which any member has committed against the society with such penalties as the law has established; whereby it is easy to discern who are, and who are not, in political society together. Those who are united into one body and have a common established law and judicature to appeal to, with authority to decide controversies between them and punish offenders, are in civil society one with another; but those who have no such common appeal, I mean on earth, are still in the state of nature, each being, where there is no other, judge for himself and executioner, which is, as I have before shown it, the perfect state of nature.

And thus the commonwealth[7] comes by a power to set down what punishment shall belong to the several transgressions which they think worthy of it committed among the members of that society—which is the power of making laws—as well as it has the power to punish any injury done unto any of its members by any one that is not of it—which is the power of war and peace—and all this for the preservation of the property of all the members of that society as far as is possible. But though every man who has entered into civil society and is become a member of any commonwealth has thereby quitted his power to punish offenses against the law of nature in prosecution of his own private judgment, yet, with the judgment of offenses which he has given up to the legislative in all cases where he can appeal to the magistrate, he has given a right to the commonwealth to employ his force for the execution of the judgments of the commonwealth, whenever he shall be called to it; which, indeed, are his own judgments, they being made by himself or his representative. And herein we have the origin of the legislative and executive power of civil society which is to judge by standing laws how far offenses are to be punished when committed within the commonwealth, and also to determine, by occasional judgments founded on the present circumstances of the fact, how far injuries from without are to be vindicated,[8] and in both these to employ all the force of all the members when there shall be need.

Whenever, therefore, any number of men are so united into one society as to quit every one his executive power of the law of nature

[7] Political community (state).
[8] Revenged, or punished.

and to resign it to the public, there and there only is a political or civil society. And this is done wherever any number of men, in the state of nature, enter into society to make one people, one body politic, under one supreme government, or else when any one joins himself to, and incorporates with, any government already made; for hereby he authorizes the society or, which is all one, the legislative thereof, to make laws for him as the public good of the society shall require, to the execution whereof his own assistance, as to his own decrees, is due. And this puts men out of a state of nature into that of a commonwealth by setting up a judge on earth, with authority to determine all the controversies and redress the injuries that may happen to any member of the commonwealth; which judge is the legislative, or magistrates appointed by it. And wherever there are any number of men, however associated, that have no such decisive power to appeal to, there they are still in the state of nature. . . .

OF THE BEGINNING OF POLITICAL SOCIETIES

Men being, as has been said, by nature all free, equal, and independent, no one can be put out of this estate and subjected to the political power of another without his own consent. The only way whereby any one divests himself of his natural liberty, and puts on the bonds of civil society, is by agreeing with other men to join and unite into a community for their comfortable, safe, and peaceable living one among another, in a secure enjoyment of their properties and a greater security against any that are not of it. This any number of men may do, because it injures not the freedom of the rest; they are left as they were in the liberty of the state of nature. When any number of men have so consented to make one community or government, they are thereby presently incorporated and make one body politic wherein the majority have a right to act and conclude the rest.

For when any number of men have, by the consent of every individual, made a community, they have thereby made that community one body, with a power to act as one body, which is only by the will and determination of the majority; for that which acts any community being only the consent of the individuals of it, and it being necessary to that which is one body to move one way, it is necessary the body should move that way whither the greater force carries it, which is the consent of the majority; or else it is impossible it should act or continue one body, one community, which the consent of every individual that united into it agreed that it should; and so every one is bound by that consent to be concluded by the majority. And therefore we see that in assemblies empowered to act by positive laws, where no number is set by that positive law which empowers them, the act of the majority passes for the act of the whole, and, of course, determines, as having by the law of nature and reason the power of the whole.

And thus every man, by consenting with others to make one body politic under one government, puts himself under an obligation to every one of that society to submit to the determination of the majority, and to be concluded by it; or else this original compact, whereby he with others incorporates into one society, would signify nothing, and be no compact, if he be left free and under no other ties than he was in before in the state of nature. For what appearance would there be of any compact? What new engagement if he were no farther tied by any decrees of the society than he himself thought fit and did actually consent to? This would be still as great a liberty as he himself had before his compact, or any one else in the state of nature has who may submit himself and consent to any acts of it if he thinks fit.

For if the consent of the majority shall not in reason be received as the act of the whole and conclude every individual, nothing but the consent of every individual can make any thing to be the act of the whole; but such a consent is next to impossible ever to be had if we consider the infirmities of health and avocations [9] of business which in a number, though much less than that of a commonwealth, will necessarily keep many away from the public assembly. To which, if we add the variety of opinions and contrariety of interests which unavoidably happen in all collections of men, the coming into society upon such terms would be only like Cato's [10] coming into the theatre, only to go out again. Such a constitution as this would make the mighty leviathan [11] of a shorter duration than the feeblest creatures,

---

[9] Regular work; duties.

[10] Marcus Porcius Cato (234–149 B.C.), also known as "Cato the Elder," was a Roman statesman and orator. He endeavored to keep alive the ancient Roman virtues such as austerity, simplicity, discipline, and obedience to authority. He loathed Greek philosophy and demonstrated his contempt for the theater by walking ostentatiously through it.

[11] A legendary monster; the term used by Hobbes and others to symbolize the awesome power of the state.

and not let it outlast the day it was born in; which cannot be supposed till we can think that rational creatures should desire and constitute societies only to be dissolved; for where the majority cannot
conclude the rest, there they cannot act as one body, and consequently will be immediately dissolved again.

Whosoever, therefore, out of a state of nature unite into a community must be understood to give up all the power necessary to the
ends for which they unite into society to the majority of the community, unless they expressly agreed in any number greater than the
majority. And this is done by barely agreeing to unite into one political society, which is all the compact that is, or needs be, between the
individuals that enter into or make up a commonwealth. And thus
that which begins and actually constitutes any political society is
nothing but the consent of any number of freemen capable of a majority to unite and incorporate into such a society. And this is that,
and that only, which did or could give beginning to any lawful government in the world. . . .

OF THE ENDS OF POLITICAL SOCIETY
AND GOVERNMENT

If man in the state of nature be so free, as has been said, if he be
absolute lord of his own person and possessions, equal to the greatest, and subject to nobody, why will he part with his freedom, why
will he give up his empire and subject himself to the dominion and
control of any other power? To which it is obvious to answer that
though in the state of nature he has such a right, yet the enjoyment
of it is very uncertain and constantly exposed to the invasion of
others; for all being kings as much as he, every man his equal, and
the greater part no strict observers of equity and justice, the enjoyment of the property he has in this state is very unsafe, very un-
secure. This makes him willing to quit a condition which, however
free, is full of fears and continual dangers; and it is not without
reason that he seeks out and is willing to join in society with others,
who are already united, or have a mind to unite, for the mutual preservation of their lives, liberties, and estates, which I call by the general name "property."

The great and chief end, therefore, of men's uniting into commonwealths and putting themselves under government, is the preservation of their property. To which in the state of nature there are many things lacking:

First, There lacks an established, settled, known law, received and allowed by common consent to be the standard of right and wrong and the common measure to decide all controversies between them; for though the law of nature be plain and intelligible to all rational creatures, yet men, being biased by their interest as well as ignorant for lack of studying it, are not apt to allow of it as a law binding to them in the application of it to their particular cases.

Secondly, In the state of nature there lacks a known and indifferent [12] judge with authority to determine all differences according to the established law; for every one in that state being both judge and executioner of the law of nature, men being partial to themselves, passion and revenge is very apt to carry them too far and with too much heat in their own cases, as well as negligence and unconcernedness to make them too remiss in other men's.

Thirdly, In the state of nature, there often lacks power to back and support the sentence when right, and to give it due execution. They who by any injustice offend will seldom fail, where they are able, by force, to make good their injustice; such resistance many times makes the punishment dangerous and frequently destructive to those who attempt it.

Thus mankind, notwithstanding all the privileges of the state of nature, being but in an ill condition while they remain in it, are quickly driven into society. Hence it comes to pass that we seldom find any number of men live any time together in this state. The inconveniences that they are therein exposed to by the irregular and uncertain exercise of the power every man has of punishing the transgressions of others make them take sanctuary under the established laws of government and therein seek the preservation of their property. It is this [that] makes them so willingly give up every one his single power of punishing, to be exercised by such alone as shall be appointed to it among them; and by such rules as the community, or those authorized by them to that purpose, shall agree on. And in this we have the original right of both the legislative and executive power, as well as of the governments and societies themselves.

---

[12] Impartial, neutral.

OF THE EXTENT OF THE LEGISLATIVE POWER

The great end of men's entering into society being the enjoyment of their properties in peace and safety, and the great instrument and means of that being the laws established in that society, the first and fundamental positive law of all commonwealths is the establishing of the legislative power; as the first and fundamental natural law which is to govern even the legislative itself, is the preservation of the society and, as far as will consist with the public good, of every person in it. This legislative is not only the supreme power of the commonwealth, but sacred and unalterable in the hands where the community have once placed it; nor can any edict of anybody else, in what form soever conceived or by what power soever backed, have the force and obligation of a law which has not its sanction from that legislative which the public has chosen and appointed; for without this the law could not have that which is absolutely necessary to its being a law: the consent of the society over whom nobody can have a power to make laws, but by their own consent and by authority received from them. And therefore all the obedience, which by the most solemn ties any one can be obliged to pay, ultimately terminates in this supreme power and is directed by those laws which it enacts; nor can any oaths to any foreign power whatsoever, or any domestic subordinate power, discharge any member of the society from his obedience to the legislative acting pursuant to their trust, nor oblige him to any obedience contrary to the laws so enacted, or farther than they do allow; it being ridiculous to imagine one can be tied ultimately to obey any power in the society which is not supreme. . . .

These are the bounds which the trust that is put in them by the society and the law of God and nature have set to the legislative power of every commonwealth, in all forms of government:

First, They are to govern by promulgated established laws, not to be varied in particular cases, but to have one rule for rich and poor, for the favorite at court and the countryman at plough.

Secondly, These laws also ought to be designed for no other end ultimately but the good of the people.

Thirdly, They must not raise taxes on the property of the people without the consent of the people, given by themselves or their deputies. And this properly concerns only such governments where the legislative is always in being, or at least where the people have not reserved any part of the legislative to deputies to be from time to time chosen by themselves.

Fourthly, The legislative neither must nor can transfer the power of making laws to anybody else, or place it anywhere but where the people have.

OF TYRANNY

As usurpation is the exercise of power which another has a right to, so tyranny is the exercise of power beyond right, which nobody can have a right to. And this is making use of the power any one has in his hands, not for the good of those who are under it, but for his own private separate advantage—when the governor, however entitled, makes not the law, but his will, the rule, and his commands and actions are not directed to the preservation of the properties of his people, but the satisfaction of his own ambition, revenge, covetousness, or any other irregular passion. . . .

Wherever law ends tyranny begins, if the law be transgressed to another's harm. And whosoever in authority exceeds the power given him by the law, and makes use of the force he has under his command to compass [13] that upon the subject which the law allows not, ceases in that to be a magistrate [14] and, acting without authority, may be opposed as any other man who by force invades the right of another. This is acknowledged in subordinate magistrates. He that has authority to seize my person in the street may be opposed as a thief and a robber if he endeavors to break into my house to execute a writ, notwithstanding that I know he has such a warrant and such a legal authority as will impower him to arrest me abroad. And why this should not hold in the highest as well as in the most inferior magistrate, I would gladly be informed. Is it reasonable that the eldest brother, because he has the greatest part of his father's estate, should thereby have a right to take away any of his younger brother's portions? Or that a rich man who possessed a whole country should from thence have a right to seize, when he pleased, the cottage and garden of his poor neighbor? The being rightfully possessed of great power and riches, exceedingly beyond the greatest part of the sons of Adam, is so far from being an excuse, much less a

[13] Enforce.
[14] A legitimate civil official.

reason, for rapine [15] and oppression, which the endamaging another without authority is, that it is a great aggravation of it; for the exceeding the bounds of authority is no more a right in a great than in a petty officer, no more justifiable in a king than a constable; [16] but is so much the worse in him in that he has more trust put in him, has already a much greater share than the rest of his brethren, and is supposed, from the advantages of his education, employment, and counsellors, to be more knowing in the measures of right and wrong. . . .

OF THE DISSOLUTION OF GOVERNMENT

The reason why men enter into society is the preservation of their property; and the end why they choose and authorize a legislative is that there may be laws made and rules set as guards and fences to the properties of all the members of the society to limit the power and moderate the dominion of every part and member of the society; for since it can never be supposed to be the will of the society that the legislative should have a power to destroy that which every one designs to secure by entering into society, and for which the people submitted themselves to legislators of their own making. Whenever the legislators endeavor to take away and destroy the property of the people, or to reduce them to slavery under arbitrary power, they put themselves into a state of war with the people who are thereupon absolved from any further obedience, and are left to the common refuge which God has provided for all men against force and violence. Whensoever, therefore, the legislative shall transgress this fundamental rule of society, and either by ambition, fear, folly, or corruption, endeavor to grasp themselves, or put into the hands of any other, an absolute power over the lives, liberties, and estates of the people, by this breach of trust they forfeit the power the people had put into their hands for quite contrary ends, and it devolves [17] to the people, who have a right to resume their original liberty, and, by the establishment of a new legislative, such as they shall think fit, provide for their own safety and security, which is the end for which they are in society. What I have said here concerning the legislative in general

[15] Plunder, pillage.
[16] A minor official, empowered to make arrests.
[17] Passes on.

holds true also concerning the supreme executor, who having a double trust put in him—both to have a part in the legislative and the supreme execution of the law—acts against both when he goes about to set up his own arbitrary will as the law of the society. He acts also contrary to his trust when he either employs the force, treasure, and offices of the society to corrupt the representatives and gain them to his purposes, or openly pre-engages the electors and prescribes to their choice such whom he has by solicitations, threats, promises, or otherwise won to his designs, and employs them to bring in such who have promised beforehand what to vote and what to enact. Thus to regulate candidates and electors, and new-model[18] the ways of election, what is it but to cut up the government by the roots, and poison the very fountain of public security? For the people, having reserved to themselves the choice of their representatives, as the fence[19] to their properties, could do it for no other end but that they might always be freely chosen, and, so chosen, freely act and advise as the necessity of the commonwealth and the public good should upon examination and mature debate be judged to require. This, those who give their votes before they hear the debate and have weighed the reasons on all sides, are not capable of doing. To prepare such an assembly as this, and endeavor to set up the declared abettors[20] of his own will for the true representatives of the people and the lawmakers of the society, is certainly as great a breach of trust and as perfect a declaration of a design to subvert the government as is possible to be met with. To which if one shall add rewards and punishments visibly employed to the same end, and all the arts of perverted law made use of to take off and destroy all that stand in the way of such a design, and will not comply and consent to betray the liberties of their country, it will be past doubt what is doing. What power they ought to have in the society who thus employ it contrary to the trust that went along with it in its first institution is easy to determine; and one cannot but see that he who has once attempted any such thing as this cannot any longer be trusted.

To this perhaps it will be said that, the people being ignorant and always discontented, to lay the foundation of government in the unsteady opinion and uncertain humor[21] of the people is to expose it to

---

[18] Alter.
[19] Protection.
[20] Supporters.
[21] Disposition, mood.

certain ruin; and no government will be able long to subsist if the people may set up a new legislative whenever they take offense at the old one. To this I answer: Quite the contrary. People are not so easily got out of their old forms as some are apt to suggest. They are hardly to be prevailed with to amend the acknowledged faults in the frame they have been accustomed to. And if there be any original defects, or adventitious [22] ones introduced by time or corruption, it is not an easy thing to get them changed, even when all the world sees there is an opportunity for it. This slowness and aversion in the people to quit their old constitutions has in the many revolutions which have been seen in this kingdom, in this and former ages, still kept us to, or after some interval of fruitless attempts still brought us back again to, our old legislative of king, lords, and commons; [23] and whatever provocations have made the crown be taken from some of our princes' heads, they never carried the people so far as to place it in another line.

But it will be said this hypothesis [24] lays a ferment for frequent rebellion. To which I answer:

First, no more than any other hypothesis; for when the people are made miserable, and find themselves exposed to the ill-usage of arbitrary power, cry up [25] their governors as much as you will for sons of Jupiter, [26] let them be sacred or divine, descended, or authorized from heaven, give them out for whom or what you please, the same will happen. The people generally ill-treated, and contrary to right, will be ready upon any occasion to ease themselves of a burden that sits heavy upon them. They will wish and seek for the opportunity, which in the change, weakness, and accidents of human affairs seldom delays long to offer itself. He must have lived but a little while in the world who has not seen examples of this in his time, and he must have read very little who cannot produce examples of it in all sorts of governments in the world.

Secondly, I answer, such revolutions happen not upon every little mismanagement in public affairs. Great mistakes in the ruling part, many wrong and inconvenient laws, and all the slips of human frailty will be borne by the people without mutiny or murmur. But

---

[22] Accidental.
[23] Representatives of the common people of England (House of Commons).
[24] Theory, argument.
[25] Praise.
[26] The principal Roman god.

if a long train of abuses, prevarications,[27] and artifices,[28] all tending the same way, make the design visible to the people, and they cannot but feel what they lie under and see where they are going, it is not to be wondered that they should then rouse themselves and endeavor to put the rule into such hands which may secure to them the ends for which government was at first erected, and without which ancient names and specious[29] forms are so far from being better that they are much worse than the state of nature or pure anarchy[30]—the inconveniences being all as great and as near, but the remedy farther off and more difficult.

Thirdly, I answer that this doctrine of a power in the people of providing for their safety anew by a new legislative, when their legislators have acted contrary to their trust by invading their property, is the best fence against rebellion, and the most likely means to hinder it; for rebellion being an opposition, not to persons, but authority which is founded only in the constitutions and laws of the government, those, whoever they be, who by force break through, and by force justify their violation of them, are truly and properly rebels; for when men, by entering into society and civil government, have excluded force and introduced laws for the preservation of property, peace, and unity among themselves, those who set up force again in opposition to the laws do *rebellare*[31]—that is, bring back again the state of war—and are properly rebels; which they who are in power, by the pretense they have to authority, the temptation of force they have in their hands, and the flattery of those about them, being likeliest to do, the best way to prevent the evil is to show them the danger and injustice of it who are under the greatest temptation to run into it. . . .

Here, it is like, the common question will be made: Who shall be judge whether the prince or legislative act contrary to their trust? This, perhaps, ill-affected and factious men may spread among the people, when the prince only makes use of his due prerogative. To this I reply: The people shall be judge; for who shall be judge whether his trustee or deputy acts well and according to the trust reposed in him but he who deputes him and must, by having de-

---

[27] Lies, misrepresentations.
[28] Tricks.
[29] Seemingly correct, but actually not.
[30] Absence of any political authority.
[31] Latin: to make war again.

puted him, have still a power to discard him when he fails in his trust? If this be reasonable in particular cases of private men, why should it be otherwise in that of the greatest moment where the welfare of millions is concerned, and also where the evil, if not prevented, is greater and the redress very difficult, dear, and dangerous? . . .

If a controversy arise between a prince and some of the people in a matter where the law is silent or doubtful, and the thing be of great consequence, I should think the proper umpire in such a case should be the body of the people; for in cases where the prince has a trust reposed in him and is dispensed from the common ordinary rules of the law, there, if any men find themselves aggrieved and think the prince acts contrary to or beyond that trust, who so proper to judge as the body of the people (who, at first, lodged that trust in him) how far they meant it should extend? But if the prince, or whoever they be in the administration, decline that way of determination, the appeal then lies nowhere but to heaven; force between either persons, who have no known superior on earth or which permits no appeal to a judge on earth, being properly a state of war wherein the appeal lies only to heaven; and in that state the injured party must judge for himself when he will think fit to make use of that appeal and put himself upon it.

To conclude, the power that every individual gave the society when he entered into it can never revert to the individuals again as long as the society lasts, but will always remain in the community, because without this there can be no community, no commonwealth, which is contrary to the original agreement; so also when the society has placed the legislative in any assembly of men, to continue in them and their successors with direction and authority for providing such successors, the legislative can never revert to the people while that government lasts, because having provided a legislative with power to continue for ever, they have given up their political power to the legislative and cannot resume it. But if they have set limits to the duration of their legislative and made this supreme power in any person or assembly only temporary, or else when by the miscarriages of those in authority it is forfeited, upon the forfeiture, or at the determination of the time set, it reverts to the society, and the people have a right to act as supreme and continue the legislative in themselves, or erect a new form, or under the old form place it in new hands, as they think good.

8

Alexander Pope

Essay on Man

The European Enlightenment, or Age of Reason, was characterized by views on God, the world, and humanity that were rooted in the scientific outlook of the seventeenth century. The leading thinkers and artists of the Age of Reason accepted the concept of a rational, benevolent, natural order, which had been created by God and whose meaning and mode of operation could be understood by rational individuals as a guide to the good life. They stated this ideal in a moderate way, inspired by ancient, classical models; thus they expressed, they felt, the old, timeless truths in a manner appropriate to their own times. One of the best representatives of this rationalistic, neoclassical tendency in literature was Alexander Pope, the English poet (1688–1744). He may, indeed, be considered the spokesman in verse of the Age of Reason. For, despite an unpleasant personality, a physical disability, and a religious handicap (he was a professing Roman Catholic in a country that still legally discriminated against that faith), Pope achieved great popular success, and the income from the sale of his works enabled him to devote his life to literature.

Above all, Pope was a poet, a great English poet. Rarely lyrical or personal, his verse was mainly a vehicle for the expression of profound moral truths and common sense about nature and humanity. Following the accepted neoclassical rules of the craft, his verse exhibited a polished elegance, yet transcended social conformity and poetic commonplaces. His carefully wrought poetic lines and balanced rhythms contain paradox, wit, satire, and even deep feeling, which raised them to the level of great, imaginative art.

Pope's Essay on Man *(1734) is a poem written in the form of four*

Alexander Pope, *Essay on Man*, in *Poetical Works of Alexander Pope* (Boston: Little, Brown, 1854), II, 36–48.

141

*epistles (letters) addressed to the English rationalist-deist Henry St. John,
Lord Bolingbroke. Its "heroic couplets"—consisting of clear, short lines—
that often balance contrasting ideas—have the effect of epigrams. The poem
deals with the problem of evil in the world and with the individual's moral
duty. Pope affirms that the universe, though rational, is not wholly intelligible, and individuals can find fulfillment in the cosmic order only if they
avoid the faulty reasoning that leads to false pride and discontent. Voicing
not only his own creed but important philosophical beliefs of his time, Pope
presents in this work a good statement of natural religion, or deism. Epistle I
and the opening stanza of Epistle II are reprinted here.*

EPISTLE I

Awake, my St. John![1] leave all meaner things
To low ambition, and the pride of Kings.
Let us (since Life can little more supply
Than just to look about us and to die)
Expatiate[2] free o'er all this scene of Man;
A mighty maze![3] but not without a plan;
A Wild, where weeds and flow'rs promiscuous shoot,
Or Garden, tempting with forbidden fruit.
Together let us beat this ample field,
Try what the open, what the covert yield;
The latent tracts,[4] the giddy heights, explore
Of all who blindly creep, or sightless soar;
Eye Nature's walks, shoot Folly as it flies,
And catch the Manners[5] living as they rise;
Laugh where we must, be candid where we can;
But vindicate[6] the ways of God to Man.

---

[1] Henry St. John, first Viscount Bolingbroke (1678–1751). He was a friend to Pope, a
guide, a philosopher, and of great inspiration to the poet.
[2] To roam or wander; to discuss at length.
[3] A confusing network of pathways.
[4] Hidden regions.
[5] Rules of behavior.
[6] Justify, defend.

I. Say first, of God above, or Man below,
What can we reason, but from what we know?
Of Man, what see we but his station here,
From which to reason, or to which refer?
Thro' worlds unnumber'd[7] tho' the God be known,
'T is ours to trace him only in our own.
He, who thro' vast immensity can pierce,
See worlds on worlds compose one universe,
Observe how system into system runs,
What other planets circle other suns,
What vary'd Being peoples ev'ry star,
May tell why Heav'n has made us as we are.
But of this frame the bearings, and the ties,
The strong connections, nice dependencies,
Gradations just, has thy pervading soul
Look'd thro'? or can a part contain the whole?
    Is the great chain, that draws all to agree,
And drawn supports, upheld by God, or thee?

II. Presumptuous Man! the reason wouldst thou find,
Why form'd so weak, so little, and so blind?
First, if thou canst, the harder reason guess,
Why form'd no weaker, blinder, and no less?
Ask of thy mother earth, why oaks are made
Taller or stronger than the weeds they shade?
Or ask of yonder argent fields[8] above,
Why Jove's satellites are less than Jove?[9]
    Of Systems possible, if 'tis confest
That Wisdom infinite must form the best,
Where all must full or not coherent be,
And all that rises, rise in due degree;
Then, in the scale of reas'ning life, 'tis plain,
There must be, somewhere, such a rank as Man;
And all the question (wrangle e'er so long)
Is only this, if God has plac'd him wrong?
    Respecting Man, whatever wrong we call,

---

[7] Endless.
[8] Silvery fields—that is, the heavens.
[9] The planet Jupiter.

May, must be right, as relative to all. [10]
In human works, tho' labour'd on with pain,
A thousand movements scarce one purpose gain;
In God's, one single can its end produce;
Yet serves to second too some other use.
So Man, who here seems principal alone,
Perhaps acts second to some sphere unknown,
Touches some wheel, or verges to some goal;
'Tis but a part we see, and not a whole.
    When the proud steed shall know why Man restrains
His fiery course, or drives him o'er the plains:
When the dull Ox, why now he breaks the clod,
Is now a victim, and now Egypt's god: [11]
Then shall Man's pride and dulness comprehend
His actions', passions', being's, use and end;
Why doing, suff'ring, check'd, impell'd; and why
This hour a slave, the next a deity.
    Then say not Man's imperfect, Heav'n in fault;
Say rather, Man's as perfect as he ought;
His knowledge measur'd to his state and place;
His time a moment, and a point his space.
If to be perfect in a certain sphere,
What matter, soon or late, or here or there?
The blest today is as completely so,
As who began a thousand years ago.

    III. Heav'n from all creatures hides the book of Fate,
All but the page prescrib'd, their present state;
From brutes [12] what men, from men what spirits [13] know:
Or who could suffer Being here below?
The lamb thy riot dooms to bleed today,
Had he thy Reason, would he skip and play?
Pleas'd to the last, he crops the flow'ry food,
And licks the hand just rais'd to shed his blood.
Oh blindness to the future! kindly giv'n,

[10] Concerning human beings, what seems defective in itself may be advantageous in relation to the hidden ends they are intended to serve.
[11] Some ancient Egyptians worshiped the sacred bull, Apis, who was connected with the god Ptah, creator of gods and humans.
[12] Animals.
[13] Angels.

That each may fill the circle mark'd by Heav'n;
Who sees with equal eye, as God of all,
A hero perish, or a sparrow fall,
Atoms or systems into ruin hurl'd,
And now a bubble burst, and now a world.
  Hope humbly then; with trembling pinions soar;
Wait the great teacher Death; and God adore!
What future bliss, he gives not thee to know,
But gives that Hope to be thy blessing now.
Hope springs eternal in the human breast:
Man never Is, but always To be blest: [14]
The soul, uneasy and confin'd from home, [15]
Rests and expatiates in a life to come.

  Lo! the poor Indian! whose untutor'd mind
Sees God in clouds, or hears him in the wind;
His soul, proud Science never taught to stray
Far as the solar walk, or milky way;
Yet simple Nature to his hope has giv'n,
Behind the cloud-topt hill, an humbler heav'n;
Some safer world in depth of woods embrac'd,
Some happier island in the wat'ry waste,
Where slaves once more their native land behold,
No fiends torment, no Christians thirst for gold!
To Be, contents his natural desire,
He asks no Angel's wing, no Seraph's [16] fire;
But thinks, admitted to that equal sky,
His faithful dog shall bear him company.

  IV. Go, wiser thou! and, in thy scale of sense,
Weigh thy Opinion against Providence; [17]
Call imperfection what thou fancy'st such,
Say, here he gives too little, there too much:
Destroy all Creatures for thy sport or gust, [18]
Yet cry, If Man's unhappy, God's unjust;
If Man alone engross not Heav'n's high care,

[14] To enjoy divine favor.
[15] The soul's origin and destination (God).
[16] The highest order of angels.
[17] Sensory perception weighed against God's wisdom.
[18] Personal pleasure.

Alone made perfect here, immortal there:
Snatch from his hand the balance [19] and the rod,[20]
Re-judge his justice, be the God of God!
In Pride, in reas'ning Pride, our error lies;
All quit their sphere, and rush into the skies.
Pride still is aiming at the blest abodes,
Men would be Angels, Angels would be Gods.
Aspiring to be Gods, if Angels fell,
Aspiring to be Angels, Men rebel:
And who but wishes to invert the laws
Of Order, sins against th' Eternal Cause.

    V. Ask for what end the heav'nly bodies shine,
Earth for whose use? Pride answers, " 'Tis for mine:
For me kind Nature wakes her genial [21] Pow'r,
Suckles each herb, and spreads out ev'ry flow'r;
Annual for me, the grape, the rose renew
The juice nectareous, and the balmy dew;
For me, the mine a thousand treasures brings;
For me, health gushes from a thousand springs;
Seas roll to waft [22] me, suns to light me rise;
My foot-stool earth, my canopy [23] the skies."
    But errs not Nature from this gracious end,
From burning suns when livid deaths descend,
When earthquakes swallow, or when tempests sweep
Towns to one grave, whole nations to the deep?
"No, ('tis reply'd) the first Almighty Cause
Acts not by partial, but by gen'ral laws;
Th' exceptions few; some change since all began,
And what created perfect?"—Why then Man?
If the great end be human Happiness,
Then Nature deviates; [24] and can Man do less?
As much that end a constant course requires
Of show'rs and sun-shine, as of Man's desires;
As much eternal springs and cloudless skies,

[19] The scales of justice.
[20] The instrument of punishment.
[21] Generative.
[22] Carry.
[23] Ornamental cover (such as that often placed above a throne).
[24] Errs.

As Men for ever temp'rate, calm, and wise.
If plagues or earthquakes break not Heav'n's design,
Why then a Borgia,[25] or a Catiline?[26]
Who knows but he, whose hand the lightning forms,
Who heaves old Ocean, and who wings the storms;
Pours fierce Ambition in a Caesar's[27] mind,
Or turns young Ammon[28] loose to scourge mankind?
From pride, from pride, our very reas'ning springs;
Account for moral, as for nat'ral[29] things:
Why charge we Heav'n in those, in these acquit?
In both, to reason right is to submit.
    Better for Us, perhaps, it might appear,
Were there all harmony, all virtue here;
That never air or ocean felt the wind;
That never passion discompos'd the mind.
But all subsists by elemental strife;
And Passions are the elements of Life.
The gen'ral Order, since the whole began,
Is kept in Nature, and is kept in Man.

    VI. What would this Man? Now upward will he soar,
And little less than Angel,[30] would be more;
Now looking downwards, just as griev'd appears
To want the strength of bulls, the fur of bears.
Made for his use all creatures if he call,
Say what their use, had he the pow'rs of all?
Nature to these, without profusion, kind,
The proper organs, proper pow'rs assign'd;

[25] Caesar Borgia (*ca.* 1476–1507), son of Pope Alexander VI, soldier, and sometime cardinal. To achieve his ends he unscrupulously used cruelty, bloodshed, terror, and assassination.

[26] Lucius Sergius Catilina (*ca.* 108–62 B.C.), a Roman politician and conspirator against the Roman government. His conspiracy did not succeed and he suffered a violent death.

[27] Gaius Julius Caesar (100–44 B.C.), Roman general and statesman, who is said to have had the ambition to be crowned King of Rome.

[28] Alexander the Great (356–323 B.C.), heir of Macedonia and conqueror of Persia and Egypt. While in Egypt, he traveled to the Siwah oasis on the western border of Egypt. During his worshiping there, it was supposedly revealed to him that his true father was not King Philip, but the Egyptian god Ammon.

[29] Natural.

[30] "Thou hast made him [man] a little lower than the angels, and hast crowned him with glory and honor." Psalm 8:5 (King James version).

Each seeming want compensated of course,
Here with degrees of swiftness, there of force;
All in exact proportion to the state;
Nothing to add, and nothing to abate.
Each beast, each insect, happy in its own;
Is Heav'n unkind to Man, and Man alone?
Shall he alone, whom rational we call,
Be pleas'd with nothing, if not bless'd with all?
   The bliss of Man (could Pride that blessing find)
Is not to act or think beyond mankind;
No pow'rs of body or of soul to share,
But what his nature and his state can bear.
Why has not Man a microscopic eye?
For this plain reason, Man is not a Fly.
Say what the use, were finer optics giv'n,
T' inspect a mite,[31] not comprehend the heav'n?
Or touch, if tremblingly alive all o'er,
To smart and agonize at every pore?
Or quick effluvia[32] darting thro' the brain,
Die of a rose in aromatic pain?
If nature thunder'd in his op'ning ears,
And stunn'd him with the music of the spheres,[33]
How would he wish that Heav'n had left him still
The whisp'ring Zephyr,[34] and the purling rill?[35]
Who finds not Providence all good and wise,
Alike in what it gives, and what denies?

   VII. Far as Creation's ample range extends,
The scale of sensual, mental pow'rs ascends:
Mark how it mounts, to Man's imperial race,[36]
From the green myriads in the peopled grass:
What modes of sight betwixt each wide extreme,
The mole's dim curtain, and the lynx's beam:

---

[31] A tiny insect.
[32] Vapors (particles) which communicate the odors to the brain.
[33] It was once held that the planets, while rolling along their spheres, emitted music. This music, should it reach the ears, was believed to be as unbearable as direct sunlight to the eye.
[34] The gentle west wind of Greek mythology.
[35] A murmuring brook.
[36] Ruling species.

Of smell, the headlong lioness between,
And hound sagacious[37] on the tainted[38] green:
Of hearing, from the life that fills the flood,[39]
To that which warbles thro' the vernal[40] wood:
The spider's touch, how exquisitely fine!
Feels at each thread, and lives along the line:
In the nice[41] bee, what sense so subtly true
From pois'nous herbs extracts the healing dew?[42]
How Instinct varies in the grov'ling swine,
Compar'd, half-reas'ning elephant, with thine!
'Twixt that, and Reason,[43] what a nice barrier,
For ever sep'rate, yet for ever near!
Remembrance[44] and Reflection[45] how ally'd;
What thin partitions Sense from Thought divide:
And Middle natures,[46] how they long to join,
Yet never pass th' insuperable line!
Without this just gradation, could they be
Subjected, these to those, or all to thee?
The pow'rs of all subdu'd by thee alone,
Is not thy Reason all these pow'rs in one?

    VIII. See, thro' this air, this ocean, and this earth,
All matter quick, and bursting into birth.
Above, how high progressive life may go!
Around, how wide! how deep extend below!
Vast chain of Being! which from God began,
Natures ethereal,[47] human, angel, man,
Beast, bird, fish, insect, what no eye can see,
No glass can reach; from Infinite to thee,

---

[37] Having a keen sense of smell.
[38] Containing the odor of the hunted animal.
[39] Ocean. (Pope thought that fish were capable of hearing.)
[40] Springlike, green.
[41] Cautious.
[42] Honey, which was supposed to possess medicinal properties—as some moderns agree.
[43] A faculty believed denied by Nature to all animals except humans.
[44] Memory, which was thought common to most animals.
[45] The power of contemplating one's own thought, believed to belong only to humans.
[46] Creatures just below humans on the biological scale.
[47] Spiritual; heavenly.

From thee to Nothing!—On superior pow'rs
Were we to press, inferior might on ours:
Or in the full creation leave a void,
Where, one step broken, the great scale's destroy'd:
From Nature's chain whatever link you strike,
Tenth or ten thousandth, breaks the chain alike.
    And, if each system in gradation roll[48]
Alike essential to th' amazing Whole,
The least confusion but in one, not all
That system only, but the Whole must fall.
Let Earth unbalanc'd from her orbit fly,
Planets and Suns run lawless thro' the sky;
Let ruling angels from their spheres be hurl'd,
Being on Being wreck'd, and world on world;
Heav'n's whole foundations to their centre nod,
And Nature tremble to the throne of God.
All this dread Order break—for whom? for thee?
Vile worm!—Oh Madness! Pride! Impiety!

    IX. What if the foot, ordain'd the dust to tread,
Or hand, to toil, aspir'd to be the head?
What if the head, the eye, or ear repin'd[49]
To serve mere engines to the ruling Mind?
Just as absurd for any part to claim
To be another, in this gen'ral frame:
Just as absurd, to mourn the tasks or pains,
The great directing Mind of All ordains.
    All are but parts of one stupendous whole,
Whose body Nature is, and God the soul;
That, chang'd thro' all, and yet in all the same;
Great in the earth, as in th' ethereal frame;
Warms in the sun, refreshes in the breeze,
Glows in the stars, and blossoms in the trees,
Lives thro' all life, extends thro' all extent,
Spreads undivided, operates unspent;
Breathes in our soul, informs our mortal part,
As full, as perfect, in a hair as heart:
As full, as perfect, in vile Man that mourns,

---

[48] The step by step progression of the interrelated parts of creation.
[49] Complained.

As the rapt Seraph that adores and burns:
To him no high, no low, no great, no small;
He fills, he bounds, connects, and equals all.

    X. Cease then, nor Order Imperfection name:
Our proper bliss depends on what we blame.
Know thy own point: This kind, this due degree
Of blindness, weakness, Heav'n bestows on thee.
Submit.—In this, or any other sphere,
Secure to be as blest as thou canst bear:
Safe in the hand of one disposing Pow'r,
Or in the natal, or the mortal hour.
All Nature is but Art,[50] unknown to thee;
All Chance, Direction, which thou canst not see;
All Discord, Harmony not understood;
All partial Evil, universal Good:
And, spite of Pride, in erring Reason's spite,
One truth is clear, WHATEVER IS, IS RIGHT.

EPISTLE II

    I. Know then thyself, presume not God to scan;[51]
The proper study of Mankind is Man.
Plac'd on this isthmus of a middle state,[52]
A Being darkly wise, and rudely great:
With too much knowledge for the Sceptic side,
With too much weakness for the Stoic's pride,[53]
He hangs between; in doubt to act, or rest;
In doubt to deem himself a God, or Beast;
In doubt his Mind or Body to prefer,
Born but to die, and reas'ning but to err;
Alike in ignorance, his reason such,

---

[50] According to the English philosopher Hobbes: "Nature is the art whereby God governs the world." This idea attributes conscious design to the physical universe.
[51] Investigate, scrutinize.
[52] Between the angels (above) and the animal kingdom (below).
[53] Scepticism and Stoicism were two philosophical schools of thought in ancient Greece. Sceptics doubted the trustworthiness of a person's senses and reason; therefore, they denied human ability to gain knowledge. Stoics demanded that a person calmly defy the trials and tribulations of life.

Whether he thinks too little, or too much:
Chaos of Thought and Passion, all confus'd;
Still by himself abus'd, or disabus'd;
Created half to rise, and half to fall;
Great lord of all things, yet a prey to all;
Sole judge of Truth, in endless Error hurl'd: [54]
The glory, jest, and riddle of the world!

• • •

[54] Cast back-and-forth.

9

Voltaire

Candide

François Marie Arouet (1694–1778), better known by his pen name, Voltaire, was perhaps the most characteristic and famous figure of the European Enlightenment. Born the son of a middle-class Parisian lawyer, he was a greatly gifted and prolific writer, creating during his long life a flood of works in history, philosophy, drama, poetry, fiction, and biography. All of Voltaire's works, in one way or another, reflect his belief in science, reason, and freedom; they also reflect his hatred of superstition, intolerance, and privilege, as the main sources of evil in the world. Voltaire eventually won fame and fortune in his lifetime, but not until after he had suffered for his views; because of them, he was imprisoned in the ancient Parisian fortress known as the Bastille and several times exiled. Amid his personal misfortunes, Voltaire devoted himself to trying to clear away what he thought was accumulated rubbish filling human minds. He popularized the faith of the Enlightenment and became the leader and symbol of the intellectual rebellion against traditional ideas and institutions. Toward the end of his life Voltaire was finally acclaimed in Paris; and in 1791, the people of France, who considered him one of the intellectual fathers of the French Revolution, enshrined his ashes in the Pantheon. At once liberal and conservative, deist and agnostic, fighter and coward, generous and miserly, Voltaire was, above all, a humanist who wished to better the world by turning nature to human use through reason.

Candide, or Optimism *(1759) was written when Voltaire was sixty-five years old and is now the most widely read of all his works. Marked by wit and irony and a clear, lively style,* Candide *is a classic story of the young innocent learning about the wickedness of the world. But as the rollicking adventures of the hero move along, he is shown to be a man of common sense. Many of the other characters are symbols of contemporary ideas and institutions, which are subjected to a withering and delightful satire. Voltaire's conclusion is that the world is mad and that sane people should concern themselves with tasks that are within their competence.*

CHAPTER 1

How Candide Was Brought Up in a Noble Castle and How He Was Expelled from the Same

In the castle of Baron Thunder-ten-tronckh[1] in Westphalia[2] there lived a youth, endowed by Nature with the most gentle character. His face was the expression of his soul. His judgment was quite honest and he was extremely simple-minded; and this was the reason, I think, that he was named Candide.[3] Old servants in the house suspected that he was the son of the Baron's sister and a decent honest gentleman of the neighborhood, whom this young lady would never marry because he could only prove seventy-one quarterings,[4] and the rest of his genealogical tree was lost, owing to the injuries of time.

The Baron was one of the most powerful lords in Westphalia, for his castle possessed a door and windows. His Great Hall was even decorated with a piece of tapestry. The dogs in his stableyards formed a pack of hounds when necessary; his grooms[5] were his

[1] Voltaire was appalled by the vast number of lesser German nobles, most of whom lorded over small pieces of land. Though ignorant and uneducated, these nobles were generally conceited and arrogant and extremely proud of their long, and sometimes questionable, bloodlines.

[2] A German province extending eastward from the point where the Rhine River crosses into Dutch territory. On traveling through that province in 1740, Voltaire was shocked by the poverty he saw.

[3] Literally, "glowing white," or pure. Voltaire chose this name to suggest innocence and honesty of character.

[4] Numbers used to indicate the chronological span of a noble family. A family of some thirty quarterings is counted among the very oldest, since each quartering represents one generation.

[5] People who feed and care for horses.

huntsmen; the village curate[6] was his Grand Almoner.[7] They all called him "My Lord," and laughed heartily at his stories.

The Baroness weighed about three hundred and fifty pounds, was therefore greatly respected, and did the honors of the house with a dignity which rendered her still more respectable. Her daughter Cunegonde,[8] aged seventeen, was rosy-cheeked, fresh, plump and tempting. The Baron's son appeared in every respect worthy of his father. The tutor Pangloss[9] was the oracle of the house, and little Candide followed his lessons with all the candor of his age and character.

Pangloss taught metaphysico–theologo–cosmolo–nigology.[10] He proved admirably that there is no effect without a cause and that, in this best of all possible worlds, My Lord the Baron's castle was the best of castles and his wife the best of all possible Baronesses.

" 'Tis demonstrated," said he, "that things cannot be otherwise; for, since everything is made for an end, everything is necessarily for the best end. Observe that noses were made to wear spectacles; and so we have spectacles. Legs were visibly instituted to be breeched, and we have breeches. Stones were formed to be quarried and to build castles; and My Lord has a very noble castle; the greatest Baron in the province should have the best house; and as pigs were made to be eaten, we eat pork all the year round; consequently, those who have asserted that all is well, talk nonsense; they ought to have said that all is for the best."

Candide listened attentively and believed innocently; for he thought Miss Cunegonde extremely beautiful, although he was never bold enough to tell her so. He decided that after the happiness of being born Baron of Thunder-ten-tronckh, the second degree of happiness was to be Miss Cunegonde; the third, to see her every day; and the fourth to listen to Dr. Pangloss, the greatest philosopher of the province and therefore of the whole world.

One day when Cunegonde was walking near the castle, in a little

---

[6] Priest.

[7] A high-ranking clergyman of the royal court, in charge of the distribution of alms.

[8] A name inspired by Kunigunde, who died in 1033 and was canonized in 1200. The wife of the medieval German Emperor Henry II, she supposedly "kept her virginity to her death"—thus abusing the sacrament of marriage.

[9] Literally (in Greek), all tongue.

[10] Voltaire uses Pangloss as a foil for his ridicule of the optimistic assumptions and statements of the English poet Alexander Pope (1688–1744), the German philosopher Gottfried Wilhelm von Leibnitz (1646–1716), and Christian von Wolff (1679–1754), who developed and popularized Leibnitz' philosophy.

wood which was called The Park, she observed Dr. Pangloss in the bushes, giving a lesson in experimental physics to her mother's waiting-maid, a very pretty and docile brunette. Miss Cunegonde had a great inclination for science and watched breathlessly the re-iterated experiments she witnessed; she observed clearly the Doctor's sufficient reason, the effects and the causes, and returned home very much excited, pensive, filled with the desire of learning, reflecting that she might be the sufficient reason of young Candide and that he might be hers.

On her way back to the castle she met Candide and blushed; Candide also blushed. She bade him good-morning in a hesitating voice; Candide replied without knowing what he was saying. Next day, when they left the table after dinner, Cunegonde and Candide found themselves behind a screen; Cunegonde dropped her handkerchief, Candide picked it up; she innocently held his hand; the young man innocently kissed the young lady's hand with remarkable vivacity, tenderness and grace; their lips met, their eyes sparkled, their knees trembled, their hands wandered. Baron Thunder-ten-tronckh passed near the screen, and, observing this cause and effect, expelled Candide from the castle by kicking him in the backside frequently and hard. Cunegonde swooned; when she recovered her senses, the Baroness slapped her in the face; and all was in consternation in the noblest and most agreeable of all possible castles.

CHAPTER 2

What Happened to Candide Among the Bulgarians [11]

Candide, expelled from the earthly paradise, wandered for a long time without knowing where he was going, turning up his eyes to Heaven, gazing back frequently at the noblest of castles which held the most beautiful of young Baronesses; he lay down to sleep sup-perless between two furrows in the open fields; it snowed heavily in large flakes. The next morning the shivering Candide, penniless, dying of cold and exhaustion, dragged himself towards the neigh-

---

[11] Fictional name for the Prussians. In Voltaire's time, Prussia and Austria were the states with the largest German-speaking populations.

boring town, which was called Waldberghoff-trarbkdikdorff.[12] He halted sadly at the door of an inn. Two men dressed in blue [13] noticed him.

"Comrade," said one, "there's a well-built young man of the right height."

They went up to Candide and very civilly invited him to dinner.

"Gentlemen," said Candide with charming modesty, "you do me a great honor, but I have no money to pay my share."

"Ah, sir," said one of the men in blue, "persons of your figure and merit never pay anything; are you not five feet five tall?"

"Yes, gentlemen," said he, bowing, "that is my height."

"Ah, sir, come to table; we will not only pay your expenses, we will never allow a man like you to be short of money; men were only made to help each other."

"You are in the right," said Candide, "that is what Dr. Pangloss was always telling me, and I see that everything is for the best."

They begged him to accept a few crowns,[14] he took them and wished to give them an IOU; they refused to take it and all sat down to table.

"Do you not love tenderly . . ."

"Oh, yes," said he. "I love Miss Cunegonde tenderly."

"No," said one of the gentlemen. "We were asking if you do not tenderly love the King of the Bulgarians." [15]

"Not a bit," said he, "for I have never seen him."

"What! He is the most charming of kings, and you must drink his health."

"Oh, gladly, gentlemen."

And he drank.[16]

"That is sufficient," he was told. "You are now the support, the aid, the defender, the hero of the Bulgarians; your fortune is made and your glory assured."

---

[12] A suggestion of how the German language sounded to Voltaire. He thought German was ugly and dissonant, fit only for soldiers and horses.

[13] Uniforms of Prussian recruiting officers. As the army suffered heavy losses in many battles, Prussian recruiters were incessantly searching for replacements.

[14] Silver coins.

[15] Frederick II (or Frederick the Great), king of Prussia from 1740 to 1786.

[16] Accepting the toast of the recruiters and having a drink with them took the place of signing up.

They immediately put irons on his legs and took him to a regiment. He was made to turn to the right and left, to raise the
ramrod [17] and return the ramrod, to take aim, to fire, to double up,
and he was given thirty strokes with a stick; the next day he drilled
not quite so badly, and received only twenty strokes; the day after,
he only had ten and was looked on as a prodigy by his comrades.

Candide was completely mystified and could not make out how he
was a hero. One fine spring day he thought he would take a walk,
going straight ahead, in the belief that to use his legs as he pleased
was a privilege of the human species as well as of animals. He had
not gone two leagues [18] when four other heroes, each six feet tall, fell
upon him, bound him and dragged him back to a cell. [19] He was
asked by his judges whether he would rather be thrashed thirty-six
times by the whole regiment or receive a dozen lead bullets at once
in his brain. Although he protested that men's wills are free and that
he wanted neither one nor the other, he had to make a choice; by virtue of that gift of God which is called *liberty,* he determined to run
the gauntlet thirty-six times and actually did so twice. There were
two thousand men in the regiment. That made four thousand strokes
which laid bare the muscles and nerves from his neck to his backside.
As they were about to proceed to a third turn, Candide, utterly
exhausted, begged as a favor that they would be so kind as to smash
his head; he obtained this favor; they bound his eyes and he was
made to kneel down. At that moment the King of the Bulgarians
came by and inquired the victim's crime; and as this King was possessed of a vast genius, he perceived from what he learned about
Candide that he was a young metaphysician very ignorant in worldly
matters, and therefore pardoned him with a clemency which will be
praised in all newspapers and all ages. An honest surgeon healed
Candide in three weeks with the ointments recommended by Dioscorides. [20] He had already regained a little skin and could walk when

[17] A rod used for ramming a powder charge into a gun, thus loading it through the
muzzle.
[18] A league is a unit of distance ranging from 2.4 to 4.6 miles, depending on country.
[19] Desertions were numerous in the armies of the eighteenth century, and punishment
for deserting was very severe. (While visiting the court of the King of Prussia, Voltaire had become acquainted with the harshness and brutality of military life.)
[20] Penadius Dioscorides, a Greek physician of the first century A.D. Voltaire was con-
temptuous of the healing arts of his age, because physicians continued to use remedies and methods that had long since become outmoded.

the King of the Bulgarians went to war with the King of the Abares.[21]

CHAPTER 3

How Candide Escaped from the Bulgarians and What Became of Him

Nothing could be smarter, more splendid, more brilliant, better drawn up than the two armies. Trumpets, fifes, hautboys,[22] drums, cannons formed a harmony such as has never been heard even in hell. The cannons first of all laid flat about six thousand men on each side; then the musketry removed from the best of worlds some nine or ten thousand blackguards[23] who infested its surface. The bayonet also was the sufficient reason for the death of some thousands of men. The whole might amount to thirty thousand souls. Candide, who trembled like a philosopher, hid himself as well as he could during this heroic butchery.

At last, while the two kings each commanded a Te Deum[24] in his camp, Candide decided to go elsewhere to reason about effects and causes. He clambered over heaps of dead and dying men and reached a neighboring village, which was in ashes; it was an Abare village which the Bulgarians had burned in accordance with international law. Here, old men dazed with blows watched the dying agonies of their murdered wives who clutched their children to their bleeding breasts; there, disembowelled girls who had been made to satisfy the natural appetites of heroes gasped their last sighs; others, half-burned, begged to be put to death. Brains were scattered on the ground among dismembered arms and legs.

Candide fled to another village as fast as he could; it belonged to the Bulgarians, and Abarian heroes had treated it in the same way. Candide, stumbling over quivering limbs or across ruins, at last es-

---

[21] The French, who in the Seven Years' War (1756–1763), sided with the Austrians against Prussia and England.

[22] Oboes.

[23] Scoundrels.

[24] *Te Deum laudamus* (We praise Thee, O God), an ancient Christian hymn of praise to God. It is used here to suggest the service of thanksgiving (for victory) in which it was a principal part.

caped from the theatre of war, carrying a little food in his knapsack, and never forgetting Miss Cunegonde. His provisions were all gone when he reached Holland; but, having heard that everyone in that country was rich and a Christian, he had no doubt at all but that he would be as well treated as he had been in the Baron's castle before he had been expelled on account of Miss Cunegonde's pretty eyes.

He asked an alms of several grave persons, who all replied that if he continued in that way he would be shut up in a house of correction to teach him how to live.[25]

He then addressed himself to a man who had been discoursing on charity in a large assembly for an hour on end. This orator, glancing at him askance, said:

"What are you doing here? Are you for the good cause?"

"There is no effect without a cause," said Candide modestly. "Everything is necessarily linked up and arranged for the best. It was necessary that I should be expelled from the company of Miss Cunegonde, that I ran the gauntlet, and that I beg my bread until I can earn it; all this could not have happened differently."

"My friend," said the orator, "do you believe that the Pope is Anti-Christ?"[26]

"I had never heard so before," said Candide, "but whether he is or isn't, I am starving."

"You don't deserve to eat," said the other. "Hence, rascal; hence, you wretch; and never come near me again."

The orator's wife thrust her head out of the window and seeing a man who did not believe that the Pope was Anti-Christ, she poured on his head a full . . . O Heavens! To what excess religious zeal is carried by ladies!

A man who had not been baptized, an honest Anabaptist[27] named

---

[25] In general, Voltaire admired the Dutch for their liberty, equality, prosperity, and tolerance, as well as for their concern for the unfortunate. On the other hand, he had also noticed that on occasion they were capable of hardheartedness and greed.

[26] At least since the days of the English reformer John Wycliffe (ca. 1320–1384), Protestant firebrands had wanted to believe that the Pope was the Antichrist (the enemy of Christ), a term that appears in the New Testament in the first two epistles of John. Voltaire thought that preoccupation with such questions was often an escape from practicing charity.

[27] A member of a religious group that in the sixteenth century attracted a number of followers in southwestern Germany and Switzerland. The Anabaptists (literally, rebaptizers) insisted upon baptism of the *adult* believer, thus rejecting infant baptism. Voltaire admired the Anabaptists for their simple piety, hard work, love of peace, and charity. (Though today they are usually listed as Protestants, in the sixteenth century they were persecuted by Catholics and Protestants alike. Many,

Jacques, saw the cruel and ignominious treatment of one of his brothers,[28] a featherless two-legged creature with a soul;[29] he took him home, cleaned him up, gave him bread and beer, presented him with two florins,[30] and even offered to teach him to work at the manufacture of Persian stuffs[31] which are made in Holland. Candide threw himself at the man's feet, exclaiming:

"Dr. Pangloss was right in telling me that all is for the best in this world, for I am vastly more touched by your extreme generosity than by the harshness of the gentleman in the black cloak and his good lady."

The next day when he walked out he met a beggar covered with sores, dull-eyed, with the end of his nose fallen away, his mouth awry, his teeth black, who talked huskily, was tormented with a violent cough and spat out a tooth at every cough.

CHAPTER 4

How Candide Met His Old Master in Philosophy, Doctor Pangloss, and What Happened

Candide, moved even more by compassion than by horror, gave this horrible beggar the two florins he had received from the honest Anabaptist, Jacques. The phantom gazed fixedly at him, shed tears and threw its arms round his neck. Candide recoiled in terror.

"Alas!" said the wretch to the other wretch, "Don't you recognise your dear Pangloss?"

"What do I hear? You, my dear master! You, in this horrible state! What misfortune has happened to you? Why are you no longer in the noblest of castles? What has become of Miss Cunegonde, the pearl of young ladies, the masterpiece of Nature?"

"I am exhausted,"[32] said Pangloss. Candide immediately took him to the Anabaptist's stable, where he gave him a little bread to eat; and when Pangloss had recovered:

therefore, fled from their homelands and settled in Holland or North America, where they became known as Mennonites or Amish.)
[28] Fellow human beings.
[29] A reference to Plato's definition of a human being.
[30] Gold coins minted in thirteenth-century Florence. They were accepted as currency throughout Europe.
[31] Persian rugs.
[32] He means that he is dying.

"Well!" said he, "Cunegonde?"

"Dead!" replied the other.

At this word Candide swooned; his friend restored him to his senses with a little bad vinegar which happened to be in the stable. Candide opened his eyes.

"Cunegonde dead! Ah! best of worlds, where are you? But what illness did she die of? Was it because she saw me kicked out of her father's noble castle?"

"No," said Pangloss. "She was disembowelled by Bulgarian soldiers, after having been raped to the limit of possibility; they broke the Baron's head when he tried to defend her; the Baroness was cut to pieces; my poor pupil was treated exactly like his sister; and as to the castle, there is not one stone standing on another, not a barn, not a sheep, not a duck, not a tree; but we were well avenged, for the Abares did exactly the same to a neighboring barony which belonged to a Bulgarian Lord."

At this, Candide swooned again; but, having recovered and having said all that he ought to say, he inquired the cause and effect, the sufficient reason which had reduced Pangloss to so piteous a state.

"Alas!" said Pangloss, " 'tis love; love, the consoler of the human race, the preserver of the universe, the soul of all tender creatures, gentle love."

"Alas!" said Candide, "I am acquainted with this love, this sovereign of hearts, this soul of our soul; it has never brought me anything but one kiss and twenty kicks in the backside. How could this beautiful cause produce in you so abominable an effect?"

Pangloss replied as follows:

"My dear Candide! You remember Paquette,[33] the maid-servant of our august Baroness; in her arms I enjoyed the delights of Paradise which have produced the tortures of Hell by which you see I am devoured; she was infected[34] and perhaps is dead. Paquette received this present from a most learned monk, who had it from the source; for he received it from an old countess, who had it from a cavalry captain, who owed it to a marchioness,[35] who derived it from a page, who had received it from a Jesuit, who, when a novice, had it in a direct line from one of the companions of Christopher Columbus. For my part, I shall not give it to anyone, for I am dying."

[33] A name derived from the French word *pâquerette,* which means daisy.
[34] With syphilis, which had been carried to Europe from the Americas.
[35] The wife or widow of a marquis, a high-ranking nobleman.

"O Pangloss!" exclaimed Candide, "this is a strange genealogy! Wasn't the devil at the root of it?"

"Not at all," replied that great man. "It was something indispensable in this best of worlds, a necessary ingredient; for, if Columbus in an island of America had not caught this disease, which poisons the source of generation, and often indeed prevents generation, we should not have chocolate and cochineal;[36] it must also be noticed that hitherto in our continent this disease is peculiar to us, like theological disputes. The Turks, the Indians, the Persians, the Chinese, the Siamese and the Japanese are not yet familiar with it; but there is a sufficient reason why they in their turn should become familiar with it in a few centuries. Meanwhile, it has made marvellous progress among us, and especially in those large armies composed of honest, well-bred stipendiaries[37] who decide the destiny of States; it may be asserted that when thirty thousand men fight a pitched battle against an equal number of troops, there are about twenty thousand with the pox[38] on either side."

"Admirable!" said Candide. "But you must get cured."

"How can I?" said Pangloss. "I haven't a sou,[39] my friend, and in the whole extent of this globe, you cannot be bled or receive an enema without paying or without someone paying for you."

This last speech determined Candide; he went and threw himself at the feet of his charitable Anabaptist, Jacques, and drew so touching a picture of the state to which his friend was reduced that the good easy man did not hesitate to succor Pangloss; he had him cured at his own expense. In this cure Pangloss only lost one eye and one ear. He could write well and knew arithmetic perfectly. The Anabaptist made him his bookkeeper. At the end of two months he was compelled to go to Lisbon[40] on business and took his two philosophers on the boat with him. Pangloss explained to him how everything was for the best. Jacques was not of this opinion.

"Men," said he, "must have corrupted nature a little, for they were not born wolves, and they have become wolves. God did not give them twenty-four-pounder cannons or bayonets, and they have made bayonets and cannons to destroy each other. I might bring

---

[36] A red dye originating in Central and South America.
[37] Mercenaries.
[38] Syphilis.
[39] A small French coin of little value.
[40] The capital city and major port of Portugal.

bankruptcies[41] into the account and Justice which seizes the goods of bankrupts in order to deprive the creditors of them."

"It was all indispensable," replied the one-eyed doctor, "and private misfortunes make the public good, so that the more private misfortunes there are, the more everything is well."

While he was reasoning, the air grew dark, the winds blew from the four quarters of the globe and the ship was attacked by the most horrible tempest in sight of the port of Lisbon.

CHAPTER 5

Storm, Shipwreck, Earthquake, and What Happened to Dr. Pangloss, to Candide and the Anabaptist Jacques

Half the enfeebled passengers, suffering from that inconceivable anguish which the rolling of a ship causes in the nerves and in all the humors[42] of bodies shaken in contrary directions, did not retain strength enough even to trouble about the danger. The other half screamed and prayed; the sails were torn, the masts broken, the vessel was leaking. Those worked who could, no one co-operated, no one commanded. The Anabaptist tried to help the crew a little; he was on the main-deck; a furious sailor struck him violently and stretched him on the deck; but the blow he delivered gave him so violent a shock that he fell head-first out of the ship. He remained hanging and clinging to part of the broken mast. The good Jacques ran to his aid, helped him to climb back, and from the effort he made was flung into the sea in full view of the sailor, who allowed him to drown without condescending even to look at him. Candide came up, saw his benefactor reappear for a moment and then be engulfed for ever. He tried to throw himself after him into the sea; he was prevented by the philosopher Pangloss, who proved to him that the Lisbon roads had been expressly created for the Anabaptist to be drowned in them. While he was proving this *a priori*,[43] the vessel sank, and everyone perished except Pangloss, Candide and the brutal

---

[41] Personal loss of money due to the bankruptcies of others had been painful to Voltaire.

[42] Prior to the advent of modern medicine it was held that four body fluids, so-called humors (blood, phlegm, yellow bile, black bile), determine a person's disposition and health.

[43] Reasoning from an accepted presumption.

sailor who had drowned the virtuous Anabaptist; the blackguard swam successfully to the shore and Pangloss and Candide were carried there on a plank.

When they had recovered a little, they walked toward Lisbon; they had a little money by the help of which they hoped to be saved from hunger after having escaped the storm.

Weeping the death of their benefactor, they had scarcely set foot in the town when they felt the earth tremble under their feet;[44] the sea rose in foaming masses in the port and smashed the ships which rode at anchor. Whirlwinds of flame and ashes covered the streets and squares; the houses collapsed, the roofs were thrown upon the foundations, and the foundations were scattered; thirty thousand inhabitants of every age and both sexes were crushed under the ruins. Whistling and swearing, the sailor said:

"There'll be something to pick up here."

"What can be the sufficient reason for this phenomenon?" said Pangloss.

"It is the last day!" cried Candide.

The sailor immediately ran among the debris, dared death to find money, found it, seized it, got drunk, and having slept off his wine, purchased the favor of the first woman of good-will he met on the ruins of the houses and among the dead and dying. Pangloss, however, pulled him by the sleeve.

"My friend," said he, "this is not well, you are disregarding universal reason, you choose the wrong time."

"Blood and 'ounds!" he retorted, "I am a sailor and I was born in Batavia;[45] four times have I stamped on the crucifix during four voyages to Japan;[46] you have found the right man for your universal reason!"

Candide had been hurt by some falling stones; he lay in the street covered with debris. He said to Pangloss:

[44] The actual Lisbon earthquake and fire occurred on November 1, 1755. The destruction of the city, with the loss of more than thirty thousand lives, confirmed for Voltaire the wisdom of his earlier rejection of philosophical optimism. The disaster also prompted him to write both *Candide* and his *Poem on the Lisbon Earthquake* (1755).

[45] A city founded by the Dutch in the early seventeenth century on the island of Java in the East Indies. Now called Djakarta, it is the capital of Indonesia.

[46] In 1638 European traders, specifically the Spanish and the Portuguese, were expelled from Japan; only the Dutch were permitted to trade there, from a small island near Nagasaki. To discourage trading and to assure that no Christian missionary might enter disguised as a trader, Dutch merchants were supposedly required to stamp on a crucifix or an image of Jesus.

"Alas! Get me a little wine and oil; I am dying."

"This earthquake is not a new thing," replied Pangloss. "The town of Lima felt the same shocks in America last year; similar causes produce similar effects; there must certainly be a train of sulphur underground from Lima to Lisbon."

"Nothing is more probable," replied Candide; "but, for God's sake, a little oil and wine."

"What do you mean, probable?" replied the philosopher; "I maintain that it is proved."

Candide lost consciousness, and Pangloss brought him a little water from a neighboring fountain.

Next day they found a little food as they wandered among the ruins and regained a little strength. Afterward they worked like others to help the inhabitants who had escaped death. Some citizens they had assisted gave them as good a dinner as could be expected in such a disaster; true, it was a dreary meal; the hosts watered their bread with their tears, but Pangloss consoled them by assuring them that things could not be otherwise.

"For," said he, "all this is for the best; for, if there is a volcano at Lisbon, it cannot be anywhere else; for it is impossible that things should not be where they are; for all is well."

A little, dark man, a familiar[47] of the Inquisition,[48] who sat beside him, politely took up the conversation, and said:

"Apparently you do not believe in original sin; for, if everything is for the best, there was neither fall nor punishment."

"I most humbly beg your excellency's pardon," replied Pangloss still more politely, "for the fall of man and the curse necessarily entered into the best of all possible worlds."

"Then you do not believe in free-will?" said the familiar.

"Your excellency will pardon me," said Pangloss; "free-will can exist with absolute necessity; for it was necessary that we should be free; for in short, limited will . . ."

Pangloss was in the middle of his phrase when the familiar nodded to his armed attendant who was pouring out port or Oporto wine for him.

[47] An undercover agent.

[48] The Inquisition, or the Congregation of the Holy Office (the official name), was a Roman Catholic tribunal charged with seeking out heresy (false beliefs) and punishing heretics. It was founded in the early thirteenth century and abolished in 1834. In the fifteenth and sixteenth centuries it raged most furiously in Spain, Portugal, and Italy.

CHAPTER 6

*How a Splendid Auto-da-Fé Was Held to Prevent Earthquakes,
and How Candide Was Flogged*

After the earthquake which destroyed three-quarters of Lisbon, the
wise men of that country could discover no more efficacious way of
preventing a total ruin than by giving the people a splendid *auto-da-
fé*.[49] It was decided by the university of Coimbre[50] that the sight of
several persons being slowly burned in great ceremony is an infallible
secret for preventing earthquakes.

Consequently they had arrested a Biscayan[51] convicted of having
married his fellow-godmother,[52] and two Portuguese who, when
eating a chicken had thrown away the bacon;[53] after dinner they
came and bound Dr. Pangloss and his disciple Candide, one because
he had spoken and the other because he had listened with an air of
approbation; they were both carried separately to extremely cool
apartments, where there was never any discomfort from the sun; a
week afterwards each was dressed in a sanbenito[54] and their heads
were ornamented with paper mitres; Candide's mitre[55] and sanbenito were painted with flames upside down and with devils who
had neither tails nor claws; but Pangloss's devils had claws and tails,
and his flames were upright.[56]

---

[49] Portuguese: act of faith. The phrase refers to the public sentencing and subsequent
punishment of convicted and hardened heretics. There were indeed several *auto-da-
fés* following the destruction of Lisbon.

[50] A city about one hundred miles north of Lisbon, boasting one of the oldest European universities.

[51] One living near the Gulf of Biscay, off the northern coast of Spain.

[52] A reference to the supposed illicit marriage of two godparents of the same child.
(Voltaire is spoofing the complicated church prohibitions regarding matrimonial
union.)

[53] Thus making themselves suspect of being Jews.

[54] A cape worn by those who were to be sentenced at the *auto-da-fé*. A yellow sanbenito with flames painted on it pointing downward indicated that the heretic's life
was spared; a person to be burned wore a black sanbenito with flames pointing
upward.

[55] A paper hat in the shape of a beehive or cone, somewhat resembling a bishop's
mitre.

[56] Candide obviously escaped the stake through confession, while Pangloss was condemned to suffer death as a stubborn heretic.

Dressed in this manner they marched in procession and listened to a most pathetic sermon, followed by lovely plain-song music. Candide was flogged in time to the music, while the singing went on; the Biscayan and the two men who had not wanted to eat bacon were burned, and Pangloss was hanged, although this is not the custom. The very same day, the earth shook again with a terrible clamor.[57]

Candide, terrified, dumbfounded, bewildered, covered with blood, quivering from head to foot, said to himself:

"If this is the best of all possible worlds, what are the others? Let it pass that I was flogged, for I was flogged by the Bulgarians, but, O my dear Pangloss! The greatest of philosophers! Must I see you hanged without knowing why! O my dear Anabaptist! The best of men! Was it necessary that you should be drowned in port! O Miss Cunegonde! The pearl of women! Was it necessary that your belly should be slit!"

He was returning, scarcely able to support himself, preached at, flogged, absolved and blessed, when an old woman accosted him and said:

"Courage, my son, follow me."

CHAPTER 7

How an Old Woman Took Care of Candide and How He Regained That Which He Loved

Candide did not take courage, but he followed the old woman to a hovel; she gave him a pot of ointment to rub on, and left him food and drink; she pointed out a fairly clean bed; near the bed there was a suit of clothes.

"Eat, drink, sleep," said she, "and may our Lady of Atocha, my Lord Saint Anthony of Padua and my Lord Saint James of Compostella take care of you; I shall come back tomorrow."

Candide, still amazed by all he had seen, by all he had suffered, and still more by the old woman's charity, tried to kiss her hand.

" 'Tis not my hand you should kiss," said the old woman, "I shall come back tomorrow. Rub on the ointment, eat and sleep."

In spite of all his misfortune, Candide ate and went to sleep. Next

---

[57] Lisbon actually suffered a second earth tremor on December 21, 1755 (some seven weeks after the leveling of the city by the first quake).

day the old woman brought him breakfast, examined his back and smeared him with another ointment; later she brought him dinner, and returned in the evening with supper. The next day she went through the same ceremony.

"Who are you?" Candide kept asking her. "Who has inspired you with so much kindness? How can I thank you?"

The good woman never made any reply; she returned in the evening without any supper.

"Come with me," said she, "and do not speak a word."

She took him by the arm and walked into the country with him for about a quarter of a mile; they came to an isolated house, surrounded with gardens and canals. The old woman knocked at a little door. It was opened; she led Candide up a back stairway into a gilded apartment, left him on a brocaded sofa, shut the door and went away. Candide thought he was dreaming, and felt that his whole life was a bad dream and the present moment an agreeable dream.

The old woman soon reappeared; she was supporting with some difficulty a trembling woman of majestic stature, glittering with precious stones and covered with a veil.

"Remove the veil," said the old woman to Candide. The young man advanced and lifted the veil with a timid hand. What a moment! What a surprise! He thought he saw Miss Cunegonde, in fact he was looking at her, it was she herself. His strength failed him, he could not utter a word and fell at her feet. Cunegonde fell on the sofa. The old woman dosed them with distilled waters; they recovered their senses and began to speak: at first they uttered only broken words, questions and answers at cross purposes, sighs, tears, exclamations. The old woman advised them to make less noise and left them alone.

"What! Is it you?" said Candide. "You are alive, and I find you here in Portugal! Then you were not raped? Your belly was not slit, as the philosopher Pangloss assured me?"

"Yes, indeed," said the fair Cunegonde; "but those two accidents are not always fatal."

"But your father and mother were killed?"

" 'Tis only too true," said Cunegonde, weeping.

"And your brother?"

"My brother was killed too." [58]

---

[58] As Candide learns later, her brother, too recovered from his wounds.

"And why are you in Portugal? And how did you know I was here? And by what strange adventure have you brought me to this house?"

"I will tell you everything," replied the lady, "but first of all you must tell me everything that has happened to you since the innocent kiss you gave me and the kicks you received."

Candide obeyed with profound respect; and, although he was bewildered, although his voice was weak and trembling, although his back was still a little painful, he related in the most natural manner all he had endured since the moment of their separation. Cunegonde raised her eyes to Heaven; she shed tears at the death of the good Anabaptist and Pangloss, after which she spoke as follows to Candide, who did not miss a word and devoured her with his eyes.

CHAPTER 8

Cunegonde's Story

"I was fast asleep in bed when it pleased Heaven to send the Bulgarians to our noble castle of Thunder-ten-tronckh; they murdered my father and brother and cut my mother to pieces. A large Bulgarian six feet tall, seeing that I had swooned at the spectacle, began to rape me; this brought me to, I recovered my senses, I screamed, I struggled, I bit, I scratched, I tried to tear out the big Bulgarian's eyes, not knowing that what was happening in my father's castle was a matter of custom; the brute stabbed me with a knife in the left side where I still have the scar."

"Alas! I hope I shall see it," said the naive Candide.

"You shall see it," said Cunegonde, "but let me go on."

"Go on," said Candide.

She took up the thread of her story as follows:

"A Bulgarian captain came in, saw me covered with blood, and the soldier did not disturb himself. The captain was angry at the brute's lack of respect to him, and killed him on my body. Afterward, he had me bandaged and took me to his billet as a prisoner of war. I washed the few shirts he had and did the cooking; I must admit he thought me very pretty; and I will not deny that he was very well built and that his skin was white and soft; otherwise he had little wit and little philosophy; it was plain that he had not been brought up by Dr. Pangloss. At the end of three months he lost all his money and got tired of me; he sold me to a Jew named Don Issachar,[59] who traded in Holland and Portugal and had a passion for women. This Jew devoted himself to my person but he could not triumph over it; I resisted him better than the Bulgarian soldier; a lady of honor may be raped once, but it strengthens her virtue. In order to subdue me, the Jew brought me to this country house. Up till then I believed that there was nothing on earth so splendid as the castle of Thunder-ten-tronckh; I was undeceived.

"One day the Grand Inquisitor noticed me at Mass; he ogled me continually and sent a message that he wished to speak to me on secret affairs. I was taken to his palace; I informed him of my birth; he pointed out how much it was beneath my rank to belong to an Israelite. A proposition was made on his behalf to Don Issachar to give me up to His Lordship. Don Issachar, who is the court banker and a man of influence, would not agree. The Inquisitor threatened him with an *auto-da-fé*. At last the Jew was frightened and made a bargain whereby the house and I belong to both in common. The Jew has Mondays, Wednesdays and the Sabbath day, and the Inquisitor has the other days of the week. This arrangement has lasted for six months. It has not been without quarrels; for it has often been debated whether the night between Saturday and Sunday belonged to the old law or the new.[60] For my part, I have hitherto resisted them both; and I think that is the reason why they still love me.

"At last My Lord the Inquisitor was pleased to arrange an *auto-da-fé* to remove the scourge of earthquakes and to intimidate Don Issachar. He honored me with an invitation. I had an excellent seat; and refreshments were served to the ladies between the Mass and the execution. I was indeed horror-stricken when I saw the burning of the two Jews and the honest Biscayan who had married his fellow-godmother; but what was my surprise, my terror, my anguish, when I saw in a sanbenito and under a mitre a face which resembled Pangloss's! I rubbed my eyes, I looked carefully, I saw him hanged; and I fainted. I had scarcely recovered my senses when I saw you stripped naked; that was the height of horror, of consternation, of grief and despair. I will frankly tell you that your skin is even whiter

---

[59] As a people, Jews were not one of Voltaire's targets. In fact, Voltaire deplored the persecution that they had endured for so many centuries. On the other hand, he was only too quick to blame his own loss of money, due to speculation and bad judgment, on Jewish bankers and financiers.

[60] The Old Testament or the New Testament.

and of a more perfect tint than that of my Bulgarian captain. This spectacle redoubled all the feelings which crushed and devoured me. I exclaimed, I tried to say: 'Stop, barbarians!' but my voice failed and my cries would have been useless. When you had been well flogged, I said to myself: 'How does it happen that the charming Candide and the wise Pangloss are in Lisbon, the one to receive a hundred lashes, and the other to be hanged, by order of My Lord the Inquisitor, whose darling I am? Pangloss deceived me cruelly when he said that all is for the best in the world.'

"I was agitated, distracted, sometimes beside myself and sometimes ready to die of faintness, and my head was filled with the massacre of my father, of my mother, of my brother, and the insolence of my horrid Bulgarian soldier, the gash he gave me, my slavery, my life as a kitchen-wench, my Bulgarian captain, my horrid Don Issachar, my abominable Inquisitor, the hanging of Dr. Pangloss, that long plain-song *miserere* [61] during which you were flogged, and above all the kiss I gave you behind the screen that day when I saw you for the last time. I praised God for bringing you back to me through so many trials, I ordered my old woman to take care of you and bring you here as soon as she could. She has carried out my commission very well; I have enjoyed the inexpressible pleasure of seeing you again, of listening to you, and of speaking to you. You must be very hungry; I have a good appetite; let us begin by having supper."

Both sat down to supper; and after supper they returned to the handsome sofa we have already mentioned; they were still there when Signor Don Issachar, one of the masters of the house, arrived. It was the day of the Sabbath. He came to enjoy his rights and to express his tender love.

CHAPTER 9

What Happened to Cunegonde, to Candide, to the Grand Inquisitor and to a Jew

This Issachar was the most choleric Hebrew who had been seen in Israel since the Babylonian captivity.[62]

---

[61] A musical composition based upon the opening phrase of Psalm 51: "Have mercy upon me, O God." It is a plea to God for pardon of deadly sins.
[62] The period (598–538 B.C.) in which Jews were held captive in Babylonia.

"What!" said he. "Bitch of a Galilean,[63] isn't it enough to have the Inquisitor? Must this scoundrel share with me too?"

So saying, he drew a long dagger which he always carried and, thinking that his adversary was unarmed, threw himself upon Candide; but our good Westphalian had received an excellent sword from the old woman along with his suit of clothes. He drew his sword, and although he had a most gentle character, laid the Israelite stone-dead on the floor at the feet of the fair Cunegonde.

"Holy Virgin!" she exclaimed, "what will become of us? A man killed in my house! If the police come we are lost."

"If Pangloss had not been hanged," said Candide, "he would have given us good advice in this extremity, for he was a great philosopher. In default of him, let us consult the old woman."

She was extremely prudent and was beginning to give her advice when another little door opened. It was an hour after midnight, and Sunday was beginning.

This day belonged to My Lord the Inquisitor. He came in and saw the flogged Candide sword in hand, a corpse lying on the ground, Cunegonde in terror, and the old woman giving advice.

At this moment, here is what happened in Candide's soul and the manner of his reasoning:

"If this holy man calls for help, he will infallibly have me burned; he might do as much to Cunegonde; he had me pitilessly lashed; he is my rival; I am in the mood to kill, there is no room for hesitation."

His reasoning was clear and swift; and, without giving the Inquisitor time to recover from his surprise, he pierced him through and through and cast him beside the Jew.

"Here's another," said Cunegonde, "there is no chance of mercy; we are excommunicated, our last hour has come. How does it happen that you, who were born so mild, should kill a Jew and a prelate in two minutes?"

"My dear young lady," replied Candide, "when a man is in love, jealous, and has been flogged by the Inquisition, he is beside himself."

The old woman then spoke up and said:

"In the stable are three Andalusian horses, with their saddles and

---

[63] A Christian. Jesus spent his childhood in Galilee, one of the three provinces of ancient Palestine.

bridles; let the brave Candide prepare them; madam has moidores[64] and diamonds; let us mount quickly, although I can only sit on one buttock, and go to Cadiz,[65] the weather is beautifully fine, and it is most pleasant to travel in the coolness of the night."

Candide immediately saddled the three horses. Cunegonde, the old woman and he rode thirty miles without stopping.

While they were riding away, the Holy Hermandad[66] arrived at the house; My Lord was buried in a splendid church and Issachar was thrown into a sewer.

Candide, Cunegonde and the old woman had already reached the little town of Aracena[67] in the midst of the mountains of the Sierra Morena,[68] and they talked in their inn as follows.

CHAPTER 10

*How Candide, Cunegonde and the Old Woman Arrived at
Cadiz in Great Distress, and How They Embarked*

"Who can have stolen my pistoles[69] and my diamonds?" said Cunegonde, weeping. "How shall we live? What shall we do? Where shall we find Inquisitors and Jews to give me others?"

"Alas!" said the old woman, "I strongly suspect a reverend Franciscan[70] father who slept in the same inn at Badajoz[71] with us; Heaven forbid that I should judge rashly! But he twice came into our room and left long before we did."

"Alas!" said Candide, "the good Pangloss often proved to me that this world's goods are common to all men and that everyone has an equal right to them. According to these principles the monk should have left us enough to continue our journey. Have you nothing left then, my fair Cunegonde?"

"Not a maravedi,"[72] said she.

---

[64] Portuguese gold coins.
[65] A maritime city in southwestern Spain; Cadiz functioned as Spain's door to the New World.
[66] The clerical police.
[67] About one hundred miles north of Cadiz.
[68] A mountain range.
[69] Spanish gold coins.
[70] A member of a Roman Catholic order.
[71] A Spanish city near the Portuguese border.
[72] A small Spanish copper coin worth less than a penny.

"What are we to do?" said Candide.

"Sell one of the horses," said the old woman. "I will ride pillion[73] behind Miss Cunegonde, although I can only sit on one buttock, and we will get to Cadiz."

In the same hotel there was a Benedictine friar. He bought the horse very cheap. Candide, Cunegonde and the old woman passed through Lucena, Chillas, Lebrixa, and at last reached Cadiz. A fleet was there being equipped and troops were being raised to bring to reason the reverend Jesuit fathers[74] of Paraguay, who were accused of causing the revolt of one of their tribes against the kings of Spain and Portugal near the town of Sacramento.[75] Candide, having served with the Bulgarians, went through the Bulgarian drill before the general of the little army with so much grace, celerity, skill, pride and agility, that he was given the command of an infantry company. He was now a captain; he embarked with Miss Cunegonde, the old woman, two servants, and the two Andalusian horses which had belonged to the Grand Inquisitor of Portugal.

During the voyage they had many discussions about the philosophy of poor Pangloss.

"We are going to a new world," said Candide, "and no doubt it is there that everything is for the best; for it must be admitted that one might lament a little over the physical and moral happenings in our own world."

"I love you with all my heart," said Cunegonde, "but my soul is still shocked by what I have seen and undergone."

"All will be well," replied Candide; "the sea in this new world already is better than the seas of our Europe; it is calmer and the winds are more constant. It is certainly the new world which is the best of all possible worlds."

"God grant it!" said Cunegonde, "but I have been so horribly unhappy in mine that my heart is nearly closed to hope."

"You complain," said the old woman to them. "Alas! you have not endured such misfortunes as mine."

Cunegonde almost laughed and thought it most amusing of the old woman to assert that she was more unfortunate.

[73] A pad or cushion attached behind a saddle to carry an extra rider.
[74] Members of the Society of Jesus, a Catholic order founded near the middle of the sixteenth century.
[75] In 1750 Spain and Portugal agreed that the city of San Sacramento in South America should pass into Portuguese hands. To forestall the transfer, the Jesuits caused the natives to rise in revolt.

"Alas! my dear," said she, "unless you have been raped by two Bulgarians, stabbed twice in the belly, have had two castles destroyed, two fathers and mothers murdered before your eyes, and have seen two of your lovers flogged in an *auto-da-fé,* I do not see how you can surpass me; moreover, I was born a Baroness with seventy-two quarterings and I have been a kitchen-wench."

"You do not know my birth," said the old woman, "and if I showed you my backside you would not talk as you do and you would suspend your judgment."

This speech aroused intense curiosity in the minds of Cunegonde and Candide. And the old woman spoke as follows.

CHAPTER 11

The Old Woman's Story

"My eyes were not always bloodshot and red-rimmed; my nose did not always touch my chin and I was not always a servant. I am the daughter of Pope Urban X [76] and the Princess of Palestrina. Until I was fourteen I was brought up in a palace to which all the castles of your German Barons would not have served as stables; and one of my dresses cost more than all the magnificence of Westphalia. I increased in beauty, in grace, in talents, among pleasures, respect and hopes; already I inspired love, my breasts were forming; and what breasts! White, firm, carved like those of the Venus de' Medici. And what eyes! What eyelids! What black eyebrows! What fire shone from my two eyeballs, and dimmed the glitter of the stars, as the local poets pointed out to me. The women who dressed and undressed me fell into ecstasy when they beheld me in front and behind; and all the men would have liked to be in their place.

"I was betrothed to a ruling prince of Massa-Carrara. [77] What a prince! As beautiful as I was, formed of gentleness and charms, brilliantly witty and burning with love; I loved him with a first love, idolatrously and extravagantly. The marriage ceremonies were ar-

---

[76] Many years after his death, the following note, left by Voltaire, was published for the first time: "Observe the author's extreme discretion, for there has not up to the present time been any pope named Urban X. He avoids attributing a bastard daughter to a known pope. What circumspection! How delicate a conscience!"

[77] A small Italian duchy, lying northwest of Pisa.

ranged with unheard-of pomp and magnificence; there were continual fêtes, revels and comic operas; all Italy wrote sonnets for me, and
not a good one among them.

"I touched the moment of my happiness when an old marchioness
who had been my prince's mistress invited him to take chocolate
with her; less than two hours afterward he died in horrible convulsions; but that is only a trifle. My mother was in despair, though less
distressed than I, and wished to absent herself for a time from a place
so disastrous. She had a most beautiful estate near Gaeta;[78] we embarked on a galley, gilded like the altar of St. Peter's at Rome. A
Sallé[79] pirate swooped down and boarded us; our soldiers defended
us like soldiers of the Pope; they threw down their arms, fell on their
knees and asked the pirates for absolution *in articulo mortis*.[80]

"They were immediately stripped as naked as monkeys and my
mother, our ladies of honor and myself as well. The diligence with
which these gentlemen strip people is truly admirable; but I was still
more surprised by their inserting a finger in a place belonging to all
of us where we women usually only allow the end of a syringe. This
appeared to me a very strange ceremony; but that is how we judge
everything when we leave our own country. I soon learned that it
was to find out if we had hidden any diamonds there; 'tis a custom
established from time immemorial among the civilized nations who
roam the seas. I have learned that the religious Knights of Malta[81]
never fail in it when they capture Turks and Turkish women; this is
an international law which has never been broken.

"I will not tell you how hard it is for a young princess to be taken
with her mother as a slave to Morocco; you will also guess all we
had to endure in the pirates' ship. My mother was still very beautiful; our ladies of honor, even our waiting-maids possessed more
charms than could be found in all Africa; and I was ravishing, I was
beauty, grace itself, and I was a virgin; I did not remain so long; the
flower which had been reserved for the handsome prince of Massa-
Carrara was ravished from me by a pirate captain; he was an abominable negro who thought he was doing me a great honor. The
Princess of Palestrina and I must indeed have been strong to bear up
against all we endured before our arrival in Morocco! But let that

[78] A coastal town near Naples.
[79] A coastal city near Rabat, Morocco, known as a pirate stronghold.
[80] A religious rite administered at the point of death.
[81] A medieval order of Christian knights.

pass; these things are so common that they are not worth mentioning.

"Morocco was swimming in blood when we arrived. The fifty sons of the Emperor Muley Ismael[82] had each a faction; and this produced fifty civil wars, of blacks against blacks, browns against browns, mulattoes against mulattoes. There was continual carnage throughout the whole extent of the empire.

"Scarcely had we landed when the blacks of a party hostile to that of my pirate arrived with the purpose of depriving him of his booty. After the diamonds and the gold, we were the most valuable possessions. I witnessed a fight such as is never seen in your European climates. The blood of the northern peoples is not sufficiently ardent; their madness for women does not reach the point which is common in Africa. The Europeans seem to have milk in their veins; but vitriol and fire flow in the veins of the inhabitants of Mount Atlas[83] and the neighboring countries. They fought with the fury of the lions, tigers[84] and serpents of the country to determine who should have us. A Moor[85] grasped my mother by the right arm, my captain's lieutenant held her by the left arm; a Moorish soldier held one leg and one of our pirates seized the other. In a moment nearly all our women were seized in the same way by four soldiers. My captain kept me hidden behind him; he had a scimitar[86] in his hand and killed everybody who opposed his fury. I saw my mother and all our Italian women torn in pieces, gashed, massacred by the monsters who disputed them. The prisoners, my companions, those who had captured them, soldiers, sailors, blacks, browns, whites, mulattoes and finally my captain were all killed and I remained expiring on a heap of corpses. As everyone knows, such scenes go on in an area of more than three hundred square leagues and yet no one ever fails to recite the five daily prayers ordered by Mahomet.[87]

"With great difficulty I extricated myself from the bloody heaps of

---

[82] Mawlay Isma'il, sultan of Morocco, from 1673 to 1727. He is generally regarded as an effective ruler, although he employed extreme measures of cruelty and brutality to secure law and order. When he died, he left five hundred male children, all of whom possessed the right to rule, which did not contribute to the country's political stability.

[83] A North African mountain range extending from Morocco to Tunisia.

[84] Voltaire is not quite accurate here. Tigers are not native to Morocco.

[85] The Moors, the principal people of northwestern Africa, are Muslim by religion and ethnically of mixed Arab and African ancestry.

[86] A curved, short sword with the cutting edge on the outside of the curve.

[87] Muhammad (570–632), Arabian prophet and founder of Islam.

corpses and dragged myself to the foot of a large orange-tree on the bank of a stream; there I fell down with terror, weariness, horror, despair and hunger. Soon afterwards, my exhausted senses fell into a sleep which was more like a swoon than repose. I was in this state of weakness and insensibility between life and death when I felt myself oppressed by something which moved on my body. I opened my eyes and saw a white man of good appearance who was sighing and muttering between his teeth: *O che sciagura d'essere senza coglioni!* [88]

CHAPTER 12

Continuation of the Old Woman's Misfortunes

"Amazed and delighted to hear my native language, and not less surprised at the words spoken by this man, I replied that there were greater misfortunes than that of which he complained. In a few words I informed him of the horrors I had undergone and then swooned again. He carried me to a neighboring house, had me put to bed, gave me food, waited on me, consoled me, flattered me, told me he had never seen anyone so beautiful as I, and that he had never so much regretted that which no one could give back to him.

" 'I was born at Naples,' he said, 'and every year they make two or three thousand children there into capons;[89] some die of it, others acquire voices more beautiful than women's, and others become the governors of States.[90] This operation was performed upon me with very great success and I was a musician in the chapel of the Princess of Palestrina.'

" 'Of my mother,' I exclaimed.

" 'Of your mother!' cried he, weeping. 'What! Are you that young princess I brought up to the age of six and who even then gave promise of being as beautiful as you are?'

" 'I am! my mother is four hundred yards from here, cut into quarters under a heap of corpses. . . .'

[88] Italian: Oh, what misfortune to have no testicles!
[89] A capon is actually a rooster that has been castrated for better fattening, thus more tasty eating.
[90] An allusion to the famous male soprano Farinelli (1705–1782). Following a successful career as a singer, he acquired substantial influence and political power, serving two Spanish kings, Philip V and Ferdinand VI. Honored with grand titles, he retired in 1761 to a castle near Bologna, Italy.

"I related all that had happened to me; he also told me his adventures and informed me how he had been sent to the King of Morocco by a Christian power to make a treaty with that monarch whereby he was supplied with powder, cannons and ships to help to exterminate the commerce of other Christians.

" 'My mission is accomplished,' said this honest eunuch, 'I am about to embark at Ceuta[91] and I will take you back to Italy. *Ma che sciagura d'essere senza coglioni!'*

"I thanked him with tears of gratitude; and instead of taking me back to Italy he conducted me to Algiers[92] and sold me to the Dey.[93] I had scarcely been sold when the plague which had gone through Africa, Asia, and Europe broke out furiously in Algiers. You have seen earthquakes; but have you ever seen the plague?"

"Never," replied the Baroness.

"If you had," replied the old women, "you would admit that it is much worse than an earthquake. It is very common in Africa; I caught it. Imagine the situation of a Pope's daughter aged fifteen, who in three months had undergone poverty and slavery, had been raped nearly every day, had seen her mother cut into four pieces, had undergone hunger and war, and was now dying of the plague in Algiers. However, I did not die; but my eunuch and the Dey and almost all the seraglio[94] of Algiers perished.

"When the first ravages of this frightful plague were over, the Dey's slaves were sold. A merchant bought me and carried me to Tunis; he sold me to another merchant who re-sold me at Tripoli: from Tripoli I was re-sold to Alexandria, from Alexandria re-sold to Smyrna, from Smyrna to Constantinople.[95] I was finally bought by an Aga[96] of the Janizaries,[97] who was soon ordered to defend Azov[98] against the Russians who were besieging it.[99]

---

[91] A maritime city at the northwestern tip of Africa, opposite Gibraltar.

[92] The capital of a province in north Africa, under Turkish rule.

[93] The title of the (Turkish) governor.

[94] Harem.

[95] The capital of the Ottoman (Turkish) Empire, which ended in 1919. The name of the city was changed to Istanbul in 1930.

[96] Title of respect for a high-ranking officer or official.

[97] An elite unit of the Turkish infantry that consisted of former slaves, natives, and sons of captured Christians. The latter were pressed into service while very young and thus quickly turned into fanatical converts to Islam.

[98] A city located at the mouth of the River Don in southern Russia.

[99] A reference to the siege of Azov (1695–96) by the Russian Tsar Peter the Great (1672–1725).

"The Aga, who was a man of great gallantry, took his whole seraglio with him, and lodged us in a little fort on the islands of Palus-Maeotis,[100] guarded by two black eunuchs and twenty soldiers. He killed a prodigious number of Russians, but they returned the compliment as well. Azov was given up to fire and blood, neither sex nor age was pardoned; only our little fort remained; and the enemy tried to reduce it by starving us. The twenty Janizaries had sworn never to surrender us. The extremities of hunger to which they were reduced forced them to eat our two eunuchs for fear of breaking their oath. Some days later they resolved to eat the women.

"We had with us a most pious and compassionate Imam[101] who delivered a fine sermon to them by which he persuaded them not to kill us altogether.

" 'Cut,' said he, 'only one buttock from each of these ladies and you will make very good cheer; if you have to return, there will still be as much left in a few days; Heaven will be pleased at so charitable an action and you will be saved.'

"He was very eloquent and persuaded them. This horrible operation was performed upon us; the Imam anointed us with the same balm that is used for children who have just been circumcized; we were all at the point of death.

"Scarcely had the Janizaries finished the meal we had supplied when the Russians arrived in flat-bottomed boats; not a Janizary escaped. The Russians paid no attention to the state we were in. There are French doctors everywhere; one of them who was very skilful, took care of us; he healed us, and I shall remember all my life that, when my wounds were cured, he made propositions to me. For the rest, he told us all to cheer up; he told us that the same thing had happened in several sieges and that it was a law of war.

"As soon as my companions could walk they were sent to Moscow. I fell to the lot of a Boyar[102] who made me his gardener and gave me twenty lashes a day. But at the end of two years this lord was broken on the wheel with thirty other Boyars owing to some court disturbance,[103] and I profited by this adventure; I fled; I crossed all Russia; for a long time I was servant in an inn at Riga,[104] then at

[100] Latin name for the Sea of Azov.
[101] Muslim official.
[102] A Russian noble of high rank.
[103] An allusion to the uprising of the Streltsy (soldiers of the Moscow garrison) in 1698.
[104] A city on the coast of Latvia.

Rostock, at Wismar, at Leipzig, at Cassel,[105] at Utrecht, at Leyden, at The Hague, at Rotterdam,[106] I have grown old in misery and in shame, with only half a backside, always remembering that I was the daughter of a Pope; a hundred times I wanted to kill myself, but I still loved life. This ridiculous weakness is perhaps the most disastrous of our inclinations; for is there anything sillier than to desire to bear continually a burden one always wishes to throw on the ground; to look upon oneself with horror and yet to cling to oneself; in short, to caress the serpent which devours us until he has eaten our heart?

"In the countries it has been my fate to traverse and in the inns where I have served I have seen a prodigious number of people who hated their lives; but I have only seen twelve who voluntarily put an end to their misery: three negroes, four Englishmen, four Genevans and a German professor named Robeck.[107] I ended up as servant to the Jew, Don Issachar; he placed me in your service, my fair young lady; I attached myself to your fate and have been more occupied with your adventures than with my own. I should never even have spoken of my misfortunes, if you had not piqued me a little and if it had not been the custom on board ship to tell stories to pass the time. In short, Miss, I have had experience, I know the world; provide yourself with an entertainment, make each passenger tell you his story; and if there is one who has not often cursed his life, who has not often said to himself that he was the most unfortunate of men, throw me head-first into the sea."

• • •

[After arriving in the New World, Candide meets with further adventures that show the stupidity, cruelty, and greed of men. Only in El Dorado, a paradise in the interior of South America, does he find a society in which people are naturally kind, courteous, generous, and reasonable. Having lost his beloved Cunegonde to a Spanish colonial noble, he makes plans to win her back by bribery and decides to return to Europe. On the way he falls in with Martin, a disillusioned pessimist, and under the latter's influence begins

---

[105] Cities in the northern half of Germany.
[106] Cities in Holland.
[107] Johann Robe(c)k (1672–1739), who maintained that the love of life was nothing but a ridiculous notion. Having written a treatise entitled "Exercise in Voluntary Death" in which he justified suicide, he faced the consequence of his conviction and drowned himself.

to doubt Pangloss's optimism, "the mania of maintaining that everything is well when we are wretched." Martin argues that their misadventures prove that the world is evil and was created only to infuriate us. Back in Europe, Candide meets with evidence for this view in the behavior of intellectuals, prostitutes, monks, and deposed kings. Nowhere can he find a truly happy man. The following two chapters bring Candide's adventures to their conclusion. *Ed.*]

CHAPTER 29

How Candide Found Cunegonde and the Old Woman Again

While Candide, the Baron,[108] Pangloss, Martin and Cacambo [109] were relating their adventures, reasoning upon contingent or non-contingent events of the universe, arguing about effects and causes, moral and physical evil, free will and necessity, and the consolations to be found in the Turkish galleys, they came to the house of the Transylvanian prince on the shores of Propontis.[110] The first objects which met their sight were Cunegonde and the old woman hanging out towels to dry on the line.

At this sight the Baron grew pale. Candide, that tender lover, seeing his fair Cunegonde sunburned, blear-eyed, flat-breasted, with wrinkles around her eyes and red, chapped arms, recoiled three paces in horror, and then advanced from mere politeness. She embraced Candide and her brother. They embraced the old woman; Candide bought them both.

In the neighborhood was a little farm; the old woman suggested that Candide should buy it, until some better fate befell the group. Cunegonde did not know that she had become ugly, for nobody had told her so; she reminded Candide of his promises in so peremptory a tone that the good Candide dared not refuse her. He therefore informed the Baron that he was about to marry his sister.

"Never," said the Baron, "will I endure such baseness on her part and such insolence on yours; nobody shall ever reproach me with

---

[108] Son of the original Baron Thunder-ten-tronckh, who appeared in Chapter 1. Candide had discovered him as a galley slave and had purchased his freedom. He was, of course, Cunegonde's long-lost brother.
[109] Candide's valet, brought from Cadiz.
[110] Sea of Marmara, situated between the Bosporus and the Dardanelles in Turkey.

this infamy; my sister's children could never enter the chapters[111] of Germany. No, my sister shall never marry anyone but a Baron of the Empire."

Cunegonde threw herself at his feet and bathed them in tears; but he was inflexible.

"Madman," said Candide, "I rescued you from the galleys, I paid your ransom and your sister's; she was washing dishes here, she is ugly, I am so kind as to make her my wife, and you pretend to oppose me! I should kill you again if I listened to my anger."

"You may kill me again," said the Baron, "but you shall never marry my sister while I am alive."

CHAPTER 30

Conclusion

At the bottom of his heart Candide had not the least wish to marry Cunegonde. But the Baron's extreme impertinence determined him to complete the marriage, and Cunegonde urged it so warmly that he could not retract. He consulted Pangloss, Martin and the faithful Cacambo. Pangloss wrote an excellent memorandum by which he proved that the Baron had no rights over his sister and that by all the laws of the empire she could make a left-handed marriage[112] with Candide. Martin advised that the Baron should be thrown into the sea; Cacambo decided that he should be returned to the Levantine[113] captain and sent back to the galleys, after which he would be returned by the first ship to the Vicar-General at Rome.[114] This was thought to be very good advice; the old woman approved it; they said nothing to the sister; the plan was carried out with the aid of a little money and they had the pleasure of duping a Jesuit and punishing the pride of a German Baron.

It would be natural to suppose that when, after so many disasters, Candide was married to his mistress, and living with the philosopher

---

[111] Knightly assemblies.
[112] A marriage between persons of unequal rank in which it was understood that the lowly spouse (and any offspring) could make no claim to the other spouse's high rank or property.
[113] Pertaining to the eastern Mediterranean region.
[114] High official of the Jesuit order.

Pangloss, the philosopher Martin, the prudent Cacambo and the old woman, having brought back so many diamonds from the country of the ancient Incas, he would lead the most pleasant life imaginable. But he was so cheated by the Jews that he had nothing left but his little farm; his wife, growing uglier every day, became shrewish and unendurable; the old woman was ailing and even more bad-tempered than Cunegonde. Cacambo, who worked in the garden and then went to Constantinople to sell vegetables, was overworked and cursed his fate. Pangloss was in despair because he did not shine in some German university. As for Martin, he was firmly convinced that people are equally uncomfortable everywhere; he accepted things patiently. Candide, Martin, and Pangloss sometimes argued about metaphysics and morals. From the windows of the farm they often watched the ships going by, filled with effendis,[115] pashas,[116] and cadis,[117] who were being exiled to Lemnos, to Mitylene[118] and Erzerum.[119] They saw other cadis, other pashas, and other effendis coming back to take the place of the exiles and to be exiled in their turn. They saw the neatly impaled heads which were taken to the Sublime Porte.[120] These sights redoubled their discussions; and when they were not arguing, the boredom was so excessive that one day the old woman dared to say to them:

"I should like to know which is worse, to be raped a hundred times by Negro pirates, to have a buttock cut off, to run the gauntlet among the Bulgarians, to be whipped and flogged in an *auto-da-fé,* to be dissected, to row in a galley, in short, to endure all the miseries through which we have passed, or to remain here doing nothing?"

" 'Tis a great question," said Candide.

These remarks led to new reflections, and Martin especially concluded that man was born to live in the convulsions of distress or in the lethargy of boredom. Candide did not agree, but he asserted nothing. Pangloss confessed that he had always suffered horribly; but, having once maintained that everything was for the best, he had continued to maintain it without believing it.

[115] Turkish title of respect for a government official.
[116] High civil or military officials.
[117] A minor magistrate.
[118] Islands in the Aegean Sea.
[119] A city in Northeastern Turkey.
[120] The main gate of the palace of the sultan in Constantinople; the heads of those who had been executed were often displayed there as a deterrent to others. The phrase "Sublime Porte" is also used as a reference to the government of the Ottoman Empire.

One thing confirmed Martin in his detestable principles, made Candide hesitate more than ever, and embarrassed Pangloss. And it was this. One day there came to their farm Paquette and Friar Giroflée,[121] who were in the most extreme misery; they had soon wasted their three thousand piastres,[122] had left each other, made up, quarreled again, been put in prison, escaped, and finally Friar Giroflée had turned Turk. Paquette continued her occupation everywhere and now earned nothing by it.

"I foresaw," said Martin to Candide, "that your gifts would soon be wasted and would only make them the more miserable. You and Cacambo were once bloated with millions of piastres and you are no happier than Friar Giroflée and Paquette."

"Ah! Ha!" said Pangloss to Paquette, "so Heaven brings you back to us, my dear child? Do you know that you cost me the end of my nose, an eye, and an ear! What a plight you are in! Ah! What a world this is!"

This new occurrence caused them to philosophize more than ever.

In the neighborhood there lived a very famous Dervish,[123] who was supposed to be the best philosopher in Turkey; they went to consult him; Pangloss was the spokesman and said:

"Master, we have come to beg you to tell us why so strange an animal as man was ever created."

"What has it to do with you?" said the Dervish. "Is it your business?"

"But, reverend father," said Candide, "there is a horrible amount of evil in the world."

"What does it matter," said the Dervish, "whether there is evil or good? When his highness sends a ship to Egypt, does he worry about the comfort or discomfort of the rats in the ship?"

"Then what should we do?" said Pangloss.

"Hold your tongue," said the Dervish.

"I flattered myself," said Pangloss, "that I should discuss with you effects and causes, this best of all possible worlds, the origin of evil, the nature of the soul and pre-established harmony."

At these words the Dervish slammed the door in their faces. During this conversation the news went round that at Constantinople

---

[121] A monk whom Candide had met in Venice. Literally (in French), wallflower.
[122] Turkish money.
[123] A member of a Muslim religious order, said to be somewhat similar to the Franciscans.

two viziers[124] and the mufti[125] had been strangled and several of their friends impaled. This catastrophe made a prodigious noise everywhere for several hours. As Pangloss, Candide, and Martin were returning to their little farm, they came upon an old man who was taking the air under a bower of orange-trees at his door. Pangloss, who was as curious as he was argumentative, asked him what was the name of the mufti who had just been strangled.

"I do not know," replied the old man. "I have never known the name of any mufti or of any vizier. I am entirely ignorant of the occurrence you mention; I presume that in general those who meddle with public affairs sometimes perish miserably and that they deserve it; but I never inquire what is going on in Constantinople; I content myself with sending there for sale the produce of the garden I cultivate."

Having spoken thus, he took the strangers into his house. His two daughters and his two sons presented them with several kinds of sherbet which they made themselves, caymac[126] flavored with candied citron peel, oranges, lemons, limes, pineapples, dates, pistachios, and Mocha coffee[127] which had not been mixed with the bad coffee of Batavia and the Isles.[128] After which this good Mussulman's two daughters perfumed the beards of Candide, Pangloss, and Martin.

"You must have a vast and magnificent estate?" said Candide to the Turk.

"I have only twenty acres," replied the Turk. "I cultivate them with my children; and work keeps at bay three great evils: boredom, vice and need."

As Candide returned to his farm he reflected deeply on the Turk's remarks. He said to Pangloss and Martin:

"That good old man seems to me to have chosen an existence preferable by far to that of the six kings with whom we had the honor to sup."

"Exalted rank," said Pangloss, "is very dangerous, according to the testimony of all philosophers; for Eglon, King of the Moabites, was murdered by Ehud; Absalom was hanged by the hair and

---

[124] Ministers of state.
[125] An official interpreter of Muslim law.
[126] Turkish word for cream.
[127] Coffee from Arabia.
[128] Presumably the East Indies.

pierced by three darts; King Nadab, son of Jeroboam, was killed by Baasha; King Elah by Zimri; Ahaziah by Jehu; Athaliah by Jehoiada; the Kings Jehoiakim, Jeconiah, and Zedekiah [129] were made slaves. You know in what manner died Croesus, Astyages, Darius, Denys of Syracuse, Pyrrhus, Perseus, Hannibal, Jugurtha, Ariovistus, Caesar, Pompey, Nero, Otho, Vitellius, Domitian, Richard II of England, Edward II, Henry VI, Richard III, Mary Stuart, Charles I, the three Henrys of France, the Emperor Henry IV. You know . . ."

"I also know," said Candide, "that we should cultivate our gardens."

"You are right," said Pangloss, "for, when man was placed in the Garden of Eden, he was placed there *ut operaretur eum,* to dress it and to keep it; which proves that man was not born for idleness."

"Let us work without theorizing," said Martin; " 'tis the only way to make life endurable."

The whole small fraternity entered into this praiseworthy plan, and each started to make use of his talents. The little farm yielded well. Cunegonde was indeed very ugly, but she became an excellent pastrycook; Paquette embroidered; the old woman took care of the linen. Even Friar Giroflée performed some service; he was a very good carpenter and even became a man of honor; and Pangloss sometimes said to Candide:

"All events are linked up in this best of all possible worlds; for, if you had not been expelled from the noble castle by hard kicks in your backside for love of Mademoiselle Cunegonde, if you had not been clapped into the Inquisition, if you had not wandered about America on foot, if you had not stuck your sword in the Baron, if you had not lost all your sheep from the land of El Dorado, you would not be eating candied citrons and pistachios here."

" 'Tis well said," replied Candide, "but we must cultivate our gardens."

---

[129] These names—of villains and victims—are mentioned in the Old Testament.

10

Jean Jacques Rousseau
The Social Contract

In the midst of the middle-class liberalism of eighteenth-century France, Jean Jacques Rousseau (1712–1778) was a startling and important exception. Though sharing some of the ideas of the Enlightenment, he was violently opposed to others. Born in Geneva into a Swiss Protestant family, Rousseau remained an outsider and a rebel, a rootless vagabond who rejected any place in French society. Privately he was unhappy and impractical, an unstable personality—nevertheless a genius—whose life would end in madness. In public matters he was an emotional democrat who spoke up sincerely for the common people, formulating ideas that would exert a paramount influence on the French Revolution, especially in its radical stage. Indeed, Rousseau has been hailed as the prophet of modern democracy and nationalism; totalitarian movements have even found inspiration in his ideas regarding the sovereignty of collective authority. Rousseau was, in addition, one of the first exponents of that combination of ideas and attitudes toward life typical of the philosophical and literary movement called romanticism.

Rousseau shared the Enlightenment belief in progress and in the goodness of human beings and their infinite perfectibility. He violently attacked the social order of his day as artificial, corrupt, and corrupting. But he refused to accept the simple equivalence of reason and nature. Nature was good, but, since reason was part of civilization, it was evil: reason was not the guide to truth. To achieve truth and justice, Rousseau advocated that human beings return to nature and trust their untaught feelings. The primitive and unsophisticated elements in people were, to him, the sources of the strength needed to remake the individual and society.

Jean Jacques Rousseau, *The Social Contract,* trans. Henry J. Tozer (New York: Scribner, 1898), 100, 103–105, 109–14, 119–20, 123–28, 131–33, 197–201.

The Social Contract (*1762*) *was written, in substance, as a prescription for the just society. In its powerful and closely reasoned exposition, Rousseau reconciled the freedom of the individual and the authority of the state in an organic community which embodied the "general will," directed to the common welfare. Such a community, originating in a "contract" among free and equal individuals, was one of democratic equality, based on the sovereignty of the people, and gave all of them a genuine sense of belonging.*

Man is born free, and everywhere he is in chains. Many a one believes himself the master of others, and yet he is a greater slave than they. How has this change come about? I do not know. What can render it legitimate? I believe that I can settle this question.

If I considered only force and the results that proceed from it, I should say that so long as a people is compelled to obey and does obey, it does well; but that, so soon as it can shake off the yoke and does shake it off, it does better; for, if men recover their freedom by virtue of the same right by which it was taken away, either they are justified in resuming it, or there was no justification for depriving them of it. But the social order is a sacred right which serves as a foundation for all others. This right, however, does not come from nature. It is therefore based on conventions. The question is to know what these conventions are. Before coming to that, I must establish what I have just laid down.

• • •

THE RIGHT OF THE STRONGEST

The strongest man is never strong enough to be always master, unless he transforms his power into right, and obedience into duty. Hence the right of the strongest—a right apparently assumed in irony, and really established in principle. But will this phrase never be explained to us? Force is a physical power; I do not see what morality can result from its effects. To yield to force is an act of necessity not of will; it is at most an act of prudence. In what sense can it be a duty?

Let us assume for a moment this pretended right. I say that nothing results from it but inexplicable nonsense; for if force constitutes right, the effect changes with the cause, and any force which overcomes the first succeeds to its rights. As soon as men can disobey with impunity, they may do so legitimately; and since the strongest is always in the right, the only thing is to act in such a way that one may be the strongest. But what sort of a right is it that perishes when force ceases? If it is necessary to obey by compulsion, there is no need to obey from duty; and if men are no longer forced to obey, obligation is at an end. We see, then, that this word *right* adds nothing to force; it here means nothing at all.

Obey the powers that be. If that means, Yield to force, the precept is good but superfluous; I reply that it will never be violated. All power comes from God, I admit; but every disease comes from him too; does it follow that we are prohibited from calling in a physician? If a brigand should surprise me in the recesses of a wood, am I bound not only to give up my purse when forced, but am I also morally bound to do so when I might conceal it? For, in effect, the pistol which he holds is a superior force.

Let us agree, then, that might does not make right, and that we are bound to obey none but lawful authorities. Thus my original question ever recurs.

SLAVERY

Since no man has any natural authority over his fellow-men, and since force is not the source of right, conventions remain as the basis of all lawful authority among men.

If an individual, says Grotius,[1] can alienate his liberty and become the slave of a master, why should not a whole people be able to alienate theirs, and become subject to a king? In this there are many equivocal terms requiring explanation; but let us confine ourselves to the word *alienate*. To alienate is to give or sell. Now, a man who becomes another's slave does not give himself; he sells himself at the very least for his subsistence. But why does a nation sell itself? So far from a king supplying his subjects with their subsistence, he draws his from them; and, according to Rabelais,[2] a king does not live on a

---

[1] Hugo Grotius (1583–1645), Dutch lawyer and theologian, who later in life served as the Swedish ambassador to France. He is considered the founder of international law.
[2] François Rabelais (1494–1553), French satirist and humorist.

little. Do subjects, then, give up their persons on condition that their property also shall be taken? I do not see what is left for them to keep.

It will be said that the despot[3] secures to his subjects civil peace. Be it so; but what do they gain by that, if the wars which his ambition brings upon them, together with his insatiable greed and the vexations of his administration, harass them more than their own dissensions would? What do they gain by it if this tranquillity is itself one of their miseries? Men live tranquilly also in dungeons; is that enough to make them contented there? The Greeks confined in the cave of the Cyclops[4] lived peacefully until their turn came to be devoured.

To say that a man gives himself for nothing is to say what is absurd and inconceivable; such an act is illegitimate and invalid, for the simple reason that he who performs it is not in his right mind. To say the same thing of a whole nation is to suppose a nation of fools; and madness does not confer rights.

Even if each person could alienate himself, he could not alienate his children; they are born free men; their liberty belongs to them, and no one has a right to dispose of it except themselves. Before they have come to years of discretion, the father can, in their name, stipulate conditions for their preservation and welfare, but not surrender them irrevocably and unconditionally; for such a gift is contrary to the ends of nature, and exceeds the rights of paternity. In order, then, that an arbitrary government might be legitimate, it would be necessary that the people in each generation should have the option of accepting or rejecting it; but in that case such a government would no longer be arbitrary.

To renounce one's liberty is to renounce one's quality as a man, the rights and also the duties of humanity. For him who renounces everything there is no possible compensation. Such a renunciation is incompatible with man's nature, for to take away all freedom from

---

[3] An autocrat using his power abusively.

[4] One of a race of giants having one eye, in the middle of the forehead, who supposedly lived on the island of Sicily. According to Greek legend, Odysseus and his companions wandered into the cave of the cyclops Polyphemus, who imprisoned them and ate two of them daily. After Polyphemus had devoured six of them, Odysseus and his comrades managed to get the cyclops drunk on wine; and while Polyphemus slept, Odysseus blinded him by plunging a stake into the one eye. With the cyclops blinded, the survivors escaped.

his will is to take away all morality from his actions. In short, a convention which stipulates absolute authority on the one side and unlimited obedience on the other is vain and contradictory. Is it not clear that we are under no obligations whatsoever towards a man from whom we have a right to demand everything? And does not this single condition, without equivalent, without exchange, involve the nullity of the act? For what right would my slave have against me, since all that he has belongs to me? His rights being mine, this right of me against myself is a meaningless phrase.

•   •   •

THE SOCIAL CONTRACT

I assume that men have reached a point at which the obstacles that endanger their preservation in the state of nature overcome by their resistance the forces which each individual can exert with a view to maintaining himself in that state. Then this primitive condition can no longer subsist, and the human race would perish unless it changed its mode of existence.

Now, as men cannot create any new forces, but only combine and direct those that exist, they have no other means of self-preservation than to form by aggregation a sum of forces which may overcome the resistance, to put them in action by a single motive power, and to make them work in concert.

This sum of forces can be produced only by the combination of many; but the strength and freedom of each man being the chief instruments of his preservation, how can he pledge them without injuring himself, and without neglecting the cares which he owes to himself? This difficulty, applied to my subject, may be expressed in these terms:

"To find a form of association which may defend and protect with the whole force of the community the person and property of every associate, and by means of which each, coalescing with all, may nevertheless obey only himself, and remain as free as before." Such is the fundamental problem of which the social contract furnishes the solution.

The clauses of this contract are so determined by the nature of the act that the slightest modification would render them vain and ineffectual; so that, although they have never perhaps been formally enunciated, they are everywhere the same, everywhere tacitly [5] admitted and recognized, until, the social pact being violated, each man regains his original rights and recovers his natural liberty, while losing the conventional liberty for which he renounced it.

These clauses, rightly understood, are reducible to one only, namely, the total alienation to the whole community of each associate with all his rights; for, in the first place, since each gives himself up entirely, the conditions are equal for all; and, the conditions being equal for all, no one has any interest in making them burdensome to others.

Further, the alienation being made without reserve, the union is as perfect as it can be, and an individual associate can no longer claim anything; for, if any rights were left to individuals, since there would be no common superior who could judge between them and the public, each, being on some point his own judge, would soon claim to be so on all; the state of nature would still subsist, and the association would necessarily become tyrannical or useless.

In short, each giving himself to all, gives himself to nobody; and as there is not one associate over whom we do not acquire the same rights which we concede to him over ourselves, we gain the equivalent of all that we lose, and more power to preserve what we have.

If, then, we set aside what is not of the essence of the social contract, we shall find that it is reducible to the following terms: "Each of us puts in common his person and his whole power under the supreme direction of the general will; and in return we receive every member as an indivisible part of the whole."

Forthwith, instead of the individual personalities of all the contracting parties, this act of association produces a moral and collective body, which is composed of as many members as the assembly has voices, and which receives from this same act its unity, its common self, its life, and its will. This public person, which is thus formed by the union of all the individual members, formerly took the name of *city,* and now takes that of *republic* or *body politic,* which is called by its members *State* when it is passive, *sovereign* when it is active, *power* when it is compared to similar bodies. With regard to the associates, they take collectively the name of *people,* and are called individually *citizens,* as participating in the sovereign power,

---

[5] Not expressed openly, but implied.

and *subjects,* as subjected to the laws of the State. But these terms are often confused and are mistaken one for another; it is sufficient to know how to distinguish them when they are used with complete precision.

THE SOVEREIGN

We see from this formula that the act of association contains a reciprocal engagement between the public and individuals, and that every individual, contracting so to speak with himself, is engaged in a double relation, namely, as a member of the sovereign towards individuals, and as a member of the State towards the sovereign. But we cannot apply here the maxim[6] of civil law that no one is bound by engagements made with himself; for there is a great difference between being bound to oneself and to a whole of which one forms part.

We must further observe that the public resolution which can bind all subjects to the sovereign in consequence of the two different relations under which each of them is regarded cannot, for a contrary reason, bind the sovereign to itself; and that accordingly it is contrary to the nature of the body politic for the sovereign to impose on itself a law which it cannot transgress. As it can only be considered under one and the same relation, it is in the position of an individual contracting with himself; whence we see that there is not, nor can be, any kind of fundamental law binding upon the body of the people, not even the social contract. This does not imply that such a body cannot perfectly well enter into engagements with others in what does not derogate from this contract; for, with regard to foreigners, it becomes a simple being, an individual.

But the body politic or sovereign, deriving its existence only from the sanctity of the contract, can never bind itself, even to others, in anything that derogates from the original act, such as alienation of some portion of itself, or submission to another sovereign. To violate the act by which it exists would be to annihilate itself; and what is nothing produces nothing.

So soon as the multitude is thus united in one body, it is impossible to injure one of the members without attacking the body, still

---

[6] Fundamental rule.

less to injure the body without the members feeling the effects. Thus duty and interest alike oblige the two contracting parties to give mutual assistance; and the men themselves should seek to combine in this twofold relationship all the advantages which are attendant on it.

Now, the sovereign, being formed only of the individuals that compose it, neither has nor can have any interest contrary to theirs; consequently the sovereign power needs no guarantee towards its subjects, because it is impossible that the body should wish to injure all its members; and we shall see hereafter that it can injure no one as an individual. The sovereign, for the simple reason that it is so, is always everything that it ought to be.

But this is not the case as regards the relation of subjects to the sovereign, which, notwithstanding the common interest, would have no security for the performance of their engagements, unless it found means to ensure their fidelity.

Indeed, every individual may, as a man, have a particular will contrary to, or divergent from, the general will which he has as citizen; his private interest may prompt him quite differently from the common interest; his absolute and naturally independent existence may make him regard what he owes to the common cause as a gratuitous[7] contribution, the loss of which will be less harmful to others than the payment of it will be burdensome to him; and, regarding the moral person that constitutes the State as an imaginary being because it is not a man, he would be willing to enjoy the rights of a citizen without being willing to fulfil the duties of a subject. The progress of such injustice would bring about the ruin of the body politic.

In order, then, that the social pact may not be a vain formulary,[8] it tacitly includes this engagement, which can alone give force to the others,—that whoever refuses to obey the general will shall be constrained to do so by the whole body; which means nothing else than that he shall be forced to be free; for such is the condition which, uniting every citizen to his native land, guarantees him from all personal dependence, a condition that ensures the control and working of the political machine, and alone renders legitimate civil engagements, which, without it, would be absurd and tyrannical, and subject to the most enormous abuses.

[7] Freely-given, not required.
[8] Collection of conventional phrases.

THE CIVIL STATE

The passage from the state of nature to the civil state produces in man a very remarkable change, by substituting in his conduct justice for instinct, and by giving his actions the moral quality that they previously lacked. It is only when the voice of duty succeeds physical impulse, and law succeeds appetite, that man, who till then had regarded only himself, sees that he is obliged to act on other principles, and to consult his reason before listening to his inclinations. Although, in this state, he is deprived of many advantages that he derives from nature, he acquires equally great ones in return; his faculties are exercised and developed; his ideas are expanded; his feelings are ennobled; his whole soul is exalted to such a degree that, if the abuses of this new condition did not often degrade him below that from which he has emerged, he ought to bless without ceasing the happy moment that released him from it for ever, and transformed him from a stupid and ignorant animal into an intelligent being and a man.

Let us reduce this whole balance to terms easy to compare. What man loses by the social contract is his natural liberty and an unlimited right to anything which tempts him and which he is able to attain; what he gains is civil liberty and property in all that he possesses. In order that we may not be mistaken about these compensations, we must clearly distinguish natural liberty, which is limited only by the powers of the individual, from civil liberty, which is limited by the general will; and possession, which is nothing but the result of force or the right of first occupancy, from property, which can be based only on a positive title.

Besides the preceding, we might add to the acquisitions of the civil state moral freedom, which alone renders man truly master of himself; for the impulse of mere appetite is slavery, while obedience to a self-prescribed law is liberty. But I have already said too much on this head, and the philosophical meaning of the term *liberty* does not belong to my present subject.

• • •

THAT SOVEREIGNTY IS INALIENABLE[9]

The first and most important consequence of the principles above established is that the general will alone can direct the forces of the State according to the object of its institution, which is the common good; for if the opposition of private interests has rendered necessary the establishment of societies, the agreement of these same interests has rendered it possible. That which is common to these different interests forms the social bond; and unless there were some point in which all interests agree, no society could exist. Now, it is solely with regard to this common interest that the society should be governed.

I say, then, that sovereignty, being nothing but the exercise of the general will, can never be alienated, and that the sovereign power, which is only a collective being, can be represented by itself alone; power indeed can be transmitted, but not will.

In fact, if it is not impossible that a particular will should agree on some point with the general will, it is at least impossible that this agreement should be lasting and constant; for the particular will naturally tends to preferences, and the general will to equality. It is still more impossible to have a security for this agreement; even though it should always exist, it would not be a result of art, but of chance. The sovereign may indeed say: "I will now what a certain man wills, or at least what he says that he wills"; but he cannot say: "What that man wills to-morrow, I shall also will," since it is absurd that the will should bind itself as regards to future, and since it is not incumbent on any will to consent to anything contrary to the welfare of the being that wills. If, then, the nation simply promises to obey, it dissolves itself by that act and loses its character as a people; the moment there is a master, there is no longer a sovereign, and forthwith the body politic is destroyed.

This does not imply that the orders of the chiefs cannot pass for decisions of the general will, so long as the sovereign, free to oppose them, refrains from doing so. In such a case the consent of the people should be inferred from the universal silence.

• • •

[9] Cannot be taken away, or transferred.

WHETHER THE GENERAL WILL CAN ERR

It follows from what precedes that the general will is always right and always tends to the public advantage; but it does not follow that the resolutions of the people have always the same rectitude. Men always desire their own good, but do not always discern it; the people are never corrupted, though often deceived, and it is only then that they seem to will what is evil.

There is often a great deal of difference between the will of all and the general will; the latter regards only the common interest, while the former has regard to private interests, and is merely a sum of particular wills; but take away from these same wills the pluses and minuses which cancel one another, and the general will remains as the sum of the differences.

If the people came to a resolution when adequately informed and without any communication among the citizens, the general will would always result from the great number of slight differences, and the resolution would always be good. But when factions, partial associations, are formed to the detriment of the whole society, the will of each of these associations becomes general with reference to its members, and particular with reference to the State; it may then be said that there are no longer as many voters as there are men, but only as many voters as there are associations. The differences become less numerous and yield a less general result. Lastly, when one of these associations becomes so great that it predominates over all the rest, you no longer have as the result a sum of small differences, but a single difference; there is then no longer a general will, and the opinion which prevails is only a particular opinion.

It is important, then, in order to have a clear declaration of the general will, that there should be no partial association in the State, and that every citizen should express only his own opinion. Such was the unique and sublime institution of the great Lycurgus.[10] But if there are partial associations, it is necessary to multiply their number and prevent inequality, as Solon,[11] Numa,[12] and Servius[13]

[10] An ancient Spartan lawgiver (ninth century B.C.).
[11] An ancient Athenian lawgiver (*ca*. 639–*ca*. 559 B.C.).
[12] Numa Pompilius (*ca*. 715–*ca*. 673 B.C.) was the second of seven legendary kings of ancient Rome. He was believed to have founded some of Rome's religious and civil institutions.
[13] Servius Tullius (578–534 B.C.), the sixth of the seven legendary kings, was credited with having begun most of the civil rights and institutions of ancient Rome.

did. These are the only proper precautions for ensuring that the general will may always be enlightened, and that the people may not be deceived.

THE LIMITS OF THE SOVEREIGN POWER

If the State or city is nothing but a moral person, the life of which consists in the union of its members, and if the most important of its cares is that of self-preservation, it needs a universal and compulsive force to move and dispose every part in the manner most expedient for the whole. As nature gives every man an absolute power over all his limbs, the social pact gives the body politic an absolute power over all its members; and it is this same power which, when directed by the general will, bears, as I said, the name of sovereignty.

But besides the public person, we have to consider the private persons who compose it, and whose life and liberty are naturally independent of it. The question, then, is to distinguish clearly between the respective rights of the citizens and of the sovereign, as well as between the duties which the former have to fulfil in their capacity as subjects and the natural rights which they ought to enjoy in their character as men.

It is admitted that whatever part of his power, property, and liberty each one alienates by the social compact is only that part of the whole of which the use is important to the community; but we must also admit that the sovereign alone is judge of what is important.

All the services that a citizen can render to the State he owes to it as soon as the sovereign demands them; but the sovereign, on its part, cannot impose on its subjects any burden which is useless to the community; it cannot even wish to do so, for, by the law of reason, just as by the law of nature, nothing is done without a cause.

The engagements which bind us to the social body are obligatory only because they are mutual; and their nature is such that in fulfilling them we cannot work for others without also working for ourselves. Why is the general will always right, and why do all invariably desire the prosperity of each, unless it is because there is no one but appropriates to himself this word *each* and thinks of himself in voting on behalf of all? This proves that equality of rights and the notion of justice that it produces are derived from the preference which each gives to himself, and consequently from man's nature;

that the general will, to be truly such, should be so in its object as well as in its essence; that it ought to proceed from all in order to be applicable to all; and that it loses its natural rectitude when it tends to some individual and determinate object, because in that case, judging of what is unknown to us, we have no true principle of equity to guide us.

Indeed, so soon as a particular fact or right is in question with regard to a point which has not been regulated by an anterior general convention, the matter becomes contentious; it is a process in which the private persons interested are one of the parties and the public the other, but in which I perceive neither the law which must be followed, nor the judge who should decide. It would be ridiculous in such a case to wish to refer the matter for an express decision of the general will, which can be nothing but the decision of one of the parties, and which, consequently, is for the other party only a will that is foreign, partial, and inclined on such an occasion to injustice as well as liable to error. Therefore, just as a particular will cannot represent the general will, the general will in turn changes its nature when it has a particular end, and cannot, as general, decide about either a person or a fact. When the people of Athens, for instance, elected or deposed their chiefs, decreed honors to one, imposed penalties on another, and by multitudes of particular decrees exercised indiscriminately all the functions of government, the people no longer had any general will properly so called; they no longer acted as a sovereign power, but as magistrates. This will appear contrary to common ideas, but I must be allowed time to expound my own.

From this we must understand that what generalises the will is not so much the number of voices as the common interest which unites them; for, under this system, each necessarily submits to the conditions which he imposes on others—an admirable union of interest and justice, which gives to the deliberations of the community a spirit of equity that seems to disappear in the discussion of any private affair, for want of a common interest to unite and identify the ruling principle of the judge with that of the party.

By whatever path we return to our principle we always arrive at the same conclusion, namely, that the social compact establishes among the citizens such an equality that they all pledge themselves under the same conditions and ought all to enjoy the same rights. Thus, by the nature of the compact, every act of sovereignty, that is, every authentic act of the general will, binds or favors equally all the citizens; so that the sovereign knows only the body of the nation, and distinguishes none of those that compose it.

What, then, is an act of sovereignty properly so called? It is not an agreement between a superior and an inferior, but an agreement of the body with each of its members; a lawful agreement, because it has the social contract as its foundation; equitable, because it is common to all; useful, because it can have no other object than the general welfare; and stable, because it has the public force and the supreme power as a guarantee. So long as the subjects submit only to such conventions,[14] they obey no one, but simply their own will; and to ask how far the respective rights of the sovereign and citizens extend is to ask up to what point the latter can make engagements among themselves, each with all and all with each.

Thus we see that the sovereign power, wholly absolute, wholly sacred, and wholly inviolable as it is, does not, and cannot, pass the limits of general conventions, and that every man can fully dispose of what is left to him of his property and liberty by these conventions; so that the sovereign never has a right to burden one subject more than another, because then the matter becomes particular and his power is no longer competent.

These distinctions once admitted, so untrue is it that in the social contract there is on the part of individuals any real renunciation, that their situation, as a result of this contract, is in reality preferable to what it was before, and that, instead of an alienation, they have only made an advantageous exchange of an uncertain and precarious mode of existence for a better and more assured one, of natural independence for liberty, of the power to injure others for their own safety, and of their strength, which others might overcome, for a right which the social union renders inviolable. Their lives, also, which they have devoted to the State, are continually protected by it; and in exposing their lives for its defence, what do they do but restore what they have received from it? What do they do but what they would do more frequently and with more risk in the state of nature, when, engaging in inevitable struggles, they would defend at the peril of their lives their means of preservation? All have to fight for their country in case of need, it is true; but then no one ever has to fight for himself. Do we not gain, moreover, by incurring,[15] for what en-

---

[14] Agreements.
[15] Taking on, assuming.

sures our safety, a part of the risks that we should have to incur for ourselves individually, as soon as we were deprived of it?

• • •

THE LAW

By the social compact we have given existence and life to the body politic; the question now is to endow it with movement and will by legislation. For the original act by which this body is formed and consolidated determines nothing in addition as to what it must do for its own preservation.

What is right and conformable to order is such by the nature of things, and independently of human conventions. All justice comes from God, He alone is the source of it; but could we receive it direct from so lofty a source, we should need neither government nor laws. Without doubt there is a universal justice emanating from reason alone; but this justice, in order to be admitted among us, should be reciprocal. Regarding things from a human standpoint, the laws of justice are inoperative among men for want of a natural sanction; they only bring good to the wicked and evil to the just when the latter observe them with every one, and no one observes them in return. Conventions and laws, then, are necessary to couple rights with duties and apply justice to its object. In the state of nature, where everything is in common, I owe nothing to those to whom I have promised nothing; I recognize as belonging to others only what is useless to me. This is not the case in the civil state, in which all rights are determined by law.

But then, finally, what is a law? So long as men are content to attach to this word only metaphysical [16] ideas, they will continue to argue without being understood; and when they have stated what a law of nature is, they will know no better what a law of the State is.

I have already said that there is no general will with reference to a particular object. In fact, this particular object is either in the State or outside of it. If it is outside the State, a will which is foreign to it is not general in relation to it; and if it is within the State, it forms part of it; then there is formed between the whole and its part a relation which makes of it two separate beings, of which the part is one, and

[16] Abstract.

the whole, less this same part, is the other. But the whole less one part is not the whole, and so long as the relation subsists, there is no longer any whole, but two unequal parts; whence it follows that the will of the one is no longer general in relation to the other.

But when the whole people decree concerning the whole people, they consider themselves alone; and if a relation is then constituted, it is between the whole object under one point of view and the whole object under another point of view, without any division at all. Then the matter respecting which they decree is general like the will that decrees. It is this act that I call a law.

When I say that the object of the laws is always general, I mean that the law considers subjects collectively, and actions as abstract, never a man as an individual nor a particular action. Thus the law may indeed decree that there shall be privileges, but cannot confer them on any person by name; the law can create several classes of citizens, and even assign the qualifications which shall entitle them to rank in these classes, but it cannot nominate such and such persons to be admitted to them; it can establish a royal government and a hereditary succession, but cannot elect a king or appoint a royal family; in a word, no function which has reference to an individual object appertains to the legislative power.

From this standpoint we see immediately that it is no longer necessary to ask whose office it is to make laws, since they are acts of the general will; nor whether the prince is above the laws, since he is a member of the State; nor whether the law can be unjust, since no one is unjust to himself; nor how we are free and yet subject to the laws, since the laws are only registers of our wills.

We see, further, that since the law combines the universality of the will with the universality of the object, whatever any man prescribes on his own authority is not a law; and whatever the sovereign itself prescribes respecting a particular object is not a law, but a decree, not an act of sovereignty, but of magistracy.

I therefore call any State a republic which is governed by laws, under whatever form of administration it may be; for then only does the public interest predominate and the commonwealth count for something. Every legitimate government is republican; I will explain hereafter what government is.

Laws are properly only the conditions of civil association. The people, being subjected to the laws, should be the authors of them; it concerns only the associates to determine the conditions of association. But how will they be determined? Will it be by a common agreement, by a sudden inspiration? Has the body politic an organ for expressing its will? Who will give it the foresight necessary to frame its acts and publish them at the outset? Or how shall it declare them in the hour of need? How would a blind multitude, which often knows not what it wishes because it rarely knows what is good for it, execute of itself an enterprise so great, so difficult, as a system of legislation? Of themselves, the people always desire what is good, but do not always discern it. The general will is always right, but the judgment which guides it is not always enlightened. It must be made to see objects as they are, sometimes as they ought to appear; it must be shown the good path that it is seeking, and guarded from the seduction of private interests, it must be made to observe closely times and places, and to balance the attraction of immediate and palpable advantages against the danger of remote and concealed evils. Individuals see the good which they reject; the public desire the good which they do not see. All alike have need of guides. The former must be compelled to conform their wills to their reason; the people must be taught to know what they require. Then from the public enlightenment results the union of the understanding and the will in the social body; and from that the close co-operation of the parts, and, lastly, the maximum power of the whole. Hence arises the need of a legislator.

* * *

THAT THE GENERAL WILL IS INDESTRUCTIBLE

So long as a number of men in combination are considered as a single body, they have but one will, which relates to the common preservation and to the general well-being. In such a case all the forces of the State are vigorous and simple, and its principles are clear and luminous,[17] it has no confused and conflicting interests; the common good is everywhere plainly manifest and only good sense is required to perceive it. Peace, union, and equality are foes to political subtleties. Upright and simple-minded men are hard to deceive because of their simplicity; allurements[18] and refined pretexts do not impose upon them; they are not even cunning enough to be dupes.

[17] Readily understood.
[18] Enticements, come-ons.

When, in the happiest nation in the world,[19] we see troops of peasants regulating the affairs of the State under an oak and always acting wisely, can we refrain from despising the refinements of other nations, who make themselves illustrious and wretched with so much art and mystery?

A State thus governed needs very few laws; and in so far as it becomes necessary to promulgate new ones, this necessity is universally recognized. The first man to propose them only gives expression to what all have previously felt, and neither factions nor eloquence will be needed to pass into law what every one has already resolved to do, so soon as he is sure that the rest will act as he does.

What deceives reasoners is that, seeing only States that are ill-constituted from the beginning, they are impressed with the impossibility of maintaining such a policy in those States; they laugh to think of all the follies to which a cunning knave, an insinuating speaker, can persuade the people of Paris or London. They know not that Cromwell[20] would have been put in irons by the people of Bern,[21] and the Duke of Beaufort[22] imprisoned by the Genevese.[23]

But when the social bond begins to be relaxed and the State weakened, when private interests begin to make themselves felt and small associations to exercise influence on the State, the common interest is injuriously affected and finds adversaries; unanimity no longer reigns in the voting; the general will is no longer the will of all; opposition and disputes arise, and the best counsel does not pass uncontested.

Lastly, when the State, on the verge of ruin, no longer subsists except in a vain and illusory form, when the social bond is broken in all hearts, when the basest interest shelters itself impudently under the sacred name of the public welfare, the general will becomes dumb; all, under the guidance of secret motives, no more express their opinions as citizens than if the State had never existed; and, under the name of laws, they deceitfully pass unjust decrees which have only private interest as their end.

---

[19] The Swiss Confederation (Switzerland). Rousseau suggests in this sentence and the following paragraphs that the self-governing Swiss are superior in judgment to the citizens of other European states, notably, England and France.

[20] Oliver Cromwell (1599–1658), the English general and statesman who became a virtual dictator.

[21] The capital of Switzerland.

[22] François de Vendôme (1616–1669), an ambitious (and sometimes conspiring) French prince.

[23] The people of Geneva, Switzerland.

Does it follow from this that the general will is destroyed or corrupted? No; it is always constant, unalterable, and pure; but it is subordinated to others which get the better of it. Each, detaching his own interest from the common interest, sees clearly that he cannot completely separate it; but his share in the injury done to the State appears to him as nothing in comparison with the exclusive advantage which he aims at appropriating to himself. This particular advantage being excepted, he desires the general welfare for his own interests quite as strongly as any other. Even in selling his vote for money, he does not extinguish in himself the general will, but eludes it. The fault that he commits is to change the state of the question, and to answer something different from what he was asked; so that, instead of saying by a vote: "It is beneficial to the State," he says: "It is beneficial to a certain man or a certain party that such or such a motion should pass." Thus the law of public order in assemblies is not so much to maintain in them the general will as to ensure that it shall always be consulted and always respond.

I might in this place make many reflections on the simple right of voting in every act of sovereignty—a right which nothing can take away from the citizens—and on that of speaking, proposing, dividing, and discussing, which the government is always very careful to leave to its members only; but this important matter would require a separate treatise, and I cannot say everything in this one.

VOTING

We see from the previous chapter that the manner in which public affairs are managed may give a sufficiently trustworthy indication of the character and health of the body politic. The more that harmony reigns in the assemblies, that is, the more the voting approaches unanimity, the more also is the general will predominant; but long discussions, dissensions, and uproar proclaim the ascendency of private interests and the decline of the State.

This is not so clearly apparent when two or more orders enter into its constitution, as, in Rome, the patricians [24] and plebeians, [25] whose

[24] Members of the founding families of the early Roman republic, who enjoyed full citizenship.

[25] The common people of the Roman republic, who enjoyed only limited rights of citizenship.

quarrels often disturbed the *comitia*, [26] even in the palmiest days of the Republic; but this exception is more apparent than real, for, at that time, by a vice inherent in the body politic, there were, so to speak, two States in one; what is not true of the two together is true of each separately. And, indeed, even in the most stormy times, the *plebiscita* [27] of the people, when the Senate [28] did not interfere with them, always passed peaceably and by a large majority of votes; the citizens having but one interest, the people had but one will.

At the other extremity of the circle unanimity returns; that is, when the citizens, fallen into slavery, have no longer either liberty or will. Then fear and flattery change votes into acclamations; men no longer deliberate, but adore or curse. Such was the disgraceful mode of speaking in the Senate under the Emperors. Sometimes it was done with ridiculous precautions. Tacitus [29] observes that under Otho [30] the senators, in overwhelming Vitellius [31] with execrations, affected to make at the same time a frightful noise, in order that, if he happened to become master, he might not know what each of them had said.

From these different considerations are deduced the principles by which we should regulate the method of counting votes and of comparing opinions, according as the general will is more or less easy to ascertain and the State more or less degenerate.

There is but one law which by its nature requires unanimous consent, that is, the social compact; for civil association is the most voluntary act in the world; every man being born free and master of himself, no one can, under any pretext whatever, enslave him without his assent. To decide that the son of a slave is born a slave is to decide that he is not born a man.

If, then, at the time of the social compact, there are opponents of it, their opposition does not invalidate the contract, but only prevents them from being included in it; they are foreigners among citi-

---

[26] The principal political assembly of the Roman republic.
[27] Resolutions passed by the plebeian assembly, which, after 287 B.C., had the force of law.
[28] The high legislative council of the Roman state, originally composed of patricians.
[29] Publius Cornelius Tacitus (*ca.* A.D. 55–*ca.* 117), a Roman historian.
[30] Marcus Salvius Otho (A.D. 32–69), Roman emperor (January–April, A.D. 69).
[31] Aulus Vitellius (A.D. 15–69), Roman emperor (January–December, A.D. 69); rival of Otho.

zens. When the State is established, consent lies in residence; to dwell in the territory is to submit to the sovereignty.

Excepting this original contract, the vote of the majority always binds all the rest, this being a result of the contract itself. But it will be asked how a man can be free and yet forced to conform to wills which are not his own. How are opponents free and yet subject to laws they have not consented to?

I reply that the question is wrongly put. The citizen consents to all the laws, even to those which are passed in spite of him, and even to those which punish him when he dares to violate any of them. The unvarying will of all the members of the State is the general will; it is through that that they are citizens and free. When a law is proposed in the assembly of the people, what is asked of them is not exactly whether they approve the proposition or reject it, but whether it is comformable or not to the general will, which is their own; each one in giving his vote expresses his opinion thereupon; and from the counting of the votes is obtained the declaration of the general will. When, therefore, the opinion opposed to my own prevails, that simply shows that I was mistaken, and that what I considered to be the general will was not so. Had my private opinion prevailed, I should have done something other than I wished; and in that case I should not have been free.

This supposes, it is true, that all the marks of the general will are still in the majority; when they cease to be so, whatever side we take, there is no longer any liberty.

In showing before how particular wills were substituted for general wills in public resolutions, I have sufficiently indicated the means practicable for preventing this abuse; I will speak of it again hereafter. With regard to the proportional number of votes for declaring this will, I have also laid down the principles according to which it may be determined. The difference of a single vote destroys unanimity; but between unanimity and equality there are many unequal divisions, at each of which this number can be fixed according to the condition and requirements of the body politic.

Two general principles may serve to regulate these proportions: the one, that the more important and weighty the resolutions, the nearer should the opinion which prevails approach unanimity; the other, that the greater the despatch requisite in the matter under discussion, the more should we restrict the prescribed difference in the division of opinions; in resolutions which must be come to immediately the majority of a single vote should suffice. The first of these principles appears more suitable to laws, the second to affairs. Be that as it may, it is by their combination that are established the best proportions which can be assigned for the decision of a majority. . . .

11

Adam Smith
The Wealth of Nations

Adam Smith (1723–1790), a Scottish professor of philosophy and one of the greatest economists of the modern era, was the apostle of liberalism in economics, as John Locke was in political theory. Eccentric in personality and unprepossessing in appearance, Smith led an outwardly uneventful life. His intellectual point of departure was his discovery of an orderly and beneficent system operating behind the cruel, haphazard economy of eighteenth-century Britain. Smith attacked the restrictive practices of mercantilism and wished to free the economy to operate in accordance with the laws of nature. His arguments served as the basis for nineteenth-century laissez-faire theories; however, proponents of those theories carried Smith's ideas to an extreme of which he would not have approved. Smith's major work, An Inquiry into the Nature and Causes of the Wealth of Nations *(1776), became the bible of free enterprise and the competitive system. It was the first great work in political economy; it was also an encyclopedic survey of the economic life of Great Britain in the eighteenth century, a treatise on how to run a colonial empire, and an assault (with revolutionary import) on the mercantilistic system. In* The Wealth of Nations, *Smith expounded his belief in a natural economic order that was responsible for progress and continuously increasing productivity. The natural laws governing the market were those of individual, enlightened self-interest and competition, which, if allowed to operate freely, would be harmonized by an "invisible hand" for the ultimate good of society. He opposed any artificial controls or restrictions on the free working of the market. Smith was not an apologist for any one system or class, but*

Adam Smith, *An Inquiry into the Nature and Causes of the Wealth of Nations,* ed. J. E. T. Rogers (Oxford: Clarendon Press, 1869), I, 128, 134–36; II, 23–24, 28–30, 63, 68–69, 71–72, 115–17, 195–98, 244–46, 258–59, 272–73.

*industrial capitalists and their supporters later used his arguments to keep in-
dustry free from any form of government regulation. The selection presented
here makes clear Smith's economic individualism and his optimistic faith in
the beneficence of free enterprise.*

OF WAGES AND PROFIT . . .

The property which every man has in his own labor, as it is the original foundation of all other property, so it is the most sacred and inviolable. The patrimony of a poor man lies in the strength and
dexterity of his hands; and to hinder him from employing this
strength and dexterity in what manner he thinks proper without injury to his neighbor, is a plain violation of this most sacred property.
It is a manifest encroachment upon the just liberty both of the workman, and of those who might be disposed to employ him. As it
hinders the one from working at what he thinks proper, so it hinders
the others from employing whom they think proper. To judge
whether he is fit to be employed, may surely be trusted to the discretion of the employers whose interest it so much concerns. The affected anxiety of the lawgiver lest they should employ an improper
person, is evidently as impertinent as it is oppressive. . . .

The superiority which the industry of the towns has everywhere in
Europe over that of the country, is not altogether owing to corporations and corporation laws. It is supported by many other regulations. The high duties upon foreign manufactures and upon all goods
imported by alien merchants, all tend to the same purpose. Corporation laws enable the inhabitants of towns to raise their prices, without fearing to be undersold by the free competition of their own
countrymen. Those other regulations secure them equally against
that of foreigners. The enhancement of price occasioned by both is
everywhere finally paid by the landlords, farmers, and laborers of the
country, who have seldom opposed the establishment of such monopolies. They have commonly neither inclination nor fitness to enter
into combinations; and the clamor and sophistry of merchants and
manufacturers easily persuade them that the private interest of a part,
and of a subordinate part of the society, is the general interest of the
whole. . . .

People of the same trade seldom meet together, even for merriment and diversion, but the conversation ends in a conspiracy against the public, or in some contrivance to raise prices. It is impossible indeed to prevent such meetings, by any law which either could be executed, or would be consistent with liberty and justice. But though the law cannot hinder people of the same trade from sometimes assembling together, it ought to do nothing to facilitate such assemblies; much less to render them necessary.

• • •

OF THE PRINCIPLES OF THE COMMERCIAL OR MERCANTILE SYSTEM[1]

The two principles being established, however, that wealth consisted in gold and silver, and that those metals could be brought into a country which had no mines only by the balance of trade, or by exporting to a greater value than it imported; it necessarily became the great object of political economy to diminish as much as possible the importation of foreign goods for home consumption, and to increase as much as possible the exportation of the produce of domestic industry. Its two great engines for enriching the country, therefore, were restraints upon importation, and encouragements to exportation.

The restraints upon importation were of two kinds.

First, Restraints upon the importation of such foreign goods for home consumption as could be produced at home, from whatever country they were imported.

Secondly, Restraints upon the importation of goods of almost all kinds from those particular countries with which the balance of trade was supposed to be disadvantageous.

Those different restraints consisted sometimes in high duties, and sometimes in absolute prohibitions.

Exportation was encouraged sometimes by drawbacks, sometimes by bounties, sometimes by advantageous treaties of commerce with foreign states, and sometimes by the establishment of colonies in distant countries.

[1] An economic system based, in large part, on the doctrine that a country's wealth is measured by the amount of gold and silver (bullion) within its borders, and that the economic interests of the state are superior to the interests of individuals or groups. Also called mercantilism.

Drawbacks were given upon two different occasions. When the home manufactures were subject to any duty or excise, either the whole or a part of it was frequently drawn back upon their exportation; and when foreign goods liable to a duty were imported in order to be exported again, either the whole or a part of this duty was sometimes given back upon such exportation.

Bounties were given for the encouragement either of some beginning manufactures, or of such sorts of industry of other kinds as were supposed to deserve particular favor.

By advantageous treaties of commerce, particular privileges were procured in some foreign state for the goods and merchants of the country, beyond what were granted to those of other countries.

By the establishment of colonies in distant countries, not only particular privileges, but a monopoly was frequently procured for the goods and merchants of the country which established them.

The two sorts of restraints upon importation above mentioned, together with these four encouragements to exportation, constitute the six principal means by which the commercial system proposes to increase the quantity of gold and silver in any country by turning the balance of trade in its favor.

• • •

OF RESTRAINTS UPON THE IMPORTATION FROM FOREIGN COUNTRIES OF SUCH GOODS AS CAN BE PRODUCED AT HOME

What is the species of domestic industry which his capital can employ, and of which the produce is likely to be of the greatest value, every individual, it is evident, can, in his local situation, judge much better than any statesman or lawgiver can do for him. The statesman, who should attempt to direct private people in what manner they ought to employ their capitals, would not only load himself with a most unnecessary attention, but assume an authority which could safely be trusted, not only to no single person, but to no council or senate whatever, and which would nowhere be so dangerous as in the hands of a man who had folly and presumption enough to fancy himself fit to exercise it.

To give the monopoly of the home market to the produce of domestic industry, in any particular art or manufacture, is in some measure to direct private people in what manner they ought to employ their capitals, and must, in almost all cases, be either a useless or a hurtful regulation. If the produce of domestic can be brought there as cheap as that of foreign industry, the regulation is evidently useless. If it cannot, it must generally be hurtful. It is the maxim[2] of every prudent master of a family, never to attempt to make at home what it will cost him more to make than to buy. The taylor does not attempt to make his own shoes, but buys them of the shoemaker. The shoemaker does not attempt to make his own clothes, but employs a taylor. The farmer attempts to make neither the one nor the other, but employs those different artificers.[3] All of them find it for their interest to employ their whole industry in a way in which they have some advantage over their neighbors, and to purchase with a part of its produce, or what is the same thing, with the price of a part of it, whatever else they have occasion for.

What is prudence in the conduct of every private family, can scarce be folly in that of a great kingdom. If a foreign country can supply us with a commodity cheaper than we ourselves can make it, better buy it of them with some part of the produce of our own industry, employed in a way in which we have some advantage. The general industry of the country, being always in proportion to the capital which employs it, will not thereby be diminished, no more than that of the above mentioned artificers; but only left to find out the way in which it can be employed with the greatest advantage. It is certainly not employed to the greatest advantage, when it is thus directed towards an object which it can buy cheaper than it can make. The value of its annual produce is certainly more or less diminished, when it is thus turned away from producing commodities evidently of more value than the commodity which it is directed to produce. According to the supposition, that commodity could be purchased from foreign countries cheaper than it can be made at home. It could, therefore, have been purchased with a part only of the commodities, or, what is the same thing, with a part only of the price of the commodities, which the industry employed by an equal capital would have produced at home, had it been left to follow its natural course. The industry of the country, therefore, is thus turned away from a more, to a less advantageous employment, and the exchangeable value of its annual produce, instead of being increased, according

[2] Fundamental rule, principle.
[3] Craftspeople.

to the intention of the lawgiver, must necessarily be diminished by every such regulation.

By means of such regulations, indeed, a particular manufacture may sometimes be acquired sooner than it could have been otherwise, and after a certain time may be made at home as cheap or cheaper than in the foreign country. But though the industry of the society may be thus carried with advantage into a particular channel sooner than it could have been otherwise, it will by no means follow that the sum total, either of its industry, or of its revenue, can ever be augmented by any such regulation. The industry of the society can augment only in proportion as its capital augments, and its capital can augment only in proportion to what can be gradually saved out of its revenue. But the immediate effect of every such regulation is to diminish its revenue, and what diminishes its revenue is certainly not very likely to augment its capital faster than it would have augmented of its own accord, had both capital and industry been left to find out their natural employments.

Though for want of such regulations the society should never acquire the proposed manufacture, it would not, upon that account, necessarily be the poorer in any one period of its duration. In every period of its duration its whole capital and industry might still have been employed, though upon different objects, in the manner that was most advantageous at the time. In every period its revenue might have been the greatest which its capital could afford, and both capital and revenue might have been augmented with the greatest possible rapidity.

. . .

OF THE UNREASONABLENESS OF THOSE EXTRAORDINARY RESTRAINTS UPON OTHER PRINCIPLES

Nothing, however, can be more absurd than this whole doctrine of the balance of trade, upon which, not only these restraints, but almost all the other regulations of commerce are founded. When two places trade with one another, this doctrine supposes that, if the balance be even, neither of them either loses or gains; but if it leans in any degree to one side, that one of them loses, and the other gains in proportion to its declension[4] from the exact equilibrium.[5] Both suppositions are false. A trade which is forced by means of bounties[6] and monopolies, may be, and commonly is disadvantageous to the country in whose favor it is meant to be established, as I shall endeavor to show hereafter. But that trade which, without force or constraint, is naturally and regularly carried on between any two places, is always advantageous, though not always equally so, to both.

By advantage or gain, I understand, not the increase of the quantity of gold and silver, but that of the exchangeable value of the annual produce of the land and labor of the country, or the increase of the annual revenue of its inhabitants. . . .

. . . The Portuguese, it is said, indeed, are better customers for our manufactures than the French, and should therefore be encouraged in preference to them. As they give us their custom, it is pretended, we should give them ours. The sneaking arts of underling tradesmen are thus erected into political maxims for the conduct of a great empire; for it is the most underling tradesmen only who make it a rule to employ chiefly their own customers. A great trader purchases his goods always where they are cheapest and best, without regard to any little interest of this kind.

By such maxims as these, however, nations have been taught that their interest consisted in beggaring[7] all their neighbors. Each nation has been made to look with an invidious[8] eye upon the prosperity of all the nations with which it trades, and to consider their gain as its own loss. Commerce, which ought naturally to be, among nations, as among individuals, a bond of union and friendship, has become the most fertile source of discord and animosity. The capricious ambition of kings and ministers has not, during the present and the preceding century, been more fatal to the repose of Europe, than the impertinent jealousy of merchants and manufacturers. The violence and injustice of the rulers of mankind is an ancient evil, for which, I am afraid, the nature of human affairs can scarce admit of a remedy. But the mean rapacity, the monopolizing spirit of merchants and

[4] Deviation, variance.
[5] Balance.
[6] Subsidies.
[7] Making poor.
[8] Envious.

manufacturers, who neither are, nor ought to be, the rulers of mankind, though it cannot perhaps be corrected, may very easily be prevented from disturbing the tranquillity of anybody but themselves.

That it was the spirit of monopoly which originally both invented and propagated this doctrine, cannot be doubted; and they who first taught it were by no means such fools as they who believed it. In every country it always is and must be the interest of the great body of the people to buy whatever they want of those who sell it cheapest. The proposition is so very manifest, that it seems ridiculous to take any pains to prove it; nor could it ever have been called in question, had not the interested sophistry of merchants and manufacturers confounded the common sense of mankind. Their interest is, in this respect, directly opposite to that of the great body of the people. As it is the interest of the freemen of a corporation to hinder the rest of the inhabitants from employing any workmen but themselves, so it is the interest of the merchants and manufacturers of every country to secure to themselves the monopoly of the home market. Hence in Great Britain, and in most other European countries, the extraordinary duties upon almost all goods imported by alien merchants. Hence the high duties and prohibitions upon all those foreign manufactures which can come into competition with our own. Hence, too, the extraordinary restraints upon the importation of almost all sorts of goods from those countries with which the balance of trade is supposed to be disadvantageous; that is, from those against whom national animosity happens to be most violently inflamed.

The wealth of a neighboring nation, however, though dangerous in war and politics, is certainly advantageous in trade. In a state of hostility it may enable our enemies to maintain fleets and armies superior to our own; but in a state of peace and commerce it must likewise enable them to exchange with us to a greater value, and to afford a better market, either for the immediate produce of our own industry, or for whatever is purchased with that produce. As a rich man is likely to be a better customer to the industrious people in his neighborhood, than a poor, so is likewise a rich nation. A rich man, indeed, who is himself a manufacturer, is a very dangerous neighbor to all those who deal in the same way. All the rest of the neighborhood, however, by far the greatest number, profit by the good market which his expence affords them. They even profit by his underselling the poorer workmen who deal in the same way with him. The manufacturers of a rich nation, in the same manner, may no doubt be very dangerous rivals to those of their neighbors. This very competition, however, is advantageous to the great body of the people, who profit greatly besides by the good market which the great expence of such a nation affords them in every other way. . . .

There is no commercial country in Europe of which the approaching ruin has not frequently been foretold by the pretended doctors of this system, from an unfavorable balance of trade. After all the anxiety, however, which they have excited about this, after all the vain attempts of almost all trading nations to turn that balance in their own favor and against their neighbors, it does not appear that any one nation in Europe has been in any respect impoverished by this cause. Every town and country, on the contrary, in proportion as they have opened their ports to all nations, instead of being ruined by this free trade, as the principles of the commercial system would lead us to expect, have been enriched by it. Though there are in Europe, indeed, a few towns which in some respects deserve the name of free ports, there is no country which does so. Holland, perhaps, approaches the nearest to this character of any, though still very remote from it; and Holland, it is acknowledged, not only derives its whole wealth, but a great part of its necessary subsistence, from foreign trade.

• • •

DIGRESSION CONCERNING THE CORN[9] TRADE AND CORN LAWS

Were all nations to follow the liberal system of free exportation and free importation, the different states into which a great continent was divided would so far resemble the different provinces of a great empire. As among the different provinces of a great empire the freedom of the inland trade appears, both from reason and experience, not only the best palliative[10] of a dearth,[11] but the most effectual preventative of a famine; so would the freedom of the exportation and importation trade be among the different states into which a

---

[9] A British term for wheat, but *not* for maize.
[10] Reliever.
[11] Scarcity (of food).

great continent was divided. The larger the continent, the easier the communication through all the different parts of it, both by land and by water, the less would any one particular part of it ever be exposed to either of these calamities, the scarcity of any one country being more likely to be relieved by the plenty of some other. But very few countries have entirely adopted this liberal system. The freedom of the corn trade is almost everywhere more or less restrained, and, in many countries, is confined by such absurd regulations, as frequently aggravate the unavoidable misfortune of a dearth, into the dreadful calamity of a famine. The demand of such countries for corn may frequently become so great and so urgent, that a small state in their neighborhood, which happened at the same time to be laboring under some degree of dearth, could not venture to supply them without exposing itself to the like dreadful calamity. The very bad policy of one country may thus render it in some measure dangerous and imprudent to establish what would otherwise be the best policy in another. The unlimited freedom of exportation, however, would be much less dangerous in great states, in which the growth being much greater, the supply could seldom be much affected by any quantity of corn that was likely to be exported. In a Swiss canton,[12] or in some of the little states of Italy, it may, perhaps, sometimes be necessary to restrain the exportation of corn. In such great countries as France or England it scarce ever can. To hinder, besides, the farmer from sending his goods at all times to the best market, is evidently to sacrifice the ordinary laws of justice to an idea of public utility, to a sort of reasons of state; an act of legislative authority which ought to be exercised only, which can be pardoned only in cases of the most urgent necessity. The price at which the exportation of corn is prohibited, if it is ever to be prohibited, ought always to be a very high price.

The laws concerning corn may everywhere be compared to the laws concerning religion. The people feel themselves so much interested in what relates either to their subsistence in this life, or to their happiness in a life to come, that government must yield to their prejudices, and, in order to preserve the public tranquillity, establish that system which they approve of. It is upon this account, perhaps, that we so seldom find a reasonable system established with regard to either of those two capital objects.

• • •

[12] A political unit, similar to a small state, of the Swiss Confederation.

OF COLONIES

It is thus that the single advantage which the monopoly procures to a single order of men, is in many different ways hurtful to the general interest of the country.

To found a great empire for the sole purpose of raising up a people of customers, may at first sight appear a project fit only for a nation of shopkeepers. It is, however, a project altogether unfit for a nation of shopkeepers; but extremely fit for a nation whose government is influenced by shopkeepers. Such statesmen, and such statesmen only, are capable of fancying that they will find some advantage in employing the blood and treasure of their fellow-citizens, to found and maintain such an empire. Say to a shopkeeper, Buy me a good estate, and I shall always buy my clothes at your shop, even though I should pay somewhat dearer than what I can have them for at other shops; and you will not find him very forward to embrace your proposal. But should any other person buy you such an estate, the shopkeeper would be much obliged to your benefactor if he would enjoin [13] you to buy all your clothes at his shop. England purchased for some of her subjects, who found themselves uneasy at home, a great estate in a distant country. The price, indeed, was very small, and instead of thirty years purchase, the ordinary price of land in the present times, it amounted to little more than the expence of the different equipments which made the first discovery, reconnoitred the coast, and took a fictitious possession of the country. The land was good and of great extent, and the cultivators having plenty of good ground to work upon, and being for some time at liberty to sell their produce where they pleased, became in the course of little more than thirty or forty years (between 1620 and 1660) so numerous and thriving a people, that the shopkeepers and other traders of England wished to secure to themselves the monopoly of their custom. Without pretending, therefore, that they had paid any part, either of the original purchase money, or of the subsequent expense of improvement, they petitioned the parliament that the cultivators of America might for the future be confined to their shop; first, for buying all the goods which they wanted from Europe; and, secondly, for selling all such parts of their own produce as those traders might find it convenient to buy. For they did not find it convenient to buy every

[13] Command.

part of it. Some parts of it imported into England might have interfered with some of the trades which they themselves carried on at home. Those particular parts of it, therefore, they were willing that the colonists should sell where they could; the farther off the better; and upon that account proposed that their market should be confined to the countries south of Cape Finisterre.[14] A clause in the famous act of navigation [15] established this truly shopkeeper proposal into a law.

The maintenance of this monopoly has hitherto been the principal, or more properly perhaps the sole end and purpose of the dominion which Great Britain assumes over her colonies. In the exclusive trade, it is supposed, consists the great advantage of provinces, which have never yet afforded either revenue or military force for the support of the civil government, or the defense of the mother country. The monopoly is the principal badge of their dependency, and it is the sole fruit which has hitherto been gathered from that dependency. Whatever expense Great Britain has hitherto laid out in maintaining this dependency, has really been laid out in order to support this monopoly. . . .

This whole expense is, in reality, a bounty which has been given in order to support a monopoly. The pretended purpose of it was to encourage the manufactures, and to increase the commerce of Great Britain. But its real effect has been to raise the rate of mercantile profit, and to enable our merchants to turn into a branch of trade, of which the returns are more slow and distant than those of the greater part of other trades, a greater proportion of their capital than they otherwise would have done; two events which if a bounty could have prevented, it might perhaps have been very well worth while to give such a bounty.

Under the present system of management, therefore, Great Britain derives nothing but loss from the dominion which she assumes over her colonies.

• • •

CONCLUSIONS ABOUT THE MERCANTILE SYSTEM

It is unnecessary, I imagine, to observe, how contrary such regulations are to the boasted liberty of the subject, of which we affect to

[14] Located at the northwestern corner of Spain.
[15] A parliamentary statute regulating all commerce between Britain and her colonies.

be so very jealous; but which, in this case, is so plainly sacrificed to the futile interests of our merchants and manufacturers.

The laudable motive of all these regulations, is to extend our own manufactures, not by their own improvement, but by the depression of those of all our neighbors, and by putting an end, as much as possible, to the troublesome competition of such odious and disagreeable rivals. Our master manufacturers think it reasonable, that they themselves should have the monopoly of the ingenuity of all their countrymen. Though by restraining, in some trades, the number of apprentices which can be employed at one time, and by imposing the necessity of a long apprenticeship in all trades, they endeavor, all of them, to confine the knowledge of their respective employments to as small a number as possible; they are unwilling, however, that any part of this small number should go abroad to instruct foreigners.

Consumption is the sole end and purpose of all production; and the interest of the producer ought to be attended to, only so far as it may be necessary for promoting that of the consumer. The maxim is so perfectly self-evident, that it would be absurd to attempt to prove it. But in the mercantile system, the interest of the consumer is almost constantly sacrificed to that of the producer; and it seems to consider production, and not consumption, as the ultimate end and object of all industry and commerce.

In the restraints upon the importation of all foreign commodities which can come into competition with those of our own growth, or manufacture, the interest of the home consumer is evidently sacrificed to that of the producer. It is altogether for the benefit of the latter, that the former is obliged to pay that enhancement of price which this monopoly almost always occasions.

It is altogether for the benefit of the producer that bounties are granted upon the exportation of some of his productions. The home consumer is obliged to pay, first, the tax which is necessary for paying the bounty, and secondly, the still greater tax which necessarily arises from the enhancement of the price of the commodity in the home market. . . .

It cannot be very difficult to determine who have been the contrivers [16] of this whole mercantile system; not the consumers, we may believe, whose interest has been entirely neglected; but the producers, whose interest has been so carefully attended to; and among

[16] Schemers, planners.

this latter class our merchants and manufacturers have been by far the principal architects. In the mercantile regulations, which have been taken notice of in this chapter, the interest of our manufacturers has been most peculiarly attended to; and the interest, not so much of the consumers, as that of some other sets of producers, has been sacrificed to it.

·   ·   ·

. . . SYSTEMS OF POLITICAL ECONOMY . . .

Mr. Colbert,[17] the famous minister of Louis XIV,[18] was a man of probity, of great industry and knowledge of detail; of great experience and acuteness in the examination of public accounts, and of abilities, in short, every way fitted for introducing method and good order into the collection and expenditure of the public revenue. That minister had unfortunately embraced all the prejudices of the mercantile system, in its nature and essence a system of restraint and regulation, and such as could scarce fail to be agreeable to a laborious and plodding man of business, who had been accustomed to regulate the different departments of public offices, and to establish the necessary checks and controls for confining each to its proper sphere. The industry and commerce of a great country he endeavored to regulate upon the same model as the departments of a public office; and instead of allowing every man to pursue his own interest his own way, upon the liberal plan of equality, liberty and justice, he bestowed upon certain branches of industry extraordinary privileges, while he laid others under as extraordinary restraints. He was not only disposed, like other European ministers, to encourage more the industry of the towns than that of the country; but, in order to support the industry of the towns, he was willing even to depress and keep down that of the country. In order to render provisions cheap to the inhabitants of the towns, and thereby to encourage manufactures and foreign commerce, he prohibited altogether the exportation of corn, and thus excluded the inhabitants of the country from every foreign market for by far the most important part of the produce of their in-

---

[17] Jean Baptiste Colbert (1619–1683), French statesman and controller-general of the finances.
[18] King of France (1638–1715).

dustry. This prohibition, joined to the restraints imposed by the ancient provincial laws of France upon the transportation of corn from one province to another, and to the arbitrary and degrading taxes which are levied upon the cultivators in almost all the provinces, discouraged and kept down the agriculture of that country very much below the state to which it would naturally have risen in so very fertile a soil and so very happy a climate. This state of discouragement and depression was felt more or less in every different part of the country, and many different inquiries were set on foot concerning the causes of it. One of those causes appeared to be the preference given, by the institutions of Mr. Colbert, to the industry of the towns above that of the country. . . .

Some speculative physicians seem to have imagined that the health of the human body could be preserved only by a certain precise regimen of diet and exercise, of which every, the smallest, violation necessarily occasioned some degree of disease or disorder proportioned to the degree of the violation. Experience, however, would seem to show, that the human body frequently preserves, to all appearance at least, the most perfect state of health under a vast variety of different regimens; even under some which are generally believed to be very far from being perfectly wholesome. But the healthful state of the human body, it would seem, contains in itself some unknown principle of preservation, capable either of preventing or of correcting, in many respects, the bad effects even of a very faulty regimen. Mr. Quesnay,[19] who was himself a physician, and a very speculative physician, seems to have entertained a notion of the same kind concerning the political body, and to have imagined that it would thrive and prosper only under a certain precise regimen, the exact regimen of perfect liberty and perfect justice. He seems not to have considered that in the political body, the natural effort which every man is continually making to better his own condition, is a principle of preservation capable of preventing and correcting, in many respects, the bad effects of a political economy, in some degree both partial and oppressive. Such a political economy, though it no doubt retards more or less, is not always capable of stopping altogether the natural progress of a nation towards wealth and prosperity, and still less of

---

[19] Francois Quesnay (1694–1774), surgeon and court physician of the French king Louis XV. Late in life, after age sixty, he published works on economics that were much appreciated by the economist Adam Smith.

making it go backwards. If a nation could not prosper without the enjoyment of perfect liberty and perfect justice, there is not in the world a nation which could ever have prospered. In the political body, however, the wisdom of nature has fortunately made ample provision for remedying many of the bad effects of the folly and in-justice of man; in the same manner as it has done in the natural body, for remedying those of his sloth and intemperance. . . .

It is thus that every system which endeavors, either, by extraordi-nary encouragements, to draw towards a particular species of in-dustry a greater share of the capital of the society than what would naturally go to it; or, by extraordinary restraints, to force from a particular species of industry some share of the capital which would otherwise be employed in it; is in reality subversive of the great pur-pose which it means to promote. It retards, instead of accelerating, the progress of the society towards real wealth and greatness; and diminishes, instead of increasing, the real value of the annual produce of its land and labor.

All systems either of preference or of restraint, therefore, being thus completely taken away, the obvious and simple system of natu-ral liberty establishes itself of its own accord. Every man, as long as he does not violate the laws of justice, is left perfectly free to pursue his own interest his own way, and to bring both his industry and capital into competition with those of any other man, or order of men. The sovereign is completely discharged from a duty, in the at-tempting to perform which he must always be exposed to innumera-ble delusions, and for the proper performance of which no human wisdom or knowledge could ever be sufficient; the duty of superin-tending the industry of private people, and of directing it towards the employments most suitable to the interest of the society. Accord-ing to the system of natural liberty, the sovereign has only three duties to attend to; three duties of great importance, indeed, but plain and intelligible to common understandings: first, the duty of protecting the society from the violence and invasion of other in-dependent societies; secondly, the duty of protecting, as far as pos-sible, every member of the society from the injustice or oppression of every other member of it, or the duty of establishing an exact ad-ministration of justice; and, thirdly, the duty of erecting and main-taining certain public works and certain public institutions, which it can never be for the interest of any individual, or small number of individuals, to erect and maintain; because the profit could never repay the expense to any individual or small number of individuals, though it may frequently do much more than repay it to a great society. . . .

12

Antoine Nicolas de Condorcet

The Progress of the Human Mind

Condemned as an enemy of the revolutionary French Republic and living as a fugitive from the Reign of Terror, Antoine Nicolas de Condorcet (1743–1794) was inspired in 1793 to put into writing the ideas for which he had lived and was prepared to die. Thus, out of the bloodstained chaos of the French Revolution came his Sketch for a Historical Picture of the Progress of the Human Mind, *a "passionate affirmation of the rationalist faith." It was to be his last testament to humanity; for soon after it was completed, he was arrested and the next day was found dead in his cell, presumably a suicide by poison. In 1795, the work was published by the more moderate government that succeeded the Terror, becoming, in effect, the new regime's declaration of revolutionary faith. Condorcet's only work of note, it is a distillation of all of his major ideas.*

An aristocratic intellectual and reformer, Condorcet was a religious skeptic and an outspoken adversary of the Church. He also fought the influence of the hereditary nobility, despite his own noble birth. His mind and efforts were devoted to scientific enlightenment and to social and political reform. He won fame as a mathematician, served as secretary of the Academy of Sciences, and became a leading member of the circle of philosopher-reformers around Voltaire. With the outbreak of the Revolution, Condorcet plunged into political activity. As a moderate, he fell afoul of the radicals, but not before he had effectively championed his proposals, chiefly in the field of education.

The Progress of the Human Mind, *an outline for a larger work that*

Antoine Nicolas de Condorcet, *Sketch for a Historical Picture of the Progress of the Human Mind,* trans. June Barraclough (London: Weidenfeld, Westport, Conn.: Greenwood Press, Inc. 1979), 4–7, 9–13, 127–28, 136–37, 139–44, 147–48, 162–65, 168–69, 173–77, 179–84, 187–95, 199–202. Reprinted by permission of George Weidenfeld & Nicolson Ltd., and Greenwood Press, Inc.

Condorcet never lived to complete, remains the best and most moving expression of the Enlightenment's gospel of progress. Suffused with a grand, historical optimism, it enshrines the idea of progress as a moral absolute and it considers the free exercise of the spirit of inquiry capable of liberating people everywhere from ignorance, poverty, and tyranny. Condorcet discerned ten stages of human development, beginning with the first, primitive stage of tribal hunters and fishers. Stage Two saw the introduction of property and slavery. In the course of each of the first nine stages, people struggled against the adversities caused by nature, their own ignorance, lack of communication, and priestly and secular tyranny. The Tenth Stage, however, he visualized to be almost totally different from the preceding nine, because this final stage would see the speedy fruition of the highest dreams of humanity.

Condorcet believed that he stood on the threshold of this Tenth Stage, the achievements of which he did not, of course, live to see. Though his grandiose prophecy is still far from fulfillment, it is remarkable that he accurately predicted many significant developments of the present epoch—among them achievements in medicine, epidemiology, genetics, geriatrics, social insurance, women's rights, education, and computer technology. He also correctly perceived that population might increase beyond the means of subsistence, but he anticipated that this calamity would be forestalled by the continuing advance of reason and science as applied to birth control. Nothing daunted Condorcet's faith in the progress of the human mind as the means to human perfectibility.

INTRODUCTION

. . .

. . . The aim of the work that I have undertaken, and its result will be to show by appeal to reason and fact that nature has set no term to the perfection of human faculties; that the perfectibility of man is truly indefinite; and that the progress of this perfectibility, from now onwards independent of any power that might wish to halt it, has no other limit than the duration of the globe upon which nature has cast us. This progress will doubtless vary in speed, but it will never be reversed as long as the earth occupies its present place in the system of the universe, and as long as the general laws of this system produce neither a general cataclysm nor such changes as will deprive the human race of its present faculties and its present resources.

The first stage of civilization observed among human beings is that of a small society whose members live by hunting and fishing, and know only how to make rather crude weapons and household utensils and to build or dig for themselves a place in which to live, but are already in possession of a language with which to communicate their needs, and a small number of moral ideas which serve as common laws of conduct; living in families, conforming to general customs which take the place of laws, and even possessing a crude system of government.

The uncertainty of life, the difficulty man experiences in providing for his needs, and the necessary cycle of extreme activity and total idleness do not allow him the leisure in which he can indulge in thought and enrich his understanding with new combinations of ideas. The means of satisfying his needs are too dependent on chance and the seasons to encourage any occupation whose progress might be handed down to later generations, and so each man confines himself to perfecting his own individual skill and talent.

Thus the progress of the human species was necessarily very slow; it could move forward only from time to time when it was favored by exceptional circumstances. However, we see hunting, fishing, and the natural fruits of the earth replaced as a source of subsistence by food obtained from animals that man domesticates and that he learns to keep and to breed. Later, a primitive form of agriculture developed; man was no longer satisfied with the fruits or plants that he came across by chance, but learned to store them, to collect them around his dwelling, to sow or plant them, and to provide them with favorable conditions under which they could spread.

Property, which at first was limited to the animals that a man killed, his weapons, his nets, and his cooking utensils, later came to include his cattle and eventually was extended to the earth that he won from its virgin state and cultivated. On the death of the owner this property naturally passed into the hands of his family, and in consequence some people came to possess a surplus that they could keep. If this surplus was absolute, it gave rise to new needs; but if it existed only in one commodity and at the same time there was a scarcity of another, this state of affairs naturally suggested the idea of exchange, and from then onwards, moral relations grew in number and increased in complexity. A life that was less hazardous and more leisured gave opportunities for meditation or, at least, for sustained observation. Some people adopted the practice of exchanging part of their surplus for labor from which they would then be absolved. In consequence there arose a class of men whose time was not wholly taken up in manual labor and whose desires extended beyond their elementary needs. Industry was born; the arts that were already known, were spread and perfected; as men became more experienced and attentive, quite casual information suggested to them new arts; the population grew as the means of subsistence became less dangerous and precarious; agriculture, which could support a greater number of people on the same amount of land, replaced the other means of subsistence; it encouraged the growth of the population and this, in its turn, favored progress; acquired ideas were communicated more quickly and were perpetuated more surely in a society that had become more sedentary,[1] more accessible, and more intimate. Already, the dawn of science had begun to break; man revealed himself to be distinct from the other species of animals and seemed no longer confined like them to a purely individual perfection.

As human relations increased in number, scope, and complexity, it became necessary to have a method of communicating with those who were absent, of perpetuating the memory of an event with greater precision than that afforded by oral tradition, of fixing the terms of an agreement with greater certainty than that assured by the testimony of witnesses, and of registering in a more enduring manner those respected customs according to which the members of a single society had agreed to regulate their conduct. So the need for writing was felt, and writing was invented. It seems to have been at first a genuine system of representation, but this gave way to a more conventional representation which preserved merely the characteristic features of objects. Finally by a sort of metaphor[2] analogous[3] to that which had already been introduced into language, the image of a physical object came to express moral ideas. The origin of these signs, like that of words, was ultimately forgotten, and writing became the art of attaching a conventional sign to every idea, to every word, and so by extension, to every modification of ideas and words. . . .

[1] Remaining in one locality.
[2] A figure of speech in which one thing represents another.
[3] Similar in certain respects.

The history of man from the time when alphabetical writing was known in Greece to the condition of the human race at the present day in the most enlightened countries of Europe is linked by an uninterrupted chain of facts and observations; and so at this point the picture of the march and progress of the human mind becomes truly historical. Philosophy has nothing more to guess, no more hypothetical surmises to make; it is enough to assemble and order the facts and to show the useful truths that can be derived from their connections and from their totality.

When we have shown all this, there will remain one last picture for us to sketch: that of our hopes, and of the progress reserved for future generations, which the constancy of the laws of nature seems to assure them. It will be necessary to indicate by what stages what must appear to us today a fantastic hope ought in time to become possible, and even likely; to show why, in spite of the transitory successes of prejudice and the support that it receives from the corruption of governments or peoples, truth alone will obtain a lasting victory; we shall demonstrate how nature has joined together indissolubly the progress of knowledge and that of liberty, virtue and respect for the natural rights of man; and how these, the only real goods that we possess, though so often separated that they have even been held to be incompatible, must on the contrary become inseparable from the moment when enlightenment has attained a certain level in a number of nations, and has penetrated throughout the whole mass of a great people whose language is universally known and whose commercial relations embrace the whole area of the globe. Once such a close accord has been established between all enlightened men, from then onwards all will be the friends of humanity, all will work together for its perfection and its happiness.

We shall reveal the origin and trace the history of those widespread errors which have somewhat retarded or suspended the progress of reason and which have, as often as forces of a political character, even caused man to fall back into ignorance.

The operations of the understanding that lead us into error or hold us there, from the subtle paralogism[4] which can deceive even the most enlightened of men, to the dreams of a madman, belong no less than the methods of right reasoning or of discourse to the theory of

[4]Faulty reasoning.

the development of our individual faculties; on the same principle, the way in which general errors are insinuated[5] among peoples and are propagated, transmitted, and perpetuated is all part of the historical picture of the progress of the human mind. Like the truths that perfect and illuminate it, they are the necessary consequences of its activity and of the disproportion that forever holds between what it knows, what it wishes to know, and what it believes it needs to know.

It can even be observed that, according to the general laws of the development of our faculties, certain prejudices have necessarily come into being at each stage of our progress, but they have extended their seductions or their empire long beyond their due season, because men retain the prejudices of their childhood, their country, and their age, long after they have discovered all the truths necessary to destroy them.

Finally, in all countries at all times there are different prejudices varying with the standard of education of the different classes of men and their professions. The prejudices of philosophers harm the progress of truth; those of the less enlightened classes retard the propagation of truths already known; those of certain eminent or powerful professions place obstacles in truth's way: here we see three enemies whom reason is obliged to combat without respite, and whom she vanquishes often only after a long and painful struggle. The history of these struggles, of the birth, triumph, and fall of prejudices, will occupy a great part of this work and will be neither the least important nor the least useful section of it . . .

Everything tells us that we are now close upon one of the great revolutions of the human race. If we wish to learn what to expect from it and to procure a certain guide to lead us in the midst of its vicissitudes,[6] what could be more suitable than to have some picture of the revolutions that have gone before it and prepared its way? The present state of enlightenment assures us that this revolution will have a favorable result, but is not this only on condition that we know how to employ our knowledge and resources to their fullest extent? And in order that the happiness that it promises may be less dearly bought, that it may be diffused more rapidly over a greater area, that it may be more complete in its effects, do we not need to

[5] Introduced slowly and indirectly.
[6] Changes of circumstances.

study the history of the human spirit to discover what obstacles we still have to fear and what means are open to us of surmounting them?

I shall divide the area that I propose to cover into nine great stages and in a tenth I shall venture to offer some observations on the future destiny of the human race.

• • •

THE NINTH STAGE: FROM DESCARTES TO THE FOUNDATION OF THE FRENCH REPUBLIC

This sketch of the progress of philosophy and of the dissemination of enlightenment, whose more general and more evident effects we have already examined, brings us up to the stage when the influence of progress upon public opinion, of public opinion upon nations or their leaders, suddenly ceases to be a slow imperceptible[7] affair, and produces a revolution in the whole order of several nations, a certain earnest of the revolution that must one day include in its scope the whole of the human race.

After long periods of error, after being led astray by vague or incomplete theories, publicists have at last discovered the true rights of man and how they can all be deduced from the single truth, that *man is a sentient*[8] *being, capable of reasoning and of acquiring moral ideas.*

They have seen that the maintenance of these rights was the sole object of men's coming together in political societies, and that the social art is the art of guaranteeing the preservation of these rights and their distribution in the most equal fashion over the largest area. It was felt that in every society the means of assuring the rights of the individual should be submitted to certain common rules, but that the authority to choose these means and to determine these rules could belong only to the majority of the members of the society itself; for in making this choice the individual cannot follow his own reason without subjecting others to it, and the will of the majority is the only mark of truth that can be accepted by all without loss of equality. . . .

Up till now we have shown the progress of philosophy only in the men who have cultivated, deepened, and perfected it. It remains for

[7] Unnoticeable.
[8] Having sensory perception, conscious.

us to show what have been its effects on public opinion; how reason, while it learned to safeguard itself against the errors into which the imagination and respect for authority had so often led it, at last found a sure method of discovering and recognizing truth; and how at the same time it destroyed the prejudices of the masses which had for so long afflicted and corrupted the human race.

At last man could proclaim aloud his right, which for so long had been ignored, to submit all opinions to his own reason and to use in the search for truth the only instrument for its recognition that he has been given. Every man learned with a sort of pride that nature had not forever condemned him to base his beliefs on the opinions of others; the superstitions of antiquity and the abasement of reason before the transports[9] of supernatural religion disappeared from society as from philosophy.

Soon there was formed in Europe a class of men who were concerned less with the discovery or development of the truth than with its propagation, men who while devoting themselves to the tracking down of prejudices in the hiding places where the priests, the schools, the governments, and all long-established institutions had gathered and protected them, made it their life-work to destroy popular errors rather than to drive back the frontiers of human knowledge—an indirect way of aiding its progress which was not less fraught with peril, nor less useful.

In England Collins[10] and Bolingbroke,[11] in France Bayle,[12] Fontenelle,[13] Voltaire,[14] Montesquieu,[15] and the schools founded by these famous men, fought on the side of truth, using in turn all the weapons with which learning, philosophy, wit, and literary talent can furnish reason; using every mood from humor to pathos,[16] every literary form from the vast erudite encyclopaedia to the novel or the

9 Influences.

10 Anthony Collins (1676–1729), English deist and friend of the political theorist John Locke.

11 Henry St. John, Lord Bolingbroke (1678–1751), English politician and statesman. A friend of Alexander Pope.

12 Pierre Bayle (1647–1706), a French philosopher who was deeply influenced by Cartesianism.

13 Bernard Le Bovier de Fontenelle (1657–1757), French man of letters, philosopher, and scientist.

14 The pen name used by François Marie Arouet (1694–1778), French man of letters, historian, and philosopher.

15 Charles Louis de Secondat Montesquieu (1689–1755), French writer on politics and law.

16 Compassion.

broadsheet of the day; covering truth with a veil that spared weaker eyes and excited one to guess what lay beyond it; skillfully flattering prejudices so as to attack them the better; seldom threatening them, and then always either only one in its entirety or several partially; sometimes conciliating the enemies of reason by seeming to wish only for a half-tolerance in religious matters, only for a half-freedom in politics; sparing despotism when tilting against the absurdities of religion, and religion when abusing tyranny; yet always attacking the principles of these two scourges [17] even when they seemed to be against only their more revolting or ridiculous abuses, and laying their axes to the very roots of these sinister [18] trees when they appeared to be lopping off a few stray branches; sometimes teaching the friends of liberty that superstition is the invincible shield behind which despotism shelters and should therefore be the first victim to be sacrificed, the first chain to be broken, and sometimes denouncing it to the despots as the real enemy of their power, and frightening them with stories of its secret machinations and its bloody persecutions; never ceasing to demand the independence of reason and the freedom of the press as the right and the salvation of mankind; protesting with indefatigable energy against all the crimes of fanaticism and tyranny; pursuing, in all matters of religion, administration, morals, and law, anything that bore the marks of tyranny, harshness, or barbarism; invoking the name of nature to bid kings, captains, magistrates, and priests to show respect for human life; laying to their charge, with vehemence [19] and severity, the blood their policy or their indifference still spilled on the battlefield or on the scaffold; and finally, taking for their battle cry—*reason, tolerance, humanity*. . . .

The salutary influence of the new truths with which genius had enriched philosophy, politics, and public economy, and which had been adopted more or less generally by enlightened men, was felt far afield.

The art of printing had spread so widely and had so greatly increased the number of books published; the books that were published catered so successfully for every degree of knowledge, or industry, or income; they were so proportioned to every taste, or cast of mind; they presented such easy and often such pleasant means

---

[17] Agents of severe suffering and punishment.
[18] Wicked, evil.
[19] Great force.

of instruction; they opened so many doors to truth that it was no longer possible that they should all of them be closed again, that there was no class and no profession from which the truth could be withheld. And so, though there remained a great number of people condemned to ignorance either voluntary or enforced, the boundary between the cultivated and the uncultivated had been almost entirely effaced, leaving an insensible[20] gradation between the two extremes of genius and stupidity.

Thus, an understanding of the natural rights of man, the belief that these rights are inalienable and indefeasible,[21] a strongly expressed desire for liberty of thought and letters, of trade and industry, and for the alleviation of the people's suffering, for the proscription of all penal laws against religious dissenters and the abolition of torture and barbarous punishments, the desire for a milder system of criminal legislation and jurisprudence which should give complete security to the innocent, and for a simpler civil code, more in conformance with reason and nature, indifference in all matters of religion which now were relegated to the status of superstitions and political impostures, a hatred of hypocrisy and fanaticism, a contempt for prejudice, zeal for the propagation of enlightenment: all these principles, gradually filtering down from philosophical works to every class of society whose education went beyond the catechism and the alphabet, became the common faith, the badges of all those who were neither Machiavellians[22] nor fools. In some countries these principles formed a public opinion sufficiently widespread for even the mass of the people to show a willingness to be guided by it and to obey it. For a feeling of humanity, a tender and active compassion for all the misfortunes that afflict the human race and a horror of anything that in the actions of public institutions, or governments, or individuals, adds new pains to those that are natural and inevitable, were the natural consequences of those principles; and this feeling exhaled from all the writings and all the speeches of the time, and already its happy influence had been felt in the laws, and the public institutions, even of those nations still subject to despotism. . . .

Force or persuasion on the part of governments, priestly intoler-

[20] Unfelt, slight.
[21] Not to be undone.
[22] Persons whose conduct matches that suggested by Niccolò Machiavelli (1469–1527), the Florentine (Italian) writer on politics and history: crafty, double-dealing, deceitful.

ance, and even national prejudices, had all lost their deadly power to smother the voice of truth, and nothing could now protect the enemies of reason or the oppressors of freedom from a sentence to which the whole of Europe would soon subscribe. . . .

A comparison of the attitude of mind I have already described with the forms of government prevalent at that time would have made it easy to foresee that a great revolution was inevitable, and that there were only two ways in which it could come about; either the people themselves would establish the reasonable and natural principles that philosophy had taught them to admire, or governments would hasten to anticipate them and carry out what was required by public opinion. If the revolution should come about in the former way it would be swifter and more thorough, but more violent; if it should come about in the latter way, it would be less swift and less thorough, but also less violent: if in the former way, then freedom and happiness would be purchased at the price of transient evils; if in the latter, then these evils would be avoided but, it might be, at the price of long delaying the harvest of the fruits that the revolution must, nevertheless, inevitably bear. The ignorance and corruption of the governments of the time saw that it came about in the former way, and the human race was avenged by the swift triumph of liberty and reason. . . .

From the moment when the genius of Descartes [23] gave men's minds that general impetus [24] which is the first principle of a revolution in the destinies of the human race, to the happy time of complete and pure social liberty when man was able to regain his natural independence only after having lived through a long series of centuries of slavery and misery, the picture of the progress of the mathematical and physical sciences reveals an immense horizon whose different parts must be distributed and ordered if we wish to grasp the significance of the whole and properly observe its relations. . . .

If we were to confine ourselves to showing the benefits that we have derived from the sciences in their immediate uses or in their applications to the arts, either for the well-being of individuals or for the prosperity of nations, we should display only a very small portion of their blessings.

The most important of these, perhaps, is to have destroyed preju-

---

[23] René Descartes (1596–1650), a noted French philosopher and mathematician.
[24] Impulse.

dices and to have redirected the human intelligence, which had been obliged to follow the false directions imposed on it by the absurd beliefs that were implanted in each generation in infancy with the terrors of superstition and the fear of tyranny.

All errors in politics and morals are based on philosophical errors and these in turn are connected with scientific errors. There is not a religious system nor a supernatural extravagance that is not founded on ignorance of the laws of nature. The inventors, the defenders of these absurdities could not foresee the successive perfection of the human mind. Convinced that men in their day knew everything that they could ever know and would always believe what they then believed, they confidently supported their idle dreams on the current opinions of their country and their age.

Advances in the physical sciences are all the more fatal to these errors in that they often destroy them without appearing to attack them, and that they can shower on those who defend them so obstinately the humiliating taunt [25] of ignorance.

At the same time the habit of correct reasoning about the objects of these sciences, the precise ideas gained by their methods, and the means of recognizing or proving the truth of a belief should naturally lead us to compare the sentiment that forces us to accept well-founded opinions credible for good reasons, with that which ties us to habitual prejudices or forces us to submit to authority. Such a comparison is enough to teach us to mistrust opinions of the latter kind, to convince us that we do not really believe them even when we boast of believing them, even when we profess them with the purest sincerity. This secret, once discovered, makes their destruction immediate and certain. . . .

Up to this stage, the sciences had been the birthright of very few; they were now becoming common property and the time was at hand when their elements, their principles, and their simpler methods would become truly popular. For it was then, as last, that their application to the arts and their influence on men's judgment would become of truly universal utility. [26]

We shall follow the progress of European nations in the education both of children and of adults. This progress may appear to have been slow, if one considers only the philosophical foundations on

[25] Ridicule.
[26] Usefulness.

which education has been based, for it is still in the grip of scholastic[27] superstition: but it appears swift enough if one considers the nature and the extent of the subjects taught, for these are now confined almost completely to genuine inquires, and include the elements of nearly all the sciences; while dictionaries, abstracts, and periodicals provide men of all ages with the information they require—even if this does not always appear in an unadulterated[28] form. We shall examine the utility of combining oral instruction in the sciences with the immediate instruction to be acquired from books and private study, and we shall also examine whether any advantage has accrued from the development of compilation[29] into an accredited profession in whose practice a man may hope to earn a livelihood; a development that has augmented the number of indifferent[30] books in circulation, but has also increased the roads to knowledge open to men of little education. We shall give an account of the influence exercised by learned societies, for these will long remain a useful bulwark against charlatanry[31] and false scholarship. Finally we shall unfold the story of the encouragement given by certain governments to the progress of knowledge, and also of the obstacles that were laid in its path often enough by these same governments, at the same time, in the same country. We shall expose, on the one hand, the prejudices and Machiavellian principles that have directed these governments in their opposition to men's progress toward the truth, and on the other, the political opinions originating either from self-interest or even from a genuine concern for the public good, that have guided them when they have seemed interested in accelerating and protecting it. . . .

Thus all the intellectual activities of man, however different they may be in their aims, their methods, or the qualities of mind they exact, have combined to further the progress of human reason. Indeed, the whole system of human labor is like a well-made machine, whose several parts have been systematically distinguished but none the less, being intimately bound together, form a single whole, and work toward a single end.

Turning now our attention to the human race in general, we shall

[27] Reflecting the educational and philosophical methods of medieval church schools.
[28] Pure, genuine.
[29] The collection of information in various fields of knowledge; for example, in an encyclopedia.
[30] Mediocre.
[31] Fraud, deception.

show how the discovery of the correct method of procedure in the sciences, the growth of scientific theories, their application to every part of the natural world, to the subject of every human need, the lines of communication established between one science and another, the great number of men who cultivate the sciences, and most important of all, the spread of printing, how together all these advances ensure that no science will ever fall below the point it has reached. We shall point out that the principles of philosophy, the slogans of liberty, the recognition of the true rights of man and his real interests, have spread through far too great a number of nations, and now direct in each of them the opinions of far too great a number of enlightened men, for us to fear that they will ever be allowed to relapse into oblivion. And indeed what reason could we have for fear, when we consider that the languages most widely spoken are the languages of the two peoples who enjoy liberty to the fullest extent and who best understand its principles, and that no league of tyrants, no political intrigues, could prevent the resolute defense, in these two languages, of the rights of reason and of liberty?

But although everything tells us that the human race will never relapse into its former state of barbarism, although everything combines to reassure us against that corrupt and cowardly political theory which would condemn it to oscillate[32] forever between truth and error, liberty and servitude, nevertheless we still see the forces of enlightenment in possession of no more than a very small portion of the globe, and the truly enlightened vastly outnumbered by the great mass of men who are still given over to ignorance and prejudice. We still see vast areas in which men groan in slavery, vast areas offering the spectacle of nations either degraded by the vices of a civilization whose progress is impeded by corruption, or still vegetating in the infant condition of early times.

We observe that the labors of recent ages have done much for the progress of the human mind, but little for the perfection of the human race; that they have done much for the honor of man, something for his liberty, but so far almost nothing for his happiness. At a few points our eyes are dazzled with a brilliant light; but thick darkness still covers an immense stretch of the horizon. There are a few circumstances from which the philosopher can take consolation, but he is still afflicted by the spectacle of the stupidity, slavery, barba-

---

[32] To swing back and forth.

rism, and extravagance of mankind; and the friend of humanity can find unmixed pleasure only in tasting the sweet delights of hope for the future.

. . .

THE TENTH STAGE: THE FUTURE PROGRESS OF THE HUMAN MIND

If man can, with almost complete assurance, predict phenomena when he knows their laws, and if, even when he does not, he can still, with great expectation of success, forecast the future on the basis of his experience of the past, why, then, should it be regarded as a fantastic undertaking to sketch, with some pretense to truth, the future destiny of man on the basis of his history? The sole foundation for belief in the natural sciences is this idea, that the general laws directing the phenomena of the universe, known or unknown, are necessary and constant. Why should this principle be any less true for the development of the intellectual and moral faculties of man than for the other operations of nature? Since beliefs founded on past experience of like conditions provide the only rule of conduct for the wisest of men, why should the philosopher be forbidden to base his conjectures on these same foundations, so long as he does not attribute to them a certainty superior to that warranted by the number, the constancy, and the accuracy of his observations?

Our hopes for the future condition of the human race can be subsumed under three important heads: the abolition of inequality between nations, the progress of equality within each nation, and the true perfection of mankind. Will all nations one day attain that state of civilization which the most enlightened, the freest, and the least burdened by prejudices, such as the French and the Anglo-Americans, have attained already? Will the vast gulf that separates these peoples from the slavery of nations under the rule of monarchs, from the barbarism of African tribes, from the ignorance of savages, little by little disappear? . . .

Is the human race to better itself, either by discoveries in the sciences and the arts, and so in the means to individual welfare and general prosperity; or by progress in the principles of conduct or practical morality; or by a true perfection of the intellectual, moral, or physical faculties of man, an improvement which may result from a perfection either of the instruments used to heighten the intensity of these faculties and to direct their use or of the natural constitution of man?

In answering these three questions we shall find in the experience of the past, in the observation of the progress that the sciences and civilization have already made, in the analysis of the progress of the human mind and of the development of its faculties, the strongest reasons for believing that nature has set no limit to the realization of our hopes.

If we glance at the state of the world today we see first of all that in Europe the principles of the French constitution are already those of all enlightened men. We see them too widely propagated, too seriously professed, for priests and despots to prevent their gradual penetration even into the hovels of their slaves; there they will soon awaken in these slaves the remnants of their common sense and inspire them with that smoldering indignation which not even constant humiliation and fear can smother in the soul of the oppressed.

As we move from nation to nation, we can see in each what special obstacles impede this revolution and what attitudes of mind favor it. We can distinguish the nations where we may expect it to be introduced gently by the perhaps belated wisdom of their governments, and those nations where its violence intensified by their resistance must involve all alike in a swift and terrible convulsion.

Can we doubt that either common sense or the senseless discords of European nations will add to the effects of the slow but inexorable progress of their colonies, and will soon bring about the independence of the New World? And then will not the European population in these colonies, spreading rapidly over that enormous land, either civilize or peacefully remove the savage nations who still inhabit vast tracts of its land?

Survey the history of our settlements and commercial undertakings in Africa or in Asia, and you will see how our trade monopolies, our treachery, our murderous contempt for men of another color or creed, the insolence of our usurpations,[33] the intrigues or the exaggerated proselytic[34] zeal of our priests, have destroyed the respect and good-will that the superiority of our knowledge and the benefits of our commerce at first won for us in the eyes of the inhabitants. But doubtless the moment approaches when, no longer pre-

[33] Unlawful seizures of rights and power.
[34] Missionary.

senting ourselves as always either tyrants or corrupters, we shall become for them the beneficent instruments of their freedom. . . .

These vast lands are inhabited partly by large tribes who need only assistance from us to become civilized, who wait only to find brothers among the European nations to become their friends and pupils; partly by races oppressed by sacred despots or dull-witted conquerors, and who for so many centuries have cried out to be liberated; partly by tribes living in a condition of almost total savagery in a climate whose harshness repels the sweet blessings of civilization and deters those who would teach them its benefits; and finally, by conquering hordes who know no other law but force, no other profession but piracy. The progress of these two last classes of people will be slower and stormier, and perhaps it will even be that, reduced in number as they are driven back by civilized nations, they will finally disappear imperceptibly before them or merge into them. . . .

The time will therefore come when the sun will shine only on free men who know no other master but their reason; when tyrants and slaves, priests and their stupid or hypocritical instruments will exist only in works of history and on the stage; and when we shall think of them only to pity their victims and their dupes; to maintain ourselves in a state of vigilance by thinking on their excesses; and to learn how to recognize and so to destroy, by force of reason, the first seeds of tyranny and superstition, should they ever dare to reappear among us.

In looking at the history of societies we shall have had occasion to observe that there is often a great difference between the rights that the law allows its citizens and the rights that they actually enjoy, and, again, between the equality established by political codes and that which in fact exists among individuals: and we shall have noticed that these differences were one of the principal causes of the destruction of freedom in the ancient republics, of the storms that troubled them, and of the weakness that delivered them over to foreign tyrants.

These differences have three main causes: inequality in wealth; inequality in status between the man whose means of subsistence are hereditary and the man whose means are dependent on the length of his life, or, rather, on that part of his life in which he is capable of work; and, finally, inequality in education.

We therefore need to show that these three sorts of real inequality must constantly diminish without however disappearing altogether:

for they are the result of natural and necessary causes which it would be foolish and dangerous to wish to eradicate; and one could not even attempt to bring about the entire disappearance of their effects without introducing even more fecund[35] sources of inequality, without striking more direct and more fatal blows at the rights of man.

It is easy to prove that wealth has a natural tendency to equality, and that any excessive disproportion could not exist or at least would rapidly disappear if civil laws did not provide artificial ways of perpetuating and uniting fortunes; if free trade and industry were allowed to remove the advantages that accrued wealth derives from any restrictive law or fiscal privilege; if taxes on covenants,[36] the restrictions placed on their free employment, their subjection to tiresome formalities, and the uncertainty and inevitable expense involved in implementing them did not hamper the activity of the poor man and swallow up his meager capital; if the administration of the country did not afford some men ways of making their fortune that were closed to other citizens; if prejudice and avarice, so common in old age, did not preside over the making of marriages; and if, in a society enjoying simpler manners and more sensible institutions, wealth ceased to be a means of satisfying vanity and ambition, and if the equally misguided notions of austerity,[37] which condemn spending money in the cultivation of the more delicate pleasures, no longer insisted on the hoarding of all one's earnings. . . .

We shall point out how [inequality] can be in great part eradicated by guaranteeing people in old age a means of livelihood produced partly by their own savings and partly by the savings of others who make the same outlay, but who die before they need to reap the reward; or, again, on the same principle of compensation, by securing for widows and orphans an income which is the same and costs the same for those families which suffer an early loss and for those which suffer it later; or again by providing all children with the capital necessary for the full use of their labor, available at the age when they start work and found a family, a capital which increases at the expense of those whom premature death prevents from reaching this age. It is to the application of the calculus to the probabilities of life and the investment of money that we owe the idea of these methods which have already been successful, although they have not been

---

[35] Prolific, fertile.
[36] Agreements.
[37] Self-denial; stinginess.

applied in a sufficiently comprehensive and exhaustive fashion to render them really useful, not merely to a few individuals, but to society as a whole, by making it possible to prevent those periodic disasters which strike at so many families and which are such a recurrent source of misery and suffering.

We shall point out that schemes of this nature, which can be organized in the name of the social authority and become one of its greatest benefits, can also be the work of private associations, which will be formed without any real risk, once the principles for the proper working of these schemes have been widely diffused and the mistakes which have been the undoing of a large number of these associations no longer hold terrors for us. . . .

The degree of equality in education that we can reasonably hope to attain, but that should be adequate, is that which excludes all dependence, either forced or voluntary. We shall show how this condition can be easily attained in the present state of human knowledge even by those who can study only for a small number of years in childhood, and then during the rest of their life in their few hours of leisure. We shall prove that, by a suitable choice of syllabus and of methods of education, we can teach the citizen everything that he needs to know in order to be able to manage his household, administer his affairs, and employ his labor and his faculties in freedom; to know his rights and to be able to exercise them; to be acquainted with his duties and fulfill them satisfactorily; to judge his own and other men's actions according to his own lights and to be a stranger to none of the high and delicate feelings which honor human nature; not to be in a state of blind dependence upon those to whom he must entrust his affairs or the exercise of his rights; to be in a proper condition to choose and supervise them; to be no longer the dupe of those popular errors which torment man with superstititious fears and chimerical[38] hopes; to defend himself against prejudice by the strength of his reason alone; and, finally, to escape the deceits of charlatans who would lay snares for his fortune, his health, his freedom of thought, and his conscience under the pretext of granting him health, wealth, and salvation.

From such time onwards the inhabitants of a single country will no longer be distinguished by their use of a crude or refined lan-

---

[38] Imaginary, fantastic.

guage; they will be able to govern themselves according to their own knowledge; they will no longer be limited to a mechanical knowledge of the procedures of the arts or of professional routine; they will no longer depend for every trivial piece of business, every insignificant matter of instruction on clever men who rule over them in virtue of their necessary superiority; and so they will attain a real equality, since differences in enlightenment or talent can no longer raise a barrier between men who understand each other's feelings, ideas, and language, some of whom may wish to be taught by others but, to do so, will have no need to be controlled by them, or who may wish to confide the care of government to the ablest of their number but will not be compelled to yield them absolute power in a spirit of blind confidence.

This kind of supervision has advantages even for those who do not exercise it, since it is employed for them and not against them. Natural differences of ability between men whose understanding has not been cultivated give rise, even in savage tribes, to charlatans and dupes, to clever men and men readily deceived. These same differences are truly universal, but now they are differences only between men of learning and upright men who know the value of learning without being dazzled by it; or between talent or genius and the common sense which can appreciate and benefit from them; so that even if these natural differences were greater, and more extensive than they are, they would be only the more influential in improving the relations between men and promoting what is advantageous for their independence and happiness.

These various causes of equality do not act in isolation; they unite, combine, and support each other and so their cumulative effects are stronger, surer, and more constant. With greater equality of education there will be greater equality in industry and so in wealth; equality in wealth necessarily leads to equality in education: and equality between the nations and equality within a single nation are mutually dependent.

So we might say that a well-directed system of education rectifies natural inequality in ability instead of strengthening it, just as good laws remedy natural inequality in the means of subsistence, and just as in societies where laws have brought about this same equality, liberty, though subject to a regular constitution, will be more widespread, more complete than in the total independence of savage life.

Then the social art will have fulfilled its aim, that of assuring and extending to all men enjoyment of the common rights to which they are called by nature.

The real advantages that should result from this progress, of which we can entertain a hope that is almost a certainty, can have no other term than that of the absolute perfection of the human race; since, as the various kinds of equality come to work in its favor by producing ampler sources of supply, more extensive education, more complete liberty, so equality will be more real and will embrace everything which is really of importance for the happiness of human beings.

It is therefore only by examining the progress and the laws of this perfection that we shall be able to understand the extent or the limits of our hopes. . . .

If we turn now to the arts,[39] whose theory depends on these same sciences, we shall find that their progress, depending as it does on that of theory, can have no other limits; that the procedures of the different arts can be perfected and simplified in the same way as the methods of the sciences; new instruments, machines, and looms can add to man's strength and can improve at once the quality and the accuracy of his productions, and can diminish the time and labor that has to be expended on them. The obstacles still in the way of this progress will disappear, accidents will be foreseen and prevented, the insanitary conditions that are due either to the work itself or to the climate will be eliminated.

A very small amount of ground will be able to produce a great quantity of supplies of greater utility or higher quality; more goods will be obtained for a smaller outlay; the manufacture of articles will be achieved with less wastage in raw materials and will make better use of them. Every type of soil will produce those things which satisfy the greatest number of needs; of several alternative ways of satisfying needs of the same order, that will be chosen which satisfies the greatest number of people and which requires least labor and least expenditure. So, without the need for sacrifice, methods of preservation and economy in expenditure will improve in the wake of progress in the arts of producing and preparing supplies and making articles from them.

So not only will the same amount of ground support more people,

[39] Crafts; production.

but everyone will have less work to do, will produce more and satisfy his wants more fully.

With all this progress in industry and welfare which establishes a happier proportion between men's talents and their needs, each successive generation will have larger possessions, either as a result of this progress or through the preservation of the products of industry; and so, as a consequence of the physical constitution of the human race, the number of people will increase. Might there not then come a moment when these necessary laws begin to work in a contrary direction; when, the number of people in the world finally exceeding the means of subsistence, there will in consequence ensue a continual diminution of happiness and population, a true retrogression, or at best an oscillation between good and bad? In societies that have reached this stage will not this oscillation be a perennial source of more or less periodic disaster? Will it not show that a point has been attained beyond which all further improvement is impossible, that the perfectibility of the human race has after long years arrived at a term beyond which it may never go?

There is doubtless no one who does not think that such a time is still very far from us; but will it ever arrive? It is impossible to pronounce about the likelihood of an event that will occur only when the human species will have necessarily acquired a degree of knowledge of which we can have no inkling. And who would take it upon himself to predict the condition to which the art of converting the elements to the use of man may in time be brought?

But even if we agree that the limit will one day arrive, nothing follows from it that is in the least alarming as far as either the happiness of the human race or its indefinite [40] perfectibility is concerned; if we consider that, before all this comes to pass, the progress of reason will have kept pace with that of the sciences, and that the absurd prejudices of superstition will have ceased to corrupt and degrade the moral code by its harsh doctrines instead of purifying and elevating it, we can assume that by then men will know that, if they have a duty toward those who are not yet born, that duty is not to give them existence but to give them happiness; their aim should be to promote the general welfare of the human race or of the society in which they live or of the family to which they belong, rather than

---

[40] Unlimited.

foolishly to encumber[41] the world with useless and wretched beings. It is, then, possible that there should be a limit to the amount of food that can be produced, and, consequently, to the size of the population of the world, without this involving that untimely destruction of some of those creatures who have been given life, which is so contrary to nature and to social prosperity.

Since the discovery, or rather the exact analysis, of the first principles of metaphysics,[42] morals, and politics is still recent and was preceded by the knowledge of a large number of detailed truths, the false notion that they have thereby attained their destination, has gained ready acceptance; men imagine that, because there are no more crude errors to refute, no more fundamental truths to establish, nothing remains to be done.

But it is easy to see how imperfect is the present analysis of man's moral and intellectual faculties; how much further the knowledge of his duties which presumes a knowledge of the influence of his actions upon the welfare of his fellow men and upon the society to which he belongs, can still be increased through a more profound, more accurate, more considered observation of that influence; how many questions have to be solved, how many social relations to be examined, before we can have precise knowledge of the individual rights of man and the rights that the state confers upon each in regard to all. Have we yet ascertained at all accurately the limits of the rights that exist between different societies in times of war, or that are enjoyed by society over its members in times of trouble and schism,[43] or that belong to individuals, or spontaneous associations at the moment of their original, free formation or of their necessary disintegration?

If we pass on to the theory which ought to direct the application of particular principles and serve as the foundation for the social art, do we not see the necessity of acquiring a precision that these elementary truths cannot possess so long as they are absolutely general? Have we yet reached the point when we can reckon as the only foundation of law either justice or a proved and acknowledged utility instead of the vague, uncertain, arbitrary views of alleged political expediency? Are we yet in possession of any precise rules for selecting out of the almost infinite variety of possible systems in which the general principles of equality and natural rights are respected, those

---

[41] Place a burden upon.
[42] Usually defined as the study of existence and fundamental causes.
[43] Division, split.

which will best secure the preservation of these rights, which will afford the freest scope for their exercise and their enjoyment, and which will moreover insure the leisure and welfare of individuals and the strength, prosperity, and peace of nations?

The application of the calculus of combinations and probabilities to these sciences promises even greater improvement, since it is the only way of achieving results of an almost mathematical exactitude and of assessing the degree of their probability or likelihood. Sometimes, it is true, the evidence upon which these results are based may lead us, without any calculation, at the first glance, to some general truth and teach us whether the effect produced by such-and-such a cause was or was not favorable, but if this evidence cannot be weighed and measured, and if these effects cannot be subjected to precise measurement, then we cannot know exactly how much good or evil they contain; or, again, if the good and evil nearly balance each other, if the difference between them is slight, we cannot pronounce with any certainty to which side the balance really inclines. Without the application of the calculus it would be almost impossible to choose with any certainty between two combinations that have the same purpose and between which there is no apparent difference in merit. Without the calculus these sciences would always remain crude and limited for want of instruments delicate enough to catch the fleeting truth, of machines precise enough to plumb the depths where so much that is of value to science lies hidden.

However, such an application, notwithstanding the happy efforts of certain geometers, is still in its earliest stages: and it will be left to the generations to come to use this source of knowledge which is as inexhaustible as the calculus itself, or as the number of combinations, relations, and facts that may be included in its sphere of operation.

There is another kind of progress within the sciences that is no less important; and that is the perfection of scientific language which is at present so vague and obscure.[44] This improvement could be responsible for making the sciences genuinely popular, even in their first rudiments. . . .[45]

Until men progress in the practice as well as in the science of morality, it will be impossible for them to attain any insight into either the nature and development of the moral sentiments, the principles of morality, the natural motives that prompt their actions, or their

[44] Clouded, difficult to understand.
[45] Simple beginnings.

own true interests either as individuals or as members of society. Is not a mistaken sense of interest the most common cause of actions contrary to the general welfare? Is not the violence of our passions often the result either of habits that we have adopted through miscalculation, or of our ignorance how to restrain them, tame them, deflect them, rule them?

Is not the habit of reflection upon conduct, of listening to the deliverances of reason and conscience upon it, of exercising those gentle feelings which identify our happiness with that of others, the necessary consequence of a well-planned study of morality and of a greater equality in the conditions of the social pact? Will not the free man's sense of his own dignity and a system of education built upon a deeper knowledge of our moral constitution, render common to almost every man those principles of strict and unsullied[46] justice, those habits of an active and enlightened benevolence, of a fine and generous sensibility which nature has implanted in the hearts of all and whose flowering waits only upon the favorable influences of enlightenment and freedom? Just as the mathematical and physical sciences tend to improve the arts that we use to satisfy our simplest needs, is it not also part of the necessary order of nature that the moral and political sciences should exercise a similar influence upon the motives that direct our feelings and our actions?

What are we to expect from the perfection of laws and public institutions, consequent upon the progress of those sciences, but the reconciliation, the identification of the interests of each with the interests of all? Has the social art any other aim save that of destroying their apparent opposition? Will not a country's constitution and laws accord best with the rights of reason and nature when the path of virtue is no longer arduous[47] and when the temptations that lead men from it are few and feeble?

Is there any vicious habit, any practice contrary to good faith, any crime, whose origin and first cause cannot be traced back to the legislation, the institutions, the prejudices of the country wherein this habit, this practice, this crime can be observed? In short will not the general welfare that results from the progress of the useful arts once they are grounded on solid theory, or from the progress of legislation once it is rooted in the truths of political science, incline mankind to humanity, benevolence, and justice? In other words, do not

[46] Unsoiled, uncorrupted.
[47] Difficult.

all these observations which I propose to develop further in my book, show that the moral goodness of man, the necessary consequence of his constitution, is capable of indefinite perfection like all his other faculties, and that nature has linked together in an unbreakable chain truth, happiness, and virtue?

Among the causes of the progress of the human mind that are of the utmost importance to the general happiness, we must number the complete annihilation of the prejudices that have brought about an inequality of rights between the sexes, an inequality fatal even to the party in whose favor it works. It is vain for us to look for a justification of this principle in any differences of physical organization, intellect, or moral sensibility between men and women. This inequality has its origin solely in an abuse of strength, and all the later sophistical attempts that have been made to excuse it are vain.

We shall show how the abolition of customs authorized, laws dictated by this prejudice, would add to the happiness of family life, would encourage the practice of the domestic virtues on which all other virtues are based, how it would favor the progress of education, and how, above all, it would bring about its wider diffusion; for not only would education be extended to women as well as to men, but it can only really be taken proper advantage of when it has the support and encouragement of the mothers of the family. Would not this belated tribute to equity and good sense put an end to a principle only too fecund of injustice, cruelty, and crime, by removing the dangerous conflict between the strongest and most irrepressible of all natural inclinations and man's duty or the interests of society? Would it not produce what has until now been no more than a dream, national manners of a mildness and purity, formed not by proud asceticism,[48] not by hypocrisy, not by the fear of shame or religious terrors but by freely contracted habits that are inspired by nature and acknowledged by reason?

Once people are enlightened they will know that they have the right to dispose of their own life and wealth as they choose; they will gradually learn to regard war as the most dreadful of scourges, the most terrible of crimes. The first wars to disappear will be those into which usurpers have forced their subjects in defense of their pretended hereditary rights.

Nations will learn that they cannot conquer other nations without

---

[48] Self-denial, self-discipline.

losing their own liberty; that permanent confederations are their only means of preserving their independence; and that they should seek not power but security. Gradually mercantile[49] prejudices will fade away: and a false sense of commercial interest will lose the fearful power it once had of drenching the earth in blood and of ruining nations under pretext of enriching them. When at last the nations come to agree on the principles of politics and morality, when in their own better interests they invite foreigners to share equally in all the benefits men enjoy either through the bounty of nature or by their own industry, then all the causes that produce and perpetuate national animosities and poison national relations will disappear one by one; and nothing will remain to encourage or even to arouse the fury of war.

Organizations more intelligently conceived than those projects of eternal peace which have filled the leisure and consoled the hearts of certain philosophers, will hasten the progress of the brotherhood of nations, and wars between countries will rank with assassinations as freakish atrocities, humiliating and vile in the eyes of nature and staining with indelible opprobrium[50] the country or the age whose annals[51] record them. . . .

All the causes that contribute to the perfection of the human race, all the means that ensure it, must by their very nature exercise a perpetual influence and always increase their sphere of action. The proofs of this we have given and in the great work they will derive additional force from elaboration. We may conclude then that the perfectibility of man is indefinite. Meanwhile we have considered him as possessing the natural faculties and organization that he has at present. How much greater would be the certainty, how much vaster the scheme of our hopes if we could believe that these natural faculties themselves and this organization could also be improved? This is the last question that remains for us to ask ourselves.

Organic perfectibility or deterioration among the various strains in the vegetable and animal kingdom can be regarded as one of the general laws of nature. This law also applies to the human race. No one can doubt that, as preventive medicine improves and food and housing become healthier, as a way of life is established that develops our physical powers by exercise without ruining them by excess, as the

---

[49] Commercial.
[50] Disgrace, shame.
[51] Histories.

two most virulent causes of deterioration, misery and excessive wealth, are eliminated, the average length of human life will be increased and a better health and a stronger physical constitution will be ensured. The improvement of medical practice, which will become more efficacious with the progress of reason and of the social order, will mean the end of infectious and heredity diseases and illnesses brought on by climate, food, or working conditions. It is reasonable to hope that all other diseases may likewise disappear as their distant causes are discovered. Would it be absurd then to suppose that this perfection of the human species might be capable of indefinite progress; that the day will come when death will be due only to extraordinary accidents or to the decay of the vital forces, and that ultimately the average span between birth and decay will have no assignable value? Certainly man will not become immortal, but will not the interval between the first breath that he draws and the time when in the natural course of events, without disease or accident, he expires, increase indefinitely? . . .

Finally may we not extend such hopes to the intellectual and moral faculties? May not our parents, who transmit to us the benefits or disadvantages of their constitution, and from whom we receive our shape and features, as well as our tendencies to certain physical affections, hand on to us also that part of the physical organization which determines the intellect, the power of the brain, the ardor [52] of the soul or the moral sensibility? Is it not probable that education, in perfecting these qualities, will at the same time influence, modify, and perfect the organization itself? Analogy, investigation of the human faculties, and the study of certain facts, all seem to give substance to such conjectures [53] which would further push back the boundaries of our hopes.

These are the questions with which we shall conclude this final stage. How consoling for the philosopher who laments the errors, the crimes, the injustices which still pollute the earth and of which he is often the victim is this view of the human race, emancipated from its shackles, released from the empire of fate and from that of the enemies of its progress, advancing with a firm and sure step along the path of truth, virtue, and happiness! It is the contemplation of this prospect that rewards him for all his efforts to assist the progress of reason and the defense of liberty. He dares to regard these striv-

---

[52] Warmth, passion.
[53] Suggestions, inferences.

ings as part of the eternal chain of human destiny; and in this persuasion he is filled with the true delight of virtue and the pleasure of
having done some lasting good which fate can never destroy by a
sinister stroke of revenge, by calling back the reign of slavery and
prejudice. Such contemplation is for him an asylum, in which the
memory of his persecutors cannot pursue him; there he lives in
thought with man restored to his natural rights and dignity, forgets
man tormented and corrupted by greed, fear, or envy; there he lives
with his peers [54] in an Elysium [55] created by reason and graced by the
purest pleasures known to the love of mankind.

[54] Equals, comrades.
[55] In Greek mythology, the region where the souls of good people enjoyed happiness.

13

Edmund Burke

Reflections on the Revolution in France

The liberal and democratic principles of the Enlightenment found explosive realization in the French Revolution, which in turn provoked a strong reaction against them. The most famous and most influential of these intellectual counterattacks was Edmund Burke's Reflections on the Revolution in France *(1790). Burke (1729–1797) was a British politician and publicist who served in the House of Commons for many years and emerged as the spokesman of the landed aristocracy. In his view, the fixed social and political order of late eighteenth-century England, based on class distinctions, upper-class rule, and parliamentary supremacy, was an excellent one, worthy of perpetuation. Burke saw the French Revolution, even as it got under way, as an attack on the whole social fabric. In the* Reflections, *written in the form of a letter to a resident of Paris, he warned that the Revolution's radical policies would lead ultimately to anarchy and military dictatorship. The essay was not merely a political pamphlet, however. It was a powerful, though unsystematic, critique of the rationalist theories of the Enlightenment and a statement of the basic principles of conservatism. Compounded of poetry, philosophy, religious mysticism, and socio-political analysis,* Reflections *elaborated a theory of society as a complex organism evolving slowly in the fixed channels of historical tradition. Burke rejected what he considered the abstract vagaries of individual reason as the guide to social progress. He thought that human beings, individually and in the mass, were*

Edmund Burke, *Reflections on the Revolution in France*, in *The Works of Edmund Burke* (Boston: Little, Brown, 1881), III, 274–76, 295–99, 308–13, 344–48, 350–52, 358–59, 454–57, 559–60. Adapted.

not basically rational, but weak creatures of irrational impulse who needed to be restrained by organized society. Property, religion, custom, and "prejudices" (or social myths) were the social controls necessary to preserve tolerable order. Burke, in short, was opposed to the rational optimism and the individualism of the Enlightenment. In time, his work became the bible of conservatism, an arsenal of arguments against social and democratic reform.

You will observe that from Magna Charta[1] to the Declaration of Right[2] it has been the uniform policy of our constitution to claim and assert our liberties as an entailed inheritance derived to us from our forefathers, and to be transmitted to our posterity—as an estate specially belonging to the people of this kingdom, without any reference whatever to any other more general or prior right. By this means our constitution preserves a unity in so great a diversity of its parts. We have an inheritable crown, an inheritable peerage,[3] and a House of Commons[4] and a people inheriting privileges, franchises, and liberties from a long line of ancestors.

This policy appears to me to be the result of profound reflection, or rather the happy effect of following nature, which is wisdom without reflection, and above it. A spirit of innovation is generally the result of a selfish temper and confined views. People will not look forward to posterity, who never look backward to their ancestors. Besides, the people of England well know that the idea of inheritance furnishes a sure principle of conservation and a sure principle of transmission, without at all excluding a principle of improvement. It leaves acquisition free, but it secures what it acquires. Whatever advantages are obtained by a state proceeding on these maxims[5] are locked fast as in a sort of family settlement, grasped as

[1] In 1215, English feudal barons forced King John to accept the Magna Charta (Great Charter). The chief significance of this document lies in the fact that the king, too, is held subject to the law and therefore required to respect it.
[2] A document passed by Parliament in 1689, guaranteeing important political and civil rights to that body and to the English people.
[3] Nobility.
[4] The lower house of Parliament. It excludes the nobility and has become the principal lawmaking body of the United Kingdom.
[5] Rules, principles.

in a kind of mortmain[6] forever. By a constitutional policy, working
after the pattern of nature, we receive, we hold, we transmit our
government and our privileges in the same manner in which we
enjoy and transmit our property and our lives. The institutions of
policy, the goods of fortune, the gifts of providence are handed
down to us, and from us, in the same course and order. Our political
system is placed in a just correspondence and symmetry with the
order of the world and with the mode of existence decreed to a permanent body composed of transitory parts, wherein, by the disposition of a stupendous wisdom, moulding together the great
mysterious incorporation of the human race, the whole, at one time,
is never old or middle-aged or young, but, in a condition of
unchangeable constancy, moves on through the varied tenor of perpetual decay, fall, renovation, and progression. Thus, by preserving
the method of nature in the conduct of the state, in what we improve
we are never wholly new; in what we retain we are never wholly
obsolete. By adhering in this manner and on those principles to our
forefathers, we are guided not by the superstition of antiquarians,
but by the spirit of philosophic analogy. In this choice of inheritance
we have given to our frame of polity the image of a relation in
blood, binding up the constitution of our country with our dearest
domestic ties, adopting our fundamental laws into the bosom of our
family affections, keeping inseparable and cherishing with the
warmth of all their combined and mutually reflected charities our
state, our hearths, our sepulchres, and our altars.

Through the same plan of a conformity to nature in our artificial
institutions, and by calling in the aid of her unerring and powerful
instincts to fortify the fallible and feeble contrivances of our reason,
we have derived several other, and those no small, benefits from
considering our liberties in the light of an inheritance. Always acting
as if in the presence of canonized[7] forefathers, the spirit of freedom,
leading in itself to misrule and excess, is tempered with an awful
gravity. This idea of a liberal descent inspires us with a sense of habitual native dignity which prevents that upstart insolence almost
inevitably adhering to and disgracing those who are the first ac-
quirers of any distinction. By this means our liberty becomes a noble

[6]Perpetual right to a property—a right that cannot be broken or transferred (literally,
a dead hand).
[7]Revered.

freedom. It carries an imposing and majestic aspect. It has a pedigree
and illustrious ancestors. It has its bearings and its ensigns armorial.[8]
It has its gallery of portraits, its monumental inscriptions, its records,
evidences, and titles. We procure reverence to our civil institutions
on the principle upon which nature teaches us to revere individual
men: on account of their age, and on account of those from whom
they are descended. All your sophisters[9] cannot produce anything
better adapted to preserve a rational and manly freedom than the
course that we have pursued, who have chosen our nature rather
than our speculations, our breasts rather than our inventions, for the
great conservatories and magazines[10] of our rights and privileges.

• • •

Believe me, Sir, those who attempt to level, never equalize. In all
societies, consisting of various descriptions of citizens, some description must be uppermost. The levellers, therefore, only change and
pervert the natural order of things; they load the edifice of society by
setting up in the air what the solidity of the structure requires to be
on the ground. The associations of tailors and carpenters, of which
the republic (of Paris, for instance) is composed, cannot be equal to
the situation into which by the worst of usurpations—and usurpation
on the prerogatives of nature—you attempt to force them.

The Chancellor of France,[11] at the opening of the States,[12] said, in
a tone of oratorical flourish, that all occupations were honorable. If
he meant only that no honest employment was disgraceful, he would
not have gone beyond the truth. But in asserting that anything is
honorable, we imply some distinction in its favor. The occupation of
a hairdresser or of a working candlemaker cannot be a matter of
honor to any person—to say nothing of a number of other more servile employments. Such descriptions of men ought not to suffer
oppression from the state; but the state suffers oppression if such as
they, either individually or collectively, are permitted to rule. In this
you think you are combating prejudice, but you are at war with nature.

[8] Symbolic designs (coats of arms) identifying family ancestors.
[9] Learned persons.
[10] Storehouses.
[11] A high official of the king's administration.
[12] Estates-General. This was the representative nationwide assembly of the three estates (social classes)—the clergy, the nobility, and the "Third Estate" (commoners:
bourgeoisie and peasants)—in the centuries preceding the French Revolution of 1789.

I do not, my dear Sir, conceive you to be of that sophistical, captious spirit, or of that uncandid dulness, as to require, for every general observation or sentiment, an explicit detail of the correctives and exceptions which reason will presume to be included in all the general propositions which come from reasonable men. You do not imagine that I wish to confine power, authority, and distinction to blood and names and titles. No, Sir. There is no qualification for government but virtue and wisdom, actual or presumptive. Wherever they are actually found, they have, in whatever state, condition, profession, or trade, the passport of Heaven to human place and honor. Woe to the country which would madly and impiously reject the service of the talents and virtues, civil, military, or religious, that are given to grace and to serve it; and would condemn to obscurity everything formed to diffuse lustre and glory around a state! Woe to that country, too, that, passing into the opposite extreme, considers a low education, a mean contracted view of things, a sordid, mercenary occupation, as a preferable title to command! Everything ought to be open, but not indifferently,[13] to every man. No rotation; no appointment by lot; no mode of election operating in the spirit of sortition[14] or rotation can be generally good in a government conversant in extensive objects. Because they have no tendency, direct or indirect, to select the man with a view to the duty, or to accommodate the one to the other. I do not hesitate to say that the road to eminence and power, from obscure condition, ought not to be made too easy, nor a thing too much of course. If rare merit be the rarest of all rare things, it ought to pass through some sort of probation. The temple of honor ought to be seated on an eminence.[15] If it be opened through virtue, let it be remembered, too, that virtue is never tried but by some difficulty and some struggle.

Nothing is a due and adequate representation of a state that does not represent its ability as well as its property. But as ability is a vigorous and active principle, and as property is sluggish, inert, and timid, it never can be safe from the invasion of ability, unless it be, out of all proportion, predominant in the representation. It must be represented, too, in great masses of accumulation, or it is not rightly protected. The characteristic essence of property, formed out of the combined principles of its acquisition and conservation, is to be *un-*

[13] Indiscriminately.
[14] Determination by lot.
[15] High or lofty ground.

equal. The great masses, therefore, which excite envy and tempt rapacity must be put out of the possibility of danger. Then they form a natural rampart about the lesser properties in all their gradations. The same quantity of property, which is by the natural course of things divided among many, has not the same operation. Its defensive power is weakened as it is diffused. In this diffusion each man's portion is less than what, in the eagerness of his desires, he may flatter himself to obtain by dissipating the accumulations of others. The plunder of the few would indeed give but a share inconceivably small in the distribution to the many. But the many are not capable of making this calculation; and those who lead them to rapine never intend this distribution.

The power of perpetuating our property in our families is one of the most valuable and interesting circumstances belonging to it, and that which tends the most to the perpetuation of society itself. It makes our weakness subservient to our virtue, it grafts benevolence even upon avarice. The possessors of family wealth, and of the distinction which attends hereditary possession (as most concerned in it), are the natural securities for this transmission. With us the House of Peers [16] is formed upon this principle. It is wholly composed of hereditary property and hereditary distinction, and made, therefore, the third of the legislature [17] and, in the last event, the sole judge of all property in all its subdivisions. The House of Commons, too, though not necessarily, yet in fact, is always so composed, in the far greater part. Let those large proprietors be what they will—and they have their chance of being among the best—they are, at the very worst, the ballast in the vessel of the commonwealth. For though hereditary wealth and the rank which goes with it are too much idolized by creeping sycophants and the blind, abject admirers of power, they are too rashly slighted in shallow speculations of the petulant, assuming, shortsighted coxcombs of philosophy. Some decent, regulated preëminence, some preference (not exclusive appropriation) given to birth is neither unnatural, nor unjust, nor impolitic.

It is said that twenty-four millions ought to prevail over two hundred thousand. True; if the constitution of a kingdom be a prob-

---

[16] The House of Peers, or House of Lords, is the upper house of Parliament. Membership in this assembly is restricted to the hereditary nobles.
[17] The first and second parts of the legislature (lawmaking procedure) are the king and the House of Commons.

lem of arithmetic. This sort of discourse does well enough with the lamppost for its second; to men who *may* reason calmly, it is ridiculous. The will of the many, and their interest must very often differ, and great will be the difference when they make an evil choice. A government of five hundred country attorneys and obscure curates is not good for twenty-four millions of men, though it were chosen by forty-eight millions, nor is it the better for being guided by a dozen of persons of quality who have betrayed their trust in order to obtain that power.[18] At present, you seem in everything to have strayed out of the high road of nature.

• • •

Far am I from denying in theory, full as far is my heart from withholding in practice (if I were of power to give or to withhold) the *real* rights of men. In denying their false claims of right, I do not mean to injure those which are real, and are such as their pretended rights would totally destroy. If civil society be made for the advantage of man, all the advantages for which it is made become his right. It is an institution of beneficence; and law itself is only beneficence acting by a rule. Men have a right to live by that rule; they have a right to do justice, as between their fellows, whether their fellows are in public function or in ordinary occupation. They have a right to the fruits of their industry and to the means of making their industry fruitful. They have a right to the acquisitions of their parents, to the nourishment and improvement of their offspring, to instruction in life and to consolation in death. Whatever each man can separately do, without trespassing upon others, he has a right to do for himself; and he has a right to a fair portion of all which society, with all its combinations of skill and force, can do in his favor. In this partnership all men have equal rights, but not to equal things. He that has but five shillings in the partnership has as good a right to it as he that has five hundred pounds has to his larger proportion. But he has not a right to an equal dividend in the product of the joint stock; and as to the share of power, authority, and direction which each individual ought to have in the management of the state, that I must deny to be among the direct original rights of man in civil society, for I have in my contemplation the civil social man, and no other. It is a thing to be settled by convention.

[18] Burke is lashing out at the small number of French noblemen who joined the cause of the Third Estate.

If civil society be the offspring of convention, that convention must be its law. That convention must limit and modify all the descriptions of constitution which are formed under it. Every sort of legislative, judicial, or executory power are its creatures. They can have no being in any other state of things; and how can any man claim, under the conventions of civil society, rights which do not so much as suppose its existence—rights which are absolutely repugnant to it? One of the first motives to civil society, and which becomes one of its fundamental rules, is, *that no man should be judge in his own cause.* By this each person has at once divested himself of the first fundamental right of uncovenanted man, that is, to judge for himself and to assert his own cause. He abdicates all right to be his own governor. He inclusively, in a great measure, abandons the right of self-defense, the first law of nature. Men cannot enjoy the rights of an uncivil and of a civil state together. That he may obtain justice, he gives up his right of determining what it is in points the most essential to him. That he may secure some liberty, he makes a surrender in trust of the whole of it.

Government is not made in virtue of natural rights, which may and do exist in total independence of it, and exist in much greater clearness and in a much greater degree of abstract perfection; but their abstract perfection is their practical defect. By having a right to everything they want everything. Government is a contrivance of human wisdom to provide for human *wants.* Men have a right that these wants should be provided for by this wisdom. Among these wants is to be reckoned the want, out of civil society, of a sufficient restraint upon their passions. Society requires not only that the passions of individuals should be subjected, but that even in the mass and body, as well as in the individuals, the inclinations of men should frequently be thwarted, their will controlled, and their passions brought into subjection. This can only be done *by a power out of themselves,* and not, in the exercise of its function, subject to that will and to those passions which it is its office to bridle and subdue. In this sense the restraints on men, as well as their liberties, are to be reckoned among their rights. But as the liberties and the restrictions vary with times and circumstances and admit of infinite modifications, they cannot be settled upon any abstract rule; and nothing is so foolish as to discuss them upon that principle.

The moment you abate anything from the full rights of men, each to govern himself, and suffer any artificial, positive limitation upon those rights, from that moment the whole organization of government becomes a consideration of convenience. This it is which makes the constitution of a state and the due distribution of its powers a matter of the most delicate and complicated skill. It requires a deep knowledge of human nature and human necessities, and of the things which facilitate or obstruct the various ends which are to be pursued by the mechanism of civil institutions. The state is to have recruits to its strength, and remedies to its distempers. What is the use of discussing a man's abstract right to food or medicine? The question is upon the method of procuring and administering them. In that deliberation I shall always advise to call in the aid of the farmer and the physician rather than the professor of metaphysics.[19]

The science of constructing a commonwealth, or renovating it, or reforming it, is, like every other experimental science, not to be taught *a priori*.[20] Nor is it a short experience that can instruct us in that practical science, because the real effects of moral causes are not always immediate; but that which in the first instance is prejudicial may be excellent in its remoter operation, and its excellence may arise even from the ill effects it produces in the beginning. The reverse also happens: and very plausible schemes, with very pleasing commencements, have often shameful and lamentable conclusions. In states there are often some obscure and almost latent causes, things which appear at first view of little moment, on which a very great part of its prosperity or adversity may most essentially depend. The science of government being therefore so practical in itself and intended for such practical purposes—a matter which requires experience, and even more experience than any person can gain in his whole life, however sagacious and observing he may be—it is with infinite caution that any man ought to venture upon pulling down an edifice which has answered in any tolerable degree for ages the common purposes of society, or on building it up again without having models and patterns of approved utility before his eyes.

These metaphysic rights entering into common life, like rays of light which pierce into a dense medium, are by the laws of nature refracted from their straight line. Indeed, in the gross and complicated mass of human passions and concerns the primitive rights of men undergo such a variety of refractions and reflections that it

---

[19] Abstract or speculative philosophy. Burke is here belittling the pro-French "liberal" philosophers.

[20] According to prior, or previous, assumptions of truth.

becomes absurd to talk of them as if they continued in the simplicity of their original direction. The nature of man is intricate; the objects of society are of the greatest possible complexity; and, therefore, no simple disposition or direction of power can be suitable either to man's nature or to the quality of his affairs. When I hear the simplicity of contrivance aimed at and boasted of in any new political constitutions, I am at no loss to decide that the artificers are grossly ignorant of their trade or totally negligent of their duty. The simple governments are fundamentally defective, to say no worse of them. If you were to contemplate society in but one point of view, all these simple modes of polity are infinitely captivating. In effect each would answer its single end much more perfectly than the more complex is able to attain all its complex purposes. But it is better that the whole should be imperfectly and anomalously answered than that, while some parts are provided for with great exactness, others might be totally neglected or perhaps materially injured by the over-care of a favorite member.

The pretended rights of these theorists are all extremes; and in proportion as they are metaphysically true, they are morally and politically false. The rights of men are in a sort of *middle,* incapable of definition, but not impossible to be discerned. The rights of men in governments are their advantages; and these are often in balances between differences of good, in compromises sometimes between good and evil, and sometimes between evil and evil. Political reason is a computing principle: adding, subtracting, multiplying, and dividing, morally and not metaphysically, or mathematically, true moral denominations.

By these theorists the right of the people is almost always sophistically confounded with their power. The body of the community, whenever it can come to act, can meet with no effectual resistance; but till power and right are the same, the whole body of them has no right inconsistent with virtue, and the first of all virtues, prudence. Men have no right to what is not reasonable and to what is not for their benefit.

•   •   •

I almost venture to affirm that not one in a hundred among us participates in the "triumph" of the Revolution Society.[21] If the king

---

[21] The Revolution Society gloried in the achievements of the English "Glorious Revolution" of 1688 to 1689. In November 1789, when meeting for the spectacular

and queen of France, and their children, were to fall into our hands by the chance of war, in the most acrimonious of all hostilities (I deprecate such an event, I deprecate such hostility), they would be treated with another sort of triumphal entry into London. We formerly have had a king of France [22] in that situation; you have read how he was treated by the victor in the field, and in what manner he was afterwards received in England. Four hundred years have gone over us, but I believe we are not materially changed since that period. Thanks to our sullen resistance to innovation, thanks to the cold sluggishness of our national character, we still bear the stamp of our forefathers. We have not (as I conceive) lost the generosity and dignity of thinking of the fourteenth century, nor as yet have we subtilized ourselves into savages. We are not the converts of Rousseau; [23] we are not the disciples of Voltaire; [24] Helvetius [25] has made no progress among us. Atheists [26] are not our preachers; madmen are not our lawgivers. We know that *we* have made no discoveries, and we think that no discoveries are to be made, in morality, nor many in the great principles of government, nor in the ideas of liberty, which were understood long before we were born, altogether as well as they will be after the grave has heaped its mould upon our presumption and the silent tomb shall have imposed its law on our pert loquacity. In England we have not yet been completely embowelled of our natural entrails; we still feel within us, and we cherish and cultivate, those inbred sentiments which are the faithful guardians, the active monitors of our duty, the true supporters of all liberal and manly morals. We have not been drawn and trussed, in order that we may be filled, like stuffed birds in a museum, with chaff and rags and paltry blurred shreds of paper about the rights of

centennial celebration of the Revolution, the Society drafted a document that congratulated the French revolutionaries on what they had achieved so far. The Revolution Society expressed its hope for the democratization of the British Parliament in the near future.

[22] John II (1319–1364), while held prisoner in England, was treated in the manner reserved for visiting royalty.

[23] Jean Jacques Rousseau (1712–1778), a philosopher and writer who promoted doctrines of human equality and democracy. He was born in Geneva, Switzerland, but lived chiefly in Paris after 1741.

[24] The literary name of François Marie Arouet (1694–1778). This French writer and historian was an untiring fighter against religious intolerance and suppression of free expression.

[25] Claude Adrien Helvetius (1715–1771), a French philosopher who taught that pleasure was the highest social good.

[26] Those who deny the existence of God.

man. We preserve the whole of our feelings still native and entire, unsophisticated by pedantry and infidelity. We have real hearts of flesh and blood beating in our bosoms. We fear God; we look up with awe to kings, with affection to parliaments, with duty to magistrates, with reverence to priests, and with respect to nobility. Why? Because when such ideas are brought before our minds, it is *natural* to be so affected; because all other feelings are false and spurious and tend to corrupt our minds, to vitiate our primary morals, to render us unfit for rational liberty, and, by teaching us a servile, licentious, and abandoned insolence, to be our low sport for a few holidays, to make us perfectly fit for, and justly deserving of, slavery through the whole course of our lives.

You see, Sir, that in this enlightened age I am bold enough to confess that we are generally men of untaught feelings, that, instead of casting away all our old prejudices,[27] we cherish them to a very considerable degree, and, to take more shame to ourselves, we cherish them because they are prejudices; and the longer they have lasted and the more generally they have prevailed, the more we cherish them. We are afraid to put men to live and trade each on his own private stock of reason, because we suspect that the stock in each man is small, and that the individuals would do better to avail themselves of the general bank and capital of nations and of ages. Many of our men of speculation, instead of exploding general prejudices, employ their sagacity to discover the latent wisdom which prevails in them. If they find what they seek, and they seldom fail, they think it more wise to continue the prejudice, with the reason involved, than to cast away the coat of prejudice and to leave nothing but the naked reason; because prejudice, with its reason, has a motive to give action to that reason, and an affection which will give it permanence. Prejudice is of ready application in the emergency; it previously engages the mind in a steady course of wisdom and virtue and does not leave the man hesitating in the moment of decision skeptical, puzzled, and unresolved. Prejudice renders a man's virtue his habit, and not a series of unconnected acts. Through just prejudice, his duty becomes a part of his nature.

Your literary men and your politicians, and so do the whole clan of the enlightened among us, essentially differ in these points. They have no respect for the wisdom of others, but they pay it off by a

---

[27] Adherence to traditions, customs, and conventions.

very full measure of confidence in their own. With them it is a sufficient motive to destroy an old scheme of things because it is an old one. As to the new, they are in no sort of fear with regard to the duration of a building run up in haste, because duration is no object to those who think little or nothing has been done before their time, and who place all their hopes in discovery. They conceive, very systematically, that all things which give perpetuity are mischievous, and therefore they are at inexpiable war with all establishments. They think that government may vary like modes of dress, and with as little ill effect; that there needs no principle of attachment, except a sense of present convenience, to any constitution of the state. They always speak as if they were of opinion that there is a singular species of compact between them and their magistrates which binds the magistrate, but which has nothing reciprocal in it, but that the majesty of the people has a right to dissolve it without any reason but its will. Their attachment to their country itself is only so far as it agrees with some of their fleeting projects; it begins and ends with that scheme of polity which falls in with their momentary opinion.

These doctrines, or rather sentiments, seem prevalent with your new statesmen. But they are wholly different from those on which we have always acted in this country.

• • •

We know, and what is better, we feel inwardly, that religion is the basis of civil society and the source of all good and of all comfort. In England we are so convinced of this, that there is no rust of superstition with which the accumulated absurdity of the human mind might have crusted it over in the course of ages, that ninety-nine in a hundred of the people of England would not prefer to impiety. We shall never be such fools as to call in an enemy to the substance of any system to remove its corruptions, to supply its defects, or to perfect its construction. If our religious tenets should ever want a further elucidation, we shall not call on atheism to explain them. We shall not light up our temple from that unhallowed fire. It will be illuminated with other lights. It will be perfumed with other incense than the infectious stuff which is imported by the smugglers of adulterated metaphysics. If our ecclesiastical establishment [28] should need a revision, it is not avarice or rapacity, public or private, that we

---

[28] The Church of England.

shall employ for the audit, or receipt, or application of its consecrated revenue. Violently condemning neither the Greek[29] nor the
Armenian,[30] nor, since heats are subsided, the Roman system of
religion,[31] we prefer the Protestant, not because we think it has less
of the Christian religion in it, but because, in our judgment, it has
more. We are Protestants, not from indifference, but from zeal.

We know, and it is our pride to know, that man is by his constitution a religious animal; that atheism is against, not only our reason,
but our instincts; and that it cannot prevail long. But if, in the moment of riot and in a drunken delirium from the hot spirit drawn out
of the alembic[32] of hell, which in France is now so furiously boiling,
we should uncover our nakedness by throwing off that Christian
religion which has hitherto been our boast and comfort, and one
great source of civilization among us, and among many other nations, we are apprehensive (being well aware that the mind will not
endure a void) that some uncouth, pernicious, and degrading superstition might take place of it.

For that reason, before we take from our establishment the natural, human means of estimation and give it up to contempt, as you
have done, and in doing it have incurred the penalties you well
deserve to suffer, we desire that some other may be presented to us
in the place of it. We shall then form our judgment.

On these ideas, instead of quarrelling with establishments, as some
do who have made a philosophy and a religion of their hostility to
such institutions, we cleave closely to them. We are resolved to keep
an established church, an established monarchy, an established aristocracy, and an established democracy, each in the degree it exists,
and in no greater.

• • •

To avoid, therefore, the evils of inconstancy and versatility, ten
thousand times worse than those of obstinacy and the blindest prejudice, we have consecrated the state that no man should approach to
look into its defects or corruptions but with due caution, that he
should never dream of beginning its reformation by its subversion,
that he should approach to the faults of the state as to the wounds of

[29] The Greek Orthodox Church.
[30] The Armenian Apostolic Church, another branch of historic Christianity.
[31] The Roman Catholic Church.
[32] Fires.

a father, with pious awe and trembling solicitude. By this wise prejudice we are taught to look with horror on those children of their country who are prompt rashly to hack that aged parent in pieces and put him into the kettle of magicians, in hopes that by their poisonous weeds and wild incantations they may regenerate the paternal constitution and renovate their father's life.[33]

Society is indeed a contract. Subordinate contracts for objects of mere occasional interest may be dissolved at pleasure—but the state ought not to be considered as nothing better than a partnership agreement in a trade of pepper and coffee, calico or tobacco, or some other such low concern, to be taken up for a little temporary interest, and to be dissolved by the fancy of the parties. It is to be looked on with other reverence, because it is not a partnership in things subservient only to the gross animal existence of a temporary and perishable nature. It is a partnership in all science; a partnership in all art; a partnership in every virtue and in all perfection. As the ends of such a partnership cannot be obtained in many generations, it becomes a partnership not only between those who are living, but between those who are living, those who are dead, and those who are to be born. Each contract of each particular state is but a clause in the great primeval contract of eternal society, linking the lower with the higher natures, connecting the visible and invisible world, according to a fixed compact sanctioned by the inviolable oath which holds all physical and all moral natures, each in their appointed place. This law is not subject to the will of those who, by an obligation above them, and infinitely superior, are bound to submit their will to that law.

• • •

It is this inability to wrestle with difficulty which has obliged the arbitrary Assembly of France[34] to commence their schemes of reform with abolition and total destruction. But is it in destroying and pulling down that skill is displayed? Your mob can do this as well at least as your assemblies. The shallowest understanding, the rudest hand is more than equal to that task. Rage and frenzy will pull down

[33] Burke is referring to the legend in which Medea, a Greek sorceress, persuades the daughters of King Pelias to hack their father to pieces and boil him with "youth-renewing" herbs. This bizarre procedure fails to achieve the father's rejuvenation.

[34] The National Assembly (1789–91), which, assuming the right to exercise sovereign power in the name of the French people, passed the reform measures that started the French Revolution.

more in half an hour than prudence, deliberation, and foresight can build up in a hundred years. The errors and defects of old establishments are visible and palpable. It calls for little ability to point them out; and where absolute power is given, it requires but a word wholly to abolish the vice and the establishment together. The same lazy, but restless disposition which loves sloth and hates quiet directs these politicians when they come to work for supplying the place of what they have destroyed. To make everything the reverse of what they have seen is quite as easy as to destroy. No difficulties occur in what has never been tried. Criticism is almost baffled in discovering the defects of what has not existed; and eager enthusiasm and cheating hope have all the wide field of imagination in which they may expatiate with little or no opposition.

At once to preserve and to reform is quite another thing. When the useful parts of an old establishment are kept, and what is superadded is to be fitted to what is retained, a vigorous mind, steady, persevering attention, various powers of comparison and combination, and the resources of an understanding fruitful in expedients are to be exercised; they are to be exercised in a continued conflict with the combined force of opposite vices, with the obstinacy that rejects all improvement and the levity that is fatigued and disgusted with everything of which it is in possession. But you may object—"A process of this kind is slow. It is not fit for an assembly which glories in performing in a few months the work of ages. Such a mode of reforming, possibly, might take up many years." Without question it might; and it ought. It is one of the excellences of a method in which time is among the assistants, that its operation is slow and in some cases almost imperceptible. If circumspection and caution are a part of wisdom when we work only upon inanimate matter, surely they become a part of duty, too, when the subject of our demolition and construction is not brick and timber but sentient [35] beings, by the sudden alteration of whose state, condition, and habits, multitudes may be rendered miserable. But it seems as if it were the prevalent opinion in Paris that an unfeeling heart and an undoubting confidence are the sole qualifications for a perfect legislator. Far different are my ideas of that high office. The true lawgiver ought to have a heart full of sensibility. He ought to love and respect his kind, and to fear himself. It may be allowed to his temperament to catch his ul-

---

[35] Living, feeling (human).

timate object with an intuitive glance, but his movements towards it ought to be deliberate. Political arrangement, as it is a work for social ends, is to be only wrought by social means. There, mind must conspire with mind. Time is required to produce that union of minds which alone can produce all the good we aim at. Our patience will achieve more than our force. If I might venture to appeal to what is so much out of fashion in Paris, I mean to experience, I should tell you that in my course I have known and, according to my measure, have cooperated with great men; and I have never yet seen any plan which has not been mended by the observations of those who were much inferior in understanding to the person who took the lead in the business. By a slow, but well-sustained progress the effect of each step is watched; the good or ill success of the first gives light to us in the second; and so, from light to light, we are conducted with safety through the whole series. We see that the parts or the system do not clash. The evils latent in the most promising contrivances are provided for as they arise. One advantage is as little as possible sacrificed to another. We compensate, we reconcile, we balance. We are enabled to unite into a consistent whole the various anomalies and contending principles that are found in the minds and affairs of men. From hence arises, not an excellence in simplicity, but one far superior, an excellence in composition. Where the great interests of mankind are concerned through a long succession of generations, that succession ought to be admitted into some share in the councils which are so deeply to affect them. If justice requires this, the work itself requires the aid of more minds than one age can furnish. It is from this view of things that the best legislators have been often satisfied with the establishment of some sure, solid, and ruling principle in government—a power like that which some of the philosophers have called a plastic nature; and having fixed the principle, they have left it afterwards to its own operation.

• • •

The effects of the incapacity shown by the popular leaders in all the great members of the commonwealth are to be covered with the "all-atoning name" of liberty. In some people I see great liberty indeed; in many, if not in the most, an oppressive, degrading servitude. But what is liberty without wisdom and without virtue? It is the greatest of all possible evils; for it is folly, vice, and madness, without tuition or restraint. Those who know what virtuous liberty is cannot bear to see it disgraced by incapable heads on account of their having high-sounding words in their mouths. Grand, swelling sentiments of liberty I am sure I do not despise. They warm the heart; they enlarge and liberalize our minds; they animate our courage in time of conflict. Old as I am, I read the fine raptures of Lucan[36] and Corneille[37] with pleasure. Neither do I wholly condemn the little arts and devices of popularity. They facilitate the carrying of many points of moment; they keep the people together; they refresh the mind in its exertions; and they diffuse occasional gaiety over the severe brow of moral freedom. Every politician ought to sacrifice to the Graces,[38] and to join compliance with reason. But in such an undertaking as that in France all these subsidiary sentiments and artifices are of little avail. To make a government requires no great prudence. Settle the seat of power, teach obedience, and the work is done. To give freedom is still more easy. It is not necessary to guide; it only requires to let go the rein. But to form a *free government,* that is, to temper together these opposite elements of liberty and restraint in one consistent work, requires much thought, deep reflection, a sagacious, powerful, and combining mind. This I do not find in those who take the lead in the National Assembly. Perhaps they are not so miserably deficient as they appear. I rather believe it. It would put them below the common level of human understanding. But when the leaders choose to make themselves bidders at an auction of popularity, their talents, in the construction of the state, will be of no service. They will become flatterers instead of legislators, the instruments, not the guides, of the people. If any of them should happen to propose a scheme of liberty, soberly limited and defined with proper qualifications, he will be immediately outbid by his competitors who will produce something more splendidly popular. Suspicions will be raised of his fidelity to his cause. Moderation will be stigmatized as the virtue of cowards, and compromise as the prudence of traitors, until, in hopes of preserving the credit which may enable him to temper and moderate, on some occasions, the popular leader is obliged to become active in propagating doctrines and establishing powers that will afterwards defeat any sober purpose at which he ultimately might have aimed. . . .

---

[36] Marcus Annaeus Lucanus (A.D. 39–65), a Roman poet.
[37] Pierre Corneille (1606–1684), a French playwright.
[38] In Greek mythology, the three sister goddesses who personified pleasure, charm, elegance, and beauty.

14

Johann Wolfgang von Goethe
Faust

Johann Wolfgang von Goethe (1749–1832), a genius whose full and varied career reflected the romantic spirit of the nineteenth century, was both a scientist and one of the greatest of the German lyric poets. In his scientific work, Goethe made important contributions to biology and advanced a theory of evolution. As political adviser to the Duke of Saxe-Weimar from 1775 to the end of his life, Goethe proved a responsible and forward-looking public servant. He also wrote novels and powerful dramas that influenced German and other European literature. In his varied activities and his changing intellectual positions, Goethe epitomized the confused strains of the transition from the neoclassicism of the eighteenth century to the romanticism of the nineteenth. Indeed, he thought of himself as a prophet of his time—an interpreter of the spiritual issues of his day; the central idea of his life was the oneness of humanity and nature.

Faust, Goethe's literary masterpiece, is a reflection of the range of the author's own intellectual career as well as a comment on the restless seeking, affirmations, and protests of his age. Part I, from which most of the following selection is taken, was written between 1774 and 1808 (when it was published), while Goethe was going through, successively, his period of youthful self-discovery and rebellion, his neoclassical phase, and his romantic phase. Part II was written during the last twenty-five years of his life and was not published until the year of his death; only its conclusion is reprinted here. Goethe presents both parts in dramatic form, but they are more suitable to reading than to performance on a stage.

From *Goethe's Faust,* translated by Louis MacNeice. Copyright 1951 by Louis MacNeice. Reprinted by permission of Oxford University Press, Inc. [Pp. 13–21, 28–31, 43–45, 47–48, 54–62, 73–76, 112–16, 146–50, 152–54, 284–91, 293–94, 298.]

Written in symbolic poetry, the drama Faust *confronts its reader with numerous situations, problems, and characters. These, however, have only as much significance as each individual finds in them. The drama's ranking among the most important pieces of Western literature is due in great measure to the fact that modern readers find themselves portrayed in it. Individuals in contemporary society, like the character Faust, are products of past civilizations, epochs, and ideas—influences that do not fuse within them into a harmonious whole but leave them disjointed and divided. Thus, from scene to scene, Faust thinks, speaks, and acts differently. For example, at some times he is a romanticist, then again a rationalist, and at times he seems thoroughly medieval. In him dwell side by side the Greek age, classical and Christian mythology, and the Reformation, as well as those deep abysses of the soul that are darkly felt but generally escape psychological and philosophical identification.*

Contemporary readers of the drama recognize themselves in the person of Faust because, like him, they rarely see their dreams and aspirations come true. Faust, for example, never learns what "girds the world together in its innermost being," nor is he privileged to spend the days of his adult life as a loving husband and father. Even his vision of a "free ground" inhabited by a "free people" remains just that—a vision. Like many present-day people, Faust does not foresee the varied and often disastrous results of his dreams and acts. Because of him, for instance, a family perishes, and his service to the Emperor climaxes in a bloody war. Later, his desire for a perfect piece of land causes a lovely old couple to perish in the flames of their small hut. Undoubtedly, the intentions of Faust are often honorable, and his efforts in pursuing them untiring and unrelenting; nonetheless the results are often disastrous, and his is a truly tragic existence.

The life of Faust also resembles many modern lives in that it consists of a number of seemingly unrelated episodes, each of which must be evaluated separately; it is a succession of experiences rather than a progression of them. In these experiences, Faust seems the modern-day Everyman condemned to a tragic existence, rather than the ideal hero. He is not fortunate enough to see even his last enterprise completed. Beholding his dream rather than reality, he speaks the fateful words that should deliver his soul to Hell. But if the drama had been written to end with Faust's death and damnation, the reader would be left with a depressing emptiness. Goethe, who confided that the ending caused him great trouble, chose instead to end the drama on a religious, conciliatory, and hopeful note: Although this world resembles a gruesome madhouse, might it not be comforting to assume that there exists yet another world whose foremost attributes are divine mercy and love? In contemplating his own death, however, Goethe emphatically rejected this comforting idea.

PROLOGUE IN HEAVEN
The Lord. The Heavenly Hosts. Mephistopheles following

(*The Three Archangels step forward*)
RAPHAEL.   The chanting sun, as ever, rivals
The chanting of his brother spheres [1]
And marches round his destined circuit—
A march that thunders in our ears.
His aspect cheers the Hosts of Heaven
Though what his essence none can say;
These inconceivable creations
Keep the high state of their first day.
GABRIEL.   And swift, with inconceivable swiftness,
The earth's full splendor rolls around,
Celestial [2] radiance alternating
With a dread night too deep to sound;
The sea against the rocks' deep bases
Comes foaming up in far-flung force,
And rock and sea go whirling onward
In the swift spheres' eternal course.
MICHAEL.   And storms in rivalry are raging
From sea to land, from land to sea,
In frenzy forge the world a girdle
From which no inmost part is free.
The blight of lightning flaming yonder
Marks where the thunder-bolt will play;
And yet Thine envoys, [3] Lord, revere
The gentle movement of Thy day.
CHOIR OF ANGELS.   Thine aspect cheers the Hosts of Heaven
Though what Thine essence none can say,

---

[1] It was held that, as the sun and planets travel through the skies, they create a loud sound. This sound was believed to be almost unbearable to the human ear.
[2] Heavenly.
[3] Messengers; angels.

And all Thy loftiest creations
Keep the high state of their first day.
(*Enter Mephistopheles*)

MEPHISTOPHELES.[4]   Since you, O Lord, once more approach and ask
If business down with us be light or heavy—
And in the past you've usually welcomed me—
That's why you see me also at your levee.[5]
Excuse me, I can't manage lofty words—
Not though your whole court jeer and find me low;
My pathos[6] certainly would make you laugh
Had you not left off laughing long ago.
Your suns and worlds mean nothing much to me;
How men torment themselves, that's all I see.
The little god of the world, one can't reshape, reshade him;
He is as strange to-day as that first day you made him.
His life would be not so bad, not quite,
Had you not granted him a gleam of Heaven's light;
He calls it Reason, uses it not the least
Except to be more beastly than any beast.
He seems to me—if your Honor does not mind—
Like a grasshopper—the long-legged kind—
That's always in flight and leaps as it flies along
And then in the grass strikes up its same old song.
I could only wish he confined himself to the grass!
He thrusts his nose into every filth, alas.

LORD.   Mephistopheles, have you no other news?
Do you always come here to accuse?
Is nothing ever right in your eyes on earth?

MEPHISTOPHELES.   No, Lord! I find things there as downright bad as
ever.
I am sorry for men's days of dread and dearth;[7]
Poor things, *my* wish to plague 'em isn't fervent.

LORD.   Do you know Faust?

MEPHISTOPHELES.   The Doctor?

LORD.   Aye, my servant.

---

[4] Medieval name for the Devil; sometimes shortened to Mephisto.
[5] Morning reception held by a person of high rank for his courtiers.
[6] Grand manners.
[7] Scarcity (of food).

MEPHISTOPHELES.   Indeed! He serves you oddly enough, I think.
　　The fool has no earthly habits in meat and drink.
　　The ferment in him drives him wide and far,
　　That he is mad he too has almost guessed;
　　He demands of heaven each fairest star
　　And of earth each highest joy and best,
　　And all that is new and all that is far
　　Can bring no calm to the deep-sea swell of his breast.
LORD.   Now he may serve me only gropingly,
　　Soon I shall lead him into the light.
　　The gardener knows when the sapling first turns green
　　That flowers and fruit will make the future bright.
MEPHISTOPHELES.   What do you wager? You will lose him yet,
　　Provided *you* give *me* permission
　　To steer him gently the course I set.
LORD.   So long as he walks the earth alive,
　　So long as you may try what enters your head;
　　Men make mistakes as long as they strive.
MEPHISTOPHELES.   I thank you for that; as regards the dead,
　　The dead have never taken my fancy.
　　I favor cheeks that are full and rosy-red;
　　No corpse is welcome to my house;
　　I work as the cat does with the mouse.
LORD.   Very well; you have my full permission.
　　Divert this soul from its primal[8] source
　　And carry it, if you can seize it,
　　Down with you upon your course—
　　And stand ashamed when you must needs admit:
　　A good man with his groping intuitions[9]
　　Still knows the path that is true and fit.
MEPHISTOPHELES.   All right—but it won't last for long.
　　I'm not afraid my bet will turn out wrong.
　　And, if my aim prove true and strong,
　　Allow me to triumph wholeheartedly.
　　Dust shall he eat—and greedily—
　　Like my cousin the Snake[10] renowned in tale and song.

[8] Original.
[9] The grasping of knowledge without learning or reasoning.
[10] The serpent that seduced Eve in the Garden of Eden. Mephistopheles intends for
　　Faust to indulge himself in vulgar, sensual pleasure.

LORD.   That too you are free to give a trial;
  I have never hated the likes of you.
  Of all the spirits of denial
  The joker is the last that I eschew.[11]
  Man finds relaxation too attractive—
  Too fond too soon of unconditional rest;
  Which is why I am pleased to give him a companion
  Who lures and thrusts and must, as devil, be active.
  But ye, true sons of Heaven, it is your duty
  To take your joy in the living wealth of beauty.
  The changing Essence which ever works and lives
  Wall you around with love, serene, secure!
  And that which floats in flickering appearance
  Fix ye it firm in thoughts that must endure.
CHOIR OF ANGELS.   Thine aspect cheers the Hosts of Heaven
  Though what Thine essence none can say,
  And all Thy loftiest creations
  Keep the high state of their first day.
  (*Heaven closes*)
MEPHISTOPHELES (*alone*).   I like to see the Old One now and then
  And try to keep relations on the level.
  It's really decent of so great a person
  To talk so humanely even to the Devil.

PART I

NIGHT

  (*In a high-vaulted narrow Gothic* [study] *Faust, restless, in a chair at
  his desk*)
FAUST.   Here stand I, ach, Philosophy
  Behind me and Law and Medicine too
  And, to my cost, Theology—
  All these I have sweated through and through
  And now you see me a poor fool
  As wise as when I entered school!
  They call me Master, they call me Doctor,
  Ten years now I have dragged my college

---

[11] Shun, avoid.

Along by the nose through zig and zag
Through up and down and round and round
And this is all that I have found—
The impossibility of knowledge!
It is this that burns away my heart;
Of course I am cleverer than the quacks,
Than master and doctor, than clerk and priest,
I suffer no scruple or doubt in the least,
I have no qualms about devil or burning,
Which is just why all joy is torn from me,
I cannot presume to make use of my learning,
I cannot presume I could open my mind
To proselytize and improve mankind.

Besides, I have neither goods nor gold,
Neither reputation nor rank in the world;
No dog would choose to continue so!
Which is why I have given myself to Magic [12]
To see if the Spirit [13] may grant me to know
Through its force and its voice full many a secret,
May spare the sour sweat that I used to pour out
In talking of what I know nothing about,
May grant me to learn what it is that girds [14]
The world together in its inmost being,
That the seeing its whole germination, the seeing
Its workings, may end my traffic in words.

O couldst thou, light of the full moon,
Look now thy last upon my pain,
Thou for whom I have sat belated
So many midnights here and waited
Till, over books and papers, thou
Didst shine, sad friend, upon my brow!
O could I but walk to and fro
On mountain heights in thy dear glow
Or float with spirits round mountain eyries [15]

---

[12] Charms, spells, and rituals which supposedly unlock natural or supernatural secrets.
[13] Supernatural.
[14] Binds, holds.
[15] Heights.

Or weave through fields thy glances glean [16]
And freed from all miasmal [17] theories
Bathe in thy dew and wash me clean!

Oh! Am I still stuck in this jail?
This God-damned dreary hole in the wall
Where even the lovely light of heaven
Breaks wanly through the painted panes!
Cooped up among these heaps of books
Gnawed by worms, coated with dust,
Round which to the top of the Gothic vault
A smoke-stained paper forms a crust.
Retorts and canisters lie pell-mell
And pyramids of instruments,
The junk of centuries, dense and mat—
Your world, man! World? They call it that!

And yet you ask why your poor heart
Cramped in your breast should feel such fear,
Why an unspecified misery
Should throw your life so out of gear?
Instead of the living natural world
For which God made all men his sons
You hold a reeking mouldering court
Among assorted skeletons.
Away! There is a world outside!
And this one book of mystic art
Which Nostradamus [18] wrote himself,
Is this not adequate guard and guide?
By this you can tell the course of the stars,
By this, once Nature gives the word,
The soul begins to stir and dawn,
A spirit by a spirit heard.
In vain your barren studies here
Construe the signs of sanctity.

[16] The shimmering moonlight.
[17] Noxious, nauseating.
[18] Nostradamus (1503–1566), a French astrologer and author of prophecies.

You Spirits, you are hovering near;
If you can hear me, answer me!

         • • •

[Faust, however, learns that the Spirits will not divulge to him the secrets of
the universe, since he is not of their kind, but merely a human being. This
rejection throws him into deepest despair, and suicide seems to him the only
way to escape such a dismal existence. *Ed.*]

I am not like the gods—that I too deeply feel—
No, I am like the worm that burrows through the dust
Which, as it keeps itself alive in the dust,
Is annulled and buried by some casual heel.

Is it not dust that on a thousand shelves
Narrows this high wall round me so?
The junk that with its thousandfold tawdriness [19]
In this moth world keeps me so low?
Shall I find here what I require?
Read maybe in a thousand books how men
Have in the general run tortured themselves,
With but a lucky one now and then?
Why do you grin at me, you hollow skull?
To point out that your brain was once, like mine, confused
And looked for the easy day but in the difficult dusk,
Lusting for truth was led astray and abused?
You instruments, I know you are mocking me
With cog and crank and cylinder.
I stood at the door, you were to be the key;
A key with intricate wards—but the bolt declines to stir.
Mysterious in the light of day
Nature lets none unveil her; if she refuse
To make some revelation to your spirit
You cannot force her with levers and with screws.
You ancient gear I have never used, it is only
Because my father used you that I retain you.
You ancient scroll, you have been turning black

---

[19] Gaudiness and cheapness.

Since first the dim lamp smoked upon this desk to stain you.
Far better to have squandered the little I have
Than loaded with that little to stay sweating here.
Whatever legacy your fathers left you,
To own it you must earn it dear.
The thing that you fail to use is a load of lead;
The moment can only use what the moment itself has bred.

But why do my eyes fasten upon that spot?
Is that little bottle a magnet to my sight?
Why do I feel of a sudden this lovely illumination
As when the moon flows round us in a dark wood at night?

Bottle, unique little bottle, I salute you
As now I devoutly lift you down. In you
I honor human invention and human skill.
You, the quintessence of all sweet narcotics,
The extract of all rare and deadly powers,
I am your master—show me your good will!
I look on you, my sorrow is mitigated,
I hold you and my struggles are abated,
The flood-tide of my spirit ebbs away, away.
The mirroring waters glitter at my feet,
I am escorted forth on the high seas,
Allured towards new shores by a new day.
A fiery chariot floats on nimble wings
Down to me and I feel myself upbuoyed
To blaze a new trail through the upper air
Into new spheres of energy unalloyed.[20]
Oh this high life, this heavenly rapture! Do *you*
Merit this, you, a moment ago a worm?
Merit it? Aye—only turn your back on the sun
Which enchants the earth, turn your back and be firm!
And brace yourself to tear asunder the gates.
Which everyone longs to shuffle past if he can;
Now is the time to act and acting prove
That God's height need not lower the merit of Man;
Nor tremble at that dark pit in which our fancy

[20] Pure, unmixed.

Condemns itself to torments of its own framing,
But struggle on and upwards to that passage
At the narrow mouth of which all hell is flaming.
Be calm and take this step, though you should fall
Beyond it into nothing—nothing at all.

And you, you loving-cup of shining crystal—
I have not given a thought to you for years—
Down you come now out of your ancient chest!
You glittered at my ancestors' junketings[21]
Enlivening the serious guest
When with you in his hand he proceeded to toast his neighbor—
But to-day no neighbor will take you from my hand.
Here is a juice that makes one drunk in a wink;
It fills you full, you cup, with its brown flood.
It was I who made this, I who had it drawn;
So let my whole soul now make my last drink
A high and gala greeting, a toast to the dawn!
(*He raises the cup to his mouth. There is an outburst of bells and choirs*)

CHORUS OF ANGELS.   Christ is arisen!
                     Joy to mortality
                     Whom its own fatally
                     Earth-bound morality
                     Bound in a prison.

FAUST.   What a deep booming, what a ringing tone
          Pulls back the cup from my lips—and with such power!
          So soon are you announcing, you deep bells,
          Easter Day's first festive hour?
          You choirs, do you raise so soon the solacing hymn
          That once round the night of the grave rang out from the seraphim[22]
          As man's new covenant[23] and dower?[24]

CHORUS OF WOMEN.   With balm and with spices
                    'Twas we laid him out,
                    We who tended him,
                    Faithful, devout;

[21] Feasts.
[22] Angels.
[23] Divine promise (in Christ).
[24] Gift.

> We wound him in linen,
> Made all clean where he lay,
> Alas—to discover
> Christ gone away.

CHORUS OF ANGELS.   Christ is arisen!
> The loving one! Blest
> After enduring the
> Grievous, the curing, the
> Chastening test.

FAUST.   You heavenly music, strong as you are kind,
> Why do you search me out in the dust?
> Better ring forth where men have open hearts!
> I hear your message, my faith it is that lags behind;
> And miracle is the favorite child of faith.
> Those spheres whence peals the gospel of forgiving,
> Those are beyond what I can dare,
> And yet, so used am I from childhood to this sound,
> It even now summons me back to living.
> Once I could feel the kiss of heavenly love
> Rain down through the calm and solemn Sabbath air,
> Could find a prophecy in the full-toned bell,
> A spasm of happiness in a prayer.
> An ineffably sweet longing bound me
> To quest at random through field and wood
> Where among countless burning tears
> I felt a world rise up around me.
> This hymn announced the lively games of youth, the lovely
> Freedom of Spring's own festival;
> Now with its childlike feelings memory holds me back
> From the last and gravest step of all.
> But you, sweet songs of heaven, keep sounding forth!
> My tears well up, I belong once more to earth.

• • •

[As is customary, Faust and his study assistant, Wagner, take a stroll on Easter Sunday. While delighting in the retreating of winter and the visible arrival of spring, Faust at some time finds himself surrounded by common folk, who praise him for the healing ability that snatched them from the fangs of a devouring epidemic. Their praise rings like mockery in Faust's ears since he was and remains ignorant regarding how to treat this illness.

Turning homeward, Faust and Wagner notice a poodle, who, it seems, has lost his master. Thereupon, Faust invites the dog to come with him and share his abode. *Ed.*]

FAUST'S STUDY

    (*He enters with the poodle*)

FAUST.   I have forsaken field and meadow
        Which night has laid in a deep bed,
        Night that wakes our better soul
        With a holy and foreboding dread.
        Now wild desires are wrapped in sleep
        And all the deeds that burn and break,
        The love of Man is waking now,
        The love of God begins to wake.

Poodle! Quiet! Don't run hither and thither!
Leave my threshold! Why are you snuffling there?
Lie down behind the stove and rest.
Here's a cushion; it's my best.
Out of doors on the mountain paths
You kept us amused by running riot;
But as my protégé at home
You'll only be welcome if you're quiet.

    Ah, when in our narrow cell
    The lamp once more imparts good cheer,
    Then in our bosom—in the heart
    That knows itself—then things grow clear.
    Reason once more begins to speak
    And the blooms of hope once more to spread;
    One hankers for the brooks of life,
    Ah, and for life's fountain head.

Don't growl, you poodle! That animal sound
Is not in tune with the holy music
By which my soul is girdled round.
We are used to human beings who jeer
At what they do not understand,
Who grouse at the good and the beautiful

Which often causes them much ado;
But must a dog snarl at it too?

But, ah, already, for all my good intentions
I feel contentment ebbing away in my breast.
Why must the stream so soon run dry
And we be left once more athirst?
I have experienced this so often;
Yet this defect has its compensation,
We learn to prize the supernatural
And hanker after revelation,
Which burns most bright and wins assent
Most in the New Testament.
I feel impelled to open the master text
And this once, with true dedication,
Take the sacred original
And make in my mother tongue my own translation.
(*He opens a Bible*)
It is written: In the beginning was the Word.[25]
Here I am stuck at once. Who will help me on?
I am unable to grant the Word such merit,
I must translate it differently
If I am truly illumined by the spirit.
It is written: In the beginning was the Mind.
But why should my pen scour
So quickly ahead? Consider that first line well.
Is it the Mind that effects and creates all things?
It *should* read: In the beginning was the Power.
Yet, even as I am changing what I have writ,
Something warns me not to abide by it.
The spirit prompts me, I see in a flash what I need,
And write: In the beginning was the Deed!

Dog! If we two are to share this room,
Leave off your baying,
Leave off your barking!
I can't have such a fellow staying
Around me causing all this bother.

---

[25] The Gospel according to John, Chapter 1, verse 1. The original uses the Greek word *Logos,* which in Hellenistic philosophy stood for "divine Reason."

One of us or the other
Will have to leave the cell.
Well?
I don't really like to eject you so
But the door is open, you may go.

But what? What do I see?
Can this really happen naturally?
Is it a fact or is it a fraud?
My dog is growing so long and broad!
He raises himself mightily,
That is not a dog's anatomy!
What a phantom have I brought to my house!
He already looks like a river horse
With fiery eyes and frightful jaws—
Aha! But I can give you pause!
For such a hybrid out of hell
Solomon's Key [26] is a good spell.

• • •

(*Mephistopheles comes forward from behind the stove, dressed like a travelling scholar*)

MEPHISTOPHELES.   What is the noise about? What might the gentleman fancy?

FAUST.   So that is what the poodle had inside him!
A travelling scholar? That casus [27] makes me laugh.

MEPHISTOPHELES.   My compliments to the learned gentleman.
You have put me in a sweat—not half!

FAUST.   What is your name?

MEPHISTOPHELES.   The question strikes me as petty
For one who holds the Word in such low repute,
Who, far withdrawn from all mere surface,
Aims only at the Essential Root. [28]

FAUST.   With you, you gentry, what is essential
The name more often than not supplies,

---

[26] A slim book of sorcery that pretends to be the testament of the Jewish King Solomon. Intended for his son Roboam (Rehoboam), it gives detailed instructions on
how to become "master over the Spirits" and how to unlock the door to "knowledge and the understanding of the magical arts and sciences."

[27] Event, situation.

[28] The inner nature of things.

As is indeed only too patent
When they call you Fly-God, Corrupter, Father of Lies.
All right, who are you then?
MEPHISTOPHELES.   A part of that Power
Which always wills evil, always procures good.
FAUST.   What do you mean by this conundrum?[29]
MEPHISTOPHELES.   I am the Spirit which always denies.
And quite rightly; whatever has a beginning
Deserves to have an undoing;
It would be better if nothing began at all.
Thus everything that you call
Sin, destruction, Evil in short,
Is my own element, my resort.

· · ·

[Following a dialogue in which Mephistopheles identifies his role more closely, spirits cast a slumber on Faust during which the devil makes his escape from Faust's study. *Ed.*]

(*The same room. Later*)
FAUST.   Who's knocking? Come in! *Now* who wants to annoy me?
MEPHISTOPHELES (*outside door*).
   It's I.
FAUST.   Come in!
MEPHISTOPHELES (*outside door*).
              You must say 'Come in' three times.
FAUST.   Come in then!
MEPHISTOPHELES (*entering*).
              Thank you; you overjoy me.
We two, I hope, we shall be good friends;
To chase those megrims[30] of yours away
I am here like a fine young squire to-day,
In a suit of scarlet trimmed with gold
And a little cape of stiff brocade,
With a cock's feather in my hat
And at my side a long sharp blade,
And the most succinct advice I can give
Is that you dress up just like me,

[29]Riddle.
[30]Depressed feelings.

So that uninhibited and free
You may find out what it means to live.
FAUST.   The pain of earth's constricted life, I fancy,
   Will pierce me still, whatever my attire;
   I am too old for mere amusement,
   Too young to be without desire.
   How can the world dispel my doubt?
   You must do without, you must do without!
   That is the everlasting song
   Which rings in every ear, which rings,
   And which to us our whole life long
   Every hour hoarsely sings.
   I wake in the morning only to feel appalled,
   My eyes with bitter tears could run
   To see the day which in its course
   Will not fulfil a wish for me, not one;
   The day which whittles away with obstinate carping
   All pleasures—even those of anticipation,
   Which makes a thousand grimaces to obstruct
   My heart when it is stirring in creation.
   And again, when night comes down, in anguish
   I must stretch out upon my bed
   And again no rest is granted me,
   For wild dreams fill my mind with dread.
   The God who dwells within my bosom
   Can make my inmost soul react;
   The God who sways my every power
   Is powerless with external fact.
   And so existence weighs upon my breast
   And I long for death and life—life I detest.
MEPHISTOPHELES.   Yet death is never a wholly welcome guest.
FAUST.   O happy is he whom death in the dazzle of victory
   Crowns with the bloody laurel in the battling swirl!
   Or he whom after the mad and breakneck dance
   He comes upon in the arms of a girl!
   O to have sunk away, delighted, deleted,
   Before the Spirit of the Earth, before his might!
MEPHISTOPHELES.   Yet I know someone who failed to drink
   A brown juice on a certain night.[31]

[31] Mephistopheles here refers to the fact that Faust, after all, did not commit suicide.

FAUST.   Your hobby is espionage—is it not?

MEPHISTOPHELES.   Oh I'm not omniscient—but I know a lot.

FAUST.   Whereas that tumult in my soul
  Was stilled by sweet familiar chimes [32]
  Which cozened [33] the child that yet was in me
  With echoes of more happy times,
  I now curse all things that encompass
  The soul with lures and jugglery
  And bind it in this dungeon of grief
  With trickery and flattery.
  Cursed in advance be the high opinion
  That serves our spirit for a cloak!
  Cursed be the dazzle of appearance
  Which bows our senses to its yoke!
  Cursed be the lying dreams of glory,
  The illusion that our name survives!
  Cursed be the flattering things we own,
  Servants and ploughs, children and wives!
  Cursed be Mammon [34] when with his treasures
  He makes us play the adventurous man
  Or when for our luxurious pleasures
  He duly spreads the soft divan!
  A curse on the balsam of the grape!
  A curse on the love that rides for a fall!
  A curse on hope! A curse on faith!
  And a curse on patience most of all!

• • •

MEPHISTOPHELES.   Stop playing with your grief which battens
  Like a vulture on your life, your mind!
  The worst of company would make you feel
  That you are a man among mankind.
  Not that it's really my proposition
  To shove you among the common men;
  Though I'm not one of the Upper Ten,
  If you would like a coalition
  With me for your career through life,

---

[32] The bells of Easter morning.
[33] Deceived.
[34] Wealth.

I am quite ready to fit in,
I'm yours before you can say knife.
I am your comrade;
If you so crave,
I am your servant, I am your slave.

FAUST.   And what have I to undertake in return?

MEPHISTOPHELES.   Oh it's early days to discuss what that is.

FAUST.   No, no, the devil is an egoist
And ready to do nothing gratis[35]
Which is to benefit a stranger.
Tell me your terms and don't prevaricate!
A servant like you in the house is a danger.

MEPHISTOPHELES.   I will bind myself to your service in this world,
To be at your beck and never rest nor slack;
When we meet again on the other side,
In the same coin you shall pay me back.

FAUST.   The other side gives me little trouble;
First batter this present world to rubble,
Then the other may rise—if that's the plan.
This earth is where my springs of joy have started,
And this sun shines on me when broken-hearted;
If I can first from them be parted,
Then let happen what will and can!
I wish to hear no more about it—
Whether there too men hate and love
Or whether in those spheres too, in the future,
There is a Below or an Above.

MEPHISTOPHELES.   With such an outlook you can risk it.
Sign on the line! In these next days you will get
Ravishing samples of my arts;
I am giving you what never man saw yet.

FAUST.   Poor devil, can *you* give anything ever?
Was a human spirit in its high endeavor
Even once understood by one of your breed?
Have you got food which fails to feed?
Or red gold which, never at rest,
Like mercury runs away through the hand?
A game at which one never wins?

---

[35] Without charge, free.

A girl who, even when on my breast,
Pledges herself to my neighbor with her eyes?
The divine and lovely delight of honor
Which falls like a falling star and dies?
Show me the fruits which, before they are plucked, decay
And the trees which day after day renew their green!

MEPHISTOPHELES.   Such a commission doesn't alarm me,
I have such treasures to purvey.
But, my good friend, the time draws on when we
Should be glad to feast at our ease on something good.

FAUST.   If ever I stretch myself on a bed of ease,
Then I am finished! Is that understood?
If ever your flatteries can coax me
To be pleased with myself, if ever you cast
A spell of pleasure that can hoax me—
Then let *that* day be my last!
That's my wager!

MEPHISTOPHELES.   Done!

FAUST.   Let's shake!
If ever I say to the passing moment
'Linger a while! Thou art so fair!'
Then you may cast me into fetters,
I will gladly perish then and there!
Then you may set the death-bell tolling,
Then from my service you are free,
The clock may stop, its hand may fall,
And that be the end of time for me!

MEPHISTOPHELES.   Think what you're saying, we shall not forget it.

FAUST.   And you are fully within your rights;
I have made no mad or outrageous claim.
If I stay as I am, I am a slave—
Whether yours or another's, it's all the same.

MEPHISTOPHELES.   I shall this very day at the College Banquet
Enter your service with no more ado,
But just one point—As a life-and-death insurance
I must trouble you for a line or two.

FAUST.   So you, you pedant, you too like things in writing?
Have you never known a man? Or a man's word? Never?
Is it not enough that my word of mouth
Puts all my days in bond for ever?

Does not the world rage on in all its streams
And shall a promise hamper *me?*
Yet this illusion reigns within our hearts
And from it who would be gladly free?
Happy the man who can inwardly keep his word;
Whatever the cost, he will not be loath to pay!
But a parchment, duly inscribed and sealed,
Is a bogey from which all wince away.
The word dies on the tip of the pen
And wax and leather lord it then.
What do you, evil spirit, require?
Bronze, marble, parchment, paper?
Quill or chisel or pencil of slate?
You may choose whichever you desire.

MEPHISTOPHELES.   How can you so exaggerate
With such a hectic rhetoric?
Any little snippet is quite good—
And you sign it with one little drop of blood.

FAUST.   If that is enough and is some use,
One may as well pander to your fad.

MEPHISTOPHELES.   Blood is a very special juice.

FAUST.   Only do not fear that I shall break this contract.
What I promise is nothing more
Than what all my powers are striving for.
I have puffed myself up too much, it is only
Your sort that really fits my case.
The great Earth Spirit has despised me
And Nature shuts the door in my face.
The thread of thought is snapped asunder,
I have long loathed knowledge in all its fashions.
In the depths of sensuality
Let us now quench our glowing passions!
And at once make ready every wonder
Of unpenetrated sorcery!
Let us cast ourselves into the torrent of time,
Into the whirl of eventfulness,
Where disappointment and success,
Pleasure and pain may chop and change
As chop and change they will and can;
It is restless action makes the man.

MEPHISTOPHELES.   No limit is fixed for you, no bound;
    If you'd like to nibble at everything
    Or to seize upon something flying round—
    Well, may you have a run for your money!
    But seize your chance and don't be funny!
FAUST.   I've told you, it is no question of happiness.
    The most painful joy, enamored hate, enlivening
    Disgust—I devote myself to all excess.
    My breast, now cured of its appetite for knowledge,
    From now is open to all and every smart,
    And what is allotted to the whole of mankind
    That will I sample in my inmost heart,
    Grasping the highest and lowest with my spirit,
    Piling men's weal and woe upon my neck,
    To extend myself to embrace all human selves
    And to founder in the end, like them, a wreck.
MEPHISTOPHELES.   O believe *me,* who have been chewing
    These iron rations many a thousand year,
    No human being can digest
    This stuff, from the cradle to the bier.
    This universe—believe a devil—
    Was made for no one but a god!
    He exists in eternal light
    But *us* he has brought into the darkness
    While *your* sole portion is day and night.

• • •

[Shortly thereafter, Faust and Mephistopheles set out on their journey, with
Mephistopheles acting as the guide, hoping to introduce Faust to the pleasures of life. The first stop on their way is Auerbach's Keller in Leipzig, a
tavern, where Faust and Mephistopheles join a company of jolly wine-bib-
bers. However, Faust finds that he has nothing in common with these people, their crude jokes, and primitive pleasures. Apparently, his lifelong
preoccupation with learning has deadened him to the pleasures of his senses.
To revive his sensuality and at the same time to rejuvenate him, Faust is
taken by Mephistopheles to the kitchen of a witch, who prepares a brew for
him. Obviously, Mephistopheles knows the potency of this brew, because
when Faust drinks it, the devil mutters:

    "With a drink like this in you, take care—
    You'll soon see Helens [36] everywhere."

[36] Helen of Troy, the ideal of feminine beauty.

Thanks to Mephistopheles's scheming, the opportunity for Faust to meet his "Helen" is close at hand. *Ed.*]

IN THE STREET

    (*Faust accosts Gretchen as she passes*)
FAUST.   My pretty young lady, might I venture
    To offer you my arm and my escort too?
GRETCHEN.   I'm not a young lady[37] nor am I pretty
    And I can get home without help from you.
    (*She releases herself and goes off*)
FAUST.   By Heaven, she's beautiful, this child!
    I have never seen her parallel.
    So decorous, so virtuous,
    And just a little pert as well.
    The light of her cheek, her lip so red,
    I shall remember till I'm dead!
    The way that she cast down her eye
    Is stamped on my heart as with a die;
    And the way that she got rid of me
    Was a most ravishing thing to see!
    (*Enter Mephistopheles*)
    Listen to me! Get me that girl!
MEPHISTOPHELES.   Which one?
FAUST.   The one that just went past.
MEPHISTOPHELES.   She? She was coming from her priest,
    Absolved from her sins one and all;
    I'd crept up near the confessional.
    An innocent thing. Innocent? Yes!
    At church with nothing to confess!
    Over that girl I have no power.
FAUST.   Yet she's fourteen if she's an hour.
MEPHISTOPHELES.   Why, you're talking like Randy Dick
    Who covets every lovely flower
    And all the favors, all the laurels,
    He fancies are for him to pick;
    But it doesn't always work out like that.
FAUST.   My dear Professor of Ancient Morals,
    Spare me your trite morality!

[37] The title "lady" was restricted to women belonging to nobility.

I tell you straight—and hear me right—
Unless this object of delight
Lies in my arms this very night,
At midnight we part company.

MEPHISTOPHELES.   Haven't you heard: more haste less speed?
A fortnight is the least I need
Even to work up an occasion.

FAUST.   If I had only seven hours clear,
I should not need the devil here
To bring *this* quest to consummation.

MEPHISTOPHELES.   It's almost French, your line of talk;
I only ask you not to worry.
Why make your conquest in a hurry?
The pleasure is less by a long chalk
Than when you first by hook and by crook
Have squeezed your doll and moulded her,
Using all manner of poppycock
That foreign novels keep in stock.

FAUST.   I am keen enough without all that.

MEPHISTOPHELES.   Now, joking apart and without aspersion,
You cannot expect, I tell you flat,
This beautiful child in quick reversion.
Immune to all direct attack—
We must lay our plots behind her back.

FAUST.   Get me something of my angel's!
Carry me to her place of rest!
Get me a garter of my love's!
Get me a kerchief from her breast!

MEPHISTOPHELES.   That you may see the diligent fashion
In which I shall abet your passion,
We won't let a moment waste away,
I will take you to her room to-day.

FAUST.   And shall I see her? Have her?

MEPHISTOPHELES.   No!
She will be visiting a neighbor.
But you in the meanwhile, quite alone,
Can stay in her aura [38] in her room
And feast your fill on joys to come.

---

[38] Surrounding atmosphere.

FAUST   Can we go now?

MEPHISTOPHELES.   It is still too soon.

FAUST.   Then a present for her! Get me one!
   (*Exit Faust*)

MEPHISTOPHELES.   Presents already? Fine. A certain hit!
   I know plenty of pretty places
   And of long-buried jewel-cases;
   I must take stock of them a bit.

• • •

[Faust succeeds in wooing Gretchen, last but not least, thanks to gifts of precious jewels supplied by Mephistopheles. Mephistopheles also arranges to have Faust and Gretchen date secretly in the garden of a neighbor woman— that is, without the knowledge of Gretchen's mother and brother Valentine. Mephistopheles tricks the neighbor woman, Mrs. Martha Schwerdtlein, supposedly a widow, into opening her house to him and Faust by pretending to be romantically interested in her. *Ed.*]

MARTHA'S GARDEN

GRETCHEN.   Promise me, Heinrich! [39]

FAUST.   If I can!

GRETCHEN.   Tell me: how do you stand in regard to religion?
   You are indeed a good, good man
   But I think you give it scant attention.

FAUST.   Leave that, my child! You feel what I feel for you;
   For those I love I would give my life and none
   Will I deprive of his sentiments and his church.

GRETCHEN.   That is not right; one must believe thereon.

FAUST.   Must one?

GRETCHEN.   If only I had some influence!
   Nor do you honor the holy sacraments.

FAUST.   I honor them.

GRETCHEN.   Yes, but not with any zest.
   When were you last at mass, when were you last confessed?
   Do you believe in God?

FAUST.   My darling, who dare say:
   I believe in God?

[39] Heinrich (Henry), Faust's first name as given by Goethe; the character's first name in the legend was Johann (John).

Ask professor or priest,
Their answers will make an odd
Mockery of you.

GRETCHEN.   You don't believe, you mean?

FAUST.   Do not misunderstand me, my love, my queen!
Who can name him?
Admit on the spot:
I believe in him?
And who can dare
To perceive and declare:
I believe in him not?
The All-Embracing One,
All-Upholding One,
Does he not embrace, uphold,
You, me, Himself?
Does not the Heaven vault itself above us?
Is not the earth established fast below?
And with their friendly glances do not
Eternal stars rise over us?
Do not my eyes look into yours,
And all things thrust
Into your head, into your heart,
And weave in everlasting mystery
Invisibly, visibly, around you?
Fill your heart with *this,* great as it is,
And when this feeling grants you perfect bliss,
Then call it what you will—
Happiness! Heart! Love! God!
I have no name for it!
Feeling is all;
Name is mere sound and reek [40]
Clouding Heaven's light.

GRETCHEN.   That sounds quite good and right;
And much as the priest might speak,
Only not word for word.

FAUST.   It is what all hearts have heard
In all the places heavenly day can reach,

[40] Smoke and vapor.

Each in his own speech;
Why not I in mine?

GRETCHEN.   I could almost accept it, you make it sound so fine,
Still there is something in it that shouldn't be;
For you have no Christianity.

FAUST.   Dear child!

• • •

GRETCHEN.   Now I must go.

FAUST.   Oh, can I never rest
One little hour hanging upon your breast,
Pressing both breast on breast and soul on soul?

GRETCHEN.   Ah, if I only slept alone!
I'd gladly leave the door unlatched for you to-night;
My mother, however, sleeps so light
And if she found us there, I own
I should fall dead upon the spot.

FAUST.   You angel, there is no fear of that.
Here's a little flask. Three drops are all
It needs—in her drink—to cover nature
In a deep sleep, a gentle pall.[41]

GRETCHEN.   What would I not do for your sake!
I hope it will do her no injury.

FAUST.   My love, do you think that of me?

GRETCHEN.   Dearest, I've only to look at you
And I do not know what drives me to meet your will
I have already done so much for you
That little more is left me to fulfil.

• • •

[The drops that were supposed to afford Gretchen's mother a deep and restful sleep do their job only too well—they dispatch the old woman into everlasting slumber. It is not long until it is rumored in town that virtuous Gretchen has a lover. On a certain night, Gretchen's brother, Valentine, a soldier, who feels greatly shamed by the rumor, hides under his sister's window to catch the villain who supposedly sneaks into Gretchen's room. As Faust and Mephistopheles arrive, Valentine draws his sword. But Mephistopheles causes Valentine's hand to go suddenly lame, allowing Faust to

---

[41] Cloak (of slumber).

deliver the fatal stab. Some time before the murder of her brother, Gretchen
learns that she is pregnant, a discovery that evokes great anxiety in her and
sends her into moments of deep depression. When her child is born, Gretchen, in a fit of despair and mental derangement, drowns it in a pond near
the village. Accused of murder, she is thrown into a dungeon. Faust, having
learned of her plight, and with the help Mephistopheles, sets out to rescue
her. *Ed.*]

DUNGEON

    (*Faust with a bunch of keys and a lamp, in front of an iron door*)
FAUST.   A long unwonted trembling seizes me,
    The woe of all mankind seizes me fast.
    It is here she lives, behind these dripping walls,
    Her crime was but a dream too good to last!
    And *you* Faust, waver at the door?
    You fear to see your love once more?
    Go in at once—or her hope of life is past.
    (*He tries the key. Gretchen starts singing inside*)
GRETCHEN.   My mother, the whore,
    Who took my life!
    My father, the rogue,
    Who ate my flesh!
    My little sister
    My bones did lay
    In a cool, cool glen;
    And there I turned to a pretty little wren;
    Fly away! Fly away!
    (*Faust opens the lock*)
FAUST.   She does not suspect that her lover is listening—
    To the chains clanking, the straw rustling.
    (*He enters*)
GRETCHEN.   Oh! They come! O death! It's hard! Hard!
FAUST.   Quiet! I come to set you free.
    (*She throws herself at his feet*)
GRETCHEN.   If you are human, feel my misery.
FAUST.   Do not cry out—you will wake the guard.
    (*He takes hold of the chains to unlock them*)
GRETCHEN (*on her knees*).   Who has given you this power,
    Hangman, so to grieve me?

To fetch me at his midnight hour!
Have pity! Oh reprieve me!
Will to-morrow not serve when the bells are rung?
(*She gets up*)
I am still so young, I am still so young!
Is my death so near?
I was pretty too, that was what brought me here.
My lover was by, he's far to-day;
My wreath[42] lies torn, my flowers have been thrown away.
Don't seize on me so violently!
What have I done to you? Let me be!
Let me not vainly beg and implore;
You know I have never seen you before.

FAUST.   Can I survive this misery?

GRETCHEN.   I am now completely in your power.
Only let me first suckle my child.
This night I cherished it, hour by hour;
To torture me they took it away
And now I murdered it, so they say.
And I shall never be happy again.
People make ballads about me—the heartless crew!
An old story ends like this—
Must mine too?
(*Faust throws himself on the ground*)

FAUST.   Look! At your feet a lover lies
To loose you from your miseries.
(*Gretchen throws herself beside him*)

GRETCHEN.   O, let us call on the saints on bended knee!
Beneath these steps—but see—
Beneath this sill
The cauldron of Hell!
And within,
The Evil One in his fury
Raising a din!

FAUST.   Gretchen! Gretchen!

GRETCHEN.   That was my lover's voice!
(*She springs up; the chains fall off*)

---

[42] The bridal wreath, made of dainty flowers and greenery, crowned the bride's head as a symbol of purity. Pregnant or formerly married brides were denied such adornment.

I heard him calling. Where can he be?
No one shall stop me. I am free!
Quick! My arms round his neck!
And lie upon his bosom! Quick!
He called 'Gretchen!' He stood at the door.
Through the whole of Hell's racket and roar,
Through the threats and jeers and from far beyond
I heard that voice so sweet, so fond.

FAUST.   It is I!

GRETCHEN.   It's you? Oh say so once again!
(*She clasps him*)
It is! It is! Where now is all my pain?
And where the anguish of my captivity?
It's you; you have come to rescue me!
I am saved!
The street is back with me straight away
Where I saw you that first day,
And the happy garden too
Where Martha and I awaited you.

FAUST.   Come! Come!

GRETCHEN.   Oh stay with me, oh do!
Where *you* stay, I would like to, too.

FAUST.   Hurry!
If you don't,
The penalty will be sore.

GRETCHEN.   What! Can you kiss no more?
So short an absence, dear, as this
And you've forgotten how to kiss!
Why do I feel so afraid, clasping your neck?
In the old days your words, your looks,
Were a heavenly flood I could not check
And you kissed me as if you would smother me—
Kiss me now!
Or I'll kiss you!
(*She kisses him*)
Oh your lips are cold as stone!
And dumb!
What has become
Of your love?
Who has robbed me of my own?

(She turns away from him)

FAUST.   Come! Follow me, my love! Be bold!
   I will cherish you after a thousandfold.
   Only follow me now! That is all I ask of you.
GRETCHEN.   And is it you then? Really? Is it true?
FAUST.   It is! But come!
GRETCHEN.   You are undoing each chain,
   You take me to your arms again.
   How comes it you are not afraid of me?
   Do you know, my love, *whom* you are setting free?
FAUST.   Come! The deep night is passing by and beyond.
GRETCHEN.   My mother, I have murdered her;
   I drowned my child in the pond.
   Was it not a gift to you and me?
   To you too—You! Are you what you seem?
   Give me your hand! It is not a dream!
   Your dear hand—but, oh, it's wet!
   Wipe it off! I think
   There is blood [43] on it.
   Oh God! What have you done?
   Put up your sword,
   I beg you to.

· · ·

FAUST.   Collect yourself!
   One step—just one—and you are free.
GRETCHEN.   If only we were past the hill!
   There sits my mother on a stone—
   My brain goes cold and dead—
   There sits my mother on a stone—
   And wags and wags her head.
   No sign, no nod, her head is such a weight
   She'll wake no more, she slept so late.
   She slept that we might sport and play.
   What a time that was of holiday!
FAUST.   If prayer and argument are no resource,
   I will risk saving you by force.
GRETCHEN.   No! I will have no violence! Let me go!

[43] The blood of Gretchen's brother Valentine.

Don't seize me in that murderous grip!
I have done everything else for you, you know.

FAUST.   My love! My love! The day is dawning!

GRETCHEN.   Day! Yes, it's growing day! The last day breaks on me!
My wedding day it was to be!
Tell no one you had been before with Gretchen.
Alas for my garland!
There's no more chance!
We shall meet again—
But not at the dance.
The people are thronging—but silently;
Street and square
Cannot hold them there.
The bell tolls—it tolls for *me*.
How they seize me, bind me, like a slave!
Already I'm swept away to the block.
Already there jabs at every neck,
The sharp blade which jabs at mine.
The world lies mute as the grave.

FAUST.   I wish I had never been born!

(*Mephistopheles appears outside*)

MEPHISTOPHELES.   Away! Or you are lost.
Futile wavering! Waiting and prating!
My horses are shivering,
The dawn's at the door.

GRETCHEN.   What rises up from the floor?
It's he! Send him away! It's he!
What does he want in the holy place?
It is I he wants!

FAUST.   You shall live!

GRETCHEN.   Judgment of God! I have given myself to Thee!

MEPHISTOPHELES (*to Faust*).   Come! Or I'll leave you both in the
lurch.

GRETCHEN.   O Father, save me! I am Thine!
You angels! Hosts of the Heavenly Church,
Guard me, stand round in serried line!
Heinrich! I shudder to look at you.

MEPHISTOPHELES.   She is condemned!

VOICE FROM ABOVE.   Redeemed!

MEPHISTOPHELES.   Follow me!
   (*He vanishes with Faust*)
VOICE (*from within, dying away*).   Heinrich! Heinrich!

PART II

[Part II, even much more than Part I, is a continuous and rapid succession of images, people, and problems. At the beginning of this part of the drama we learn that Faust took up services with the "Emperor," which, however, did not usher in better days, but rather caused upheavals and climaxed in war. As a reward for these services the Emperor gave Faust a useless stretch of land near the sea—a swamp, to be precise. Next, Faust entered the world of classical Greece where, with beautiful Helen, he sired a son, Euphorion. Like the mythological Icarus, Euphorion rose into the air and then perished when he suddenly fell to the ground. Faust's former assistant, Wagner—now a scientist in his own right, returns in Part II. He has succeeded in creating Homunculus, an artificial man, by means of chemistry and fire. Near the close of the drama, Faust, blinded by age and nearly one hundred years old, sets out to shore up his own domain by draining the very swamp he received from the Emperor. Mephistopheles supplies him with cheap labor, so-called Lemurs, "half-alives patched up with thin sinews and skulls and femurs." [44] While the Lemurs are actually digging a grave for his body, Faust imagines that they are building an earthen dam to protect his land from the sea. *Ed.*]

FAUST (*blinded*).   The night seems pressing in more thickly, thickly,
   Yet in my inmost heart a light shines clear;
   What I have planned, I must complete it quickly;
   Only the master's word is weighty here.
   Up and to work, my men! Each man of you!
   And bring my bold conception to full view.
   Take up your tools and toil with pick and spade!
   What has been outlined must at once be *made*.
   Good order, active diligence,
   Ensure the fairest recompense;
   That this vast work completion find,
   A thousand hands need but one mind.
MEPHISTOPHELES (*leading the way, as foreman*).   Come on, come on!
   Come in, come in!

[44] Thigh-bones.

You gangling gang of Lemurs,
You half-alives patched up with thin
Sinews and skulls and femurs.

LEMURS (*in chorus*).   You call us, here we are at hand;
And, as we understand it,
We stand to win a stretch of land
Intended as our mandate.

Our pointed staves we have them here,
Our chain to measure sections,
But why you called on us, we fear,
Has slipped our recollections.

MEPHISTOPHELES.   Artistic efforts we can spare;
And just let each one's nature guide him!
Let now the longest lie his length down there,
You others prise away the turf beside him;
As for your forebears long asleep,
Dig you an oblong, long and deep.
To narrow house from palace hall
Is such a stupid way to end it all.

(*The Lemurs begin to dig, with mocking gestures*)

LEMURS.   When I was young and lived and loved,
Methought it was passing sweet;
In the merry rout and roundabout
There would I twirl my feet.

But sneaking Age has upped his crutch
And downed me unaware;
I stumbled over the door of the grave—
Why was it open *there*?

FAUST (*groping his way*).   Oh how this clink of spades rejoices me!
For that is my conscripted labor,
The earth is now her own good neighbor
And sets the waves a boundary—
Confinement strict and strenuous.

MEPHISTOPHELES (*aside*).   And yet you've only toiled for *us*
With all your damning, all your dyking—
Spreading a feast to Neptune's liking
To glut that water-demon's maw.[45]
In all respects you're lost and stranded,

[45] Stomach.

The elements with us have banded—
Annihilation is the law.

FAUST.   Foreman!

MEPHISTOPHELES.   Here!

FAUST.   Use every means you can;
Bring all your gangs up and exhort them—
Threaten them if you like or court them—
But pay or woo or force each man!
And day by day send word to me, assessing
How my intended earthworks are progressing.

MEPHISTOPHELES (*half aloud*).   The word to-day, from what I've heard,
Is not 'intended' but 'interred'.

FAUST.   A swamp along the mountains' flank
Makes all my previous gains contaminate;
My deeds, if I could drain this sink,
Would culminate as well as terminate:
To open to the millions living space,
Not danger-proof but free to run their race.
Green fields and fruitful; men and cattle hiving
Upon this newest earth at once and thriving,
Settled at once beneath this sheltering hill
Heaped by the masses' brave and busy skill.
With such a heavenly land behind this hedge,
The sea beyond may bluster to its edge
And, as it gnaws to swamp the work of masons,
To stop the gap one common impulse hastens.
Aye! Wedded to this concept like a wife,
I find this wisdom's final form:
He only earns his freedom and his life
Who takes them every day by storm.
And so a man, beset by dangers here,
As child, man, old man, spends his manly year.
Oh to see such activity,
Treading free ground with people that are free!
Then could I bid the passing moment:
'Linger a while, thou art so fair!' [46]

---

[46] Legalists will forever debate whether or not Faust lost the bet because, when he spoke these fateful words (see Part I, page 294), he beheld a vision, rather than reality.

The traces of my earthly days can never
Sink in the aeons [47] unaware.
And I, who feel ahead such heights of bliss,
At last enjoy my highest moment—this.
(*Faust sinks back* [*and dies*]; *the Lemurs seize him and lay him on the
ground*)

MEPHISTOPHELES.   By no joy sated, filled by no success,
  Still whoring after shapes that flutter past,
  This last ill moment of sheer emptiness—
  The poor man yearns to hold it fast.
  He who withstood me with such strength,
  Time masters him and here he lies his length.
  The clock stands still—

CHORUS.   Stands still! Like
  midnight . . . silent . . . stilled.
  Its hand drops down.

MEPHISTOPHELES.   Drops down; it is fulfilled.

LEMURS.   It is gone by.

MEPHISTOPHELES.   Gone by! A stupid phrase.
  Why say gone by?
  Gone by—pure naught—complete monotony.
  What use these cycles of creation!
  Or snatching off the creatures to negation!
  'It is gone by!'—and we can draw the inference:
  If it had *not* been, it would make no difference;
  The wheel revolves the same, no more, no less.
  I should prefer eternal emptiness.

                             •   •   •

MEPHISTOPHELES.   Here lies the corpse and if the soul would flee
  At once I show the bond, the blood-signed scroll;
  Though now, alas, they have so many means
  To cheat the devil of a soul.
  Our old procedure gives offense,
  Our new has not yet found endorsement;
  Once I'd have managed it alone,
  Now I must look for reinforcement.
  Come up, you devils! Make it double quick!

[47] Ages.

You straight-horned peers and crooked-horned as well,
You old and sterling devil-stock,
Come up—and bring with you the jaws of Hell!
(*The Jaws of Hell open upon the left*)
The eye-teeth gape; the throat's enormous vault
Spews forth a raging fiery flow
And through the smoking cyclone of the gullet
I see the infernal city's eternal glow.
You do right well to make the sinner quake;
And yet they think it all a dream, a fake.
Now, devils, watch this body! How does it seem?
See if you see a phosphorescent gleam.
That is the little soul, Psyche with wings—
Pull out her wings and it's a noisome worm;
With my own seal I'll set my stamp upon her,
Then forth with her into the fiery storm!
Come, claw and comb the air, strain every nerve
To catch her though she flutter, though she swerve.
To stay in her old lodging gives her pain;
The genius is about to leave the brain.
(*Glory, from above, on the right*)

THE HOST OF HEAVEN.   Fly, as directed,
    Heaven's elected,
    Serenely whereby
    Sin shall have pardon,
    Dust become garden;
    Stay your progression,
    Make intercession,
    Trace for all natures
    A path to the sky.

MEPHISTOPHELES.   Discords I hear, a filthy strumming tumbling
    Down from the sky with the unwelcome day;
    That is the angels' boyish-girlish fumbling,
    Their canting taste *likes* it to sound that way.
    You know how we, in hours of deep damnation,
    Have schemed annihilation for mankind;
    Those angels use for adoration
    The greatest stigma[48] we could find.

---

[48] Mark of shame.

They come so fawningly, the milksops!
They've kidnapped many souls before our eyes,
They fight us back with our own weapons;
They too are devils—in disguise.
Defeat to-day would mean disgrace eternal;
So stand around the grave and stand infernal![49]

*   *   *

ANGEL.   See, we approach—why do you shrink away?
     We come; if you can face us—why, then, stay!
     (*The Angels, closing in, occupy all the space*)
CHOIR OF ANGELS.   Flames of dear feeling,
     Rise beyond seeing!
     Self-condemned being—
     Truth be its healing!
     Blessed transition
     Forth from perdition,[50]
     Into Eternity,
     Into the One!
MEPHISTOPHELES (*collecting himself*).   Look! The damned flames are
   out that caused my fall.
     Now I become myself and curse you one and all!
CHOIR OF ANGELS.   Light of Creation!
     Whom it embraces
     Finds all the graces
     Found in salvation.
     Praising in unison
     Rise to your goal!
     Purged is the air now—
     Breathe now the soul!
     (*They soar up, carrying away the immortal part of Faust*)
MEPHISTOPHELES (*looking around him*).   But how is this? Where have
   they moved away to?
     You juveniles, to take me by surprise!
     Flying off heavenwards—and with my prey too;
     They nibbled at this grave to win this prize.
     Wresting from me a great and matchless treasure,
     That noble soul which gave me right of seizure

---

[49] Immovable.
[50] Eternal damnation.

They've filched by throwing rose-dust in my eyes.
Who is there now to lend an ear to
My wrong, restore my hard-earned right?
You have been hoaxed—so late in your career too—
It's your own fault, you're in a lurid[51] plight.
Such gross mismanagement—outrageous!
Such a great outlay squandered! Oh the shame!
Erotic folly, vulgar lust, contagious
To an old devil at the game!
Experience has indulged its appetite
On such a childish-foolish level;
When all is said, the folly is not slight
Which in the end has seized the devil.

• • •

ANGELS (*floating in the higher air, carrying the immortal part of Faust*).   Saved, saved now is that precious part
Of our spirit world from evil:
'Should a man strive with all his heart,
Heaven can foil the devil.'
And if love also from on high
Has helped him through his sorrow,
The hallowed legions of the sky
Will give him glad good morrow.

• • •

[51] Horrible.

15

Romantic Poetry

Romanticism, an intellectual style that flourished in the Western world from about 1780 to 1850, was generally based on a faith in the value of the unseen and the ability of human beings to discover and express hidden truth by the use of imagination, emotion, and inspiration. Great art, in the romantic credo, was the expression, in new, appropriate language, of the basic moral and aesthetic, rather than factual, truths that would bring happiness to human beings. Specifically, this imaginative faith held to a belief in the surpassing goodness and glory of physical nature, in the primacy of the individual, and in the truth of the individual's subjective feelings. Romanticism was, at the same time, fascinated with the remote in space and time, with the dramatic and violent, and with the melancholy and terrible. Along with these affirmations, the romantics rejected the world as it was and rebelled against the social, intellectual, and aesthetic standards of their time.

Lyric poetry was the greatest literary expression of romanticism, and it has seldom been equaled in color, sensuousness, and imaginative scope. For the romantic rebels, the poem was an organic whole, expressing more than any paraphrase, and to be grasped only in terms of the unique world it had created. The poem sprang from the individual creator's mystical experience and had no basis in common social discourse.

The three poems reprinted below are prime examples of romantic lyric poetry. "Lines Composed a Few Miles Above Tintern Abbey" (1798), by William Wordsworth (1770–1850), reflects the poet's lifelong conviction that truth and joy lay in the union of the individual with external nature and that this experience could be made clear to others in artistic, symbolic forms. The

William Wordsworth, "Lines Composed a Few Miles Above Tintern Abbey," in *The Poetical Works of William Wordsworth* (Boston: Houghton, Osgood, 1880), II, 186–91.

poem itself is a quiet meditation expressed in smooth, rolling phrases of blank verse. It describes the development of the poet's responses to nature, from childhood experiences of it to a culminating religious communion with its beauty and harmony.

"Ode on a Grecian Urn," by John Keats (1795–1821), has as its themes art and life. Written in 1820, near the end of the short, tragic life of the poet, it is an example of his self-discipline and craftsmanship as well as his sensuous appeal and richness of color and forms. Keats finds, in the scenes of life carved on an ancient urn, an expression of transcendent art that resolved the paradoxes of the arrested action: the life in death, past and present, poetry and reality, beauty and truth.

The third poem is by Walt Whitman (1819–1892), a great American poet, robust man of the people, and romantic rebel. In the free-flowing verse and large rhythms of "Out of the Cradle Endlessly Rocking" (1859), he recaptures the intense melancholy of the childhood experience of lost love. This memory calls him to a poetic destiny whose fulfillment is death, which he joyfully hails as the continuum of life.

WILLIAM WORDSWORTH

Lines Composed a Few Miles Above Tintern Abbey,[1] on Revisiting the Banks of the Wye During a Tour. July 13, 1798

Five years have past; five summers, with the length
Of five long winters! and again I hear
These waters, rolling from their mountain-springs
With a soft inland murmur.—Once again
Do I behold these steep and lofty cliffs,
That on a wild, secluded scene impress
Thoughts of more deep seclusion, and connect
The landscape with the quiet of the sky.
The day is come when I again repose
Here, under this dark sycamore, and view

---

[1] A medieval monastery, whose ruins are found on a wooded hillside of the River Wye, about ten miles from its mouth. The river rises from springs in the mountains of Wales and flows southeasterly to the Bristol Channel.

These plots of cottage-ground, these orchard-tufts,
Which at this season, with their unripe fruits,
Are clad in one green hue, and lose themselves
'Mid groves and copses. Once again I see
These hedge-rows, hardly hedge-rows, little lines
Of sportive wood run wild: these pastoral farms,
Green to the very door; and wreaths of smoke
Sent up, in silence, from among the trees!
With some uncertain notice, as might seem
Of vagrant dwellers in the houseless woods,
Or of some Hermit's cave, where by his fire
The Hermit sits alone.
These beauteous forms,
Through a long absence, have not been to me
As is a landscape to a blind man's eye:
But oft, in lonely rooms, and 'mid the din
Of towns and cities, I have owed to them,
In hours of weariness, sensations sweet,
Felt in the blood, and felt along the heart;
And passing even into my purer mind,
With tranquil restoration:—feelings too
Of unremembered pleasure: such, perhaps,
As have no slight or trivial influence
On the best portion of a good man's life,
His little, nameless, unremembered acts
Of kindness and of love. Nor less, I trust,
To them I may have owed another gift,
Of aspect more sublime: that blessed mood,
In which the burden of the mystery,
In which the heavy and the weary weight
Of all this unintelligible world,
Is lightened:—that serene and blessed mood,
In which the affections gently lead us on,—
Until, the breath of this corporeal frame
And even the motion of our human blood
Almost suspended, we are laid asleep
In body, and become a living soul:
While with an eye made quiet by the power
Of harmony, and the deep power of joy,
We see into the life of things!

If this
Be but a vain belief, yet, oh! how oft—
In darkness and amid the many shapes
Of joyless daylight; when the fretful stir
Unprofitable, and the fever of the world,
Have hung upon the beatings of my heart—
How oft, in spirit, have I turned to thee,
O sylvan Wye! thou wanderer through the woods,
How often has my spirit turned to thee!

   And now, with gleams of half-extinguished thought,
With many recognitions dim and faint,
And somewhat of a sad perplexity,
The picture of the mind revives again:
While here I stand, not only with the sense
Of present pleasure, but with pleasing thoughts
That in this moment there is life and food
For future years. And so I dare to hope,
Though changed, no doubt, from what I was when first
I came among these hills; when like a roe
I bounded o'er the mountains, by the sides
Of the deep rivers, and the lonely streams,
Wherever nature led: more like a man
Flying from something that he dreads, than one
Who sought the thing he loved. For nature then
(The coarser pleasures of my boyish days
And their glad animal movements all gone by)
To me was all in all.—I cannot paint
What then I was. The sounding cataract
Haunted me like a passion: the tall rock,
The mountain, and the deep and gloomy wood,
Their colors and their forms, were then to me
An appetite; a feeling and a love,
That had no need of a remoter charm
By thoughts supplied, nor any interest
Unborrowed from the eye.—That time is past,
And all its aching joys are now no more,
And all its dizzy raptures. Not for this
Faint I, nor mourn nor murmur; other gifts
Have followed; for such loss, I would believe,

Abundant recompense. For I have learned
To look on nature, not as in the hour
Of thoughtless youth; but hearing oftentimes
The still, sad music of humanity,
Nor harsh nor grating, though of ample power
To chasten and subdue. And I have felt
A presence that disturbs me with the joy
Of elevated thoughts; a sense sublime
Of something far more deeply interfused,
Whose dwelling is the light of setting suns,
And the round ocean, and the living air,
And the blue sky, and in the mind of man:
A motion and a spirit, that impels
All thinking things, all objects of all thought,
And rolls through all things. Therefore am I still
A lover of the meadows and the woods,
And mountains; and of all that we behold
From this green earth; of all the mighty world
Of eye, and ear,—both what they half create,
And what perceive; well pleased to recognize
In nature and the language of the sense,
The anchor of my purest thoughts, the nurse,
The guide, the guardian of my heart, and soul
Of all my moral being.
                              Nor perchance,
If I were not thus taught, should I the more
Suffer my genial spirits to decay:
For thou art with me here upon the banks
Of this fair river; thou my dearest Friend,
My dear, dear Friend; and in thy voice I catch
The language of my former heart, and read
My former pleasures in the shooting lights
Of thy wild eyes. O yet a little while
May I behold in thee what I was once,
My dear, dear Sister! and this prayer I make,
Knowing that Nature never did betray
The heart that loved her; 'tis her privilege,
Through all the years of this our life, to lead
From joy to joy: for she can so inform
The mind that is within us, so impress

With quietness and beauty, and so feed
With lofty thoughts, that neither evil tongues,
Rash judgments, nor the sneers of selfish men,
Nor greetings where no kindness is, nor all
The dreary intercourse of daily life,
Shall e'er prevail against us, or disturb
Our cheerful faith, that all which we behold
Is full of blessings. Therefore let the moon
Shine on thee in thy solitary walk;
And let the misty mountain-winds be free
To blow against thee: and, in after years,
When these wild ecstasies shall be matured
Into a sober pleasure; when thy mind
Shall be a mansion for all lovely forms,
Thy memory be as a dwelling-place
For all sweet sounds and harmonies; O, then,
If solitude, or fear, or pain, or grief,
Should be thy portion, with what healing thoughts
Of tender joy wilt thou remember me,
And these my exhortations! Nor, perchance,—
If I should be where I no more can hear
Thy voice, nor catch from thy wild eyes these gleams
Of past existence,—wilt thou then forget
That on the banks of this delightful stream
We stood together; and that I, so long
A worshipper of Nature, hither came
Unwearied in that service: rather say
With warmer love,—O with far deeper zeal
Of holier love. Nor wilt thou then forget,
That after many wanderings, many years
Of absence, these steep woods and lofty cliffs,
And this green pastoral landscape, were to me
More dear, both for themselves and for thy sake!

JOHN KEATS

Ode on a Grecian Urn

Thou still unravish'd bride of quietness!
  Thou foster-child of Silence and slow Time,
Sylvan historian,[2] who canst thus express
  A flowery tale more sweetly than our rhyme:
What leaf-fringed legend haunts about thy shape
  Of deities or mortals, or of both,
    In Tempe[3] or the dales of Arcady?[4]
  What men or gods are these? What maidens loath?
What mad pursuit? What struggle to escape?
    What pipes and timbrels? What wild ecstasy?

Heard melodies are sweet, but those unheard
  Are sweeter; therefore, ye soft pipes, play on;
Not to the sensual ear, but, more endear'd,
  Pipe to the spirit ditties of no tone:
Fair youth, beneath the trees, thou canst not leave
  Thy song, nor ever can those trees be bare;
    Bold Lover, never, never canst thou kiss,
Though winning near the goal—yet, do not grieve;
    She cannot fade, though thou hast not thy bliss,
  Forever wilt thou love, and she be fair!

Ah, happy, happy boughs! that cannot shed
  Your leaves, nor ever bid the Spring adieu;
And, happy melodist, unwearièd,
  Forever piping songs forever new;
More happy love! more happy, happy love!
  Forever warm and still to be enjoy'd,
    Forever panting and forever young;
All breathing human passion far above,
  That leaves a heart high sorrowful and cloy'd,
    A burning forehead, and a parching tongue.

John Keats, "Ode on a Grecian Urn," in the *Poetical Works of John Keats* (Boston: Little, Brown, 1854), 310–12.

[2] The pictures on the urn are a record of history.
[3] Valley along the Tempe River in northern Greece.
[4] The central region of the Peloponnesus (southern Greece).

Who are these coming to the sacrifice?
    To what green altar, O mysterious priest,
Lead'st thou that heifer lowing at the skies,
    And all her silken flanks with garlands drest?
What little town by river or sea-shore,
    Or mountain-built with peaceful citadel,
      Is emptied of its folk, this pious morn?
And, little town, thy streets forevermore
    Will silent be; and not a soul to tell
      Why thou art desolate, can e'er return.

O Attic[5] shape! Fair attitude! with brede[6]
    Of marble men and maidens overwrought.[7]
With forest branches and the trodden weed;
    Thou, silent form! dost tease us out of thought
As doth eternity: Cold Pastoral!
    When old age shall this generation waste,
      Thou shalt remain, in midst of other woe
Than ours, a friend to man, to whom thou say'st,
"Beauty is truth, truth beauty,"—that is all
    Ye know on earth, and all ye need to know.

WALT WHITMAN

Out of the Cradle Endlessly Rocking

Out of the cradle endlessly rocking,
Out of the mocking-bird's throat, the musical shuttle,
Out of the Ninth-month midnight,
Over the sterile sands and the fields beyond, where the child leaving
  his bed wander'd alone, bareheaded, barefoot,
Down from the shower'd halo,
Up from the mystic play of shadows twining and twisting as if they
  were alive,
Out from the patches of briers and blackberries,

[5] Classical, refined.
[6] As if interwoven, flowing.
[7] Moving around the surface of the urn.
Walt Whitman, "Out of the Cradle Endlessly Rocking," in *Leaves of Grass* (Philadelphia: McKay, 1884), 196–201.

From the memories of the bird that chanted to me,
From your memories sad brother, from the fitful risings and fallings
    I heard,
From under that yellow half-moon late-risen and swollen as if with
    tears,
From those beginning notes of yearning and love there in the mist,
From the thousand responses of my heart never to cease,
From the myriad thence-arous'd words,
From the word stronger and more delicious than any,
From such as now they start the scene revisiting,
As a flock, twittering, rising, or overhead passing,
Borne hither, ere all eludes me, hurriedly,
A man, yet by these tears a little boy again,
Throwing myself on the sand, confronting the waves,
I, chanter of pains and joys, uniter of here and hereafter,
Taking all hints to use them, but swiftly leaping beyond them,
A reminiscence sing.

Once Paumanok,[8]
When the lilac-scent was in the air and Fifth-month grass was grow-
    ing,
Up this seashore in some briers,
Two feather'd guests from Alabama, two together,
And their nest, and four light-green eggs spotted with brown,
And every day the he-bird to and fro near at hand,
And every day the she-bird crouch'd on her nest, silent, with bright
    eyes,
And every day I, a curious boy, never too close, never disturbing
    them,
Cautiously peering, absorbing, translating.

Shine! shine! shine!
Pour down your warmth, great sun!
While we bask, we two together.

Two together!
Winds blow south, or winds blow north,
Day come white, or night come black,

---

[8] The Indian name for Long Island, New York, a place which for Whitman held strong
  childhood memories.

Home, or rivers and mountains from home,
Singing all time, minding no time,
While we two keep together.

Till of a sudden,
May-be kill'd, unknown to her mate,
One forenoon the she-bird crouch'd not on the nest,
Nor return'd that afternoon, nor the next,
Nor ever appear'd again.

And thenceforward all summer in the sound of the sea,
And at night under the full of the moon in calmer weather,
Over the hoarse surging of the sea,
Or flitting from brier to brier by day,
I saw, I heard at intervals the remaining one, the he-bird,
The solitary guest from Alabama.

Blow! blow! blow!
Blow up sea-winds along Paumanok's shore;
I wait and I wait till you blow my mate to me.

Yes, when the stars glisten'd,
All night long on the prong of a moss-scallop'd stake,
Down almost amid the slapping waves,
Sat the lone singer wonderful causing tears.

He call'd on his mate,
He pour'd forth the meanings which I of all men know.

Yes my brother I know,
The rest might not, but I have treasur'd every note,
For more than once dimly down to the beach gliding,
Silent, avoiding the moonbeams, blending myself with the shadows,
Recalling now the obscure shapes, the echoes, the sounds and sights
    after their sorts,
The white arms out in the breakers tirelessly tossing,
I, with bare feet, a child, the wind wafting my hair,
Listen'd long and long.

Listen'd to keep, to sing, now translating the notes,
Following you my brother.

Soothe! soothe! soothe!
Close on its wave soothes the wave behind,

And again another behind embracing and lapping, every one close,
But my love soothes not me, not me.

Low hangs the moon, it rose late,
It is lagging—O I think it is heavy with love, with love.

O madly the sea pushes upon the land,
With love, with love.

O night! do I not see my love fluttering out among the breakers?
What is that little black thing I see there in the white?

Loud! loud! loud!
Loud I call to you, my love!
High and clear I shoot my voice over the waves,
Surely you must know who is here, is here,
You must know who I am, my love.

Low-hanging moon!
What is that dusky spot in your brown yellow?
O it is the shape, the shape of my mate!
O moon do not keep her from me any longer.

Land! land! O land!
Whichever way I turn, O I think you could give me my mate back again if
    you only would,
For I am almost sure I see her dimly whichever way I look.

O rising stars!
Perhaps the one I want so much will rise, will rise with some of you.

O throat! O trembling throat!
Sound clearer through the atmosphere!
Pierce the woods, the earth,
Somewhere listening to catch you must be the one I want.

Shake out carols!
Solitary here, the night's carols!
Carols of lonesome love! death's carols!
Carols under that lagging, yellow, waning moon!
O under that moon where she droops almost down into the sea!
O reckless despairing carols.

But soft! sink low!
Soft! let me just murmur,

And do you wait a moment you husky-nois'd sea,
For somewhere I believe I heard my mate responding to me,
So faint, I must be still, be still to listen,
But not altogether still, for then she might not come immediately to me.

Hither my love!
Here I am! here!
With this just-sustain'd note I announce myself to you,
This gentle call is for you my love, for you.

Do not be decoy'd elsewhere,
That is the whistle of the wind, it is not my voice,
That is the fluttering, the fluttering of the spray,
Those are the shadows of leaves.

O darkness! O in vain!
O I am very sick and sorrowful.

O brown halo in the sky near the moon, drooping upon the sea!
O troubled reflection in the sea!
O throat! O throbbing heart!
And I singing uselessly, uselessly all the night.

O past! O happy life! O songs of joy!
In the air, in the woods, over fields,
Loved! loved! loved! loved! loved!
But my mate no more, no more with me!
We two together no more.

The aria sinking,
All else continuing, the stars shining,
The winds blowing, the notes of the bird continuous echoing,
With angry moans the fierce old mother incessantly moaning,
On the sands of Paumanok's shore gray and rustling,
The yellow half-moon enlarged, sagging down, drooping, the face
    of the sea almost touching,
The boy ecstatic, with his bare feet the waves, with his hair the at-
    mosphere dallying,
The love in the heart long pent, now loose, now at last tumultuously
    bursting,
The aria's meaning, the ears, the soul, swiftly depositing,
The strange tears down the cheeks coursing,
The colloquy there, the trio, each uttering,

The undertone, the savage old mother incessantly crying,
To the boy's soul's questions sullenly timing, some drown'd secret
  hissing,
To the outsetting bard.

Demon or bird! (said the boy's soul),
Is it indeed toward your mate you sing? or is it really to me?
For I, that was a child, my tongue's use sleeping, now I have heard
  you,
Now in a moment I know what I am for, I awake,
And already a thousand singers, a thousand songs, clearer, louder
  and more sorrowful than yours,
A thousand warbling echoes have started to life within me, never to
  die.

O you singer solitary, singing by yourself, projecting me,
O solitary me listening, never more shall I cease perpetuating you,
Never more shall I escape, never more the reverberations,
Never more the cries of unsatisfied love be absent from me,
Never again leave me to be the peaceful child I was before what there
  in the night,
By the sea under the yellow and sagging moon,
The messenger there arous'd, the fire, the sweet hell within,
The unknown want, the destiny of me.

O give me the clew![9] (it lurks in the night here somewhere,)
O if I am to have so much, let me have more!

A word then, (for I will conquer it,)
The word final, superior to all,
Subtle, sent up—what is it?—I listen;
Are you whispering it, and have been all the time, you sea-waves?
Is that it from your liquid rims and wet sands?

Whereto answering, the sea,
Delaying not, hurrying not,
Whisper'd me through the night, and very plainly before daybreak,
Lisp'd to me the low and delicious word death,
And again death, death, death, death,

---

[9] Variant of clue.

Hissing melodious, neither like the bird nor like my arous'd child's
    heart,
But edging near as privately for me rustling at my feet,
Creeping thence steadily up to my ears and laving me softly all over,
Death, death, death, death, death.

Which I do not forget,
But fuse the song of my dusky demon and brother,
That he sang to me in the moonlight on Paumanok's gray beach,
With the thousand responsive songs at random,
My own songs awaked from that hour,
And with them the key, the word up from the waves,
The word of the sweetest song and all songs,
That strong and delicious word which, creeping to my feet,
(Or like some old crone rocking the cradle, swathed in sweet gar-
    ments, bending aside,)
The sea whisper'd me.

16

Alexis de Tocqueville
Democracy in America

Political and social democracy, as a logical extension of the principles of
liberalism, developed in the Western world in the course of the nineteenth
century and thereafter. The earliest and fullest manifestation of this concept
was the United States of America. Alexis de Tocqueville (1805–1859), a
French aristocrat, recognized this fact and, in 1830, left his minor government post under the French monarchy to visit the United States and, for some
eighteen months, see the new society at work. Ostensibly, his specific purpose was to survey the American penal system; and, indeed, he later produced a report on this subject. But the major products of his visit were the
two volumes of Democracy in America (1835, 1840), his thorough survey of American society during the Age of Jackson.

Democracy in America was well received in both Europe and America,
and it is still the best work on the subject by any European observer. More
than a scholarly travelogue, it is a shrewd and prophetic analysis of democracy in action—the practical problems and implications of social equality,
public opinion, majority rule, democratic leadership, and emerging industrialization. Tocqueville not only describes but analyzes what he observed.
He judges democratic society by the standards of a moderate, enlightened aristocrat; he appreciates the new order as the wave of the future but is troubled
by some of its aspects. Like Burke, Tocqueville values the conservative
ideals of freedom and order, but, unlike Burke, accepts the value of an open
society based on popular liberty. His central concern, therefore, is to reconcile
individual freedom with the conformity, materialism, and potential tyranny

Alexis de Tocqueville, *Democracy in America*, trans. Henry Reeve, rev. ed. (London
and New York: Colonial, 1900), I, 3, 6–7, 9–11, 13–14, 263–70; II, 11–13, 99–103,
336–37, 339–44. Adapted.

of an egalitarian order. As the following excerpts suggest, Tocqueville's solution is an enlightened and tempered self-interest on the part of individuals and the diffusion of power among many interest groups in a pluralistic system.

Among the novel objects that attracted my attention during my stay in the United States, nothing struck me more forcibly than the general equality of conditions. I readily discovered the prodigious influence which this primary fact exercises on the whole course of society, by giving a certain direction to public opinion, and a certain tenor to the laws; by imparting new maxims to the governing powers, and peculiar habits to the governed. I speedily perceived that the influence of this fact extends far beyond the political character and the laws of the country, and that it has no less empire over civil society than over the Government; it creates opinions, engenders sentiments, suggests the ordinary practices of life, and modifies whatever it does not produce. The more I advanced in the study of American society, the more I perceived that the equality of conditions is the fundamental fact from which all others seem to be derived, and the central point at which all my observations constantly terminated.

I then turned my thoughts to our own hemisphere, where I imagined that I discerned something analogous to the spectacle which the New World presented to me. I observed that the equality of conditions is daily progressing toward those extreme limits which it seems to have reached in the United States, and that the democracy which governs the American communities appears to be rapidly rising into power in Europe. I hence conceived the idea of the book which is now before the reader. . . .

Nor is this phenomenon at all peculiar to France. Wherever we turn our eyes we shall witness the same continual revolution throughout the whole of Christendom. The various occurrences of national existence have everywhere turned to the advantage of democracy; all men have aided it by their exertions: those who have intentionally labored in its cause, and those who have served it unwittingly; those who have fought for it and those who have declared themselves its opponents, have all been driven along in the same track, have all labored to one end, some ignorantly and some unwillingly; all have been blind instruments in the hands of God.

The gradual development of the equality of conditions is therefore a providential fact, and it possesses all the characteristics of a divine decree: it is universal, it is durable, it constantly eludes all human interference, and all events as well as all men contribute to its progress. Would it, then, be wise to imagine that a social impulse which dates from so far back can be checked by the efforts of a generation? Is it credible that the democracy which has annihilated the feudal system and vanquished kings will respect the citizen and the capitalist? Will it stop now that it has grown so strong and its adversaries so weak? None can say which way we are going, for all terms of comparison are wanting: the equality of conditions is more complete in the Christian countries of the present day than it has been at any time or in any part of the world; so that the extent of what already exists prevents us from foreseeing what may be yet to come.

The whole book which is here offered to the public has been written under the impression of a kind of religious dread produced in the author's mind by the contemplation of so irresistible a revolution, which has advanced for centuries in spite of such amazing obstacles, and which is still proceeding in the midst of the ruins it has made. . . .

The scene is now changed . . . ; the divisions which once severed mankind are lowered, property is divided, power is held in common, the light of intelligence spreads, and the capacities of all classes are equally cultivated; the State becomes democratic, and the empire of democracy is slowly and peaceably introduced into the institutions and the manners of the nation. I can conceive a society in which all men would profess an equal attachment and respect for the laws of which they are the common authors; in which the authority of the State would be respected as necessary, though not as divine; and the loyalty of the subject to the chief magistrate would not be a passion, but a quiet and rational persuasion. Every individual being in the possession of rights which he is sure to retain, a kind of manly reliance and reciprocal courtesy would arise between all classes, alike removed from pride and meanness. The people, well acquainted with its true interests, would allow that in order to profit by the advantages of society it is necessary to satisfy its demands. In this state of things the voluntary association of the citizens might supply the individual exertions of the nobles, and the community would be alike protected from anarchy and from oppression.

I admit that, in a democratic State thus constituted, society will not be stationary; but the impulses of the social body may be regulated and directed forwards; if there be less splendor than in the halls of an aristocracy, the contrast of misery will be less frequent also; the pleasures of enjoyment may be less excessive, but those of comfort will be more general; the sciences may be less perfectly cultivated, but ignorance will be less common; the impetuosity of the feelings will be repressed, and the habits of the nation softened; there will be more vices and fewer crimes. In the absence of enthusiasm and of an ardent faith, great sacrifices may be obtained from the members of the commonwealth by an appeal to their understandings and their experience; each individual will feel the same necessity for uniting with his fellow citizens to protect his own weakness; and as he knows that if they are to assist he must co-operate, he will readily perceive that his personal interest is identified with the interest of the community. The nation, taken as a whole, will be less brilliant, less glorious, and perhaps less strong; but the majority of the citizens will enjoy a greater degree of prosperity, and the people will remain quiet not because it despairs of amelioration but because it is conscious of the advantages of its condition. If all the consequences of this state of things were not good or useful, society would at least have appropriated all such as were useful and good; and having once and for ever renounced the social advantages of aristocracy, mankind would enter into possession of all the benefits which democracy can afford.

But here it may be asked what we have adopted in the place of those institutions, those ideas, and those customs of our forefathers which we have abandoned. The spell of royalty is broken, but it has not been succeeded by the majesty of the laws; the people have learned to despise all authority, but fear now extorts a larger tribute of obedience than that which was formerly paid by reverence and by love.

I perceive that we have destroyed those independent beings which were able to cope with tyranny single-handed; but it is the Government that has inherited the privileges of which families, corporations, and individuals have been deprived; the weakness of the whole community has therefore succeeded that influence of a small body of citizens, which, if it was sometimes oppressive, was often conservative. The division of property has lessened the distance which separated the rich from the poor; but it would seem that the nearer they draw to each other, the greater is their mutual hatred, and the more vehement the envy and the dread with which they resist each other's claims to power; the notion of right is alike insensible to both classes, and force affords to both the only argument for the present, and the only guarantee for the future. The poor man retains the prejudices of his forefathers without their faith, and their ignorance without their virtues; he has adopted the doctrine of self-interest as the rule of his actions, without understanding the science which controls it, and his egotism is no less blind than his devotedness was formerly. If society is tranquil, it is not because it relies upon its strength and its well-being, but because it knows its weakness and its infirmities; a single effort may cost it its life; everybody feels the evil, but no one has courage or energy enough to seek the cure; the desires, the regrets, the sorrows, and the joys of the time produce nothing that is visible or permanent, like the passions of old men, which terminate in impotence.

We have, then, abandoned whatever advantages the old state of things afforded, without receiving any compensation from our present condition; we have destroyed an aristocracy, and we seem inclined to survey its ruins with complacency, and to fix our abode in the midst of them. . . .

There is a country in the world where the great revolution which I am speaking of seems nearly to have reached its natural limits; it has been effected with ease and simplicity, say rather that this country has attained the consequences of the democratic revolution which we are undergoing without having experienced the revolution itself. The emigrants who fixed themselves on the shores of America in the beginning of the seventeenth century severed the democratic principle from all the principles which repressed it in the old communities of Europe, and transplanted it unalloyed to the New World. It has there been allowed to spread in perfect freedom, and to put forth its consequences in the laws by influencing the manners of the country.

It appears to me beyond a doubt that sooner or later we shall arrive, like the Americans, at an almost complete equality of conditions. But I do not conclude from this that we shall ever be necessarily led to draw the same political consequences which the Americans have derived from a similar social organization. I am far from supposing that they have chosen the only form of government which a democracy may adopt; but the identity of the efficient cause of laws and manners in the two countries is sufficient to account for the immense interest we have in becoming acquainted with its effects in each of them.

It is not, then, merely to satisfy a legitimate curiosity that I have examined America; my wish has been to find instruction by which we may ourselves profit. Whoever should imagine that I have intended to write a panegyric[1] will perceive that such was not my design; nor has it been my object to advocate any form of government in particular, for I am of opinion that absolute excellence is rarely to be found in any legislation; I have not even affected to discuss whether the social revolution, which I believe to be irresistible, is advantageous or prejudicial to mankind; I have acknowledged this revolution as a fact already accomplished or on the eve of its accomplishment; and I have selected the nation, from among those which have undergone it, in which its development has been the most peaceful and the most complete, in order to discern its natural consequences, and, if it be possible, to distinguish the means by which it may be rendered profitable. I confess that in America I saw more than America; I sought the image of democracy itself, with its inclinations, its character, its prejudices, and its passions, in order to learn what we have to fear or to hope from its progress.

• • •

TYRANNY OF THE MAJORITY

I hold it to be an impious and an execrable maxim that, politically speaking, a people has a right to do whatsoever it pleases, and yet I have asserted that all authority originates in the will of the majority. Am I, then, in contradiction with myself?

A general law—which bears the name of Justice—has been made and sanctioned, not only by a majority of this or that people, but by a majority of mankind. The rights of every people are consequently confined within the limits of what is just. A nation may be considered in the light of a jury which is empowered to represent society at large, and to apply the great and general law of justice. Ought such a jury, which represents society, to have more power than the society in which the laws it applies originate?

---

[1] A speech or script of praise.

When I refuse to obey an unjust law, I do not contest the right which the majority has of commanding, but I simply appeal from the sovereignty of the people to the sovereignty of mankind. It has been asserted that a people can never entirely outstep the boundaries of justice and of reason in those affairs which are more peculiarly its own, and that consequently full power may fearlessly be given to the majority by which it is represented. But this language is that of a slave.

A majority taken collectively may be regarded as a being whose opinions, and most frequently whose interests, are opposed to those of another being, which is styled a minority. If it be admitted that a man, possessing absolute power, may misuse that power by wronging his adversaries, why should a majority not be liable to the same reproach? Men are not apt to change their characters by agglomeration; nor does their patience in the presence of obstacles increase with the consciousness of their strength. And for these reasons I can never willingly invest any number of my fellow creatures with that unlimited authority which I should refuse to any one of them.

I do not think that it is possible to combine several principles in the same government, so as at the same time to maintain freedom, and really to oppose them to one another. The form of government which is usually termed mixed has always appeared to me to be a mere chimera.[2] Accurately speaking, there is no such thing as a mixed government (with the meaning usually given to that word), because in all communities some one principle of action may be discovered which preponderates over the others. England in the last century, which has been more especially cited as an example of this form of government, was in point of fact an essentially aristocratic state, although it comprised very powerful elements of democracy; for the laws and customs of the country were such that the aristocracy could not but preponderate in the end, and subject the direction of public affairs to its own will. The error arose from too much attention being paid to the actual struggle which was going on between the nobles and the people, without considering the probable issue of the contest, which was in reality the important point. When a community really has a mixed government, that is to say, when it is equally divided between two adverse principles, it must either pass through a revolution, or fall into complete dissolution.

[2] An imaginary creation.

I am therefore of opinion that some one social power must always be made to predominate over the others; but I think that liberty is endangered when this power is checked by no obstacles which may retard its course, and force it to moderate its own vehemence.

Unlimited power is in itself a bad and dangerous thing; human beings are not competent to exercise it with discretion, and God alone can be omnipotent, because his wisdom and his justice are always equal to his power. But no power upon earth is so worthy of honor for itself, or of reverential obedience to the rights which it represents, that I would consent to admit its uncontrolled and all-predominant authority. When I see that the right and the means of absolute command are conferred on a people or upon a king, upon an aristocracy or a democracy, a monarchy or a republic, I recognize the germ of tyranny, and I journey onward to a land of more hopeful institutions.

In my opinion the main evil of the present democratic institutions of the United States does not arise, as is often asserted in Europe, from their weakness, but from their overpowering strength; and I am not so much alarmed at the excessive liberty which reigns in that country as at the very inadequate securities which exist against tyranny.

When an individual or a party is wronged in the United States, to whom can he apply for redress? If to public opinion, public opinion constitutes the majority; if to the legislature, it represents the majority, and implicitly obeys its injunctions; if to the executive power, it is appointed by the majority, and remains a passive tool in its hands; the public troops consist of the majority under arms; the jury is the majority invested with the right of hearing judicial cases; and in certain States even the judges are elected by the majority. However iniquitous or absurd the evil of which you complain may be, you must submit to it as well as you can.

If, on the other hand, a legislative power could be so constituted as to represent the majority without necessarily being the slave of its passions; an executive, so as to retain a certain degree of uncontrolled authority; and a judiciary, so as to remain independent of the two other powers; a government would be formed which would still be democratic without incurring any risk of tyannical abuse.

I do not say that tyrannical abuses frequently occur in America at the present day, but I maintain that no sure barrier is established against them, and that the causes which mitigate the government are to be found in the circumstances and the manners of the country more than in its laws.

. . .

POWER EXERCISED BY THE MAJORITY IN AMERICA UPON OPINION

It is in the examination of the display of public opinion in the United States that we clearly perceive how far the power of the majority surpasses all the powers with which we are acquainted in Europe. Intellectual principles exercise an influence which is so invisible, and often so inappreciable, that they baffle the toils of oppression. At the present time the most absolute monarchs in Europe are unable to prevent certain notions, which are opposed to their authority, from circulating in secret throughout their dominions, and even in their courts. Such is not the case in America; as long as the majority is still undecided, discussion is carried on; but as soon as its decision is irrevocably pronounced, a submissive silence is observed, and the friends, as well as the opponents, of the measure unite in assenting to its propriety. The reason of this is perfectly clear: no monarch is so absolute as to combine all the powers of society in his own hands, and to conquer all opposition with the energy of a majority which is invested with the right of making and of executing the laws.

The authority of a king is purely physical, and it controls the actions of the subject without subduing his private will; but the majority possesses a power which is physical and moral at the same time; it acts upon the will as well as upon the actions of men, and it represses not only all contest, but all controversy.

I know no country in which there is so little true independence of mind and freedom of discussion as in America. In any constitutional state in Europe every sort of religious and political theory may be advocated and propagated abroad; for there is no country in Europe so subdued by any single authority as not to contain citizens who are ready to protect the man who raises his voice in the cause of truth from the consequences of his boldness. If he is unfortunate enough to live under an absolute government, the people are upon his side; if he inhabits a free country, he may find a shelter behind the authority of the throne, if he require one. The aristocratic part of society supports him in some countries, and the democracy in others. But in a nation where democratic institutions exist, organized like those of the United States, there is but one sole authority, one single element of strength and of success, with nothing beyond it.

In America, the majority raises very formidable barriers to the liberty of opinion: within these barriers an author may write whatever he pleases, but he will repent it if he ever step beyond them. Not that he is exposed to the terrors of an auto-da-fé,[3] but he is tormented by the slights and persecutions of daily obloquy.[4] His political career is closed forever, since he has offended the only authority which is able to promote his success. Every sort of compensation, even that of celebrity, is refused to him. Before he published his opinions he imagined that he held them in common with many others; but no sooner has he declared them openly than he is loudly censured by his overbearing opponents, while those who think like him, without having the courage to speak, abandon him in silence. He yields at length, oppressed by the daily efforts he has been making, and he subsides into silence, as if he was tormented by remorse for having spoken the truth.

Fetters and headsmen were the coarse instruments which tyranny formerly employed; but the civilization of our age has refined the arts of despotism, which seemed, however, to have been sufficiently perfected before. The excesses of monarchical power had devised a variety of physical means of oppression: the democratic republics of the present day have rendered it as entirely an affair of the mind as that will which it is intended to coerce. Under the absolute sway of an individual despot the body was attacked in order to subdue the soul, and the soul escaped the blows which were directed against it and rose superior to the attempt; but such is not the course adopted by tyranny in democratic republics; there the body is left free, and the soul is enslaved. The sovereign can no longer say, "You shall think as I do on pain of death"; but he says, "You are free to think differently from me, and to retain your life, your property, and all that you possess; but if such be your determination, you are henceforth an alien among your people. You may retain your civil rights, but they will be useless to you, for you will never be chosen by your fellow citizens if you solicit their suffrages,[5] and they will

[3] A ceremony sentencing and punishing heretics (believers in false doctrines).
[4] Censure, disgrace.
[5] Votes.

affect to scorn you if you solicit their esteem. You will remain among men, but you will be deprived of the rights of mankind. Your fellow creatures will shun you like an impure being, and those who are most persuaded of your innocence will abandon you too, lest they should be shunned in their turn. Go in peace! I have given you your life, but it is an existence incomparably worse than death."

Monarchical institutions have thrown an odium upon despotism; let us beware lest democratic republics should restore oppression, and should render it less odious and less degrading in the eyes of the many, by making it still more onerous to the few.

Works have been published in the proudest nations of the Old World expressly intended to censure the vices and deride the follies of the times: Labruyère[6] inhabited the palace of Louis XIV[7] when he composed his chapter upon the Great, and Molière[8] criticized the courtiers in the very pieces which were acted before the court. But the ruling power in the United States is not to be made game of; the smallest reproach irritates its sensibility, and the slightest joke which has any foundation in truth renders it indignant; from the style of its language to the more solid virtues of its character, everything must be made the subject of encomium.[9] No writer, whatever be his eminence, can escape from this tribute of adulation to his fellow citizens. The majority lives in the perpetual practice of self-applause, and there are certain truths which the Americans can only learn from strangers or from experience.

If great writers have not at present existed in America, the reason is very simply given in these facts; there can be no literary genius without freedom of opinion, and freedom of opinion does not exist in America. The Inquisition[10] has never been able to prevent a vast number of anti-religious books from circulating in Spain. The empire of the majority succeeds much better in the United States, since it actually removes the wish of publishing them. Unbelievers are to be met with in America, but, to say the truth, there is no public organ of infidelity. Attempts have been made by some governments to protect the morality of nations by prohibiting licentious books. In the United States no one is punished for this sort of works, but no

---

[6] Jean de Labruyère (1645–1696), a French moralist.
[7] Louis XIV (1638–1715), absolute king of France, called the Great.
[8] Jean Baptiste Molière (1622–1673), French actor and playwright.
[9] High praise.
[10] An office of the medieval Roman Catholic Church, established to seek out heretics and assure their punishment.

one is induced to write them; not because all the citizens are immaculate in their manners, but because the majority of the community is decent and orderly.

In these cases the advantages derived from the exercise of this power are unquestionable, and I am simply discussing the nature of the power itself. This irresistible authority is a constant fact, and its judicious exercise is an accidental occurrence.

• • •

OF THE PRINCIPAL SOURCE OF BELIEF AMONG DEMOCRATIC NATIONS

When the ranks of society are unequal, and men unlike each other in condition, there are some individuals invested with all the power of superior intelligence, learning, and enlightenment, while the multitude is sunk in ignorance and prejudice. Men living at these aristocratic periods are therefore naturally induced to shape their opinions by the superior standard of a person or a class of persons, while they are averse to recognize the infallibility of the mass of the people.

The contrary takes place in ages of equality. The nearer the citizens are drawn to the common level of an equal and similar condition, the less prone does each man become to place implicit faith in a certain man or a certain class of men. But his readiness to believe the multitude increases, and opinion is more than ever mistress of the world. Not only is common opinion the only guide which private judgment retains among a democratic people, but among such a people it possesses a power infinitely beyond what it has elsewhere. At periods of equality men have no faith in one another, by reason of their common resemblance; but this very resemblance gives them almost unbounded confidence in the judgment of the public; for it would not seem probable, as they are all endowed with equal means of judging, but that the greater truth should go with the greater number.

When the inhabitant of a democratic country compares himself individually with all those about him, he feels with pride that he is the equal of any one of them; but when he comes to survey the totality of his fellows, and to place himself in contrast to so huge a body, he is instantly overwhelmed by the sense of his own insignificance and weakness. The same equality which renders him independent of each of his fellow citizens taken separately, exposes him alone and unpro-

tected to the influence of the greater number. The public has therefore among a democratic people a singular power, of which
aristocratic nations could never so much as conceive an idea; for it
does not persuade to certain opinions, but it enforces them, and in-
fuses them into the faculties by a sort of enormous pressure of the
minds of all upon the reason of each.

In the United States the majority undertakes to supply a multitude
of ready-made opinions for the use of individuals, who are thus relieved from the necessity of forming opinions of their own. Everybody there adopts great numbers of theories, on philosophy, morals,
and politics, without inquiry, upon public trust; and if we look to it
very narrowly, it will be perceived that religion herself holds her
sway there, much less as a doctrine of revelation than as a commonly
received opinion. The fact that the political laws of the Americans
are such that the majority rules the community with sovereign sway,
materially increases the power which that majority naturally exercises over the mind. For nothing is more customary in man than to
recognize superior wisdom in the person of his oppressor. This political omnipotence of the majority in the United States doubtless augments the influence which public opinion would obtain without it
over the mind of each member of the community; but the foundations of that influence do not rest upon it. They must be sought for
in the principle of equality itself, not in the more or less popular institutions which men living under that condition may give themselves. The intellectual dominion of the greater number would
probably be less absolute among a democratic people governed by a
king than in the sphere of a pure democracy, but it will always be
extremely absolute; and by whatever political laws men are governed
in the ages of equality, it may be foreseen that faith in public opinion
will become a species of religion there, and the majority its minister-
ing prophet.

Thus intellectual authority will be different, but it will not be
diminished; and far from thinking that it will disappear, I predict that
it may readily acquire too much preponderance, and confine the action of private judgment within narrower limits than are suited either
to the greatness or the happiness of the human race. In the principle
of equality I very clearly discern two tendencies: the one leading the
mind of every man to untried thoughts, the other inclined to prohibit him from thinking at all. And I perceive how, under the dominion of certain laws, democracy would extinguish that liberty of

the mind to which a democratic social condition is favorable; so that, after having broken all the bondage once imposed on it by ranks or by men, the human mind would be closely fettered to the general will of the greatest number.

If the absolute power of the majority were to be substituted by democratic nations, for all the different powers which checked or retarded too much the energy of individual minds, the evil would only have changed its symptoms. Men would not have found the means of independent life; they would simply have invented (no easy task) a new dress for servitude. There is—and I cannot repeat it too often— there is in this matter for profound reflection for those who look on freedom as a holy thing, and who hate not only the despot, but despotism. For myself, when I feel the hand of power lie heavy on my brow, I care but little to know who oppresses me; and I am not the more disposed to pass beneath the yoke, because it is held out to me by the arms of a million of men.

• • •

WHY DEMOCRATIC NATIONS SHOW A MORE ARDENT AND ENDURING LOVE OF EQUALITY THAN OF LIBERTY

The first and most intense passion which is engendered by the equality of conditions is, I need hardly say, the love of that same equality. My readers will therefore not be surprised that I speak of it before all others. Everybody has remarked that in our time, and especially in France, this passion for equality is every day gaining ground in the human heart. It has been said a hundred times that our contemporaries are far more ardently and tenaciously attached to equality than to freedom; but as I do not find that the causes of the fact have been sufficiently analyzed, I shall endeavor to point them out.

It is possible to imagine an extreme point at which freedom and equality would meet and be confounded together. Let us suppose that all the members of the community take a part in the government, and that each one of them has an equal right to take a part in it. As none is different from his fellows, none can exercise a tyrannical power: men will be perfectly free, because they will all be entirely equal; and they will all be perfectly equal, because they will be entirely free. To this ideal state democratic nations tend. Such is the most complete form that equality can assume upon earth; but there are a thousand others which, without being equally perfect, are not less cherished by those nations.

The principle of equality may be established in civil society, without prevailing in the political world. Equal rights may exist of indulging in the same pleasures, of entering the same professions, of frequenting the same places—in a word, of living in the same manner and seeking wealth by the same means, although all men do not take an equal share in the government. A kind of equality may even be established in the political world, though there should be no political freedom there. A man may be the equal of all his countrymen save one, who is the master of all without distinction, and who selects equally from among them all the agents of his power. Several other combinations might be easily imagined, by which very great equality would be united to institutions more or less free, or even to institutions wholly without freedom. Although men cannot become absolutely equal unless they be entirely free, and consequently equality, pushed to its furthest extent, may be confounded with freedom, yet there is good reason for distinguishing the one from the other. The taste which men have for liberty, and that which they feel for equality, are, in fact, two different things; and I am not afraid to add that, among democratic nations, they are two unequal things.

Upon close inspection, it will be seen that there is in every age some peculiar and preponderating fact with which all others are connected; this fact almost always gives birth to some pregnant idea or some ruling passion, which attracts to itself, and bears away in its course, all the feelings and opinions of the time: it is like a great stream, towards which each of the surrounding rivulets seems to flow. Freedom has appeared in the world at different times and under various forms; it has not been exclusively bound to any social condition, and it is not confined to democracies. Freedom cannot, therefore, form the distinguishing characteristic of democratic ages. The peculiar and preponderating fact which marks those ages as its own is the equality of conditions; the ruling passion of men in those periods is the love of this equality. Ask not what singular charm the men of democratic ages find in being equal, or what special reasons they may have for clinging so tenaciously to equality rather than to the other advantages which society holds out to them: equality is the distinguishing characteristic of the age they live in; that, of itself, is enough to explain that they prefer it to all the rest.

But independently of this reason there are several others, which will at all times habitually lead men to prefer equality to freedom. If a people could ever succeed in destroying, or even in diminishing, the equality which prevails in its own body, this could only be accomplished by long and laborious efforts. Its social condition must be modified, its laws abolished, its opinions superseded, its habits changed, its manners corrupted. But political liberty is more easily lost; to neglect to hold it fast is to allow it to escape. Men therefore not only cling to equality because it is dear to them; they also adhere to it because they think it will last forever.

That political freedom may compromise in its excesses the tranquillity, the property, the lives of individuals, is obvious to the narrowest and most unthinking minds. But, on the contrary, none but attentive and clear-sighted men perceive the perils with which equality threatens us, and they commonly avoid pointing them out. They know that the calamities they apprehend are remote, and flatter themselves that they will only fall upon future generations, for which the present generation takes but little thought. The evils which freedom sometimes brings with it are immediate; they are apparent to all, and all are more or less affected by them. The evils which extreme equality may produce are slowly disclosed; they creep gradually into the social frame; they are only seen at intervals, and at the moment at which they become most violent habit already causes them to be no longer felt. The advantages which freedom brings are only shown by length of time; and it is always easy to mistake the cause in which they originate. The advantages of equality are instantaneous, and they may constantly be traced from their source. Political liberty bestows exalted pleasures, from time to time, upon a certain number of citizens. Equality every day confers a number of small enjoyments on every man. The charms of equality are every instant felt, and are within the reach of all; the noblest hearts are not insensible to them, and the most vulgar souls exult in them. The passion which equality engenders must therefore be at once strong and general. Men cannot enjoy political liberty unpurchased by some sacrifices, and they never obtain it without great exertions. But the pleasures of equality are self-proffered: each of the petty incidents of life seems to occasion them, and in order to taste them nothing is required but to live.

Democratic nations are at all times fond of equality, but there are certain epochs at which the passion they entertain for it swells to the height of fury. This occurs at the moment when the old social system, long menaced, completes its own destruction after a last internal struggle, and when the barriers of rank are at length thrown down. At such times men pounce upon equality as their booty, and they cling to it as to some precious treasure which they fear to lose. The passion for equality penetrates on every side into men's hearts, expands there, and fills them entirely. Tell them not that by this blind surrender of themselves to an exclusive passion they risk their dearest interests: they are deaf. Show them not freedom escaping from their grasp, while they are looking another way: they are blind—or rather, they can discern but one sole object to be desired in the universe.

What I have said is applicable to all democratic nations: what I am about to say concerns the French alone. Among most modern nations, and especially among all those of the Continent of Europe, the taste and the idea of freedom only began to exist and to extend themselves at the time when social conditions were tending to equality, and as a consequence of that very equality. Absolute kings were the most efficient levellers of ranks among their subjects. Among these nations equality preceded freedom: equality was therefore a fact of some standing when freedom was still a novelty: the one had already created customs, opinions, and laws belonging to it, when the other, alone and for the first time, came into actual existence. Thus the latter was still only an affair of opinion and of taste, while the former had already crept into the habits of the people, possessed itself of their manners, and given a particular turn to the smallest actions of their lives. Can it be wondered that the men of our own time prefer the one to the other?

I think that democratic communities have a natural taste for freedom: left to themselves, they will seek it, cherish it, and view any privation of it with regret. But for equality, their passion is ardent, insatiable, incessant, invincible: they call for equality in freedom; and if they cannot obtain that, they still call for equality in slavery. They will endure poverty, servitude, barbarism—but they will not endure aristocracy. This is true at all times, and especially true in our own. All men and all powers seeking to cope with this irresistible passion, will be overthrown and destroyed by it. In our age, freedom cannot be established without it, and despotism itself cannot reign without its support.

• • •

WHAT SORT OF DESPOTISM
DEMOCRATIC NATIONS HAVE TO FEAR

I believe that it is easier to establish an absolute and despotic government among a people in which the conditions of society are equal, than among any other; and I think that if such a government were once established among such a people, it would not only oppress men, but would eventually strip each of them of several of the highest qualities of humanity. Despotism, therefore, appears to me peculiarly to be dreaded in democratic ages. I should have loved freedom, I believe, at all times, but in the time in which we live I am ready to worship it. On the other hand, I am persuaded that all who shall attempt, in the ages upon which we are entering, to base freedom upon aristocratic privilege, will fail—that all who shall attempt to draw and to retain authority within a single class, will fail. At the present day no ruler is skilful or strong enough to found a despotism, by re-establishing permanent distinctions of rank among his subjects; no legislator is wise or powerful enough to preserve free institutions, if he does not take equality for his first principle and his watchword. All those of our contemporaries who would establish or secure the independence and the dignity of their fellow men, must show themselves the friends of equality; and the only worthy means of showing themselves as such, is to be so: upon this depends the success of their holy enterprise. Thus the question is not how to reconstruct aristocratic society, but how to make liberty proceed out of that democratic state of society in which God has placed us.

These two truths appear to me simple, clear, and fertile in consequences; and they naturally lead me to consider what kind of free government can be established among a people in which social conditions are equal.

It results from the very constitution of democratic nations and from their necessities, that the power of government among them must be more uniform, more centralized, more extensive, more searching, and more efficient than in other countries. Society at large is naturally stronger and more active, individuals more subordinate and weak; the former does more, the latter less; and this is inevitably the case. It is not therefore to be expected that the range of private independence will ever be as extensive in democratic as in aristocratic countries—nor is this to be desired; for, among aristocratic nations, the mass is often sacrificed to the individual, and the prosperity of the greater number to the greatness of the few. It is both necessary and desirable that the government of a democratic people should be active and powerful: and our object should not be to render it weak or indolent, but solely to prevent it from abusing its aptitude and its strength. . . .

I think that men living in aristocracies may, strictly speaking, do without the liberty of the press: but such is not the case with those who live in democratic countries. To protect their personal independence I trust not to great political assemblies, to parliamentary privilege, or to the assertion of popular sovereignty. All these things may, to a certain extent, be reconciled with personal servitude—but that servitude cannot be complete if the press is free: the press is the chiefest democratic instrument of freedom.

Something analogous may be said of the judicial power. It is a part of the essence of judicial power to attend to private interests, and to fix itself with predilection on minute objects submitted to its observation; another essential quality of judicial power is never to volunteer its assistance to the oppressed, but always to be at the disposal of the humblest of those who solicit it; their complaint, however feeble they may themselves be, will force itself upon the ear of justice and claim redress, for this is inherent in the very constitution of the courts of justice. A power of this kind is therefore peculiarly adapted to the wants of freedom, at a time when the eye and finger of the government are constantly intruding into the minutest details of human actions, and when private persons are at once too weak to protect themselves, and too much isolated for them to reckon upon the assistance of their fellows. The strength of the courts of law has ever been the greatest security which can be offered to personal independence; but this is more especially the case in democratic ages: private rights and interests are in constant danger, if the judicial power does not grow more extensive and more strong to keep pace with the growing equality of conditions.

Equality awakens in men several propensities extremely dangerous to freedom, to which the attention of the legislator ought constantly to be directed. I shall only remind the reader of the most important among them. Men living in democratic ages do not readily comprehend the utility of forms: they feel an instinctive contempt for them—I have elsewhere shown for what reasons. Forms excite their contempt and often their hatred; as they commonly aspire to none but easy and present gratifications, they rush onwards to the object of their desires, and the slightest delay exasperates them. This same temper, carried with them into political life, renders them hostile to forms, which perpetually retard or arrest them in some of their projects. Yet this objection which the men of democracies make to forms is the very thing which renders forms so useful to freedom; for their chief merit is to serve as a barrier between the strong and the weak, the ruler and the people, to retard the one, and give the other time to look about him. Forms become more necessary in proportion as the government becomes more active and more powerful, while private persons are becoming more indolent and more feeble. Thus democratic nations naturally stand more in need of forms than other nations, and they naturally respect them less. This deserves most serious attention. Nothing is more pitiful than the arrogant disdain of most of our contemporaries for questions of form; for the smallest questions of form have acquired in our time an importance which they never had before: many of the greatest interests of mankind depend upon them. I think that if the statesmen of aristocratic ages could sometimes scorn forms with impunity, and frequently rise above them, the statesmen to whom the government of nations is now confided ought to treat the very least among them with respect, and not neglect them without imperious necessity. In aristocracies the observance of forms was superstitious; among us they ought to be kept with a deliberate and enlightened deference.

Another tendency, which is extremely natural to democratic nations and extremely dangerous, is that which leads them to despise and undervalue the rights of private persons. The attachment which men feel to a right, and the respect which they display for it, is generally proportioned to its importance, or to the length of time during which they have enjoyed it. The rights of private persons among democratic nations are commonly of small importance, of recent growth, and extremely precarious—the consequence is that they are often sacrificed without regret, and almost always violated without remorse. But it happens that at the same period and among the same nations in which men conceive a natural contempt for the rights of private persons, the rights of society at large are naturally extended and consolidated: in other words, men become less attached to private rights at the very time at which it would be most necessary to retain and to defend what little remains of them. It is therefore most especially in the present democratic ages, that the true friends of the liberty and the greatness of man ought constantly to be on the alert to prevent the power of government from lightly sacrificing the private rights of individuals to the general execution of its designs. At such times no citizen is so obscure that it is not very dangerous to allow him to be oppressed—no private rights are so unimportant that they can be surrendered with impunity to the caprices of a government. The reason is plain:—if the private right of an individual is violated at a time when the human mind is fully impressed with the importance and the sanctity of such rights, the injury done is confined to the individual whose right is infringed; but to violate such a right, at the present day, is deeply to corrupt the manners of the nation and to put the whole community in jeopardy, because the very notion of this kind of right constantly tends among us to be impaired and lost. . . .

I shall conclude by one general idea, which comprises not only all the particular ideas which have been expressed in the present chapter, but also most of those which it is the object of this book to treat. In the ages of aristocracy which preceded our own, there were private persons of great power, and a social authority of extreme weakness. The outline of society itself was not easily discernible, and constantly confounded with the different powers by which the community was ruled. The principal efforts of the men of those times were required to strengthen, aggrandize, and secure the supreme power; and on the other hand, to circumscribe individual independence within narrower limits, and to subject private interests to the interests of the public. Other perils and other cares await the men of our age. Among the greater part of modern nations, the government, whatever may be its origin, its constitution, or its name, has become almost omnipotent, and private persons are falling, more and more, into the lowest stage of weakness and dependence. In past society everything was different; unity and uniformity were nowhere to be met with. In modern society everything threatens to become so much alike, that the peculiar characteristics of each individual will soon be entirely lost in the general aspect of the world. Our forefathers were ever prone to make an improper use of the notion, that private rights ought to be respected; and we are naturally prone on the other hand to exaggerate the idea that the interest of a private individual ought always to bend to the interest of the many. The political world is subject to change: new remedies must henceforth be sought for new disorders. To lay down extensive, but distinct and settled limits, to the action of the government; to confer certain rights on private persons, and to secure to them the undisputed enjoyment of those rights; to enable individual man to maintain whatever independence, strength, and original power he still possesses; to raise him by the side of society at large, and uphold him in that position—these appear to me the main objects of legislators in the ages upon which we are now entering. It would seem as if the rulers of our time sought only to use men in order to make things great; I wish that they would try a little more to make great men; that they would set less value on the work, and more upon the workman; that they would never forget that a nation cannot long remain strong when every man belonging to it is individually weak, and that no form or combination of social polity has yet been devised, to make an energetic people out of a community of pusillanimous and enfeebled citizens.

I trace among our contemporaries two contrary notions which are equally injurious. One set of men can perceive nothing in the principle of equality but the anarchical tendencies which it engenders: they dread their own free agency—they fear themselves. Other thinkers, less numerous but more enlightened, take a different view: besides that track which starts from the principle of equality to terminate in anarchy, they have at last discovered the road which seems to lead men to inevitable servitude. They shape their souls beforehand to this necessary condition; and, despairing of remaining free, they already do obeisance in their hearts to the master who is soon to appear. The former abandon freedom, because they think it dangerous; the latter, because they hold it to be impossible. If I had entertained the latter conviction, I should not have written this book, but I should have confined myself to deploring in secret the destiny of mankind. I have sought to point out the dangers to which the principle of equality exposes the independence of man, because I firmly believe that these dangers are the most formidable, as well as the least foreseen, of all those which futurity holds in store: but I do not think that they are insurmountable. The men who live in the democratic ages upon which we are entering have naturally a taste for independence: they are naturally impatient of regulation, and they are wearied by the permanence even of the condition they themselves prefer. They are fond of power; but they are prone to despise and hate those who wield it, and they easily elude its grasp by their own mobility and insignificance. These propensities will always manifest themselves, because they originate in the groundwork of society, which will undergo no change: for a long time they will prevent the establishment of any despotism, and they will furnish fresh weapons to each succeeding generation which shall struggle in favor of the liberty of mankind. Let us then look forward to the future with that salutary fear which makes men keep watch and ward for freedom, not with that faint and idle terror which depresses and enervates the heart.

17

John Stuart Mill
On Liberty

The full flowering of liberal thought came in the work of John Stuart Mill (1806–1873), known as "the Aristotle of the Victorian Age" because of his versatility and the reasonableness of his views. Mill was a liberal in politics who favored a democratic base for representation, an economist who balanced laissez faire and positive government, an empiricist in philosophy, and a secular humanist in religion. He was, in short, representative of middle-class England at its intellectual best in the mid-nineteenth century. Mill came to symbolize liberalism as a way of life, with its broad sympathies and its dedication to the improvement of human beings through freedom.

The views Mill held were rooted in the doctrinaire rationalism of his father, James Mill, who rigidly directed his son's education in the principles of Jeremy Bentham's utilitarianism. In his twenties, however, the younger Mill underwent a psychological crisis induced by his reading of romantic poets and philosophers. Exposed to their works, he rebelled against what seemed to him the barren, calculating rationalism of Bentham and adopted a more positive, complex, and flexible point of view. While receptive to the romantic and democratic currents of mid-century European thought, Mill remained dedicated to objective, rational methods and never forsook his belief in individualism. He was, at the same time, an active social reformer who worked for all the "good causes" of his day.

On Liberty (1859), Mill's greatest contribution to social thought, is an eloquent essay on "the nature and limits of the power which can be legitimately exercised by society over the individual," and it offers a rational defense of a balanced position between individual freedom and social neces-

John Stuart Mill, *On Liberty* (London: John W. Parker & Son, 1859), 21–44, 94–99, 134–38, 140–41, 207. Adapted.

sity. For Mill, positive, individual liberty was necessary to both the personal happiness of self-realization and the advancement of the welfare of society. He insisted, moreover, on the necessity of unrestricted competition of ideas as the social means for discovery of truth. Although the image of society offered by Mill—an atomistic aggregation of individuals—is no longer consonant with reality, his views on intellectual freedom are enduring ideals of the Western world.

INTRODUCTORY

• • •

The object of this essay is to assert one very simple principle, as entitled to govern absolutely the dealings of society with the individual in the way of compulsion and control, whether the means used be physical force in the form of legal penalties or the moral coercion of public opinion. That principle is that the sole end for which mankind are warranted, individually or collectively, in interfering with the liberty of action of any of their number is self-protection. That the only purpose for which power can be rightfully exercised over any member of a civilized community, against his will, is to prevent harm to others. His own good, either physical or moral, is not a sufficient warrant. He cannot rightfully be compelled to do or forbear because it will be better for him to do so, because it will make him happier, because, in the opinions of others, to do so would be wise or even right. These are good reasons for remonstrating with him, or reasoning with him, or persuading him, or entreating him, but not for compelling him or visiting him with any evil in case he do otherwise. To justify that, the conduct from which it is desired to deter him must be calculated to produce evil to some one else. The only part of the conduct of anyone for which he is amenable to society is that which concerns others. In the part which merely concerns himself, his independence is, of right, absolute. Over himself, over his own body and mind, the individual is sovereign. . . .

It is proper to state that I forego any advantage which could be derived to my argument from the idea of abstract right as a thing independent of utility. I regard utility as the ultimate appeal on all ethical questions; but it must be utility in the largest sense, grounded on the permanent interests of man as a progressive being. Those interests, I contend, authorize the subjection of individual spontaneity to external control only in respect to those actions of each which concern the interest of other people. If anyone does an act hurtful to others, there is a *prima facie* [1] case for punishing him by law or, where legal penalties are not safely applicable, by general disapprobation. There are also many positive acts for the benefit of others which he may rightfully be compelled to perform, such as to give evidence in a court of justice, to bear his fair share in the common defense or in any other joint work necessary to the interest of the society of which he enjoys the protection, and to perform certain acts of individual beneficence, such as saving a fellow creature's life or interposing to protect the defenseless against ill usage—things which, whenever it is obviously a man's duty to do, he may rightfully be made responsible to society for not doing. A person may cause evil to others not only by his actions but by his inaction, and in either case he is justly accountable to them for the injury. The latter case, it is true, requires a much more cautious exercise of compulsion than the former. To make anyone answerable for doing evil to others is the rule; to make him answerable for not preventing evil is, comparatively speaking, the exception. Yet there are many cases clear enough and grave enough to justify that exception. In all things which regard the external relations of the individual, he is *de jure* [2] amenable to those whose interests are concerned, and, if need be, to society as their protector. There are often good reasons for not holding him to the responsibility; but these reasons must arise from the special expediencies of the case: either because it is a kind of case in which he is on the whole likely to act better when left to his own discretion than when controlled in any way in which society have it in their power to control him; or because the attempt to exercise control would produce other evils, greater than those which it would prevent. When such reasons as these preclude the enforcement of responsibility, the conscience of the agent himself should step into the vacant judgment seat and protect those interests of others which have no external protection; judging himself all the more rigidly, because the case does not

[1] At first view, on first impression.
[2] By law, by right.

admit of his being made accountable to the judgment of his fellow creatures.

But there is a sphere of action in which society, as distinguished from the individual, has, if any, only an indirect interest: comprehending all that portion of a person's life and conduct which affects only himself or, if it also affects others, only with their free, voluntary, and undeceived consent and participation. When I say only himself, I mean directly and in the first instance; for whatever affects himself may affect others *through* himself; and the objection which may be grounded on this contingency, will receive consideration in the sequel. This, then, is the appropriate region of human liberty. It comprises, first, the inward domain of consciousness, demanding liberty of conscience in the most comprehensive sense, liberty of thought and feeling, absolute freedom of opinion and sentiment on all subjects, practical or speculative, scientific, moral, or theological. The liberty of expressing and publishing opinions may seem to fall under a different principle, since it belongs to that part of the conduct of an individual which concerns other people, but, being almost of as much importance as the liberty of thought itself and resting in great part on the same reasons, is practically inseparable from it. Secondly, the principle requires liberty of tastes and pursuits, of framing the plan of our life to suit our own character, of doing as we like, subject to such consequences as may follow, without impediment from our fellow creatures, so long as what we do does not harm them, even though they should think our conduct foolish, perverse, or wrong. Thirdly, from this liberty of each individual follows the liberty, within the same limits, of combination among individuals; freedom to unite for any purpose not involving harm to others: the persons combining being supposed to be of full age and not forced or deceived.

No society in which these liberties are not, on the whole, respected is free, whatever may be its form of government; and none is completely free in which they do not exist absolute and unqualified. The only freedom which deserves the name is that of pursuing our own good in our own way, so long as we do not attempt to deprive others of theirs or impede their efforts to obtain it. Each is the proper guardian of his own health, whether bodily or mental and spiritual. Mankind are greater gainers by suffering each other to live as seems good to themselves than by compelling each to live as seems good to the rest.

Though this doctrine is anything but new and, to some persons, may have the air of a truism,[3] there is no doctrine which stands more directly opposed to the general tendency of existing opinion and practice. Society has expended fully as much effort in the attempt (according to its lights) to compel people to conform to its notions of personal as of social excellence. The ancient commonwealths thought themselves entitled to practice, and the ancient philosophers countenanced,[4] the regulation of every part of private conduct by public authority, on the ground that the State had a deep interest in the whole bodily and mental discipline of every one of its citizens—a mode of thinking which may have been admissible in small republics surrounded by powerful enemies, in constant peril of being subverted by foreign attack or internal commotion, and to which even a short interval of relaxed energy and self-command might so easily be fatal that they could not afford to wait for the salutary permanent effects of freedom. In the modern world, the greater size of political communities and, above all, the separation between spiritual and temporal authority (which placed the direction of men's consciences in other hands than those which controlled their worldly affairs) prevented so great an interference by law in the details of private life; but the engines of moral repression have been wielded more strenuously against divergence from the reigning opinion in self-regarding then even in social matters; religion, the most powerful of the elements which have entered into the formation of moral feeling, having almost always been governed either by the ambition of a hierarchy seeking control over every department of human conduct, or by the spirit of Puritanism. . . .

Apart from the peculiar tenets of individual thinkers, there is also in the world at large an increasing inclination to stretch unduly the powers of society over the individual, both by the force of opinion and even by that of legislation; and as the tendency of all the changes taking place in the world is to strengthen society and diminish the power of the individual, this encroachment is not one of the evils which tend spontaneously to disappear, but, on the contrary, to grow more and more formidable. The disposition of mankind, whether as rulers or as fellow citizens, to impose their own opinions and inclinations as a rule of conduct on others is so energetically supported by some of the best and by some of the worst feelings in-

[3] A truth so obvious that it scarcely calls for elaboration.
[4] Condoned, allowed.

cident to human nature that it is hardly ever kept under restraint by anything but want of power; and as the power is not declining, but growing, unless a strong barrier of moral conviction can be raised against the mischief, we must expect, in the present circumstances of the world, to see it increase.

It will be convenient for the argument if, instead of at once entering upon the general thesis, we confine ourselves in the first instance to a single branch of it on which the principle here stated is, if not fully, yet to a certain point, recognized by the current opinions. This one branch is the Liberty of Thought, from which it is impossible to separate the cognate liberty of speaking and of writing. Although these liberties, to some considerable amount, form part of the political morality of all countries which profess religious toleration and free institutions, the grounds, both philosophical and practical, on which they rest are perhaps not so familiar to the general mind, nor so thoroughly appreciated by many, even of the leaders of opinion, as might have been expected. Those grounds, when rightly understood, are of much wider application than to only one division of the subject, and a thorough consideration of this part of the question will be found the best introduction to the remainder. Those to whom nothing which I am about to say will be new may therefore, I hope, excuse me if on the subject which for now three centuries has been so often discussed I venture on one discussion more.

OF THE LIBERTY OF THOUGHT AND DISCUSSION

The time, it is to be hoped, is gone by when any defense would be necessary of the "liberty of the press" as one of the securities against corrupt or tyrannical government. No argument, we may suppose, can now be needed against permitting a legislature or an executive, not identified in interest with the people, to prescribe opinions to them and determine what doctrines or what arguments they shall be allowed to hear. This aspect of the question, besides, has been so often and so triumphantly enforced by preceding writers that it needs not be specially insisted on in this place. Though the law of England, on the subject of the press, is as servile to this day as it was in the time of the Tudors,[5] there is little danger of its being actually put in

[5] The Tudor royal house ruled England from 1485 to 1603.

force against political discussion except during some temporary panic when fear of insurrection drives ministers and judges from their propriety; and, speaking generally, it is not, in constitutional countries, to be apprehended that the government, whether completely responsible to the people or not, will often attempt to control the expression of opinion, except when in doing so it makes itself the organ of the general intolerance of the public. Let us suppose, therefore, that the government is entirely at one with the people, and never thinks of exerting any power of coercion unless in agreement with what it conceives to be their voice. But I deny the right of the people to exercise such coercion, either by themselves or by their government. The power itself is illegitimate. The best government has no more title to it than the worst. It is as noxious, or more noxious, when exerted in accordance with public opinion than when in opposition to it. If all mankind minus one were of one opinion, and only one person were of the contrary opinion, mankind would be no more justified in silencing that one person, than he, if he had the power, would be justified in silencing mankind. Were an opinion a personal possession of no value except to the owner, if to be obstructed in the enjoyment of it were simply a private injury, it would make some difference whether the injury was inflicted only on a few persons or on many. But the peculiar evil of silencing the expression of an opinion is that it is robbing the human race, posterity as well as the existing generation—those who dissent from the opinion, still more than those who hold it. If the opinion is right, they are deprived of the opportunity of exchanging error for truth; if wrong, they lose, what is almost as great a benefit, the clearer perception and livelier impression of truth produced by its collision with error.

It is necessary to consider separately these two hypotheses, each of which has a distinct branch of the argument corresponding to it. We can never be sure that the opinion we are endeavoring to stifle is a false opinion; and if we were sure, stifling it would be an evil still.

First, the opinion which it is attempted to suppress by authority may possibly be true. Those who desire to suppress it, of course, deny its truth; but they are not infallible. They have no authority to decide the question for all mankind and exclude every other person from the means of judging. To refuse a hearing to an opinion because they are sure that it is false is to assume that their certainty is the same thing as absolute certainty. All silencing of discussion is an assumption of infallibility. Its condemnation may be allowed to rest on this common argument, not the worse for being common.

Unfortunately for the good sense of mankind, the fact of their fallibility is far from carrying the weight in their practical judgment which is always allowed to it in theory; for while every one well knows himself to be fallible, few think it necessary to take any precautions against their own fallibility, or admit the supposition that any opinion of which they feel very certain may be one of the examples of the error to which they acknowledge themselves to be liable. Absolute princes, or others who are accustomed to unlimited deference, usually feel this complete confidence in their own opinions on nearly all subjects. People more happily situated, who sometimes hear their opinions disputed and are not wholly unused to be set right when they are wrong, place the same unbounded reliance only on such of their opinions as are shared by all who surround them, or to whom they habitually defer; for in proportion to a man's want of confidence in his own solitary judgment does he usually repose, with implicit trust, on the infallibility of "the world" in general. And the world, to each individual, means the part of it with which he comes in contact: his party, his sect, his church, his class of society; the man may be called, by comparison, almost liberal and large-minded to whom it means anything so comprehensive as his own country or his own age. Nor is his faith in this collective authority at all shaken by his being aware that other ages, countries, sects, churches, classes, and parties have thought, and even now think, the exact reverse. He devolves upon his own world the responsibility of being in the right against the dissentient worlds of other people; and it never troubles him that mere accident has decided which of these numerous worlds is the object of his reliance, and that the same causes which make him a churchman[6] in London would have made him a Buddhist[7] or a Confucian[8] in Peking. Yet it is as evident in itself, as any amount of argument can make it, that ages are no more infallible than individuals—every age having held many opinions which subsequent ages have deemed not only false but absurd; and it is as certain that many opinions, now general, will

[6] A member of the Church of England.
[7] A follower of the Indian religious philosopher Buddha (Gautama Siddhartha, ca. 563–ca. 483 B.C.).
[8] A follower of the Chinese philosopher Confucius (ca. 551–479 B.C.).

be rejected by future ages, as it is that many, once general, are rejected by the present.

The objection likely to be made to this argument would probably take some such form as the following. There is no greater assumption of infallibility in forbidding the propagation of error than in any other thing which is done by public authority on its own judgment and responsibility. Judgment is given to men that they may use it. Because it may be used erroneously, are men to be told that they ought not to use it at all? To prohibit what they think pernicious, is not claiming exemption from error, but fulfilling the duty incumbent on them, although fallible, of acting on their conscientious conviction. If we were never to act on our opinions, because those opinions may be wrong, we should leave all our interests uncared for, and all our duties unperformed. An objection which applies to all conduct can be no valid objection to any conduct in particular. It is the duty of governments, and of individuals, to form the truest opinions they can; to form them carefully, and never impose them upon others unless they are quite sure of being right. But when they are sure (such reasoners may say), it is not conscientiousness but cowardice to shrink from acting on their opinions and allow doctrines which they honestly think dangerous to the welfare of mankind, either in this life or in another, to be scattered abroad without restraint, because other people, in less enlightened times, have persecuted opinions now believed to be true. Let us take care, it may be said, not to make the same mistake; but governments and nations have made mistakes in other things which are not denied to be fit subjects for the exercise of authority: they have laid on bad taxes, made unjust wars. Ought we therefore to lay on no taxes and, under whatever provocation, make no wars? Men and governments must act to the best of their ability. There is no such thing as absolute certainty, but there is assurance sufficient for the purposes of human life. We may, and must, assume our opinion to be true for the guidance of our own conduct; and it is assuming no more when we forbid bad men to pervert society by the propagation of opinions which we regard as false and pernicious.

I answer, that it is assuming very much more. There is the greatest difference between presuming an opinion to be true because, with every opportunity for contesting it, it has not been refuted, and assuming its truth for the purpose of not permitting its refutation.

Complete liberty of contradicting and disproving our opinion is the very condition which justifies us in assuming its truth for purposes of action; and on no other terms can a being with human faculties have any rational assurance of being right.

When we consider either the history of opinion or the ordinary conduct of human life, to what is it to be ascribed that the one and the other are no worse than they are? Not certainly to the inherent force of the human understanding, for on any matter not self-evident there are ninty-nine persons totally incapable of judging of it for one who is capable; and the capacity of the hundredth person is only comparative, for the majority of the eminent men of every past generation held many opinions now known to be erroneous, and did or approved numerous things which no one will now justify. Why is it, then, that there is on the whole a preponderance among mankind of rational opinions and rational conduct? If there really is this preponderance—which there must be unless human affairs are, and have always been, in an almost desperate state—it is owing to a quality of the human mind, the source of everything respectable in man either as an intellectual or as a moral being, namely, that his errors are corrigible. He is capable of rectifying his mistakes by discussion and experience. Not by experience alone. There must be discussion to show how experience is to be interpreted. Wrong opinions and practices gradually yield to fact and argument; but facts and arguments, to produce any effect on the mind, must be brought before it. Very few facts are able to tell their own story, without comments to bring out their meaning. The whole strength and value, then, of human judgment depending on the one property, that it can be set right when it is wrong, reliance can be placed on it only when the means of setting it right are kept constantly at hand. In the case of any person whose judgment is really deserving of confidence, how has it become so? Because he has kept his mind open to criticism of his opinions and conduct. Because it has been his practice to listen to all that could be said against him; to profit by as much of it as was just, and to expound to himself, and upon occasion to others, the fallacy of what was fallacious. Because he has felt that the only way in which a human being can make some approach to knowing the whole of a subject is by hearing what can be said about it by persons of every variety of opinion, and studying all modes in which it can be looked at by every character of mind. No wise man ever acquired his wisdom in any mode but this; nor is it in the nature of human intellect to become wise in any other manner. The steady habit of correcting and completing his own opinion by collating it with those of others, so far from causing doubt and hesitation in carrying it into practice, is the only stable foundation for a just reliance on it; for, being cognizant of all that can, at least obviously, be said against him, and having taken up his position against all gain-sayers—knowing that he has sought for objections and difficulties instead of avoiding them, and has shut out no light which can be thrown upon the subject from any quarter—he has a right to think his judgment better than that of any person, or any multitude, who have not gone through a similar process.

It is not too much to require that what the wisest of mankind, those who are best entitled to trust their own judgment, find necessary to warrant their relying on it, should be submitted to by that miscellaneous collection of a few wise and many foolish individuals called the public. The most intolerant of churches, the Roman Catholic Church, even at the canonization of a saint admits, and listens patiently to, a "devil's advocate." The holiest of men, it appears, cannot be admitted to posthumous honors until all that the devil could say against him is known and weighed. If even the Newtonian philosophy[9] were not permitted to be questioned, mankind could not feel as complete assurance of its truth as they now do. The beliefs which we have most warrant for have no safeguard to rest on but a standing invitation to the whole world to prove them unfounded. If the challenge is not accepted, or is accepted and the attempt fails, we are far enough from certainty still, but we have done the best that the existing state of human reason admits of: we have neglected nothing that could give the truth a chance of reaching us; if the lists are kept open, we may hope that, if there be a better truth, it will be found when the human mind is capable of receiving it; and in the meantime we may rely on having attained such approach to truth as is possible in our own day. This is the amount of certainty attainable by a fallible being, and this the sole way of attaining it.

Strange it is that men should admit the validity of the arguments for free discussion, but object to their being "pushed to an extreme," not seeing that unless the reasons are good for an extreme case, they are not good for any case. Strange that they should imagine that they are not assuming infallibility when they acknowledge that there

[9] Isaac Newton (1642–1727), an English mathematician, physicist, and philosopher, is famous for his "Laws of Motion" and for his principles of scientific reasoning.

should be free discussion on all subjects which can possibly be *doubtful*, but think that some particular principle or doctrine should be forbidden to be questioned because it is *so certain*, that is, because *they are certain* that it is certain. To call any proposition certain, while there is any one who would deny its certainty if permitted, but who is not permitted, is to assume that we ourselves, and those who agree with us, are the judges of certainty, and judges without hearing the other side.

In the present age—which has been described as "destitute of faith, but terrified at scepticism"—in which people feel sure, not so much that their opinions are true as that they should not know what to do without them—the claims of an opinion to be protected from public attack are rested not so much on its truth as on its importance to society. There are, it is alleged, certain beliefs so useful, not to say indispensable, to well-being that it is as much the duty of governments to uphold those beliefs as to protect any other of the interests of society. In a case of such necessity, and so directly in the line of their duty, something less than infallibility may, it is maintained, warrant, and even bind, governments to act on their own opinion confirmed by the general opinion of mankind. It is also often argued, and still oftener thought, that none but bad men would desire to weaken these salutary beliefs; and there can be nothing wrong, it is thought, in restraining bad men and prohibiting what only such men would wish to practice. This mode of thinking makes the justification of restraints on discussion not a question of the truth of doctrines but of their usefulness, and flatters itself by that means to escape the responsibility of claiming to be an infallible judge of opinions. But those who thus satisfy themselves do not perceive that the assumption of infallibility is merely shifted from one point to another. The usefulness of an opinion is itself matter of opinion—as disputable, as open to discussion, and requiring discussion as much as the opinion itself. There is the same need of an infallible judge of opinions to decide an opinion to be noxious as to decide it to be false, unless the opinion condemned has full opportunity of defending itself. And it will not do to say that the heretic may be allowed to maintain the utility or harmlessness of his opinion, though forbidden to maintain its truth. The truth of an opinion is part of its utility. It we would know whether or not it is desirable that a proposition should be believed, is it possible to exclude the consideration of whether or not it is true? In the opinion, not of bad men, but of the best men, no belief which is contrary to truth can be really useful; and can you prevent such men from urging that plea when they are charged with culpability for denying some doctrine which they are told is useful, but which they believe to be false? Those who are on the side of received opinions never fail to take all possible advantage of this plea; you do not find *them* handling the question of utility as if it could be completely abstracted from that of truth; on the contrary, it is, above all, because their doctrine is "the truth," that the knowledge or the belief of it is held to be so indispensable. There can be no fair discussion of the question of usefulness when an argument so vital may be employed on one side, but not on the other. And in point of fact, when law or public feeling do not permit the truth of an opinion to be disputed, they are just as little tolerant of a denial of its usefulness. The utmost they allow is an extenuation of its absolute necessity, or of the positive guilt of rejecting it.

· · ·

We have now recognized the necessity to the mental well-being of mankind (on which all their other well-being depends) of freedom of opinion, and freedom of the expression of opinion, on four distinct grounds, which we will now briefly recapitulate:

First, if any opinion is compelled to silence, that opinion may, for aught we can certainly know, be true. To deny this is to assume our own infallibility.

Secondly, though the silenced opinion be an error, it may, and very commonly does, contain a portion of truth; and since the general or prevailing opinion on any subject is rarely or never the whole truth, it is only by the collision of adverse opinions that the remainder of the truth has any chance of being supplied.

Thirdly, even if the received opinion be not only true, but the whole truth; unless it is suffered to be, and actually is, vigorously and earnestly contested, it will, by most of those who receive it, be held in the manner of a prejudice, with little comprehension or feeling of its rational grounds. And not only this, but, fourthly, the meaning of the doctrine itself will be in danger of being lost or enfeebled, and deprived of its vital effect on the character and conduct: the dogma becoming a mere formal profession, inefficacious for good, but cumbering the ground and preventing the growth of any real and heartfelt conviction from reason or personal experience.

Before quitting the subject of freedom of opinion, it is fit to take some notice of those who say that the free expression of all opinions should be permitted on condition that the manner be temperate and do not pass the bounds of fair discussion. Much might be said on the impossibility of fixing where these supposed bounds are to be placed; for if the test be offense to those whose opinion is attacked, I think experience testifies that this offense is given whenever the attack is telling and powerful, and that every opponent who pushes them hard, and whom they find it difficult to answer, appears to them, if he shows any strong feeling on the subject, an intemperate opponent. But this, though an important consideration in a practical point of view, merges in a more fundamental objection. Undoubtedly, the manner of asserting an opinion, even though it be a true one, may be very objectionable and may justly incur severe censure. But the principal offenses of the kind are such as it is mostly impossible, unless by accidental self-betrayal, to bring home to conviction. The gravest of them is, to argue sophistically, to suppress facts or arguments, to misstate the elements of the case, or misrepresent the opposite opinion. But all this, even to the most aggravated degree, is so continually done in perfect good faith by persons who are not considered, and in many other respects may not deserve to be considered, ignorant or incompetent, that it is rarely possible, on adequate grounds, conscientiously to stamp the misrepresentation as morally culpable, and still less could law presume to interfere with this kind of controversial misconduct. With regard to what is commonly meant by intemperate discussion, namely invective, sarcasm, personality, and the like, the denunciation of these weapons would deserve more sympathy if it were ever proposed to interdict them equally to both sides; but it is only desired to restrain the employment of them against the prevailing opinion; against the unprevailing they may not only be used without general disapproval, but will be likely to obtain for him who uses them the praise of honest zeal and righteous indignation. Yet whatever mischief arises from their use, is greatest when they are employed against the comparatively defenseless; and whatever unfair advantage can be derived by any opinion from this mode of asserting it accrues almost exclusively to received opinions. The worst offense of this kind which can be committed by a polemic is to stigmatize those who hold the contrary opinion as bad and immoral men. To calumny[10] of this sort, those who hold

---

[10] Slander.

any unpopular opinion are peculiarly exposed, because they are in general few and uninfluential, and nobody but themselves feels much interest in seeing justice done them; but this weapon is, from the nature of the case, denied to those who attack a prevailing opinion: they can neither use it with safety to themselves, nor, if they could, would it do anything but recoil on their own cause. In general, opinions contrary to those commonly received can only obtain a hearing by studied moderation of language and the most cautious avoidance of unnecessary offense, from which they hardly ever deviate even in a slight degree without losing ground, while unmeasured vituperation employed on the side of the prevailing opinion really does deter people from professing contrary opinions and from listening to those who profess them. For the interest, therefore, of truth and justice it is far more important to restrain this employment of vituperative language than the other; and, for example, if it were necessary to choose, there would be much more need to discourage offensive attacks on infidelity than on religion. It is, however, obvious that law and authority have no business with restraining either, while opinion ought, in every instance, to determine its verdict by the circumstances of the individual case—condemning everyone, on whichever side of the argument he places himself, in whose mode of advocacy either want of candor, or malignity, bigotry, or intolerance of feeling manifest themselves; but not inferring these vices from the side which a person takes, though it be the contrary side of the question to our own; and giving merited honor to everyone, whatever opinion he may hold, who has calmness to see and honesty to state what his opponents, and their opinions really are, exaggerating nothing to their discredit, keeping nothing back which tells, or can be supposed to tell, in their favor. This is the real morality of public discussion; and if often violated, I am happy to think that there are many controversialists who to a great extent observe it, and a still greater number who conscientiously strive towards it.

• • •

OF THE LIMITS TO THE AUTHORITY OF SOCIETY OVER THE INDIVIDUAL

What, then, is the rightful limit to the sovereignty of the individual over himself? Where does the authority of society begin? How much of human life should be assigned to individuality, and how much to society?

Each will receive its proper share if each has that which more particularly concerns it. To individuality should belong the part of life in which it is chiefly the individual that is interested; to society, the part which chiefly interests society.

Though society is not founded on a contract, and though no good purpose is answered by inventing a contract in order to deduce social obligations from it, every one who receives the protection of society owes a return for the benefit, and the fact of living in society renders it indispensable that each should be bound to observe a certain line of conduct towards the rest. This conduct consists, first, in not injuring the interests of one another, or rather certain interests which, either by express legal provision or by tacit understanding, ought to be considered as rights; and secondly, in each person's bearing his share (to be fixed on some equitable principle) of the labors and sacrifices incurred for defending the society or its members from injury and molestation. These conditions society is justified in enforcing at all costs to those who endeavor to withhold fulfillment. Nor is this all that society may do. The acts of an individual may be hurtful to others or wanting in due consideration for their welfare, without going to the length of violating any of their constituted rights. The offender may then be justly punished by opinion, though not by law. As soon as any part of a person's conduct affects prejudicially the interests of others, society has jurisdiction over it, and the question whether the general welfare will or will not be promoted by interfering with it becomes open to discussion. But there is no room for entertaining any such question when a person's conduct affects the interests of no persons besides himself, or needs not affect them unless they like (all the persons concerned being of full age and the ordinary amount of understanding). In all such cases, there should be perfect freedom, legal and social, to do the action and stand the consequences.

It would be a great misunderstanding of this doctrine to suppose that it is one of selfish indifference which pretends that human beings have no business with each other's conduct in life, and that they should not concern themselves about the well-doing or well-being of one another, unless their own interest is involved. Instead of any diminution, there is need of a great increase of disinterested exertion to promote the good of others. But disinterested benevolence can find other instruments to persuade people to their good than whips and scourges,[11] either of the literal or the metaphorical sort. I am the last person to undervalue the self-regarding virtues; they are only second in importance, if even second, to the social. It is equally the business of education to cultivate both. But even education works by conviction and persuasion as well as by compulsion, and it is by the former only that, when the period of education is past, the self-regarding virtues should be inculcated. Human beings owe to each other help to distinguish the better from the worse, and encouragement to choose the former and avoid the latter. They should be forever stimulating each other to increased exercise of their higher faculties and increased direction of their feelings and aims towards wise instead of foolish, elevating instead of degrading, objects and contemplations. But neither one person, nor any number of persons, is warranted in saying to another human creature of ripe years that he shall not do with his life for his own benefit what he chooses to do with it. He is the person most interested in his own well-being: the interest which any other person, except in cases of strong personal attachment, can have in it is trifling compared with that which he himself has; the interest which society has in him individually (except as to his conduct to others) is fractional and altogether indirect, while with respect to his own feelings and circumstances the most ordinary man or woman has means of knowledge immeasurably surpassing those that can be possessed by any one else. The interference of society to overrule his judgment and purposes in what only regards himself must be grounded on general presumptions which may be altogether wrong and, even if right, are as likely as not to be misapplied to individual cases, by persons no better acquainted with the circumstances of such cases than those are who look at them merely from without. In this department, therefore, of human affairs, individuality has its proper field of action. In the conduct of human beings towards one another it is necessary that general rules should for the most part be observed in order that people may know what they have to expect; but in each person's own concerns his individual spontaneity is entitled to free exercise. Considerations to aid his judgment, exhortations to strengthen his will may be offered to

[11] Various instruments of physical punishment.

him, even obtruded on him, by others; but he himself is the final judge. All errors which he is likely to commit against advice and warning are far out-weighed by the evil of allowing others to constrain him to what they deem his good. . . .

What I contend for is, that the inconveniences which are strictly inseparable from the unfavorable judgment of others, are the only ones to which a person should ever be subjected for that portion of his conduct and character which concerns his own good, but which does not affect the interests of others in their relations with him. Acts injurious to others require a totally different treatment. Encroachment on their rights; infliction on them of any loss or damage not justified by his own rights; falsehood or duplicity in dealing with them; unfair or ungenerous use of advantages over them; even selfish abstinence from defending them against injury—these are fit objects of moral reprobation and, in grave cases, of moral retribution and punishment. And not only these acts, but the dispositions which lead to them, are properly immoral and fit subjects of disapprobation which may rise to abhorrence. Cruelty of disposition; malice and ill-nature; that most antisocial and odious of all passions, envy; dissimulation and insincerity, irascibility on insufficient cause, and resentment disproportioned to the provocation; the love of domineering over others; the desire to engross more than one's share of advantages (the *pleonexía* [12] of the Greeks); the pride which derives gratification from the abasement of others; the egotism which thinks self and its concerns more important than everything else, and decides all doubtful questions in its own favor—these are moral vices, and constitute a bad and odious moral character; unlike the self-regarding faults previously mentioned, which are not properly immoralities and, to whatever pitch they may be carried, do not constitute wickedness. They may be proofs of any amount of folly or want of personal dignity and self-respect, but they are only a subject of moral reprobation when they involve a breach of duty to others, for whose sake the individual is bound to have care for himself. What are called duties to ourselves are not socially obligatory unless circumstances render them at the same time duties to others. The term duty to oneself, when it means anything more than prudence, means self-respect or self-development, and for none of these is anyone ac-

---

[12] The claim to more than one deserves, greediness.

countable to his fellow creatures, because for none of them is it for the good of mankind that he be held accountable to them.

• • •

APPLICATIONS

The worth of a State, in the long run, is the worth of the individuals composing it; and a State which postpones the interests of *their* mental expansion and elevation to a little more of administrative skill, or of that semblance of it which practice gives in the details of business; a State which dwarfs its men, in order that they may be more docile instruments in its hands even for beneficial purposes—will find that with small men no great thing can really be accomplished; and that the perfection of machinery to which it has sacrificed everything will in the end avail it nothing, for want of the vital power which, in order that the machine might work more smoothly, it has preferred to banish.

18

Georg Wilhelm Friedrich Hegel
Reason in History

*Georg Wilhelm Friedrich Hegel (1770–1831), the most influential philoso-
pher of the nineteenth century, incorporated into his written work many elements of romanticism. His philosophical idealism, his emphasis on change
and the sweep of history, his organic theory of society, and his rejection of
the abstract, mechanical rationalism of the Enlightenment—all stamp Hegel
as a child of the romantic age. A university professor in Germany for most of
his life, he wrote in a complex and difficult style, but nevertheless dominated
European philosophy in his lifetime by reason of the universal scope and
power of his intellectual system. Since that era, almost all great Western
philosophies—whether idealist or materialist, pragmatic or existentialist, radical or conservative—have had to come to terms with Hegel's ideas. In this respect, the philosophy of Hegel may be considered an intellectual bridge
between the eighteenth and twentieth centuries.*

*Through his philosophy Hegel hoped to prove this universe to be actually
one—even if views, phenomena, and facts seemed to contradict one another.
He derived his conviction concerning the oneness of the world from his Lu-
theran faith, which taught that all creation was of divine origin; therefore,
all the world, he reasoned, had to be of one divine nature. Hegel went a step
further, asserting that God, or Spirit, the term he used, had become history—
and not merely interfered in history. The process in which the Spirit became
history had been set in motion because the Spirit sought knowledge of its own*

From Georg Wilhelm Friedrich Hegel, *Reason in History*, edited by Robert S. Hart-
man, copyright 1953 by the Liberal Arts Press, Inc., reprinted by permission of the
Liberal Arts Press Division of The Bobbs-Merrill Company, Inc. [This work is a new
translation of Hegel's *The Philosophy of History*, 11–12, 20, 22–23, 25–29, 49–50,
52–53, 68–71, 87–89, 94–95.]

nature or potential. In order to achieve it, the Spirit had to incorporate itself into its opposite, that is, physical creation. In incorporating itself into its opposite, the Spirit became "estranged" or "alienated." World development from that moment onward, Hegel maintained, has been a creative clash between two opposites thesis and antithesis, out of which emerges a synthesis (containing elements of the former thesis and antithesis). Each synthesis becomes in turn, a new thesis, calling forth its own antithesis; and this "dialectical" process is repeated, each time on a higher level, endlessly. Thus, world development is not to be understood as simple and unopposed growth, but as unwilling labor against itself, that is, struggle by which the Spirit, or Idea, may more completely realize itself. To Hegel, the objects of nature were visible monuments of the various steps of the struggle. But once they become locked in their places, their subsequent history merely shows constant, though perhaps varied, cycles of repetition. Only in the realm of historic [struggling] Ideas is the new to be found. As Ideas struggle within the arena of human events, another element enters the picture: human passions and interest. Although necessarily a continuous upward movement, world history nevertheless rocks back and forth constantly within the confines of the "warp and woof" of divine Idea and human passions.

Hegel believed that the State was the highest and purest level the divine Idea had achieved up to his time. Thus the State was not to be understood as an organization formed at will and forged by chance, but as the highest expression of divine morality. It followed that the laws of the State were of divine origin, and therefore the duty of a citizen was to submit to them. It also was prudent to be obedient to the laws because all value that people have, all spiritual morality, all chance for self-realization, they have through the State alone. Only in fusing their subjective will with the rational will of the State could citizens find true freedom. Freedom thus could never be synonymous with a person's individualistic choices and preferences ("caprice"). Hegel held that the national bourgeois states of nineteenth-century Europe in general, and the Prussian State in particular, had arrived near the last stage of the unfolding of the divine Idea: State and morality had become virtually synonymous and interchangeable terms. That a government (State) in the next century might demand obedience while performing criminal and inhuman acts was unimaginable to Hegel. Since its premise was progression, the Hegelian dialectic allowed no room for retrogression or relapse into a barbarous past.

The Philosophy of History *was not written by Hegel himself. But it is a compilation of notes written by him and by students present at lectures he delivered at the University of Berlin between 1822 and 1831; it was first published in 1837, several years after his death. The following selection, taken from the introduction to the work, summarizes its general ideas.*

REASON AS THE BASIS OF HISTORY

The sole thought which philosophy brings to the treatment of history is the simple concept of *Reason:* that Reason is the law of the world and that, therefore, in world history, things have come about rationally. This conviction and insight is a presupposition of history as such; in philosophy itself it is not presupposed. Through its speculative reflection philosophy has demonstrated that Reason—and this term may be accepted here without closer examination of its relation to God—is both *substance and infinite power,* in itself the infinite material of all natural and spiritual life as well as the *infinite form,* the actualization of itself as content. It is *substance,* that is to say, that by which and in which all reality has its being and subsistence. It is infinite *power,* for Reason is not so impotent as to bring about only the ideal, the ought, and to remain in an existence outside of reality—who knows where—as something peculiar in the heads of a few people. It is the infinite *content* of all essence and truth, for it does not require, as does finite activity, the condition of external materials, of given data from which to draw nourishment and objects of its activity; it supplies its own nourishment and is its own reference. And it is infinite *form,* for only in its image and by its fiat[1] do phenomena arise and begin to live. It is its own exclusive presupposition and absolutely final purpose, and itself works out this purpose from potentiality into actuality, from inward source to outward appearance, not only in the natural but also in the spiritual universe, in world history. That this *Idea* or *Reason* is the True, the Eternal, the Absolute Power and that it and nothing but it, its glory and majesty, manifests itself in the world—this, as we said before, has been proved in philosophy and is being presupposed here as proved.

Those among you . . . who are not yet acquainted with philosophy could perhaps be asked to come to these lectures on world history with the belief in Reason, with a desire, a thirst for its insight. It

[1] Order, authorization.

is indeed this desire for rational insight, for cognition, and not merely for a collection of various facts, which ought to be presupposed as a subjective aspiration in the study of the sciences. For even though one were not approaching world history with the thought and knowledge of Reason, at least one ought to have the firm and invincible faith that there is Reason in history and to believe that the world of intelligence and of self-conscious willing is not abandoned to mere chance, but must manifest itself in the light of the rational Idea. Actually, however, I do not have to demand such belief in advance. What I have said here provisionally, and shall have to say later on, must, even in our branch of science, be taken as a summary view of the whole. It is not a presupposition of study; it is a *result* which happens to be known to myself because I already know the whole. Therefore, only the study of world history itself can show that it has proceeded rationally, that it represents the rationally necessary course of the World Spirit, the Spirit whose nature is indeed always one and the same, but whose one nature unfolds in the course of the world. This, as I said, must be the result of history. History itself must be taken as it is; we have to proceed historically, empirically.[2] . . .

THE IDEA OF HISTORY AND ITS REALIZATION

The question of how Reason is determined in itself and what its relation is to the world coincides with the question, *What is the ultimate purpose of the world?* This question implies that the purpose is to be actualized and realized. Two things, then, must be considered: first, the content of this ultimate purpose, the determination as such, and, secondly, its realization.

To begin with, we must note that world history goes on within the realm of Spirit. The term "world" includes both physical and psychical nature. Physical nature does play a part in world history, and from the very beginning we shall draw attention to the fundamental natural relations thus involved. But Spirit, and the course of its development, is the substance of history. We must not contemplate nature as a rational system in itself, in its own particular domain, but only in its relation to Spirit. . . .

---

[2] Relying on practical experience.

. . . Spirit, on the stage on which we observe it, that of world history, is in its most concrete reality. But nevertheless—or rather in order to understand also the general idea of this concrete existence of Spirit—we must set forth, first, some general definition of the *nature of Spirit*. . . .

THE IDEA OF FREEDOM

The nature of Spirit may be understood by a glance at its direct opposite—Matter. The essence of matter is gravity, the essence of Spirit—its substance—is Freedom. It is immediately plausible to everyone that, among other properties, Spirit also possesses Freedom. But philosophy teaches us that *all* the properties of Spirit exist only through Freedom. All are but means of attaining Freedom; all seek and produce this and this alone. It is an insight of speculative philosophy that Freedom is the sole truth of Spirit. Matter possesses gravity by virtue of its tendency toward a central point; it is essentially composite, consisting of parts that exclude each other. It seeks its unity and thereby its own abolition; it seeks its opposite. If it would attain this it would be matter no longer, but would have perished. It strives toward ideality, for in unity it exists ideally. Spirit, on the contrary, is that which has its center in itself. It does not have unity outside of itself but has found it; it is in itself and with itself. Matter has its substance outside of itself; Spirit is Being-within-itself (self-contained existence). But this, precisely, is Freedom. For when I am dependent, I refer myself to something else which I am not; I cannot exist independently of something external. I am free when I am within myself. This self-contained existence of Spirit is self-consciousness, consciousness of self.

Two things must be distinguished in consciousness, first *that* I know and, secondly, *what* I know. In self-consciousness the two coincide, for Spirit knows itself. It is the judgment of its own nature and, at the same time, the operation of coming to itself, to produce itself, to make itself (actually) into that which it is in itself (potentially). Following this abstract definition it may be said that world history is the exhibition of spirit striving to attain knowledge of its own nature. As the germ bears in itself the whole nature of the tree, the taste and shape of its fruit, so also the first traces of Spirit virtually contain the whole of history. . . .

THE IDEA AND THE INDIVIDUAL

The question of the *means* whereby Freedom develops itself into a world leads us directly to the phenomenon of history. Although Freedom as such is primarily an internal idea, the means it uses are the external phenomena which in history present themselves directly before our eyes. The first glance at history convinces us that the actions of men spring from their needs, their passions, their interests, their characters, and their talents. Indeed, it appears as if in this drama of activities these needs, passions, and interests are the sole springs of action and the main efficient cause. It is true that this drama involves also universal purposes, benevolence, or noble patriotism. But such virtues and aims are insignificant on the broad canvas of history. We may, perhaps, see the ideal of Reason actualized in those who adopt such aims and in the spheres of their influence; but their number is small in proportion to the mass of the human race and their influence accordingly limited. Passions, private aims, and the satisfaction of selfish desires are, on the contrary, tremendous springs of action. Their power lies in the fact that they respect none of the limitations which law and morality would impose on them; and that these natural impulses are closer to the core of human nature than the artificial and troublesome discipline that tends toward order, self-restraint, law, and morality. . . .

The first thing we notice—something which has been stressed more than once before but which cannot be repeated too often, for it belongs to the central point of our inquiry—is the merely general and abstract nature of what we call principle, final purpose, destiny, or the nature and concept of Spirit. A principle, a law is something implicit, which as such, however true in itself, is not completely real (actual). Purposes, principles, and the like, are at first in our thoughts, our inner intention. They are not yet in reality. That which is in itself is a possibility, a faculty. It has not yet emerged out of its implicitness into existence. A second element must be added for it to become reality, namely, activity, actualization. The principle of this is the will, man's activity in general. It is only through this activity that the concept and its implicit ("being-in-themselves") determinations can be realized, actualized; for of themselves they have no immediate efficacy. The activity which puts them in operation and in existence is the need, the instinct, the inclination, and passion of man. When I have an idea I am greatly interested in transforming it into action, into actuality. In its realization through my participation I want to find my own satisfaction. A purpose for which I shall be active must in some way be my purpose; I must thereby satisfy my own desires, even though it may have ever so many aspects which do not concern me. This is the infinite right of the individual to find itself satisfied in its activity and labor. If men are to be interested in anything they must have "their heart" in it. Their feelings of self-importance must be satisfied. . . .

Two elements therefore enter into our investigation: first, the Idea, secondly, the complex of human passions; the one the warp, the other the woof of the vast tapestry of world history. Their contact and concrete union constitutes moral liberty in the state. We have already spoken of the Idea of freedom as the essence of Spirit and absolutely final purpose of history.

• • •

THE STATE AS REALIZATION OF THE IDEA

The [final] point, then, concerns the end to be attained by these means, that is, the form it assumes in the realm of the actual. We have spoken of means; but the carrying out of a subjective, limited aim also requires a *material* element, either already present or to be procured or to serve this actualization. Thus the question would arise: What is the material in which the final end of Reason is to be realized? It is first of all the subjective agent itself, human desires, subjectivity in general. In human knowledge and volition,[3] as its material basis, the rational attains existence. We have considered subjective volition with its purpose, namely, the truth of reality, insofar as moved by a great world-historical passion. As a subjective will in limited passions it is dependent; it can gratify its particular desires only within this dependence. But the subjective will has also a substantial life, a reality where it moves in the region of essential being and has the essential itself as the object of its existence. This essential being is the union of the subjective with the rational will; it is the moral whole, the *State*. It is that actuality in which the individual has and enjoys his freedom, but only as knowing, believing, and willing the universal. This must not be understood as if the subjective will of the individual attained its gratification and enjoyment through the

[3] Will.

common will and the latter were a means for it—as if the individual limited his freedom among the other individuals, so that this common limitation, the mutual constraint of all, might secure a small space of liberty for each. (This would only be negative freedom.) Rather, law, morality, the State, and they alone, are the positive reality and satisfaction of freedom. The caprice of the individual is not freedom. It is this caprice which is being limited, the license of particular desires.

The subjective will, passion, is the force which actualizes and realizes. The Idea is the interior; the State is the externally existing, genuinely moral life. It is the union of the universal and essential with the subjective will, and as such it is *Morality*. The individual who lives in this unity has a moral life, a value which consists in this substantiality alone. Sophocles' Antigone[4] says: "The divine commands are not of yesterday nor of today; no, they have an infinite existence, and no one can say whence they came." The laws of ethics are not accidental, but are rationality itself. It is the end of the State to make the substantial prevail and maintain itself in the actual doings of men and in their convictions. It is the absolute interest of Reason that this moral whole exist; and herein lies the justification and merit of heroes who have founded states, no matter how crude. . . .

[The State] is the realization of Freedom, of the absolute, final purpose, and exists for its own sake. All the value man has, all spiritual reality, he has only through the State. For his spiritual reality is the knowing presence to him of his own essence, of rationality, of its objective, immediate actuality present in and for him. Only thus is he truly a consciousness, only thus does he partake in morality, in the legal and moral life of the state. For the True is the unity of the universal and particular will. And the universal in the State is in its laws, its universal and rational provisions. The State is the divine Idea as it exists on earth.

Thus the State is the definite object of world history proper. In it freedom achieves its objectivity and lives in the enjoyment of this objectivity. For law is the objectivity of Spirit; it is will in its true form. Only the will that obeys the law is free, for it obeys itself and, being in itself, is free. In so far as the state, our country, constitutes a community of existence, and as the subjective will of man subjects

---

[4] The protagonist (heroine) of the play, *Antigone,* by the Greek dramatist Sophocles (*ca.* 496–406 B.C.).

itself to the laws, the antithesis of freedom and necessity disappears. The rational, like the substantial, is necessary. We are free when we recognize it as law and follow it as the substance of our own being. The objective and the subjective will are then reconciled and form one and the same harmonious whole. For the ethos[5] of the state is not of the moral, the reflective kind in which one's own conviction rules supreme. This latter is rather the peculiarity of the modern world. The true and antique morality is rooted in the principle that everybody stands in his place of duty. An Athenian citizen[6] did what was required of him, as it were from instinct. But if I reflect on the object of my activity, I must have the consciousness that my will counts. Morality, however, is the duty, the substantial law, the second nature, as it has been rightly called; for the first nature of man is his immediate, animalic existence.

• • •

THE COURSE OF WORLD HISTORY: THE PRINCIPLE OF DEVELOPMENT

We have now learned the abstract characteristics of the nature of Spirit, the means which it uses to realize its Idea, and the form which its complete realization assumes in external existence, namely, the State. All that remains for this introduction is to consider the *course of world history*.

Historical change, seen abstractly, has long been understood generally as involving a progress toward the better, the more perfect. Change in nature, no matter how infinitely varied it is, shows only a cycle of constant repetition. In nature nothing new happens under the sun, and in this respect the multiform play of her products leads to boredom. One and the same permanent character continuously reappears, and all change reverts to it. Only the changes in the realm of Spirit create the novel. This characteristic of Spirit suggested to man a feature entirely different from that of nature—the desire toward *perfectibility*. This principle, which brings change itself under laws, has been badly received by religions such as the Catholic and also by states which desire as their true right to be static or at least

---

[5] Distinguishing attitude and character.
[6] That is, a citizen of Athens during its "Great Age" (fifth century B.C.).

stable. When the mutability[7] of secular things, such as states, is conceded on principle, then religion, as religion of truth, is excluded. On the other hand, one leaves undecided whether changes, revolutions, and destructions of legitimate conditions are not due to accidents, blunders, and, in particular, the license and evil passions of men. Actually, perfectibility is something almost as undetermined as mutability in general; it is without aim and purpose and without a standard of change. The better, the more perfect toward which it is supposed to attain, is entirely undetermined.

The principle of *development* implies further that it is based on an inner principle, a presupposed potentiality, which brings itself into existence. This formal determination is essentially the Spirit whose scene, property, and sphere of realization is world history. It does not flounder about in the external play of accidents. On the contrary, it is absolutely determined and firm against them. It uses them for its own purposes and dominates them. But development is also a property of organic natural objects. Their existence is not merely dependent, subject to external influences. It proceeds from an inner immutable principle, a simple essence, which first exists as germ. From this simple existence it brings forth out of itself differentiations which connect it with other things. Thus it lives a life of continuous transformation. On the other hand, we may look at it from the opposite point of view and see in it the preservation of the organic principle and its form. Thus the organic individual produces itself; it makes itself actually into that which it is in itself (potentially). In the same way, Spirit is only that into which it makes itself, and it makes itself actually into that which it is in itself (potentially). The development of the organism proceeds in an immediate, direct (undialectic), unhindered manner. Nothing can interfere between the concept and its realization, the inherent nature of the germ and the adaptation of its existence to this nature. It is different with Spirit. The transition of its potentiality into actuality is mediated through consciousness and will. These are themselves first immersed in their immediate organic life; their first object and purpose is this natural existence as such. But the latter, through its animation by Spirit, becomes itself infinitely demanding, rich, and strong. Thus Spirit is at war with itself. It must overcome itself as its own enemy and formidable ob-

[7] Changeability.

stacle. Development, which in nature is a quiet unfolding, is in Spirit a hard, infinite struggle against itself. What Spirit wants is to attain its own concept. But it hides it from itself and is proud and full of enjoyment in this alienation from itself.

Historical development, therefore, is not the harmless and unopposed simple growth of organic life but hard, unwilling labor against itself. Furthermore, it is not mere formal self-development in general, but the production of an end of determined content. This end we have stated from the beginning: it is Spirit in its essence, the concept of freedom. This is the fundamental object and hence the leading principle of development. Through it the development receives meaning and significance—just as in Roman history Rome is the object and hence the guiding principle of the inquiry into past events. At the same time, however, the events arise out of this object and have meaning and content only with reference to it.

There are in world history several large periods which have passed away, apparently without further development. Their whole enormous gain of culture has been annihilated and, unfortunately, one had to start all over from the beginning in order to reach again one of the levels of culture which had been reached long ago—assisted, perhaps, by some ruins saved of old treasures—with a new, immeasurable effort of power and time, of crime and suffering. On the other hand, there are continuing developments, structures, and systems of culture in particular spheres, rich in kind and well-developed in every direction. The merely formal view of development can give preference neither to one course nor the other; nor can it account for the purpose of that decline of older periods. It must consider such events, and in particular such reversals, as external accidents. It can judge the relative advantages only according to indefinite viewpoints—viewpoints which are relative precisely because development *in general* is viewed as the one and only purpose.

World history, then, represents the phases in the development of the principle whose *content* is the consciousness of freedom. The analysis of its stages in general belongs to Logic. That of its particular, its concrete nature, belongs to the Philosophy of Spirit. Let us only repeat here that the first stage is the immersion of Spirit in natural life, the second its stepping out into the consciousness of its freedom. This first emancipation from nature is incomplete and partial; it issues from immediate naturalness, still refers to it, and hence is still incumbered by it as one of its elements. The third stage is the rising out of this still particular form of freedom into pure universality of freedom, where the spiritual essence attains the consciousness and feeling of itself. These stages are the fundamental principles of the universal process. Each is again, within itself, a process of its own formation. But the detail of this inner dialectic of transition must be left to the sequel.

All we have to indicate here is that Spirit begins with its infinite possibility, but *only* its possibility. As such it contains its absolute content within itself, as its aim and goal, which it attains only as result of its activity. Then and only then has Spirit attained its reality. Thus, in existence, progress appears as an advance from the imperfect to the more perfect. But the former must not only be taken in abstraction as the merely imperfect, but as that which contains at the same time its own opposite, the so-called perfect, as germ, as urge within itself. In the same way, at least in thought, possibility points to something which shall become real; more precisely, the Aristotelian *dynamis* is also *potentia,* force and power. The imperfect, thus, as the opposite of itself in itself, is its own antithesis, which on the one hand exists, but, on the other, is annulled and resolved. It is the urge, the impulse of spiritual life in itself, to break through the hull of nature, of sensuousness, of its own self-alienation, and to attain the light of consciousness, namely, its own self.

• • •

THE DIALECTIC OF NATIONAL PRINCIPLES

World history in general is the development of Spirit in *Time,* just as nature is the development of the Idea in *Space.*

When we cast a glance at world history in general, we see a tremendous picture of transformations and actions, an infinite of varied formations of peoples, states, individuals, in restless succession. Everything that can enter and interest the mind of man, every sentiment of goodness, beauty, greatness is called into play. Everywhere aims are adopted and pursued which we recognize, whose accomplishment we desire; we hope and fear for them. In all these events and accidents we see human activity and suffering in the foreground, everywhere something which is part and parcel of ourselves, and therefore everywhere our interest takes sides for or against. At times we are attracted by beauty, freedom, and richness, at others by energy, by which even vice knows how to make itself important. At other times we see the large mass of a universal interest move heavily along, only to be abandoned to and pulverized by an infinite complexity of trifling circumstances. Then again we see trivial results from gigantic expenditures of forces or tremendous results from seemingly insignificant causes. Everywhere the motliest throng which draws us into its circle; when the one disappears, the other swiftly takes its place. . . .

We must, then, consider the Spirit in this respect. Its transformations are not merely rejuvenating transitions, returns to the same form. They are elaborations upon itself, by which it multiplies the material for its endeavors. Thus it experiments in a multitude of dimensions and directions, developing itself, exercising itself, enjoying itself in inexhaustible abundance. For each of its creations, satisfying for the moment, presents new material, a new challenge for further elaboration. The abstract thought of mere change gives place to the thought of Spirit manifesting, developing, and differentiating its powers in all the directions of its plenitude. What powers it possesses in itself we understand by the multiplicity of its products and formations. In this lust of activity it only deals with itself. Though involved with the conditions of nature, both inner and outer, it not only meets in them opposition and hindrance, but often failure and defeat through the complications into which it becomes involved through them or through itself. But even when it perishes it does so in the course of its function and destiny, and even then it offers the spectacle of having proved itself as spiritual activity. . . .

Spirit is essentially the result of its own activity. Its activity is transcending the immediately given, negating it, and returning into itself. We can compare it with the seed of a plant, which is both beginning and result of the plant's whole life. The powerlessness of life manifests itself precisely in this falling apart of beginning and end. Likewise in the lives of individuals and peoples. The life of a people brings a fruit to maturity, for its activity aims at actualizing its principle. But the fruit does not fall back into the womb of the people which has produced and matured it. On the contrary, it turns into a bitter drink for this people. The people cannot abandon it, for it has an unquenchable thirst for it. But imbibing the drink is the drinker's destruction, yet, at the same time the rise of a new principle.

We have already seen what the final purpose of this process is. The principles of the national spirits progressing through a necessary succession of stages are only moments of the one universal Spirit which through them elevates and completes itself into a self-comprehending *totality*.

Thus, in dealing with the idea of Spirit only and in considering the whole of world history as nothing but its manifestation, we are dealing only with the *present*—however long the past may be which we survey. The Idea is ever present, the Spirit immortal. This implies that the present stage of Spirit contains all previous stages within itself. These, to be sure, have unfolded themselves successively and separately, but Spirit still is what it has in itself always been. The differentiation of its stages is but the development of what it is in itself. The life of the ever-present Spirit is a cycle of stages, which, on the one hand, co-exist side by side, but, on the other hand, seem to be past. The moments which Spirit seems to have left behind, it still possesses in the depth of its present.

19

Charles Darwin

The Origin of Species

Charles Darwin (1809–1882) has, with good reason, been called "the New-
ton of Biology." His ideas not only revolutionized that discipline but re-
formed most social thought around the concepts of evolutionary biology. Like
Newton, Darwin is one of the giant figures in the intellectual development of
the Western world; however, his central concept, it is important to note, was
not original with him. The idea of evolution was already "in the air" during
the years in which this young English naturalist surveyed the results of his
five-year trip to South America in the H.M.S. "Beagle" (1831–1836).
Geologists and biologists, as well as philosophers and social thinkers, had al-
ready advanced the concept of developmental growth in their fields. Darwin,
however, was to give the theory a solid scientific basis and establish it beyond
quibbling by marshaling voluminous evidence in its favor. For a time he was
extremely diffident about publishing his conclusions, fearing that they would
offend religious scruples. But the simultaneous work and independent exposi-
tion of organic evolution in 1858 by another biologist, Alfred Russel Wal-
lace, prodded Darwin into action. In 1859 he published the results of his
own findings, The Origin of Species by Means of Natural Selection,
or the Preservation of the Favored Races in the Struggle for Life.

The title underlined Darwin's novel thesis that organic evolution had
taken place by natural selection and competitive struggle, in which successive
small variations that made for survival eventually produced new species.
Even this explanation of the process had been suggested to Darwin, for in
1838 he had read Thomas Malthus's Essay on Population, *which describes*
the pressure of population on the food supply. The Origin of Species, *as*

Charles Darwin, *The Origin of Species by Means of Natural Selection, or the Preservation of*
the Favored Races in the Struggle for Life, 6th ed. (New York: Appleton, 1892), II,
267–68, 270–82, 287–306.

well as Darwin's later work The Descent of Man *(1871), caused a great outcry. Contradicting the Christian belief in special creation, it held humans to be part of nature and subject to all its laws, and it seemed to obliterate the distinction between body and mind. Darwin stood firm, however, and evolution was soon widely accepted both by scientists and by the general public.*

The implications of the evolutionary theory were equally important for political, economic, and moral thought. By analogy, all ideas, beliefs, and institutions were conceived to be in a state of flux, a view that seemed to destroy any rational basis for absolute standards and to equate the natural and the good. By making human beings a part of nature engaged in a dramatic struggle for survival, Darwinism reinforced the perspectives of romanticism and encouraged the irrationalism of the last century. Some social thinkers used the theory to justify the competitive economic system, while others, like Marx, saw in it a rationale for the class struggle and progress toward socialism. Darwin himself never made these broader applications or ever went beyond the limits of his biological hypothesis. The organic theory of evolution still stands essentially as he stated it, with only those modifications made necessary by new discoveries in genetics, ecology, and paleontology.

As this whole volume is one long argument, it may be convenient to the reader to have the leading facts and inferences briefly recapitulated.

That many and serious objections may be advanced against the theory of descent with modification through variation and natural selection, I do not deny. I have endeavored to give to them their full force. Nothing at first can appear more difficult to believe than that the more complex organs and instincts have been perfected, not by means superior to, though analogous with, human reason, but by the accumulation of innumerable slight variations, each good for the individual possessor. Nevertheless, this difficulty, though appearing to our imagination insuperably great, cannot be considered real if we admit the following propositions, namely, that all parts of the organization and instincts offer, at least, individual differences—that there is a struggle for existence leading to the preservation of profitable deviations of structure or instinct—and, lastly, that gradations in the state of perfection of each organ may have existed, each good of its kind. The truth of these propositions cannot, I think, be disputed.

It is, no doubt, extremely difficult even to conjecture by what gradations many structures have been perfected, more especially among broken and failing groups of organic beings, which have suffered much extinction; but we see so many strange gradations in nature, that we ought to be extremely cautious in saying that any organ or instinct, or any whole structure, could not have arrived at its present state by many graduated steps. There are, it must be admitted, cases of special difficulty opposed to the theory of natural selection; and one of the most curious of these is the existence in the same community of two or three defined castes of workers or sterile female ants; but I have attempted to show how these difficulties can be mastered. . . .

Turning to geographical distribution, the difficulties encountered on the theory of descent with modification are serious enough. All the individuals of the same species, and all the species of the same genus, or even higher group, are descended from common parents; and therefore, in however distant and isolated parts of the world they may now be found, they must in the course of successive generations have travelled from some one point to all the others. We are often wholly unable even to conjecture how this could have been effected. Yet, as we have reason to believe that some species have retained the same specific form for very long periods of time, immensely long as measured by years, too much stress ought not to be laid on the occasional wide diffusion of the same species; for during very long periods there will always have been a good chance for wide migration by many means. A broken or interrupted range may often be accounted for by the extinction of the species in the intermediate regions. It cannot be denied that we are as yet very ignorant as to the full extent of the various climatic and geographical changes which have affected the earth during modern periods; and such changes will often have facilitated migration. As an example, I have attempted to show how potent has been the influence of the Glacial period on the distribution of the same and of allied species throughout the world. We are as yet profoundly ignorant of the many occasional means of transport. With respect to distinct species of the same genus inhabiting distant and isolated regions, as the process of modification has necessarily been slow, all the means of migration will have been possible during a very long period; and consequently the difficulty of the wide diffusion of the species of the same genus is in some degree lessened.

As according to the theory of natural selection an interminable number of intermediate forms must have existed, linking together all the species in each group by gradations as fine as are our existing varieties, it may be asked, Why do we not see these linking forms all around us? Why are not all organic beings blended together in an inextricable chaos? With respect to existing forms, we should remember that we have no right to expect (excepting in rare cases) to discover *directly* connecting links between them, but only between each and some extinct and supplanted form. Even on a wide area, which has during a long period remained continuous, and of which the climatic and other conditions of life change insensibly in proceeding from a district occupied by one species into another district occupied by a closely allied species, we have no just right to expect often to find intermediate varieties in the intermediate zones. For we have reason to believe that only a few species of a genus ever undergo change; the other species becoming utterly extinct and leaving no modified progeny. Of the species which do change, only a few within the same country change at the same time; and all modifications are slowly effected. I have also shown that the intermediate varieties which probably at first existed in the intermediate zones, would be liable to be supplanted by the allied forms on either hand; for the latter, from existing in greater numbers, would generally be modified and improved at a quicker rate than the intermediate varieties, which existed in lesser numbers; so that the intermediate varieties would, in the long run, be supplanted and exterminated.

On this doctrine of the extermination of an infinitude of connecting links, between the living and extinct inhabitants of the world, and at each successive period between the extinct and still older species, why is not every geological formation charged with such links? Why does not every collection of fossil remains afford plain evidence of the gradation and mutation of the forms of life? Although geological research has undoubtedly revealed the former existence of many links, bringing numerous forms of life much closer together, it does not yield the infinitely many fine gradations between past and present species required on the theory; and this is the most obvious of the many objections which may be urged against it. Why, again, do whole groups of allied species appear, though this appearance is often false, to have come in suddenly on the successive geological stages? Although we now know that organic beings appeared on this globe, at a period incalculably remote, long before the lowest bed of the Cambrian system was deposited, why do we not find beneath this system great piles of strata stored with the remains of the progenitors of the Cambrian fossils? For on the theory, such strata must somewhere have been deposited at these ancient and utterly unknown epochs of the world's history.

I can answer these questions and objections only on the supposition that the geological record is far more imperfect than most geologists believe. The number of specimens in all our museums is absolutely as nothing compared with the countless generations of countless species which have certainly existed. The parent-form of any two or more species would not be in all its characters directly intermediate between its modified offspring, any more than the rock-pigeon is directly intermediate in crop and tail between its descendants, the pouter and fantail pigeons. We should not be able to recognize a species as the parent of another and modified species, if we were to examine the two ever so closely, unless we possessed most of the intermediate links; and owing to the imperfection of the geological record, we have no just right to expect to find so many links. If two or three, or even more linking forms were discovered, they would simply be ranked by many naturalists as so many new species, more especially if found in different geological sub-stages, let their differences be ever so slight. Numerous existing doubtful forms could be named which are probably varieties; but who will pretend that in future ages so many fossil links will be discovered, that naturalists will be able to decide whether or not these doubtful forms ought to be called varieties? Only a small portion of the world has been geologically explored. Only organic beings of certain classes can be preserved in a fossil condition, at least in any great number. Many species when once formed never undergo any further change but become extinct without leaving modified descendants; and the periods, during which species have undergone modification, though long as measured by years, have probably been short in comparison with the periods during which they retained the same form. It is the dominant and widely ranging species which vary most frequently and vary most, and varieties are often at first local—both causes rendering the discovery of intermediate links in any one formation less likely. Local varieties will not spread into other and distant regions until they are considerably modified and improved; and when they have spread, and are discovered in a geological formation, they appear as if suddenly created there, and will be simply classed as new species. Most formations have been intermittent in their accumulation; and their duration has probably been shorter than the average duration of specific forms. Successive formations are in most cases separated from each other by blank intervals of time of great length; for fossiliferous formations thick enough to resist future degradation can as a general rule be accumulated only where much sediment is deposited on the subsiding bed of the sea. During the alternate periods of elevation and of stationary level the record will generally be blank. During these latter periods there will probably be more variability in the forms of life; during periods of subsidence, more extinction.

With respect to the absence of strata rich in fossils beneath the Cambrian formation, I can recur only to the hypothesis given in the tenth chapter; namely, that though our continents and oceans have endured for an enormous period in nearly their present relative positions, we have no reason to assume that this has always been the case; consequently formations much older than any now known may lie buried beneath the great oceans. With respect to the lapse of time not having been sufficient since our planet was consolidated for the assumed amount of organic change, and this objection, as urged by Sir William Thompson,[1] is probably one of the gravest as yet advanced, I can only say, firstly, that we do not know at what rate species change as measured by years, and secondly, that many philosophers are not as yet willing to admit that we know enough of the constitution of the universe and of the interior of our globe to speculate with safety on its past duration.

That the geological record is imperfect all will admit; but that it is imperfect to the degree required by our theory, few will be inclined to admit. If we look at long enough intervals of time, geology plainly declares that species have all changed; and they have changed in the manner required by the theory, for they have changed slowly and in a graduated manner. We clearly see this in the fossil remains from consecutive formations invariably being much more closely related to each other, than are the fossils from widely separated formations.

Such is the sum of the several chief objections and the difficulties which may be justly urged against the theory; and I have now briefly recapitulated the answers and explanations which, as far as I can see, may be given. I have felt these difficulties far too heavily during

[1] A British physicist and geologist (1824–1907).

many years to doubt their weight. But it deserves special notice that the more important objections relate to questions on which we are confessedly ignorant; nor do we know how ignorant we are. We do not know all the possible transitional gradations between the simplest and the most perfect organs; it cannot be pretended that we know all the varied means of Distribution during the long lapse of years, or that we know how imperfect is the Geological Record. Serious as these several objections are, in my judgment they are by no means sufficient to overthrow the theory of descent with subsequent modification.

Now let us turn to the other side of the argument. Under domestication we see much variability, caused, or at least excited, by changed conditions of life; but often in so obscure a manner, that we are tempted to consider the variations as spontaneous. Variability is governed by many complex laws,—by correlated growth, compensation, the increased use and disuse of parts, and the definite action of the surrounding conditions. There is much difficulty in ascertaining how largely our domestic productions have been modified; but we may safely infer that the amount has been large, and that modifications can be inherited for long periods. As long as the conditions of life remain the same, we have reason to believe that a modification, which has already been inherited for many generations, may continue to be inherited for an amost infinite number of generations. On the other hand, we have evidence that variability when it has once come into play, does not cease under domestication for a very long period; nor do we know that it ever ceases, for new varieties are still occasionally produced by our oldest domesticated productions.

Variability is not actually caused by man; he only unintentionally exposes organic beings to new conditions of life, and then nature acts on the organization and causes it to vary. But man can and does select the variations given to him by nature, and thus accumulates them in any desired manner. He thus adapts animals and plants for his own benefit or pleasure. He may do this methodically, or he may do it unconsciously by preserving the individuals most useful or pleasing to him without any intention of altering the breed. It is certain that he can largely influence the character of a breed by selecting, in each successive generation, individual differences so slight as to be inappreciable except by an educated eye. This unconscious process of selection has been the great agency in the formation of the most distinct and useful domestic breeds. That many breeds produced by man have to a large extent the character of natural species, is shown by the inextricable doubts whether many of them are varieties or aboriginally distinct species.

There is no reason why the principles which have acted so efficiently under domestication should not have acted under nature. In the survival of favored individuals and races, during the constantly recurrent Struggle for Existence, we see a powerful and everacting form of Selection. The struggle for existence inevitably follows from the high geometrical ratio of increase which is common to all organic beings. This high rate of increase is proved by calculation,—by the rapid increase of many animals and plants during a succession of peculiar seasons, and when naturalized in new countries. More individuals are born than can possibly survive. A grain in the balance may determine which individuals shall live and which shall die,—which variety or species shall increase in number, and which shall decrease, or finally become extinct. As the individuals of the same species come in all respects into the closest competition with each other, the struggle will generally be most severe between them; it will be almost equally severe between the varieties of the same species, and next in severity between the species of the same genus. On the other hand the struggle will often be severe between beings remote in the scale of nature. The slightest advantage in certain individuals, at any age or during any season, over those with which they come into competition, or better adaptation in however slight a degree to the surrounding physical conditions, will, in the long run, turn the balance.

With animals having separated sexes, there will be in most cases a struggle between the males for the possession of the females. The most vigorous males, or those which have most successfully struggled with their conditions of life, will generally leave most progeny. But success will often depend on the males having special weapons, or means of defense, or charms; and a slight advantage will lead to victory.

As geology plainly proclaims that each land has undergone great physical changes, we might have expected to find that organic beings have varied under nature, in the same way as they have varied under domestication. And if there has been any variability under nature, it would be an unaccountable fact if natural selection had not come into play. It has often been asserted, but the assertion is incapable of proof, that the amount of variation under nature is a strictly limited quantity. Man, though acting on external characters alone and often capriciously, can produce within a short period a great result by adding up mere individual differences in his domestic productions; and every one admits that species present individual differences. But, besides such differences, all naturalists admit that natural varieties exist which are considered sufficiently distinct to be worthy of record in systematic works. No one has drawn any clear distinction between individual differences and slight varieties; or between more plainly marked varieties and sub-species, and species. On separate continents, and on different parts of the same continent when divided by barriers of any kind, and on outlying islands, what a multitude of forms exist, which some experienced naturalists rank as varieties, others as geographical races or sub-species, and others as distinct, though closely allied species!

If, then, animals and plants do vary, let it be ever so slightly or slowly, why should not variations or individual differences, which are in any way beneficial, be preserved and accumulated through natural selection, or the survival of the fittest? If man can by patience select variations useful to him, why, under changing and complex conditions of life, should not variations useful to nature's living products often arise, and be preserved or selected? What limit can be put to this power, acting during long ages and rigidly scrutinizing the whole constitution, structure, and habits of each creature,— favoring the good and rejecting the bad? I can see no limit to this power, in slowly and beautifully adapting each form to the most complex relations of life. The theory of natural selection, even if we look no farther than this, seems to be in the highest degree probable. I have already recapitulated, as fairly as I could, the opposed difficulties and objections: now let us turn to the special facts and arguments in favor of the theory.

On the view that species are only strongly marked and permanent varieties, and that each species first existed as a variety, we can see why it is that no line of demarcation can be drawn between species, commonly supposed to have been produced by special acts of creation, and varieties which are acknowledged to have been produced by secondary laws. On this same view we can understand how it is that in a region where many species of a genus have been produced, and where they now flourish, these same species should present many varieties; for where the manufactory of species has been active, we might expect, as a general rule, to find it still in action; and this is the case if varieties be incipient species. Moreover, the species of the larger genera, which afford the greater number of varieties or incipient species, retain to a certain degree the character of varieties; for they differ from each other by a less amount of difference than do the species of smaller genera. The closely allied species also of the larger genera apparently have restricted ranges, and in their affinities they are clustered in little groups round other species—in both respects resembling varieties. These are strange relations on the view that each species was independently created, but are intelligible if each existed first as a variety.

As each species tends by its geometrical rate of reproduction to increase inordinately in number; and as the modified descendants of each species will be enabled to increase by as much as they become more diversified in habits and structure, so as to be able to seize on many and widely different places in the economy of nature, there will be a constant tendency in natural selection to preserve the most divergent offspring of any one species. Hence, during a long-continued course of modification, the slight differences characteristic of varieties of the same species, tend to be augmented into the greater differences characteristic of the species of the same genus. New and improved varieties will inevitably supplant and exterminate the older, less improved, and intermediate varieties; and thus species are rendered to a large extent defined and distinct objects. Dominant species belonging to the larger groups within each class tend to give birth to new and dominant forms; so that each large group tends to become still larger, and at the same time more divergent in character. But as all groups cannot thus go on increasing in size, for the world would not hold them, the more dominant groups beat the less dominant. This tendency in the large groups to go on increasing in size and diverging in character, together with the inevitable contingency of much extinction, explains the arrangement of all the forms of life in groups subordinate to groups, all within a few great classes, which has prevailed throughout all time. This grand fact of the grouping of all organic beings under what is called the Natural System, is utterly inexplicable on the theory of creation.

As natural selection acts solely by accumulating slight, successive, favorable variations, it can produce no great or sudden modifications; it can act only by short and slow steps. Hence, the canon of

"Natura non facit saltum,"[2] which every fresh addition to our knowledge tends to confirm, is on this theory intelligible. We can see why throughout nature the same general end is gained by an almost infinite diversity of means, for every peculiarity when once acquired is long inherited, and structures already modified in many different ways have to be adapted for the same general purpose. We can, in short, see why nature is prodigal in variety, though niggard in innovation. But why this should be a law of nature if each species has been independently created, no man can explain. . . .

If we admit that the geological record is imperfect to an extreme degree, then the facts, which the record does give, strongly support the theory of descent with modification. New species have come on the stage slowly and at successive intervals; and the amount of change, after equal intervals of time, is widely different in different groups. The extinction of species and of whole groups of species, which has played so conspicuous a part in the history of the organic world, almost inevitably follows from the principle of natural selection; for old forms are supplanted by new and improved forms. Neither single species nor groups of species reappear when the chain of ordinary generation is once broken. The gradual diffusion of dominant forms, with the slow modification of their descendants, causes the forms of life, after long intervals of time, to appear as if they had changed simultaneously throughout the world. The fact of the fossil remains of each formation being in some degree intermediate in character between the fossils in the formations above and below, is simply explained by their intermediate position in the chain of descent. The grand fact that all extinct beings can be classed with all recent beings, naturally follows from the living and the extinct being the offspring of common parents. As species have generally diverged in character during their long course of descent and modification, we can understand why it is that the more ancient forms, or early progenitors of each group, so often occupy a position in some degree intermediate between existing groups. Recent forms are generally looked upon as being, on the whole, higher in the scale of organization than ancient forms; and they must be higher, in so far as the later and more improved forms have conquered the older and less improved forms in the struggle for life; they have also generally had their organs more specialized for different functions. This fact is per-

[2] Latin: nature makes no leap—that is, there are no large gaps, or jumps, in natural development.

fectly compatible with numerous beings still retaining simple and but little improved structures, fitted for simple conditions of life; it is likewise compatible with some forms having retrograded in organization, by having become at each stage of descent better fitted for new and degraded habits of life. Lastly, the wonderful law of the long endurance of allied forms on the same continent,—of marsupials in Australia, of edentata in America, and other such cases,—is intelligible, for within the same country the existing and the extinct will be closely allied by descent.

Looking to geographical distribution, if we admit that there has been during the long course of ages much migration from one part of the world to another, owing to former climatic and geographical changes and to the many occasional and unknown means of dispersal, then we can understand, on the theory of descent with modification, most of the great leading facts in Distribution. We can see why there should be so striking a parallelism in the distribution of organic beings throughout space, and in their geological succession throughout time; for in both cases the beings have been connected by the bond of ordinary generation, and the means of modification have been the same. We see the full meaning of the wonderful fact, which has struck every traveller, namely, that on the same continent, under the most diverse conditions, under heat and cold, on mountain and lowland, on deserts and marshes, most of the inhabitants within each great class are plainly related; for they are the descendants of the same progenitors and early colonists. On this same principle of former migration, combined in most cases with modification, we can understand, by the aid of the Glacial period, the identity of some few plants, and the close alliance of many others, on the most distant mountains, and in the northern and southern temperate zones; and likewise the close alliance of some of the inhabitants of the sea in the northern and southern temperate latitudes, though separated by the whole intertropical ocean. Although two countries may present physical conditions as closely similar as the same species ever require, we need feel no surprise at their inhabitants being widely different, if they have been for a long period completely sundered from each other; for as the relation of organism to organism is the most important of all relations, and as the two countries will have received colonists at various periods and in different proportions, from some other country or from each other, the course of modification in the two areas will inevitably have been different. . . .

The fact, as we have seen, that all past and present organic beings can be arranged within a few great classes, in groups subordinate to groups, and with the extinct groups often falling in between the recent groups, is intelligible on the theory of natural selection with its contingencies of extinction and divergence of character. On these same principles we see how it is, that the mutual affinities of the forms within each class are so complex and circuitous. We see why certain characters are far more serviceable than others for classification;—why adaptive characters, though of paramount importance to the beings, are of hardly any importance in classification; why characters derived from rudimentary parts, though of no service to the beings, are often of high classificatory value; and why embryological characters are often the most valuable of all. The real affinities of all organic beings, in contradistinction to their adaptive resemblances, are due to inheritance or community of descent. The Natural System is a genealogical arrangement, with the acquired grades of difference, marked by the terms, varieties, species, genera, families, and so forth; and we have to discover the lines of descent by the most permanent characters whatever they may be and of however slight vital importance.

The similar framework of bones in the hand of a man, wing of a bat, fin of the porpoise, and leg of the horse,—the same number of vertebrae forming the neck of the giraffe and of the elephant,—and innumerable other such facts, at once explain themselves on the theory of descent with slow and slight successive modifications. The similarity of pattern in the wing and in the leg of a bat, though used for such different purpose,—in the jaws and legs of a crab,—in the petals, stamens, and pistils of a flower, is likewise, to a large extent, intelligible on the view of the gradual modification of parts or organs which were aboriginally alike in an early progenitor in each of these classes. On the principle of successive variations not always supervening at an early age, and being inherited at a corresponding not early period of life, we clearly see why the embryos of mammals, birds, reptiles, and fishes should be so closely similar, and so unlike the adult forms. We may cease marvelling at the embryo of an air-breathing mammal or bird having branchial slits and arteries running in loops, like those of a fish which has to breathe the air dissolved in water by the aid of well-developed branchiae.

Disuse, aided sometimes by natural selection, will often have reduced organs when rendered useless under changed habits or conditions of life; and we can understand on this view the meaning of rudimentary organs. But disuse and selection will generally act on each creature, when it has come to maturity and has to play its full part in the struggle for existence, and will thus have little power on an organ during early life; hence the organ will not be reduced or rendered rudimentary at this early age. The calf, for instance, has inherited teeth, which never cut through the gums of the upper jaw, from an early progenitor having well-developed teeth; and we may believe that the teeth in the mature animal were formerly reduced by disuse, owing to the tongue and palate, or lips, having become excellently fitted through natural selection to browse without their aid; whereas in the calf, the teeth have been left unaffected, and on the principle of inheritance at corresponding ages have been inherited from a remote period to the present day. On the view of each organism with all its separate parts having been specially created, how utterly inexplicable is it that organs bearing the plain stamp of inutility, such as the teeth in the embryonic calf or the shrivelled wings under the soldered wing-covers of many beetles, should so frequently occur. Nature may be said to have taken pains to reveal her scheme of modification, by means of rudimentary organs, of embryological and homologous structures, but we are too blind to understand her meaning.

I have now recapitulated the facts and considerations which have thoroughly convinced me that species have been modified, during a long course of descent. This has been effected chiefly through the natural selection of numerous successive, slight, favorable variations; aided in an important manner by the inherited effects of the use and disuse of parts; and in an unimportant manner, that is in relation to adaptive structures, whether past or present, by the direct action of external conditions, and by variations which seem to us in our ignorance to arise spontaneously. It appears that I formerly underrated the frequency and value of these latter forms of variation, as leading to permanent modifications of structure independently of natural selection. But as my conclusions have lately been much misrepresented, and it has been stated that I attribute the modification of species exclusively to natural selection, I may be permitted to remark that in the first edition of this work, and subsequently, I placed in a most conspicuous position—namely, at the close of the Introduction—the following words: "I am convinced that natural selection has been the main but not the exclusive means of modification."

This has been of no avail. Great is the power of steady misrepresentation; but the history of science shows that fortunately this power does not long endure.

It can hardly be supposed that a false theory would explain, in so satisfactory a manner as does the theory of natural selection, the several large classes of facts above specified. It has recently been objected that this is an unsafe method of arguing; but it is a method used in judging of the common events of life, and has often been used by the greatest natural philosophers. The undulatory theory of light has thus been arrived at; and the belief in the revolution of the earth on its own axis was until lately supported by hardly any direct evidence. It is no valid objection that science as yet throws no light on the far higher problem of the essence or origin of life. Who can explain what is the essence of the attraction of gravity? No one now objects to following out the results consequent on this unknown element of attraction; notwithstanding that Leibnitz[3] formerly accused Newton[4] of introducing "occult qualities and miracles into philosophy."

I see no good reason why the views given in this volume should shock the religious feelings of any one. It is satisfactory, as showing how transient such impressions are, to remember that the greatest discovery ever made by man, namely the law of the attraction of gravity, was also attacked by Leibnitz, "as subversive of natural, and inferentially of revealed, religion." A celebrated author and divine has written to me that "he has gradually learned to see that it is just as noble a conception of the Deity to believe that He created a few original forms capable of self-development into other and needful forms, as to believe that He required a fresh act of creation to supply the voids caused by the action of His laws."

Why, it may be asked, until recently did nearly all the most eminent living naturalists and geologists disbelieve in the mutability of species. It cannot be asserted that organic beings in a state of nature are subject to no variation; it cannot be proved that the amount of variation in the course of long ages is a limited quantity; no clear distinction has been, or can be, drawn between species and well-marked varieties. It cannot be maintained that species when intercrossed are invariably sterile, and varieties invariably fertile; or that sterility is a

[3] Gottfried Wilhelm von Leibnitz (1646–1716), German philosopher and mathematician.
[4] Isaac Newton (1642–1727), English philosopher, mathematician, and physicist.

special endowment and sign of creation. The belief that species were immutable productions was almost unavoidable as long as the history of the world was thought to be of short duration; and now that we have acquired some idea of the lapse of time, we are too apt to assume, without proof, that the geological record is so perfect that it would have afforded us plain evidence of the mutation of species, if they had undergone mutation.

But the chief cause of our natural unwillingness to admit that one species has given birth to other and distinct species, is that we are always slow in admitting great changes of which we do not see the steps. The difficulty is the same as that felt by so many geologists, when Lyell[5] first insisted that long lines of inland cliffs had been formed, and great valleys excavated, by the agencies which we see still at work. The mind cannot possibly grasp the full meaning of the term of even a million years; it cannot add up and perceive the full effects of many slight variations, accumulated during an almost infinite number of generations.

Although I am fully convinced of the truth of the views given in this volume under the form of an abstract, I by no means expect to convince experienced naturalists whose minds are stocked with a multitude of facts all viewed, during a long course of years, from a point of view directly opposite to mine. It is so easy to hide our ignorance under such expressions as the "plan of creation," "unity of design," and so forth, and to think that we give an explanation when we only re-state a fact. Any one whose disposition leads him to attach more weight to unexplained difficulties than to the explanation of a certain number of facts will certainly reject the theory. A few naturalists, endowed with much flexibility of mind, and who have already begun to doubt the immutability of species, may be influenced by this volume; but I look with confidence to the future,—to young and rising naturalists, who will be able to view both sides of the question with impartiality. Whoever is led to believe that species are mutable will do good service by conscientiously expressing his conviction; for thus only can the load of prejudice by which this subject is overwhelmed be removed.

Several eminent naturalists have of late published their belief that a multitude of reputed species in each genus are not real species; but that other species are real, that is, have been independently created.

[5] Charles Lyell (1797–1875), British geologist.

This seems to me a strange conclusion to arrive at. They admit that a multitude of forms, which till lately they themselves thought were special creations, and which are still thus looked at by the majority of naturalists, and which consequently have all the external characteristic features of true species,—they admit that these have been produced by variation, but they refuse to extend the same view to other and slightly different forms. Nevertheless they do not pretend that they can define, or even conjecture, which are the created forms of life, and which are those produced by secondary laws. They admit variation as a *vera causa* [6] in one case, they arbitrarily reject it in another, without assigning any distinction in the two cases. The day will come when this will be given as a curious illustration of the blindness of preconceived opinion. These authors seem no more startled at a miraculous act of creation than at an ordinary birth. But do they really believe that at innumerable periods in the earth's history certain elemental atoms have been commanded suddenly to flash into living tissues? Do they believe that at each supposed act of creation one individual or many were produced? Were all the infinitely numerous kinds of animals and plants created as eggs or seed, or as full grown? And in the case of mammals, were they created bearing the false marks of nourishment from the mother's womb? Undoubtedly some of these same questions cannot be answered by those who believe in the appearance or creation of only a few forms of life, or of some one form alone. It has been maintained by several authors that it is as easy to believe in the creation of a million beings as of one; but Maupertuis' [7] philosophical axiom "of least action" leads the mind more willingly to admit the smaller number; and certainly we ought not to believe that innumerable beings within each great class have been created with plain, but deceptive, marks of descent from a single parent.

As a record of a former state of things, I have retained in the foregoing paragraphs, and elsewhere, several sentences which imply that naturalists believe in the separate creation of each species; and I have been much censured for having thus expressed myself. But undoubtedly this was the general belief when the first edition of the present

[6] Latin: true cause.

[7] Pierre Louis de Maupertuis (1698–1759) was a French mathematician, astronomer, and philosopher, who from 1745 to 1753 served as president of the Prussian Academy of Sciences in Berlin. In 1740, he formulated the *"principle of least action,"* which he later used to prove the existence of God. For this and other views, Voltaire satirized him heavily.

work appeared. I formerly spoke to very many naturalists on the subject of evolution, and never once met with any sympathetic agreement. It is probable that some did then believe in evolution, but they were either silent, or expressed themselves so ambiguously that it was not easy to understand their meaning. Now things are wholly changed, and almost every naturalist admits the great principle of evolution. There are, however, some who still think that species have suddenly given birth, through quite unexplained means, to new and totally different forms: but, as I have attempted to show, weighty evidence can be opposed to the admission of great and abrupt modifications. Under a scientific point of view, and as leading to further investigation, but little advantage is gained by believing that new forms are suddenly developed in an inexplicable manner from old and widely different forms, over the old belief in the creation of species from the dust of the earth.

It may be asked how far I extend the doctrine of the modification of species. The question is difficult to answer, because the more distinct the forms are which we consider, by so much the arguments in favor of community of descent become fewer in number and less in force. But some arguments of the greatest weight extend very far. All the members of whole classes are connected together by a chain of affinities, and all can be classed on the same principle, in groups subordinate to groups. Fossil remains sometimes tend to fill up very wide intervals between existing orders.

Organs in a rudimentary condition plainly show that an early progenitor had the organ in a fully developed condition; and this in some cases implies an enormous amount of modification in the descendants. Throughout whole classes various structures are formed on the same pattern, and at a very early age the embryos closely resemble each other. Therefore I cannot doubt that the theory of descent with modification embraces all the members of the same great class or kingdom. I believe that animals are descended from at most only four or five progenitors, and plants from an equal or lesser number.

Analogy would lead me one step farther, namely, to the belief that all animals and plants are descended from some one prototype. But analogy may be a deceitful guide. Nevertheless all living things have much in common, in their chemical composition, their cellular structure, their laws of growth, and their liability to injurious influences. We see this even in so trifling a fact as that the same poison often similarly affects plants and animals; or that the poison secreted by the gall-fly produces monstrous growths on the wild rose or oak-tree. With all organic beings, excepting perhaps some of the very lowest, sexual reproduction seems to be essentially similar. With all, as far as is at present known, the germinal vesicle is the same; so that all organisms start from a common origin. If we look even to the two main divisions—namely, to the animal and vegetable kingdoms—certain low forms are so far intermediate in character that naturalists have disputed to which kingdom they should be referred. As Professor Asa Gray[8] has remarked, "the spores and other reproductive bodies of many of the lower algae may claim to have first a characteristically animal, and then an unequivocally vegetable existence." Therefore, on the principle of natural selection with divergence of character, it does not seem incredible that, from some such low and intermediate form, both animals and plants may have been developed; and, if we admit this, we must likewise admit that all the organic beings which have ever lived on this earth may be descended from some one primordial form. But this inference is chiefly grounded on analogy, and it is immaterial whether or not it be accepted. No doubt it is possible, as Mr. G. H. Lewes[9] has urged, that at the first commencement of life many different forms were evolved; but if so, we may conclude that only a very few have left modified descendants. For, as I have recently remarked in regard to the members of each great kingdom, such as the Vertebrata, Articulata, and so forth, we have distinct evidence in their embryological, homologous, and rudimentary structures, that within each kingdom all the members are descended from a single progenitor.

When the views advanced by me in this volume, and by Mr. Wallace,[10] or when analogous views on the origin of species are generally admitted, we can dimly foresee that there will be a considerable revolution in natural history. Systematists will be able to pursue their labors as at present; but they will not be incessantly haunted by the shadowy doubt whether this or that form be a true species. This, I feel sure and I speak after experience, will be no slight relief. The endless disputes whether or not some fifty species of British brambles are good species will cease. Systematists will have only to decide

---

[8] Asa Gray (1810–1888), American botanist.
[9] George Henry Lewes (1817–1878), English philosopher and literary critic.
[10] Alfred Russel Wallace (1823–1913), an English biologist who advanced, independently, an evolutionary view similar to that of Darwin.

(not that this will be easy) whether any form be sufficiently constant and distinct from other forms, to be capable of definition; and if definable, whether the differences be sufficiently important to deserve a specific name. This latter point will become a far more essential consideration than it is at present; for differences, however slight, between any two forms, if not blended by intermediate gradations, are looked at by most naturalists as sufficient to raise both forms to the rank of species.

Hereafter we shall be compelled to acknowledge that the only distinction between species and well-marked varieties is, that the latter are known, or believed, to be connected at the present day by intermediate gradations, whereas species were formerly thus connected. Hence, without rejecting the consideration of the present existence of intermediate gradations between any two forms, we shall be led to weigh more carefully and to value higher the actual amount of difference between them. It is quite possible that forms now generally acknowledged to be merely varieties may hereafter be thought worthy of specific names; and in this case scientific and common language will come into accordance. In short, we shall have to treat species in the same mannner as those naturalists treat genera, who admit that genera are merely artificial combinations made for convenience. This may not be a cheering prospect; but we shall at least be freed from the vain search for the undiscovered and undiscoverable essence of the term species.

The other and more general departments of natural history will rise greatly in interest. The terms used by naturalists, of affinity, relationship, community of type, paternity, morphology, adaptive characters, rudimentary and aborted organs, and so forth, will cease to be metaphorical, and will have a plain signification. When we no longer look at an organic being as a savage looks at a ship, as something wholly beyond his comprehension; when we regard every production of nature as one which has had a long history; when we contemplate every complex structure and instinct as the summing up of many contrivances, each useful to the possessor, in the same way as any great mechanical invention is the summing up of the labor, the experience, the reason, and even the blunders of numerous workmen; when we thus view each organic being, how far more interesting,—I speak from experience,—does the study of natural history become!

A grand and almost untrodden field of inquiry will be opened, on the causes and laws of variation, on correlation, on the effects of use and disuse, on the direct action of external conditions, and so forth. The study of domestic productions will rise immensely in value. A new variety raised by man will be a more important and interesting subject for study than one more species added to the infinitude of already recorded species. Our classifications will come to be, as far as they can be so made, genealogies; and will then truly give what may be called the plan of creation. The rules for classifying will no doubt become simpler when we have a definite object in view. We possess no pedigrees or armorial bearings; [11] and we have to discover and trace the many diverging lines of descent in our natural genealogies, by characters of any kind which have long been inherited. Rudimentary organs will speak infallibly with respect to the nature of long-lost structures. Species and groups of species which are called aberrant, and which may fancifully be called living fossils, will aid us in forming a picture of the ancient forms of life. Embryology will often reveal to us the structure, in some degree obscured, of the prototypes of each great class.

When we can feel assured that all the individuals of the same species, and all the closely allied species of most genera, have within a not very remote period descended from one parent, and have migrated from some one birth-place; and when we better know the many means of migration, then, by the light which geology now throws, and will continue to throw, on former changes of climate and of the level of the land, we shall surely be enabled to trace in an admirable manner the former migrations of the inhabitants of the whole world. Even at present, by comparing the differences between the inhabitants of the sea on the opposite sides of a continent, and the nature of the various inhabitants on that continent in relation to their apparent means of immigration, some light can be thrown on ancient geography.

The noble science of Geology loses glory from the extreme imperfection of the record. The crust of the earth with its imbedded remains must not be looked at as a well-filled museum, but as a poor collection made at hazard and at rare intervals. The accumulation of each great fossiliferous formation will be recognized as having depended on an unusual concurrence of favorable circumstances, and the blank intervals between the successive stages as having been of

[11] Heraldic designs on a coat of arms.

vast duration. But we shall be able to gauge with some security the duration of these intervals by a comparison of the preceding and succeeding organic forms. We must be cautious in attempting to correlate as strictly contemporaneous two formations, which do not include many identical species, by the general succession of the forms of life. As species are produced and exterminated by slowly acting and still existing causes, and not by miraculous acts of creation; and as the most important of all causes of organic change is one which is almost independent of altered and perhaps suddenly altered physical conditions, namely, the mutual relation of organism to organism,— the improvement of one organism entailing the improvement or the extermination of others; it follows, that the amount of organic change in the fossils of consecutive formations probably serves as a fair measure of the relative, though not actual lapse of time. A number of species, however, keeping in a body might remain for a long period unchanged, while within the same period, several of these species, by migrating into new countries and coming into competition with foreign associates, might become modified; so that we must not overrate the accuracy of organic change as a measure of time.

In the future I see open fields for far more important researches. Psychology will be securely based on the foundation already well laid by Mr. Herbert Spencer,[12] that of the necessary acquirement of each mental power and capacity by gradation. Much light will be thrown on the origin of man and his history.

Authors of the highest eminence seem to be fully satisifed with the view that each species has been independently created. To my mind it accords better with what we know of the laws impressed on matter by the Creator, that the production and extinction of the past and present inhabitants of the world should have been due to secondary causes, like those determining the birth and death of the individual. When I view all beings not as special creations, but as the lineal descendants of some few beings which lived long before the first bed of the Cambrian system was deposited, they seem to me to become ennobled. Judging from the past, we may safely infer that not one living species will transmit its unaltered likeness to a distant futurity. And of the species now living very few will transmit progeny of any kind to a far distant futurity; for the manner in which all organic

[12] Herbert Spencer (1820–1903), an English philosopher, was a strong supporter of Darwin's theories and the founder of what came to be called Social Darwinism.

beings are grouped, shows that the greater number of species in each genus, and all the species in many genera, have left no descendants, but have become utterly extinct. We can so far take a prophetic glance into futurity as to foretell that it will be the common and widely-spread species, belonging to the larger and dominant groups within each class, which will ultimately prevail and procreate new and dominant species. As all the living forms of life are the lineal descendants of those which lived long before the Cambrian epoch, we may feel certain that the ordinary succession by generation has never once been broken, and that no cataclysm has desolated the whole world. Hence we may look with some confidence to a secure future of great length. And as natural selection works solely by and for the good of each being, all corporeal and mental endowments will tend to progress towards perfection.

It is interesting to contemplate a tangled bank, clothed with many plants of many kinds, with birds singing on the bushes, with various insects flitting about, and with worms crawling through the damp earth, and to reflect that these elaborately constructed forms, so different from each other, and dependent upon each other in so complex a manner, have all been produced by laws acting around us. These laws, taken in the largest sense, being Growth with Reproduction; Inheritance which is almost implied by reproduction; Variability from the indirect and direct action of the conditions of life, and from use and disuse: a Ratio of Increase so high as to lead to a Struggle for Life, and as a consequence to Natural Selection, entailing Divergence of Character and the Extinction of less-improved forms. Thus, from the war of nature, from famine and death, the most exalted object which we are capable of conceiving, namely, the production of the higher animals, directly follows. There is grandeur in this view of life, with its several powers, having been originally breathed by the Creator into a few forms or into one; and that, while this planet has gone cycling on according to the fixed law of gravity, from so simple a beginning endless forms most beautiful and most wonderful have been, and are being evolved.

20

Karl Marx and *Friedrich Engels*
The Communist Manifesto

The development of the Industrial Revolution in the first half of the nineteenth century, with its gross exploitation of factory labor, gave rise to criticisms of the prevailing social and economic systems. The most thoroughgoing
and influential attack was mounted in the 1840s by two young Germans,
Karl Marx (1818–1883) and Friedrich Engels (1820–1895). Marx was a
philosophy student turned journalist and revolutionary agitator, who was
forced to flee from Germany and France. He finally settled in London in
1849, where he devoted the rest of his life to radical activities on an international scale and to writing a critical analysis of the capitalist economy. Marx
worked in close collaboration with his friend and fellow radical Engels, who
used his inherited wealth to underwrite his impecunious colleague's activities.
The two dedicated their lives to the overthrow of capitalist society and to its
replacement by a new socialist or communist order. Their chief weapon was
the ideology that has come to be known as Marxism—a combination of philosophical, economic, and historical theory and revolutionary practice. Marxism has since become the official doctrine of the international socialist and
communist movements and has also influenced the thought and practice of
many non-Marxists.

The underlying philosophy of Marxism was dialectical materialism,
which, like Hegel's thought, viewed all existence as a process evolving in a
rational pattern according to the "dialectic," the real "laws of motion" of nature, society, and thought. But it rejected Hegel's idealist contention that
"ideas" (spirit) are superior to "matter" and held matter to be the ultimate
stuff of reality. It embodied a theory of history that saw all social change as

Karl Marx and Friedrich Engels, *Manifesto of the Communist Party*, trans. Samuel
Moore (New York: Socialist Labor Party, 1888), 7–21, 28.

basically determined by technological-economic forces ("the modes of produc-
tion") and moving inevitably through conflict to the resolution of all contra-
dictions in the final stage of communism.

Marx and Engels wished, however, to do more than understand the
world; they wished to change it. The Communist Manifesto, which they
wrote in Brussels in 1847 as a platform for a radical organization, was a call
to arms as well as a summary of the two men's basic social views. Its revolu-
tionary appeal was made in the context of an outline of the history of West-
ern Europe. Marx and Engels traced the evolution of socio-political systems
in the past and projected this evolution into the future. For them, all histori-
cal change was characterized by the struggle of economic classes. The in-
strument for the final transformation of society was the proletariat, the class
of industrial wage-earners. Once the proletariat achieved full consciousness of
its role, it would organize economically and politically to overthrow the capi-
talist system. Though falling short of predictive accuracy, the Manifesto, *as*
well as Marxism generally, has had wide appeal because of the cogency of its
analysis, its apocalyptic quality, and its assurances of inevitable success.

A spectre[1] is haunting Europe—the spectre of Communism. All the
powers of old Europe have entered into a holy alliance to exorcise
this spectre; Pope and Czar, Metternich[2] and Guizot,[3] French radicals[4] and German police spies.

Where is the party in opposition that has not been decried as communistic by its opponents in power? Where the opposition that has
not hurled back the branding reproach of Communism, against the
more advanced opposition parties, as well as against its reactionary
adversaries?

Two things result from this fact.

1. Communism is already acknowledged by all European powers
to be itself a power.

---

[1] A frightening, ghost-like image.
[2] Prince von Metternich (1773–1859), an Austrian statesman and diplomat, was largely
responsible for the concept of Europe that emerged from the Congress of Vienna
(1814–15). In March 1848 a rebellious Vienna mob forced Metternich to resign as
minister of foreign affairs, an office that he had held since 1809.
[3] François Pierre Guillaume Guizot (1787–1874), a French historian and statesman, was
prime minister (1840–48) under King Louis Philippe.
[4] Radical republicans.

2. It is high time that Communists should openly, in the face of the whole world, publish their views, their aims, their tendencies, and meet this nursery tale of the spectre of Communism with a Manifesto of the party itself.

To this end Communists of various nationalities have assembled in London, and sketched the following manifesto, to be published in the English, French, German, Italian, Flemish and Danish languages.

BOURGEOIS AND PROLETARIANS

The history of all hitherto existing society is the history of class struggles.

Freeman and slave, patrician and plebeian,[5] lord and serf, guildmaster and journeyman, in a word, oppressor and oppressed, stood in constant opposition to one another, carried on an uninterrupted, now hidden, now open fight, a fight that each time ended, either in a revolutionary reconstitution of society at large, or in the common ruin of the contending classes.

In the earlier epochs of history we find almost everywhere a complicated arrangement of society into various orders, a manifold graduation of social rank. In ancient Rome we have patricians, knights, plebeians, slaves; in the Middle Ages, feudal lords, vassals,[6] guildmasters, journeymen, apprentices, serfs; in almost all of these classes, again, subordinate gradations.

The modern bourgeois society that has sprouted from the ruins of feudal society, has not done away with class antagonisms. It has but established new classes, new conditions of oppression, new forms of struggle in place of the old ones.

Our epoch, the epoch of the bourgeoisie,[7] possesses, however, this distinctive feature: it has simplified the class antagonisms. Society as a whole is more and more splitting up into two great hostile camps, into two great classes directly facing each other: Bourgeoisie and Proletariat.[8]

[5] A person of the lower class of freemen in ancient Rome.
[6] Medieval lords and their vassals (subordinates) made up the ruling military and landholding aristocracy.
[7] The small class of entrepreneurs and capitalists who own and control the means of production.
[8] The large and ever-increasing number of wage earners who neither own nor control the means of production.

From the serfs of the Middle Ages sprang the chartered burghers of the earliest towns. From these burgesses[9] the first elements of the bourgeoisie were developed.

The discovery of America, the rounding of the Cape,[10] opened up fresh ground for the rising bourgeoisie. The East Indian and Chinese markets, the colonization of America, trade with the colonies, the increase in the means of exchange and in commodities generally, gave to commerce, to navigation, to industry, an impulse never before known, and thereby, to the revolutionary element in the tottering feudal society, a rapid development.

The feudal system of industry, under which industrial production was monopolized by closed guilds,[11] now no longer sufficed for the growing wants of the new markets. The manufacturing system took its place. The guildmasters were pushed on one side by the manufacturing middle class; division of labor between the different corporate guilds vanished in the face of division of labor in each single workshop.

Meantime the markets kept ever growing, the demand, ever rising. Even manufacture no longer sufficed. Thereupon, steam and machinery revolutionized industrial production. The place of manufacture was taken by the giant, Modern Industry, the place of the industrial middle class, by industrial millionaires, the leaders of whole industrial armies, the modern bourgeois.

Modern industry has established the world market, for which the discovery of America paved the way. This market has given an immense development to commerce, to navigation, to communication by land. This development has, in its turn, reacted on the extension of industry; and in proportion as industry, commerce, navigation and railways extended, in the same proportion the bourgeoisie developed, increased its capital, and pushed into the background every class handed down from the Middle Ages.

We see, therefore, how the modern bourgeoisie is itself the product of a long course of development, of a series of revolutions in the modes of production and of exchange.

Each step in the development of the bourgeoisie was accompanied by a corresponding political advance of that class. An oppressed class

[9] Shopkeepers; townspeople.
[10] The Cape of Good Hope, at the southern tip of Africa.
[11] Medieval "unions" of craftsmen or merchants; they limited their own numbers and fixed prices.

under the sway of the feudal nobility, an armed and self-governing association in the medieval commune, here independent urban republic (as in Italy and Germany), there taxable "third estate" of the monarchy (as in France), afterwards, in the period of manufacture proper, serving either the semi-feudal or the absolute monarchy as a counterpoise against the nobility, and, in fact, cornerstone of the great monarchies in general, the bourgeoisie has at last, since the establishment of Modern Industry and of the world market, conquered for itself, in the modern representative State, exclusive political sway. The executive of the modern State is but a committee for managing the common affairs of the whole bourgeoisie.

The bourgeoisie, historically, has played a most revolutionary part.

The bourgeoisie, wherever it has got the upper hand, has put an end to all feudal, patriarchal, idyllic relations. It has pitilessly torn asunder the motley feudal ties that bound man to his "natural superiors," and has left remaining no other nexus between man and man than naked self-interest, callous "cash payment." It has drowned the most heavenly ecstasies of religious fervor, of chivalrous enthusiasm, of philistine sentimentalism, in the icy water of egotistical calculation. It has resolved personal worth into exchange value, and in place of the numberless indefeasible chartered freedoms, has set up that single, unconscionable freedom—Free Trade. In one word, for exploitation, veiled by religious and political illusions, it has substituted naked, shameless, direct, brutal exploitation.

The bourgeoisie has stripped of its halo every occupation hitherto honored and looked up to with reverent awe. It has converted the physician, the lawyer, the priest, the poet, the man of science, into its paid wage laborers.

The bourgeoisie has torn away from the family its sentimental veil, and has reduced the family relation to a mere money relation.

The bourgeoisie has disclosed how it came to pass that the brutal display of vigor in the Middle Ages, which Reactionists so much admire, found its fitting complement in the most slothful indolence. It has been the first to show what man's activity can bring about. It has accomplished wonders far surpassing Egyptian pyramids, Roman aqueducts, and Gothic cathedrals; it has conducted expeditions that put in the shade all former Exoduses of nations and crusades.

The bourgeoisie cannot exist without constantly revolutionizing the instruments of production, and thereby the relations of production, and with them the whole relations of society. Conservation of the old modes of production in unaltered form, was, on the contrary, the first condition of existence for all earlier industrial classes. Constant revolutionizing of production, uninterrupted disturbance of all social conditions, everlasting uncertainty and agitation, distinguish the bourgeois epoch from all earlier ones. All fixed, fast-frozen relations, with their train of ancient and venerable prejudices and opinions, are swept away, all new-formed ones become antiquated before they can ossify. All that is solid melts into air, all that is holy is profaned, and man is at last compelled to face with sober senses his real conditions of life and his relations with his kind.

The need of a constantly expanding market for its products chases the bourgeoisie over the whole surface of the globe. It must nestle everywhere, settle everywhere, establish connections everywhere.

The bourgeoisie has through its exploitation of the world market given a cosmopolitan character to production and consumption in every country. To the great chagrin of Reactionists, it has drawn from under the feet of industry the national ground on which it stood. All old-established national industries have been destroyed or are daily being destroyed. They are dislodged by new industries, whose introduction becomes a life and death question for all civilized nations, by industries that no longer work up indigenous raw material, but raw material drawn from the remotest zones, industries whose products are consumed, not only at home, but in every quarter of the globe. In place of the old wants, satisfied by the productions of the country, we find new wants, requiring for their satisfaction the products of distant lands and climes. In place of the old local and national seclusion and self-sufficiency, we have intercourse in every direction, universal inter-dependence of nations. And as in material, so also in intellectual production. The intellectual creations of individual nations become common property. National one-sidedness and narrow-mindedness become more and more impossible, and from the numerous national and local literatures there arises a world literature.

The bourgeoisie, by the rapid improvement of all instruments of production, by the immensely facilitated means of communication, draws all, even the most barbarian, nations into civilization. The cheap prices of its commodities are the heavy artillery with which it batters down all Chinese walls, with which it forces the barbarians' intensely obstinate hatred of foreigners to capitulate. It compels all nations, on pain of extinction, to adopt the bourgeois mode of production; it compels them to introduce what it calls civilization into their midst, namely, to become bourgeois themselves. In a word, it creates a world after its own image.

The bourgeoisie has subjected the country to the rule of the towns. It has created enormous cities, has greatly increased the urban population as compared with the rural, and has thus rescued a considerable part of the population from the idiocy of rural life. Just as it has made the country dependent on the towns, so it has made barbarian and semi-barbarian countries dependent on the civilized ones, nations of peasants on nations of bourgeois, the East on the West.

The bourgeoisie keeps more and more doing away with the scattered state of the population, of the means of production, and of property. It has agglomerated population, centralized means of production, and has concentrated property in a few hands. The necessary consequence of this was political centralization. Independent, or but loosely connected provinces, with separate interests, laws, governments, and systems of taxation, became lumped together in one nation, with one government, one code of laws, one national class-interest, one frontier and one customs tariff.

The bourgeoisie, during its rule of scarce one hundred years, has created more massive and more colossal productive forces than have all preceding generations together. Subjection of Nature's forces to man, machinery, application of chemistry to industry and agriculture, steam navigation, railways, electric telegraphs, clearing of whole continents for cultivation, canalization of rivers, whole populations conjured out of the ground—what earlier century had even a presentiment that such productive forces slumbered in the lap of social labor?

We see then: the means of production and of exchange on whose foundation the bourgeoisie built itself up, were generated in feudal society. At a certain stage in the development of these means of production and of exchange, the conditions under which feudal society produced and exchanged, the feudal organization of agriculture and manufacturing industry, in one word, the feudal relations of property, became no longer compatible with the already developed productive forces; they became so many fetters. They had to burst asunder; they were burst asunder.

Into their place stepped free competition, accompanied by a social and political constitution adapted to it, and by the economical and political sway of the bourgeois class.

A similar movement is going on before our own eyes. Modern bourgeois society with its relations of production, of exchange, and of property, a society that has conjured up such gigantic means of production and of exchange, is like the sorcerer, who is no longer able to control the powers of the nether world whom he has called up by his spells. For many a decade past the history of industry and commerce is but the history of the revolt of modern productive forces against modern conditions of production, against the property relations that are the conditions for the existence of the bourgeoisie and of its rule. It is enough to mention the commercial crises that by their periodical return put on its trial, each time more threateningly, the existence of the entire bourgeois society. In these crises a great part not only of the existing products, but also of the previously created productive forces, is periodically destroyed. In these crises there breaks out an epidemic that, in all earlier epochs, would have seemed an absurdity—the epidemic of overproduction. Society suddenly finds itself put back into a state of momentary barbarism; it appears as if a famine, a universal war of devastation had cut off the supply of every means of subsistence; industry and commerce seem to be destroyed; and why? Because there is too much civilization, too much means of subsistence, too much industry, too much commerce. The productive forces at the disposal of society no longer tend to further the development of the conditions of bourgeois property; on the contrary, they have become too powerful for these conditions, by which they are fettered, and so soon as they overcome these fetters, they bring disorder into the whole of bourgeois society, endanger the existence of bourgeois property. The conditions of bourgeois society are too narrow to comprise the wealth created by them. And how does the bourgeoisie get over these crises? On the one hand by enforced destruction of a mass of productive forces; on the other, by the conquest of new markets, and by the more thorough exploitation of the old ones. That is to say, by paving the way for more extensive and more destructive crises, and by diminishing the means whereby crises are prevented.

The weapons with which the bourgeoisie felled feudalism to the ground are now turned against the bourgeoisie itself.

But not only has the bourgeoisie forged the weapons that bring death to itself; it has also called into existence the men who are to wield those weapons—the modern working class—the proletarians.

In proportion as the bourgeoisie, that is, capital, is developed, in the same proportion is the proletariat, the modern working class, developed; a class of laborers, who live only so long as they find work, and who find work only so long as their labor increases capital. These laborers, who must sell themselves piecemeal, are a commodity, like every other article of commerce, and are consequently exposed to all the vicissitudes of competition, to all the fluctuations of the market.

Owing to the extensive use of machinery and to division of labor, the work of the proletarians has lost all individual character, and, consequently, all charm for the workman. He becomes an appendage of the machine, and it is only the most simple, most monotonous, and most easily acquired knack that is required of him. Hence, the cost of production of a workman is restricted, almost entirely, to the means of subsistence that he requires for his maintenance, and for the propagation of his race. But the price of a commodity, and also of labor, is equal to its cost of production. In proportion, therefore, as the repulsiveness of the work increases, the wage decreases. Nay, more, in proportion as the use of machinery and division of labor increases, in the same proportion the burden of toil also increases, whether by prolongation of the working hours, by increase of the work exacted in a given time, or by increased speed of the machinery, and so forth.

Modern industry has converted the little workshop of the patriarchal master into the great factory of the industrial capitalist. Masses of laborers, crowded into the factory, are organized like soldiers. As privates of the industrial army they are placed under the command of a perfect hierarchy of officers and sergeants. Not only are they slaves of the bourgeois class, and of the bourgeois State, they are daily and hourly enslaved by the machine, by the over-seer, and, above all, by the individual bourgeois manufacturer himself. The more openly this despotism proclaims gain to be its end and aim, the more petty, the more hateful and the more embittering it is.

The less the skill and exertion or strength is implied in manual labor, in other words, the more modern industry becomes developed, the more is the labor of men superseded by that of women.

Differences of age and sex have no longer any distinctive social validity for the working class. All are instruments of labor, more or less expensive to use, according to age and sex.

No sooner is the exploitation of the laborer by the manufacturer so far at an end that he receives his wages in cash, than he is set upon by the other portions of the bourgeoisie, the landlord, the shopkeeper, the pawnbroker, and so forth.

The lower strata of the middle class—the small tradespeople, shopkeepers, and retired tradesmen generally, the handicraftsmen and peasants—all these sink gradually into the proletariat, partly because their diminutive capital does not suffice for the scale on which modern industry is carried on, and is swamped in the competition with the large capitalists, partly because their specialized skill is rendered worthless by new methods of production. Thus the proletariat is recruited from all classes of the population.

The proletariat goes through various stages of development. With its birth begins its struggle with the bourgeoisie. At first the contest is carried on by individual laborers, then by the workpeople of a factory, then by the operatives of one trade, in one locality, against the individual bourgeois who directly exploits them. They direct their attacks not against the bourgeois conditions of production, but against the instruments of production themselves; they destroy imported wares that compete with their labor, they smash to pieces machinery, they set factories ablaze, they seek to restore by force the vanished status of the workman of the Middle Ages.

At this stage the laborers still form an incoherent mass scattered over the whole country, and broken up by their mutual competition. If anywhere they unite to form more compact bodies, this is not yet the consequence of their own active union, but of the union of the bourgeoisie, which class, in order to attain its own political ends, is compelled to set the whole proletariat in motion, and is moreover yet, for a time, able to do so. At this stage, therefore, the proletarians do not fight their enemies, but the enemies of their enemies, the remnants of absolute monarchy, the landowners, the non-industrial bourgeois, the petty bourgeoisie. Thus the whole historical movement is concentrated in the hands of the bourgeoisie; every victory so obtained is a victory for the bourgeoisie.

But with the development of industry the proletariat not only increases in number; it becomes concentrated in greater masses, its strength grows and it feels that strength more. The various interests and conditions of life within the ranks of the proletariat are more and more equalized, in proportion as machinery obliterates all distinctions of labor, and nearly everywhere reduces wages to the same low level. The growing competition among the bourgeois, and the resulting commercial crises, make the wages of the workers ever more fluctuating. The unceasing improvement of machinery, ever more rapidly developing, makes their livelihood more and more precarious; the collisions between individual workmen and individual bourgeois take more and more the character of collisions between two classes. Thereupon the workers begin to form combinations (Trades' Unions) against the bourgeois; they club together in order to keep up the rate of wages; they found permanent associations in order to make provision beforehand for these occasional revolts. Here and there the contest breaks out into riots.

Now and then the workers are victorious, but only for a time. The real fruit of their battles lies not in the immediate result, but in the ever-expanding union of the workers. This union is furthered by the improved means of communication that are created in modern industry and that place the workers of different localities in contact with one another. It was just this contact that was needed to centralize the numerous local struggles, all of the same character, into one national struggle between classes. But every class struggle is a political struggle. And that union, to attain which the burghers of the Middle Ages, with their miserable highways, required centuries, the modern proletarians, thanks to railways, achieve in a few years.

This organization of the proletarians into a class and consequently into a political party, is continually being upset again by the competition between the workers themselves. But it ever rises up again; stronger, firmer, mightier. It compels legislative recognition of particular interests of the workers, by taking advantage of the divisions among the bourgeoisic itself. Thus the ten-hour bill in England was carried.

Altogether collisions between the classes of the old society further, in many ways, the course of development of the proletariat. The bourgeoisie finds itself involved in a constant battle. At first with the aristocracy; later on, with those portions of the bourgeoisie itself whose interests have become antagonistic to the progress of industry; at all times with the bourgeoisie of foreign countries. In all these battles it sees itself compelled to appeal to the proletariat, to ask for its help, and thus to drag it into the political arena. The bourgeoisie itself, therefore, supplies the proletariat with its own elements of political and general education, in other words, it furnishes the proletariat with weapons for fighting the bourgeoisie.

Further, as we have already seen, entire sections of the ruling classes are, by the advance of industry, precipitated into the proletariat, or are at least threatened in their conditions of existence. These also supply the proletariat with fresh elements of enlightenment and progress.

Finally, in times when the class struggle nears the decisive hour, the process of dissolution going on within the ruling class, in fact within the whole range of old society, assumes such a violent, glaring character, that a small section of the ruling class cuts itself adrift, and joins the revolutionary class, the class that holds the future in its hands. Just as, therefore, at an earlier period, a section of the nobility went over to the bourgeoisie, so now a portion of the bourgeoisie goes over to the proletariat, and in particular, a portion of the bourgeois ideologists, who have raised themselves to the level of comprehending theoretically the historical movement as a whole.

Of all the classes that stand face to face with the bourgeoisie today, the proletariat alone is a really revolutionary class. The other classes decay and finally disappear in the face of modern industry; the proletariat is its special and essential product.

The lower middle class, the small manufacturer, the shopkeeper, the artisan, the peasant, all these fight against the bourgeoisie to save from extinction their existence as fractions of the middle class. They are, therefore, not revolutionary, but conservative. Nay, more, they are reactionary, for they try to roll back the wheel of history. If by chance they are revolutionary, they are so only in view of their impending transfer into the proletariat, they thus defend not their present, but their future interests, they desert their own standpoint to place themselves at that of the proletariat.

The "dangerous class," the social scum, that passively rotting mass thrown off by the lowest layers of old society, may, here and there, be swept into the movement by a proletarian revolution; its conditions of life, however, prepare it far more for the part of a bribed tool of reactionary intrigue.

In the conditions of the proletariat, those of old society at large are already virtually swamped. The proletarian is without property; his relation to his wife and children has no longer anything in common with the bourgeois family relations; modern industrial labor, modern subjection to capital, the same in England as in France, in America as in Germany, has stripped him of every trace of national character. Law, morality, religion, are to him so many bourgeois prejudices, behind which lurk in ambush just as many bourgeois interests.

All the preceding classes that got the upper hand sought to fortify their already acquired status by subjecting society at large to their conditions of appropriation. The proletarians cannot become masters of the productive forces of society, except by abolishing their own previous mode of appropriation, and thereby also every other previous mode of appropriation. They have nothing of their own to secure and to fortify; their mission is to destroy all previous securities for, and insurances of, individual property.

All previous historical movements were movements of minorities, or in the interest of minorities. The proletarian movement is the self-conscious, independent movement of the immense majority, in the interest of the immense majority. The proletariat, the lowest stratum of our present society, cannot stir, cannot raise itself up, without the whole superincumbent strata of official society being sprung into the air.

Though not in substance, yet in form, the struggle of the proletariat with the bourgeoisie is at first a national struggle. The proletariat of each country must, of course, first of all settle matters with its own bourgeoisie.

In depicting the most general phases of the development of the proletariat, we traced the more or less veiled civil war, raging within existing society, up to the point where that war breaks out into open revolution, and where the violent overthrow of the bourgeoisie lays the foundation for the sway of the proletariat.

Hitherto every form of society has been based, as we have already seen, on the antagonism of oppressing and oppressed classes. But in order to oppress a class certain conditions must be assured to it under which it can, at least, continue its slavish existence. The serf, in the period of serfdom, raised himself to membership in the commune, just as the petty bourgeois, under the yoke of feudal absolutism, managed to develop into a bourgeois. The modern laborer, on the contrary, instead of rising with the progress of industry, sinks deeper and deeper below the conditions of existence of his own class. He becomes a pauper, and pauperism develops more rapidly than population and wealth. And here it becomes evident that the bourgeoisie is unfit any longer to be the ruling class in society and to impose its

conditions of existence upon society as an over-riding law. It is unfit
to rule because it is incompetent to assure an existence to its slave
within his slavery, because it cannot help letting him sink into such a
state that it has to feed him instead of being fed by him. Society can
no longer live under this bourgeoisie; in other words, its existence is
no longer compatible with society.

The essential condition for the existence, and for the sway of the
bourgeois class, is the formation and augmentation of capital; the
condition for capital is wage-labor. Wage-labor rests exclusively on
competiton between the laborers. The advance of industry, whose
involuntary promoter is the bourgeoisie, replaces the isolation of the
laborers, due to competition, by their revolutionary combination,
due to association. The development of modern industry, therefore,
cuts from under its feet the very foundation on which the bourgeoisie produces and appropriates products. What the bourgeoisie therefore produces, above all, are its own gravediggers. Its fall and the
victory of the proletariat are equally inevitable.

PROLETARIANS AND COMMUNISTS

In what relation do the Communists stand to the proletarians as a
whole?

The Communists do not form a separate party opposed to other
working class parties.

They have no interests separate and apart from those of the proletariat as a whole.

They do not set up any sectarian principles of their own by which
to shape and mould the proletarian movement.

The Communists are distinguished from the other working class
parties by this only: 1. In the national struggles of the proletarians of
the different countries, they point out and bring to the front the
common interests of the entire proletariat, independently of all nationality. 2. In the various stages of development which the struggle
of the working class against the bourgeoisie has to pass through,
they always and everywhere represent the interests of the movement
as a whole.

The Communists, therefore, are on the one hand, practically, the
most advanced and resolute section of the working class parties of
every country, that section which pushes forward all others; on the

other hand, theoretically, they have over the great mass of the proletariat the advantage of clearly understanding the line of march, the conditions, and the ultimate general results of the proletarian movement.

The immediate aim of the Communists is the same as that of all the other proletarian parties: formation of the proletariat into a class, overthrow of the bourgeois supremacy, conquest of political power by the proletariat.

The theoretical conclusions of the Communists are in no way based on ideas or principles that have been invented, or discovered, by this or that would-be universal reformer.

They merely express, in general terms, actual relations springing from an existing class struggle, from a historical movement going on under our very eyes. The abolition of existing property relations is not at all a distinctive feature of Communism.

All property relations in the past have continually been subject to historical change, consequent upon the change in historical conditions.

The French revolution, for example, abolished feudal property in favor of bourgeois property.

The distinguishing feature of Communism is not the abolition of property generally, but the abolition of bourgeois property. But modern bourgeois private property is the final and most complete expression of the system of producing and appropriating products, that is based on class antagonism, on the exploitation of the many by the few.

In this sense the theory of the Communists may be summed up in the single sentence: Abolition of private property.

We Communists have been reproached with the desire of abolishing the right of personally acquiring property as the fruit of a man's own labor, which property is alleged to be the ground work of all personal freedom, activity and independence.

Hard-won, self-acquired, self-earned property! Do you mean the property of the petty artisan and of the small peasant, a form of property that preceded the bourgeois form? There is no need to abolish that; the development of industry has to a great extent already destroyed it, and is still destroying it daily.

Or do you mean modern bourgeois private property?

But does wage-labor create any property for the laborer? Not a bit. It creates capital, namely, that kind of property which exploits wage-labor, and which cannot increase except upon condition of getting a new supply of wage-labor for fresh exploitation. Property, in its present form, is based on the antagonism of capital and wage-labor. Let us examine both sides of this antagonism.

To be a capitalist, is to have not only a purely personal, but a social status in production. Capital is a collective product, and only by the united action of many members, nay, in the last resort, only by the united action of all members of society, can it be set in motion.

Capital is therefore not a personal, it is a social power.

When, therefore, capital is converted into common property, into the property of all members of society, personal property is not thereby transformed into social property. It is only the social character of the property that is changed. It loses its class character.

Let us now take wage-labor.

The average price of wage-labor is the minimum wage, namely, that quantum of the means of subsistence, which is absolutely requisite to keep the laborer in bare existence as a laborer. What, therefore, the wage-laborer appropriates by means of his labor, merely suffices to prolong and reproduce a bare existence. We by no means intend to abolish this personal appropriation of the products of labor, an appropriation that is made for the maintenance and reproduction of human life, and that leaves no surplus wherewith to command the labor of others. All that we want to do away with is the miserable character of this appropriation, under which the laborer lives merely to increase capital, and is allowed to live only in so far as the interest of the ruling class requires it.

In bourgeois society, living labor is but a means to increase accumulated labor. In communist society, accumulated labor is but a means to widen, to enrich, to promote the existence of the laborer.

In bourgeois society, therefore, the past dominates the present; in communist society, the present dominates the past. In bourgeois society capital is independent and has individuality, while the living person is dependent and has no individuality.

And the abolition of this state of things is called by the bourgeois, abolition of individuality and freedom! And rightly so. The abolition of bourgeois individuality, bourgeois independence, and bourgeois freedom is undoubtedly aimed at.

By freedom is meant, under the present bourgeois conditions of production, free trade, free selling and buying.

But if selling and buying disappears, free selling and buying disappears also. This talk about free selling and buying, and all the other "brave words" of our bourgeoisie about freedom in general, have a meaning, if any, only in contrast with restricted selling and buying, with the fettered traders of the Middle Ages, but have no meaning when opposed to the Communistic abolition of buying and selling, of the bourgeois conditions of production, and of the bourgeoisie itself.

You are horrified at our intending to do away with private property. But in your existing society private property is already done away with for nine-tenths of the population; its existence for the few is solely due to its non-existence in the hands of those nine-tenths. You reproach us, therefore, with intending to do away with a form of property, the necessary condition for whose existence is the non-existence of any property for the immense majority of society.

In one word, you reproach us with intending to do away with your property. Precisely so: that is just what we intend.

From the moment when labor can no longer be converted into capital, money, or rent, into a social power capable of being monopolized, that is, from the moment when individual property can no longer be transformed into bourgeois property, into capital, from that moment, you say, individuality vanishes!

You must, therefore, confess that by "individual" you mean no other person than the bourgeois, than the middle class owner of property. This person must, indeed, be swept out of the way, and made impossible.

Communism deprives no man of the power to appropriate the products of society: all that it does is to deprive him of the power to subjugate the labor of others by means of such appropriation.

It has been objected, that upon the abolition of private property all work will cease, and universal laziness will overtake us.

According to this, bourgeois society ought long ago to have gone to the dogs through sheer idleness; for those of its members who work, acquire nothing, and those who acquire anything, do not work. The whole of this objection is but another expression of the tautology: that there can no longer be any wage-labor when there is no longer any capital.

All objections against the Communistic mode of producing and appropriating material products, have, in the same way, been urged against the Communistic modes of producing and appropriating intellectual products. Just as, to the bourgeois the disappearance of class property is the disappearance of production itself, so the disappearance of class culture is to him identical with the disappearance of all culture.

That culture, the loss of which he laments, is, for the enormous majority, a mere training to act as a machine.

But don't wrangle with us so long as you apply to our intended abolition of bourgeois property, the standard of your bourgeois notions of freedom, culture, law, and so forth. Your very ideas are but the outgrowth of the conditions of your bourgeois production and bourgeois property, just as your jurisprudence is but the will of your class made into a law for all, a will, whose essential character and direction are determined by the economic conditions of existence of your class.

The selfish misconception that induces you to transform into eternal laws of nature and of reason, the social forms springing from your present mode of production and form of property—historical relations that rise and disappear in the progress of production—this misconception you share with every ruling class that has preceded you. What you see clearly in the case of ancient property, what you admit in the case of feudal property, you are of course forbidden to admit in the case of your own bourgeois form of property.

Abolition of the family! Even the most radical flare up at this infamous proposal of the Communists.

On what foundation is the present family, the bourgeois family, based? On capital, on private gain. In its completely developed form this family exists only among the bourgeoisie. But this state of things finds its complement in the practical absence of the family among the proletarians, and in public prostitution.

The bourgeois family will vanish as a matter of course when its complement vanishes, and both will vanish with the vanishing of capital.

Do you charge us with wanting to stop the exploitation of children by their parents? To this crime we plead guilty.

But, you will say, we destroy the most hallowed of relations, when we replace home education by social.

And your education! Is not that also social, and determined by the social conditions under which you educate, by the intervention, direct or indirect, of society by means of schools, and so forth? The Communists have not invented the intervention of society in education; they do but seek to alter the character of that intervention, and to rescue education from the influence of the ruling class.

The bourgeois clap-trap about the family and education, about the hallowed co-relation of parent and child, become all the more disgusting, the more, by the action of modern industry, all family ties among the proletarians are torn asunder, and their children transformed into simple articles of commerce and instruments of labor.

But you Communists would introduce community of women, screams the whole bourgeoisie in chorus.

The bourgeois sees in his wife a mere instrument of production. He hears that the instruments of production are to be exploited in common, and, naturally, can come to no other conclusion than that the lot of being common to all will likewise fall to the women.

He has not even a suspicion that the real point aimed at is to do away with the status of women as mere instruments of production.

For the rest nothing is more ridiculous than the virtuous indignation of our bourgeois at the community of women which, they pretend, is to be openly and officially established by the Communists. The Communists have no need to introduce community of women; it has existed almost from time immemorial.

Our bourgeois, not content with having the wives and daughters of their proletarians at their disposal, not to speak of common prostitutes, take the greatest pleasure in seducing each other's wives.

Bourgeois marriage is in reality a system of wives in common, and thus, at the most, what the Communists might possibly be reproached with, is that they desire to introduce, in substitution for a hypocritically concealed, an openly legalized community of women. For the rest it is self-evident that the abolition of the present system of production must bring with it the abolition of the community of women springing from that system, namely, of prostitution both public and private.

The Communists are further reproached with desiring to abolish countries and nationality.

The working men have no country. We cannot take from them what they have not got. Since the proletariat must first of all acquire political supremacy, must rise to be the leading class of the nation, must constitute itself *the* nation, it is, so far, itself national, though not in the bourgeois sense of the word.

National differences and antagonisms between peoples are daily more and more vanishing, owing to the development of the bourgeoisie, to freedom of commerce, to the world market, to uniformity in the mode of production and in the conditions of life corresponding thereto.

The supremacy of the proletariat will cause them to vanish still faster. United action, of the leading civilized countries at least, is one of the first conditions for the emancipation of the proletariat.

In proportion as the exploitation of one individual by another is put an end to, the exploitation of one nation by another will also be put an end to. In proportion as the antagonism between classes within the nation vanishes, the hostility of one nation to another will come to an end.

The charges against Communism made from a religious, a philosophical, and generally, from an ideological standpoint are not deserving of serious examination.

Does it require deep intuition to comprehend that man's ideas, views, and conceptions, in one word, man's consciousness changes with every change in the conditions of his material existence, in his social relations and in his social life?

What else does the history of ideas prove, than that intellectual production changes its character in proportion as material production is changed? The ruling ideas of each age have ever been the ideas of its ruling class.

When people speak of ideas that revolutionize society, they do but express the fact that within the old society the elements of a new one have been created, and that the dissolution of the old ideas keeps even pace with the dissolution of the old conditions of existence.

When the ancient world was in its last throes, the ancient religions were overcome by Christianity. When Christian ideas succumbed in the 18th century to rationalist ideas, feudal society fought its death battle with the then revolutionary bourgeoisie. The ideas of religious liberty and freedom of conscience merely gave expression to the sway of free competition within the domain of knowledge.

"Undoubtedly," it will be said, "religious, moral, philosophical and juridical ideas have been modified in the course of historical development. But religion, morality, philosophy, political science, and law, constantly survived this change."

"There are, besides, eternal truths, such as Freedom, Justice, and so forth, that are common to all states of society. But Communism abolishes eternal truths, it abolishes all religion, and all morality, instead of constituting them on a new basis; it therefore acts in contradiction to all past historical experience."

What does this accusation reduce itself to? The history of all past society has consisted in the development of class antagonisms, antagonisms that assume different forms at different epochs.

But whatever form they may have taken, one fact is common to all past ages, namely, the exploitation of one part of society by the other. No wonder, then, that the social consciousness of past ages, despite all the multiplicity and variety it displays, moves within certain common forms, or general ideas, which cannot completely vanish except with the total disappearance of class antagonisms.

The Communist revolution is the most radical rupture with traditional property relations; no wonder that its development involves the most radical rupture with traditional ideas.

But let us have done with the bourgeois objections to Communism.

We have seen above that the first step in the revolution by the working class is to raise the proletariat to the position of ruling class; to win the battle of democracy.

The proletariat will use its political supremacy to wrest, by degrees, all capital from the bourgeoisie; to centralize all instruments of production in the hands of the State, that is, of the proletariat organized as the ruling class; and to increase the total productive forces as rapidly as possible.

Of course, in the beginning this cannot be effected except by means of despotic inroads on the rights of property and on the conditions of bourgeois production; by means of measures, therefore, which appear economically insufficient and untenable, but which, in the course of the movement, outstrip themselves, necessitate further inroads upon the old social order and are unavoidable as a means of entircly revolutionizing the mode of production.

These measures will, of course, be different in different countries.

Nevertheless in the most advanced countries the following will be pretty generally applicable:

1. Abolition of property in land and application of all rents of land to public purposes.

2. A heavy progressive or graduated income tax.

3. Abolition of all right of inheritance.

4. Confiscation of the property of all emigrants and rebels.

5. Centralization of credit in the hands of the State, by means of a national bank with State capital and an exclusive monopoly.

6. Centralization of the means of communication and transport in the hands of the State.

7. Extension of factories and instruments of production owned by the State; the bringing into cultivation of waste lands, and the improvement of the soil generally in accordance with a common plan.

8. Equal liability of all to labor. Establishment of industrial armies, especially for agriculture.

9. Combination of agriculture with manufacturing industries: gradual abolition of the distinction between town and country, by a more equable distribution of population over the country.

10. Free education for all children in public schools. Abolition of children's factory labor in its present form. Combination of education with industrial production, and so forth.

When, in the course of development, class distinctions have disappeared and all production has been concentrated in the hands of a vast association of the whole nation, the public power will lose its political character. Political power, properly so called, is merely the organized power of one class for oppressing another. If the proletariat during its contest with the bourgeoisie is compelled, by the force of circumstances, to organize itself as a class, if, by means of a revolution, it makes itself the ruling class, and, as such, sweeps away by force the old conditions of production, then it will, along with these conditions, have swept away the conditions for the existence of class antagonisms, and of classes generally, and will thereby have abolished its own supremacy as a class.

In place of the old bourgeois society with its classes and class antagonisms we shall have an association in which the free development of each is the condition for the free development of all.

• • •

POSITION OF THE COMMUNISTS IN RELATION TO THE VARIOUS EXISTING OPPOSITION PARTIES

The Communists fight for the attainment of the immediate aims, for the enforcement of the momentary interests of the working class; but in the movement of the present, they also represent and take care of the future of that movement. In France the Communists ally themselves with the Social-Democrats, against the conservative and radical bourgeoisie, reserving, however, the right to take up a critical position in regard to phrases and illusions traditionally handed down from the great Revolution.[12] . . .

In Germany they fight with the bourgeoisie whenever it acts in a revolutionary way, against the absolute monarchy, the feudal squirearchy,[13] and the petty bourgeoisie.[14]

But they never cease, for a single instant, to instill into the working class the clearest possible recognition of the hostile antagonism between bourgeoisie and proletariat, in order that the German workers may straightway use, as so many weapons against the bourgeoisie, the social and political conditions that the bourgeoisie must necessarily introduce along with its supremacy, and in order that, after the fall of the reactionary classes in Germany, the fight against the bourgeoisie itself may immediately begin.

The Communists turn their attention chiefly to Germany, because that country is on the eve of a bourgeois revolution[15] that is bound to be carried out under more advanced conditions of European civilization, and with a more developed proletariat, than that of England was in the seventeenth, and of France in the eighteenth century, and because the bourgeois revolution in Germany will be but the prelude to an immediately following proletarian revolution.

In short, the Communists everywhere support every revolutionary movement against the existing social and political order of things.

In all these movements they bring to the front, as the leading question in each, the property question, no matter what its degree of development at the time.

Finally, they labor everywhere for the union and agreement of the democratic parties of all countries.

The Communists disdain to conceal their views and aims. They openly declare that their ends can be attained only by the forcible overthrow of all existing social conditions. Let the ruling classes tremble at a Communistic revolution. The proletarians have nothing to lose but their chains. They have a world to win.

Working men of all countries, unite!

[12] The French Revolution (1789–95).
[13] The landed gentry (small landowners).
[14] Small shopkeepers and craftspeople.
[15] The ill-fated national and liberal revolution of 1848 to 1849.

21

Michael Bakunin

Anarchism

*Marx and Engels were not the only important social agitators of the mid-
and late-nineteenth century. Of a different mold but similarly influential was
the anarchist Michael Bakunin (1814–1876). His birth into a Russian family of rank and privilege assured Bakunin of a good education and prospects
for a distinguished career; upon completing his education as a cadet, he became an officer of the Russian army. But after only two years of service he
resigned his commission in order to pursue studies at the University of Berlin, where for a short time he studied Hegelian philosophy. Just as abruptly
as he had cut his ties with the army, however, he discontinued and even
repudiated his formal studies in order to throw himself into the revolutionary
struggles of his day. From age thirty, he devoted his entire existence to activities related to the cause of revolution: writing, traveling, agitating, organizing—and paying for his dedication to the cause by spending over a decade
either in prison or in exile.*

*More than a political theorist, Bakunin was a revolutionary activist who
threw himself into every situation that had even the semblance of a rebellious
disturbance. Social rebellion drew him so often from his desk that most of his
written legacy consists of unfinished articles, books, pamphlets, and proposed
programs for action. His prime and lasting aim was revolutionary work that
would bring about, at last, the total annihilation of the existing order. He
was the forerunner of the anarchic "terrorist" bands that frighten and perplex
the present-day world.*

The anarchistic ideas of Bakunin rested upon his perception that the masses of his day were deprived of liberty and locked into servitude and exploitation. He felt that those in power would continue to use any and all means to keep the rest of the people down—laws, courts, police, conventions, morality and, above all else, religion. Consequently, Bakunin's struggle was against every manifestation of power and privilege, even the minutest expression and vestige of the bourgeois world. Unlike Marx, Bakunin did not hope and labor for a grand day of world revolution, when the existing power structure would be overturned. Rather, whenever an opportunity presented itself to weaken the existing order, he sought to deliver the hardest blow possible against it.

The unceasing struggle against authority brought Bakunin into frequent (but temporary) comradeship with the Marxian socialists. Though the target of their revolt was the same, the goals of socialists and anarchists were vastly different. Whereas the Marxists' foremost aim was economic equality for all, Bakunin's overwhelming concern was for liberty—that is, everlasting freedom from every constituted power, monopoly, regimentation, and control. Consequently, while the Marxist proletariat—being petty bourgeois in spirit—in reality sought economic and politcal re-enfranchisement, Bakunin and his followers aimed at the destruction of all established institutions. Before the new society could be built, the old had to be turned into rubble. Bakunin was convinced, further, that only those people who had been completely rejected by bourgeois society, such as the landless laborers and the much reviled Lumpenproletariat (the Marxian term for the very lowest of the proletariat—that is, riff-raff, or rabble), were capable of a genuine rebellion or revolution. He discerned such people only in southern Europe (Italy and Spain) and in eastern Europe (Russia). Differing with Marx, Bakunin held the industrial proletariat of England and Germany to be incapable of truly revolutionary action.

Bakunin maintained that in their struggle for liberty the truly revolutionary masses would find themselves assisted by "that intelligent and genuinely noble section of youth whose open-hearted convictions and burning aspirations lead it to embrace the cause of the people despite being born into the privileged classes." These educated idealists (he among them) would supply leadership and guidance while at all times remaining one with the people. At no time would they allow themselves to become a ruling elite of any sort and in this way deprive the people of the choicest fruit of their rebellion—liberty. Bakunin suspected that after a socialist revolution, the party elite would transform itself into a new ruling class of government officials, functionaries, and technocrats. If this were to happen, the people would have merely exchanged one ruling class for another. The romantic ide-

alist Bakunin demanded that following the anarchist *revolution, his elite should relinquish all positions of power, because liberty for everyone was assured only when people lived together in free associations of equals. Individuals, he visualized, would collaborate voluntarily, because they would perceive it to be in their own best interest to do so. On the other hand, everyone would have the right to refuse collaboration or to secede from the association. The words* force, coercion, *and* compulsion *would be totally absent from the vocabulary of the future.*

While Marx viewed history as a dialectic process, Bakunin was unable to discern any blueprint for historical development. Accordingly, he felt that events happen because of human volition, certain conditions, or chance. In the 1860s Bakunin believed that the masses were intent upon making sweeping revolutionary changes in the near future. But he was sobered by the unification of Germany in 1871, which appeared to postpone the fruition of his dreams. He then adopted the view that no large-scale revolutionary changes would take place until after the mighty nation-states of Europe had clashed in a general and bloody war.

The following selection is taken from one of Bakunin's proposed programs of action, entitled "Principles and Organization of the International Brotherhood." It was written in the mid-1860s.

PRINCIPLES AND ORGANIZATION OF THE INTERNATIONAL BROTHERHOOD

I. *Aim of the Society*

1. The aim of this society is the triumph of the principle of revolution in the world, and consequently the radical overthrow of all presently existing religious, political, economic and social organizations and institutions and the reconstitution first of European and subsequently of world society on the basis of *liberty, reason, justice* and *work.*

2. This kind of task cannot be achieved overnight. The association is therefore constituted for an indefinite period, and will cease to exist only on the day when the triumph of its principle throughout the world removes its *raison d'être.* [1]

---

[1] French: reason for being.

II. *Revolutionary Catechism* [2]

1. Denial of the existence of a real, extra-terrestrial, individual God, and consequently also of any revelation and any divine intervention in the affairs of the human world. *Abolition of the service and worship of divinity.*

2. In replacing the worship of God by *respect* and *love for humanity,* we assert *human reason* as the one criterion of truth; *human conscience* as the basis of justice; *individual and collective liberty* as the only creator of order for mankind.

3. *Liberty* is the absolute right of all adult men and women to seek no sanction for their actions except their own conscience and their own reason, to determine them only of their own free will, and consequently to be responsible for them to themselves first of all, and then to the society of which they are a part, but only in so far as they freely consent to be a part of it.

4. It is quite untrue that the freedom of the individual is bounded by that of every other individual. Man is truly free only to the extent that his own freedom, freely acknowledged and reflected as in a mirror by the free conscience of all other men, finds in their freedom the confirmation of its infinite scope. Man is truly free only among other equally free men, and since he is free only in terms of mankind, the enslavement of any one man on earth, being an offence against the very principle of humanity, is a denial of the liberty of all.

5. Every man's *liberty* can be realized, therefore, only by the *equality* of all. The realization of liberty in legal and actual equality is *justice.*

6. There is only one dogma, one law, one moral basis for men, and *that is liberty.* To respect your neighbor's liberty *is duty;* to love, help and serve him, *virtue.*

7. *Absolute rejection of any principle of authority and of raison d'État.* [3] *Human society,* which was originally a natural fact, prior to liberty and the awakening of the human mind, and which later became a religious fact, organized on the principle of divine and human authority, must now be reconstituted on the basis of liberty, henceforward to be the sole determinant of its organization, both political and economic. *Order in society must be the outcome of the greatest possible development of all local, collective and individual liberties.*

[2] Summary of doctrines and principles.

[3] Literally, reason of State; a measure taken by a government to ensure the very continuance of the state—sometimes contrary to individual liberty and justice.

8. The political and economic organization of society must therefore not flow downwards, from high to low, and outwards, from centre to circumference, as it does today on the principle of unity and enforced centralization, *but upwards* and *inwards,* on the principle of free association and free federation.

9. *Political organization.*

It is impossible to determine a concrete, universal and compulsory norm for the internal development and political organization of nations, since the existence of each is subordinate to a host of variable historical, geographical and economic factors which never permit of the establishment of an organizational model equally applicable and acceptable to all. Furthermore, any undertaking of this nature, being utterly devoid of practical utility, would militate against the richness and spontaneity of life, which delights in infinite diversity, and would in addition be contrary to the very principle of liberty. Nevertheless, there do exist *essential, absolute conditions* without which the practical realization and organization of liberty will always be impossible. These conditions are:

9(a). *The radical abolition of all official religion and every privileged or state-protected, -financed or -maintained church.* Absolute freedom of conscience and propaganda for all, each man having the unlimited option of building as many temples as he pleases to his gods, whatever their denomination, and of paying and maintaining the priests of his religion.

9(b). Seen as religious corporations, churches shall enjoy none of the political rights which will belong to productive associations, shall be unable to inherit or possess wealth in common, excepting their houses or establishments of prayer, and shall never be allowed to participate in the upbringing of children, since their sole aim in life is the systematic negation of morality and liberty, and the practice of sorcery for profit.

9(c). *Abolition of monarchy, republic.*

9(d). *Abolition of class, rank, privilege and distinction in all its forms. Complete equality of political rights for all men and all women; universal suffrage.*

9(e). *Abolition,* dissolution, and moral, political, legal, bureaucratic and social bankruptcy of the *custodial, transcendental,* centralist *state,* lackey and alter ego[4] of the church, and as such the permanent source of poverty, degradation and subjugation among the people.

[4] Another self.

As a natural consequence, *abolition of all state universities*—public education must be the exclusive prerogative of the free communes and associations; *abolition* of *state magistracy*—all judges to be elected by the people; *abolition* of the *criminal and civil codes currently in force in Europe*—because all of these, being equally inspired by the worship of God, state, family as a religious and political entity, and property, are contrary to human rights, and because *only by liberty* can the code of liberty be created. *Abolition* of *banks, and all other state credit institutions. Abolition* of *all central administration, bureaucracies, standing armies* and *state police.*

9(*f*). Immediate and direct election of all public officials, both civil and judicial, as well of all national, provincial and communal councillors or representatives, by popular vote, which is to say by the universal suffrage of all adult men and women.

9(*g*). *Reorganization* of each region, taking as its basis and starting point *the absolute freedom of individual, productive association and commune.*

9(*h*). *Individual rights.*

(i). The right of every man or woman to be completely supported, cared for, protected, brought up and educated from birth to coming of age in all public, primary, secondary, higher, industrial, artistic and scientific schools at the expense of society.

(ii). The equal right of each to be advised and assisted by the latter, as far as possible, at the outset of the career which each new adult will freely choose, after which the society which has declared him completely free will exercise no further supervision or authority over him, decline all responsibility towards him, and owe him nothing more than respect and if necessary protection for his liberty.

(iii). The liberty of every adult man and woman must be absolute and complete freedom to come and go, openly to profess any shade of opinion, to be idle or active, immoral or moral, in other words to dispose of his own person and his own belongings as he pleases and to be answerable to no one; freedom either to live honestly, by their own labor, or shamefully, by exploiting charity or individual trust, given that such charity and trust be voluntary and be proffered by adults only.

(iv). Unconditional freedom for every variety of propaganda, whether through conversation, the press or in public or private meetings, without any constraint but the natural corrective power of public opinion. Absolute liberty of associations, not excepting those whose aims may be or seem to be immoral, and even including those whose aim is the corruption and [destruction] of individual and public liberty.

(v). Liberty cannot and should not defend itself except by means of liberty, and it is a dangerous misconception to advocate its limitation under the specious pretext of protection. Since morality has no other source, incentive, cause and object than liberty, and is itself inseparable from liberty, all restrictions imposed on the latter with the intention of safeguarding the former have always turned against it. Psychology, statistics and the entire course of history prove that individual and social immorality have always been the necessary consequence of bad public and private education, of the absence or breakdown of public opinion, which never develops or improves its moral level except by way of liberty alone, and above all of defective social organization. As the famous French statistician Quételet[5] has pointed out, experience shows that it is always society which prepares the ground for crime, and that the wrong-doer is only the predestined instrument of its commission. It is pointless, therefore, to level against social immorality the rigors of a legislation which would encroach upon the freedom of the individual. On the contrary, experience shows that repression and authoritarianism, far from preventing its excesses, have always deepened and extended it in those countries so afflicted, and that private and public morality have always gained or lost to the extent that the freedom of individuals has broadened or narrowed. So that in order to moralize present-day society, we must first embark upon the outright destruction of that entire political and social organization which is based upon inequality, privilege, divine authority and contempt for humanity. And once having rebuilt it on the basis of the utmost equality, justice, work and an education inspired exclusively by respect for humanity, we should provide it for its guardian with public opinion, and for its soul with the most absolute liberty.

(vi). Yet society must not remain totally defenseless against parasitic, mischievous and dangerous individuals. Since labor is to be the basis of all political rights, society—a province, a nation, each within its individual borders—will have the power to remove

[5] Adolphe Lambert Jacques Quételet (1796–1874), Belgian statistician and astronomer.

[these rights] from all adult individuals who, being neither sick, disabled nor old, live at the expense of public or private charity, together with the obligation to restore them as soon as they begin to live by their own labor once again.

(vii). Since the freedom of every individual is inalienable, society shall never allow any individual whatsoever legally to alienate his freedom or to engage upon any contract with another individual on any footing but the utmost equality and reciprocity. It shall not, however, have the power to disbar a man or woman so devoid of any sense of personal dignity as to contract a relationship of voluntary servitude with another individual, but it will consider them as living off private charity and therefore unfit to enjoy political rights *throughout the duration of that servitude.*

(viii). All persons who have been deprived of their political rights shall likewise lose the right to rear and keep their children. In case of infidelity to a freely contracted commitment, or in the event of an overt or proven infringement of the property, the person or especially the liberty of a citizen, whether native or foreign, society shall apply those penalties specified by its laws against the offending native or foreigner.

(ix). Absolute abolition of all cruel and degrading sentences, corporal, punishment and the death penalty as sanctioned and enforced by the law. Abolition of all those indefinite or protracted punishments which leave no hope and no real possibility of rehabilitation, since crime ought to be considered as sickness, and punishment as cure rather than social retaliation.

(x). Any individual condemned by the laws of any society, commune, province or nation shall retain the right not to submit to the sentence imposed on him, by declaring that he no longer wishes to be part of that society. But in such a case the society in question shall have the concomitant right to expel him from its midst and to declare him outside its warrant and protection.

(xi). Having thus reverted to the natural law of an eye for an eye, a tooth for a tooth, at least inside the territory occupied by that society, the individual shall be liable to robbery, ill-treatment and even death without any cause for alarm. Any person will be able to dispose of him like a dangerous animal, although never to subject him or use him as a slave. . . .

10. *Social organization.*

Without political equality there is no true political liberty, but political equality will only become possible when there is *economic and social equality*.

10(*a*). Equality does not mean the levelling down of individual differences, nor intellectual, moral and physical uniformity among individuals. This diversity of ability and strength, and these differences of race, nation, sex, age and character, far from being a social evil, constitute the treasurehouse of mankind. Nor do economic and social equality mean the levelling down of individual fortunes, in so far as these are products of the ability, productive energy and thrift of an individual.

10(*b*). The sole prerequisite for equality and justice is *a form of social organization such that each human individual born into it may find—to the extent that these are dependent upon society rather than upon nature—equal means for his development from infancy and adolescence to coming of age, first in upbringing and education, then in the exercise of the various capacities with which each is endowed by nature. This equality at the outset,* which justice requires for all, will never be feasible as long as the right of succession survives.

10(*c*). Justice, as well as human dignity, demands that *each individual should be the child of his own achievements, and only those achievements.* We hotly reject the doctrine of hereditary sin,[6] disgrace and responsibility. By the same token, we must reject the illusory heredity of virtue, honors and rights—*and of wealth also.* The heir to any kind of wealth is no longer the complete child of his own achievements, and in terms of initial circumstance he is privileged.

10(*d*). *Abolition of the right of inheritance.* As long as this right continues, hereditary differences of class, rank and wealth—in other words, social inequality and privilege—will survive in fact, if not in law. But it is an inescapable social law that *de facto* inequality always produces inequality of rights: social inequality necessarily becomes political. And we have already stated that without political equality there is no liberty in the universal, human and truly democratic sense, while society will always remain split into two uneven halves, with one vast section, including the entire mass of the people, suffering the oppression and exploitation of the other. Therefore *the right of*

---

[6] Hereditary, or original, sin (in traditional Christian doctrine) is the guilt or weakness implanted in every human being at conception, due to the sinful disobedience of Adam, the first man.

succession is contrary to the triumph of liberty, and a society wishing to become free must abolish it.

10(*e*). *This right must be abolished because, relying as it does upon a fiction, it runs counter to the very spirit of liberty.* All individual, political and social rights belong to the real, the living individual. Once dead, his will does not exist any more than he himself does, and it is a fictitious will that oppresses the living in the name of the dead. If the dead person sets such store by the enforcement of his wishes, let him stand up and enforce them himself, if he can, but he has no right to ask society to bend all its strength and law to the service of his non-existence.

10(*f*). The legitimate and positive function of the right of succession has always been that of securing for subsequent generations the means to grow and to become men. Consequently, *only the trust for public upbringing and education will have the right to inherit,* with the matching obligation to make equal provision for the maintenance, upbringing and education of every child from birth to coming of age and emancipation. In this way, all parents will be equally confident in their children's future, and since equality for all is a fundamental precondition of morality for all, and all privilege is a cradle of immorality, parents whose love for their children is rational enough to be inspired not by vanity but by human dignity will prefer them to be brought up in strict equality, even if they do have the means to leave an inheritance which would place them in a privileged position.

10(*g*). Once the inequality produced by the right of inheritance has been abolished, there will still remain (but to a far lesser degree) the inequality that arises from differences in individual ability, strength and productive capacity—a difference which, while never disappearing altogether, will be of diminishing importance under the influence of an egalitarian upbringing and social system, and which in addition will never weigh upon future generations once there is no more right of inheritance.

10(*h*). Labor is the sole producer of wealth. Everybody is free, of course, either to die of starvation or to dwell among the wild beasts of the desert or the forest, but anybody who wants to live within society should earn his living by his own work, or run the risk of being considered a parasite, an exploiter of the wealth (that is, the labor) of others, and a thief.

10(*i*). *Labor* is the fundamental basis of dignity and human rights, for it is only by means of his own free, intelligent work that man becomes a creator in his turn, wins from the surrounding world and his own animal nature his humanity and rights, and creates the world of civilization. . . .

The unequal line drawn between intellectual and manual labor must therefore be removed. The economic output of society is itself considerably impaired, because mind cut off from physical activity weakens, withers and fades, whereas the physical vigor of humanity cut off from intelligence is brutalized, and in this state of artificial divorce neither produces the half of what could and should be produced once they are restored by a new social synthesis to form an indivisible productive process. When the thinker works and the worker thinks, free, intelligent labor will emerge as humanity's highest aspiration, the basis of its dignity and law and the embodiment of its human power on earth—and humanity will be instituted.

10(k).[7] *Intelligent free labor will necessarily be associated labor.* Everybody will be free to associate or not to associate in labor, but there can be no doubt that with the exception of works of imagination, whose nature requires the inner concentration of the individual mind, in all those industrial and even scientific and artistic enterprises whose nature admits of associated labor, such association will be generally preferred for the simple reason that it would miraculously increase the productive energies of each associate member of a productive association, who will earn a great deal more in less time and with far less trouble. Once the free productive associations stop being slaves and become their own masters and the owners of the necessary capital, once they include all the specialist minds required by each enterprise as members cooperating side by side with the labor force, and once they amalgamate among themselves—still freely, in accordance with their needs and natures—then sooner or later they will expand beyond national frontiers. They will form one vast economic federation, with a parliament informed by precise, detailed statistics on a world scale, such as are not yet possible today, and will both offer and demand to control, decide and distribute the output of world industry among the various countries, so that there will no longer, or hardly ever, be commercial or industrial crises, enforced stagnation, disasters and waste of energy and capital. Human labor emancipating each and every man, will regenerate the world.

[7] There is no sub-entry (j) in the original text.

10(l). The land, with all its natural resources, belongs to all, but will be held only by those who work it.

10(m). Woman, *differing from man* but *not inferior to him, intelligent, industrious and free like him, is declared his equal both in rights and in all political and social functions and duties.*

10(n). Abolition not of the natural but of the *legal* family, based on civil law and ownership. Religious and civil marriage are replaced by *free marriage.* Two *adult* individuals of opposite sex have the right to unite and separate in accordance with their desires and mutual interests and the promptings of their hearts, nor does society have any right either to prevent their union or to hold them to it against their will. Once the right of succession is abolished and society guarantees the upbringing of all its children, every reason previously advanced for the political and civil backing given to marital indissolubility disappears, and the union of the sexes reverts to the complete liberty which, here as elsewhere, is always the *sine qua non*[8] of genuine morality. In free marriage, man and woman must enjoy equal measure of liberty. Neither violence, passion nor the rights freely granted in the past may excuse any infringement by one party of the other's liberty, and any such infringement shall be considered criminal.

10(o). From the moment of conception until her child is born, a woman is entitled to a social subvention paid not for her benefit but for her child's. Any mother wishing to feed and rear her children will also receive all the costs of their maintenance and care from society.

10(p). Parents will have the right to keep their children at their side and to attend to their upbringing, under the guardianship and supreme supervision of society, which will always retain the right and duty to part children from their parents whenever the latter may be in a position to demoralize or even hamper their children's development, either by example or by brutal, inhuman precepts or treatment.

10(q). Children belong neither to their parents nor to society but to themselves and their future liberty. From infancy to coming of age they are only potentially free, and must therefore find themselves under the aegis[9] of *authority*. It is true that their parents are their natural protectors, but *the legal and ultimate protector is society,* which has the right and duty to tend them because its own future depends on

[8] Latin: without which, not—that is, the absolutely necessary prerequisite.
[9] Protective shield or cover.

the intellectual and moral guidance they receive. Society can only give liberty to adults provided it supervises the upbringing of minors.

10(r). School must take the place of church, with the immense difference that the religious education provided by the latter has no other purpose than to perpetuate the rule of human ignorance or so-called divine authority, whereas school upbringing and education will have no other purpose than the true emancipation of the children upon reaching the age of majority, and will consist of nothing less than their progressive initiation into liberty by the threefold development of their physical and mental powers and their will. Reason, truth, justice, human respect, awareness of personal dignity (inseparable from the human dignity of another), love of liberty for one's own sake and for others', belief in work as the basis and condition of all rights; contempt for unreason, falsehood, injustice, cowardice, slavery and idleness—these must be the keystones of public education. First it must shape men, then specialists and citizens, and, in step with the children's growth, authority must naturally make more and more room for liberty, so that by the time the adolescent has come of age and become lawfully emancipated he will have forgotten how his infancy was controlled and guided by something other than liberty. Human respect, the seed of liberty, must be present even in the harshest and most absolute behavior of authority. This is the touchstone of all moral education: inculcate that respect in children, and you create men.

After completing their primary and secondary education the children will be advised, informed, but not coerced, by their superiors with a view to choosing some higher or specialist school, according to their abilities and inclinations. At the same time, each will apply himself to the theoretical and practical study of that branch of industry which most attracts him, and whatever sums he earns by working during his apprenticeship will be made available when he comes of age.

10(s). As soon as he comes of age, the adolescent will be declared a free citizen and absolute master of his actions. In exchange for the care it has exercised during his infancy, society will ask for three things: that he remain *free,* that he *live by his own labor,* and that he *respect the liberty of others.* And because the crimes and vices by which present-day society is afflicted are the sole outcome of defective social organization, we may be sure that given a form of organization and upbringing based on reason, justice, liberty, human respect and complete equality, good will become the rule and evil a morbid exception, ever decreasing under the all-powerful influence of moralized public opinion.

10(t). The old, the disabled and the sick will be cared for and respected, enjoy all public and social rights, and be generously maintained at the common expense. . . .

III. *Requisite Qualities for Membership of the International Family:*

He must be an atheist. On behalf of the earth and of mankind, he must join us in laying claim to everything which religions have hauled off into the heavens and bestowed upon their gods: truth, liberty, happiness, justice, goodness. He must recognize that *morality* is totally independent of theology and divine metaphysics and has no other source than the collective conscience of man.

He must, like ourselves, be the adversary of the principle of authority and loathe all its applications and consequences in the intellectual and moral as well as in the political, economic and social spheres. . . .

He must be a revolutionary. He must understand that such a complete and radical transformation of society, which must necessarily involve the downfall of all privilege, monopoly and constituted power, will naturally not occur by peaceful means. That for the same reason it will be opposed by the rich and powerful, and supported, in every land, only by the people, together with that intelligent and genuinely noble section of youth whose open-hearted convictions and burning aspirations lead it to embrace the cause of the people despite being born into the privileged classes.

He must understand that the sole and final purpose of this revolution is the true political, economic and social emancipation of the people, and that while it may be assisted and largely organized by the above-mentioned section of youth, in the long run it will only come through the people. That history has completely exhausted all other religious, national and political questions, and that only one question remains outstanding today, subsuming all the rest and uniquely capable of mobilizing the people—*the social question.* That any so-called revolution—whether it resembles the recent Polish insurrection, [10] or the doctrine which Mazzini [11] now preaches, whether it is exclusively political, constitutional, monarchist or even republican, like the last abortive move of the Spanish progressives [12]—any such revolution, working as it does apart from the people, and consequently unable to succeed without drawing upon some privileged class and representing the interests of the latter, will necessarily work against the people and will be a retrograde, harmful, counter-revolutionary movement.

He will therefore despise any secondary movement whose immediate, direct aim is other than the political and social emancipation of the working classes, in other words the people, and will see it either as a fatal error or a shabby trick. Hostile to all compromise and conciliation—henceforward impossible—and to any false coalition with those whose interests make them the natural enemies of the people, *he must see that the only salvation for his own country and for the entire world lies in social revolution.*

He must also understand that this revolution, being essentially cosmopolitan, like justice and liberty themselves, will only be able to triumph by sweeping like a universal holocaust across the flimsy barriers of nations and bringing all states tumbling in its wake, embracing first the whole of Europe, and then the world. *He must understand that the social revolution will necessarily become a European and worldwide revolution.*

That the world will inevitably split into two camps, that of the new life and of the old privileges, and that between these two opposing camps, created as in the time of the wars of religion not by national sympathies but by community of ideas and interests, a war of extermination is bound to erupt, with no quarter and no respite. That in the very interest of its own security and self-preservation the social revolution—contrary in its whole essence to that hypocritical policy of non-intervention, which is fit only for the moribund and the impotent—cannot live and thrive except by growing, and will not lay down the sword until it has destroyed all states and all the old religious, political and economic institutions both in Europe and throughout the civilized world.

[10] The Second Polish Revolution (1863–64), a futile uprising of zealous Polish nationalists attempting to gain complete independence from czarist (Russian) rule.

[11] Giuseppe Mazzini (1805–1872), an Italian patriot and devoted republican who labored a lifetime on behalf of the unification of Italy.

[12] Nineteenth-century Spanish liberals who tried and failed to overthrow the monarchy and establish a republic.

That this will not be a war of conquest, but of emancipation—sometimes enforced, perhaps, but salutary all the same—because its purpose and outcome will be nothing more nor less than the destruction of states and their secular roots, which have always been the basis of all slavery, with the blessing of religion.

That even in the most apparently hostile countries, once the social revolution breaks out at one point it will find keen and tenacious allies in the popular masses, who will be unable to do other than rally to its banner as soon as they understand and come in contact with its activities and purpose. That it will consequently be necessary to choose the most fertile soil for its beginning, where it has only to withstand the first assault of reaction before expanding to overwhelm the frenzies of its enemies, federalizing all the lands it has absorbed and welding them into a single indomitable revolutionary alliance. . . .

22

Pope Leo XIII

Rerum Novarum

The response of the papacy to the spread of industrialization and its consequent problems and disturbances was long awaited. At last in 1891 Pope Leo XIII stated the official Roman Catholic position in an encyclical known as Rerum Novarum (Of New Things)*. The pontiff's declaration was greeted joyously by most Roman Catholics. Both clergy and laity had for some time been concerned about the plight of the industrial working classes and had sought alleviation of labor's distress; they welcomed guidance from the pope himself.*

Beyond that, even many non-Catholic humanitarians soon came to appreciate Rerum Novarum *as a document that retained the positive elements of the past while, at the same time, furnishing a guide for the humane development of industrial society. The papal letter repudiated the two economic theories that had dominated much of the nineteenth century, economic liberalism and Marxian socialism. The evil fruits of the former were visible everywhere. (The pope, while serving as a prelate in Belgium, had witnessed the blight and deprivation wrought upon the population by industrialization—just as Karl Marx had observed it a few decades earlier.) The pursuit of selfish interests had not resulted in "the advantage of each and all." Rather, economic liberalism had created a small group of very rich entrepreneurs and financiers while, on the other hand, a vast number of people had been reduced to abject poverty and virtual slavery. Marxian socialism, the opposing economic theory that had made converts among the laboring masses, was criticized by the pope for preaching class hatred and for predicting that the two remaining classes of historical consequence, the proletariat*

Pope Leo XIII, *Rerum Novarum* (New York: The Paulist Press, 1939), 3–5, 8–13, 15, 19–20, 23–31, 36–37. Reprinted by permission of the Paulist Press.

and the capitalists, would meet in a clash of cataclysmic dimensions. Such a gospel of hatred, destruction, and bloodshed was abhorrent to Christian teaching. Was not reconciliation one of the noblest tasks of the Christian Church?

The appeal of Rerum Novarum *lies in the fact that it deals with the relationship between past, present, and future. Leo himself was deeply influenced by the teachings of St. Thomas Aquinas, who saw society as a living body whose members perform different functions but at the same time have a right to receive a just reward for their labor. Accordingly, Leo spoke of the right of everyone to procure for self and family what is necessary for a life of "reasonable and frugal comfort." The earnings that can be saved a laborer must be able to invest in property. Indeed, the pope desired property to be spread as widely as possible. Yet, at the same time, he accepted the fact that the amount of property people possess will vary because their abilities, circumstances, and luck vary greatly. Though all are equal before God's judgment, this life produces a fruitful inequality relative to rank and property. However, concluded the pope, the possession of any amount of property always carries the obligation of good stewardship and generosity to the poor.*

To insure that their interests were well represented, the pope encouraged workers to form labor unions. These, then, would negotiate with the employers so that each laborer might receive a fair share. The state, in turn, was to assure the peaceful and fair process of the employee-employer relationship. Leo expected the state to protect the weak from abuse by the strong whenever the need arose. At all times, however, the state was to guarantee the inviolate possession of private property.

When Rerum Novarum *first appeared, Marxian socialists as well as economic liberals saw nothing new or noteworthy in it. Even many Catholic employers paid scant attention to it. Yet, as time progressed,* Rerum Novarum *was increasingly perceived as a principal guide in the development of industrial capitalism in the West. As years and decades passed, employers and employees learned to shun class warfare and to live together and bargain together with a degree of mutual respect. Leo's letter, upheld by succeeding pontiffs, contributed to this outcome.*

It is not surprising that the spirit of revolutionary change, which has long been predominant in the nations of the world, should have passed beyond politics and made its influence felt in the cognate field of practical economy. The elements of a conflict are unmistakable: the growth of industry, and the surprising discoveries of science; the changed relations of masters and workmen; the enormous fortunes of individuals and the poverty of the masses; the increased self-reliance and the closer mutual combination of the working population; and, finally, a general moral deterioration. The momentous seriousness of the present state of things just now fills every mind with painful apprehension; wise men discuss it; practical men propose schemes; popular meetings, legislatures, and sovereign princes, all are occupied with it—and there is nothing which has a deeper hold on public attention.

Therefore, Venerable Brethren,[1] as on former occasions, when it seemed opportune to refute false teaching, We[2] have addressed you in the interests of the Church and of the commonwealth, and have issued Letters on Political Power, on Human Liberty, on the Christian Constitution of the State, and on similar subjects, so now We have thought it useful to speak on the Condition of Labor.

It is a matter on which we have touched once or twice already. But in this letter the responsibility of the apostolic office urges Us to treat the question expressly and at length, in order that there may be no mistake as to the principles which truth and justice dictate for its settlement. The discussion is not easy, nor is it free from danger. It is not easy to define the relative rights and the mutual duties of the wealthy and of the poor, of capital and of labor. And the danger lies in this, that crafty agitators constantly make use of these disputes to pervert men's judgments and to stir up the people to sedition.

But all agree, and there can be no question whatever, that some remedy must be found, and quickly found, for the misery and wretchedness which press so heavily at this moment on the large majority of the very poor. The ancient workmen's guilds[3] were destroyed in the last century, and no other organization took their place. Public institutions and the laws have repudiated the ancient religion.[4] Hence by degrees it has come to pass that working men have been given over, isolated and defenseless, to the callousness of

[1] Patriarchs, primates, archbishops, and bishops of the Catholic world and other prelates in communion with the Roman papacy.
[2] Pope Leo XIII. It has been common for persons of royal or papal authority to refer to themselves in this plural form.
[3] Medieval associations of craftsmen.
[4] Christian religion. Leo is referring to the secularization of life in a number of countries as well as to the separation of Church and State.

employers and the greed of unrestrained competition. The evil has been increased by rapacious usury,[5] which, although more than once condemned by the Church, is nevertheless, under a different form but with the same guilt, still practiced by avaricious and grasping men. And to this must be added the custom of working by contract, and the concentration of so many branches of trade in the hands of a few individuals, so that a small number of very rich men have been able to lay upon the masses of the poor a yoke little better than slavery itself.

To remedy these evils the *Socialists,* working on the poor man's envy of the rich, endeavor to destroy private property, and maintain that individual possessions should become the common property of all, to be administered by the State or by municipal bodies. They hold that, by thus transferring property from private persons to the community, the present evil state of things will be set to rights, because each citizen will then have his equal share of whatever there is to enjoy. But their proposals are so clearly futile for all practical purposes, that if they were carried out the working man himself would be among the first to suffer. Moreover they are emphatically unjust, because they would rob the lawful possessor, bring the State into a sphere that is not its own, and cause complete confusion in the community.

It is surely undeniable that, when a man engages in remunerative labor, the very reason and motive of his work is to obtain property, and to hold it as his own private possession. If one man hires out to another his strength or his industry, he does this for the purpose of receiving in return what is necessary for food and living; he thereby expressly proposes to acquire a full and real right, not only to the remuneration, but also to the disposal of that remuneration as he pleases. Thus, if he lives sparingly, saves money, and invests his savings, for greater security, in land, the land in such a case is only his wages in another form; and, consequently, a working man's little estate thus purchased should be as completely at his own disposal as the wages he receives for his labor. But it is precisely in this power of disposal that ownership consists, whether the property be land or movable goods. The *Socialists,* therefore, in endeavoring to transfer the possessions of individuals to the community, strike at the interests of every wage earner, for they deprive him of the liberty of

[5] Rates of interest in excess of what the law allows or what can be justified.

disposing of his wages, and thus of all hope and possibility of increasing his stock and of bettering his condition in life.

What is of still greater importance, however, is that the remedy they propose is manifestly against justice. For every man has by nature the right to possess property as his own. . . .

. . . The same principle is confirmed and enforced by the civil laws—laws which, as long as they are just, derive their binding force from the law of nature. The authority of the divine law adds its sanction, forbidding us in the gravest terms even to covet that which is another's: "You shall not covet your neighbor's wife; nor his house, nor his field, nor his man-servant, nor his maid-servant, nor his ox, nor his ass, nor anything which is his."[6] . . .

The idea, then, that the civil government should, at its own discretion, penetrate and pervade the family and the household, is a great and pernicious mistake. True, if a family finds itself in great difficulty, utterly friendless, and without prospect of help, it is right that extreme necessity be met by public aid; for each family is a part of the commonwealth. In like manner, if within the walls of the household there occur grave disturbance of mutual rights, the public power must interfere to force each party to give the other what is due; for this is not to rob citizens of their rights, but justly and properly to safeguard and strengthen them. But the rulers of the State must go no further: nature bids them stop here. . . .

And such interference is not only unjust, but is quite certain to harass and disturb all classes of citizens, and to subject them to odious and intolerable slavery. It would open the door to envy, to evil speaking, and to quarrelling; the sources of wealth would themselves run dry, for no one would have any interest in exerting his talents or his industry; and that ideal equality of which so much is said would, in reality, be the leveling down of all of the same condition of misery and dishonor.

Thus it is clear *that the main tenet of Socialism, the community of goods, must be utterly rejected;* for it would injure those whom it is intended to benefit, it would be contrary to the natural rights of mankind, and it would introduce confusion, and disorder into the commonwealth. Our first and most fundamental principle, therefore, when we undertake to alleviate the condition of the masses, must be the in-

[6] Deuteronomy 5:21.

violability of private property. This laid down, We go on to show where we must find the remedy that we seek.

We approach the subject with confidence, and in the exercise of the rights which belong to Us. For no practical solution of this question will ever be found without the assistance of religion and the Church. It is We who are the chief guardian of religion, and the chief dispenser of what belongs to the Church, and we must not by silence neglect the duty which lies upon Us. Doubtless this most serious question demands the attention and the efforts of others besides Ourselves—of the rulers of States, of employers of labor, of the wealthy, and of the working population themselves for whom We plead. . . .

Let it be laid down, in the first place, that humanity must remain as it is. It is impossible to reduce human society to a level. The *Socialists* may do their utmost, but all striving against nature is vain. There naturally exists among mankind innumerable differences of the most important kind; people differ in capability, in diligence, in health, and in strength; and unequal fortune is a necessary result of inequality in condition. Such inequality is far from being disadvantageous either to individuals or to the community; social and public life can only go on by the help of various kinds of capacity and the playing of many parts, and each man, as a rule, chooses the part which peculiarly suits his case. As regards bodily labor, even had man never fallen from the state of innocence, he would not have been wholly unoccupied; but that which would then have been his free choice, his delight, became afterwards compulsory, and the painful expiation of his sin. "Cursed be the earth in your work; in your labor you shall eat of it all the days of your life."[7] In like manner, the other pains and hardships of life will have no end or cessation on this earth; for the consequences of sin are bitter and hard to bear, and they must be with man as long as life lasts. To suffer and to endure, therefore, is the lot of humanity; let men try as they may, no strength and no artifice will ever succeed in banishing from human life the ills and troubles which beset it. If any there are who pretend differently—who hold out to a hard-pressed people freedom from pain and trouble, undisturbed repose, and constant enjoyment—they cheat the people and impose upon them, and their

---

[7] Genesis 3:17.

lying promises will only make the evil worse than before. There is nothing more useful than to look at the world as it really is—and at the same time look elsewhere for a remedy to its troubles.

The great mistake that is made in the matter now under consideration, is to possess oneself of the idea that class is naturally hostile to class; that rich and poor are intended by nature to live at war with one another. So irrational and so false is this view, that the exact contrary is the truth. Just as the symmetry of the human body is the result of the disposition of the members of the body, so in a State it is ordained by nature that these two classes should exist in harmony and agreement, and should, as it were, fit into one another, so as to maintain the equilibrium of the body politic. Each requires the other; capital cannot do without labor, nor labor without capital. Mutual agreement results in pleasantness and good order; perpetual conflict necessarily produces confusion and outrage. Now, in preventing such strife as this, and in making it impossible, the efficacy of Christianity is marvelous and manifold. First of all, there is nothing more powerful than religion (of which the Church is the interpreter and guardian) in drawing rich and poor together, by reminding each class of its duties to the other, and especially of the duties of justice. Thus religion teaches the laboring man and the workman to carry out honestly and well all equitable agreements freely made, never to injure capital, nor to outrage the person of an employer; never to employ violence in representing his own cause, nor to engage in riot and disorder; and to have nothing to do with men of evil principles, who work upon the people with artful promises, and raise foolish hopes which usually end in disaster and in repentance when too late. Religion teaches the rich man and the employer that their work-people are not their slaves; that they must respect in every man his dignity as a man and as a Christian; that labor is nothing to be ashamed of, if we listen to right reason and to Christian philosophy, but is an honorable employment, enabling a man to sustain his life in an upright and creditable way, and that it is shameful and inhuman to treat men like chattels to make money by, or to look upon them merely as so much muscle or physical power. Thus, again, religion teaches that, as among the workmen's concerns are religion herself, and things spiritual and mental, the employer is bound to see that he has time for the duties of piety; that he be not exposed to corrupting influences and dangerous occasions; and that he be not led away to neglect his home and family or to squander his wages. Then, again, the employer must never tax his work-people beyond their strength, nor employ them in work unsuited to their sex or age. His great and principal obligation is to give to every one that which is just. Doubtless before we can decide whether wages are adequate many things have to be considered; but rich men and masters should remember this—that to exercise pressure for the sake of gain, upon the indigent and destitute, and to make one's profit out of the need of another, is condemned by all laws, human and divine. To defraud any one of wages that are his due is a crime which cries to the avenging anger of heaven. "Behold, the hire of the laborers . . . which by fraud has been kept back by you, cries; and the cry of them has entered the ears of the Lord of Sabaoth."[8] Finally, the rich must religiously refrain from cutting down the workman's earnings, either by force, fraud, or by usurious dealing; and with the more reason because the poor man is weak and unprotected, and because his slender means should be sacred in proportion to their scantiness.

Were these precepts carefully obeyed and followed would not strife die out and cease? . . .

. . . Private ownership, as we have seen, is the natural right of man; and to exercise that right, especially as members of society, is not only lawful but absolutely necessary. "It is lawful," says St. Thomas of Aquin, "for a man to hold private property; and it is also necessary for the carrying on of human life."[9] But if the question be asked, How must one's possessions be used? the Church replies without hesitation in the words of the same holy Doctor.[10] "Man should not consider his outward possessions as his own, but as common to all, so as to share them without difficulty when others are in need. Whence the Apostle says, Command the rich of this world . . . to give with ease, to communicate."[11] True, no one is commanded to distribute to others that which is required for his own necessities and those of his household; nor even to give away what is reasonably required to keep up becomingly his condition in life; "for no one ought to live unbecomingly."[12] But when necessity has been supplied, and one's position fairly considered, it is a duty to give to the indigent out of that which is over. "That which remains give

[8] James 5:4.
[9] Thomas Aquinas, *Summa Theologica*, Book Two, Part Two, Question 66, Article 2.
[10] St. Thomas Aquinas (*ca.* 1225–1274), a leading medieval philosopher, is sometimes referred to as the "Angelic Doctor."
[11] Aquinas, *Summa Theologica*, Book Two, Part Two, Question 65, Article 2.
[12] Ibid., Question 32, Article 6.

alms."[13] It is a duty, not of justice (except in extreme cases), but of Christian charity—a duty which is not enforced by human law. . . .

It cannot, however, be doubted that to attain the purpose of which We treat, not only the Church, but all human means must conspire. All who are concerned in the matter must be of one mind and must act together. It is in this, as in the Providence which governs the world; results do not happen save where all the causes cooperate. . . .

. . . The first duty, therefore, of the rulers of the State should be to make sure that the laws and institutions, the general character and administration of the commonwealth, shall be such as to produce of themselves public well-being and private prosperity. This is the proper office of wise statesmanship and the work of the heads of the State. Now a State chiefly prospers and flourishes by morality, well-regulated family life, by respect for religion and justice, by the moderation and equal distribution of public burdens, by the progress of the arts and of trade, by the abundant yield of the land—by everything which makes the citizens better and happier. . . .

Rights must be religiously respected wherever they are found; and it is the duty of the public authority to prevent and punish injury, and to protect each one in the possession of his own. Still, when there is question of protecting the rights of individuals, the poor and helpless have a claim to special consideration. The richer population have many ways of protecting themselves, and stand less in need of help from the State; those who are badly off have no resources of their own to fall back upon, and must chiefly rely upon the assistance of the State. And it is for this reason that wage-earners, who are, undoubtedly, among the weak and necessitous, should be specially cared for and protected by the commonwealth.

Here, however, it will be advisable to advert expressly to one or two of the more important details.

It must be borne in mind that the chief thing to be secured is the safeguarding, by legal enactment and policy, of private property. Most of all it is essential in these times of covetous greed, to keep the multitude within the line of duty; for if all may justly strive to better their condition, yet neither justice nor the common good allows anyone to seize that which belongs to another, or, under the pretext of

[13] Luke 11:41.

futile and ridiculous equality, to lay hands on other people's fortunes. It is most true that by far the larger part of the people who work prefer to improve themselves by honest labor rather than by doing wrong to others. But there are not a few who are imbued with bad principles and are anxious for revolutionary change, and whose great purpose it is to stir up tumult and bring about a policy of violence. The authority of the State should intervene to put restraint upon these disturbers, to save the workmen from their seditious arts, and to protect lawful owners from spoliation. . . .

When work-people have recourse to a strike, it is frequently because the hours of labor are too long, or the work too hard, or because they consider their wages insufficient. The grave inconvenience of this not uncommon occurrence should be obviated by public remedial measures; for such paralysis of labor not only affects the masters and their work-people, but is extremely injurious to trade, and to the general interests of the public; moreover, on such occasions, violence and disorder are generally not far off, and thus it frequently happens that the public peace is threatened. The laws should be beforehand, and prevent these troubles from arising; they should lend their influence and authority to the removal in good time of the causes which lead to conflicts between masters and those whom they employ. . . .

If we turn now to things exterior and corporal, the first concern of all is to save the poor workers from the cruelty of grasping speculators, who use human beings as mere instruments for making money. It is neither justice nor humanity so to grind men down with excessive labor as to stupefy their minds and wear out their bodies. Man's powers, like his general nature, are limited, and beyond these limits he cannot go. His strength is developed and increased by use and exercise, but only on condition of due intermission and proper rest. Daily labor, therefore, must be so regulated that it may not be protracted during longer hours than strength admits. How many and how long the intervals of rest should be, will depend upon the nature of the work, on circumstances of time and place, and on the health and strength of the workman. Those who labor in mines and quarries, and in work within the bowels of the earth, should have shorter hours in proportion, as their labor is more severe and more trying to health. Then, again, the season of the year must be taken in account; for not unfrequently a kind of labor is easy at one time which at another is intolerable or very difficult. Finally, work which is suitable for a strong man cannot reasonably be required from a woman or a child.

And, in regard to children, great care should be taken not to place them in workshops and factories until their bodies and minds are sufficiently mature. For just as rough weather destroys the buds of spring, so too early an experience of life's hard work blights the young promise of a child's powers, and makes any real education impossible. Women, again, are not suited to certain trades; for a woman is by nature fitted for home-work, and it is that which is best adapted at once to preserve her modesty, and to promote the good bringing up of children and the well-being of the family. As a general principle, it may be laid down, that a workman ought to have leisure and rest in proportion to the wear and tear of his strength; for the waste of strength must be repaired by the cessation of work.

In all agreements between masters and work-people, there is always the condition, expressed or understood, that there be allowed proper rest for soul and body. To agree in any other sense would be against what is right and just; for it can never be right or just to require on the one side, or to promise on the other, the giving up of those duties which a man owes to his God and to himself.

We now approach a subject of very great importance and one on which, if extremes are to be avoided, right ideas are absolutely necessary. Wages, we are told, are fixed by free consent; and, therefore, the employer when he pays what was agreed upon, has done his part, and is not called upon for anything further. The only way, it is said, in which injustice could happen, would be if the master refused to pay the whole of the wages, or the workman would not complete the work undertaken; when this happens the State should intervene, to see that each obtains his own, but not under any other circumstances. . . .

Let it be granted, then, that, as a rule, workman and employer should make free agreements, and in particular should freely agree as to wages; nevertheless, there is a dictate of nature more imperious and more ancient than any bargain between man and man, that the remuneration must be enough to support the wage-earner in reasonable and frugal comfort. If through necessity or fear of a worse evil, the workman accepts harder conditions because an employer or contractor will give him no better, he is the victim of force and injustice. . . .

If a workman's wages be sufficient to enable him to maintain himself, his wife, and his children in reasonable comfort, he will not find it difficult, if he is a sensible man, to study economy; and he will not fail, by cutting down expenses, to put by a little property: nature and reason would urge him to do this. We have seen that this great labor question cannot be solved except by assuming as a principle that private ownership must be held sacred and inviolable. The law, therefore, should favor ownership, and its policy should be to induce as many people as possible to become owners.

Many excellent results will follow from this; and first of all, property will certainly become more equitably divided. For the effect of civil change and revolution has been to divide society into two widely different castes. On the one side there is the party which holds the power because it holds the wealth; which has in its grasp all labor and all trade; which manipulates for its own benefit and its own purposes all the sources of supply, and which is powerfully represented in the councils of the State itself. On the other side there is the needy and powerless multitude, sore and suffering, always ready for disturbance. If working people can be encouraged to look forward to obtaining a share in the land, the result will be that the gulf between vast wealth and deep poverty will be bridged over, and the two orders will be brought nearer together. Another consequence will be the great abundance of the fruits of the earth. Men always work harder and more readily when they work on that which is their own; nay, they learn to love the very soil which yields in response to the labor of their hands, not only food to eat, but an abundance of the good things for themselves and those that are dear to them. It is evident how such a spirit of willing labor would add to the produce of the earth and to the wealth of the community. And a third advantage would arise from this: men would cling to the country in which they were born; for no one would exchange his country for foreign land if his own afforded him the means of living a tolerable and happy life. These three important benefits, however, can only be expected on the condition that a man's means be not drained and exhausted by excessive taxation. The right to possess private property is from nature, not from man; and the State has only the right to regulate its use in the interests of the public good, but by no means to abolish it altogether. The State is, therefore, unjust and cruel, if, in the name of taxation, it deprives the private owner of more than is just.

In the first place—employers and workmen may themselves effect much in the matter of which We treat, by means of those institutions and organizations which afford opportune assistance to those in need, and which draw the two orders more closely together. Among these may be enumerated: societies for mutual help; various foundations established by private persons for providing for the workman, and for his widow or his orphans, in sudden calamity, in sickness, and in the event of death; and what are called "patronages," or institutions for the care of boys and girls, for young people, and also for those of more mature age.

The most important of all are workmen's associations; for these virtually include all the rest. History attests what excellent results were affected by the craftsman's guilds of a former day. They were the means not only of many advantages to the workmen, but in no small degree of the advancement of craft, as numerous monuments remain to prove. Such associations should be adapted to the requirements of the age in which we live—an age of greater instruction, of different customs, and of more numerous requirements in daily life. It is gratifying to know that there are actually in existence not a few societies of this nature, consisting either of workmen alone, or of workmen and employers together; but it were greatly to be desired that they should multiply and become more effective. We have spoken of them more than once; but it will be well to explain here how much they are needed, to show that they exist by their own right, and to enter into their organization and their work.

The experience of his own weakness urges man to call in help from without. We read in the pages of Holy Writ: "It is better that two should be together than one; for they have the advantage of their society. If one fall he shall be supported by the other. Woe to him that is alone, for when he falls he has none to lift him up." [14] And further: "A brother that is helped by his brother is like a strong city." [15] It is this natural impulse which unites men in civil society; and it is this also which makes them band themselves together in associations of citizen with citizen; associations which, it is true, cannot be called societies in the complete sense of the word, but which are societies nevertheless. . . .

. . . Particular societies, then, although they exist within the State, and are each a part of the State, nevertheless cannot be prohib-

[14] Ecclesiastes 4:9–10.
[15] Proverbs 18:19.

ited by the State absolutely and as such. For to enter into a "society" of this kind is the natural right of man; and the State must protect natural rights, not destroy them; and if it forbids its citizens to form associations, it contradicts the very principle of its own existence; for both they and it exist in virtue of the same principle, which is, the natural propensity of man to live in society. . . .

We have now laid before you, Venerable Brethren, who are the persons, and what are the means, by which this most difficult question must be solved. Every one must put his hand to work which falls to his share, and that at once and immediately, lest the evil which is already so great may by delay become absolutely beyond remedy. Those who rule the State must use the law and the institutions of the country; masters and rich men must remember their duty; the poor, whose interests are at stake, must make every lawful and proper effort; since religion alone, as We said at the beginning, can destroy the evil at its root, all men must be persuaded that the primary thing needful is to return to real Christianity, in the absence of which all the plans and devices of the wisest will be of little avail.

As far as regards the Church, its assistance will never be wanting, be the time or the occasion what it may; and it will intervene with great effect in proportion as its liberty of action is the more unfettered; let this be carefully noted by those whose office it is to provide for the public welfare. Every minister of holy religion must throw into the conflict all the energy of his mind, and all the strength of his endurance; with your authority, Venerable Brethren, and by your example, they must never cease to urge upon all men of every class, upon the high as well as the lowly, the gospel doctrines of Christian life; by every means in their power they must strive for the good of the people; and above all they must earnestly cherish in themselves, and try to arouse in others, charity, the mistress and queen of virtues. For the happy results we all long for must be chiefly brought about by the plenteous outpouring of charity; of that true Christian charity which is the fulfilling of the whole gospel law, which is always ready to sacrifice itself for other's sake, and which is man's surest antidote against worldly pride and immoderate love of self; that charity whose office is described and whose God-like features are drawn by the apostle St. Paul in these words: "Charity is patient, is kind, . . . seeks not her own, . . . suffers all things, . . . endures all things." [16] . . .

[16] I Corinthians 13:4–7.

23

Fyodor Dostoevsky

The Brothers Karamazov: The Grand Inquisitor

The contemporary era, with its concern for the irrational, unconscious springs of human behavior, with its doubts and rejection of the old certainties, may be said to have begun in the last quarter of the nineteenth century. Fyodor Dostoevsky (1821–1881), the great Russian novelist, was the literary herald of the new age, and it is significant that his genius was not truly appreciated until half a century after his death. Today he is considered one of the greatest artists and thinkers of the Western world, the writer who first laid bare the confusion in human minds and souls that grew into the intellectual chaos of the twentieth century.

The artistry of Dostoevsky is inseparable from his ideas. In his novels, he cast these ideas in artistic form, making his characters symbols of universal truths. Although he wrote in a simple, direct style, the novels have an intricate, agitated quality that produces a disturbing emotional effect in the reader. Dostoevsky was a literary realist, but he probed beneath the surface of realistic detail into the tortured, innermost recesses of his characters. His work thus focused on the morbid aspects of human behavior and feeling, on evil and suffering. Dostoevsky saw human beings as both corrupt and capable of greatness; he felt that their salvation lay in faith in God and in His revelation through suffering, forgiveness, and love. Dostoevsky was, however, no simple believer. His faith arose from doubts and contradictions and was shaped by a sense of humanity's unending tragic quest.

In his novels, Dostoevsky suggests the tragic course of his own life and the

Reprinted with permission of The Macmillan Company from *The Brothers Karamazov* by F. Dostoevsky. [Trans. Constance Garnett (New York, 1951), 253–72.] First published in 1912 by William Heinemann Ltd.

torments of his restless mind and passionate nature. From childhood on, death, disease, and suffering pervaded his life. While in exile in Siberia as a result of his radical social views, he experienced a religious conversion. His religious feelings led him to identify with the masses of Russian peasants and to preach a gospel of mystical Russian nationalism. At the same time, he attacked the bourgeois civilization of Western Europe, with its rationalism and materialism, as decadent and doomed to destruction. Dostoevsky was not only the prophet of the irrational: he was the enemy of reason.

The Brothers Karamazov (1880), Dostoevsky's greatest novel and the tragic tale of a middle-class Russian family, has as its theme the search for faith through struggle against evil. Presented in the following selection is the portion known as "The Grand Inquisitor," after a legend composed by one character, a rationalist and unbeliever, and told to his brother, a saintly figure living in a monastery. Essentially, the story is an allegory of the human predicament, in which individuals strive for true freedom but fear and reject it in favor of the ease and security of obedience to authority. Some have also considered the story Dostoevsky's prophetic attack on authoritarian ideologies and systems and growing secular rationalism.

[The setting is a tavern, where two of the brothers Karamazov, Ivan and Aloysha, are seated at a table. Ivan begins telling Aloysha about a "poem" he wrote. *Ed.*]

"Even this must have a preface—that is, a literary preface," laughed Ivan, "and I am a poor hand at making one. You see, my action takes place in the sixteenth century, and at that time, as you probably learnt at school, it was customary in poetry to bring down heavenly powers on earth. Not to speak of Dante,[1] in France clerks, as well as the monks in the monasteries, used to give regular performances in which the Madonna,[2] the saints, the angels, Christ, and God Himself were brought on the stage. In those days it was done in all simplicity. In Victor Hugo's[3] 'Notre Dame de Paris' an edifying and gratuitous spectacle was provided for the people in the Hotel de Ville[4] of

---

[1] Dante Alighieri (1265–1321), the Florentine poet who wrote the *Divine Comedy,* one of the great works of literature.
[2] The Virgin Mary, the mother of Jesus.
[3] Victor Marie Hugo (1802–1885), a prolific French writer, published his novel *Notre Dame de Paris* in 1831.
[4] City Hall.

Paris in the reign of Louis XI[5] in honor of the birth of the dauphin.[6] It was called *Le bon jugement de la très sainte et gracieuse Vierge Marie,*[7] and she appears herself on the stage and pronounces her *bon jugement.* Similar plays, chiefly from the Old Testament, were occasionally performed in Moscow, too, up to the times of Peter the Great.[8] But besides plays there were all sorts of legends and ballads scattered about the world, in which the saints and angels and all the powers of Heaven took part when required. In our monasteries the monks busied themselves in translating, copying, and even composing such poems—and even under the Tartars.[9] There is, for instance, one such poem (of course, from the Greek), 'The Wanderings of Our Lady Through Hell,' with descriptions as bold as Dante's. Our Lady[10] visits Hell, and the Archangel Michael leads her through the torments. She sees the sinners and their punishment. There she sees among others one noteworthy set of sinners in a burning lake; some of them sink to the bottom of the lake so that they can't swim out, and 'these God forgets'—an expression of extraordinary depth and force. And so Our Lady, shocked and weeping, falls before the throne of God and begs for mercy for all in Hell—for all she has seen there, indiscriminately. Her conversation with God is immensely interesting. She beseeches Him, she will not desist, and when God points to the hands and feet of her Son, nailed to the Cross, and asks, 'How can I forgive His tormentors?' she bids all the saints, all the martyrs, all the angels and archangels to fall down with her and pray for mercy on all without distinction. It ends by her winning from God a respite of suffering every year from Good Friday till Trinity day,[11] and the sinners at once raise a cry of thankfulness from Hell, chanting, 'Thou art just, O Lord, in this judgment.' Well, my poem would have been of that kind if it had appeared at that time. He comes on the scene in my poem, but He says nothing, only appears and passes on. Fifteen centuries have passed since He promised to come in His glory, fifteen centuries since His prophet wrote, 'Behold, I come quickly'; 'Of that day and that hour knoweth no man,

---

[5] Louis XI (1423–1483) was king of France from 1461 to 1483.
[6] Title of the eldest son of the king.
[7] French: The good judgment of the very holy and gracious Virgin Mary.
[8] Peter the Great (1672–1725), czar of Russia.
[9] A people of Mongol origin who controlled much of Russia during the Middle Ages.
[10] The Virgin Mary.
[11] Trinity Sunday (the Sunday after Pentecost).

neither the Son, but the Father,' as He Himself predicted on earth.[12] But humanity awaits him with the same faith and with the same love. Oh, with greater faith, for it is fifteen centuries since man has ceased to see signs from Heaven.

> No signs from Heaven come today
> To add to what the heart doth say.

There was nothing left but faith in what the heart doth say. It is true there were many miracles in those days. There were saints who performed miraculous cures; some holy people, according to their biographies, were visited by the Queen of Heaven[13] herself. But the devil did not slumber, and doubts were already arising among men of the truth of these miracles. And just then there appeared in the north of Germany a terrible new heresy. 'A huge star like to a torch' (that is, to a church) 'fell on the sources of the waters and they became bitter.'[14] These heretics began blasphemously denying miracles. But those who remained faithful were all the more ardent in their faith. The tears of humanity rose up to Him as before, awaiting His coming, loved Him, hoped for Him, yearned to suffer and die for Him as before. And so many ages mankind had prayed with faith and fervor, 'O Lord our God, hasten Thy coming,' so many ages called upon Him, that in His infinite mercy He deigned to come down to His servants. Before that day He had come down, He had visited some holy men, martyrs, and hermits, as is written in their 'Lives.'[15] Among us, Tyutchev,[16] with absolute faith in the truth of his words, bore witness that

> Bearing the Cross, in slavish dress,
> Weary and worn, the Heavenly King
> Our mother, Russia, came to bless,
> And through our land went wandering.

And that certainly was so, I assure you.

"And behold, He deigned to appear for a moment to the people, to the tortured, suffering people, sunk in iniquity, but loving Him like children. My story is laid in Spain, in Seville, in the most terrible

[12] Jesus' prophecy concerning his Second Coming (Matthew 24:36 and Mark 13:32).
[13] The Virgin Mary.
[14] Revelation 8:10–11.
[15] Biographies.
[16] Fyodor Tyutchev (1803–1873), a Russian lyric poet.

time of the Inquisition,[17] when fires were lighted every day to the glory of God, and 'in the splendid *auto-da-fé*[18] the wicked heretics were burnt.' Oh, of course, this was not the coming in which He[19] will appear according to His promise at the end of time in all His heavenly glory, and which will be sudden 'as lightning flashing from east to west.' No, He visited His children only for a moment, and there where the flames were crackling round the heretics. In His infinite mercy He came once more among men in that human shape in which He walked among men for three years fifteen centuries ago.

"He came down to the 'hot pavement' of the southern town in which on the day before almost a hundred heretics had, *ad majorem gloriam Dei,*[20] been burnt by the cardinal, the Grand Inquisitor,[21] in a magnificent *auto-da-fé,* in the presence of the king, the court, the knights, the cardinals, the most charming ladies of the court, and the whole population of Seville.

"He came softly, unobserved, and yet, strange to say, every one recognized Him. That might be one of the best passages in the poem. I mean, why they recognized Him. The people are irresistibly drawn to Him, they surround Him, they flock about Him, follow Him. He moves silently in their midst with a gentle smile of infinite compassion. The sun of love burns in His heart, light and power shine from His eyes, and their radiance, shed on the people, stirs their hearts with responsive love. He holds out His hands to them, blesses them, and a healing virtue comes from contact with Him, even with His garments. An old man in the crowd, blind from childhood, cries out, 'O Lord, heal me and I shall see Thee!' and, as it were, scales fall from his eyes and the blind man sees Him. The crowd weeps and kisses the earth under His feet. Children throw flowers before Him, sing, and cry hosannah.[22] 'It is He—it is He!' all repeat. 'It must be He, it can be no one but Him!' He stops at the steps of the Seville cathedral at the moment when the weeping mourners are bringing in a little open white coffin. In it lies a child of

---

[17] The Inquisition, or the Congregation of the Holy Office (the official name), was charged with seeking out heresy (false beliefs) and punishing heretics. (The Inquisition was founded in the early thirteenth century and abolished in 1834. In the fifteenth and sixteenth centuries it raged most furiously in Spain, Portugal, and Italy.)

[18] Portuguese: act of faith. The phrase refers to the public sentencing and subsequent punishment of convicted (repentant and unrepentant) heretics.

[19] Jesus.

[20] Latin: to the greater glory of God.

[21] The high-ranking clergyman in charge of the Inquisition within a certain territory.

[22] A shout of praise to God: "Save, we pray!"

seven, the only daughter of a prominent citizen. The dead child lies hidden in flowers. 'He will raise your child,' the crowd shouts to the weeping mother. The priest, coming to meet the coffin, looks perplexed and frowns, but the mother of the dead child throws herself at His feet with a wail. 'If it is Thou, raise my child!' she cries, holding out her hands to Him. The procession halts, the coffin is laid on the steps at His feet. He looks with compassion, and His lips once more softly pronounce, 'Maiden, arise!' and the maiden arises. The little girl sits up in the coffin and looks round, smiling with wide-open wondering eyes, holding a bunch of white roses they had put in her hand.

"There are cries, sobs, confusion among the people, and at that moment the cardinal himself, the Grand Inquisitor, passes by the cathedral. He is an old man, almost ninety, tall and erect, with a withered face and sunken eyes, in which there is still a gleam of light. He is not dressed in his gorgeous cardinal's robes, as he was the day before, when he was burning the enemies of the Roman Church [23]—at that moment he was wearing his coarse, old, monk's cassock. At a distance behind him come his gloomy assistants and slaves and the 'holy guard.' [24] He stops at the sight of the crowd and watches it from a distance. He sees everything; he sees them set the coffin down at His feet, sees the child rise up, and his face darkens. He knits his thick grey brows and his eyes gleam with a sinister fire. He holds out his finger and bids the guards take Him. And such is his power, so completely are the people cowed into submission and trembling obedience to him, that the crowd immediately makes way for the guards, and in the midst of death-like silence they lay hands on Him and lead Him away. The crowd instantly bows down to the earth, like one man, before the old inquisitor. He blesses the people in silence and passes on. The guards lead their prisoner to the close, gloomy, vaulted prison in the ancient palace of the Holy Inquisition and shut Him in it. The day passes and is followed by the dark, burning 'breathless' night of Seville. The air is 'fragrant with laurel and lemon.' In the pitch darkness the iron door of the prison is suddenly opened and the Grand Inquisitor himself comes in with a light in his hand. He is alone; the door is closed at once behind him. He stands in the doorway and for a minute or two gazes into His face. At last he goes up slowly, sets the light on the table and speaks.

[23] Roman Catholic Church.
[24] Bodyguard.

" 'Is it Thou? Thou?' but receiving no answer, he adds at once, 'Don't answer, be silent. What canst Thou say, indeed? I know too well what Thou wouldst say. And Thou hast no right to add anything to what Thou hadst said of old. Why, then, art Thou come to hinder us? For Thou hast come to hinder us, and Thou knowest that. But dost Thou know what will be tomorrow? I know not who Thou art and care not to know whether it is Thou or only a semblance of Him, but tomorrow I shall condemn Thee and burn Thee at the stake as the worst of heretics. And the very people who have today kissed Thy feet, tomorrow at the faintest sign from me will rush to heap up the embers of Thy fire. Knowest Thou that? Yes, maybe Thou knowest it,' he added with thoughtful penetration, never for a moment taking his eyes off the Prisoner."

"I don't quite understand, Ivan. What does it mean?" Alyosha, who had been listening in silence, said with a smile. "Is it simply a wild fantasy, or a mistake on the part of the old man—some impossible *quid pro quo?*" [25]

"Take it as the last," said Ivan, laughing, "if you are so corrupted by modern realism and can't stand anything fantastic. If you like it to be a case of mistaken identity, let it be so. It is true," he went on, laughing, "the old man was ninety, and he might well be crazy over his set idea. He might have been struck by the appearance of the Prisoner. It might, in fact, be simply his ravings, the delusion of an old man of ninety, over-excited by the *auto-da-fé* of a hundred heretics the day before. But does it matter to us after all whether it was a mistake of identity or a wild fantasy? All that matters is that the old man should speak out, should speak openly of what he has thought in silence for ninety years."

"And the Prisoner too is silent? Does He look at him and not say a word?"

"That's inevitable in any case," Ivan laughed again. "The old man has told Him He hasn't the right to add anything to what He has said of old. One may say it is the most fundamental feature of Roman Catholicism, in my opinion at least. 'All has been given by Thee to the Pope,' they say, 'and all, therefore, is still in the Pope's hands, and there is no need for Thee to come now at all. Thou must not meddle for the time, at least.' That's how they speak and write,

---

[25] One thing in exchange for another; a trade-off.

too—the Jesuits,[26] at any rate. I have read it myself in the works of their theologians. 'Hast Thou the right to reveal to us one of the mysteries of that world from which Thou hast come?' my old man asks Him, and answers the question for Him. 'No, Thou hast not; that Thou mayest not add to what has been said of old, and mayest not take from men the freedom which Thou didst exalt when Thou wast on earth. Whatsoever Thou revealest anew will encroach on men's freedom of faith; for it will be manifest as a miracle, and the freedom of their faith was dearer to Thee than anything in those days fifteen hundred years ago. Didst Thou not often say then, "I will make you free"? But now Thou hast seen these "free" men,' the old man adds suddenly, with a pensive smile. 'Yes, we've paid dearly for it,' he goes on, looking sternly at Him, 'but at last we have completed that work in Thy name. For fifteen centuries we have been wrestling with Thy freedom, but now it is ended and over for good. Dost Thou not believe that it's over for good? Thou lookest meekly at me and deignest not even to be wroth with me. But let me tell Thee that now, today, people are more persuaded than ever that they have perfect freedom, yet they have brought their freedom to us and laid it humbly at our feet. But that has been our doing. Was this what Thou didst? Was this Thy freedom?' "

"I don't understand again," Alyosha broke in. "Is he ironical, is he jesting?"

"Not a bit of it! He claims it as a merit for himself and his Church that at last they have vanquished freedom and have done so to make men happy. 'For now' (he is speaking of the Inquisition, of course) 'for the first time it has become possible to think of the happiness of men. Man was created a rebel; and how can rebels be happy? Thou wast warned,' he says to Him. 'Thou hast had no lack of admonitions, and warnings, but Thou didst not listen to those warnings; Thou didst reject the only way by which men might be made happy. But, fortunately, departing Thou didst hand on the work to us. Thou hast promised, Thou hast established by Thy word, Thou hast given to us the right to bind and to unbind, and now, of course, Thou canst not think of taking it away. Why, then, hast Thou come to hinder us?' "

---

[26] Members of the Society of Jesus, which was viewed as the most aggressive and militant order of the Roman Catholic Church. The order was founded in 1534 by a former soldier, the Spaniard Ignatius of Loyola (1491–1556).

"And what's the meaning of 'no lack of admonitions and warnings'?" asked Alyosha.

"Why, that's the chief part of what the old man must say."

" 'The wise and dread Spirit,[27] the spirit of self-destruction and nonexistence,' the old man goes on, 'the great spirit talked with Thee in the wilderness, and we are told in the books that he "tempted" Thee. Is that so? And could anything truer be said than what he revealed to Thee in three questions and what Thou didst reject, and what in the books is called "the temptation"?[28] And yet if there has ever been on earth a real stupendous miracle, it took place on that day, on the day of the three temptations. The statement of those three questions was itself the miracle. If it were possible to imagine simply for the sake of argument that those three questions of the dread spirit had perished utterly from the books, and that we had to restore them and to invent them anew, and to do so had gathered together all the wise men of the earth—rulers, chief priests, learned men, philosophers, poets—and had set them the task to invent three questions, such as would not only fit the occasion, but express in three words, three human phrases, the whole future history of the world and of humanity—dost Thou believe that all the wisdom of the earth united could have invented anything in depth and force equal to the three questions which were actually put to Thee then by the wise and mighty spirit in the wilderness? From those questions alone, from the miracle of their statement, we can see that we have here to do not with the fleeting human intelligence, but with the absolute and eternal. For in those three questions the whole subsequent history of mankind is, as it were, brought together into one whole, and foretold, and in them are united all the unsolved historical contradictions of human nature. At the time it could not be so clear, since the future was unknown; but now that fifteen hundred years have passed, we see that everything in those three questions was so justly divined and foretold, and has been so truly fulfilled, that nothing can be added to them or taken from them.

" 'Judge Thyself who was right—Thou or he who questioned Thee then? Remember the first question; its meaning, in other words, was this: "Thou wouldst go into the world, and art going with empty hands, with some promise of freedom which men in

---

[27] Devil.

[28] The three temptations of Jesus as related in the gospels: Matthew 4:1–11; Luke 4:1–13; Mark 1:12–13.

their simplicity and their natural unruliness cannot even understand, which they fear and dread—for nothing has ever been more insupportable for a man and a human society than freedom. But seest Thou these stones in this parched and barren wilderness? Turn them into bread, and mankind will run after Thee like a flock of sheep, grateful and obedient, though forever trembling, lest Thou withdraw Thy hand and deny them Thy bread." But Thou wouldst not deprive man of freedom and didst reject the offer, thinking, what is that freedom worth, if obedience is bought with bread? Thou didst reply that man lives not by bread alone. But dost Thou know that for the sake of that earthly bread the spirit of the earth will rise up against Thee and will strive with Thee and overcome Thee, and all will follow him, crying, "Who can compare with this beast? He has given us fire from heaven!" Dost Thou know that the ages will pass, and humanity will proclaim by the lips of their sages that there is no crime, and therefore no sin; there is only hunger? "Feed men, and then ask of them virtue!" that's what they'll write on the banner which they will raise against Thee, and with which they will destroy Thy temple. Where Thy temple stood will rise a new building; the terrible tower of Babel [29] will be built again, and though, like the one of old, it will not be finished, yet Thou mightest have prevented that new tower and have cut short the sufferings of men for a thousand years; for they will come back to us after a thousand years of agony with their tower. They will seek us again, hidden underground in the catacombs, for we shall be again persecuted and tortured. They will find us and cry to us, "Feed us, for those who have promised us fire from heaven haven't given it!" And then we shall finish building their tower, for he finishes the building who feeds them. And we alone shall feed them in Thy name, declaring falsely that it is in Thy name. Oh, never, never can they feed themselves without us! No science will give them bread so long as they remain free. In the end they will lay their freedom at our feet, and say to us, "Make us your slaves, but feed us." They will understand themselves, at last, that freedom and bread enough for all are inconceivable together, for never, never will they be able to share between them! They will be

---

[29] According to the Old Testament (Genesis 11:1–9), a tower (and city) built in the plain of Shinar. The tower was to be so tall as to reach into heaven. However, God punished the builders for their pride by replacing their single language with many diverse tongues. Now unable to understand one another, the builders had to abandon their project.

convinced, too, that they can never be free, for they are weak, vicious, worthless and rebellious. Thou didst promise them the bread of Heaven, but, I repeat again, can it compare with earthly bread in the eyes of the weak, ever-sinful and ignoble race of man? And if for the sake of the bread of Heaven thousands and tens of thousands shall follow Thee, what is to become of the millions and tens of thousands of millions of creatures who will not have the strength to forego the earthly bread for the sake of the heavenly? Or dost Thou care only for the tens of thousands of the great and strong, while the millions, numerous as the sands of the sea, who are weak but love Thee, must exist only for the sake of the great and strong? No, we care for the weak, too. They are sinful and rebellious, but in the end they too will become obedient. They will marvel at us and look on us as gods, because we are ready to endure the freedom which they have found so dreadful and to rule over them—so awful it will seem to them to be free. But we shall tell them that we are Thy servants and rule them in Thy name. We shall deceive them again, for we will not let Thee come to us again. That deception will be our suffering, for we shall be forced to lie.

" 'This is the significance of the first question in the wilderness, and this is what Thou hast rejected for the sake of that freedom which Thou hast exalted above everything. Yet in this question lies hidden the great secret of this world. Choosing "bread," Thou wouldst have satisfied the universal and everlasting craving of humanity—to find someone to worship. So long as man remains free he strives for nothing so incessantly and so painfully as to find someone to worship. But man seeks to worship what is established beyond dispute, so that all men would agree at once to worship it. For these pitiful creatures are concerned not only to find what one or the other can worship, but to find something that all would believe in and worship; what is essential is that all may be *together* in it. This craving for *community* of worship is the chief misery of every man individually and of all humanity from the beginning of time. For the sake of common worship they've slain each other with the sword. They have set up gods and challenged one another, "Put away your gods and come and worship ours, or we will kill you and your gods!" And so it will be to the end of the world, even when gods disappear from the earth; they will fall down before idols just the same. Thou didst know, Thou couldst not but have known, this fundamental secret of human nature, but Thou didst reject the one infallible banner which was offered Thee to make all men bow down to Thee alone—the banner of earthly bread; and Thou hast rejected it for the sake of freedom and the bread of Heaven. Behold what Thou didst further. And all again in the name of freedom! I tell Thee that man is tormented by no greater anxiety than to find someone quickly to whom he can hand over the gift of freedom with which the ill-fated creature is born. But only one who can appease their conscience can take over their freedom. In bread there was offered Thee an invincible banner; give bread, and man will worship Thee, for nothing is more certain than bread. But if someone else gains possession of his conscience—oh! then he will cast away Thy bread and follow after him who has ensnared his conscience. In that Thou wast right. For the secret of man's being is not only to live but to have something to live for. Without a stable conception of the object of life, man would not consent to go on living, and would rather destroy himself than remain on earth, though he had bread in abundance. That is true. But what happened? Instead of taking men's freedom from them, Thou didst make it greater than ever! Didst Thou forget that man prefers peace, and even death, to freedom of choice in the knowledge of good and evil? Nothing is more seductive for man than his freedom of conscience, but nothing is a greater cause of suffering. And behold, instead of giving a firm foundation for setting the conscience of man at rest forever, Thou didst choose all that is exceptional, vague and enigmatic; Thou didst choose what was utterly beyond the strength of men, acting as though Thou didst not love them at all—Thou who didst come to give Thy life for them! Instead of taking possession of man's freedom, Thou didst increase it, and burdened the spiritual kingdom of mankind with its sufferings forever. Thou didst desire man's free love, that he should follow Thee freely, enticed and taken captive by Thee. In place of the rigid, ancient law, man must hereafter with free heart decide for himself what is good and what is evil, having only Thy image before him as his guide. But didst Thou not know he would at last reject even Thy image and Thy truth, if he is weighed down with the fearful burden of free choice? They will cry aloud at last that the truth is not in Thee, for they could not have been left in greater confusion and suffering than Thou hast caused, laying upon them so many cares and unanswerable problems.

" 'So that, in truth, Thou didst Thyself lay the foundation for the destruction of Thy kingdom, and no one is more to blame for it. Yet what was offered Thee? There are three powers, three powers alone, able to conquer and to hold captive forever the conscience of these impotent rebels for their happiness—those forces are miracle, mystery and authority. Thou hast rejected all three and hast set the example for doing so. When the wise and dread spirit set Thee on the pinnacle of the temple and said to Thee, "If Thou wouldst know whether Thou art the son of God then cast Thyself down, for it is written: the angels shall hold him up lest he fall and bruise himself, and Thou shalt know then whether Thou art the Son of God and shalt prove then how great is Thy faith in Thy Father." But Thou didst refuse and wouldst not cast Thyself down. Oh! of course, Thou didst proudly and well like God; but the weak, unruly race of men, are they gods? Oh, Thou didst know then that in taking one step, in making one movement to cast Thyself down, Thou wouldst be tempting God and have lost all Thy faith in Him, and wouldst have been dashed to pieces against that earth which Thou didst come to save. And the wise spirit that tempted Thee would have rejoiced. But I ask again, are there many like Thee? And couldst Thou believe for one moment that men, too, could face such a temptation? Is the nature of men such that they can reject miracle, and at the great moments of their life, the moments of their deepest, most agonizing spiritual difficulties, cling only to the free verdict of the heart? Oh, Thou didst know that Thy deed would be recorded in books, would be handed down to remote times and the utmost ends of the earth, and Thou didst hope that man, following Thee, would cling to God and not ask for a miracle. But Thou didst not know that when man rejects miracles he rejects God too; for man seeks not so much God as the miraculous. And as man cannot bear to be without the miraculous, he will create new miracles of his own for himself, and will worship deeds of sorcery and witchcraft, though he might be a hundred times over a rebel, heretic and infidel. Thou didst not come down from the Cross when they shouted to Thee, mocking and reviling Thee, "Come down from the Cross and we will believe that Thou art He." Thou didst not come down, for again Thou wouldst not enslave man by a miracle, and didst crave faith given freely, not based on miracle. Thou didst crave for free love and not the base raptures of the slave before the might that has overawed him forever. But Thou didst think too highly of men therein, for they are slaves, of course, though rebellious by nature. Look round and judge; fifteen centuries have passed; look upon them. Whom hast Thou raised up to Thyself? I swear, man is weaker and baser by nature than Thou hast believed him! Can he, can he do what Thou didst? By showing him so much respect, Thou didst, as it were, cease to feel for him, for Thou didst ask far too much from him—Thou who hast loved him more than Thyself! Respecting him less, Thou wouldst have asked less of him. That would have been more like love, for his burden would have been lighter. He is weak and vile. What though he is everywhere now rebelling against our power, and proud of his rebellion? It is the pride of a child and a schoolboy. They are little children rioting and barring out the teacher at school. But their childish delight will end; it will cost them dear. They will cast down temples and drench the earth with blood. But they will see at last, the foolish children, that, though they are rebels, they are impotent rebels, unable to keep up their own rebellion. Bathed in their foolish tears, they will recognize at last that He who created them rebels must have meant to mock at them. They will say this in despair, and their utterance will be a blasphemy which will make them more unhappy still, for man's nature cannot bear blasphemy, and in the end always avenges it on itself. And so unrest, confusion and unhappiness—that is the present lot of man after Thou didst bear so much for their freedom! Thy great prophet tells in vision and in image that he saw all those who took part in the first resurrection and that there were of each tribe twelve thousand.[30] But if there were so many of them, they must have been not men but gods. They had borne Thy cross, they had endured scores of years in the barren, hungry wilderness, living upon locusts and roots—and Thou mayest indeed point with pride at those children of freedom, of free love, of free and splendid sacrifice for Thy name. But remember that they were only some thousands; and what of the rest? And how are the other weak ones to blame, because they could not endure what the strong have endured? How is the weak soul to blame that it is unable to receive such terrible gifts? Canst Thou have simply come to the elect and for the elect? But if so, it is a mystery and we cannot understand it. And if it is a mystery, we too have a right to preach a mystery, and to teach them that it's not the free judgment of their hearts, not love, that matters, but a mystery which they must follow blindly, even against their conscience. So we have done. We have corrected Thy work and have founded it upon *miracle, mystery* and *authority*. And

[30] A reference to a passage in the Book of Revelation (ascribed to John, the Evangelist), 7:4–8.

men rejoiced that they were again led like sheep, and that the terrible gift that had brought them such suffering was, at last, lifted from their hearts. Were we right teaching them this? Speak! Did we not love mankind, so meekly acknowledging their feebleness, lovingly lightening their burden, and permitting their weak nature even sin with our sanction? Why hast Thou come now to hinder us? And why dost Thou look silently and searchingly at me with Thy mild eyes? Be angry. I don't want Thy love, for I love Thee not. And what use is it for me to hide anything from Thee? Don't I know to Whom I am speaking? All that I can say is known to Thee already. And is it for me to conceal from Thee our mystery? Perhaps it is Thy will to hear it from my lips. Listen, then. We are not working with Thee, but with *him*—that is our mystery. It's long—eight centuries— since we have been on *his* side and not on Thine. Just eight centuries ago, we took from him what Thou didst reject with scorn, that last gift he offered Thee, showing Thee all the kingdoms of the earth. We took from him Rome and the sword of Caesar, and proclaimed ourselves sole rulers of the earth, though hitherto we have not been able to complete our work. But whose fault is that? Oh, the work is only beginning, but it has begun. It has long to await completion and the earth has yet much to suffer, but we shall triumph and shall be Caesars, and then we shall plan the universal happiness of man. But Thou mightest have taken even then the sword of Caesar. Why didst Thou reject that last gift? Hadst Thou accepted that last counsel of the mighty spirit, Thou wouldst have accomplished all that man seeks on earth—that is, someone to worship, someone to keep his conscience, and some means of uniting all in one unanimous and har- monious ant heap, for the craving for universal unity is the third and last anguish of men. Mankind as a whole has always striven to orga- nize a universal state. There have been many great nations with great histories, but the more highly they were developed the more un- happy they were, for they felt more acutely than other people the craving for world-wide union. The great conquerors, Timours[31] and Genghis Khans,[32] whirled like hurricanes over the face of the earth, striving to subdue its people, and they too were but the unconscious

---

[31] Timour, or Tamerlane (*ca.* 1336–1405), was a Mongol conqueror, who, after he had made himself lord of Turkestan, took control of Persia and Central Asia and led armies deep into Russia, India, Syria and Asia Minor.

[32] Genghis Khan (1162–1227) was a Mongol conqueror whose hordes overran north- ern China, Korea, northern India, Iran, Iraq and parts of Russia.

expression of the same craving for universal unity. Hadst Thou taken the world and Caesar's purple,[33] Thou wouldst have founded the universal state and have given universal peace. For who can rule men if not he who holds their conscience and their bread in his hands? We have taken the sword of Caesar, and in taking it, of course, have rejected Thee and followed *him*. Oh, ages are yet to come of the confusion of free thought, of their science and cannibalism. For having begun to build their tower of Babel without us, they will end, of course, with cannibalism. But then the beast will crawl to us and lick our feet and spatter them with tears of blood. And we shall sit upon the beast and raise the cup, and on it will be written, "Mystery." But then, and only then, the reign of peace and happiness will come for men. Thou art proud of Thine elect, but Thou hast only the elect, while we give rest to all. And besides, how many of those elect, those mighty ones who could become elect, have grown weary waiting for Thee, and have transferred and will transfer the powers of their spirit and the warmth of their heart to the other camp, and end by raising their *free* banner against Thee. Thou didst Thyself lift up that banner. But with us all will be happy and will no more rebel, nor destroy one another as under Thy freedom. Oh, we shall persuade them that they will only become free when they renounce their freedom to us and submit to us. And shall we be right or shall we be lying? They will be convinced that we are right, for they will remember the horrors of slavery and confusion to which Thy freedom brought them. Freedom, free thought and science, will lead them into such straits and will bring them face to face with such marvels and insoluble mysteries that some of them, the fierce and rebellious, will destroy themselves; others, rebellious but weak, will destroy one another, while the rest, weak and unhappy, will crawl fawning to our feet and whine to us: "Yes, you were right, you alone possess His mystery, and we come back to you, save us from ourselves!"

" 'Receiving bread from us, they will see clearly that we take the bread made by their hands from them, to give it to them, without any miracle. They will see that we do not change the stones to bread, but in truth they will be more thankful for taking it from our hands than for the bread itself! For they will remember only too well that in old days, without our help, even the bread they made turned to stones in their hands, while since they have come back to us, the very stones have turned to bread in their hands. Too, too well they

[33] The symbol of imperial power in ancient Rome.

know the value of complete submission! And until men know that, they will be unhappy. Who is most to blame for their not knowing it, speak? Who scattered the flock and sent it astray on unknown paths? But the flock will come together again and will submit once more, and then it will be once for all. Then we shall give them the quiet humble happiness of weak creatures such as they are by nature. Oh, we shall persuade them at last not to be proud, for Thou didst lift them up and thereby taught them to be proud. We shall show them that they are weak, that they are only pitiful children, but that childlike happiness is the sweetest of all. They will become timid and will look to us and huddle close to us in fear, as chicks to the hen. They will marvel at us and will be awe-stricken before us, and will be proud at our being so powerful and clever, that we have been able to subdue such a turbulent flock of thousands of millions. They will tremble impotently before our wrath, their minds will grow fearful, they will be quick to shed tears like women and children, but they will be just as ready at a sign from us to pass to laughter and rejoicing, to happy mirth and childish song. Yes, we shall set them to work, but in their leisure hours we shall make their life like a child's game, with children's songs and innocent dance. Oh, we shall allow them even sin; they are weak and helpless, and they will love us like children because we allow them to sin. We shall tell them that every sin will be expiated, if it is done with our permission, that we allow them to sin because we love them, and the punishment for these sins we take upon ourselves. And we shall take it upon ourselves, and they will adore us as their saviors who have taken on themselves their sins before God. And they will have no secrets from us. We shall allow or forbid them to live with their wives and mistresses, to have or not to have children—according to whether they have been obedient or disobedient—and they will submit to us gladly and cheerfully. The most painful secrets of their conscience, all, all they will bring to us, and we shall have an answer for all. And they will be glad to believe our answer, for it will save them from the great anxiety and terrible agony they endure at present in making a free decision for themselves. And all will be happy, all the millions of creatures, except the hundred thousand who rule over them. For only we, we who guard the mystery, shall be unhappy. There will be thousands of millions of happy babes, and a hundred thousand sufferers who have taken upon themselves the curse of the knowledge of good and evil. Peacefully they will die, peacefully they will expire in Thy name, and beyond the grave they will find nothing but death. But we shall keep the secret, and for their happiness we shall allure them with the reward of heaven and eternity. Though if there were anything in the other world, it certainly would not be for such as they. It is prophesied that Thou wilt come again in victory, Thou wilt come with Thy chosen, the proud and strong, but we will say that they have only saved themselves, but we have saved all. We are told that the harlot who sits upon the beast, and holds in her hands the *mystery,* shall be put to shame, that the weak will rise up again, and will rend her royal purple and will strip naked her loathsome body. But then I will stand up and point out to Thee the thousand millions of happy children who have known no sin. And we who have taken their sins upon us for their happiness will stand up before Thee and say: "Judge us if Thou canst and darest." Know that I fear Thee not. Know that I too have been in the wilderness, I too have lived on roots and locusts, I too prized the freedom with which Thou hast blessed men, and I too was striving to stand among Thy elect, among the strong and powerful, thirsting "to make up the number." But I awakened and would not serve madness. I turned back and joined the ranks of those *who have corrected Thy work.* I left the proud and went back to the humble, for the happiness of the humble. What I say to Thee will come to pass, and our dominion will be built up. I repeat, tomorrow Thou shalt see that obedient flock who at a sign from me will hasten to heap up the hot cinders about the pile on which I shall burn Thee for coming to hinder us. For if anyone has ever deserved our fires, it is Thou. Tomorrow I shall burn Thee. *Dixi.' "* [34]

Ivan stopped. He was carried away as he talked and spoke with excitement; when he had finished, he suddenly smiled.

Alyosha had listened in silence; toward the end he was greatly moved and seemed several times on the point of interrupting, but restrained himself. Now his words came with a rush.

"But . . . that's absurd!" he cried, flushing. "Your poem is in praise of Jesus, not in blame of Him—as you meant it to be. And who will believe you about freedom? Is that the way to understand it? That's not the idea of it in the Orthodox Church.[35] . . . That's

---

[34] Latin: I have said (all that I am going to); I have spoken.

[35] Russian Orthodox Church, the national church of czarist Russia. (After the division of the ancient Roman Empire, the Christian Church, too, split into two main branches: Roman Catholicism in the West, and the Orthodox churches in the East.

Rome, and not even the whole of Rome, it's false—those are the worst of the Catholics, the Inquisitors, the Jesuits! . . . And there could not be such a fantastic creature as your Inquisitor. What are these sins of mankind they take on themselves? Who are these keepers of the mystery who have taken some curse upon themselves for the happiness of mankind? When have they been seen? We know the Jesuits, they are spoken ill of, but surely they are not what you describe? They are not that at all, not at all. . . . They are simply the Romish army for the earthly sovereignty of the world in the future, with the Pontiff[36] of Rome for Emperor . . . that's their ideal, but there's no sort of mystery or lofty melancholy about it. . . . It's simple lust of power, of filthy earthly gain, of domination—something like a universal serfdom with them as masters—that's all they stand for. They don't even believe in God, perhaps. Your suffering Inquisitor is a mere fantasy."

"Stay, stay," laughed Ivan, "how hot you are! A fantasy you say, let it be so! Of course it's a fantasy. But allow me to say: do you really think that the Roman Catholic movement of the last centuries is actually nothing but the lust of power, of filthy earthly gain? Is that Father Paissy's[37] teaching?"

"No, no, on the contrary, Father Paissy did once say something rather the same as you . . . but of course it's not the same, not a bit the same," Alyosha hastily corrected himself.

"A precious admission, in spite of your 'not a bit the same.' I ask you why your Jesuits and Inquisitors have united simply for vile material gain? Why can there not be among them one martyr oppressed by great sorrow and loving humanity? You see, only suppose that there was one such man among all those who desire nothing but filthy material gain—if there's only one like my old Inquisitor, who had himself eaten roots in the desert and made frenzied efforts to subdue his flesh to make himself free and perfect. But yet all his life he loved humanity, and suddenly his eyes were opened, and he saw that it is no great moral blessedness to attain perfection and freedom, if at the same time one gains the conviction that millions of God's creatures have been created as a mockery, that they will never be capable of using their freedom, that these poor rebels can never turn into giants to complete the tower, that it was not for such geese that the great idealist dreamt his dream of harmony. Seeing all that, he

[36] The pope.
[37] Father Paissy, a learned monk.

turned back and joined—the clever people. Surely that could have happened?"

"Joined whom, what clever people?" cried Alyosha, completely carried away. "They have no such great cleverness and no mysteries and secrets. . . . Perhaps nothing but atheism,[38] that's all their secret. Your Inquisitor does not believe in God, that's his secret!"

"What if it is so! At last you have guessed it. It's perfectly true that that's the whole secret, but isn't that suffering, at least for a man like that, who has wasted his whole life in the desert and yet could not shake off his incurable love of humanity? In his old age he reached the clear conviction that nothing but the advice of the great dread spirit could build up any tolerable sort of life for the feeble, unruly, 'incomplete, empirical creatures created in jest.' And so, convinced of this, he sees that he must follow the counsel of the wise spirit, the dread spirit of death and destruction, and therefore accept lying and deception, and lead men consciously to death and destruction, and yet deceive them all the way so that they may not notice where they are being led, that the poor, blind creatures may at least on the way think themselves happy. And note, the deception is in the name of Him in Whose ideal the old man had so fervently believed all his life long. Is not that tragic? And if only one such stood at the head of the whole army 'filled with the lust of power only for the sake of filthy gain'—would not one such be enough to make a tragedy? More than that, one such standing at the head is enough to create the actual leading idea of the Roman Church with all its armies and Jesuits, its highest idea. I tell you frankly that I firmly believe that there has always been such a man among those who stood at the head of the movement. Who knows, there may have been some such even among the Roman Popes. Who knows, perhaps the spirit of that accursed old man who loves mankind so obstinately in his own way is to be found even now in a whole multitude of such old men, existing not by chance but by agreement, as a secret league formed long ago for the guarding of the mystery, to guard it from the weak and the unhappy, so as to make them happy. No doubt it is so, and so it must be indeed. I fancy that even among the Masons[39] there's something of the same mystery at the bottom, and that that's why the Catholics so detest the Masons as their rivals breaking up the unity of the idea, while it is so essential that there should be one flock and

[38] Denial of God's existence.
[39] Freemasons, a secret society formed for fraternal (and religious) purposes.

one shepherd. . . . But from the way I defend my idea I might be an author impatient of your criticism. Enough of it."

"You are perhaps a Mason yourself!" broke suddenly from Alyosha. "You don't believe in God," he added, speaking this time very sorrowfully. He fancied besides that his brother was looking at him ironically. "How does your poem end?" he asked, suddenly looking down. "Or was it the end?"

"I meant it to end like this: When the Inquisitor ceased speaking, he waited some time for his Prisoner to answer him. His silence weighed down upon him. He saw the Prisoner had listened intently all the time, looking gently in his face and evidently not wishing to reply. The old man longed for Him to say something, however bitter and terrible. But He suddenly approached the old man in silence and softly kissed him on his bloodless, aged lips. That was all His answer. The old man shuddered. His lips moved. He went to the door, opened it, and said to Him 'Go, and come no more. . . . Come not at all, never, never!' And he let Him out into the dark alleys of the town. The Prisoner went away."

"And the old man?"

"The kiss glows in his heart, but the old man adheres to his idea."

"And you with him, you too?" cried Alyosha, mournfully.

Ivan laughed.

"Why, it's all nonsense, Alyosha. It's only a senseless poem of a senseless student, who could never write two lines of verse. Why do you take it so seriously? Surely you don't suppose I am going straight off to the Jesuits, to join the men who are correcting His work? Good Lord, it's no business of mine. I told you, all I want is to live on to thirty, and then . . . dash the cup to the ground!"

"But the little sticky leaves, and the precious tombs, and the blue sky, and the woman you love! How will you live, how will you love them?" Alyosha cried sorrowfully. "With such a hell in your heart and your head, how can you? No, that's just what you are going away for, to join them . . . if not, you will kill yourself, you can't endure it!"

"There is a strength to endure everything," Ivan said with a cold smile.

"What strength?"

"The strength of the Karamazovs—the strength of the Karamazov baseness."

"To sink into debauchery, to stifle your soul with corruption, yes?"

"Possibly even that . . . only perhaps till I am thirty I shall escape it, and then—"

"How will you escape it? By what will you escape it? That's impossible with your ideas."

"In the Karamazov way, again."

" 'Everything is lawful,' you mean? Everything is lawful, is that it?"

Ivan scowled, and all at once turned strangely pale.

"Ah, you've caught up yesterday's phrase, which so offended Miusov[40]—and which Dmitri[41] pounced upon so naively and paraphrased!" he smiled queerly. "Yes, if you like, 'everything is lawful' since the word has been said. I won't deny it. And Mitya's[42] version isn't bad."

Alyosha looked at him in silence.

"I thought that going away from here I have you at least," Ivan said suddenly, with unexpected feeling; "but now I see that there is no place for me even in your heart, my dear hermit. The formula, 'all is lawful,' I won't renounce—will you renounce me for that, yes?"

Alyosha got up, went to him and softly kissed him on the lips.

"That's plagiarism," cried Ivan, highly delighted. "You stole that from my poem. Thank you, though. Get up, Alyosha, it's time we were going, both of us."

They went out, but stopped when they reached the entrance of the tavern.

"Listen, Alyosha," Ivan began in a resolute voice, "if I am really able to care for the sticky little leaves, I shall only love them remembering you. It's enough for me that you are somewhere here, and I shan't lose my desire for life yet. Is that enough for you? Take it as a declaration of love if you like. And now you go to the right and I to the left. And it's enough, do you hear—enough! I mean even if I don't go away tomorrow (I think I certainly shall go) and we meet again, don't say a word more on these subjects. I beg that particularly. And about Dmitri, too, I ask you especially never speak to me

---

[40] Peter Miusov, a relative of Ivan and Alyosha; a man of enlightened ideas.
[41] Half-brother of Ivan and Alyosha.
[42] Mitya is a variant name of Dmitri.

again," he added, with sudden irritation; "it's all exhausted, it has all been said over and over again, hasn't it? And I'll make you one promise in return for it. When, at thirty, I want to 'dash the cup to the ground,' wherever I may be I'll come to have one more talk with you, even though it were from America—you may be sure of that. I'll come on purpose. It will be very interesting to have a look at you, to see what you'll be by that time. It's rather a solemn promise, you see. And we really may be parting for seven years or ten. Come, go now to your Pater Seraphicus,[43] he is dying. If he dies without you, you will be angry with me for having kept you. Good-bye, kiss me once more; that's right, now go." . . .

---

[43] Father Zossima, the beloved and renowned elder at the monastery, was of great influence upon Alyosha.

24

Friedrich Nietzsche

The Genealogy of Morals

Friedrich Nietzsche (1844–1900) considered Dostoevsky the only one who had taught him anything about human nature. And, as was the case with the Russian novelist, the true greatness of this German philosopher has been recognized only in recent years, when he has been acclaimed as the prophet of existentialism and psychoanalytic doctrine. The earlier views of Nietzsche as a brilliant but incoherent iconoclast and as the mad prophet of German Nazism have been abandoned as distortions. Today, he is accorded a place as one of the original thinkers of the Western tradition; he was one of the first to recognize the absurdity of human existence as the necessary basis for creative life and to stress the importance of irrational and illusional factors in shaping human behavior.

Nietzsche did not put forward a grand philosophical system. His ideas were expressed in an elusive style, as brilliant aphorisms or in short paragraphs; nevertheless, they framed a consistent and searching point of view. His writings are the work of a lonely, sensitive man with profound convictions and integrity, whose later life was marked by suffering and disease culminating in insanity. It was as though Nietzsche strove by intellectual energy to overcome the obstacles of his life and to derive bold, new visions from his plight. In any case, his work has a supercharged quality that does not always make for clarity, but allows him to strike off brilliant insights into the nature and condition of human beings.

Looking at the previous two thousand years of European history, Nietzsche was certain that Europe had undergone a most harmful develop-

Friedrich Nietzsche, *The Genealogy of Morals,* from *The Birth of Tragedy and the Genealogy of Morals,* trans. Francis Golffing. Copyright © 1956 by Doubleday & Company, Inc., 166–82, 185–87. Reprinted by permission of Doubleday & Company, Inc.

ment and was convinced that conditions had never been worse than in his own time, the late nineteenth century. He believed that all kinds of institutions and movements were engaged in reducing human beings to a still lower level of existence, making everything ever smaller and more common; and that, accordingly, any individual who displayed such qualities as strength, boldness, aggressiveness, and power could expect to be vilified and shackled. Thus it was no wonder, suggested Nietzsche, that people living in the nineteenth century, as well as those of preceding ages, had not produced the many and mighty monuments they were capable of creating.

Nietzsche attributed the "wrong turn" in Western civilization to the influence of those Jews who, in the sixth century B.C., *were held in captivity by the Babylonians. Rather than admit that their powerful captors must be the beloved of the deities, the subjugated Jews claimed that being a slave was a sure sign of divine favor and that thus they—powerless, humiliated, trampled, and weak—were the chosen people of God. Nietzsche saw in this claim the beginning of "slave" morality, the religious sanction under which slaves and losers of all sorts had ever since been ganging up on the strong and attempting to destroy the only genuine morality—"master" morality. Christianity, Judaism's successor, Nietzsche considered the embodiment of slave morality* par excellence: *it had not only succeeded in annihilating the Roman Empire but had held Europe in shackles ever afterward. Indeed, in Nietzsche's view of European history, whenever master morality had attempted to reassert itself, some embodiment of slave morality had sought to obliterate it. Thus, as Christianity had triumphed over the ideals of ancient warriors, the Reformation had triumphed over the Renaissance, and liberalism and socialism over feudal aristocracy. The* Genealogy of Morals *(1887), from which the following selection is taken, is Nietzsche's elaboration of these ideas.*

Given the horrible uses made of his treatise by others, it is important to realize that, although he blamed the invention of slave morality on the ancient Jews, Nietzsche was never a religious persecutor. Nor did his heroes, among them the Renaissance soldier Cesare Borgia (1476–1507) and the French emperor Napoleon I (1769–1821), persecute or eliminate the weak and powerless. Those twentieth-century leaders who have dealt monstrously with Jews and other national minorities would have been abhorrent to Nietzsche.

7

By now the reader will have got some notion how readily the priestly system of valuations can branch off from the aristocratic and develop into its opposite. An occasion for such a division is furnished whenever the priest caste and the warrior caste jealously clash with one another and find themselves unable to come to terms. The chivalrous and aristocratic valuations presuppose a strong physique, blooming, even exuberant health, together with all the conditions that guarantee its preservation: combat, adventure, the chase, the dance, war games, etc. The value system of the priestly aristocracy is founded on different presuppositions. So much the worse for them when it becomes a question of war! As we all know, priests are the most evil enemies to have—why should this be so? Because they are the most impotent. It is their impotence which makes their haste so violent and sinister, so cerebral and poisonous. The greatest haters in history—but also the most intelligent haters—have been priests. Beside the brilliance of priestly vengeance all other brilliance fades. Human history would be a dull and stupid thing without the intelligence furnished by its impotents. Let us begin with the most striking example. Whatever else has been done to damage the powerful and great of this earth seems trivial compared with what the Jews have done, that priestly people who succeeded in avenging themselves on their enemies and oppressors by radically inverting all their values, that is, by an act of the most spiritual vengeance.[1] This was a strategy entirely appropriate to a priestly people in whom vindictiveness had gone most deeply underground. It was the Jew who, with frightening consistency, dared to invert the aristocratic value equations good/noble/powerful/beautiful/happy/favored-of-the-gods and maintain, with the furious hatred of the underprivileged and impotent, that "only the poor, the powerless, are good; only the suffering, sick, and ugly, truly blessed. But you noble and mighty ones of the earth will be, to all eternity, the evil, the cruel, the avaricious, the godless, and thus the cursed and damned!" . . . We know who has

---

[1] Nietzsche accused the ancient Jews of having undertaken a transformation of values while in Babylonian Captivity. (On three occasions, beginning with the year 597 B.C., the Babylonian king Nebuchadrezzar II [reigned 605–562 B.C.], having conquered Jerusalem, had its leading Jews deported to Babylon. This enforced stay of some fifty to seventy years is known as the Babylonian Captivity of the Jews. After conquering Babylon in 539 B.C., the Persian king Cyrus the Great [600–529 B.C.] permitted the Jews to return to their homeland.)

fallen heir to this Jewish inversion of values. . . . In reference to the grand and unspeakably disastrous initiative which the Jews have launched by this most radical of all declarations of war, I wish to repeat a statement I made in a different context (*Beyond Good and Evil*),[2] to wit, that it was the Jews who started the slave revolt in morals; a revolt with two millennia of history behind it, which we have lost sight of today simply because it has triumphed so completely.

8

You find that difficult to understand? You have no eyes for something that took two millennia to prevail? . . . There is nothing strange about this: all long developments are difficult to see in the round. From the tree trunk of Jewish vengeance and hatred—the deepest and sublimest hatred in human history, since it gave birth to ideals and a new set of values—grew a branch that was equally unique: a new love, the deepest and sublimest of loves. From what other trunk could this branch have sprung? But let no one surmise that this love represented a denial of the thirst for vengeance, that it contravened the Jewish hatred. Exactly the opposite is true. Love grew out of hatred as the tree's crown, spreading triumphantly in the purest sunlight, yet having, in its high and sunny realm, the same aims—victory, aggrandizement, temptation—which hatred pursued by digging its roots ever deeper into all that was profound and evil. Jesus of Nazareth, the gospel of love made flesh, the "redeemer," who brought blessing and victory to the poor, the sick, the sinners— what was he but temptation in its most sinister and irresistible form, bringing men by a roundabout way to precisely those Jewish values and renovations of the ideal? Has not Israel, precisely by the detour of this "redeemer," this seeming antagonist and destroyer of Israel, reached the final goal of its sublime vindictiveness? Was it not a necessary feature of a truly brilliant politics of vengeance, a farsighted, subterranean, slowly and carefully planned vengeance, that Israel had to deny its true instrument publicly and nail him to the cross like a mortal enemy, so that "the whole world" (meaning all the enemies of Israel) might naïvely swallow the bait? And could one, by straining every resource, hit upon a bait more dangerous than this? What

[2] One of Nietzsche's books, published in the preceding year, 1886.

could equal in debilitating narcotic power the symbol of the "holy cross," the ghastly paradox of a crucified god, the unspeakably cruel mystery of God's self-crucifixion for the benefit of mankind? One thing is certain, that in this sign Israel has by now triumphed over all other, nobler values.

9

—"But what is all this talk about nobler values? Let us face facts: the people have triumphed—or the slaves, the mob, the herd, whatever you wish to call them—and if the Jews brought it about, then no nation ever had a more universal mission on this earth. The lords are a thing of the past, and the ethics of the common man is completely triumphant. I don't deny that this triumph might be looked upon as a kind of blood poisoning, since it has resulted in a mingling of the races, but there can be no doubt that the intoxication has succeeded. The 'redemption' of the human race (from the lords, that is) is well under way; everything is rapidly becoming Judaized, or Christianized, or mob-ized—the word makes no difference. The progress of this poison throughout the body of mankind cannot be stayed; as for its tempo, it can now afford to slow down, become finer, barely audible—there's all the time in the world. . . . Does the Church any longer have a necessary mission or even a *raison d'être?* [3] Or could it be done without? *Quaeritur.* [4] It would almost seem that it retards rather than accelerates that progress. In which case we might consider it useful. But one thing is certain, it has gradually become something crude and lumpish, repugnant to a sensitive intelligence, a truly modern taste. Should it not, at least, be asked to refine itself a bit? . . . It alienates more people today than it seduces. . . . Who among us would be a freethinker, were it not for the Church? It is the Church which offends us, not its poison. . . . Apart from the Church we, too, like the poison. . . ." This was a "freethinker's" reaction to my argument—an honest fellow, as he has abundantly proved, and a democrat to boot. He had been listening to me until that moment, and could not stand to hear my silence. For I have a great deal to be silent about in this matter.

---

[3] Reason (or justification) for being.
[4] The question arises.

10

The slave revolt in morals begins by rancor turning creative and giving birth to values—the rancor of beings who, deprived of the direct outlet of action, compensate by an imaginary vengeance. All truly noble morality grows out of triumphant self-affirmation. Slave ethics, on the other hand, begins by saying *no* to an "outside," an "other," a non-self, and that *no* is its creative act. This reversal of direction of the evaluating look, this invariable looking outward instead of inward, is a fundamental feature of rancor. Slave ethics requires for its inception a sphere different from and hostile to its own. Physiologically speaking, it requires an outside stimulus in order to act at all; all its action is reaction. The opposite is true of aristocratic valuations: such values grow and act spontaneously, seeking out their contraries only in order to affirm themselves even more gratefully and delightedly. Here the negative concepts, *humble, base, bad,* are late, pallid counterparts of the positive, intense and passionate credo,[5] "We noble, good, beautiful, happy ones." Aristocratic valuations may go amiss and do violence to reality, but this happens only with regard to spheres which they do not know well, or from the knowledge of which they austerely guard themselves: the aristocrat will, on occasion, misjudge a sphere which he holds in contempt, the sphere of the common man, the people. On the other hand we should remember that the emotion of contempt, of looking down, provided that it falsifies at all, is as nothing compared with the falsification which suppressed hatred, impotent vindictiveness, effects upon its opponent, though only in effigy. There is in all contempt too much casualness and nonchalance, too much blinking of facts and impatience, and too much inborn gaiety for it ever to make of its object a downright caricature and monster. Hear the almost benevolent nuances the Greek aristocracy, for example, puts into all its terms for the commoner; how emotions of compassion, consideration, indulgence, sugar-coat these words until, in the end, almost all terms referring to the common man survive as expressions for "unhappy," "pitiable" (compare *deilos, deilaios, poneros, mochtheros,*[6] the last two of which properly characterize the common man

---

[5] Creed (statement of beliefs).

[6] In sore distress, in sorry plight, wretched, villainous, rascally. This and the preceding descriptive Greek words have fine shades of meaning, extending from miserable to cowardly to villainous.

as a drudge and beast of burden); how, on the other hand, the words *bad, base, unhappy* have continued to strike a similar note for the Greek ear, with the timbre "unhappy" preponderating. The "well-born" really felt that they were also the "happy." They did not have to construct their happiness factitiously by looking at their enemies, as all rancorous men are wont to do, and being fully active, energetic people they were incapable of divorcing happiness from action. They accounted activity a necessary part of happiness (which explains the origin of the phrase *eu prattein*).[7]

All this stands in utter contrast to what is called happiness among the impotent and oppressed, who are full of bottled-up aggressions. Their happiness is purely passive and takes the form of drugged tranquillity, stretching and yawning, peace, "sabbath," emotional slackness. Whereas the noble lives before his own conscience with confidence and frankness (*gennaîos* "nobly bred" emphasizes the nuance "truthful" and perhaps also "ingenuous"), the rancorous person is neither truthful nor ingenuous nor honest and forthright with himself. His soul squints; his mind loves hide-outs, secret paths, and back doors; everything that is hidden seems to him his own world, his security, his comfort; he is expert in silence, in long memory, in waiting, in provisional self-depreciation, and in self-humiliation. A race of such men will, in the end, inevitably be cleverer than a race of aristocrats, and it will honor sharp-wittedness to a much greater degree, i.e., as an absolutely vital condition for its existence. Among the noble, mental acuteness always tends slightly to suggest luxury and overrefinement. The fact is that with them it is much less important than is the perfect functioning of the ruling, unconscious instincts or even a certain temerity to follow sudden impulses, court danger, or indulge spurts of violent rage, love, worship, gratitude, or vengeance. When a noble man feels resentment, it is absorbed in his instantaneous reaction and therefore does not poison him. Moreover, in countless cases where we might expect it, it never arises, while with weak and impotent people it occurs without fail. It is a sign of strong, rich temperaments that they cannot for long take seriously their enemies, their misfortunes, their *misdeeds;* for such characters have in them an excess of plastic curative power, and also a power of oblivion. (A good modern example of the latter is Mira-

---

[7] To deal well, to do well.

beau,[8] who lacked all memory for insults and meannesses done him, and who was unable to forgive because he had forgotten). Such a man simply shakes off vermin which would get beneath another's skin—and only here, if anywhere on earth, is it possible to speak of "loving one's enemy." The noble person will respect his enemy, and respect is already a bridge to love. . . . Indeed he requires his enemy for himself, as his mark of distinction, nor could he tolerate any other enemy than one in whom he finds nothing to despise and much to esteem. Imagine, on the other hand, the "enemy" as conceived by the rancorous man! For this is his true creative achievement: he has conceived the "evil enemy," the Evil One, as a fundamental idea, and then as a pendant he has conceived a Good One—himself.

11

The exact opposite is true of the noble-minded, who spontaneously creates the notion *good,* and later derives from it the conception of the *bad.* How ill-matched these two concepts look, placed side by side: the bad of noble origin, and the *evil* that has risen out of the cauldron[9] of unquenched hatred! The first is a by-product, a complementary color, almost an afterthought; the second is the beginning, the original creative act of slave ethics. But neither is the conception of good the same in both cases, as we soon find out when we ask ourselves who it is that is really evil according to the code of rancor. The answer is: precisely the good one of the opposite code, that is the noble, the powerful—only colored, reinterpreted, reenvisaged by the poisonous eye of resentment. And we are the first to admit that anyone who knew these "good" ones only as enemies would find them evil enemies indeed. For these same men who, amongst themselves, are so strictly constrained by custom, worship, ritual, gratitude, and by mutual surveillance and jealousy, who are so resourceful in consideration, tenderness, loyalty, pride and friendship, when once they step outside their circle become little better than uncaged beasts of prey. Once abroad in the wilderness, they revel in the freedom from social constraint and compensate for their long confinement in the quietude of their own community. They revert to the innocence of wild animals: we can imagine them return-

---

[8] Comte de Mirabeau (1749–91), an aristocratic French orator who was a leader in the French Revolution.
[9] Boiling pot.

ing from an orgy of murder, arson, rape, and torture, jubilant and at peace with themselves as though they had committed a fraternity prank—convinced, moreover, that the poets for a long time to come will have something to sing about and to praise. Deep within all these noble races there lurks the beast of prey, bent on spoil and conquest. This hidden urge has to be satisfied from time to time, the beast let loose in the wilderness. This goes as well for the Roman, Arabian, German, Japanese nobility as for the Homeric heroes [10] and the Scandinavian vikings. The noble races have everywhere left in their wake the catchword "barbarian." And even their highest culture shows an awareness of this trait and a certain pride in it (as we see, for example, in Pericles' [11] famous funeral oration, when he tells the Athenians: "Our boldness has gained us access to every land and sea, and erected monuments to itself *for both good and evil.*") This "boldness" of noble races, so headstrong, absurd, incalculable, sudden, improbable (Pericles commends the Athenians especially for their *rathumia*), [12] their utter indifference to safety and comfort, their terrible pleasure in destruction, their taste for cruelty—all these traits are embodied by their victims in the image of the "barbarian," the "evil enemy," the Goth or the Vandal. [13] The profound and icy suspicion which the German arouses as soon as he assumes power (we see it happening again today) harks back to the persistent horror with which Europe for many centuries witnessed the raging of the blond Teutonic [14] beast (although all racial connection between the old Teutonic tribes and ourselves has been lost). I once drew attention to the embarrassment Hesiod [15] must have felt when he tried to embody the cultural epochs of mankind in the gold, silver, and iron ages. He could cope with the contradictions inherent in Homer's world, so marvelous on the one hand, so ghastly and brutal on the other, only by making two ages out of one and presenting them in temporal sequence; first, the age of the heroes and demigods of Troy [16] and

---

[10] The ancient heroes of Greek legend described by the poet Homer (*ca.* 800 B.C.) in his *Iliad* and *Odyssey*.

[11] Pericles was an Athenian general and statesman (died 429 B.C.)

[12] Relaxed temperament, nonchalance.

[13] The Goths and the Vandals were barbarian Germanic tribes that ravaged the Roman Empire during the fourth and fifth centuries.

[14] Germanic.

[15] A Greek poet of the eighth century B.C.

[16] A famous ancient city located on the strait called Dardanelles, separating Europe from Asia Minor (near Istanbul); scene of the epic war between the Greeks and Trojans (*ca.* 1200 B.C.).

Thebes,[17] as that world was still remembered by the noble tribes who traced their ancestry to it; and second, the iron age, which presented the same world as seen by the descendants of those who had been crushed, despoiled, brutalized, sold into slavery. If it were true, as passes current nowadays, that the real meaning of culture resides in its power to domesticate man's savage instincts, then we might be justified in viewing all those rancorous machinations by which the noble tribes, and their ideals, have been laid low as the true instruments of culture. But this would still not amount to saying that the *organizers* themselves represent culture. Rather, the exact opposite would be true, as is vividly shown by the current state of affairs. These carriers of the leveling and retributive instincts, these descendants of every European and extra-European slavedom, and especially of the pre-Aryan populations,[18] represent human retrogression most flagrantly. Such "instruments of culture" are a disgrace to man and might make one suspicious of culture altogether. One might be justified in fearing the wild beast lurking within all noble races and in being on one's guard against it, but who would not a thousand times prefer fear when it is accompanied with admiration to security accompanied by the loathsome sight of perversion, dwarfishness, degeneracy? And is not the latter our predicament today? What accounts for our repugnance to man—for there is no question that he makes us suffer? Certainly not our fear of him, rather the fact that there is no longer anything to be feared from him; that the vermin "man" occupies the entire stage; that, tame, hopelessly mediocre, and savorless, he considers himself the apex of historical evolution; and not entirely without justice, since he is still somewhat removed from the mass of sickly and effete creatures whom Europe is beginning to stink of today.

12

Here I want to give vent to a sigh and a last hope. Exactly what is it that I, especially, find intolerable; that I am unable to cope with; that asphyxiates me? A bad smell. The smell of failure, of a soul that has gone stale. God knows it is possible to endure all kinds of misery—vile weather, sickness, trouble, isolation. All this can be coped with,

---

[17] An ancient city in Greece, some forty miles north of Athens; home of the ill-fated royal house of Laius and Oedipus.
[18] Those that lived in Europe before (about) 3000 B.C.

if one is born to a life of anonymity and battle. There will always be moments of re-emergence into the light, when one tastes the golden hour of victory and once again stands foursquare, unshakable, ready to face even harder things, like a bowstring drawn taut against new perils. But, you divine patronesses—if there are any such in the realm beyond good and evil—grant me now and again the sight of something perfect, wholly achieved, happy, magnificently triumphant, something still capable of inspiring fear! Of a man who will justify the existence of mankind, for whose sake one may continue to believe in mankind! . . . The leveling and diminution of European man is our greatest danger; because the sight of him makes us despond. . . . We no longer see anything these days that aspires to grow greater; instead, we have a suspicion that things will continue to go downhill, becoming ever thinner, more placid, smarter, cosier, more ordinary, more indifferent, more Chinese, more Christian— without doubt man is getting "better" all the time. . . . This is Europe's true predicament: together with the fear of man we have also lost the love of man, reverence for man, confidence in man, indeed the *will to man*. Now the sight of man makes us despond. What is nihilism [19] today if not that?

13

But to return to business: our inquiry into the origins of that other notion of goodness, as conceived by the resentful, demands to be completed. There is nothing very odd about lambs disliking birds of prey, but this is no reason for holding it against large birds of prey that they carry off lambs. And when the lambs whisper among themselves, "These birds of prey are evil, and does not this give us a right to say that whatever is the opposite of a bird of prey must be good?" there is nothing intrinsically wrong with such an argument— though the birds of prey will look somewhat quizzically and say, "*We* have nothing against these good lambs; in fact, we love them; nothing tastes better than a tender lamb."—To expect that strength will not manifest itself as strength, as the desire to overcome, to appropriate, to have enemies, obstacles, and triumphs, is every bit as absurd as to expect that weakness will manifest itself as strength. A quantum of strength is equivalent to a quantum of urge, will, activ-

---

[19] The rejection of the certainties offered by religion and morality; in politics, the desire to overturn institutions and reduce them to nothing (Latin, *nihil*).

ity, and it is only the snare of language (of the arch-fallacies of reason petrified in language), presenting all activity as conditioned by an agent—the "subject"—that blinds us to this fact. For, just as popular superstition divorces the lightning from its brilliance, viewing the latter as an activity whose subject is the lightning, so does popular morality divorce strength from its manifestations, as though there were behind the strong a neutral agent, free to manifest its strength or contain it. But no such agent exists; there is no "being" behind the doing, acting, becoming; the "doer" has simply been added to the deed by the imagination—the doing is everything. The common man actually doubles the doing by making the lightning flash; he states the same event once as cause and then again as effect. The natural scientists are no better when they say that "energy *moves,*" "energy *causes.*" For all its detachment and freedom from emotion, our science is still the dupe of linguistic habits; it has never yet got rid of those changelings called "subjects." The atom is one such changeling, another is the Kantian "thing-in-itself." [20] Small wonder, then, that the repressed and smoldering emotions of vengeance and hatred have taken advantage of this superstition and in fact espouse no belief more ardently than that it is within the discretion of the strong to be weak, of the bird of prey to be a lamb. Thus they assume the right of calling the bird of prey to account for being a bird of prey. We can hear the oppressed, downtrodden, violated whispering among themselves with the wily vengefulness of the impotent, "Let us be unlike those evil ones. Let us be good. And the good shall be he who does not do violence, does not attack or retaliate, who leaves vengeance to God, who, like us, lives hidden, who shuns all that is evil, and altogether asks very little of life—like us, the patient, the humble, the just ones." Read in cold blood, this means nothing more than "We weak ones are, in fact, weak. It is a good thing that we do nothing for which we are not strong enough." But this plain fact, this basic prudence, which even the insects have (who, in circumstances of great danger, sham death in order not to have to "do" too much) has tricked itself out in the garb of quiet, virtuous resignation, thanks to the duplicity of impotence—as though the weakness of the weak, which is after all his essence, his natural way of being, his sole and inevitable reality, were a spontaneous act, a meritorious deed. This

---

[20] Immanuel Kant (1724–1804) was a German philosopher who desired to know what an object really was ("thing-in-itself"), rather than what human perception declared it to be.

sort of person requires the belief in a "free subject" able to choose in-differently, out of that instinct of self-preservation which notoriously justifies every kind of lie. It may well be that to this day the subject, or in popular language the soul, has been the most viable of all ar-ticles of faith simply because it makes it possible for the majority of mankind—i.e., the weak and oppressed of every sort—to practice the sublime sleight of hand which gives weakness the appearance of free choice and one's natural disposition the distinction of merit.

<h2 style="text-align:center">14</h2>

Would anyone care to learn something about the way in which ideals are manufactured? Does anyone have the nerve? . . . Well then, go ahead! There's a chink through which you can peek into this murkey shop. But wait just a moment, Mr. Foolhardy; your eyes must grow accustomed to the fickle light. . . . All right, tell me what's going on in there, audacious fellow; now I am the one who is listening.

"I can't see a thing, but I hear all the more. There's a low, cautious whispering in every nook and corner. I have a notion these people are lying. All the sounds are sugary and soft. No doubt you were right; they are transmuting weakness into merit."

"Go on."

"Impotence, which cannot retaliate, into kindness; pusillanimity into humility; submission before those one hates into obedience to One of whom they say that he has commanded this submission—they call him God. The inoffensiveness of the weak, his cowardice, his ineluctable standing and waiting at doors, are being given honori-fic titles such as patience; to be *unable* to avenge oneself is called to be *unwilling* to avenge oneself—even forgiveness ('for they know not what *they* do—we alone know what *they* do.') Also there's some talk of loving one's enemy—accompanied by much sweat."

"Go on."

"I'm sure they are quite miserable, all these whisperers and small-time counterfeiters, even though they huddle close together for warmth. But they tell me that this very misery is the sign of their election by God, that one beats the dogs one loves best, that this misery is perhaps also a preparation, a test, a kind of training, per-haps even more than that: something for which eventually they will be compensated with tremendous interest—in gold? No, in happi-ness. They call this *bliss*."

"Go on."

"Now they tell me that not only are they better than the mighty of this earth, whose spittle they must lick (not from fear—by no means—but because God commands us to honor our superiors), but they are even better off, or at least they will be better off someday. But I've had all I can stand. The smell is too much for me. This shop where they manufacture ideals seem to me to stink of lies."

"But just a moment. You haven't told me anything about the greatest feat of these black magicians, who precipitate the white milk of loving-kindness out of every kind of blackness. Haven't you noticed their most consummate sleight of hand, their boldest, finest, most brilliant trick? Just watch! These vermin, full of vindictive hatred, what are they brewing out of their own poisons? Have you ever heard vengeance and hatred mentioned? Would you ever guess, if you only listened to their words, that these are men bursting with hatred?"

"I see what you mean. I'll open my ears again—and stop my nose. Now I can make out what they seem to have been saying all along: 'We, the good ones, are also the just ones.' They call the thing they seek not retribution but the triumph of justice; the thing they hate is not their enemy, by no means—they hate injustice, ungodliness; the thing they hope for and believe in is not vengeance, the sweet exultation of vengeance ('sweeter than honey' as Homer said) but 'the triumph of God, who is just, over the godless'; what remains to them to love on this earth is not their brothers in hatred, but what they call their 'brothers in love'—all who are good and just."

"And what do they call that which comforts them in all their sufferings—their phantasmagoria[21] of future bliss?"

"Do I hear correctly? They call it Judgment Day, the coming of *their* kingdom, the 'Kingdom of God.' Meanwhile they live in 'faith,' in 'love,' in 'hope.' "

"Stop! I've heard enough."

· · ·

16

Let us conclude. The two sets of valuations, good/bad and good/evil, have waged a terrible battle on this earth, lasting many millennia; and just as surely as the second set has for a long time now been in

---

[21] Fantastic and idle dreams.

the ascendant, so surely are there still places where the battle goes on and the issue remains in suspension. It might even be claimed that by being raised to a higher plane the battle has become much more profound. Perhaps there is today not a single intellectual worth his salt who is not divided on that issue, a battleground for those opposites. The watchwords of the battle, written in characters which have remained legible throughout human history, read: "Rome vs. Israel, Israel vs. Rome." No battle has ever been more momentous than this one. Rome viewed Israel as a monstrosity; the Romans regarded the Jews as *convicted* of hatred against the whole of mankind—and rightly so if one is justified in associating the welfare of the human species with absolute supremacy of aristocratic values. But how did the Jews, on their part, feel about Rome? A thousand indications point to the answer. It is enough to read once more the Revelations of St. John,[22] the most rabid outburst of vindictiveness in all recorded history. (We ought to acknowledge the profound consistency of the Christian instinct in assigning this book of hatred and the most extravagantly doting of the Gospels to the same disciple. There is a piece of truth hidden here, no matter how much literary skulduggery may have gone on.) The Romans were the strongest and most noble people who ever lived. Every vestige of them, every least inscription, is a sheer delight, provided we are able to read the spirit behind the writing. The Jews, on the contrary, were the priestly, rancorous nation *par excellence,* though possessed of an unequaled ethical genius; we need only compare with them nations of comparable endowments, such as the Chinese or the Germans, to sense which occupies the first rank. Has the victory so far been gained by the Romans or by the Jews? But this is really an idle question. Remember who it is before whom one bows down, in Rome itself, as before the essence of all supreme values—and not only in Rome but over half the globe, wherever man has grown tame or desires to grow tame: before three Jews and one Jewess (Jesus of Nazareth, the fisherman Peter, the rug weaver Paul, and Maria, the mother of that Jesus). This is very curious: Rome, without a doubt, has capitulated. It is true that during the Renaissance men witnessed a strange and splendid awakening of the classical ideal; like one buried alive, Rome stirred under the weight of a new Judaic Rome that looked like an ecumenical synagogue and was called the Church.

[22] The last book of the New Testament, supposedly written by St. John the Evangelist, who traditionally is also credited with writing the Gospel according to John.

But presently Israel triumphed once again, thanks to the plebeian rancor of the German and English Reformation, together with its natural corollary, the restoration of the Church—which also meant the restoration of ancient Rome to the quiet of the tomb. In an even more decisive sense did Israel triumph over the classical ideal through the French Revolution. For then the last political nobleness Europe had known, that of seventeenth- and eighteenth-century France, collapsed under the weight of vindictive popular instincts. A wilder enthusiasm was never seen. And yet, in the midst of it all, something tremendous, something wholly unexpected happened: the ancient classical ideal appeared incarnate and in unprecedented splendor before the eyes and conscience of mankind. Once again, stronger, simpler, more insistent than ever, over against the lying shibboleth [23] of the rights of the majority, against the furious tendency toward leveling out and debasement, sounded the terrible yet exhilarating shibboleth of the "prerogative of the few." Like a last signpost to an *alternative* route Napoleon [24] appeared, most isolated and anachronistic of men, the embodiment of the noble ideal. It might be well to ponder what exactly Napoleon, that synthesis of the brutish with the more than human, did represent. . . .

---

[23] A slogan or phrase associated with a particular group.
[24] Napoleon I (1769–1821), French emperor.

25

Sigmund Freud

The Sexual Life Of Human Beings

Like Marx and Darwin, Sigmund Freud (1856–1939) was a major influence on the contemporary view of human existence. What others had offered as poetic insights, Freud established by clinical observation and persuasive reasoning, as well as by speculative leaps of the imagination. He provided a naturalistic explanation of the vital role of unconscious elements in human behavior and destroyed the old view of the self as a conscious rational entity. His great influence is apparent in modern psychiatry, literature, art, and social thought.

An Austrian neurologist, who was himself zealous in the observance of conventional middle-class moralities, Freud began his career in a rather unrevolutionary manner: in his treatment of the mentally disturbed, he used methods that were firmly in the tradition of nineteenth-century positivistic science. Increasingly, however, Freud came to rely on imaginative insights and on literary myths and symbols to clarify the deepest springs of behavior. He nevertheless maintained his faith in reason as the indispensable means of finding the truths that would make people free.

Freud applied his findings in the study of neurotics to normal individuals and to society as a whole. He explained all human behavior as the result of instinctual drives, such as the sexual and aggressive urges, that are suppressed because they are unpleasant or socially disapproved. He saw the conscious mind as a battleground of warring impulses, where only a compromise

effected by the suppression of some of them can produce the realistic adjust-
ment necessary for "normal" living.

One of the greatest contributions made by Freud to the understanding of
human behavior was his discovery of the importance the instinctual develop-
ment that occurs in infancy can have in adult life. Freud's declaration that the
basic traits of personality are set before age five was received initially with
great disbelief. His contemporaries were convinced that the later years of ado-
lescence and, especially, the years of young adulthood play the most impor-
tant role in personality development. Another Freudian "discovery,"
infantile sexuality, provoked outright rejection and scorn. In the nineteenth
century it was universally held that infants and preadolescents are asexual
and that sexuality begins between ages twelve and fourteen. But observations
made in the course of his clinical work led Freud to believe that sexuality is
an aspect of human beings from almost the first day of life. He felt that those
who claimed that human sexual life begins in the early teens made the mis-
take of considering only sexuality directly related to genital areas. He main-
tained not only that infantile sexuality exists but that it passes through stages
linked with different functions and developmental changes in the human
body. Since he felt that any disturbances of instinctual development in in-
fancy would have an impact in adult life, Freud concluded that a frank and
fearless examination of infantile sexuality was a prerequisite to under-
standing adult norms and perversions.

The following selection, which explains his views on some previously
"taboo" subjects, is taken from a series of lectures that Freud gave on psycho-
analysis. This particular lecture was given before students at the University
of Vienna near the end of 1916, and it was first published in May 1917.
Much of it remains controversial, but it demonstrates the path-breaking na-
ture of Freud's work.

Ladies and gentlemen,—One would certainly have supposed that
there could be no doubt as to what is to be understood by 'sexual'.
First and foremost, what is sexual is something improper, something
one ought not to talk about. I have been told that the pupils of a celebrated psychiatrist made an attempt once to convince their teacher of
how frequently the symptoms of hysterical patients represent sexual
things. For this purpose they took him to the bedside of a female
hysteric, whose attacks were an unmistakable imitation of the pro-

cess of childbirth. But with a shake of his head he remarked: 'Well, there's nothing sexual about childbirth.' Quite right. Childbirth need not in every case be something improper.

I see that you take offence at my joking about such serious things. But it is not altogether a joke. Seriously, it is not easy to decide what is covered by the concept 'sexual'. Perhaps the only suitable definition would be 'everything that is related to the distinction between the two sexes'. But you will regard that as colourless and too comprehensive. If you take the fact of the sexual act as the central point, you will perhaps define as sexual everything which, with a view to obtaining pleasure, is concerned with the body, and in particular with the sexual organs, of someone of the opposite sex, and which in the last resort aims at the union of the genitals and the performance of the sexual act. But if so you will really not be very far from the equation of what is sexual with what is improper, and childbirth will really not be anything sexual. If, on the other hand, you take the reproductive function as the nucleus of sexuality, you risk excluding a whole number of things which are not aimed at reproduction but which are certainly sexual, such as masturbation and perhaps even kissing. But we are already prepared to find that attempts at a definition always lead to difficulties; so let us renounce the idea of doing better in this particular case. We may suspect that in the course of the development of the concept 'sexual' something has happened which has resulted in what Silberer has aptly called an 'error of superimposition'.[1]

On the whole, indeed, when we come to think of it, we are not quite at a loss in regard to what it is that people call sexual. Something which combines a reference to the contrast between the sexes, to the search for pleasure, to the reproductive function and to the characteristic of something that is improper and must be kept secret—some such combination will serve for all practical purposes in everyday life. But for science that is not enough. By means of careful investigations (only made possible, indeed, by disinterested self-discipline) we have come to know groups of individuals whose 'sexual life' deviates in the most striking way from the usual picture of the average. Some of these 'perverse' people have, we might say,

---

[1] H. Silberer, *Problems of Mysticism and its Symbolism* (New York, 1917). What Silberer suggested was that individuals may think they are looking at a *single* thing when, actually, they are viewing *two different* things, one superimposed upon the other.

struck the distinction between the sexes off their programme. Only members of their own sex can rouse their sexual wishes; those of the other sex, and especially their sexual parts, are not a sexual object for them at all, and in extreme cases are an object of disgust. This implies, of course, that they have abandoned any share in reproduction. We call such people homosexuals or inverts. They are men and women who are often, though not always, irreproachably fashioned in other respects, of high intellectual and ethical development, the victims only of this one fatal deviation. Through the mouth of their scientific spokesmen they represent themselves as a special variety of the human species—a 'third sex' which has a right to stand on an equal footing beside the other two. We shall perhaps have an opportunity of examining their claims critically. Of course they are not, as they also like to assert, an *'élite'* of mankind; there are at least as many inferior and useless individuals among them as there are among those of a different sexual kind.

This class of perverts at any rate behave to their sexual objects in approximately the same way as normal people do to theirs. But we now come to a long series of abnormal people whose sexual activity diverges more and more widely from what seems desirable to a sensible person. In their multiplicity and strangeness they can only be compared to the grotesque monsters painted by Breughel[2] for the temptation of St. Anthony or to the long procession of vanished gods and believers which Flaubert leads past, before the eyes of his pious penitent.[3] Such a medley calls for some kind of arrangement if it is not to confuse our senses. We accordingly divide them into those in whom, like the homosexuals, the sexual *object* has been changed, and others in whom the sexual *aim* is what has primarily been altered. The first group includes those who have renounced the union of the two genitals and who replace the genitals of one of the couple engaged in the sexual act by some other part or region of the body; in this they disregard the lack of suitable organic arrangements as well as any impediment offered by feelings of disgust. (They replace the vulva, for instance, by the mouth or anus.) Others follow, who, it is true, still retain the genitals as an object—not, however, on account of their sexual function but of other functions in which the genital plays a part either for anatomical reasons or be-

[2] Pieter Breughel, the Elder (*ca.* 1520–1569), a Flemish painter.
[3] In *La Tentation de Saint Antoine,* Part V of the final version (1874), by the French novelist Gustave Flaubert (1821–1880).

cause of its propinquity. We find from them that the excretory functions, which have been put aside as improper during the upbringing of children, retain the ability to attract the whole of sexual interest. Then come others again, who have abandoned the genital as an object altogether, and have taken some other part of the body as the object they desire—a woman's breast, a foot or a plait of hair. After them come others for whom parts of the body are of no importance but whose every wish is satisfied by a piece of clothing, a shoe, a piece of underclothing—the fetishists. Later in the procession come people who require the whole object indeed, but make quite definite demands of it—strange or horrible—even that it must have become a defenceless corpse, and who, using criminal violence, make it into one so that they may enjoy it. But enough of this kind of horror!

The second group is led by perverts who have made what is normally only an introductory or preparatory act into the aim of their sexual wishes. They are people whose desire it is to look at the other person or to feel him or to watch him in the performance of his intimate actions, or who expose parts of their own bodies which should be covered, in the obscure expectation that they may be rewarded by a corresponding action in return. Next come the sadists, puzzling people whose tender endeavors have no other aim than to cause pain and torment to their object, ranging from humiliation to severe physical injuries; and, as though to counterbalance them, their counterparts, the masochists, whose only pleasure it is to suffer humiliations and torments of every kind from their loved object either symbolically or in reality. There are still others in whom several of these abnormal preconditions are united and intertwined; and lastly, we must learn that each of these groups is to be found in two forms: alongside of those who seek their sexual satisfaction in reality are those who are content merely to *imagine* that satisfaction, who need no real object at all, but can replace it by their phantasies.

Now there cannot be the slightest doubt that all these crazy, eccentric and horrible things really constitute the sexual activity of these people. Not only do they themselves regard them as such and are aware that they are substitutes for each other, but we must admit that they play the same part in their lives as normal sexual satisfaction does in ours; they make the same, often excessive sacrifices for them, and we can trace both in the rough and in finer detail the points at which these abnormalities are based on what is normal and the points at which they diverge from it. Nor can you fail to notice that here once again you find the characteristic of being improper, which clings to sexual activity, though here it is for the most part intensified to the point of being abominable.

Well, Ladies and Gentlemen, what attitude are we to adopt to these unusual kinds of sexual satisfaction? Indignation, an expression of our personal repugnance and an assurance that we ourselves do not share these lusts will obviously be of no help. Indeed, that is not what we have been asked for. When all is said and done, what we have here is a field of phenomena like any other. A denial in the form of an evasive suggestion that after all these are only rarities and curiosities would be easy to refute. On the contrary, we are dealing with quite common and widespread phenomena. If, however, it is argued that we need not allow our views of sexual life to be misled by them because they are one and all aberrations and deviations of the sexual instinct, a serious answer is called for. Unless we can understand these pathological forms of sexuality and can co-ordinate them with normal sexual life, we cannot understand normal sexuality either. In short, it remains an unavoidable task to give a complete theoretical account of how it is that these perversions can occur and of their connection with what is described as normal sexuality.

We shall be helped in this by a piece of information and two fresh observations. We owe the former to Iwan Bloch.[4] It corrects the view that all these perversions are 'signs of degeneracy' by showing that aberrations of this kind from the sexual aim, lossenings like these of the tie with the sexual object, have occurred from time immemorial, in all periods known to us, among all peoples, the most primitive and the most civilized, and have occasionally obtained toleration and general recognition. The two observations were derived from the psycho-analytic investigation of neurotics; they are bound to have a decisive influence on our view of the sexual perversions.

I have said that neurotic symptoms are substitutes for sexual satisfaction, and I indicated to you that the confirmation of this assertion by the analysis of symptoms would come up against a number of difficulties. For it can only be justified if under 'sexual satisfaction' we include the satisfaction of what are called perverse sexual needs, since an interpretation of symptoms of that kind is forced upon us with surprising frequency. The claim made by homosexuals or in-

[4] Pseudonym of Eugen Dühren (1872–1922), a dermatologist and one of the founders of the study of human sexuality.

verts to being exceptions collapses at once when we learn that homosexual impulses are invariably discovered in every single neurotic, and that a fair number of symptoms give expression to this latent inversion. Those who call themselves homosexuals are only the conscious and manifest inverts, whose number is nothing compared to that of the *latent* homosexuals. We are compelled, however, to regard choice of an object of one's own sex as a divergence in erotic life which is of positively habitual occurrence, and we are learning more and more to ascribe an especially high importance to it. No doubt this does not do away with the differences between manifest homosexuality and a normal attitude; their practical significance remains, but their theoretical value is greatly diminished. We have even found that a particular disease, paranoia, which is not to be counted among the transference neuroses, regularly arises from an attempt to fend off excessively strong homosexual impulses. You will perhaps recall that one of our patients behaved in her obsessional action like a man, her own husband whom she had left; neurotic women very commonly produce symptoms in this way in the character of a man. Even if this is not actually to be regarded as homosexuality, it is closely related to its preconditions.

As you probably know, the hysterical neurosis can produce its symptoms in any system of organs and so disturb any function. Analysis shows that in this way all the so-called perverse impulses which seek to replace the genital by some other organ manifest themselves: these organs are then behaving like substitutive genitals. The symptoms of hysteria have actually led us to the view that the bodily organs, besides the functional part they play, must be recognized as having a sexual (erotogenic) significance, and that the execution of the first of these tasks is disturbed if the second of them makes too many claims. Countless sensations and innervations which we come across as symptoms of hysteria in organs that have no apparent connection with sexuality are in this way revealed to us as being in the nature of fulfilments of perverse sexual impulses in relation to which other organs have acquired the significance of the sexual parts. We learn too to what a large extent the organs for the intake of nourishment and for excretion can in particular become the vehicles of sexual excitation. Here, then, we have the same thing that we were shown by the perversions; only in their case it was visible easily and unmistakably, whereas in hysteria we have to take a circuitous path by way of the interpretation of symptoms, and do not then ascribe the perverse sexual impulses concerned to the subject's consciousness but locate them in his unconscious.

Of the many symptomatic pictures in which obsessional neurosis appears, the most important turn out to be those provoked by the pressure of excessively strong sadistic sexual impulses (perverse, therefore, in their aim). The symptoms, indeed, in accordance with the structure of an obsessional neurosis, serve predominantly as a *defense* against these wishes or give expression to the struggle between satisfaction and defense. But satisfaction does not come off too badly either; it succeeds in roundabout ways in putting itself into effect in the patients' behaviour and is preferably directed against themselves and makes them into self-tormentors. Other forms of the neurosis, the brooding kinds, correspond to an excessive sexualization of actions which ordinarily have their place on the path to normal sexual satisfaction—an excessive sexualization of wanting to look or to touch or to explore. Here we have the explanation of the great importance of the fear of touching and of the obsession for washing. An unsuspectedly large proportion of obsessional actions may be traced back to masturbation, of which they are disguised repetitions and modifications; it is a familiar fact that masturbation, though a single and uniform action, accompanies the most various forms of sexual phantasying.

I should not have much difficulty in giving you a far more intimate picture of the relations between perversion and neurosis; but I think what I have already said will serve our purpose. We must however guard against being misled by what I have told you of the meaning of symptoms into over-estimating the frequency and intensity of people's perverse inclinations. It is possible, as you have heard, to fall ill of a neurosis as a result of a frustration of normal sexual satisfaction. But when a real frustration like this occurs, the need moves over on to abnormal methods of sexual excitation. . . You will realize that as a result of this 'collateral' damming-back [of the normal sexual current] the perverse impulses must emerge more strongly than they would have if normal sexual satisfaction had met with no obstacle in the real world. Moreover a similar influence is to be recognized also as affecting the *manifest* perversions. In some cases they are provoked or made active if the normal satisfaction of the sexual instinct encounters too great difficulties for temporary reasons or because of permanent social regulations. In other cases, it is true, the inclination to perversions is quite independent of such favouring conditions; they are, we might say, the normal species of sexual life for those particular individuals.

For the moment, perhaps, you may have an impression that I have confused rather than explained the relation between normal and perverse sexuality. But you must bear the following consideration in mind. If it is true that increased difficulty in obtaining normal sexual satisfaction in real life, or deprivation of that satisfaction, brings out perverse inclinations in people who had not shown any previously, we must suppose that there was something in these people which came half-way to meet the perversions; or, if you prefer it, the perversions must have been present in them in a latent form.

And this brings us to the second novelty that I announced to you [before]. For psycho-analytic research has had to concern itself, too, with the sexual life of children, and this is because the memories and associations arising during the analysis of symptoms [in adults] regularly led back to the early years of childhood. What we inferred from these analyses was later confirmed point by point by direct observations of children. And it then turned out that all these inclinations to perversion had their roots in childhood, that children have a predisposition to all of them and carry them out to an extent corresponding to their immaturity—in short, that perverse sexuality is nothing else than a magnified infantile sexuality split up into its separate impulses.

At all events you will now see the perversions in a new light and no longer fail to realize their connection with the sexual life of human beings: but at the price of what surprises and of what feelings of distress over these incongruities! No doubt you will feel inclined at first to deny the whole business: the fact that children have anything that can be described as sexual life, the correctness of our observations and the justification for finding any kinship between the behaviour of children and what is later condemned as perversion. So allow me to begin by explaining to you the motives for your opposition, and then to present you with the sum of our observations. To suppose that children have no sexual life—sexual excitations and needs and a kind of satisfaction—but suddenly acquire it between the ages of twelve and fourteen, would (quite apart from any observations) be as improbable, and indeed senseless, biologically as to suppose that they brought no genitals with them into the world and only grew them at the time of puberty. What *does* awaken in them at this time is the reproductive function, which makes use for its purposes of physical and mental material already present. You are committing the error of confusing sexuality and reproduction and by doing so you are blocking your path to an understanding of sexuality, the perversions and the neuroses. This error is, however, a tendentious one. Strangely enough, it has its source in the fact that you yourselves were once children and, while you were children, came under the influence of education. For society must undertake as one of its most important educative tasks to tame and restrict the sexual instinct when it breaks out as an urge to reproduction, and to subject it to an individual will which is identical with the bidding of society. It is also concerned to postpone the full development of the instinct till the child shall have reached a certain degree of intellectual maturity, for, with the complete irruption of the sexual instinct, educability is for practical purposes at an end. Otherwise, the instinct would break down every dam and wash away the laboriously erected work of civilization. Nor is the task of taming it ever an easy one; its success is sometimes too small, sometimes too great. The motive of human society is in the last resort an economic one; since it does not possess enough provisions to keep its members alive unless they work, it must restrict the number of its members and divert their energies from sexual activity to work. It is faced, in short, by the eternal, primaeval exigencies of life, which are with us to this day.

Experience must no doubt have taught the educators that the task of making the sexual will of the new generation tractable could only be carried out if they began to exercise their influence very early, if they did not wait for the storm of puberty but intervened already in the sexual life of children which is preparatory to it. For this reason almost all infantile sexual activities were forbidden to children and frowned upon; an ideal was set up of making the life of children asexual, and in course of time things came to the point at which people really believed they were asexual and thereafter science pronounced this as its doctrine. To avoid contradicting their belief and their intentions, people since then overlook the sexual activities of children (no mean achievement) or are content in science to take a different view of them. Children are pure and innocent, and anyone who describes them otherwise can be charged with being an infamous blasphemer against the tender and sacred feelings of mankind.

Children are alone in not falling in with these conventions. They assert their animal rights with complete *naïveté* and give constant evidence that they have still to travel the road to purity. Strangely enough, the people who deny the existence of sexuality in children do not on that account become milder in their educational efforts but pursue the manifestations of what they deny exists with the utmost severity—describing them as 'childish naughtinesses'. It is also of the highest theoretical interest that the period of life which contradicts the prejudice of an asexual childhood most glaringly—the years of a child's life up to the age of five or six—is afterwards covered in most people by the veil of amnesia which is only completely torn away by an analytic enquiry, though it has been permeable earlier for the construction of a few dreams.

I will now set out before you what is most definitely known about the sexual life of children. Let me at the same time, for convenience sake, introduce the concept of 'libido'. On the exact analogy of 'hunger', we use 'libido' as the name of the force (in this case that of the sexual instinct, as in the case of hunger that of the nutritive instinct) by which the instinct manifests itself. Other concepts, such as sexual 'excitation' and 'satisfaction', call for no explanation. You yourselves will easily perceive that the sexual activities of infants in arms are mostly a matter of interpretation, or you will probably use that as a ground of objection. These interpretations are arrived at on the basis of analytic examinations made by tracing from the symptoms backwards. In an infant the first impulses of sexuality make their appearance attached to other vital functions. His main interest is, as you know, directed to the intake of nourishment; when children fall asleep after being sated at the breast, they show an expression of blissful satisfaction which will be repeated later in life after the experience of a sexual orgasm. This would be too little on which to base an inference. But we observe how an infant will repeat the action of taking in nourishment without making a demand for further food; here, then, he is not actuated by hunger. We describe this as sensual sucking, and the fact that in doing this he falls asleep once more with a blissful expression shows us that the act of sensual sucking has in itself alone brought him satisfaction. Soon, as we know, things come to a point at which he cannot go to sleep without having sucked. A paediatrician in Budapest, Dr. Lindner, was the first to point out long ago the sexual nature of this activity. Those who are in charge of children, and who have no theoretical views on the subject, seem to form a similar judgement of sucking. They have no doubt of its only purpose being to obtain pleasure, class it as one of a child's 'naughtinesses' and compel him to abandon it by causing him distress, if he will not give it up of his own accord. Thus we learn that infants perform actions which have no purpose other than obtaining pleasure. It is our belief that they first experience this pleasure in connection with taking nourishment but that they soon learn to separate it from that accompanying condition. We can only refer this pleasure to an excitation of the areas of the mouth and lips; we call those parts of the body 'erotogenic zones' and describe the pleasure derived from sucking as a sexual one. We shall no doubt have to discuss further whether this description is justifiable.

If an infant could speak, he would no doubt pronounce the act of sucking at his mother's breast by far the most important in his life. He is not far wrong in this, for in this single act he is satisfying at once the two great vital needs. We are therefore not surprised to learn from psycho-analysis how much psychical importance the act retains all through life. Sucking at the mother's breast is the starting-point of the whole of sexual life, the unmatched prototype of every later sexual satisfaction, to which phantasy often enough recurs in times of need. This sucking involves making the mother's breast the first object of the sexual instinct. I can give you no idea of the important bearing of this first object upon the choice of every later object, of the profound effects it has in its transformations and substitutions in even the remotest regions of our sexual life. But at first the infant, in his sucking activity, gives up this object and replaces it by a part of his own body. He begins to suck his thumbs or his own tongue. In this way he makes himself independent of the consent of the external world as regards gaining pleasure, and besides this he increases it by adding the excitation of a second area of his body. The erotogenic zones are not all equally generous in yielding pleasure; it is therefore an important experience when the infant, as Lindner reports, discovers, in the course of feeling around, the specially excitable regions afforded by his genitals and so finds his way from sucking to masturbation.

In forming this opinion of sensual sucking we have already become acquainted with two decisive characteristics of infantile sexuality. It makes its appearance attached to the satisfaction of the major organic needs, and it behaves *auto-erotically*—that is, it seeks and finds its objects in the infant's own body. What has been shown most clearly in connection with the intake of nourishment is repeated in part with the excretions. We conclude that infants have feelings of pleasure in the process of evacuating urine and faeces and that they soon contrive to arrange those actions in such a way as to bring them the greatest possible yield of pleasure through the corresponding excitations of the erotogenic zones of the mucous membrane. It is here for the first time (as Lou Andreas-Salomé[5] has subtly perceived) that they encounter the external world as an inhibiting power, hostile to their desire for pleasure, and have a glimpse of later conflicts both external and internal. An infant must not produce his excreta at whatever moment he chooses, but when other people decide that he shall. In order to induce him to forgo these sources of pleasure, he is told that everything that has to do with these functions is improper and must be kept secret. This is where he is first obliged to exchange pleasure for social respectability. To begin with, his attitude to his excreta themselves is quite different. He feels no disgust at his faeces, values them as a portion of his own body with which he will not readily part, and makes use of them as his first 'gift', to distinguish people whom he values especially highly. Even after education has succeeded in its aim of making these inclinations alien to him, he carries on his high valuation of faeces in his estimate of 'gifts' and 'money'. On the other hand he seems to regard his achievements in urinating with peculiar pride.[6]

I know you have been wanting for a long time to interrupt me and exclaim: 'Enough of these atrocities! You tell us that defaecating is a source of sexual satisfaction, and already exploited in infancy! that faeces is a valuable substance and that the anus is a kind of genital! We don't believe all that—but we do understand why paediatricians and educationists have given a wide berth to psycho-analysis and its findings.' No, Gentlemen. You have merely forgotten that I have been trying to introduce the facts of infantile sexual life to you in connection with the facts of the sexual perversions. Why should you not be aware that for a large number of adults, homosexual and heterosexual alike, the anus does really take over the role of the vagina in sexual intercourse? And that there are many people who retain a voluptuous feeling in defaecating all through their lives and describe

[5] A novelist (1861–1937) who had connections with the Vienna circle of psychoanalysts and with Freud.

[6] The relationships between faeces and money were discussed by Freud in a paper called "Character and Anal Eroticism" (1908) and in a later one, almost contemporary with the present lecture, called "On Transformations of Instinct as Exemplified in Anal Eroticism" (1917). The connection between urination and pride had been shown in a dream-analysis that appeared in *The Interpretation of Dreams* (1900).

it as being far from small? As regards interest in the act of defaeca-
tion and enjoyment in watching someone else defaecating, you can
get children themselves to confirm the fact when they are a few years
older and able to tell you about it. Of course, you must not have systematically intimidated them beforehand, or they will quite understand that they must be silent on the subject. And as to the other
things that you are anxious not to believe, I will refer you to the
findings of analysis and of the direct observation of children and will
add that it calls for real ingenuity not to see all this or to see it differently. Nor do I complain if you find the kinship between infantile
sexual activity and sexual perversions something very striking. But it
is in fact self-evident: if a child has a sexual life at all it is bound to be
of a perverse kind; for, except for a few obscure hints, children are
without what makes sexuality into the reproductive function. On the
other hand, the abandonment of the reproductive function is the
common feature of all perversions. We actually describe a sexual activity as perverse if it has given up the aim of reproduction and pursues the attainment of pleasure as an aim independent of it. So, as
you will see, the breach and turning-point in the development of
sexual life lies in its becoming subordinate to the purposes of reproduction. Everything that happens before this turn of events and
equally everything that disregards it and that aims solely at obtaining
pleasure is given the uncomplimentary name of 'perverse' and as such
is proscribed.

Allow me, therefore, to proceed with my brief account of infantile
sexuality. What I have already reported of two systems of organs
[nutritional and excretory] might be confirmed in reference to the
others. A child's sexual life is indeed made up entirely of the activities of a number of component instincts which seek, independently
of one another, to obtain pleasure, in part from the subject's own
body and in part already from an external object. Among these
organs the genitals come into prominence very soon. There are people in whom obtaining pleasure from their own genitals, without the
assistance of any other genitals or of an object, continues uninterrup-
tedly from infantile masturbation to the unavoidable masturbation of
puberty and persists for an indefinite length of time afterwards. In-
cidentally, the topic of masturbation is not one that can be so easily
disposed of: it is something that calls for examination from many
angles.

Though I am anxious to cut short this discussion still further, I must nevertheless tell you a little about the sexual researches of children: they are too characteristic of infantile sexuality and of too great significance for the symptomatology of the neuroses to be passed over. Infantile sexual researches begin very early, sometimes before the third year of life. They do not relate to the distinction between the sexes, for this means nothing to children, since they (or at any rate boys) attribute the same male genital to both sexes. If, afterwards, a boy makes the discovery of the vagina from seeing his little sister or a girl playmate, he tries, to begin with, to disavow the evidence of his senses, for he cannot imagine a human creature like himself who is without such a precious portion. Later on, he takes fright at the possibility thus presented to him; and any threats that may have been made to him earlier, because he took too intense an interest in his little organ, now produce a deferred effect. He comes under the sway of the castration complex, the form of which plays a great part in the construction of his character if he remains normal, in his neurosis if he falls ill, and in his resistances if he comes into analytic treatment. As regards little girls, we can say of them that they feel greatly at a disadvantage owing to their lack of a big, visible penis, that they envy boys for possessing one and that, in the main for this reason, they develop a wish to be a man—a wish that reemerges later on, in any neurosis that may arise if they meet with a mishap in playing a feminine part. In her childhood, moreover, a girl's clitoris takes on the role of a penis entirely: it is characterized by special excitability and is the area in which auto-erotic satisfaction is obtained. The process of a girl's becoming a woman depends very much on the clitoris passing on this sensitivity to the vaginal orifice in good time and completely. In cases of what is known as sexual anaesthesia in women the clitoris has obstinately retained its sensitivity.

The sexual interest of children begins by turning, rather, to the problem of where babies come from—the same problem which underlies the question put by the Theban Sphinx [7]—and it is most often raised by egoistic fears on the arrival of a new baby. The reply which is ready to hand in the nursery, that babies are brought by the stork,

---

[7] In Greek mythology, a terrible-looking monster that lived on a rock outside the Grecian city of Thebes. Those who passed by her were asked a certain riddle. If they could not solve it, she either devoured or dashed them against the rock. Her question was: What creature walks on four legs in the morning, two at noon, and three in the evening? (The answer: man.)

comes up against disbelief on the part even of small children far oftener than we are aware. The sense of being defrauded of the truth by the grown-ups contributes much to making children feel lonely and to developing their independence. But a child is not in a position to solve this problem by his own means. His undeveloped sexual constitution sets definite limits to his power of perception. He begins by supposing that babies come from people taking in something special in their food, nor does he know that only women can have babies. Later he becomes aware of this limitation and ceases to regard eating as the origin of babies—though the theory persists in fairy tales. When the child is grown bigger, he soon notices that his father must play some part in getting babies, but he cannot guess what. If he happens to witness a sexual act, he regards it as an attempt at subjugation, a struggle, and this is the sadistic misunderstanding of coition. But at first he does not connect this act with the coming into being of a baby. So, too, if he finds traces of blood on his mother's bed or on her underclothes, he takes it as a sign that she has been injured by his father. Still later in childhood, he no doubt suspects that the man's sexual organ has an essential share in producing babies, but the only function he can attribute to that part of the body is micturition.[8]

From the very first, children are at one in thinking that babies must be born through the bowel; they must make their appearance like lumps of faeces. This theory is not abandoned until all anal interests have been deprived of their value, and it is then replaced by the hypothesis that the navel comes open or that the area of the breast between the nipples is where birth takes place. In this way the child in the course of his researches comes nearer to the facts about sex, or, feeling at a loss owing to his ignorance, he passes them by till, usually in the years before puberty, he is given what is as a rule a depreciatory and incomplete explanation, which often produces traumatic effects.

You will no doubt have heard, Gentlemen, that in psychoanalysis the concept of what is sexual has been unduly extended in order to support the theses of the sexual causation of the neuroses and the sexual meaning of symptoms. You are now in a position to judge for yourselves whether this extension is unjustified. We have only extended the concept of sexuality far enough to be able to comprise the

---

[8] Urination.

sexual life of perverts and of children. We have, that is to say, given it back its true compass. What is called sexuality outside psychoanalysis relates only to a restricted sexual life, which serves the purpose of reproduction and is described as normal.

26

Carl G. Jung

Autobiography

As Freud is esteemed for his keen ability to observe, and his intellectual courage, Carl G. Jung (1875–1961) must be admired for his open mind and freedom from shackling dogmatism. Born in Switzerland to the family of a Swiss Reformed pastor, and blessed with a number of gifted ancestors, he became aware of himself and the world around him while still very young. At an age when children ordinarily absorb their experiences in a matter-of-fact fashion, Jung pondered his observations and dreams, seeking an explanation for them. Even as a child he contemplated the existence of two worlds. One was the world of facts, the realm of the sciences, which in school demanded his attention. The other was the world of value, which gave meaning to what he had learned and experienced. Though endowed with a dual personality, of complementary aspects rather than contradictory ones, Jung eventually had to choose between the sciences and the humanities. Though both were appealing, the sciences prevailed; and he decided to study medicine rather than archaeology or religion.

In 1900, while preparing for his final medical exam, Jung realized that psychiatry was the field to which he wanted to devote his life. Psychiatry was then still in its infancy—groping for answers rather than offering them—and among those who were also captivated by it was the Viennese physician Sigmund Freud. When, in the same year, Freud's pioneering work came to his attention, Jung was at once fascinated by Freud's penetrating perceptions and daring speculations. In 1906 the two men met for the first time, and shortly thereafter Freud decided that this younger man should be the person to preserve and continue his work. Jung, however, who meanwhile had begun his research into mythology, soon came to the conclusion that Freud's dogmatic nature and their differing intellectual orientations, would keep him from assuming the Freudian intellectual heritage.

Indeed, indications of disharmony between Jung and Freud were discernible as early as 1912. The break came over a number of issues: for example, the role of sexuality in infant behavior, and Freud's insistence that sexuality is the prime psychological force in the life of a human being. Jung judged the latter an unwarranted dogmatism, especially in view of the fact that inquiry into the human psyche was of very recent date and, in his view, needed to be pursued without restrictions. Another reason for disagreement was the fact that Freud focused on certain key events in a person's life, rather than considering them in relation to the person's cultural heritage. Elements of this heritage, especially myth, philosophy, and religion, were of primary importance to Jung; whereas Freud consigned them to the realm of the occult.

Even from his recollections of childhood experiences, it is clear that Jung possessed an unusual ability to grasp and understand meanings that lie beneath the surface. As a young man, he was shocked that his father and members of their parish performed the rituals of religion without being gripped by them. While pursuing his studies, Jung perceived that all individuals in the West engage in many visible acts whose meaning has been either lost or forgotten. He attributed this loss to the fact that Western culture has valued thought and experience over feeling and intuition, or result and process over meaning and vision. Jung made the rediscovery of meaning and vision the center of his life's work. He believed that as one progresses in unlocking myth, religion, and philosophy, one discovers an evolving pattern of instincts, potentials, and needs common to all humankind—which he termed archetypes. One of the conclusions he came to was that dreams can indicate that a particular psyche is out of harmony with the inherited patterns of human culture. Consequently, he saw dreams as pointers toward psychic growth—unlike Freud, who saw them as indicators of unresolved crises of one's past.

Some have found Jung's work too elusive and esoteric—more like Plato's philosophy of two thousand years ago than like modern science. Yet it seems that, as time goes on, Jung's influence on psychological study increases and the Jungian viewpoint reaches an ever larger portion of society.

PROLOGUE

My life is a story of the self-realization of the unconscious. Everything in the unconscious seeks outward manifestation, and the personality too desires to evolve out of its unconscious conditions and to experience itself as a whole. I cannot employ the language of science to trace this process of growth in myself, for I cannot experience myself as a scientific problem.

What we are to our inward vision, and what man appears to be *sub specie aeternitatis,*[1] can only be expressed by way of myth. Myth is more individual and expresses life more precisely than does science. Science works with concepts of averages which are far too general to do justice to the subjective variety of an individual life.

Thus it is that I have now undertaken, in my eighty-third year, to tell my personal myth. I can only make direct statements, only "tell stories." Whether or not the stories are "true" is not the problem. The only question is whether what I tell is *my* fable, *my* truth.

An autobiography is so difficult to write because we possess no standards, no objective foundation, from which to judge ourselves. There are really no proper bases for comparison. I know that in many things I am not like others, but I do not know what I really am like. Man cannot compare himself with any other creature; he is not a monkey, not a cow, not a tree. I am a man. But what is it to be that? Like every other being, I am a splinter of the infinite deity, but I cannot contrast myself with any animal, any plant or any stone. Only a mythical being has a range greater than man's. How then can a man form any definite opinions about himself?

We are a psychic process which we do not control, or only partly direct. Consequently, we cannot have any final judgment about ourselves or our lives. If we had, we would know everything—but at most that is only a pretense. At bottom we never know how it has all come about. The story of a life begins somewhere, at some particular point we happen to remember; and even then it was already highly complex. We do not know how life is going to turn out. Therefore the story has no beginning, and the end can only be vaguely hinted at.

The life of man is a dubious experiment. It is a tremendous phenomenon only in numerical terms. Individually, it is so fleeting, so

[1] Latin: under the aspect of eternity.

insufficient, that it is literally a miracle that anything can exist and develop at all. I was impressed by that fact long ago, as a young medical student, and it seemed to me miraculous that I should not have been prematurely annihilated.

Life has always seemed to me like a plant that lives on its rhizome.[2] Its true life is invisible, hidden in the rhizome. The part that appears above ground lasts only a single summer. Then it withers away—an ephemeral apparition. When we think of the unending growth and decay of life and civilizations, we cannot escape the impression of absolute nullity. Yet I have never lost a sense of something that lives and endures underneath the eternal flux. What we see is the blossom, which passes. The rhizome remains.

In the end the only events in my life worth telling are those when the imperishable world irrupted into this transitory one. That is why I speak chiefly of inner experiences, amongst which I include my dreams and visions. These form the *prima materia*[3] of my scientific work. They were the fiery magma out of which the stone that had to be worked was crystallized.

• • •

FIRST YEARS

At about the same time—I could not say with absolute certainty whether it preceded this experience or not—I had the earliest dream I can remember, a dream which was to preoccupy me all my life. I was then between three and four years old.

The vicarage[4] stood quite alone near Laufen castle, and there was a big meadow stretching back from the sexton's[5] farm. In the dream I was in this meadow. Suddenly I discovered a dark, rectangular, stone-lined hole in the ground. I had never seen it before. I ran forward curiously and peered down into it. Then I saw a stone stairway leading down. Hesitantly and fearfully, I descended. At the bottom was a doorway with a round arch, closed off by a green curtain. It was a big, heavy curtain of worked stuff like brocade, and it

[2] A plant with roots below and shoots above the ground, with a thickened subterranean stem where reserve food material is stored.
[3] Primary source.
[4] Parsonage.
[5] Church custodian's.

looked very sumptuous. Curious to see what might be hidden behind, I pushed it aside. I saw before me in the dim light a rectangular chamber about thirty feet long. The ceiling was arched and of hewn stone. The floor was laid with flagstones, and in the center a red carpet ran from the entrance to a low platform. On this platform stood a wonderfully rich golden throne. I am not certain, but perhaps a red cushion lay on the seat. It was a magnificent throne, a real king's throne in a fairy tale. Something was standing on it which I thought at first was a tree trunk twelve to fifteen feet high and about one and a half to two feet thick. It was a huge thing, reaching almost to the ceiling. But it was of a curious composition: it was made of skin and naked flesh, and on top there was something like a rounded head with no face and no hair. On the very top of the head was a single eye, gazing motionlessly upward.

It was fairly light in the room, although there were no windows and no apparent source of light. Above the head, however, was an aura of brightness. The thing did not move, yet I had the feeling that it might at any moment crawl off the throne like a worm and creep toward me. I was paralyzed with terror. At that moment I heard from outside and above me my mother's voice. She called out, "Yes, just look at him. That is the man-eater!" That intensified my terror still more, and I awoke sweating and scared to death. For many nights afterward I was afraid to go to sleep, because I feared I might have another dream like that.

This dream haunted me for years. Only much later did I realize that what I had seen was a phallus, and it was decades before I understood that it was a ritual phallus.[6] I could never make out whether my mother meant, "*That* is the man-eater," or, "That is the *man-eater.*" In the first case she would have meant that not Lord Jesus or the Jesuit[7] was the devourer of little children, but the phallus; in the second case that the "man-eater" in general was symbolized by the phallus, so that the dark Lord Jesus, the Jesuit, and the phallus were identical.

· · ·

[6] A representation of the penis.
[7] A member of the Society of Jesus, a Roman Catholic order founded in the sixteenth century.

SCHOOL YEARS

My twelfth year was indeed a fateful one for me. One day in the early summer of 1887 I was standing in the cathedral square, waiting for a classmate who went home by the same route as myself. It was twelve o'clock, and the morning classes were over. Suddenly another boy gave me a shove that knocked me off my feet. I fell, striking my head against the curbstone so hard that I almost lost consciousness. For about half an hour afterward I was a little dazed. At the moment I felt the blow the thought flashed through my mind: "Now you won't have to go to school any more." I was only half unconscious, but I remained lying there a few moments longer than was strictly necessary, chiefly in order to avenge myself on my assailant. Then people picked me up and took me to a house nearby, where two elderly spinster aunts lived.

From then on I began to have fainting spells whenever I had to return to school, and whenever my parents set me to doing my homework. For more than six months I stayed away from school, and for me that was a picnic. I was free, could dream for hours, be anywhere I liked, in the woods or by the water, or draw. I resumed my battle pictures and furious scenes of war, of old castles that were being assaulted or burned, or drew page upon page of caricatures. Similar caricatures sometimes appear to me before falling asleep to this day, grinning masks that constantly move and change, among them familiar faces of people who soon afterward died.

Above all, I was able to plunge into the world of the mysterious. To that realm belonged trees, a pool, the swamp, stones and animals, and my father's library. But I was growing more and more away from the world, and had all the while faint pangs of conscience. I frittered away my time with loafing, collecting, reading, and playing. But I did not feel any happier for it; I had the obscure feeling that I was fleeing from myself.

I forgot completely how all this had come about, but I pitied my parents' worries. They consulted various doctors, who scratched their heads and packed me off to spend the holidays with relatives in Winterthur. This city had a railroad station that proved a source of endless delight to me. But when I returned home everything was as before. One doctor thought I had epilepsy. I knew what epileptic fits were like and I inwardly laughed at such nonsense. My parents became more worried than ever. Then one day a friend called on my father. They were sitting in the garden and I hid behind a shrub, for I was possessed of an insatiable curiosity. I heard the visitor saying to my father, "And how is your son?" "Ah, that's a sad business," my father replied. "The doctors no longer know what is wrong with him. They think it may be epilepsy. It would be dreadful if he were incurable. I have lost what little I had, and what will become of the boy if he cannot earn his own living?"

I was thunderstruck. This was the collision with reality. "Why, then, I must get to work!" I thought suddenly.

From that moment on I became a serious child. I crept away, went to my father's study, took out my Latin grammar, and began to cram with intense concentration. After ten minutes of this I had the finest of fainting fits. I almost fell off the chair, but after a few minutes I felt better and went on working. "Devil take it, I'm not going to faint," I told myself, and persisted in my purpose. This time it took about fifteen minutes before the second attack came. That, too, passed like the first. "And now you must really get to work!" I stuck it out, and after an hour came the third attack. Still I did not give up, and worked for another hour, until I had the feeling that I had overcome the attacks. Suddenly I felt better than I had in all the months before. And in fact the attacks did not recur. From that day on I worked over my grammar and other schoolbooks every day. A few weeks later I returned to school, and never suffered another attack, even there. The whole bag of tricks was over and done with! That was when I learned what a neurosis is.

Gradually the recollection of how it had all come about returned to me, and I saw clearly that I myself had arranged this whole disgraceful situation. That was why I had never been seriously angry with the schoolmate who pushed me over. I knew that he had been put up to it, so to speak, and that the whole affair was a diabolical plot on my part. I knew, too, that this was never going to happen to me again. I had a feeling of rage against myself, and at the same time was ashamed of myself. For I knew that I had wronged myself and made a fool of myself in my own eyes. Nobody else was to blame; I was the cursed renegade! From then on I could no longer endure my parents' worrying about me or speaking of me in a pitying tone.

The neurosis became another of my secrets, but it was a shameful secret, a defeat. Nevertheless it induced in me a studied punctiliousness and an unusual diligence. Those days saw the beginnings of my conscientiousness, practiced not for the sake of appearances, so that I would amount to something, but for my own sake. Regularly I would get up at five o'clock in order to study, and sometimes I worked from three in the morning till seven, before going to school. . . .

I compensated my inner insecurity by an outward show of security, or—to put it better—the defect compensated itself without the intervention of my will. That is, I found myself being guilty and at the same time wishing to be innocent. Somewhere deep in the background I always knew that I was two persons. One was the son of my parents, who went to school and was less intelligent, attentive, hard-working, decent, and clean than many other boys. The other was grown up—old, in fact—skeptical, mistrustful, remote from the world of men, but close to nature, the earth, the sun, the moon, the weather, all living creatures, and above all close to the night, to dreams, and to whatever "God" worked directly in him. I put "God" in quotation marks here. For nature seemed, like myself, to have been set aside by God as non-divine, although created by Him as an expression of Himself. Nothing could persuade me that "in the image of God" applied only to man. In fact it seemed to me that the high mountains, the rivers, lakes, trees, flowers, and animals far better exemplified the essence of God than men with their ridiculous clothes, their meanness, vanity, mendacity, and abhorrent egotism— all qualities with which I was only too familiar from myself, that is, from personality No. 1, the schoolboy of 1890. Besides his world there existed another realm, like a temple in which anyone who entered was transformed and suddenly overpowered by a vision of the whole cosmos, so that he could only marvel and admire, forgetful of himself. Here lived the "Other," who knew God as a hidden personal, and at the same time suprapersonal secret. Here nothing separated man from God; indeed, it was as though the human mind looked down upon Creation simultaneously with God.

What I am here unfolding, sentence by sentence, is something I was then not conscious of in any articulate way, though I sensed it with an overpowering premonition and intensity of feeling. At such times I *knew* I was worthy of myself, that I was my true self. As soon as I was alone, I could pass over into this state. I therefore sought the peace and solitude of this "Other," personality No. 2.

The play and counterplay between personalities No. 1 and No. 2, which has run through my whole life, has nothing to do with a "split" or dissociation in the ordinary medical sense. On the contrary, it is played out in every individual. In my life No. 2 has been of prime importance, and I have always tried to make room for anything that wanted to come to me from within. He is a typical figure, but he is perceived only by the very few. Most people's conscious understanding is not sufficient to realize that he is also what they are. . . .

I would have liked to lay my religious difficulties before [my father] and ask him for advice, but I did not do so because it seemed to me that I knew in advance what he would be obliged to reply out of respect for his office. How right I was in this assumption was demonstrated to me soon afterward. My father personally gave me my instruction for confirmation. It bored me to death. . . .

In spite of the boredom, I made every effort to believe without understanding—an attitude which seemed to correspond with my father's—and prepared myself for Communion, on which I had set my last hopes. This was, I thought, merely a memorial meal, a kind of anniversary celebration for Lord Jesus who had died $1890 - 30 = 1860$ years ago. But still, he had let fall certain hints such as, "Take, eat, this is my body," meaning that we should eat the Communion bread as if it were his body, which after all had originally been flesh. Likewise we were to drink the wine which had originally been blood. It was clear to me that in this fashion we were to incorporate him into ourselves. This seemed to me so preposterous an impossibility that I was sure some great mystery must lie behind it, and that I would participate in this mystery in the course of Communion, on which my father seemed to place so high a value.

As was customary, a member of the church committee stood godfather to me. He was a nice, taciturn old man, a wheelwright in whose workshop I had often stood, watching his skill with lathe and adze. Now he came, solemnly transformed by frock coat and top hat, and took me to church, where my father in his familiar robes stood behind the altar and read prayers from the liturgy. On the white cloth covering the altar lay large trays filled with small pieces of bread. I could see that the bread came from our baker, whose baked goods were generally poor and flat in taste. From a pewter jug, wine was poured into a pewter cup. My father ate a piece of the bread, took a swallow of the wine—I knew the tavern from which it had come—and passed the cup to one of the old men. All were stiff, solemn, and, it seemed to me, uninterested. I looked on in suspense, but could not see or guess whether anything unusual was going on inside the old men. The atmosphere was the same as that of all other performances in church—baptisms, funerals, and so on. . . .

Suddenly my turn came. I ate the bread; it tasted flat, as I had expected. The wine, of which I took only the smallest sip, was thin and rather sour, plainly not the best. Then came the final prayer, and the people went out, neither depressed nor illumined with joy, but with faces that said, "So that's that. . . ."

Only gradually, in the course of the following days, did it dawn on me that nothing had happened. I had reached the pinnacle of religious initiation, had expected something—I knew not what—to happen, and nothing at all had happened. I knew that God could do stupendous things to me, things of fire and unearthly light; but this ceremony contained no trace of God—not for me, at any rate. To be sure, there had been talk about Him, but it had all amounted to no more than words. Among the others I had noticed nothing of the vast despair, the overpowering elation and outpouring of grace which for me constituted the essence of God. I had observed no sign of "communion," of "union, becoming one with . . ." With whom? With Jesus? Yet he was only a man who had died 1860 years ago. Why should a person become one with him? He was called the "Son of God"—a demigod, therefore, like the Greek heroes: how then could an ordinary person become one with him? This was called the "Christian religion," but none of it had anything to do with God as I had experienced Him. On the other hand it was quite clear that Jesus, the man, did have to do with God; he had despaired in Gethsemane and on the cross, after having taught that God was a kind and loving father. He too, then, must have seen the fearfulness of God. That I could understand, but what was the purpose of this wretched memorial service with the flat bread and the sour wine? Slowly I came to understand that this communion had been a fatal experience for me. It had proved hollow; more than that, it had proved to be a total loss. I knew that I would never again be able to participate in this ceremony. "Why, that is not religion at all," I thought. "It is an absence of God; the church is a place I should not go to. It is not life which is there, but death."

I was seized with the most vehement pity for my father. All at once I understood the tragedy of his profession and his life. He was struggling with a death whose existence he could not admit. An abyss had opened between him and me, and I saw no possibility of ever bridging it, for it was infinite in extent. . . .

STUDENT YEARS

During the summer holidays, however, something happened that was destined to influence me profoundly. One day I was sitting in my room, studying my textbooks. In the adjoining room, the door to which stood ajar, my mother was knitting. That was our dining room, where the round walnut dining table stood. The table had come from the dowry of my paternal grandmother, and was at this time about seventy years old. My mother was sitting by the window, about a yard away from the table. My sister was at school and our maid in the kitchen. Suddenly there sounded a report like a pistol shot. I jumped up and rushed into the room from which the noise of the explosion had come. My mother was sitting flabbergasted in her armchair, the knitting fallen from her hands. She stammered out, "W-w-what's happened? It was right beside me!" and stared at the table. Following her eyes, I saw what had happened. The table top had split from the rim to beyond the center, and not along any joint; the split ran right through the solid wood. I was thunderstruck. How could such a thing happen? A table of solid walnut that had dried out for seventy years—how could it split on a summer day in the relatively high degree of humidity characteristic of our climate? . . .

Some two weeks later I came home at six o'clock in the evening and found the household—my mother, my fourteen-year-old sister, and the maid—in a great state of agitation. About an hour earlier there had been another deafening report. This time it was not the already damaged table; the noise had come from the direction of the sideboard, a heavy piece of furniture dating from the early nineteenth century. They had already looked all over it, but had found no trace of a split. I immediately began examining the sideboard and the entire surrounding area, but just as fruitlessly. Then I began on the interior of the sideboard. In the cupboard containing the bread basket I found a loaf of bread, and, beside it, the bread knife. The greater part of the blade had snapped off in several pieces. The handle lay in one corner of the rectangular basket, and in each of the other corners lay a piece of the blade. The knife had been used shortly before, at four-o'clock tea, and afterward put away. Since then no one had gone to the sideboard.

The next day I took the shattered knife to one of the best cutlers in the town. He examined the fractures with a magnifying glass, and shook his head. "This knife is perfectly sound," he said. "There is no fault in the steel. Someone must have deliberately broken it piece by piece. It could be done, for instance, by sticking the blade into the crack of the drawer and breaking off a piece at a time. Or else it might have been dropped on stone from a great height. But good steel can't explode. Someone has been pulling your leg." I have carefully kept the pieces of the knife to this day. . . .

A few weeks later I heard of certain relatives who had been engaged for some time in table-turning, and also had a medium, a young girl of fifteen and a half. The group had been thinking of having me meet the medium, who produced somnambulistic[8] states and spiritualistic phenomena. When I heard this, I immediately thought of the strange manifestations in our house, and I conjectured that they might be somehow connected with this medium. I therefore began attending the regular séances[9] which my relatives held every Saturday evening. We had results in the form of communications and tapping noises from the walls and the table. Movements of the table independently of the medium were questionable, and I soon found out that limiting conditions imposed on the experiment generally had an obstructive effect. I therefore accepted the obvious autonomy of the tapping noises and turned my attention to the content of the communications. I set forth the results of these observations in my doctoral thesis. After about two years of experimentation we all became rather weary of it. I caught the medium trying to produce phenomena by trickery, and this made me break off the experiments—very much to my regret, for I had learned from this example how a No. 2 personality is formed, how it enters into a child's consciousness and finally integrates it into itself. . . .

All in all, this was the one great experience which wiped out all my earlier philosophy and made it possible for me to achieve a psychological point of view. I had discovered some objective facts about the human psyche. Yet the nature of the experience was such that once again I was unable to speak of it. I knew no one to whom I

[8] Characteristic of sleepwalking.
[9] Spiritualist meetings.

could have told the whole story. Once more I had to lay aside an unfinished problem. It was not until two years later that my dissertation appeared. . . .

Though I had attended psychiatric lectures and clinics, the current instructor in psychiatry was not exactly stimulating, and when I recalled the effects which the experience of asylums had had on my father, this was not calculated to prepossess me in favor of psychiatry. In preparing myself for the state examination, therefore, the textbook on psychiatry was the last I attacked. I expected nothing of it, and I still remember that as I opened the book by Krafft-Ebing [10] the thought came to me: "Well, now let's see what a psychiatrist has to say for himself." The lectures and clinical demonstrations had not made the slightest impression on me. I could not remember a single one of the cases I had seen in the clinic, but only my boredom and disgust.

I began with the preface, intending to find out how a psychiatrist introduced his subject or, indeed, justified his reason for existing at all. By way of excuse for this high and mighty attitude I must make it clear that in the medical world at that time psychiatry was quite generally held in contempt. No one really knew anything about it, and there was no psychology which regarded man as a whole and included his pathological variations in the total picture. The director was locked up in the same institution with his patients, and the institution was equally cut off, isolated on the outskirts of the city like an ancient lazaret with its lepers. No one liked looking in that direction. The doctors knew almost as little as the layman and therefore shared his feelings. Mental disease was a hopeless and fatal affair which cast its shadow over psychiatry as well. The psychiatrist was a strange figure in those days, as I was soon to learn from personal experience.

Beginning with the preface, I read: "It is probably due to the peculiarity of the subject and its incomplete state of development that psychiatric textbooks are stamped with a more or less subjective character." A few lines further on, the author called the psychoses "diseases of the personality." My heart suddenly began to pound. I had to stand up and draw a deep breath. My excitement was intense, for it had become clear to me, in a flash of illumination, that for me the only possible goal was psychiatry. Here alone the two currents of my interest could flow together and in a united stream dig their own

[10] Richard von Krafft-Ebing (1840–1902), a German neurologist who wrote about neurology, forensic psychiatry, and psychopathology.

bed. Here was the empirical field common to biological and spiritual facts, which I had everywhere sought and nowhere found. Here at last was the place where the collision of nature and spirit became a reality.

My violent reaction set in when Krafft-Ebing spoke of the "subjective character" of psychiatric textbooks. So, I thought, the textbook is in part the subjective confession of the author. With his specific prejudice, with the totality of his being, he stands behind the objectivity of his experiences and responds to the "disease of the personality" with the whole of his own personality. Never had I heard anything of this sort from my teacher at the clinic. In spite of the fact that Krafft-Ebing's textbook did not differ essentially from other books of the kind, these few hints cast such a transfiguring light on psychiatry that I was irretrievably drawn under its spell.

The decision was taken. When I informed my teacher in internal medicine of my intention, I could read in his face his amazement and disappointment. My old wound, the feeling of being an outsider and of alienating others, began to ache again. But now I understood why. No one, not even I myself, had ever imagined I could become interested in this obscure bypath. My friends were astounded and put out, thinking me a fool for throwing up the enviable chance of a sensible career in internal medicine, which dangled so temptingly before my nose, in favor of this psychiatric nonsense.

I saw that once again I had obviously got myself into a side alley where no one could or would follow me. But I knew—and nothing and nobody could have deflected me from my purpose—that my decision stood, and that it was fate. It was as though two rivers had united and in one grand torrent were bearing me inexorably toward distant goals. This confident feeling that I was a "united double nature" carried me as if on a magical wave through the examination, in which I came out at the top.

· · ·

PSYCHIATRIC ACTIVITIES

I am often asked about my psychotherapeutic or analytic method. I cannot reply unequivocally to the question. Therapy is different in every case. When a doctor tells me that he adheres strictly to this or that method, I have my doubts about his therapeutic effect. So much is said in the literature about the resistance of the patient that it would almost seem as if the doctor were trying to put something over on him, whereas the cure ought to grow naturally out of the patient himself. Psychotherapy and analysis are as varied as are human individuals. I treat every patient as individually as possible, because the solution of the problem is always an individual one. Universal rules can be postulated only with a grain of salt. A psychological truth is valid only if it can be reversed. A solution which would be out of the question for me may be just the right one for someone else.

Naturally, a doctor must be familiar with the so-called "methods." But he must guard against falling into any specific, routine approach. In general one must guard against theoretical assumptions. Today they may be valid, tomorrow it may be the turn of other assumptions. In my analyses they play no part. I am unsystematic very much by intention. To my mind, in dealing with individuals, only individual understanding will do. We need a different language for every patient. In one analysis I can be heard talking the Adlerian dialect, in another the Freudian.[11]

The crucial point is that I confront the patient as one human being to another. Analysis is a dialogue demanding two partners. Analyst and patient sit facing one another, eye to eye; the doctor has something to say, but so has the patient.

Since the essence of psychotherapy is not the application of a method, psychiatric study alone does not suffice. I myself had to work for a very long time before I possessed the equipment for psychotherapy. As early as 1909 I realized that I could not treat latent psychoses if I did not understand their symbolism. It was then that I began to study mythology.

With cultivated and intelligent patients the psychiatrist needs more than merely professional knowledge. He must understand, aside from all theoretical assumptions, what really motivates the patient. Otherwise he stirs up unnecessary resistances. What counts, after all, is not whether a theory is corroborated, but whether the patient grasps himself as an individual. This, however, is not possible with-

[11] Sigmund Freud (1856–1939) was an Austrian neurologist and founder of psychoanalysis. Alfred Adler (1870–1937), an Austrian psychologist and psychiatrist, was a disciple and supporter of Freud until 1911, when he broke with the psychoanalytical school and became the founder of "individual" psychology.

out reference to the collective views, concerning which the doctor ought to be informed. For that, mere medical training does not suffice, for the horizon of the human psyche embraces infinitely more than the limited purview of the doctor's consulting room. . . .

The psychotherapist, however, must understand not only the patient; it is equally important that he should understand himself. For that reason the *sine qua non* [12] is the analysis of the analyst, what is called the training analysis. The patient's treatment begins with the doctor, so to speak. Only if the doctor knows how to cope with himself and his own problems will he be able to teach the patient to do the same. Only then. In the training analysis the doctor must learn to know his own psyche and to take it seriously. If he cannot do that, the patient will not learn either. He will lose a portion of his psyche, just as the doctor has lost that portion of his psyche which he has not learned to understand. It is not enough, therefore, for the training analysis to consist in acquiring a system of concepts. The analysand must realize that it concerns himself, that the training analysis is a bit of real life and is not a method which can be learned by rote. The student who does not grasp that fact in his own training analysis will have to pay dearly for the failure later on.

Though there is treatment known as "minor psychotherapy," in any thoroughgoing analysis the whole personality of both patient and doctor is called into play. There are many cases which the doctor cannot cure without committing himself. When important matters are at stake, it makes all the difference whether the doctor sees himself as a part of the drama, or cloaks himself in his authority. In the great crises of life, in the supreme moments when to be or not to be is the question, little tricks of suggestion do not help. Then the doctor's whole being is challenged.

The therapist must at all times keep watch over himself, over the way he is reacting to his patient. For we do not react only with our consciousness. Also we must always be asking ourselves: How is our unconscious experiencing this situation? We must therefore observe our dreams, pay the closest attention and study ourselves just as carefully as we do the patient. Otherwise the entire treatment may go off the rails. I shall give a single example of this.

• • •

---

[12] Latin: the indispensable condition, a necessity.

SIGMUND FREUD

At the beginning it was not easy for me to assign Freud the proper place in my life, or to take the right attitude toward him. When I became acquainted with his work I was planning an academic career, and was about to complete a paper that was intended to advance me at the university. But Freud was definitely *persona non grata* [13] in the academic world at the time, and any connection with him would have been damaging in scientific circles. "Important people" at most mentioned him surreptitiously, and at congresses he was discussed only in the corridors, never on the floor. Therefore the discovery that my association experiments were in agreement with Freud's theories was far from pleasant to me.

Once, while I was in my laboratory and reflecting again upon these questions, the devil whispered to me that I would be justified in publishing the results of my experiments and my conclusions without mentioning Freud. After all, I had worked out my experiments long before I understood his work. But then I heard the voice of my second personality: "If you do a thing like that, as if you had no knowledge of Freud, it would be a piece of trickery. You cannot build your life upon a lie." With that, the question was settled. From then on I became an open partisan of Freud's and fought for him.

I first took up the cudgels for Freud at a congress in Munich where a lecturer discussed obsessional neuroses but studiously forbore to mention the name of Freud. In 1906, in connection with this incident, I wrote a paper for the *Münchner Medizinische Wochenschrift* [14] on Freud's theory of the neuroses, which had contributed a great deal to the understanding of obsessional neuroses. In response to this article, two German professors wrote to me, warning that if I remained on Freud's side and continued to defend him, I would be endangering my academic career. I replied: "If what Freud says is the truth, I am with him. I don't give a damn for a career if it has to be based on the premise of restricting research and concealing the truth." And I went on defending Freud and his ideas. But on the basis of my own findings I was still unable to feel that all neuroses were caused by sexual repression or sexual traumata. In certain cases that was so, but not in others. Nevertheless, Freud had opened up a

[13] Latin: an unacceptable person.
[14] A medical journal published in Munich, Germany.

new path of investigation, and the shocked outcries against him at the time seemed to me absurd.

I had not met with much sympathy for the ideas expressed in "The Psychology of Dementia Praecox." [15] In fact, my colleagues laughed at me. But through this book I came to know Freud. He invited me to visit him, and our first meeting took place in Vienna in March 1907. We met at one o'clock in the afternoon and talked virtually without a pause for thirteen hours. Freud was the first man of real importance I had encountered; in my experience up to that time, no one else could compare with him. There was nothing the least trivial in his attitude. I found him extremely intelligent, shrewd, and altogether remarkable. And yet my first impressions of him remained somewhat tangled; I could not make him out.

What he said about his sexual theory impressed me. Nevertheless, his words could not remove my hesitations and doubts. I tried to advance these reservations of mine on several occasions, but each time he would attribute them to my lack of experience. Freud was right; in those days I had not enough experience to support my objections. I could see that his sexual theory was enormously important to him, both personally and philosophically. This impressed me, but I could not decide to what extent this strong emphasis upon sexuality was connected with subjective prejudices of his, and to what extent it rested upon verifiable experiences.

Above all, Freud's attitude toward the spirit seemed to me highly questionable. Wherever, in a person or in a work of art, an expression of spirituality (in the intellectual, not the supernatural sense) came to light, he suspected it, and insinuated that it was repressed sexuality. Anything that could not be directly interpreted as sexuality he referred to as "psychosexuality." I protested that this hypothesis, carried to its logical conclusion, would lead to an annihilating judgment upon culture. Culture would then appear as a mere farce, the morbid consequence of repressed sexuality. "Yes," he assented, "so it is, and that is just a curse of fate against which we are powerless to contend." I was by no means disposed to agree, or to let it go at that, but still I did not feel competent to argue it out with him.

There was something else that seemed to me significant at that

[15] Published in 1907. The Latin phrase *dementia praecox* means prematurely deteriorated mentality.

first meeting. It had to do with things which I was able to think out and understand only after our friendship was over. There was no mistaking the fact that Freud was emotionally involved in his sexual theory to an extraordinary degree. When he spoke of it, his tone became urgent, almost anxious, and all signs of his normally critical and skeptical manner vanished. A strange, deeply moved expression came over his face, the cause of which I was at a loss to understand. I had a strong intuition that for him sexuality was a sort of *numinosum*.[16] This was confirmed by a conversation which took place some three years later (in 1910), again in Vienna.

I can still recall vividly how Freud said to me, "My dear Jung, promise me never to abandon the sexual theory. That is the most essential thing of all. You see, we must make a dogma of it, an unshakable bulwark." He said that to me with great emotion, in the tone of a father saying, "And promise me this one thing, my dear son: that you will go to church every Sunday." In some astonishment I asked him, "A bulwark—against what?" To which he replied, "Against the black tide of mud"—and here he hesitated for a moment, then added—"of occultism." First of all, it was the words "bulwark" and "dogma" that alarmed me; for a dogma, that is to say, an undisputable confession of faith, is set up only when the aim is to suppress doubts once and for all. But that no longer has anything to do with scientific judgment; only with a personal power drive.

This was the thing that struck at the heart of our friendship. I knew that I would never be able to accept such an attitude. What Freud seemed to mean by "occultism" was virtually everything that philosophy and religion, including the rising contemporary science of parapsychology, had learned about the psyche. To me the sexual theory was just as occult, that is to say, just as unproven as an hypothesis, as many other speculative views. As I saw it, a scientific truth was a hypothesis which might be adequate for the moment but was not to be preserved as an article of faith for all time. . . .

It interested me to hear Freud's views on precognition and on parapsychology in general. When I visited him in Vienna in 1909 I asked him what he thought of these matters. Because of his materialistic prejudice, he rejected this entire complex of questions as nonsensical, and did so in terms of so shallow a positivism that I had

[16] Latin: higher reality, creative force.

difficulty in checking the sharp retort on the tip of my tongue. It was some years before he recognized the seriousness of parapsychology and acknowledged the factuality of "occult" phenomena.

While Freud was going on this way, I had a curious sensation. It was as if my diaphragm were made of iron and were becoming red-hot—a glowing vault. And at that moment there was such a loud report in the bookcase, which stood right next to us, that we both started up in alarm, fearing the thing was going to topple over on us. I said to Freud: "There, that is an example of a so-called catalytic exteriorization phenomenon."

"Oh come," he exclaimed. "That is sheer bosh."

"It is not," I replied. "You are mistaken, Herr Professor.[17] And to prove my point I now predict that in a moment there will be another such loud report!" Sure enough, no sooner had I said the words than the same detonation went off in the bookcase.

To this day I do not know what gave me this certainty. But I knew beyond all doubt that the report would come again. Freud only stared aghast at me. I do not know what was in his mind, or what his look meant. In any case, this incident aroused his mistrust of me, and I had the feeling that I had done something against him. I never afterward discussed the incident with him.

The year 1909 proved decisive for our relationship. I had been invited to lecture on the association experiment at Clark University in Worcester, Massachusetts. Independently, Freud had also received an invitation, and we decided to travel together. We met in Bremen, where Ferenczi[18] joined us. In Bremen the much-discussed incident of Freud's fainting fit occurred. It was provoked—indirectly—by my interest in the "peat-bog corpses." I knew that in certain districts of Northern Germany these so-called bog corpses were to be found. They are the bodies of prehistoric men who either drowned in the marshes or were buried there. . . .

Having read about these peat-bog corpses, I recalled them when we were in Bremen, but, being a bit muddled, confused them with the mummies in the lead cellars of the city. This interest of mine got on Freud's nerves. "Why are you so concerned with these corpses?" he asked me several times. He was inordinately vexed by the whole thing and during one such conversation, while we were having din-

[17] Professor Freud.
[18] Sandor Ferenczi (1873–1933), a Hungarian neurologist and one of Freud's earliest supporters.

ner together, he suddenly fainted. Afterward he said to me that he was convinced that all this chatter about corpses meant I had death-wishes toward him. I was more than surprised by this interpretation. I was alarmed by the intensity of his fantasies—so strong that, obviously, they could cause him to faint.

In a similar connection Freud once more suffered a fainting fit in my presence. This was during the Psychoanalytic Congress in Munich in 1912. Someone had turned the conversation to Amenophis IV (Ikhnaton).[19] The point was made that as a result of his negative attitude toward his father he had destroyed his father's cartouches[20] on the steles,[21] and that at the back of his great creation of monotheistic religion there lurked a father complex. This sort of thing irritated me, and I attempted to argue that Amenophis had been a creative and profoundly religious person whose acts could not be explained by personal resistances toward his father. On the contrary, I said, he had held the memory of his father in honor, and his zeal for destruction had been directed only against the name of the god Amon, which he had everywhere annihilated; it was also chiseled out of the cartouches of his father Amon-hotep. Moreover, other pharaohs had replaced the names of their actual or divine forefathers on monuments and statues by their own, feeling that they had a right to do so since they were incarnations of the same god. Yet they, I pointed out, had inaugurated neither a new style nor a new religion.

At that moment Freud slid off his chair in a faint. Everyone clustered helplessly around him. I picked him up, carried him into the next room, and laid him on a sofa. As I was carrying him, he half came to, and I shall never forget the look he cast at me. In his weakness he looked at me as if I were his father. Whatever other causes may have contributed to this faint—the atmosphere was very tense—the fantasy of father-murder was common to both cases.

At the time Freud frequently made allusions indicating that he

---

[19] Pharaoh (ruler) of ancient Egypt from about 1375 to 1358 B.C. A religious innovator and reformer, Ikhnaton rejected the god Amon in favor of the new sun god Aton. The pharaoh himself changed his name from Amenophis, or Amenhotep, to Ikhnaton, which means "Aton is satisfied." He chose a new Egyptian capital, named Akhetaton (Horizon of Aton), and ordered the name of his father Amenhotep III (also spelled Amon-hotep) removed from all monuments, because it contained the name of the old god Amon (Amen).

[20] Oval or oblong frames enclosing the name of an Egyptian ruler.

[21] Commemorative stone monuments (usually tombstones).

regarded me as his successor. These hints were embarrassing to me, for I knew that I would never be able to uphold his views properly, that is to say, as he intended them. On the other hand I had not yet succeeded in working out my criticisms in such a manner that they would carry any weight with him, and my respect for him was too great for me to want to force him to come finally to grips with my own ideas. I was by no means charmed by the thought of being burdened, virtually over my own head, with the leadership of a party. In the first place that sort of thing was not in my nature; in the second place I could not sacrifice my intellectual independence; and in the third place such luster was highly unwelcome to me since it would only deflect me from my real aims. I was concerned with investigating truth, not with questions of personal prestige.

The trip to the United States which began in Bremen in 1909 lasted for seven weeks. We were together every day, and analyzed each other's dreams. At the time I had a number of important ones, but Freud could make nothing of them. I did not regard that as any reflection upon him, for it sometimes happens to the best analyst that he is unable to unlock the riddle of a dream. It was a human failure, and I would never have wanted to discontinue our dream analyses on that account. On the contrary, they meant a great deal to me, and I found our relationship exceedingly valuable. I regarded Freud as an older, more mature and experienced personality, and felt like a son in that respect. But then something happened which proved to be a severe blow to the whole relationship.

Freud had a dream—I would not think it right to air the problem it involved. I interpreted it as best I could, but added that a great deal more could be said about it if he would supply me with some additional details from his private life. Freud's response to these words was a curious look—a look of the utmost suspicion. Then he said, "But I cannot risk my authority!" At that moment he lost it altogether. That sentence burned itself into my memory; and in it the end of our relationship was already foreshadowed. Freud was placing personal authority above truth.

As I have already said, Freud was able to interpret the dreams I was then having only incompletely or not at all. They were dreams with collective contents, containing a great deal of symbolic material. One in particular was important to me, for it led me for the first time to the concept of the "collective unconscious" and thus formed a kind of prelude to my book, *Wandlungen und Symbole der Libido*. [22]

This was the dream. I was in a house I did not know, which had two stories. It was "my house." I found myself in the upper story, where there was a kind of salon furnished with fine old pieces in rococo style. On the walls hung a number of precious old paintings. I wondered that this should be my house, and thought, "Not bad." But then it occurred to me that I did not know what the lower floor looked like. Descending the stairs, I reached the ground floor. There everything was much older, and I realized that this part of the house must date from about the fifteenth or sixteenth century. The furnishings were medieval; the floors were of red brick. Everywhere it was rather dark. I went from one room to another, thinking, "Now I really must explore the whole house." I came upon a heavy door, and opened it. Beyond it, I discovered a stone stairway that led down into the cellar. Descending again, I found myself in a beautifully vaulted room which looked exceedingly ancient. Examining the walls, I discovered layers of brick among the ordinary stone blocks, and chips of brick in the mortar. As soon as I saw this I knew that the walls dated from Roman times. My interest by now was intense. I looked more closely at the floor. It was of stone slabs, and in one of these I discovered a ring. When I pulled it, the stone slab lifted, and again I saw a stairway of narrow stone steps leading down into the depths. These, too, I descended, and entered a low cave cut into the rock. Thick dust lay on the floor, and in the dust were scattered bones and broken pottery, like remains of a primitive culture. I discovered two human skulls, obviously very old and half disintegrated. Then I awoke.

What chiefly interested Freud in this dream were the two skulls. He returned to them repeatedly, and urged me to find a *wish* in connection with them. What did I think about these skulls? And whose were they? I knew perfectly well, of course, what he was driving at: that secret death-wishes were concealed in the dream. "But what does he really expect of me?" I thought to myself. Toward whom would I have death-wishes? I felt violent resistance to any such interpretation. I also had some intimation of what the dream might really mean. But I did not then trust my own judgment, and wanted to

[22] Published in 1912; English title: "Psychology of the Unconscious" (1916).

hear Freud's opinion. I wanted to learn from him. Therefore I submitted to his intention and said, "My wife and my sister-in-law"—after all, I had to name someone whose death was worth the wishing!

I was newly married at the time and knew perfectly well that there was nothing within myself which pointed to such wishes. But I would not have been able to present to Freud my own ideas on an interpretation of the dream without encountering incomprehension and vehement resistance. I did not feel up to quarreling with him, and I also feared that I might lose his friendship if I insisted on my own point of view. On the other hand, I wanted to know what he would make of my answer, and what his reaction would be if I deceived him by saying something that suited his theories. And so I told him a lie.

I was quite aware that my conduct was not above reproach, but *à la guerre, comme à la guerre!* [23] It would have been impossible for me to afford him any insight into my mental world. The gulf between it and his was too great. In fact Freud seemed greatly relieved by my reply. I saw from this that he was completely helpless in dealing with certain kinds of dreams and had to take refuge in his doctrine. I realized that it was up to me to find out the real meaning of the dream.

It was plain to me that the house represented a kind of image of the psyche—that is to say, of my then state of consciousness, with hitherto unconscious additions. Consciousness was represented by the salon. It had an inhabited atmosphere, in spite of its antiquated style.

The ground floor stood for the first level of the unconscious. The deeper I went, the more alien and the darker the scene became. In the cave, I discovered remains of a primitive culture, that is, the world of the primitive man within myself—a world which can scarcely be reached or illuminated by consciousness. The primitive psyche of man borders on the life of the animal soul, just as the caves of prehistoric times were usually inhabited by animals before men laid claim to them.

During this period I became aware of how keenly I felt the difference between Freud's intellectual attitude and mine. I had grown

---

[23] French: in war, [do] as in war!

up in the intensely historical atmosphere of Basel at the end of the nineteenth century, and had acquired, thanks to reading the old philosophers, some knowledge of the history of psychology. When I thought about dreams and the contents of the unconscious, I never did so without making historical comparisons. . . .

27

V. I. Lenin

Imperialism
AND
State and Revolution

V. I. Lenin (1870–1924), one of the most influential political figures of the twentieth century, was the architect of the Russian Bolshevik Revolution of 1917 and, from that time until his death, the prime mover of the Soviet state. His radical, incisive ideas and dynamic leadership have made him a guiding spirit of twentieth-century communism and an inspiration for revolutionary movements throughout the world.

Lenin was trained to be a lawyer, but at age twenty-three he threw himself into the revolutionary movement, becoming in time one of the leaders of the Russian Socialist party. After imprisonment and exile in Siberia, he fled Russia, not to return until after the outbreak of revolution in 1917. As the head of the Bolsheviks, the left-wing faction of the socialists, he fought uncompromisingly against the theories and tactics of the moderate, revisionist socialists and organized the Bolshevik seizure of power. From 1918 on, he led the party and the nation in the building of a soviet political and economic system.

Leninism was an adaptation of Marxism to Russian conditions and the Russian revolutionary tradition. In developing the ideas and organization of the revolution, Lenin stressed the role of a professional revolutionary elite, organized in a centralized party, in leading the proletariat in the struggle

V. I. Lenin, *Imperialism, the Highest Stage of Capitalism* (New York: International Publishers, 1939), 88–89, 95–97, 123–27. Copyright 1939. *State and Revolution* (New York: International Publishers, 1932, 1943), 8–10, 15–17, 71–80. Copyright 1932, 1943. Reprinted by permission of International Publishers Co., Inc.

against capitalism. This struggle, he insisted, was an expression of irreconcilable class interests and was to be carried on in both the political and the economic spheres and by violent as well as peaceful means. Once victorious, the communists were to institute a dictatorship of the proletariat in order to effect the violent suppression of the bourgeoisie and the destruction of the capitalist state necessary to the organization of a socialist and, eventually, a communist society.

Lenin also applied his theories to the advanced industrial countries. He contended that capitalism has reached its final stage in such countries when industrial and financial monopolies dominated the economy. After exhausting the possibilities for economic growth at the domestic level, monopoly capitalists, or imperialists, are forced to seek political and economic control in backward areas of the world. According to Lenin, imperialistic rivalries result that inevitably lead to wars and the destruction of capitalism. Lenin elaborated these ideas in Imperialism, the Highest Stage of Capitalism *(1916), from which the first excerpt is taken.*

In his State and Revolution *(1917), from which the second excerpt is taken, Lenin expounds his theory of the state as the result of irreconcilable class conflict and as a coercive instrument of the ruling class. He saw revolution as the victory of the working-class state over the capitalistic state. Eventually, he predicted, when classes had been abolished in the communist society, the state as such would wither away.*

Imperialism

IMPERIALISM AS A SPECIAL STAGE OF CAPITALISM

We must now try to sum up and put together what has been said on the subject of imperialism. Imperialism emerged as the development and direct continuation of the fundamental attributes of capitalism in general. But capitalism only became capitalist imperialism at a definite and very high stage of its development, when certain of its fundamental attributes began to be transformed into their opposites, when the features of a period of transition from capitalism to a higher social and economic system began to take shape and reveal themselves all along the line. Economically, the main thing in this process is the substitution of capitalist monopolies for capitalist free competition. Free competition is the fundamental attribute of capitalism, and of commodity production generally. Monopoly is exactly the opposite of free competition; but we have seen the latter being transformed into monopoly before our very eyes, creating large-scale industry and eliminating small industry, replacing large-scale industry by still larger-scale industry, finally leading to such a concentration of production and capital that monopoly has been and is the result: cartels, syndicates and trusts, and, merging with them, the capital of a dozen or so banks manipulating thousands of millions. At the same time monopoly, which has grown out of free competition, does not abolish the latter, but exists over it and alongside of it, and thereby gives rise to a number of very acute, intense antagonisms, friction and conflicts. Monopoly is the transition from capitalism to a higher system.

If it were necessary to give the briefest possible definition of imperialism we should have to say that imperialism is the monopoly stage of capitalism. Such a definition would include what is most important, for, on the one hand, finance capital is the bank capital of a few big monopolist banks, merged with the capital of the monopolist combines of manufacturers; and, on the other hand, the division of the world is the transition from a colonial policy which has extended without hindrance to territories unoccupied by any capitalist power, to a colonial policy of monopolistic possession of the territory of the world which has been completely divided up.

But very brief definitions, although convenient, for they sum up the main points, are nevertheless inadequate, because very important features of the phenomenon that has to be defined have to be especially deduced. And so, without forgetting the conditional and relative value of all definitions, which can never include all the concatenations of a phenomenon in its complete development, we must give a definition of imperialism that will embrace the following five essential features:

1) The concentration of production and capital developed to such a high stage that it created monopolies which play a decisive role in economic life.

2) The merging of bank capital with industrial capital, and the creation, on the basis of this "finance capital," of a "financial oligarchy."

3) The export of capital, which has become extremely important, as distinguished from the export of commodities.

4) The formation of international capitalist monopolies which share the world among themselves.

5) The territorial division of the whole world among the greatest capitalist powers is completed. . . .

We notice three areas of highly developed capitalism with a high development of means of transport, of trade and of industry, the Central European, the British and the American areas. Among these are three states which dominate the world: Germany, Great Britain, the United States. Imperialist rivalry and the struggle between these countries have become very keen because Germany has only a restricted area and few colonies (the creation of "Central Europe" is still a matter for the future; it is being born in the midst of desperate struggles). For the moment the distinctive feature of Europe is political disintegration. In the British and American areas, on the other hand, political concentration is very highly developed, but there is a tremendous disparity between the immense colonies of the one and the insignificant colonies of the other. In the colonies, capitalism is only beginning to develop. The struggle for South America is becoming more and more acute.

There are two areas where capitalism is not strongly developed: Russia and Eastern Asia. In the former, the density of population is very low, in the latter it is very high; in the former political concentration is very high, in the latter it does not exist. The partition of China is only beginning, and the struggle between Japan, U.S.A., and so forth, in connection therewith is continually gaining in intensity. . . .

Finance capital and the trusts are increasing instead of diminishing the differences in the rate of development of the various parts of world economy. When the relation of forces is changed, how else, *under capitalism,* can the solution of contradictions be found, except by resorting to *violence?*

・ ・ ・

THE PLACE OF IMPERIALISM IN HISTORY

We have seen that the economic quintessence of imperialism is monopoly capitalism. This very fact determines its place in history, for monopoly that grew up on the basis of free competition, and precisely out of free competition, is the transition from the capitalist system to a higher social-economic order. We must take special note of the four principal forms of monopoly, or the four principal manifestations of monopoly capitalism, which are characteristic of the epoch under review.

Firstly, monopoly arose out of the concentration of production at a very advanced stage of development. This refers to the monopolist capitalist combines, cartels, syndicates and trusts. We have seen the important part that these play in modern economic life. At the beginning of the twentieth century, monopolies acquired complete supremacy in the advanced countries. And although the first steps towards the formation of the cartels were first taken by countries enjoying the protection of high tariffs (Germany, America), Great Britain, with her system of free trade, was not far behind in revealing the same basic phenomenon, namely, the birth of monopoly out of the concentration of production.

Secondly, monopolies have accelerated the capture of the most important sources of raw materials, especially for the coal and iron industries, which are the basic and most highly cartelized industries in capitalist society. The monopoly of the most important sources of raw materials has enormously increased the power of big capital, and has sharpened the antagonism between cartelized and non-cartelized industry.

Thirdly, monopoly has sprung from the banks. The banks have developed from modest intermediary enterprises into the monopolists of finance capital. Some three or five of the biggest banks in each of the foremost capitalist countries have achieved the "personal union" of industrial and bank capital, and have concentrated in their hands the disposal of thousands upon thousands of millions which form the greater part of the capital and income of entire countries. A financial oligarchy, which throws a close net of relations of dependence over all the economic and political institutions of contemporary bourgeois society without exception—such is the most striking manifestation of this monopoly.

Fourthly, monopoly has grown out of colonial policy. To the numerous "old" motives of colonial policy, finance capital has added the struggle for the sources of raw materials, for the export of capital, for "spheres of influence," namely, for spheres for profitable deals, concessions, monopolist profits and so on; in fine, for economic territory in general. When the colonies of the European powers in Africa, for instance, comprised only one-tenth of that territory (as was the case in 1876), colonial policy was able to develop by methods other than those of monopoly—by the "free grabbing" of territories, so to speak. But when nine-tenths of Africa had been seized (approximately by 1900), when the whole world had been divided up, there was inevitably ushered in a period of colonial monopoly and, consequently, a period of particularly intense struggle for the division and the redivision of the world.

The extent to which monopolist capital has intensified all the contradictions of capitalism is generally known. It is sufficient to mention the high cost of living and the oppression of the cartels. This intensification of contradictions constitutes the most powerful driving force of the transitional period of history, which began from the time of the definite victory of world finance capital.

Monopolies, oligarchy, the striving for domination instead of the striving for liberty, the exploitation of an increasing number of small or weak nations by an extremely small group of the richest or most powerful nations—all these have given birth to those distinctive characteristics of imperialism which compel us to define it as parasitic or decaying capitalism. More and more prominently there emerges, as one of the tendencies of imperialism, the creation of the "bondholding" (rentier) state, the usurer state, in which the bourgeoisie lives on the proceeds of capital exports and by "clipping coupons." It would be a mistake to believe that this tendency to decay precludes the possibility of the rapid growth of capitalism. It does not. In the epoch of imperialism, certain branches of industry, certain strata of the bourgeoisie and certain countries betray, to a more or less degree, one or other of these tendencies. On the whole, capitalism is growing far more rapidly than before. But this growth is not only becoming more and more uneven in general; its unevenness also manifests itself, in particular, in the decay of the countries which are richest in capital (such as England). . . .

In its turn, this finance capital which has grown so rapidly is not unwilling (precisely because it has grown so quickly) to pass on to a more "tranquil" possession of colonies which have to be seized—and not only by peaceful methods—from richer nations. In the United States, economic development in the last decades has been even more rapid than in Germany, and *for this very reason* the parasitic character of modern American capitalism has stood out with particular prominence. On the other hand, a comparison of, say, the republican American bourgeoisie with the monarchist Japanese or German bourgeoisie shows that the most pronounced political distinctions diminish to an extreme degree in the epoch of imperialism—not because they are unimportant in general, but because in all these cases we are discussing a bourgeoisie which has definite features of parasitism.

The receipt of high monopoly profits by the capitalists in one of the numerous branches of industry, in one of numerous countries, and so forth, makes it economically possible for them to corrupt certain sections of the working class, and for a time a fairly considerable minority, and win them to the side of the bourgeoisie of a given industry or nation against all the others. The intensification of antagonisms between imperialist nations for the division of the world increases this striving. And so there is created that bond between imperialism and opportunism, which revealed itself first and most clearly in England, owing to the fact that certain features of imperialist development were observable there much earlier than in other countries. . . .

From all that has been said on the economic nature of imperialism, it follows that we must define it as capitalism in transition, or, more precisely, as moribund capitalism. It is very instructive in this respect to note that the bourgeois economists, in describing modern capitalism, frequently employ terms like "interlocking," "absence of isolation," and so forth; "in conformity with their functions and course of development," banks are "not purely private business enterprises; they are more and more outgrowing the sphere of purely private business regulation." . . .

. . . But the underlying factor of this interlocking, its very base, is the changing social relations of production. When a big enterprise assumes gigantic proportions, and, on the basis of exact computation of mass data, organizes according to plan the supply of primary raw materials to the extent of two-thirds, or three-fourths of all that is necessary for tens of millions of people; when the raw materials are transported to the most suitable place of production, sometimes hundreds or thousands of miles away, in a systematic and organized manner; when a single centre directs all the successive stages of work right up to the manufacture of numerous varieties of finished articles; when these products are distributed according to a single plan among tens and hundreds of millions of consumers (as in the case of the distribution of oil in America and Germany by the American "oil trust")—then it becomes evident that we have socialization of production, and not mere "interlocking"; that private economic relations and private property relations constitute a shell which is no longer suitable for its contents, a shell which must inevitably begin to decay if its destruction be delayed by artificial means; a shell which may continue in a state of decay for a fairly long period (particularly if the cure of the opportunist abscess is protracted), but which will inevitably be removed. . . .

State and Revolution

• • •

THE STATE AS THE PRODUCT OF THE
IRRECONCILABILITY OF CLASS ANTAGONISMS

Let us begin with the most popular of Engels'[1] works, *The Origin of the Family, Private Property, and the State.* . . . Summarizing his historical analysis Engels says:

> The state is therefore by no means a power imposed on society from the outside; just as little is it "the reality of the moral idea," "the image and reality of reason," as Hegel[2] asserted. Rather, it is a product of society at a certain stage of development; it is the admission that this society has become entangled in an insoluble contradiction with itself, that it is cleft into irreconcilable antagonisms which it is powerless to dispel. But in order that these antagonisms, classes with conflicting economic interests, may not consume themselves and society in sterile struggle, a power apparently standing above society becomes necessary, whose purpose is to moderate the conflict and keep it within the bounds of "order"; and this power arising out of society, but placing itself above it, and increasingly separating itself from it, is the state.

Here we have, expressed in all its clearness, the basic idea of Marxism on the question of the historical role and meaning of the state. The state is the product and the manifestation of the *irreconcilability* of class antagonisms. The state arises when, where, and to the extent that the class antagonisms *cannot* be objectively reconciled. And, conversely, the existence of the state proves that the class antagonisms *are* irreconcilable.

[1] Friedrich Engels (1820–1895) was a German socialist and manufacturer.
[2] Georg Friedrich Wilhelm Hegel (1770–1831), a German idealist philosopher.

It is precisely on this most important and fundamental point that distortions of Marxism arise along two main lines.

On the one hand, the bourgeois, and particularly the petty-bourgeois, ideologists, compelled under the pressure of indisputable historical facts to admit that the state only exists where there are class antagonisms and the class struggle, "correct" Marx[3] in such a way as to make it appear that the state is an organ for *reconciling* the classes. According to Marx, the state could neither arise nor maintain itself if a reconciliation of classes were possible. But with the petty-bourgeois[4] and philistine[5] professors and publicists, the state—and this frequently on the strength of benevolent references to Marx!—becomes a conciliator of the classes. According to Marx, the state is an organ of class *domination,* an organ of *oppression* of one class by another; its aim is the creation of "order" which legalizes and perpetuates this oppression by moderating the collisions between the classes. But in the opinion of the petty-bourgeois politicians, order means reconciliation of the classes, and not oppression of one class by another; to moderate collisions does not mean, they say, to deprive the oppressed classes of certain definite means and methods of struggle for overthrowing the oppressors, but to practice reconciliation. . . .

On the other hand, the "Kautskyist"[6] distortion of Marx is far more subtle. "Theoretically," there is no denying that the state is the organ of class domination, or that class antagonisms are irreconcilable. But what is forgotten or glossed over is this: if the state is the product of the irreconcilable character of class antagonisms, if it is a force standing *above* society and "increasingly separating itself from it," then it is clear that the liberation of the oppressed class is impossible not only without a violent revolution, *but also without the destruction* of the apparatus of state power, which was created by the ruling class and in which this "separation" is embodied.

* * *

[3] Karl Marx (1818–1883), a German socialist philosopher and writer—sometimes with Engels—on economics and political philosophy.

[4] Shopkeeping class.

[5] Smugly conventional and narrow.

[6] Karl Johann Kautsky (1854–1938) was a German Social Democratic leader and writer. (Kautsky argued that state power could be "taken over" by the working classes through political means. It was chiefly to refute this "revisionist" view that Lenin argues in this document for the necessity of the forceful *seizure* of power.)

THE "WITHERING AWAY" OF THE STATE AND VIOLENT REVOLUTION

Engels' words regarding the "withering away" of the state enjoy such popularity, they are so often quoted, and they show so clearly the essence of the usual adulteration by means of which Marxism is made to look like opportunism, that we must dwell on them in detail. Let us quote the whole passage [from *Anti-Duehring*][7] from which they are taken.

The proletariat seizes state power, and then transforms the means of production into state property. But in doing this, it puts an end to itself as the proletariat, it puts an end to all class differences and class antagonisms, it puts an end also to the state as the state. Former society, moving in class antagonisms, had need of the state, that is, an organization of the exploiting class at each period for the maintenance of its external conditions of production; therefore, in particular, for the forcible holding down of the exploited class in the conditions of oppression (slavery, bondage or serfdom, wage-labor) determined by the existing mode of production. The state was the official representative of society as a whole, its embodiment in a visible corporate body; but it was this only in so far as it was the state of that class which itself, in its epoch, represented society as a whole: in ancient times, the state of the slave-owning citizens; in the Middle Ages, of the feudal nobility; in our epoch, of the bourgeoisie. When ultimately it becomes really representative of society as a whole, it makes itself superfluous. As soon as there is no longer any class of society to be held in subjection; as soon as, along with class domination and the struggle for individual existence based on the former anarchy of production, the collisions and excesses arising from these have also been abolished, there is nothing more to be repressed, and a special repressive force, a state, is no longer necessary. The first act in which the state really comes forward as the representative of society as a whole—the seizure of the means of production in the name of society—is at the same time its last independent act as a state. The interference of a state power in social relations becomes superfluous in one sphere after another, and then becomes dormant of itself. Government over persons is replaced by the administration of things and the direction of the processes of production. The state is not "abolished," *it withers away*. It is from this standpoint that we must appraise the phrase "people's free state"—both its justification at times

[7] Friedrich Engels, *Herr Eugen Duehring's Revolution in Science* (1878), a work commonly known as *Anti-Duehring*.

for agitational purposes, and its ultimate scientific inadequacy—and also the demand of the so-called Anarchists[8] that the state should be abolished overnight. . . .

In the first place, Engels at the very outset of his argument says that, in assuming state power, the proletariat by that very act "puts an end to the state as the state." One is "not accustomed" to reflect on what this really means. Generally, it is either ignored altogether, or it is considered as a piece of "Hegelian weakness" on Engels' part. As a matter of fact, however, these words express succinctly the experience of one of the greatest proletarian revolutions—the Paris Commune of 1871,[9] of which we shall speak in greater detail in its proper place. As a matter of fact, Engels speaks here of the destruction of the bourgeois state by the proletarian revolution, while the words about its withering away refer to the remains of *proletarian* statehood *after* the Socialist revolution. The bourgeois state does not "wither away," according to Engels, but is "put an end to" by the proletariat in the course of the revolution. What withers away after the revolution is the proletarian state or semistate.

Secondly, the state is a "special repressive force." This splendid and extremely profound definition of Engels is given by him here with complete lucidity. It follows from this that the "special repressive force" of the bourgeoisie for the suppression of the proletariat, of the millions of workers by a handful of the rich, must be replaced by a "special repressive force" of the proletariat for the suppression of the bourgeoisie (the dictatorship of the proletariat). It is just this that constitutes the destruction of "the state as the state." It is just this that constitutes the "act" of "the seizure of the means of production in the name of society." And it is obvious that such a substitution of one (proletarian) "special repressive force" for another (bourgeois) "special repressive force" can in no way take place in the form of a "withering away."

Thirdly, as to the "withering away" or, more expressively and

[8] The anarchists struggled against and endeavored to abolish any and all forms of power of human beings over human beings. (They were so called after the Greek word *anarchos,* meaning without a ruler—hence, absence of government.)

[9] An uprising, in March 1871, of radical, republican, and "socialist" Paris against the pro-monarchistic National Assembly and the kind of France it seemed to foreshadow. The lower classes were further enraged by the fact that the Assembly had too readily accepted the peace terms ending the Franco-Prussian war. The uprising was ruthlessly stamped out by troops of the National Assembly before the end of May 1871.

colorfully, as to the state "becoming dormant," Engels refers quite clearly and definitely to the period *after* "the seizure of the means of production [by the state] in the name of society," that is, *after* the Socialist revolution. We all know that the political form of the "state" at that time is complete democracy. But it never enters the head of any of the opportunists who shamelessly distort Marx that when Engels speaks here of the state "withering away," or "becoming dormant," he speaks of *democracy*. At first sight this seems very strange. But it is "unintelligible" only to one who has not reflected on the fact that democracy is *also* a state and that, consequently, democracy will *also* disappear when the state disappears. The bourgeois state can only be "put an end to" by a revolution. The state in general, that is, most complete democracy, can only "wither away."

• • •

TRANSITION FROM CAPITALISM TO COMMUNISM

> Between capitalist and Communist society—Marx [writes]—lies the period of the revolutionary transformation of the former into the latter. To this also corresponds a political transition period, in which the state can be no other than *the revolutionary dictatorship of the proletariat.*

This conclusion Marx bases on an analysis of the role played by the proletariat in modern capitalist society, on the data concerning the evolution of this society, and on the irreconcilability of the opposing interests of the proletariat and the bourgeoisie.

Earlier the question was put thus: to attain its emancipation, the proletariat must overthrow the bourgeoisie, conquer political power and establish its own revolutionary dictatorship.

Now the question is put somewhat differently: the transition from capitalist society, developing towards Communism, towards a Communist society, is impossible without a "political transition period," and the state in this period can only be the revolutionary dictatorship of the proletariat.

What, then, is the relation of this dictatorship to democracy?

We have seen that the *Communist Manifesto* simply places side by side the two ideas: the "transformation of the proletariat into the ruling class" and the "establishment of democracy." On the basis of all that has been said above, one can define more exactly how democracy changes in the transition from capitalism to Communism.

In capitalist society, under the conditions most favorable to its development, we have more or less complete democracy in the democratic republic. But this democracy is always bound by the narrow framework of capitalist exploitation, and consequently always remains, in reality, a democracy for the minority, only for the possessing classes, only for the rich. Freedom in capitalist society always remains just about the same as it was in the ancient Greek republics: freedom for the slave-owners. The modern wage-slaves, owing to the conditions of capitalist exploitation, are so much crushed by want and poverty that "democracy is nothing to them," "politics is nothing to them"; that, in the ordinary peaceful course of events, the majority of the population is debarred from participating in social and political life. . . .

Democracy for an insignificant minority, democracy for the rich— that is the democracy of capitalist society. If we look more closely into the mechanism of capitalist democracy, everywhere, both in the "petty"—so-called petty—details of the suffrage (residential qualification, exclusion of women, and so forth), and in the technique of the representative institutions, in the actual obstacles to the right of assembly (public buildings are not for "beggars"!), in the purely capitalist organization of the daily press, and so forth—on all sides we see restriction after restriction upon democracy. These restrictions, exceptions, exclusions, obstacles for the poor, seem slight, especially in the eyes of one who has himself never known want and has never been in close contact with the oppressed classes in their mass life (and nine-tenths, if not ninety-nine hundredths, of the bourgeois publicists and politicians are of this class), but in their sum total these restrictions exclude and squeeze out the poor from politics and from an active share in democracy.

Marx splendidly grasped this *essence* of capitalist democracy, when, in analyzing the experience of the Commune,[10] he said that the oppressed were allowed, once every few years, to decide which particular representatives of the oppressing class should be in parliament to represent and repress them!

But from this capitalist democracy—inevitably narrow, subtly rejecting the poor, and therefore hypocritical and false to the core— progress does not march onward, simply, smoothly and directly, to "greater and greater democracy," as the liberal professors and petty-

[10] The Paris Commune (see footnote 9).

bourgeois opportunists would have us believe. No, progress marches onward, that is, towards Communism, through the dictatorship of the proletariat; it cannot do otherwise, for there is no one else and no other way to *break the resistance* of the capitalist exploiters.

But the dictatorship of the proletariat—that is, the organization of the vanguard of the oppressed as the ruling class for the purpose of crushing the oppressors—cannot produce merely an expansion of democracy. *Together* with an immense expansion of democracy which *for the first time* becomes democracy for the poor, democracy for the people, and not democracy for the rich folk, the dictatorship of the proletariat produces a series of restrictions of liberty in the case of the oppressors, the exploiters, the capitalists. We must crush them in order to free humanity from wage-slavery; their resistance must be broken by force; it is clear that where there is suppression there is also violence, there is no liberty, no democracy.

Engels expressed this splendidly in his letter to Bebel[11] when he said, as the reader will remember, that "as long as the proletariat still *needs* the state, it needs it not in the interests of freedom, but for the purpose of crushing its antagonists; and as soon as it becomes possible to speak of freedom, then the state, as such, ceases to exist."

Democracy for the vast majority of the people, and suppression by force, namely, exclusion from democracy, of the exploiters and oppressors of the people—this is the modification of democracy during the *transition* from capitalism to Communism.

Only in Communist society, when the resistance of the capitalists has been completely broken, when the capitalists have disappeared, when there are no classes (that is, there is no difference between the members of society in their relation to the social means of production), *only then* "the state ceases to exist," and *"it becomes possible to speak of freedom."* Only then a really full democracy, a democracy without any exceptions, will be possible and will be realized. And only then will democracy itself begin to *wither away* due to the simple fact that, freed from capitalist slavery, from the untold horrors, savagery, absurdities and infamies of capitalist exploitation, people will gradually *become accustomed* to the observance of the elementary rules of social life that have been known for centuries and repeated for thousands of years in all school books; they will become accustomed to observing them without force, without compulsion, with-

---

[11] August Bebel (1840–1913), a German Social Democratic leader who shared the political position of Karl Kautsky (see footnote 6).

out subordination, without the *special apparatus* for compulsion which is called the state.

The expression "the state *withers away,*" is very well chosen, for it indicates both the gradual and the elemental nature of the process. Only habit can, and undoubtedly will, have such an effect; for we see around us millions of times how readily people get accustomed to observe the necessary rules of life in common, if there is no exploitation, if there is nothing that causes indignation, that calls forth protest and revolt and has to be *suppressed.*

Thus, in capitalist society, we have a democracy that is curtailed, poor, false; a democracy only for the rich, for the minority. The dictatorship of the proletariat, the period of transition to Communism, will, for the first time, produce democracy for the people, for the majority, side by side with the necessary suppression of the minority—the exploiters. Communism alone is capable of giving a really complete democracy, and the more complete it is the more quickly will it become unnecessary and wither away of itself.

In other words: under capitalism we have a state in the proper sense of the word, that is, special machinery for the suppression of one class by another, and of the majority by the minority at that. Naturally, for the successful discharge of such a task as the systematic suppression by the exploiting minority of the exploited majority, the greatest ferocity and savagery of suppression are required, seas of blood are required, through which mankind is marching in slavery, serfdom, and wage-labor.

Again, during the *transition* from capitalism to Communism, suppression is *still* necessary; but it is the suppression of the minority of exploiters by the majority of the exploited. A special apparatus, special machinery for suppression, the "state," is *still* necessary, but this is now a transitional state, no longer a state in the usual sense, for the suppression of the minority of exploiters, by the majority of the wage slaves *of yesterday,* is a matter comparatively so easy, simple and natural that it will cost far less bloodshed than the suppression of the risings of slaves, serfs or wage laborers, and will cost mankind far less. This is compatible with the diffusion of democracy among such an overwhelming majority of the population, that the need for *special machinery* of suppression will begin to disappear. The exploiters are, naturally, unable to suppress the people without the most complex machinery for performing this task; but *the people* can suppress the exploiters even with very simple "machinery," almost without any "machinery," without any special apparatus, by the simple *organization of the armed masses*. . . .

Finally, only Communism renders the state absolutely unnecessary, for there is *no one* to be suppressed—"no one" in the sense of a *class,* in the sense of a systematic struggle with a definite section of the population. We are not Utopians,[12] and we do not in the least deny the possibility and inevitability of excesses on the part of *individual persons,* nor the need to suppress *such* excesses. But, in the first place, no special machinery, no special apparatus of repression is needed for this; this will be done by the armed people itself, as simply and as readily as any crowd of civilized people, even in modern society, parts a pair of combatants or does not allow a woman to be outraged. And, secondly, we know that the fundamental social cause of excesses which consist in violating the rules of social life is the exploitation of the masses, their want and their poverty. With the removal of this chief cause, excesses will inevitably begin to *"wither away."* We do not know how quickly and in what succession, but we know that they will wither away. With their withering away, the state will also *wither away*.

Without going into Utopias, Marx defined more fully what can *now* be defined regarding this future, namely, the difference between the lower and higher phases (degrees, stages) of Communist society.

FIRST PHASE OF COMMUNIST SOCIETY

. . . Marx gives a sober estimate of exactly how a Socialist society will have to manage its affairs. Marx undertakes a *concrete* analysis of the conditions of life of a society in which there is no capitalism, and says:

> What we are dealing with here [analyzing the programme of the party] is not a Communist society which has *developed* on its own foundations, but, on the contrary, one which is just *emerging* from capitalist society, and which therefore in all respects—economic, moral and intellectual—still bears the birthmarks of the old society from whose womb it sprung.

And it is this Communist society—a society which has just come into the world out of the womb of capitalism, and which, in all re-

[12] Idealists dreaming of a society of perfect harmony.

spects, bears the stamp of the old society—that Marx terms the "first," or lower, phase of Communist society.

The means of production are no longer the private property of individuals. The means of production belong to the whole of society. Every member of society, performing a certain part of socially-necessary work, receives a certificate from society to the effect that he has done such and such a quantity of work. According to this certificate, he receives from the public warehouses, where articles of consumption are stored, a corresponding quantity of products. Deducting that proportion of labor which goes to the public fund, every worker, therefore, receives from society as much as he has given it.

"Equality" seems to reign supreme. . . .

"Equal right," says Marx, we indeed have here; but it is *still* a "bourgeois right," which, like every right, *presupposes inequality*. Every right is an application of the *same* measure to *different* people who, in fact, are not the same and are not equal to one another; this is why "equal right" is really a violation of equality, and an injustice. In effect, every man having done as much social labor as every other, receives an equal share of the social products (with the above-mentioned deductions).

But different people are not alike: one is strong, another is weak; one is married, the other is not; one has more children, another has less, and so on.

> With equal labor—Marx concludes—and therefore an equal share in the social consumption fund, one man in fact receives more than the other, one is richer than the other, and so forth. In order to avoid all these defects, rights, instead of being equal, must be unequal.

The first phase of Communism, therefore, still cannot produce justice and equality; differences, and unjust differences, in wealth will still exist, but the *exploitation* of man by man will have become impossible, because it will be impossible to seize as private property the *means of production,* the factories, machines, land, and so on. In tearing down Lassalle's [13] petty-bourgeois, confused phrase about "equality" and "justice" *in general,* Marx shows the *course of development* of Communist society, which is forced at first to destroy *only* the "injustice" that consists in the means of production having been

[13] Ferdinand Lassalle (1825–1864) was a German socialist and the founder of the German Social Democratic Party.

seized by private individuals, and which *is not capable* of destroying at once the further injustice consisting in the distribution of the articles of consumption "according to work performed" (and not according to need). . . .

Marx not only takes into account with the greatest accuracy the inevitable inequality of men; he also takes into account the fact that the mere conversion of the means of production into the common property of the whole of society ("Socialism" in the generally accepted sense of the word) *does not remove* the defects of distribution and the inequality of "bourgeois right" which *continue to rule* as long as the products are divided "according to work performed."

> But these defects—Marx continues—are unavoidable in the first phase of Communist society, when, after long travail, it first emerges from capitalist society. Justice can never rise superior to the economic conditions of society and the cultural development conditioned by them.

And so, in the first phase of Communist society (generally called Socialism) "bourgeois right" is *not* abolished in its entirety, but only in part, only in proportion to the economic transformation so far attained, that is, only in respect of the means of production. "Bourgeois right" recognizes them as the private property of separate individuals. Socialism converts them into common property. *To that extent,* and to that extent alone, does "bourgeois right" disappear.

However, it continues to exist as far as its other part is concerned; it remains in the capacity of regulator (determining factor) distributing the products and allotting labor among the members of society. "He who does not work, shall not eat"—this Socialist principle is *already* realized; "for an equal quantity of labor, an equal quantity of products"—this Socialist principle is also *already* realized. However, this is not yet Communism, and this does not abolish "bourgeois right," which gives to unequal individuals, in return for an unequal (in reality unequal) amount of work, an equal quantity of products.

This is a "defect," says Marx, but it is unavoidable during the first phase of Communism; for, if we are not to fall into Utopianism, we cannot imagine that, having overthrown capitalism, people will at once learn to work for society *without any standards of right;* indeed, the abolition of capitalism *does not immediately lay* the economic foundations for *such* a change.

And there is no other standard yet than that of "bourgeois right."

To this extent, therefore, a form of state is still necessary, which, while maintaining public ownership of the means of production, would preserve the equality of labor and equality in the distribution of products.

The state is withering away in so far as there are no longer any capitalists, any classes, and, consequently, no *class* can be suppressed.

But the state has not yet altogether withered away, since there still remains the protection of "bourgeois right" which sanctifies actual inequality. For the complete extinction of the state, complete Communism is necessary.

HIGHER PHASE OF COMMUNIST SOCIETY

Marx continues:

> In a higher phase of Communist society, when the enslaving subordi-
> nation of individuals in the division of labor has disappeared, and with it
> also the antagonism between mental and physical labor; when labor has
> become not only a means of living, but itself the first necessity of life;
> when, along with the all-round development of individuals, the produc-
> tive forces too have grown, and all the springs of social wealth are
> flowing more freely—it is only at that stage that it will be possible to
> pass completely beyond the narrow horizon of bourgeois rights, and for
> society to inscribe on its banners: from each according to his ability; to
> each according to his needs!

Only now can we appreciate the full correctness of Engels' re-marks in which he mercilessly ridiculed all the absurdity of combin-ing the words "freedom" and "state." While the state exists there is no freedom. When there is freedom, there will be no state.

The economic basis for the complete withering away of the state is that high stage of development of Communism when the antago-nism between mental and physical labor disappears, that is to say, when one of the principal sources of modern *social* inequality dis-appears—a source, moreover, which it is impossible to remove im-mediately by the mere conversion of the means of production into public property, by the mere expropriation of the capitalists.

This expropriation will make a gigantic development of the pro-ductive forces *possible*. And seeing how incredibly, even now, capi-talism *retards* this development, how much progress could be made even on the basis of modern technique at the level it has reached, we have a right to say, with the fullest confidence, that the expropriation of the capitalists will inevitably result in a gigantic development of the productive forces of human society. But how rapidly this development will go forward, how soon it will reach the point of breaking away from the division of labor, of removing the antagonism between mental and physical labor, of transforming work into the "first necessity of life"—this we do not and *cannot* know.

Consequently, we have a right to speak solely of the inevitable withering away of the state, emphasizing the protracted nature of this process and its dependence upon the rapidity of development of the *higher phase* of Communism; leaving quite open the question of lengths of time, or the concrete forms of withering away, since material for the solution of such questions is *not available*.

The state will be able to wither away completely when society has realized the rule: "From each according to his ability; to each according to his needs," namely, when people have become accustomed to observe the fundamental rules of social life, and their labor is so productive, that they voluntarily work *according to their ability*. "The narrow horizon of bourgeois rights," which compels one to calculate, with the hard-heartedness of a Shylock,[14] whether he has not worked half an hour more than another, whether he is not getting less pay than another—this narrow horizon will then be left behind. There will then be no need for any exact calculation by society of the quantity of products to be distributed to each of its members; each will take freely "according to his needs."

From the bourgeois point of view, it is easy to declare such a social order "a pure Utopia," and to sneer at the Socialists for promising each the right to receive from society, without any control of the labor of the individual citizen, any quantity of truffles, automobiles, pianos, and so forth. Even now, most bourgeois "savants"[15] deliver themselves of such sneers, thereby displaying at once their ignorance and their self-seeking defense of capitalism.

Ignorance—for it has never entered the head of any Socialist to "promise" that the highest phase of Communism will arrive; while the great Socialists, in *foreseeing* its arrival, presupposed both a productivity of labor unlike the present and a person not like the present man in the street, capable of spoiling, without reflection, like the

---

[14] The greedy and merciless moneylender in Shakespeare's play *The Merchant of Venice*.
[15] Learned men; here used satirically, as "wiseacres."

seminary students in Pomyalovsky's [16] book, the stores of social wealth, and of demanding the impossible.

Until the "higher" phase of Communism arrives, the Socialists demand the *strictest* control, *by society and by the state,* of the quantity of labor and the quantity of consumption; only this control must *start* with the expropriation of the capitalists, with the control of the workers over the capitalists, and must be carried out, not by a state of bureaucrats, but by a state of *armed workers.* . . .

---

[16] Nikolai Pomyalovsky (1835–1863) was a Russian writer who had been a theology student before turning to literature. In his *Sketches from the Seminary,* published in 1859, he rendered a shocking and disenchanting description of life in a theological school.

28

Adolf Hitler

Mein Kampf

The First World War and the Bolshevik Revolution were severe blows to the European liberal order. The destruction of the traditional social system and its values and the spiritual uprooting of the European masses gave rise to a widespread popular reaction against liberalism, democracy, and the complex urban-industrial revolution that had nurtured them. Adolf Hitler (1889– 1945) became the demonic prophet and leader of this counterrevolution.

As a young man, Hitler led an aimless existence in prewar Austria and Germany. After the war, in which he served with great personal satisfaction, he devoted his life to political affairs, joining the National Socialist (Nazi) German Workers' Party and soon becoming its leader (Führer). In 1923 he led an unsuccessful revolt against the government, for which he served a short term in prison; but he went on to transform the Nazi party into the mass movement that would, within a decade, dominate Germany. In doing so, he played on the frustrations of a people in defeat and economic depression and, for the most part, in distress over the dislocations brought on by indus- trialization and urbanization. The party he headed won allegiance through mass propaganda and terror, and in 1933 he became dictator of the nation. As head of state he instituted a nationalist, collectivist, and militarist regime based on romantic notions of people (Volk) and race, and led the Germans into a series of annexations and invasions that developed into the Second World War.

Hitler had expounded his program in an exciting but confused book called Mein Kampf (My Struggle), *which was written during his prison term and*

Adolf Hitler, *Mein Kampf,* trans. Ralph Manheim (Boston: Houghton Mifflin, 1943), 51, 64–65, 107, 118–19, 177–81, 214–15, 231, 286, 288, 290, 294, 305–306, 314–16, 318–20, 324–27, 382–85, 623, 642–43, 645–46, 652–54, 661, 682.

published sometime between 1925 and 1927. Supposedly the story of his early life and the development of his ideas and the Nazi movement, the book is a mixture of half truths, big lies, scurrilous attacks, and idealistic emotional appeals. He denounces Marxism, Jews, bourgeois liberals, and democracy as the sources of Germany's ills; and he calls for a "regenerated" German nation, attached to its sacred soil, purified in its racial make-up, and devotedly following its leaders to world supremacy. The bible of Nazi Germany, the book remains a classic exhibition of violent hatred and irrationality.

The following selection from Mein Kampf—*in which sections have been rearranged for the sake of clarity—illustrates Hitler's views on what he believed to be a Marxist-Jewish conspiracy against the German people; the natural inequality of races and the superiority of the Aryan race; the* Volk *as the natural human unit and the primacy of the German* Volk; *the nature and purposes of propaganda in the creation of a successful mass movement dedicated to the achievement of Nazi objectives; and the need for Germany to conquer more soil for its people. Though largely discredited at present, some of Hitler's ideas still have appeal among those disenchanted with the course of Western civilization and desirous of a return to a simpler past.*

MARXISM

I began to make myself familiar with the founders of [Marxism] in order to study the foundations of the movement. If I reached my goal more quickly than at first I had perhaps ventured to believe, it was thanks to my newly acquired, though at that time not very profound, knowledge of the Jewish question. This alone enabled me to draw a practical comparison between the reality and the theoretical flim-flam of the founding fathers of Social Democracy, since it taught me to understand the language of the Jewish people, who speak in order to conceal or at least to veil their thoughts; their real aim is not therefore to be found in the lines themselves, but slumbers well concealed between them.

For me this was the time of the greatest spiritual upheaval I have ever had to go through.

I had ceased to be a weak-kneed cosmopolitan and become an anti-Semite.[1] . . .

---

[1] One who hates Jews and Jewish things.

The Jewish doctrine of Marxism rejects the aristocratic principle of Nature and replaces the eternal privilege of power and strength by the mass of numbers and their dead weight. Thus it denies the value of personality in man, contests the significance of nationality and race, and thereby withdraws from humanity the premise of its existence and its culture. As a foundation of the universe, this doctrine would bring about the end of any order intellectually conceivable to man. And as, in this greatest of all recognizable organisms, the result of an application of such a law could only be chaos, on earth it could only be destruction for the inhabitants of this planet.

If, with the help of his Marxist creed, the Jew is victorious over the other peoples of the world, his crown will be the funeral wreath of humanity and this planet will, as it did thousands of years ago, move through the ether devoid of men.

Eternal Nature inexorably avenges the infringement of her commands.

Hence today I believe that I am acting in accordance with the will of the Almighty Creator: *by defending myself against the Jew, I am fighting for the work of the Lord. . . .*

Only a knowledge of the Jews provides the key with which to comprehend the inner, and consequently real, aims of Social Democracy.

The erroneous conceptions of the aim and meaning of this party fall from our eyes like veils, once we come to know this people, and from the fog and mist of social phrases rises the leering grimace of Marxism. . . .

Marxist doctrine is a brief spiritual extract of the philosophy of life that is generally current today. And for this reason alone any struggle of our so-called bourgeois world against it is impossible, absurd in fact, since this bourgeois world is also essentially infected by these poisons, and worships a view of life which in general is distinguished from the Marxists only by degrees and personalities. The bourgeois world is Marxist, but believes in the possibility of the rule of certain groups of men (bourgeoisie), while Marxism itself systematically plans to hand the world over to the Jews. . . .

. . . A Germany saved from these mortal enemies of her existence and her future would possess forces which the whole world could no longer have stifled. *On the day when Marxism is smashed in Germany, her fetters will in truth be broken forever.* For never in our history have we been defeated by the strength of our foes, but always by our own vices and by the enemies in our own camp. . . .

JEWS

The Jew of all times has lived in the states of other peoples, and there formed his own state, which, to be sure, habitually sailed under the disguise of 'religious community' as long as outward circumstances made a complete revelation of his nature seem inadvisable. But as soon as he felt strong enough to do without the protective cloak, he always dropped the veil and suddenly became what so many of the others previously did not want to believe and see: the Jew.

The Jew's life as a parasite in the body of other nations and states explains a characteristic which once caused Schopenhauer[2]. . . to call him the 'great master in lying.' Existence impels the Jew to lie, and to lie perpetually, just as it compels the inhabitants of the northern countries to wear warm clothing.

His life within other peoples can only endure for any length of time if he succeeds in arousing the opinion that he is not a people but a 'religious community,' though of a special sort.

And this is the first great lie. . . .

The Jew has always been a people with definite racial characteristics and never a religion; only in order to get ahead he early sought for a means which could distract unpleasant attention from his person. And what would have been more expedient and at the same time more innocent than the 'embezzled' concept of a religious community? For here, too, everything is borrowed or rather stolen. Due to his own original special nature, the Jew cannot possess a religious institution, if for no other reason because he lacks idealism in any form, and hence belief in a hereafter is absolutely foreign to him. And a religion in the Aryan[3] sense cannot be imagined which lacks the conviction of survival after death in some form. . . .

---

[2] Arthur Schopenhauer (1788–1860), a German philosopher and chief expounder of pessimism.

[3] Indo-European, as differentiated from Jewish. (The Indo-European peoples, as a large *language* group, were believed to have originated in north-central Europe and to

The Jew also becomes liberal and begins to rave about the necessary progress of mankind.

Slowly he makes himself the spokesman of a new era.

Also, of course, he destroys more and more thoroughly the foundations of any economy that will really benefit the people. By way of stock shares he pushes his way into the circuit of national production which he turns into a purchasable or rather tradable object, thus robbing the enterprises of the foundations of a personal ownership. Between employer and employee there arises that inner estrangement which later leads to political class division.

Finally, the Jewish influence on economic affairs grows with terrifying speed through the stock exchange. He becomes the owner, or at least the controller, of the national labor force.

To strengthen his political position he tries to tear down the racial and civil barriers which for a time continue to restrain him at every step. To this end he fights with all the tenacity innate in him for religious tolerance. . . .

He always represents himself personally as having an infinite thirst for knowledge, praises all progress, mostly, to be sure, the progress that leads to the ruin of others; for he judges all knowledge and all development only according to its possibilities for advancing his nation, and where this is lacking, he is the inexorable mortal enemy of all light, a hater of all true culture. He uses all the knowledge he acquires in the schools of other peoples, exclusively for the benefit of his race. . . .

His ultimate goal . . . is the victory of 'democracy,' or, as he understands it: the rule of parliamentarianism. It is most compatible with his requirements; for it excludes the personality—and puts in its place the majority characterized by stupidity, incompetence, and last but not least, cowardice. . . .

. . . While on the one hand he organizes capitalistic methods of human exploitation to their ultimate consequence, [the Jew] approaches the very victims of his spirit and his activity and in a short time becomes the leader of their struggle against himself. 'Against

have dispersed westward, southward, and eastward around 3000 B.C. Some race theorists, followed by Hitler, insisted that the Indo-Europeans constituted a distinctive and superior *racial* group, which they called "Aryans.")

himself' is only figuratively speaking; for the great master of lies understands as always how to make himself appear to be the pure one and to load the blame on others. Since he has the gall to lead the masses, it never even enters their heads that this might be the most infamous betrayal of all times.

And yet it was.

Scarcely has the [proletariat] grown out of the general economic shift than the Jew, clearly and distinctly, realizes that it can open the way for his own further advancement. First, he used the bourgeoisie as a battering-ram against the feudal world, then the worker against the bourgeois world. If formerly he knew how to swindle his way to civil rights in the shadow of the bourgeoisie, now he hopes to find the road to his own domination in the worker's struggle for existence.

From now on the worker has no other task but to fight for the future of the Jewish people. Unconsciously he is harnessed to the service of the power which he thinks he is combating. He is seemingly allowed to attack capital, and this is the easiest way of making him fight for it. In this the Jew keeps up an outcry against international capital and in truth he means the national economy which must be demolished in order that the international stock exchange can triumph over its dead body. . . .

Thus there arises a pure movement entirely of manual workers under Jewish leadership, apparently aiming to improve the situation of the worker, but in truth planning the enslavement and with it the destruction of all non-Jewish peoples.

The general pacifistic paralysis of the national instinct of self-preservation . . . in the circles of the so-called intelligentsia [4] is transmitted to the broad masses and above all to the bourgeoisie by the activity of the big papers which today are always Jewish. Added to these two weapons of disintegration comes a third and by far the most terrible, the organization of brute force. As a shock and storm troop, Marxism is intended to finish off what the preparatory softening up with the first two weapons has made ripe for collapse. . . .

Here [the Jew] stops at nothing, and in his vileness he becomes so gigantic that no one need be surprised if among our people the per-

---

[4] The educated class, the intellectuals.

sonification of the devil as the symbol of all evil assumes the living shape of the Jew.

The ignorance of the broad masses about the inner nature of the Jew, the lack of instinct and narrow-mindedness of our upper classes, make the people an easy victim for this Jewish campaign of lies. . . .

With satanic joy in his face, the black-haired Jewish youth lurks in wait for the unsuspecting girl whom he defiles with his blood, thus stealing her from her people. With every means he tries to destroy the racial foundations of the people he has set out to subjugate. Just as he himself systematically ruins women and girls, he does not shrink back from pulling down the blood barriers for others, even on a large scale. It was and it is Jews who bring the Negroes into the Rhineland,[5] always with the same secret thought and clear aim of ruining the hated white race by the necessarily resulting bastardization, throwing it down from its cultural and political height, and himself rising to be its master.

For a racially pure people which is conscious of its blood can never be enslaved by the Jew. In this world he will forever be master over bastards and bastards alone.

And so he tries systematically to lower the racial level by a continuous poisoning of individuals.

And in politics he begins to replace the idea of democracy by the dictatorship of the proletariat.

In the organized mass of Marxism he has found the weapon which lets him dispense with democracy and in its stead allows him to subjugate and govern the peoples with a dictatorial and brutal fist.

He works systematically for revolutionization in a twofold sense: economic and political.

Around peoples who offer too violent a resistance to attack from within he weaves a net of enemies, thanks to his international influence, incites them to war, and finally, if necessary, plants the flag of revolution on the very battlefields.

In economics he undermines the states until the social enterprises which have become unprofitable are taken from the state and subjected to his financial control.

In the political field he refuses the state the means for its self-preser-

---

[5] A reference to the French occupation of the Rhineland after the First World War; some of the French troops were blacks from French colonial Africa.

vation, destroys the foundations of all national self-maintenance and defense, destroys faith in the leadership, scoffs at its history and past, and drags everything that is truly great into the gutter.

Culturally he contaminates art, literature, the theater, makes a mockery of natural feeling, overthrows all concepts of beauty and sublimity, of the noble and the good, and instead drags men down into the sphere of his own base nature.

Religion is ridiculed, ethics and morality represented as outmoded, until the last props of a nation in its struggle for existence in this world have fallen.

Now begins the great last revolution. In gaining political power the Jew casts off the few cloaks that he still wears. The democratic people's Jew becomes the blood-Jew and tyrant over peoples. In a few years he tries to exterminate the national intelligentsia and by robbing the peoples of their natural intellectual leadership makes them ripe for the slave's lot of permanent subjugation.

The most frightful example of this kind is offered by Russia, where he killed or starved about thirty million people with positively fanatical savagery, in part amid inhuman tortures, in order to give a gang of Jewish journalists and stock exchange bandits domination over a great people.

The end is not only the end of freedom of the peoples oppressed by the Jew, but also the end of this parasite upon the nations. After the death of his victim, the vampire sooner or later dies too. . . .

The Jewish train of thought in all this is clear. The Bolshevization of Germany[6]—that is, the extermination of the national folkish . . . intelligentsia to make possible the sweating of the German working class under the yoke of Jewish world finance—is conceived only as a preliminary to the further extension of this Jewish tendency of world conquest. As often in history, Germany is the great pivot in the mighty struggle. If our people and our state become the victim of these bloodthirsty and avaricious Jewish tyrants of nations, the whole earth will sink into the snares of this octopus; if Germany frees herself from this embrace, this greatest of dangers to nations may be regarded as broken for the whole world. . . .

. . . The striving of the Jewish people for world domination . . . is just as natural as the urge of the Anglo-Saxon to seize domination

---

[6] The turning of Germany into a communist state on the Russian Bolshevik model.

of the earth. And just as the Anglo-Saxon pursues this course in his own way and carries on the fight with his own weapons, likewise the Jew. He goes his way, the way of sneaking in among the nations and boring from within, and he fights with his weapons, with lies and slander, poison and corruption, intensifying the struggle to the point of bloodily exterminating his hated foes. *In Russian Bolshevism* [7] *we must see the attempt undertaken by the Jews in the twentieth century to achieve world domination. . . .*

RACE AND THE FOLKISH PHILOSOPHY

For me and all true National Socialists there is but one doctrine: people and fatherland.

What we must fight for is to safeguard the existence and reproduction of our race and our people, the sustenance of our children and the purity of our blood, the freedom and independence of the fatherland, so that our people may mature for the fulfillment of the mission allotted it by the creator of the universe.

Every thought and every idea, every doctrine and all knowledge, must serve this purpose. And everything must be examined from this point of view and used or rejected according to its utility. Then no theory will stiffen into a dead doctrine, since it is life alone that all things must serve. . . .

No more than Nature desires the mating of weaker with stronger individuals, even less does she desire the blending of a higher with a lower race, since, if she did, her whole work of higher breeding, over perhaps hundreds of thousands of years, might be ruined with one blow.

Historical experience offers countless proofs of this. It shows with terrifying clarity that in every mingling of Aryan blood with that of lower peoples the result was the end of the cultured people. North America, whose population consists in by far the largest part of Germanic elements who mixed but little with the lower colored peoples, shows a different humanity and culture from Central and South America, where the predominantly Latin immigrants often mixed with the aborigines on a large scale. By this one example, we can

---

[7] Communism.

clearly and distinctly recognize the effect of racial mixture. The Germanic inhabitant of the American continent, who has remained racially pure and unmixed, rose to be master of the continent; he will remain the master as long as he does not fall a victim to defilement of the blood.

The result of all racial crossing is therefore in brief always the following:

(a) Lowering of the level of the higher race;

(b) Physical and intellectual regression and hence the beginning of a slowly but surely progressing sickness.

To bring about such a development is, then, nothing else but to sin against the will of the eternal creator. . . .

Everything we admire on this earth today—science and art, technology and inventions—is only the creative product of a few peoples and originally perhaps of *one* race. On them depends the existence of this whole culture. If they perish, the beauty of this earth will sink into the grave with them. . . .

It is idle to argue which race or races were the original representative of human culture and hence the real founders of all that we sum up under the word 'humanity.' It is simpler to raise this question with regard to the present, and here an easy, clear answer results. All the human culture, all the results of art, science, and technology that we see before us today, are almost exclusively the creative product of the Aryan. This very fact admits of the not unfounded inference that he alone was the founder of all higher humanity, therefore representing the prototype of all that we understand by the word 'man.' He is the Prometheus[8] of mankind from whose bright forehead the divine spark of genius has sprung at all times, forever kindling anew that fire of knowledge which illumined the night of silent mysteries and thus caused man to climb the path to mastery over the other beings of this earth. Exclude him—and perhaps after a few thousand years darkness will again descend on the earth, human culture will pass, and the world turn to a desert.

If we were to divide mankind into three groups, the founders of culture, the bearers of culture, the destroyers of culture, only the Aryan could be considered as the representative of the first group.

[8] In Greek mythology, an ancient god who stole fire from heaven and gave it to humankind.

From him originate the foundations and walls of all human creation, and only the outward form and color are determined by the changing traits of character of the various peoples. He provides the mightiest building stones and plans for all human progress and only the execution corresponds to the nature of the varying men and races. . . .

. . . Just as in the life of the outstanding individual, genius or extraordinary ability strives for practical realization only when spurred on by special occasions, likewise in the life of nations the creative forces and capacities which are present can often be exploited only when definite preconditions invite.

We see this most distinctly in connection with the race which has been and is the bearer of human cultural development—the Aryans. As soon as Fate leads them toward special conditions, their latent abilities begin to develop in a more and more rapid sequence and to mold themselves into tangible forms. The cultures which they found in such cases are nearly always decisively determined by the existing soil, the given climate, and—the subjected people. This last item, to be sure, is almost the most decisive. The more primitive the technical foundations for a cultural activity, the more necessary is the presence of human helpers who, organizationally assembled and employed, must replace the force of the machine. Without this possibility of using lower human beings, the Aryan would never have been able to take his first steps toward his future culture; just as without the help of various suitable beasts which he knew how to tame, he would not have arrived at a technology which is now gradually permitting him to do without these beasts. . . .

The folkish[9] philosophy finds the importance of mankind in its basic racial elements. In the state it sees on principle only a means to an end and construes its end as the preservation of the racial existence of man. Thus, it by no means believes in an equality of the races, but along with their difference it recognizes their higher or lesser value and feels itself obligated, through this knowledge, to promote the victory of the better and stronger, and demand the subordination of the inferior and weaker in accordance with the eternal will that dominates this universe. Thus, in principle, it serves the basic aristocratic

[9] Originating from the people (*Volk*) and benefiting them.

idea of Nature and believes in the validity of this law down to the last individual. It sees not only the different value of the races, but also the different value of individuals. From the mass it extracts the importance of the individual personality, and thus, in contrast to disorganizing Marxism, it has an organizing effect. It believes in the necessity of an idealization of humanity, in which alone it sees the premise for the existence of humanity. But it cannot grant the right to existence even to an ethical idea if this idea represents a danger for the racial life of the bearers of a higher ethics; for in a bastardized and niggerized world all the concepts of the humanly beautiful and sublime, as well as all ideas of an idealized future of our humanity, would be lost forever. . . .

And so the folkish philosophy of life corresponds to the innermost will of Nature, since it restores that free play of forces which must lead to a continuous mutual higher breeding, until at last the best of humanity, having achieved possession of this earth, will have a free path for activity in domains which will lie partly above it and partly outside it.

We all sense that in the distant future humanity must be faced by problems which only a highest race, become master people and supported by the means and possibilities of an entire globe, will be equipped to overcome. . . .

It is self-evident that so general a statement of the meaningful content of a folkish philosophy can be interpreted in thousands of ways. And actually we find hardly a one of our newer political formations which does not base itself in one way or another on this world view. And, by its very existence in the face of the many others, it shows the difference of its conceptions. And so the Marxist world view, led by a unified top organization, is opposed by a hodge-podge of views which even as ideas are not very impressive in face of the solid, hostile front. Victories are not gained by such feeble weapons! Not until the international world view—politically led by organized Marxism—is confronted by a folkish world view, organized and led with equal unity, will success, supposing the fighting energy to be equal on both sides, fall to the side of eternal truth.

A philosophy can only be organizationally comprehended on the basis of a definite formulation of that philosophy, and what dogmas represent for religious faith, party principles are for a political party in the making.

Hence an instrument must be created for the folkish world view which enables it to fight, just as the Marxist party organization creates a free path for internationalism.

This is the goal pursued by the National Socialist German Workers' Party. . . .

PROPAGANDA

The broad masses of the people can be moved only by the power of speech. And all great movements are popular movements, volcanic eruptions of human passions and emotional sentiments, stirred either by the cruel Goddess of Distress or by the firebrand of the word hurled among the masses; they are not the lemonade-like outpourings of literary aesthetes and drawing-room heroes.

Only a storm of hot passion can turn the destinies of peoples, and he alone can arouse passion who bears it within himself.

It alone gives its chosen one the words which like hammer blows can open the gates to the heart of a people.

But the man whom passion fails and whose lips are sealed—he has not been chosen by Heaven to proclaim its will. . . .

In general the art of all truly great national leaders at all times consists among other things primarily in not dividing the attention of a people, but in concentrating it upon a single foe. The more unified the application of a people's will to fight, the greater will be the magnetic attraction of a movement and the mightier will be the impetus of the thrust. It belongs to the genius of a great leader to make even adversaries far removed from one another seem to belong to a single category, because in weak and uncertain characters the knowledge of having different enemies can only too readily lead to the beginning of doubt in their own right.

Once the wavering mass sees itself in a struggle against too many enemies, objectivity will put in an appearance, throwing open the question whether all others are really wrong and only their own people or their own movement are in the right.

And this brings about the first paralysis of their own power. Hence a multiplicity of different adversaries must always be combined so that in the eyes of the masses of one's own supporters the struggle is directed against only one enemy. This strengthens their faith in their own right and enhances their bitterness against those who attack it. . . .

The function of propaganda does not lie in the scientific training of the individual, but in calling the masses' attention to certain facts, processes, necessities, and so forth, whose significance is thus for the first time placed within their field of vision.

The whole art consists in doing this so skillfully that everyone will be convinced that the fact is real, the process necessary, the necessity correct, and so forth. But since propaganda is not and cannot be the necessity in itself, since its function, like the poster, consists in attracting the attention of the crowd, and not in educating those who are already educated or who are striving after education and knowledge, its effect for the most part must be aimed at the emotions and only to a very limited degree at the so-called intellect.

All propaganda must be popular and its intellectual level must be adjusted to the most limited intelligence among those it is addressed to. Consequently, the greater the mass it is intended to reach, the lower its purely intellectual level will have to be. But if, as in propaganda for sticking out a war, the aim is to influence a whole people, we must avoid excessive intellectual demands on our public, and too much caution cannot be exerted in this direction.

The more modest its intellectual ballast, the more exclusively it takes into consideration the emotions of the masses, the more effective it will be. And this is the best proof of the soundness or unsoundness of a propaganda campaign, and not success in pleasing a few scholars or young aesthetes.

The art of propaganda lies in understanding the emotional ideas of the great masses and finding, through a psychologically correct form, the way to the attention and thence to the heart of the broad masses. The fact that our bright boys do not understand this merely shows how mentally lazy and conceited they are.

Once we understand how necessary it is for propaganda to be adjusted to the broad mass, the following rule results:

It is a mistake to make propaganda many-sided, like scientific instruction, for instance.

The receptivity of the great masses is very limited, their intelligence is small, but their power of forgetting is enormous. In consequence of these facts, all effective propaganda must be limited to a very few points and must harp on these in slogans until the last member of the public understands what you want him to understand by your slogan. As soon as you sacrifice this slogan and try to be many-sided, the effect will piddle away, for the crowd can neither digest nor retain the material offered. In this way the result is weakened and in the end entirely cancelled out.

Thus we see that propaganda must follow a simple line and correspondingly the basic tactics must be psychologically sound. . . .

. . . The magnitude of a lie always contains a certain factor of credibility, since the great masses of the people in the very bottom of their hearts tend to be corrupted rather than consciously and purposely evil, and that, therefore, in view of the primitive simplicity of their minds, they more easily fall a victim to a big lie than to a little one, since they themselves lie in little things, but would be ashamed of lies that were too big. . . .

FOREIGN POLICY AND WAR

When the nations on this planet fight for existence—when the question of destiny, 'to be or not to be,' cries out for a solution—than all considerations of humanitarianism or aesthetics crumble into nothingness; for all these concepts do not float about in the ether, they arise from man's imagination and are bound up with man. When he departs from this world, these concepts are again dissolved into nothingness, for Nature does not know them. . . .

But all such concepts become secondary when a nation is fighting for its existence; in fact, they become totally irrelevant to the forms of the struggle as soon as a situation arises where they might paralyze a struggling nation's power of self-preservation. And that has always been their only visible result.

As for humanitarianism, Moltke[10] said years ago that in war it lies in the brevity of the operation, and that means that the most aggressive fighting technique is the most humane.

But when people try to approach these questions with drivel about aesthetics, and so forth, really only one answer is possible: where the destiny and existence of a people are at stake, all obligation toward

[10] Helmuth von Moltke (1800–1891), a German field marshal (top-ranking military commander).

beauty ceases. The most unbeautiful thing there can be in human life is and remains the yoke of slavery. . . .

The foreign policy of the folkish state must safeguard the existence on this planet of the race embodied in the state, by creating a healthy, viable natural relation between the nation's population and growth on the one hand and the quantity and quality of its soil on the other hand.

As a healthy relation we may regard only that condition which assures the sustenance of a people on its own soil. Every other condition, even if it endures for hundreds, nay, thousands of years, is nevertheless unhealthy and will sooner or later lead to the injury if not annihilation of the people in question.

Only an adequately large space on this earth assures a nation of freedom of existence.

Moreover, the necessary size of the territory to be settled cannot be judged exclusively on the basis of present requirements, not even in fact on the basis of the yield of the soil compared to the population. For . . . *in addition to its importance as a direct source of a people's food, another significance, that is, a military and political one, must be attributed to the area of a state.* If a nation's sustenance as such is assured by the amount of its soil, the safeguarding of the existing soil itself must also be borne in mind. This lies in the general power-political strength of the state, which in turn to no small extent is determined by geo-military considerations.

Hence, the German nation can defend its future only as a world power. . . .

If the National Socialist movement really wants to be consecrated by history with a great mission for our nation, it must be permeated by knowledge and filled with pain at our true situation in this world; boldly and conscious of its goal, it must take up the struggle against the aimlessness and incompetence which have hitherto guided our German nation in the line of foreign affairs. Then, without consideration of 'traditions' and prejudices, it must find the courage to gather our people and their strength for an advance along the road that will lead this people from its present restricted living space to new land and soil, and hence also free it from the danger of vanishing from the earth or of serving others as a slave nation.

The National Socialist movement must strive to eliminate the disproportion between our population and our area—viewing this latter as a source of food as well as a basis for power politics—between our historical past and the hopelessness of our present impotence. . . .

And I must sharply attack those folkish pen-pushers who claim to regard such an acquisition of soil as a 'breach of sacred human rights' and attack it as such in their scribblings. One never knows who stands behind these fellows. But one thing is for certain, that the confusion they can create is desirable and convenient to our national enemies. By such an attitude they help to weaken and destroy from within our people's will for the only correct way of defending their vital needs. For no people on this earth possesses so much as a square yard of territory on the strength of a higher will or superior right. Just as Germany's frontiers are fortuitous frontiers, momentary frontiers in the current political struggle of any period, so are the boundaries of other nations' living space. And just as the shape of our earth's surface can seem immutable as granite only to the thoughtless soft-head, but in reality only represents at each period an apparent pause in a continuous development, created by the mighty forces of Nature in a process of continuous growth, only to be transformed or destroyed tomorrow by greater forces, likewise the boundaries of living spaces in the life of nations.

State boundaries are made by man and changed by man. . . .

But we National Socialists must go further. *The right to possess soil can become a duty if without extension of its soil a great nation seems doomed to destruction.* And most especially when not some little nigger[11] nation or other is involved, but the Germanic mother of life, which has given the present-day world its cultural picture. *Germany will either be a world power or there will be no Germany.* And for world power she needs that magnitude which will give her the position she needs in the present period, and life to her citizens. . . .

---

[11] Hitler's term of contempt for any small, non-Aryan country.

29

Jean-Paul Sartre

Existentialism

*Existentialism is a contemporary intellectual movement that has found ex-
pression in philosophy, literature, religion, and politics. Though its roots lie
in the nineteenth century, in the writings of Sören Kierkegaard, Dostoevsky,
and Nietzsche, it flowered in the years after the Second World War. Essentially, it is a response of Westerners to an age of anxiety, an age in which
war, collectivism, and technological innovation have weakened the traditional belief in progress and destroyed the generally accepted standards for determining the good and the true. The existentialist movement is an attempt
to find new grounds of truth and value for the modern human being—"a
lonely anguished being in an ambiguous world."*

*The most popular and influential exponent of existentialism is Jean-Paul
Sartre (1905–), a French philosopher, novelist, playwright, and political
activist. Sartre's form of existentialism has a secular orientation; it rejects
any belief in God or the supernatural. Starting from and centered on the
human situation, it may be characterized as a contemporary version of humanism.*

*Like all existentialists, Sartre rejects abstract, rationalistic views of the
world that are concerned with defining human essence or being and then
deducing the purpose and values of human existence. He insists that existence is prior to essence. It is our condition—our actions and total experience—that define human nature. We are what we make of ourselves.
Individual humans are the creators of all values and whatever meaning there
may be in human life. But they must act; they must exercise their choice.
Only by so acting, in the face of preponderant force, evil, despair, and death,*

Jean-Paul Sartre, *Existentialism,* trans. Bernard Frechtman (New York: Philosophical
Library, 1947), 10, 12–40, 49–51.

can individuals be truly free. And freedom for Sartre is the greatest good. It is not, however, merely a negative release. It is a dreadful responsibility, for individuals by their choices not only determine their own existence but legislate for all. They endow the universe with values by their actions. Sartre, in short, proposes a courageous, irrational affirmation of responsible life and truth against meaninglessness and death.

His own life has been a heady and controversial amalgam of belief and action. A professor of philosophy at the outset of the Second World War, Sartre later fought in the French resistance and was taken prisoner by the Germans. After his release he wrote Being and Nothingness *(1943), his major philosophical work. He later expounded his existentialist concepts in a number of plays, the best known and most performed being* No Exit *(1945). In 1964, Sartre declined the coveted Nobel Prize for literature because of what he believed to be the political implications of the award. An unorthodox Marxist, he has been a critical supporter of postwar communist causes.*

The following selection is taken from lectures Sartre gave in Paris in 1945. It is a pointed response to his critics and a popular and stimulating exposition of his existentialist views.

. . . What can be said from the very beginning is that by existentialism we mean a doctrine which makes human life possible and, in addition, declares that every truth and every action implies a human setting and a human subjectivity. . . .

. . . What complicates matters is that there are two kinds of existentialist; first, those who are Christian, among whom I would include Jaspers[1] and Gabriel Marcel,[2] both Catholic; and on the other hand the atheistic existentialists, among whom I class Heidegger,[3] and then the French existentialists and myself. What they have in common is that they think that existence precedes essence, or, if you prefer, that subjectivity must be the starting point.

Just what does that mean? Let us consider some object that is man-

---

[1] Karl Jaspers (1883–1969), a German philosopher and psychologist who (after 1948) taught at Basel, Switzerland.

[2] Gabriel Marcel (1889–1973), a French writer and an exponent of a form of Christian existentialism. His philosophy stands in sharp opposition to Sartre's, especially regarding the problem of death.

[3] Martin Heidegger (1889–1976), a German philosopher; his important work *Being and Time* was published in 1927.

ufactured, for example, a book or a paper-cutter: here is an object which has been made by an artisan whose inspiration came from a concept. He referred to the concept of what a paper-cutter is and likewise to a known method of production, which is part of the concept, something which is, by and large, a routine. Thus, the paper-cutter is at once an object produced in a certain way and, on the other hand, one having a specific use; and one can not postulate a man who produces a paper-cutter but does not know what it is used for. Therefore, let us say that, for the paper-cutter, essence—that is, the ensemble of both the production routines and the properties which enable it to be both produced and defined—precedes existence. Thus, the presence of the paper-cutter or book in front of me is determined. Therefore, we have here a technical view of the world whereby it can be said that production precedes existence.

When we conceive God as the Creator, He is generally thought of as a superior sort of artisan. Whatever doctrine we may be considering, whether one like that of Descartes[4] or that of Leibnitz,[5] we always grant that will more or less follows understanding or, at the very least, accompanies it, and that when God creates He knows exactly what He is creating. Thus, the concept of man in the mind of God is comparable to the concept of paper-cutter in the mind of the manufacturer, and, following certain techniques and a conception, God produces man, just as the artisan, following a definition and a technique, makes a paper-cutter. Thus, the individual man is the realization of a certain concept in the divine intelligence.

In the eighteenth century, the atheism of the *philosophes*[6] discarded the idea of God, but not so much the notion that essence precedes existence. To a certain extent, this idea is found everywhere; we find it in Diderot,[7] in Voltaire,[8] and even in Kant.[9] Man has a human nature; this human nature, which is the concept of the human, is found in all men, which means that each man is a particular example of a universal concept, man. In Kant, the result of this universality is that

[4] René Descartes (1596–1650), a French philosopher and mathematician.
[5] Gottfried Wilhelm von Leibnitz (1646–1716), a German philosopher, scientist, and mathematician.
[6] The philosophers of the French Enlightenment.
[7] Denis Diderot (1713–1784), a French philosopher and author who was a co-editor of the monumental *Encyclopedia*.
[8] The literary name of François Marie Arouet (1694–1778), French writer, historian, and philosopher.
[9] Immanual Kant (1724–1804), a German critical and moral philosopher.

the wild-man, the natural man, as well as the bourgeois, are circumscribed by the same definition and have the same basic qualities. Thus, here too the essence of man precedes the historical existence that we find in nature.

Atheistic existentialism, which I represent, is more coherent. It states that if God does not exist, there is at least one being in whom existence precedes essence, a being who exists before he can be defined by any concept, and that this being is man, or, as Heidegger says,. human reality. What is meant here by saying that existence precedes essence? It means that, first of all, man exists, turns up, appears on the scene, and, only afterwards, defines himself. If man, as the existentialist conceives him, is indefinable, it is because at first he is nothing. Only afterward will he be something, and he himself will have made what he will be. Thus, there is no human nature, since there is no God to conceive it. Not only is man what he conceives himself to be, but he is also only what he wills himself to be after this thrust toward existence.

Man is nothing else but what he makes of himself. Such is the first principle of existentialism. It is also what is called subjectivity, the name we are labeled with when charges are brought against us. But what do we mean by this, if not that man has a greater dignity than a stone or table? For we mean that man first exists, that is, that man first of all is the being who hurls himself toward a future and who is conscious of imagining himself as being in the future. Man is at the start a plan which is aware of itself, rather than a patch of moss, a piece of garbage, or a cauliflower; nothing exists prior to this plan; there is nothing in heaven; man will be what he will have planned to be. Not what he will want to be. Because by the word "will" we generally mean a conscious decision, which is subsequent to what we have already made of ourselves. I may want to belong to a political party, write a book, get married; but all that is only a manifestation of an earlier, more spontaneous choice that is called "will." But if existence really does precede essence, man is responsible for what he is. Thus, existentialism's first move is to make every man aware of what he is and to make the full responsibility of his existence rest on him. And when we say that a man is responsible for himself, we do not only mean that he is responsible for his own individuality, but that he is responsible for all men.

The word subjectivism has two meanings, and our opponents play on the two. Subjectivism means, on the one hand, that an individual chooses and makes himself; and, on the other, that it is impossible for man to transcend human subjectivity. The second of these is the essential meaning of existentialism. When we say that man chooses his own self, we mean that every one of us does likewise; but we also mean by that that in making this choice he also chooses all men. In fact, in creating the man that we want to be, there is not a single one of our acts which does not at the same time create an image of man as we think he ought to be. To choose to be this or that is to affirm at the same time the value of what we choose, because we can never choose evil. We always choose the good, and nothing can be good for us without being good for all.

If [moreover] existence precedes essence, and if we grant that we exist and fashion our image at one and the same time, the image is valid for everybody and for our whole age. Thus, our responsibility is much greater than we might have supposed, because it involves all mankind. If I am a workingman and choose to join a Christian trade union rather than be a communist, and if by being a member I want to show that the best thing for man is resignation, that the kingdom of man is not of this world, I am not only involving my own case—I want to be resigned for everyone. As a result, my action has involved all humanity. To take a more individual matter, if I want to marry, to have children; even if this marriage depends solely on my own circumstances or passion or wish, I am involving all humanity in monogamy and not merely myself. Therefore, I am responsible for myself and for everyone else. I am creating a certain image of man of my own choosing. In choosing myself, I choose man.

This helps us understand what the actual content is of such rather grandiloquent words as anguish, forlornness, despair. As you will see, it's all quite simple.

First, what is meant by anguish? The existentialists say at once that man is anguish. What that means is this: the man who involves himself and who realizes that he is not only the person he chooses to be, but also a lawmaker who is, at the same time, choosing all mankind as well as himself, can not help escape the feeling of his total and deep responsibility. Of course, there are many people who are not anxious; but we claim that they are hiding their anxiety, that they are fleeing from it. Certainly, many people believe that when they do something, they themselves are the only ones involved, and when someone says to them, "What if everyone acted that way?" they shrug their shoulders and answer, "Everyone doesn't act that way."

But really, one should always ask himself, "What would happen if everybody looked at things that way?" There is no escaping this disturbing thought except by a kind of double-dealing. A man who lies and makes excuses for himself by saying "not everybody does that" is someone with an uneasy conscience, because the act of lying implies that a universal value is conferred upon the lie.

Anguish is evident even when it conceals itself. This is the anguish that Kierkegaard[10] called the anguish of Abraham. You know the story:[11] an angel has ordered Abraham to sacrifice his son; if it really were an angel who has come and said, "You are Abraham, you shall sacrifice your son," everything would be all right. But everyone might first wonder, "Is it really an angel, and am I really Abraham? What proof do I have?"

There was a madwoman who had hallucinations; someone used to speak to her on the telephone and give her orders. Her doctor asked her, "Who is it who talks to you?" She answered, "He says it's God." What proof did she really have that it was God? If an angel comes to me, what proof is there that it's an angel? And if I hear voices, what proof is there that they come from heaven and not from hell, or from the subconscious, or a pathological condition? What proves that they are addressed to me? What proof is there that I have been appointed to impose my choice and my conception of man on humanity? I'll never find any proof or sign to convince me of that. If a voice addresses me, it is always for me to decide that this is the angel's voice; if I consider that such an act is a good one, it is I who will choose to say that it is good rather than bad.

Now, I'm not being singled out as an Abraham, and yet at every moment I'm obliged to perform exemplary acts. For every man, everything happens as if all mankind had its eyes fixed on him and were guiding itself by what he does. And every man ought to say to himself, "Am I really the kind of man who has the right to act in such a way that humanity might guide itself by my actions?" And if he does not say that to himself, he is masking his anguish.

There is no question here of the kind of anguish which would lead to quietism,[12] to inaction. It is a matter of a simple sort of anguish

---

[10] Sören Kierkegaard (1813–1855), a Danish theologian and philosopher. Sartre is referring to Kierkegaard's important work *Fear and Trembling,* published in 1843.

[11] The story of the readiness of Abraham to kill his son, Isaac, if it is God's will that he do so (Genesis 22:1–14).

[12] A kind of mysticism that demanded that a person surrender totally to God. The extinction of human will and passion was considered a prerequisite for God's entrance

that anybody who has had responsibilities is familiar with. For example, when a military officer takes the responsibility for an attack and sends a certain number of men to death, he chooses to do so, and in the main he alone makes the choice. Doubtless, orders come from above, but they are too broad; he interprets them, and on this interpretation depend the lives of ten or fourteen or twenty men. In making a decision he can not help having a certain anguish. All leaders know this anguish. That doesn't keep them from acting; on the contrary, it is the very condition of their action. For it implies that they envisage a number of possibilities, and when they choose one, they realize that it has value only because it is chosen. We shall see that this kind of anguish, which is the kind that existentialism describes, is explained, in addition, by a direct responsibility to the other men whom it involves. It is not a curtain separating us from action, but is part of action itself.

When we speak of forlornness, a term Heidegger was fond of, we mean only that God does not exist and that we have to face all the consequences of this. The existentialist is strongly opposed to a certain kind of secular ethics which would like to abolish God with the least possible expense. About 1880, some French teachers tried to set up a secular ethics which went something like this: God is a useless and costly hypothesis; we are discarding it; but, meanwhile, in order for there to be an ethics, a society, a civilization, it is essential that certain values be taken seriously and that they be considered as having an *a priori* [13] existence. It must be obligatory, *a priori,* to be honest, not to lie, not to beat your wife, to have children, and so forth. So we're going to try a little device which will make it possible to show that values exist all the same, inscribed in a heaven of ideas, though otherwise God does not exist. In other words—and this, I believe, is the tendency of everything called reformism in France—nothing will be changed if God does not exist. We shall find ourselves with the same norms of honesty, progress, and humanism, and we shall have made of God an outdated hypothesis which will peacefully die off by itself.

The existentialist, on the contrary, thinks it very distressing that God does not exist, because all possibility of finding values in a heaven of ideas disappears along with Him; there can no longer be an

---

into the human vessel. Those who separated themselves from this world and calmly and passively meditated on God and divine things received divine grace.

[13] Preceding and independent.

a priori Good, since there is no infinite and perfect consciousness to think it. Nowhere is it written that the Good exists, that we must be honest, that we must not lie because the fact is we are on a plane where there are only men. Dostoevsky [14] said, "If God didn't exist, everything would be possible." That is the very starting point of existentialism. Indeed, everything is permissible if God does not exist, and as a result man is forlorn, because neither within him nor without does he find anything to cling to. He can't start making excuses for himself.

If existence really does precede essence, there is no explaining things away by reference to a fixed and given human nature. In other words, there is no determinism, man is free, man is freedom. On the other hand, if God does not exist, we find no values or commands to turn to which legitimize our conduct. So, in the bright realm of values, we have no excuse behind us, nor justification before us. We are alone, with no excuses.

That is the idea I shall try to convey when I say that man is condemned to be free. Condemned, because he did not create himself, yet, in other respects is free; because, once thrown into the world, he is responsible for everything he does. The existentialist does not believe in the power of passion. He will never agree that a sweeping passion is a ravaging torrent which fatally leads a man to certain acts and is therefore an excuse. He thinks that man is responsible for his passion.

The existentialist does not think that man is going to help himself by finding in the world some omen by which to orient himself. Because he thinks that man will interpret the omen to suit himself. Therefore, he thinks that man, with no support and no aid, is condemned every moment to invent man. Ponge, [15] in a very fine article, has said, "Man is the future of man." That's exactly it. But if it is taken to mean that this future is recorded in heaven, that God sees it, then it is false, because it would really no longer be a future. If it is taken to mean that, whatever a man may be, there is a future to be forged, a virgin future before him, then this remark is sound. But then we are forlorn.

To give you an example which will enable you to understand forlornness better, I shall cite the case of one of my students who came to see me under the following circumstances: his father was on

---

[14] Fyodor Dostoevsky (1821–1881), a Russian novelist.
[15] Francis Ponge (1899–   ), a French writer and poet.

bad terms with his mother, and, moreover, was inclined to be a col-laborationist,[16] his older brother had been killed in the German of-fensive of 1940, and the young man, with somewhat immature but generous feelings, wanted to avenge him. His mother lived alone with him, very much upset by the half-treason of her husband and the death of her older son; the boy was her only consolation.

The boy was faced with the choice of leaving for England and joining the Free French Forces[17]—that is, leaving his mother be-hind—or remaining with his mother and helping her to carry on. He was fully aware that the woman lived only for him and that his going-off—and perhaps his death—would plunge her into despair. He was also aware that every act that he did for his mother's sake was a sure thing, in the sense that it was helping her to carry on, whereas every effort he made toward going off and fighting was an uncertain move which might run aground and prove completely useless; for example, on his way to England he might, while passing through Spain, be detained indefinitely in a Spanish camp; he might reach England or Algiers and be stuck in an office at a desk job. As a result, he was faced with two very different kinds of action: one, concrete, immediate, but concerning only one individual; the other concerned an incomparably vaster group, a national collectivity, but for that very reason was dubious, and might be interrupted en route. And, at the same time, he was wavering between two kinds of ethics. On the one hand, an ethics of sympathy, of personal devo-tion; on the other, a broader ethics, but one whose efficacy was more dubious. He had to choose between the two.

Who could help him choose? Christian doctrine? No. Christian doctrine says, "Be charitable, love your neighbor, take the more rugged path, and so forth." But which is the more rugged path? Whom should he love as a brother? The fighting man or his mother? Which does the greater good, the vague act of fighting in a group, or the concrete one of helping a particular human being to go on living? Who can decide *a priori?* [18] Nobody. No book of ethics can tell him. The Kantian ethics says, "Never treat any person as a means, but as an end." Very well, if I stay with my mother, I'll treat her as an end

---

[16] One of a minority of French people, who, following the fall of France in the Second World War (1940), willingly collaborated (cooperated) with the German occupation forces.

[17] French people who, from places outside France (either England or North Africa), continued to struggle against the German occupation until the end of the war.

[18] Without knowing all the facts or the final result.

and not as a means; but by virtue of this very fact, I'm running the risk of treating the people around me who are fighting, as means; and, conversely, if I go to join those who are fighting, I'll be treating them as an end, and, by doing that, I run the risk of treating my mother as a means.

If values are vague, and if they are always too broad for the concrete and specific case that we are considering, the only thing left for us is to trust our instincts. That's what this young man tried to do; and when I saw him, he said, "In the end, feeling is what counts. I ought to choose whichever pushes me in one direction. If I feel that I love my mother enough to sacrifice everything else for her—my desire for vengeance, for action, for adventure—then I'll stay with her. If, on the contrary, I feel that my love for my mother isn't enough, I'll leave."

But how is the value of a feeling determined? What gives his feeling for his mother value? Precisely the fact that he remained with her. I may say that I like so-and-so well enough to sacrifice a certain amount of money for him, but I may say so only if I've done it. I may say "I love my mother well enough to remain with her" if I have remained with her. The only way to determine the value of this affection is, precisely, to perform an act which confirms and defines it. But, since I require this affection to justify my act, I find myself caught in a vicious circle.

On the other hand, Gide[19] has well said that a mock feeling and a true feeling are almost indistinguishable; to decide that I love my mother and will remain with her, or to remain with her by putting on an act, amount somewhat to the same thing. In other words, the feeling is formed by the acts one performs; so, I can not refer to it in order to act upon it. Which means that I can neither seek within myself the true condition which will impel me to act, nor apply to a system of ethics for concepts which will permit me to act. You will say, "At least, he did go to a teacher for advice." But if you seek advice from a priest, for example, you have chosen this priest; you already knew, more or less, just about what advice he was going to give you. In other words, choosing your adviser is involving yourself. The proof of this is that if you are a Christian, you will say, "Consult a priest." But some priests are collaborating, some are just marking time, some are resisting. Which to choose? If the young

[19] André Gide (1869–1951), a French writer and moralist.

man chooses a priest who is resisting or collaborating, he has already decided on the kind of advice he's going to get. Therefore, in coming to see me he knew the answer I was going to give him, and I had only one answer to give: "You're free, choose, that is, invent." No general ethics can show you what is to be done; there are no omens in the world. The Catholics will reply, "But there are." Granted—but, in any case, I myself choose the meaning they have.

When I was a prisoner, I knew a rather remarkable young man who was a Jesuit.[20] He had entered the Jesuit order in the following way: he had had a number of very bad breaks; in childhood, his father died, leaving him in poverty, and he was a scholarship student at a religious institution where he was constantly made to feel that he was being kept out of charity; then, he failed to get any of the honors and distinctions that children like; later on, at about eighteen, he bungled a love affair; finally, at twenty-two, he failed in military training, a childish enough matter, but it was the last straw.

This young fellow might well have felt that he had botched everything. It was a sign of something, but of what? He might have taken refuge in bitterness or despair. But he very wisely looked upon all this as a sign that he was not made for secular triumphs, and that only the triumphs of religion, holiness, and faith were open to him. He saw the hand of God in all this, and so he entered the order. Who can help seeing that he alone decided what the sign meant?

Some other interpretation might have been drawn from this series of setbacks; for example, that he might have done better to turn carpenter or revolutionist. Therefore, he is fully responsible for the interpretation. Forlornness implies that we ourselves choose our being. Forlornness and anguish go together.

As for despair, the term has a very simple meaning. It means that we shall confine ourselves to reckoning only with what depends upon our will, or on the ensemble of probabilities which make our action possible. When we want something, we always have to reckon with probabilities. I may be counting on the arrival of a friend. The friend is coming by rail or street-car; this supposes that the train will arrive on schedule, or that the street-car will not jump the track. I am left in the realm of possibility; but possibilities are to be reckoned with only to the point where my action comports with the ensemble of these possibilities, and no further. The moment the

---

[20] A member of the Society of Jesus, a Roman Catholic religious order.

possibilities I am considering are not rigorously involved by my action, I ought to disengage myself from them, because no God, no scheme, can adapt the world and its possibilities to my will. When Descartes said, "Conquer yourself rather than the world," he meant essentially the same thing.

The Marxists[21] to whom I have spoken reply, "You can rely on the support of others in your action, which obviously has certain limits because you're not going to live forever. That means: rely on both what others are doing elsewhere to help you, in China, in Russia, and what they will do later on, after your death, to carry on the action and lead it to its fulfillment, which will be the revolution. You even *have* to rely upon that, otherwise you're immoral." I reply at once that I will always rely on fellow fighters insofar as these comrades are involved with me in a common struggle, in the unity of a party or a group in which I can more or less make my weight felt; that is, one whose ranks I am in as a fighter and whose movements I am aware of at every moment. In such a situation, relying on the unity and will of the party is exactly like counting on the fact that the train will arrive on time or that the car won't jump the track. But, given that man is free and that there is no human nature for me to depend on, I can not count on men whom I do not know by relying on human goodness or man's concern for the good of society. I don't know what will become of the Russian revolution;[22] I may make an example of it to the extent that at the present time it is apparent that the proletariat plays a part in Russia that it plays in no other nation. But I can't swear that this will inevitably lead to a triumph of the proletariat. I've got to limit myself to what I see.

Given that men are free and that tomorrow they will freely decide what man will be, I can not be sure that, after my death, fellow fighters will carry on my work to bring it to its maximum perfection. Tomorrow, after my death, some men may decide to set up Fascism,[23] and the others may be cowardly and muddled enough to

---

[21] Marxian socialists.

[22] The Russian revolution began as a bourgeois revolution in the spring of 1917 and climaxed with the seizure of power by the Bolsheviks (Communists) in early November of that year. Its ultimate form is, of course, unknown to Sartre.

[23] A twentieth-century political ideology that is characterized by elitism, one-party rule and dictatorship, and persecution of racial and religious minorities. Its growth was most pronounced after the First World War in the states of Italy and Germany. Fascism (called Nazism in Germany) was crushed militarily in the course of the Second World War.

let them do it. Fascism will then be the human reality, so much the worse for us.

Actually, things will be as man will have decided they are to be. Does that mean that I should abandon myself to quietism? No. First, I should involve myself; then, act on the old saw, "Nothing ventured, nothing gained." Nor does it mean that I shouldn't belong to a party, but rather that I shall have no illusions and shall do what I can. For example, suppose I ask myself, "Will socialization, as such, ever come about?" I know nothing about it. All I know is that I'm going to do everything in my power to bring it about. Beyond that, I can't count on anything. Quietism is the attitude of people who say, "Let others do what I can't do." The doctrine I am presenting is the very opposite of quietism, since it declares, "There is no reality except in action." Moreover, it goes further, since it adds, "Man is nothing else than his plan; he exists only to the extent that he fulfills himself; he is therefore nothing else than the ensemble of his acts, nothing else than his life."

According to this, we can understand why our doctrine horrifies certain people. Because often the only way they can bear their wretchedness is to think, "Circumstances have been against me. What I've been and done doesn't show my true worth. To be sure, I've had no great love, no great friendship, but that's because I haven't met a man or woman who was worthy. The books I've written haven't been very good because I haven't had the proper leisure. I haven't had children to devote myself to because I didn't find a man with whom I could have spent my life. So there remains within me, unused and quite viable, a host of propensities, inclinations, possibilities, that one wouldn't guess from the mere series of things I've done."

Now, for the existentialist there is really no love other than one which manifests itself in a person's being in love. There is no genius other than one which is expressed in works of art; the genius of Proust[24] is the sum of Proust's works; the genius of Racine[25] is his series of tragedies. Outside of that, there is nothing. Why say that Racine could have written another tragedy, when he didn't write it? A man is involved in life, leaves his impress on it, and outside of that there is nothing. To be sure, this may seem a harsh thought to some-

---

[24] Marcel Proust (1871–1922), a French novelist renowned for his work *Remembrance of Things Past.*
[25] Jean Baptiste Racine (1639–1699), a French dramatist.

one whose life hasn't been a success. But, on the other hand, it prompts people to understand that reality alone is what counts, that dreams, expectations, and hopes warrant no more than to define a man as a disappointed dream, as miscarried hopes, as vain expectations. In other words, to define him negatively and not positively. However, when we say, "You are nothing else than your life," that does not imply that the artist will be judged solely on the basis of his works of art; a thousand other things will contribute toward summing him up. What we mean is that a man is nothing else than a series of undertakings, that he is the sum, the organization, the ensemble of the relationships which make up these undertakings.

When all is said and done, what we are accused of, at bottom, is not our pessimism, but an optimistic toughness. If people throw up to us our works of fiction in which we write about people who are soft, weak, cowardly, and sometimes even downright bad, it's not because these people are soft, weak, cowardly, or bad; because if we were to say, as Zola[26] did, that they are that way because of heredity, the workings of environment, society, because of biological or psychological determinism, people would be reassured. They would say, "Well, that's what we're like, no one can do anything about it." But when the existenialist writes about a coward, he says that this coward is responsible for his cowardice. He's not like that because he has a cowardly heart or lung or brain; he's not like that on account of his physiological make-up; but he's like that because he has made himself a coward by his acts. There's no such thing as a cowardly constitution; there are nervous constitutions; there is poor blood, as the common people say, or strong constitutions. But the man whose blood is poor is not a coward on that account, for what makes cowardice is the act of renouncing or yielding. A constitution is not an act; the coward is defined on the basis of the acts he performs. People feel, in a vague sort of way, that this coward we're talking about is guilty of being a coward, and the thought frightens them. What people would like is that a coward or a hero be born that way.

One of the complaints most frequently made about *The Ways of Freedom*[27] can be summed up as follows: "After all, these people are

---

[26] Émile Zola (1840–1902), a French novelist whose main theme is that people are the helpless creatures of their biological make-up and their physical and social environment. Zola is also remembered for his courageous defense of Alfred Dreyfus, a captain in the French army.

[27] *Les Chemins de la liberté,* M. Sartre's trilogy of novels: *L'Âge de raison* (*The Age of*

so spineless, how are you going to make heroes out of them?" This objection almost makes me laugh, for it assumes that people are born heroes. That's what people really want to think. If you're born cowardly, you may set your mind perfectly at rest; there's nothing you can do about it; you'll be cowardly all your life, whatever you may do. If you're born a hero, you may set your mind just as much at rest; you'll be a hero all your life; you'll drink like a hero and eat like a hero. What the existentialist says is that the coward makes himself cowardly, that the hero makes himself heroic. There's always a possibility for the coward not to be cowardly any more and for the hero to stop being heroic. What counts is total involvement; some one particular action or set of circumstances is not total involvement.

Thus, I think we have answered a number of the charges concerning existentialism. You see that it can not be taken for a philosophy of quietism, since it defines man in terms of action; nor for a pessimistic description of man—there is no doctrine more otpimistic, since man's destiny is within himself; nor for an attempt to discourage man from acting, since it tells him that the only hope is in his acting and that action is the only thing that enables a man to live. Consequently, we are dealing here with an ethics of action and involvement.

Nevertheless, on the basis of a few notions like these, we are still charged with immuring man in his private subjectivity. There again we're very much misunderstood. Subjectivity of the individual is indeed our point of departure, and this for strictly philosophic reasons. Not because we are bourgeois, but because we want a doctrine based on truth and not a lot of fine theories, full of hope but with no real basis. There can be no other truth to take off from than this: *I think; therefore, I exist.*[28] There we have the absolute truth of consciousness becoming aware of itself. Every theory which takes man out of the moment in which he becomes aware of himself is, at its very beginning, a theory which confounds truth, for outside the Cartesian[29] *cogito,*[30] all views are only probable, and a doctrine of probability which is not bound to a truth dissolves into thin air. In order to describe the probable, you must have a firm hold on the

<hr>

Reason; 1945), *Le Sursis* (*The Reprieve;* 1945), and *La Mort dans l'âme* (*Troubled Sleep;* 1949). [Translator's note.]

[28] The starting point in Descartes' philosophical search for certainty and truth.

[29] From Cartesius, a latinized form of Descartes' name.

[30] Latin: I think.

true. Therefore, before there can be any truth whatsoever, there must be an absolute truth; and this one is simple and easily arrived at; it's on everyone's doorstep; it's a matter of grasping it directly.

Secondly, this theory is the only one which gives man dignity, the only one which does not reduce him to an object. The effect of all materialism is to treat all men, including the one philosophizing, as objects, that is, as an ensemble of determined reactions in no way distinguished from the ensemble of qualities and phenomena which constitute a table or a chair or a stone. We definitely wish to establish the human realm as an ensemble of values distinct from the material realm. But the subjectivity that we have thus arrived at, and which we have claimed to be truth, is not a strictly individual subjectivity, for we have deomonstrated that one discovers in the *cogito* not only himself, but others as well.

The philosophies of Descartes and Kant to the contrary, through the *I think* we reach our own self in the presence of others, and the others are just as real to us as our own self. Thus, the man who becomes aware of himself through the *cogito* also perceives all others, and he perceives them as the condition of his own existence. He realizes that he can not be anything (in the sense that we say that someone is witty or nasty or jealous) unless others recognize it as such. In order to get any truth about myself, I must have contact with another person. The other is indispensable to my own existence, as well as to my knowledge about myself. This being so, in discovering my inner being I discover the other person at the same time, like a freedom placed in front of me which thinks and wills only for or against me. Hence, let us at once announce the discovery of a world which we shall call intersubjectivity; this is the world in which man decides what he is and what others are.

Besides, if it is impossible to find in every man some universal essence which would be human nature, yet there does exist a universal human condition. It's not by chance that today's thinkers speak more readily of man's condition than of his nature. By condition they mean, more or less definitely, the a priori [31] limits which outline man's fundamental situation in the universe. Historical situations vary; a man may be born a slave in a pagan society or a feudal lord or a proletarian. What does not vary is the necessity for him to exist in the world, to be at work there, to be there in the midst of other

[31] Predetermined.

people, and to be mortal there. The limits are neither subjective nor objective, or, rather, they have an objective and a subjective side. Objective because they are to be found everywhere and are recognizable everywhere; subjective because they are *lived* and are nothing if man does not live them, that is, freely determine his existence with reference to them. And though the configurations may differ, at least none of them are completely strange to me, because they all appear as attempts either to pass beyond these limits or recede from them or deny them or adapt to them. Consequently, every configuration, however individual it may be, has a universal value.

Every configuration, even the Chinese, the Indian, or the Negro, can be understood by a Westerner. "Can be understood" means that by virtue of a situation that he can imagine, a European of 1945 can, in like manner, push himself to his limits and reconstitute within himself the configuration of the Chinese, the Indian, or the African. Every configuration has universality in the sense that every configuration can be understood by every man. This does not at all mean that this configuration defines man forever, but that it can be met with again. There is always a way to understand the idiot, the child, the savage, the foreigner, provided one has the necessary information.

In this sense we may say that there is a universality of man; but it is not given, it is perpetually being made. I build the universal in choosing myself; I build it in understanding the configuration of every other man, whatever age he might have lived in. This absoluteness of choice does not do away with the relativeness of each epoch. At heart, what existentialism shows is the connection between the absolute character of free involvement, by virtue of which every man realizes himself in realizing a type of mankind, an involvement always comprehensible in any age whatsoever and by any person whosoever, and the relativeness of the cultural ensemble which may result from such a choice; it must be stressed that the relativity of Cartesianism and the absolute character of Cartesian involvement go together. In this sense, you may, if you like, say that each of us performs an absolute act in breathing, eating, sleeping, or behaving in any way whatever. There is no difference between being free, like a configuration, like an existence which chooses its essence, and being absolute. There is no difference between being an absolute temporarily localized, that is, localized in history, and being universally comprehensible.

• • •

I've been reproached for asking whether existentialism is humanistic. It's been said, "But you said in *Nausea* [32] that the humanists were all wrong. You made fun of a certain kind of humanist. Why come back to it now?" Actually, the world humanism has two very different meanings. By humanism one can mean a theory which takes man as an end and as a higher value. Humanism in this sense can be found in Cocteau's [33] tale *Around the World in Eighty Hours* when a character, because he is flying over some mountains in an airplane, declares, "Man is simply amazing." That means that I, who did not build the airplanes, shall personally benefit from these particular inventions, and that I, as man, shall personally consider myself responsible for, and honored by, acts of a few particular men. This would imply that we ascribe a value to man on the basis of the highest deeds of certain men. This humanism is absurd, because only the dog or the horse would be able to make such an over-all judgment about man, which they are careful not to do, at least to my knowledge.

But it can not be granted that a man may make a judgment about man. Existentialism spares him from any such judgment. The existentialist will never consider man as an end because he is always in the making. Nor should we believe that there is a mankind to which we might set up a cult in the manner of Auguste Comte. [34] The cult of mankind ends in the self-enclosed humanism of Comte, and, let it be said, of fascism. This kind of humanism we can do without.

But there is another meaning of humanism. Fundamentally, it is this: man is constantly outside of himself; in projecting himself, in losing himself outside of himself, he makes for man's existing; and, on the other hand, it is by pursuing transcendent goals that he is able to exist; man, being in this state of passing-beyond, and seizing upon things only as they bear upon this passing-beyond, is at the heart, at the center of this passing-beyond. There is no universe other than a human universe, the universe of human subjectivity. This connection between transcendency, as a constituent element of man—not in the sense that God is transcendent, but in the sense of passing beyond—

[32] *La Nausée,* a philosophical novel by Sartre published in 1938.
[33] Jean Cocteau (1889–1963), a French novelist and playwright.
[34] A French philosopher and mathematician (1798–1857), who was the founder of the "religion of humanity," a cult that establishes *humanity* as the Supreme Being.

and subjectivity, in the sense that man is not closed in on himself but is always present in a human universe, is what we call existentialist humanism. Humanism, because we remind man that there is no law-maker other than himself, and that in his forlornness he will decide by himself; because we point out that man will fulfill himself as man, not in turning toward himself, but in seeking outside of himself a goal which is just this liberation, just this particular fulfillment.

From these few reflections it is evident that nothing is more unjust than the objections that have been raised against us. Existentialism is nothing else than an attempt to draw all the consequences of a coherent atheistic position. It isn't trying to plunge man into despair[35] at all. But if one calls every attitude of unbelief despair, like the Christians, then the word is not being used in its original sense. Existentialism isn't so atheistic that it wears itself out showing that God doesn't exist. Rather, it declares that even if God did exist, that would change nothing. There you've got our point of view. Not that we believe that God exists, but we think that the problem of His existence is not the issue; [what man needs is to find himself again, and to understand that nothing can save him from himself, not even a valid proof of the existence of God]. In this sense existentialism is optimistic, a doctrine of action, and it is plain dishonesty for Christians to make no distinction between their own despair and ours and then to call us despairing.

[35] A key concept in Christian existentialism.

30

Max Frisch
The Firebugs

Max Frisch (1911–   ), a Swiss writer, conceived the idea for The Firebugs
at least five years before it was presented as a radio play and ten years before
it was first produced for the theatre. The idea for the play grew out of certain
events he witnessed in Czechoslovakia in early 1948. In that year the
Czech communists, having infiltrated key positions in the state, pressured
President Eduard Beneš to admit them to participation in the top level of
government. Even with Beneš still in office—he resigned in June of
1949—the communists set about transforming democratic Czechoslovakia
into a communist state.

With this transformation of Czechoslovakia, it was apparent that totali-
tarianism had once again won out over the liberal-bourgeois order, recalling
the prewar triumphs of Mussolini in Italy and Hitler in Germany. Frisch
made these parallels the framework of his play. Neither Hitler nor Mussolini
came to power through his own cunning and brutality alone; each was helped
by the very citizens whose way of life he sought to destroy. Thus, in the
play, the prosperous citizen Biedermann (the German equivalent of Everyman) offers shelter and hospitality to two men, Schmitz and Eisenring, who
scarcely conceal the fact that they are firebugs (arsonists) bent on preparing
his house for a conflagration. Rather than expel them from his home at once,
Biedermann foolishly tries to befriend them.

Biedermann has good reason for not asking the police to rid him of these
criminals; the police would not be of help. The historical tyrannies again
serve as models: not in Italy, Germany, nor Czechoslovakia were the police

able to protect the citizenry from those who aimed to destroy the state. Rather, the civil authority of each country stood by, pretending not to notice, until matters were beyond control. Thus, in the play, the firemen act only after the fire has been started and has spread—that is, when it is too late. Also among those that Frisch portrays as collaborators of the firebugs is an academic called Ph.D. When the time for effective action has slipped away, this intellectual attempts to read a weak statement intended to free him of blame. Having uttered his disapproval of the recent events, he seats himself in the audience, thereby suggesting that the members of the audience are similarly accomplices of the firebugs.

In interpreting The Firebugs exclusively as a political play, one can miss much of Frisch's message and forfeit many significant insights into the play's characters and circumstances. Biedermann is not merely the self-satisfied and comfortable citizen who, as appears superficially, is easily duped into contributing to his own destruction. He is also the modern person living in a tragic setting that restricts individual power, limits information, subjects one to countless fears, and causes one to make wrong judgments. His wife, Babette, seems to be hemmed in by the conventions of the world in which she grew up. Undoubtedly, students of the social sciences will also find much to ponder in the family background and childhood attributed to Schmitz and in his and Eisenring's narrow chances for success in life. Is it so remarkable that these men feel compelled to destroy a society that has rejected them?

In 1959, a year after its opening in a Zurich theatre, the play was staged in Frankfurt, Germany, and for that production an epilog was added. While the first eight scenes project black humor meant as a warning, the ninth scene is a grotesque and cynical parody—a comic mimicry in the form and style of Dante's Inferno. But in Dante's great work, hell is a place of suffering and punishment for most of humankind; the hell visualized by Frisch's modern bourgeois characters displays no semblance of torment. Those sent to this hell are only everyday people or small-time crooks. The high and mighty, especially those who kill while clad in uniform, so Frisch tells us, are saved. Biedermann and Babette are surprised to find themselves in hell and demand compensation, instead of asking for divine justice. "Ph.D." is present, too, and functions as the Monkey; Schmitz is Beelzebub (the Devil's assistant), and Eisenring is the Devil (disguised as the "Personage"). Hell, however, is not to remain open for just a bunch of small fry. The Devil puts hell on strike, and its inmates are released. The fires are extinguished, and Eisenring and Schmitz return to earth. There, Biedermann's city has been rebuilt richer and shinier than ever before. Forgotten are the anguished cries and mortal terror of the fires' victims. But with Schmitz and

Eisenring roaming the world once again, can the future be any better than the past?

Characters

GOTTLIEB BIEDERMANN
BABETTE, *his wife*
ANNA, *a maidservant*
SEPP SCHMITZ, *a wrestler*
WILLI EISENRING, *a waiter*
A POLICEMAN
A PH.D.
MRS. KNECHTLING
THE CHORUS OF FIREMEN

SCENE—*A simultaneous setting, showing the living room and the attic of* BIEDER-
MANN'S *house.*

TIME—*Now.*

SCENE ONE

The stage is dark; then a match flares, illuminating the face of HERR
BIEDERMANN. *He is lighting a cigar, and as the stage grows more visible he looks about him. He is surrounded by* FIREMEN *wearing their
helmets.*

BIEDERMANN.   You can't even light a cigar any more without think-
ing of houses on fire . . . It's disgusting!
   (He hides the burning cigar and exits. The FIREMEN *come forward in
the manner of an antique* CHORUS. *The town clock booms the quarter-
hour)*
CHORUS.   Fellow-citizens, we,
   Guardians of the city.
   Watchers, listeners,
   Friends of the friendly town.
LEADER.   Which pays our salaries.
CHORUS.   Uniformed, equipped,
   We guard your homes,
   Patrol your streets,
   Vigilant, tranquil.

LEADER.   Resting from time to time,
But alert, unsleeping.
CHORUS.   Watching, listening,
Lest hidden danger
Come to light
Too late.
(*The clock strikes half-hour*)
LEADER.   Much goes up in flames,
But not always
Because of fate.
CHORUS.   Call it fate, they tell you,
And ask no questions.
But mischief alone
Can destroy whole cities.
LEADER.   Stupidity alone—
CHORUS.   Stupidity, all-too-human—
LEADER.   Can undo our citizens,
Our all-too-mortal citizens.
(*The clock strikes three-quarters*)
CHORUS.   Use your head;
A stitch in time saves nine.
LEADER.   Exactly.
CHORUS.   Just because it happened,
Don't put the blame on God,
Nor on our human nature,
Nor on our fruitful earth,
Nor on our radiant sun . . .
Just because it happened,
Must you call the damned thing Fate?
(*The clock strikes four-quarters*)
LEADER.   Our watch begins.
(*The* CHORUS *sits. The clock strikes nine o'clock*)

SCENE TWO

The Living Room

GOTTLIEB BIEDERMANN *is reading the paper and smoking a cigar.*
ANNA, *the maid-servant, in a white apron, brings him a bottle of wine.*

ANNA.   Herr Biedermann? (*No answer*) Herr Biedermann—(*He puts down his paper*)

BIEDERMANN.   They ought to hang them! I've said so all along! Another fire! And always the same story: another peddler shoe-horning his way into somebody's attic—another "harmless" peddler— (*He picks up the bottle*) They ought to hang every one of them! (*He picks up the corkscrew*)

ANNA.   He's still here, Herr Biedermann. The peddler. He wants to talk to you.

BIEDERMANN.   I'm not in!

ANNA.   Yes, sir, I told him—an hour ago. He says he knows you. I can't throw him out, Herr Biedermann.

BIEDERMANN.   Why not?

ANNA.   He's too strong.

BIEDERMANN.   Let him come to the office tomorrow.

ANNA.   Yes sir. I told him three times. He says he's not interested. He doesn't want any hair tonic.[1]

BIEDERMANN.   What *does* he want?

ANNA.   Kindness, he says. Humanity.

BIEDERMANN. (*Sniffs at the cork*)   Tell him I'll throw him out myself if he doesn't get going at once. (*He fills his glass carefully*) Humanity! (*He tastes the wine*) Let him wait in the hall for me. If he's selling suspenders or razors . . . I'm not inhuman, you know, Anna. But they mustn't come into the house—I've told you that a hundred times! Even if we have three vacant beds, it's out of the question! Where a thing like that can lead to, these days— (ANNA *is about to go when* SCHMITZ *enters. He is athletic, in a costume reminiscent partly of the prison, partly of the circus; his arms are tattooed and there are leather straps on his wrists.* ANNA *edges out.* BIEDERMANN *sips his wine, unaware of* SCHMITZ, *who waits until he turns around*)

SCHMITZ.   Good evening. (BIEDERMANN *drops his cigar in surprise*) Your cigar, Herr Biedermann. (*He picks up the cigar and hands it to* BIEDERMANN)

BIEDERMANN.   Look here—

SCHMITZ.   Good evening.

BIEDERMANN.   What is this? I told the girl distinctly to have you wait in the hall.

---

[1] Biedermann is a small manufacturer of hair tonic.

SCHMITZ.   My name is Schmitz.

BIEDERMANN.   Without even knocking!

SCHMITZ.   Sepp Schmitz. (*Silence*)   Good evening.

BIEDERMANN.   What do you want?

SCHMITZ.   You needn't worry, Herr Biedermann. I'm not a peddler.

BIEDERMANN.   No?

SCHMITZ.   A heavyweight wrestler. I mean I *used* to be.

BIEDERMANN.   And now?

SCHMITZ.   Unemployed. (*Pause*) Don't worry, sir, I'm not looking
for a job—I'm fed up with wrestling. I came in here because it's
raining hard outside. (*Pause*) It's warm in here. (*Pause*) I hope
I'm not intruding . . . (*Pause*)

BIEDERMANN.   Cigar? (*He offers one*)

SCHMITZ.   You know, it's awful, Herr Biedermann—with a build
like mine, everybody gets scared—Thank you. (BIEDERMANN
gives him a light) Thank you. (*They stand there, smoking*)

BIEDERMANN.   Get to the point.

SCHMITZ.   My name is Schmitz.

BIEDERMANN.   You've said that . . . Delighted.

SCHMITZ.   I have no place to sleep. (*He holds the cigar to his nose, enjoying the aroma*) No place to sleep.

BIEDERMANN.   Would you like—some bread?

SCHMITZ.   If that's all there is.

BIEDERMANN.   A glass of wine?

SCHMITZ.   Bread and wine . . . If it's no trouble, sir; if it's no
trouble. (BIEDERMANN *goes to the door*)

BIEDERMANN.   Anna! (*He comes back*)

SCHMITZ.   The girl said you were going to throw me out personally,
Herr Biedermann, but I knew you didn't mean it. (ANNA *has entered*)

BIEDERMANN.   Anna, bring another glass.

ANNA.   Yes sir.

BIEDERMANN.   And some bread.

SCHMITZ.   And if you don't mind, Fräulein, a little butter. Some
cheese or cold cuts. Only don't go to any trouble. Some pickles,
a tomato or something, some mustard—whatever you have,
Fräulein.

ANNA.   Yes sir.

SCHMITZ.   If it's no trouble. (ANNA *exits*)

BIEDERMANN.   You told the girl you knew me.

SCHMITZ.   That's right, sir.

BIEDERMANN.   How do you know me?

SCHMITZ.   I know you at your best, sir. Last night at the pub—you didn't see me; I was sitting in the corner. The whole place liked the way you kept banging at the table.

BIEDERMANN.   What did I say?

SCHMITZ.   Exactly the right thing, Herr Biedermann! (*He takes a puff at his cigar*) "They ought to hang them all! The sooner the better—the whole bunch! All those firebugs!" (BIEDERMANN *offers him a chair*)

BIEDERMANN.   Sit down. (SCHMITZ *sits*)

SCHMITZ.   This country needs men like you, sir.

BIEDERMANN.   I know, but—

SCHMITZ.   No buts, Herr Biedermann, no buts. You're the old-time type of solid citizen. That's why your slant on things—

BIEDERMANN.   Certainly, but—

SCHMITZ.   That's why.

BIEDERMANN.   Why what?

SCHMITZ.   You have a conscience. Everybody in the pub could see that. A solid conscience.

BIEDERMANN.   Naturally, but—

SCHMITZ.   Herr Biedermann, it's not natural at all. Not these days. In the circus, where I did my wrestling, for instance—before it burned down, the whole damned circus—our manager, for instance; you know what he told me? "Sepp," he says (They call me Sepp), "You know me. Will you tell me what I need a conscience for?" Just like that! "What my animals need is a whip," he says. That's the sort of character he is! "A conscience!" He'd laugh out loud. "If anybody has a conscience, you can make a bet it's a bad one." (*Enjoying his cigar*) God rest him!

BIEDERMANN.   Is he dead?

SCHMITZ.   Burned to a frazzle, with everything he owned. (*A pendulum clock strikes nine*)

BIEDERMANN.   I don't know what's keeping that girl so long.

SCHMITZ.   I've got time. (*Their eyes meet*) You haven't an empty bed in the house, Herr Biedermann. The girl told me.

BIEDERMANN.   Why do you laugh?

SCHMITZ.   "Sorry, no empty bed." That's what they all say . . . What's the result? Somebody like me, with no place to sleep— Anyway I don't want a bed.

BIEDERMANN.   No?

SCHMITZ.   Oh, I'm used to sleeping on the floor. My father was a miner. I'm used to it. (*He puffs at his cigar*) No apologies necessary, sir. You're not one of those birds who crap off in public—when *you* say something I believe it. What are things coming to if people can't believe each other any more? Nothing but suspicion all over! Am I right? But *you* still believe in yourself and others. Right? You're about the only man left in this town who doesn't say right off that people like us are firebugs.

BIEDERMANN.   Here's an ash-tray.

SCHMITZ.   Or am I wrong? (*He taps the ash off his cigar carefully*) People don't believe in God any more—they believe in the Fire Department.

BIEDERMANN.   What do you mean by that?

SCHMITZ.   Nothing but the truth. (ANNA *comes in with a tray*)

ANNA.   We have no cold cuts.

SCHMITZ.   This will do fine, Fräulein, this will do. Only you forgot the mustard.

ANNA.   Excuse me. (*Exits*)

BIEDERMANN.   Eat. (*He fills the glasses*)

SCHMITZ.   You don't get a reception like this every place you go, Herr Biedermann, let me tell you that! I've had some experiences! Somebody like me comes to the door—no necktie, no place to stay, hungry; "Sit down," they say, "Have a seat"—and meanwhile they call the police. How do you like that? All I ask for is a place to sleep, that's all. A good wrestler who's wrestled all his life—and some bird who never wrestled at all grabs me by the collar! "What's this?" I ask myself. I turn around just to look, and first thing you know he's broken his shoulder! (*Picks up his glass*) Prosit![2] (*They drink, and* SCHMITZ *starts eating*)

BIEDERMANN.   That's how it goes, these days. You can't open a newspaper without reading about another arson case. The same old story: another peddler asking for a place to sleep, and next morning the house is in flames. I mean to say . . . well, frankly, I can understand a certain amount of distrust . . . (*Reaches for his newspaper*) Look at this! (*He lays the paper next to* SCHMITZ's *plate*)

[2] To your health!

SCHMITZ.   I saw it.

BIEDERMANN.   A whole district in flames. (*He gets up to show it to* SCHMITZ) Just read that! (SCHMITZ *eats, reads and drinks*)

SCHMITZ.   Is this wine Beaujolais?

BIEDERMANN.   Yes.

SCHMITZ.   Could be a little warmer. (*He reads, over his plate*) "Apparently the fire was planned and executed in the same way as the previous one." (*They exchange a glance*)

BIEDERMANN.   Isn't that the limit?

SCHMITZ.   That's why I don't care to read newspapers. Always the same thing.

BIEDERMANN.   Yes, yes, naturally . . . But that's no answer to the problem, to stop reading the papers. After all you have to know what you're up against.

SCHMITZ.   What for?

BIEDERMANN.   Why, because.

SCHMITZ.   It'll happen anyway, Herr Biedermann, it'll happen anyway. (*He sniffs the sausage*) God's will. (*He slices the sausage*)

BIEDERMANN.   You think so? (ANNA *brings the mustard*)

SCHMITZ.   Thank you, Fräulein, thank you.

ANNA.   Anything else you'd like?

SCHMITZ.   Not today. (ANNA *stops at the door*) Mustard is my favorite dish. (*He squeezes mustard out of the tube*)

BIEDERMANN.   How do you mean, God's will?

SCHMITZ.   God knows . . . (*He continues to eat with his eye on the paper*) "Expert opinion is that apparently the fire was planned and executed in the same way as the previous one." (*He laughs shortly, and fills his glass*)

ANNA.   Herr Biedermann?

BIEDERMANN.   What is it now?

ANNA.   Herr Knechtling would like to speak to you.

BIEDERMANN.   Knechtling? Now? Knechtling?

ANNA.   He says—

BIEDERMANN.   Out of the question.

ANNA.   He says he simply can't understand you.

BIEDERMANN.   Why must he understand me?

ANNA.   He has a sick wife and three children, he says—

BIEDERMANN.   Out of the question! (*He gets up impatiently*) Herr Knechtling! Herr Knechtling! Let Herr Knechtling leave me alone, dammit! Or let him get a lawyer! Please—let him! I'm through for the day . . . Herr Knechtling! All this to-do because I gave him his notice! Let him get a lawyer, by all means! I'll get one, too . . . Royalties on his invention! Let him put his head over the gas jet or get a lawyer! If Herr Knechtling can afford indulging in lawyers! Please—let him! (*Controlling himself, with a glance at* SCHMITZ) Tell Herr Knechtling I have a visitor. (ANNA *exits*) Excuse me.

SCHMITZ.   This is your house, Herr Biedermann.

BIEDERMANN.   How is the food? (*He sits, observing* SCHMITZ, *who attacks his food with enthusiasm*)

SCHMITZ.   Who'd have thought you could still find it, these days?

BIEDERMANN.   Mustard?

SCHMITZ.   Humanity! (*He screws the top of the mustard tube back on*) Here's what I mean: you don't grab me by the collar and throw me out in the rain, Herr Biedermann—*That's* what we need, Herr Biedermann! Humanity! (*He pours himself a drink*) God will reward you! (*He drinks with gusto*)

BIEDERMANN.   You mustn't think I'm inhuman, Herr Schmitz.

SCHMITZ.   Herr Biedermann!

BIEDERMANN.   That's what Frau Knechtling thinks.

SCHMITZ.   Would you be giving me a place to sleep tonight if you were inhuman?—Ridiculous!

BIEDERMANN.   Of course!

SCHMITZ.   Even if it's a bed in the attic. (*He puts down his glass*) Now our wine's the right temperature. (*The doorbell rings*) Police?

BIEDERMANN.   My wife. (*The doorbell rings again*) Come along, Herr Schmitz . . . But mind you, no noise! My wife has a heart condition—(WOMEN's *voices are heard offstage.* BIEDERMANN *motions to* SCHMITZ *to hurry. They pick up the tray, bottles and glasses and tiptoe toward stage right, where the* CHORUS *is sitting*)

BIEDERMANN.   Excuse me! (*He steps over the bench*)

SCHMITZ.   Excuse me! (*He steps over the bench. He and* BIEDERMANN *disappear.* FRAU BIEDERMANN *enters, left, accompanied by* ANNA, *who takes her wraps*)

BABETTE.   Where's my husband?—You know, Anna, we're not narrow-minded, and I don't mind your having a boy friend. But if you're going to park him in the house—

ANNA.   But I don't have a boy friend, Frau Biedermann.

BABETTE.   Then whose rusty bicycle is that, outside the front door? It scared me to death!

The Attic

(BIEDERMANN *switches on the light and gestures for* SCHMITZ *to come in. They speak in whispers*)

BIEDERMANN.   Here's the light-switch. If you get cold there's an old sheepskin around here somewhere. Only for Heaven's sake be quiet! Take off your shoes! (SCHMITZ *puts down the tray, takes off one shoe*) Herr Schmitz?

SCHMITZ.   Herr Biedermann?

BIEDERMANN.   You promise me, though, you're not a firebug? (SCHMITZ *starts to laugh*) Sh!! (*He nods goodnight and exits, closing the door.* SCHMITZ *takes off his other shoe*)

The Living Room

(BABETTE *has heard something; she listens, frightened. Then, relieved, she turns to the audience*)

BABETTE.   Gottlieb, my husband, promised to go up to the attic every evening, personally, to see if there is any firebug up there. I'm so thankful! Otherwise I'd lie awake half the night.

The Attic

(SCHMITZ, *now in his socks, goes to the light-switch and snaps out the light*)

CHORUS.   Fellow-citizens, we,
  Shield of the innocent.
  Guardians ever-tranquil,
  Shield of the sleeping city.
  Standing or
  Sitting,
  Ever on guard.

LEADER.   Taking a quiet smoke, now and again, to pass the time.

CHORUS.   Watching,
  Listening,
  Lest malignant fire leap out
  Above these cozy rooftops
  To undo our city.
  (*The town clock strikes three*)

LEADER.   Everyone knows we're here,
   Ready on call.
   (*He fills his pipe*)
CHORUS.   Who turns the light on at this wee, small hour?
   Woe!
   Nerve-shattered,
   Uncomforted by sleep,
   The wife appears.
   (BABETTE *enters in a bathrobe*)
BABETTE.   Somebody coughed! (*A snore*) Gottlieb, did you hear that?
   (*A cough*) Somebody's there! (*A snore*) That's men for you! A
   sleeping pill is all they need!
   (*The town clock strikes four*)
LEADER.   Four o'clock.
   (BABETTE *turns off the light again*)
   We were not called.
   (*He puts away his pipe. The stage lightens*)
CHORUS.   O radiant sun!
   O godlike eye!
   Light up the day above our cozy roofs!
   Thanks be!
   No harm has come to our sleeping town.
   Not yet.
   Thanks be!
   (*The* CHORUS *sits*)

SCENE THREE

The Living Room

BIEDERMANN, *his hat and coat on, his briefcase under his arm, is drinking a cup of coffee standing up, and is speaking to* BABETTE, *who is offstage.*
BIEDERMANN.   For the last time—he's not a firebug!
BABETTE'S VOICE.   How do you know?
BIEDERMANN.   I asked him myself, point blank— Can't you think of
   anything else in this world? You and your firebugs—you're
   enough to drive a man insane! (BABETTE *enters with the cream
   pitcher*)

BABETTE.   Don't yell at me.

BIEDERMANN.   I'm not yelling at you, Babette, I'm merely yelling. (*She pours cream into his cup*) I have to go. (*He drinks his coffee. It's too hot*) If everybody goes around thinking everybody else is an arsonist— You've got to have a little trust in people, Babette, just a little! (*He looks at his watch*)

BABETTE.   I don't agree. You're too good-hearted, Gottlieb. You listen to the promptings of your heart, but I'm the one who can't sleep all night . . . I'll give him some breakfast and then I'll send him on his way, Gottlieb.

BIEDERMANN.   Do that.

BABETTE.   In a nice way, of course, without offending him.

BIEDERMANN.   Do that. (*He puts his cup down*) I have to see my lawyer. (*He gives* BABETTE *a perfunctory kiss. They do not notice* SCHMITZ, *who enters, the sheepskin around his shoulders*)

BABETTE.   Why did you give Knechtling his notice?

BIEDERMANN. I don't need him any more.

BABETTE.   But you were always so pleased with him!

BIEDERMANN.   That's just what he's presuming on, now! Royalties on his invention—that's what he wants! Invention! Our hair tonic is merchandise, that's all—it's no invention! All those good folk who pour our tonic on their domes could use their own piss for all the good it does them!

BABETTE.   Gottlieb!

BIEDERMANN.   It's true, though. (*He checks to see if he has everything in his briefcase*) I'm too goodhearted—you're right. But I'll take care of this Knechtling! (*He is about to go when he sees* SCHMITZ)

SCHMITZ.   Good morning, everybody.

BIEDERMANN.   Herr Schmitz— (SCHMITZ *offers his hand*)

SCHMITZ.   Call me Sepp.

BIEDERMANN.   (*Ignores his hand*) My wife will speak with you, Herr Schmitz. I have to go, I'm sorry. Good luck . . . (*Changes his mind and shakes hands*) Good luck, Sepp. (BIEDERMANN *exits*)

SCHMITZ.   Good luck, Gottlieb. (BABETTE *looks at him*) That's your husband's name, isn't it—Gottlieb?

BABETTE.   How did you sleep?

SCHMITZ.   Thank you, madam—kind of freezing. But I made use of this sheepskin. Reminded me of old days in the mines. I'm used to the cold.

BABETTE.   Your breakfast is ready.

SCHMITZ.   Really, madam! (*She motions for him to sit*) No, really, I—
(*She fills his cup*)

BABETTE.   You must pitch in, Sepp. You have a long way to go, I'm
sure.

SCHMITZ.   How do you mean? (*She points to the chair again*)

BABETTE.   Would you care for a soft-boiled egg?

SCHMITZ.   Two.

BABETTE.   Anna!

SCHMITZ.   I feel right at home, madam. (*He sits.* ANNA *enters*)

BABETTE.   Two soft-boiled eggs.

ANNA.   Yes ma'am.

SCHMITZ.   Three and a half minutes.

ANNA.   Very well. (ANNA *starts to leave*)

SCHMITZ.   Fräulein—(ANNA *stops at the door*) Good morning.

ANNA.   Morning. (*She exits*)

SCHMITZ.   The look she gave me! If it was up to her I'd still be out
there in the pouring rain. (BABETTE *fills his cup*)

BABETTE.   Herr Schmitz—

SCHMITZ.   Yeah?

BABETTE.   If I may speak frankly—

SCHMITZ.   Aren't you kind of shaky, madam?

BABETTE.   Herr Schmitz—

SCHMITZ.   What's troubling you?

BABETTE.   Here's some cheese.

SCHMITZ.   Thank you.

BABETTE.   Marmalade.

SCHMITZ.   Thank you.

BABETTE.   Honey.

SCHMITZ.   One at a time, madam, one at a time. (*He leans back, eating his bread and butter; attentively*) Well?

BABETTE.   Frankly, Herr Schmitz—

SCHMITZ.   Just call me Sepp.

BABETTE.   Frankly—

SCHMITZ.   You'd like to get rid of me.

BABETTE.   No, Herr Schmitz, no! I wouldn't put it that way—

SCHMITZ.   How would you put it? (*He takes some cheese*) Tilsit cheese
is my dish. (*He leans back, eating; attentively*) Madam thinks I'm a
firebug.

BABETTE.   Please don't misunderstand me. What did I say? The last
thing I want to do is hurt your feelings, Herr Schmitz . . .

You've got me all confused now. Who ever mentioned firebugs? Even your manners, Herr Schmitz; I'm not complaining.

SCHMITZ.   I know. I have no manners.

BABETTE.   That's not it, Herr Schmitz—

SCHMITZ.   I smack my lips when I eat.

BABETTE.   Nonsense.

SCHMITZ.   That's what they used to tell me at the orphanage: "Schmitz, don't smack your lips when you eat!" (BABETTE *is about to pour more coffee*)

BABETTE.   You don't understand me. Really, you don't in the least! (SCHMITZ *places his hand over his cup*)

SCHMITZ.   I'm going.

BABETTE.   Herr Schmitz—

SCHMITZ.   I'm going.

BABETTE.   Another cup of coffee? (*He shakes his head*) Half a cup? (*He shakes his head*) You mustn't take it like that, Herr Schmitz. I didn't mean to hurt your feelings. I didn't say a single word about you making noises while you eat. (*He gets up*) Have I hurt your feelings? (*He folds his napkin*)

SCHMITZ.   It's not your lookout, madam, if I have no manners. My father was a coal-miner. Where would people like us get any manners? Starving and freezing, madam—that's something I don't mind; but no education, madam, no manners, madam, no refinement—

BABETTE.   I understand.

SCHMITZ.   I'm going.

BABETTE.   Where?

SCHMITZ.   Out in the rain.

BABETTE.   Oh, no!

SCHMITZ.   I'm used to it.

BABETTE.   Herr Schmitz . . . don't look at me like that. Your father was a miner—I can understand it. You had an unfortunate childhood—

SCHMITZ.   No childhood at all, madam. (*He looks down at his fingers*) None at all. My mother died when I was seven . . . (*He turns away to wipe his eyes*)

BABETTE.   Sepp!— But Sepp—
(ANNA *brings the soft-boiled eggs*)

ANNA.   Anything else you'd like? (*She gets no answer; exits*)

BABETTE.   I haven't ordered you to leave, Herr Schmitz. I never said

that. After all, what did I say? You misunderstand me, Herr
Schmitz. Really, I mean it—won't you believe me? (*She takes his
sleeve—with some hesitation*) Come, Sepp—finish eating! (SCHMITZ
sits down again) What do you take us for? I haven't even noticed
that you smack your lips. Honestly! Even if I did—we don't
care a bit about external things. We're not like that at all, Herr
Schmitz . . . (*He cracks his egg*)
SCHMITZ. God will reward you!
BABETTE. Here's the salt. (*He eats the egg with a spoon*)
SCHMITZ. It's true, madam, you didn't order me away. You didn't
say a word about it. That's true. Pardon me, madam, for not
understanding.
BABETTE. Is the egg all right?
SCHMITZ. A little soft . . . Do pardon me, won't you? (*He has finished the egg*) What were you going to say, madam, when you
started to say, very frankly—
BABETTE. Well, I was going to say . . . (*He cracks the second egg*)
SCHMITZ. God will reward you. (*He starts on the second egg*) My
friend Willi says you can't find it any more, he says. Private
charity. No fine people left; everything State-controlled. No real
people left, these days . . . He says. The world is going to the
dogs—that's why! (*He salts his egg*) Wouldn't he be surprised to
get a breakfast like this! Wouldn't he open his eyes, my friend,
Willi! (*The doorbell rings*) That could be him. (*It rings again*)
BABETTE. Who is Willi?
SCHMITZ. You'll see, madam. Willi's refined. Used to be a waiter at
the Metropol. Before it burned down . . .
BABETTE. Burned down?
SCHMITZ. Head waiter. (ANNA *enters*)
BABETTE. Who is it?
ANNA. A gentleman.
BABETTE. What does he want?
ANNA. From the fire insurance, he says. To look over the house.
(BABETTE *gets up*) He's wearing a frock coat—
SCHMITZ. My friend Willi!
CHORUS. Now two of them dismay us—
Two bicycles, both rusty.
To whom do they belong?
LEADER. One yesterday's arrival.
One today's.

CHORUS.   Woe!

LEADER.   Night once again, and our watch.
   (*The town clock strikes*)

CHORUS.   How much the coward fears where nothing threatens!
   Dreading his own shadow,
   Whirling at each sound,
   Until his fears overtake him
   At his own bedside!
   (*The town clock strikes*)

LEADER.   They never leave their room, these two.
   What is the reason?
   (*The town clock strikes*)

CHORUS.   Blind, ah, blind is the weakling!
   Trembling, expectant of evil,
   Yet hoping somehow to avoid it!
   Defenseless!
   Ah, weary of menacing evil,
   With open arms he receives it!
   (*The town clock strikes*)
   Woe!
   (*The CHORUS sits*)

SCENE FOUR

The Attic

SCHMITZ *is dressed as before.* EISENRING *has removed the jacket of his frock coat and is in a white vest and shirtsleeves. He and* SCHMITZ *are rolling tin barrels into a corner of the attic. The barrels are the type used for storing gasoline. Both vagabonds are in their socks and are working as quietly as they can.*

EISENRING.   Quiet! Quiet!

SCHMITZ.   Suppose he calls the police?

EISENRING.   Keep going.

SCHMITZ.   What then?

EISENRING.   Easy! Easy! (*They roll the barrels up to those already stacked in the shadows.* EISENRING *wipes his fingers with some cotton waste*)

EISENRING.   Why would he call the police?

SCHMITZ.   Why not?

EISENRING.   Because he's guilty himself—that's why. (*Doves are heard cooing*) It's morning. Bed-time! (*He throws away the rag*) Above a certain income every citizen is guilty one way or another. Have no fear. (*There is a sudden knocking on the locked door*)

BIEDERMANN'S VOICE.   Open up! Open up, there! (*He pounds on the door and shakes it*)

EISENRING.   That's no call for breakfast.

BIEDERMANN.   Open, I say! Immediately!

SCHMITZ.   He was never like that before. (*The banging on the door gets louder. Without haste, but briskly,* EISENRING *puts on his jacket, straightens his tie and flicks the dust from his trousers. Then he opens the door.* BIEDERMANN *enters. He is in his bathrobe. He does not see* EISENRING, *who is now behind the open door*)

BIEDERMANN.   Herr Schmitz!

SCHMITZ.   Good morning, sir. I hope this noise didn't wake you.

BIEDERMANN.   Herr Schmitz—

SCHMITZ.   It won't happen again, I assure you.

BIEDERMANN.   Leave this house! (*Pause*) I say leave this house!

SCHMITZ.   When?

BIEDERMANN.   At once!

SCHMITZ.   But—

BIEDERMANN.   Or my wife will call the police. And I can't and won't stop her.

SCHMITZ.   Hm . . .

BIEDERMANN.   I said right away, and I mean it. What are you waiting for? (SCHMITZ *picks up his shoes*) I'll have no discussion about it!

SCHMITZ.   Did I say anything?

BIEDERMANN.   If you think you can do as you like here because you're a wrestler—A racket like that, all night—(*Points to the door*) Out, I say! Get out! (SCHMITZ *turns to* EISENRING)

SCHMITZ.   He was never like that before . . . (BIEDERMANN *sees* EISENRING *and is speechless*)

EISENRING.   My name is Eisenring.

BIEDERMANN.   What's the meaning of this?

EISENRING.   Willi Maria Eisenring.

BIEDERMANN.   Why are there two of you suddenly? (SCHMITZ *and* EISENRING *look at each other*) Without even asking!

EISENRING.   There, you see!

BIEDERMANN.   What's going on here?

EISENRING.   (*To* SCHMITZ) Didn't I tell you? Didn't I say it's no way to act, Sepp? Where are your manners? Without even asking! Suddenly two of us!

BIEDERMANN.   I'm beside myself!

EISENRING.   There, you see! (*He turns to* BIEDERMANN) That's what I told him! (*Back to* SCHMITZ) Didn't I? (SCHMITZ *hangs his head*)

BIEDERMANN.   Where do you think you are? Let's get one thing clear, gentlemen—I'm the owner of this house! I ask you— where do you think you are? (*Pause*)

EISENRING.   Answer when the gentleman asks you something! (*Pause*)

SCHMITZ.   Willi is a friend of mine . . .

BIEDERMANN.   And so?

SCHMITZ.   We were schoolmates together.

BIEDERMANN.   And so?

SCHMITZ.   And so I thought . . .

BIEDERMANN.   What?

SCHMITZ.   I thought . . . (*Pause*)

EISENRING.   You didn't think! (*He turns to* BIEDERMANN) I understand fully, Herr Biedermann. All you want to do is what's right— let's get that clear! (*He shouts at* SCHMITZ) You think the owner of this house is going to be pushed around? (*He turns to* BIEDER- MANN *again*) Sepp didn't consult you at all?

BIEDERMANN.   Not one word!

EISENRING.   Sepp—

BIEDERMANN.   Not a word!

EISENRING.   (*To* SEPP) And then you're surprised when people throw you out in the street! (*He laughs contemptuously*)

BIEDERMANN.   There's nothing to laugh at, gentlemen! I'm serious! My wife has a heart condition—

EISENRING.   There, you see!

BIEDERMANN.   She didn't sleep half the night because of your noise. And anyway, what are you doing here? (*He looks around*) What the devil are these barrels doing here? (SCHMITZ *and* EISENRING *look hard where there are no barrels*) If you don't mind—what are these? (*He raps on a barrel*)

SCHMITZ.   Barrels . . .

BIEDERMANN.   Where did *they* come from?

SCHMITZ.   Do you know, Willi? Where they came from?

EISENRING.   It says "Imported" on the label.

BIEDERMANN.   Gentlemen—

EISENRING.   It says so on them somewhere! (EISENRING *and* SCHMITZ *look for a label*)

BIEDERMANN.   I'm speechless! What do you think you're doing? My whole attic is full of barrels—floor to ceiling! All the way from floor to ceiling!

EISENRING.   I knew it! (EISENRING *swings around*) Sepp had it figured out all wrong. (*To* SCHMITZ) Twelve by fifteen meters, you said. There's not a hundred square meters in this attic!—I couldn't leave my barrels in the street, Herr Biedermann; you can understand that—

BIEDERMANN.   I don't understand a thing! (SCHMITZ *shows him a label*)

SCHMITZ.   Here, Herr Biedermann—here's the label.

BIEDERMANN.   I'm speechless! (*He inspects the label*)

Downstairs

(ANNA *leads a* POLICEMAN *into the living room*)

ANNA.   I'll call him. (*She exits. The* POLICEMAN *waits*)

Upstairs

BIEDERMANN.   Gasoline?

Downstairs

(ANNA *returns*)

ANNA.   What's it about, officer?

POLICEMAN.   Official business. (ANNA *goes out again. The* POLICEMAN *waits*)

Upstairs

BIEDERMANN.   Is it true, sirs? Is it true?

EISENRING.   Is what true?

BIEDERMANN.   What's printed on this label? (*He shows them the label*) What do you take me for? I've never in my life been through anything like this! Do you think I can't read? (*They look at the label*) If you don't mind! (*He laughs sourly*) Gasoline! (*In the voice of a district attorney*) What is in those barrels?

EISENRING.   Gasoline!

BIEDERMANN.   Never mind your jokes! I'm asking you for the last time—what's in those barrels? You know as well as I do—this attic is no place for gasoline! (*He runs his finger over one of the barrels*) If you don't mind—just smell that for yourselves! (*He waves his finger under their noses*) Is that gasoline or isn't it? (*They sniff and exchange glances*)

EISENRING.   It is.

SCHMITZ.   It is.

BOTH.   No doubt whatever.

BIEDERMANN.   Are you insane? My whole attic full of gasoline—

SCHMITZ.   That's just why we don't smoke up here, Herr Biedermann.

BIEDERMANN.   What do you think you're doing? A thing like that—when every single newspaper is warning people to watch out for fires! My wife will have a heart attack!

EISENRING.   There, you see!

BIEDERMANN.   Don't keep saying, "There, you see!"

EISENRING.   You can't do that to a lady, Sepp. Not to a housewife. I know housewives. (ANNA *calls up the stairs*)

ANNA.   Herr Biedermann! Herr Biedermann! (BIEDERMANN *shuts the door*)

BIEDERMANN.   Herr Schmitz! Herr—

EISENRING.   Eisenring.

BIEDERMANN.   If you don't get these barrels out of the house this instant—and I mean this instant—

EISENRING.   You'll call the police.

BIEDERMANN.   Yes!

SCHMITZ.   There, you see! (ANNA *calls up the stairs*)

ANNA.   Herr Biedermann!

BIEDERMANN.   (*Lowers his voice*) That's my last word.

EISENRING.   What word?

BIEDERMANN.   I won't stand for it! I won't stand for gasoline in my attic! Once for all! (*There is a knock at the door*) I'm coming down! (*He opens the door. The* POLICEMAN *enters*)

POLICEMAN.   Ah, there you are, Herr Biedermann! You don't have to come down; I won't take much of your time.

BIEDERMANN.   Good morning!

POLICEMAN.   Good morning!

EISENRING.   Morning!

SCHMITZ.   Morning! (SCHMITZ *and* EISENRING *nod courteously*)

POLICEMAN.   There's been an accident.

BIEDERMANN.   Good Heavens!

POLICEMAN.   An elderly man. His wife says he used to work for you . . . An inventor. Put his head over the gas jet of his kitchen stove last night. (*He consults his notebook*) Knechtling, Johann. Number 11 Rossgasse. (*He puts his notebook away*) Did you know anybody by that name?

BIEDERMANN.   I—

POLICEMAN.   Maybe you'd rather we talked about this privately, Herr Biedermann?

BIEDERMANN.   Yes.

POLICEMAN.   It doesn't concern these employees of yours.

BIEDERMANN.   No . . . (*He stops at the door*) If anyone wants me, gentlemen, I'll be at the police station. I'll be right back. (SCHMITZ *and* EISENRING *nod)*

POLICEMAN.   Herr Biedermann—

BIEDERMANN.   I'm ready.

POLICEMAN.   What have you got in those barrels?

BIEDERMANN.   These?

POLICEMAN.   If I may ask?

BIEDERMANN.   . . . Hair tonic . . . (*He looks at* SCHMITZ *and* EISENRING)

EISENRING.   Hormotone.

SCHMITZ.   Science's gift to the well-groomed.

EISENRING.   Hormotone.

SCHMITZ.   Try a bottle today.

EISENRING.   You won't regret it.

BOTH.   Hormotone. Hormotone. Hormotone. (*The* POLICEMAN *laughs*)

BIEDERMANN.   Is he dead? (BIEDERMANN *and the* POLICEMAN *exit*)

EISENRING.   A real sweetheart!

SCHMITZ.   Didn't I tell you?

EISENRING.   But he didn't mention breakfast.

SCHMITZ.   He was never like that before. (EISENRING *reaches in his pants pocket*)

EISENRING.   Have you the detonator cap? (SCHMITZ *reaches in his pants pocket*)

SCHMITZ.   He was never that way before.

CHORUS.   O radiant sun!
  O godlike eye!
  Light up the day again above our cozy roofs!
LEADER.   Today same as yesterday.
CHORUS.   Hail!
LEADER.   No harm has come to our sleeping city.
CHORUS.   Hail!
LEADER.   Not yet . . .
CHORUS.   Hail!
  (*Traffic noises offstage; honking, streetcars*)
LEADER.   Wise is man,
  And able to ward off most perils,
  If, sharp of mind and alert,
  He heeds signs of coming disaster
  In time.
CHORUS.   And if he does not?
LEADER.   He, who
  Attentive to possible dangers,
  Studies his newspaper daily—
  Is daily, at breakfast, dismayed
  By distant tidings, whose meaning
  Is daily digested to spare him
  Fatigue of his own stressful brain work—
  Learning daily what's happened afar—
  Can he so quickly discern
  What is happening under his roof-tree?
  Things that are—
CHORUS.   Unpublished!
LEADER.   Disgraceful!
CHORUS.   Inglorious!
LEADER.   Real!
CHORUS.   Things not easy to face! For, if he—
  (*The* LEADER *interrupts with a gesture*)
LEADER.   He's coming.
  (*The* CHORUS *breaks formation*)
CHORUS.   No harm has come to the sleeping city.
  No harm yesterday or today.
  Ignoring all omens,
  The freshly-shaved citizen
  Speeds to his office . . .

(*Enter* BIEDERMANN *in hat and coat, his briefcase under his arm*)

BIEDERMANN.   Taxi! . . . Taxi! . . . Taxi! (*The* CHORUS *is in his way*)
What's the trouble?

CHORUS.   Woe!

BIEDERMANN.   What's up?

CHORUS.   Woe!

BIEDERMANN.   You've said that!

CHORUS.   Three times woe!

BIEDERMANN.   But why?

LEADER.   All-too-strangely a fiery prospect
Unfolds to our eyes.
And to yours.
Shall I be plainer?
Gasoline in the attic—

BIEDERMANN.   (*Shouts*) Is that *your* business? (*Silence*) Let me through—
I have to see my lawyer—What do you want of me? I'm not
guilty . . . (*Unnerved*) What's this—an inquest? (*Masterfully*) Let
me through, please! (*The* CHORUS *remains motionless*)

CHORUS.   Far be it from us, the Chorus,
To judge a hero of drama—

LEADER.   But we *do* see the oncoming peril,
See clearly the menacing danger!

CHORUS.   Making a simple inquiry
About an impending disaster—
Uttering, merely, a warning—
Civic-minded, the Chorus comes forward,
Bathed, alas, in cold sweat,
In half-fainting fear of that moment
That calls for the hoses of firemen!

(BIEDERMANN *looks at his wrist watch*)

BIEDERMANN.   I'm in a hurry.

CHORUS.   Woe!

LEADER.   All that gasoline, Gottlieb
Biedermann!
How could you take it?

BIEDERMANN.   Take it?

LEADER.   You know very well,
The world is a brand for the burning!
Yet, knowing it, what did you think?

BIEDERMANN.   Think? (*He appraises the* CHORUS) My dear sirs, I am a

free and independent citizen. I can think anything I like. What
are all these questions? I have the right, my dear sirs, not to
think at all if I feel like it! Aside from the fact that whatever goes
on under my own roof—Let's get one thing clear, gentlemen:
I am the owner of the house!

CHORUS.   Sacred, sacred to us
Is property,
Whatever befall!
Though we be scorched,
Though we be cindered—
Sacred, sacred to us!

BIEDERMANN.   Well, then—(*Silence*) Why can't I go through? (*Silence*)
Why must you always imagine the worst? Where will that get
you? All I want is some peace and quiet, not a thing more . . . As
for those two gentlemen—aside from the fact that I have other
troubles right now . . . (BABETTE *enters in street clothes*) What do
you want here?

BABETTE.   Am I interrupting?

BIEDERMANN.   Can't you see I'm in conference? (BABETTE *nods to the*
CHORUS, *then whispers in* BIEDERMANN's *ear*) With ribbons, of
course. Never mind the cost. As long as it's a wreath. (BABETTE
nods to the CHORUS)

BABETTE.   Excuse me, sirs. (*She exits*)

BIEDERMANN.   To cut it short, gentlemen, I'm fed up! You and your
firebugs! I don't even go to the pub any more—that's how fed
up I am! Is there nothing else to talk about these days? Let's get
one thing straight—if you go around thinking everybody except
yourself is an arsonist, how are things ever going to improve? A
little trust in people, for Heaven's sake! A little good will! Why
keep looking at the bad side? Why go on the assumption that
everybody else is a firebug? A little confidence, a little—
(*Pause*) You can't go on living in fear! (*Pause*) You think I closed
my eyes last night for one instant? I'm not an imbecile, you
know! Gasoline is gasoline! I had the worst kind of thoughts
running through my head last night . . . I climbed up on the
table to listen—even got up on the bureau and put my ear to the
ceiling! They were snoring, mind you—snoring! At least four
times I climbed up on that bureau. Peacefully snoring! Just the
same I got as far as the stairs, once—believe it or not—in my
pajamas—and frantic, I tell you—frantic! I was all ready to wake

up those two scoundrels and throw them out in the street, along with their barrels. Single-handedly, without compunction, in the middle of the night!

CHORUS.   Single-handedly?

BIEDERMANN.   Yes.

CHORUS.   Without compunction?

BIEDERMANN.   Yes.

CHORUS.   In the middle of the night?

BIEDERMANN.   Just about to! If my wife hadn't come after me, afraid I'd catch cold—(*Embarrassed, he reaches for a cigar*)

LEADER.   How shall I put it?
Sleepless he passed the night.
That they'd take advantage of a man's good nature—
Was that conceivable?
Suspicion came over him. Why?
(BIEDERMANN *lights his cigar*)

CHORUS.   No it's not easy for the citizen,
Tough in business
But really soft of heart,
Always ready,
Ready always to do good.

LEADER.   If that's how he happens to feel.

CHORUS.   Hoping that goodness
Will come of goodness.
How mistaken can you be?

BIEDERMANN.   What are you getting at?

CHORUS.   It seems to us there's a stink of gasoline. (BIEDERMANN *sniffs*)

BIEDERMANN.   I don't smell anything.

CHORUS.   Woe to us!

BIEDERMANN.   Not a thing.

CHORUS.   Woe to us!

LEADER.   How soon he's got accustomed to bad smells!

CHORUS.   Woe to us!

BIEDERMANN.   And don't keep giving us that defeatism, gentlemen. Don't keep saying all the time, "Woe to us!" (*A car honks off-stage*) Taxi!—Taxi! (*A car stops offstage*) If you'll excuse me—(*He hurries off*)

CHORUS.   Citizen—where to?
(*The car drives off*)

LEADER.   What is his recourse, poor wretch?
   Forceful, yet fearful,
   Milk-white of face,
   Fearful yet firm—
   Against what?
   (*The car is heard honking*)
CHORUS.   So soon accustomed to bad smells!
   (*The car is heard distantly honking*)
   Woe to us!
LEADER.   Woe to you!
   (*The* CHORUS *retires. All but the* LEADER, *who takes out his pipe*)
   He who dreads change
   More than disaster,
   How can he fight
   When disaster impends?
   (*He follows the* CHORUS *out*)

SCENE FIVE

The Attic

EISENRING *is alone, unwinding cord from a reel and singing "Lily Marlene"* [3] *while he works. He stops whistling, wets his forefinger and holds it up to the dormer window to test the wind.*

The Living Room

(BIEDERMANN *enters, cigar in mouth, followed by* BABETTE. *He takes off his coat and throws down his briefcase*)
BIEDERMANN.   Do as I say.
BABETTE.   A goose?
BIEDERMANN.   A goose! (*He takes off his tie without removing his cigar*)
BABETTE.   Why are you taking off your necktie, Gottlieb?
BIEDERMANN.   If I report those two boys to the police I'll make them my enemies. What good will that do me? Just one match and the whole house is up in flames! What good will that do us? On the other hand, if I go up there and invite them to dinner, why—
BABETTE.   Why, what?

---

[3] A rather sentimental song that was popular in Germany during the Second World War.

BIEDERMANN.   Why, then we'll be friends. (*He takes off his jacket, hands it to* BABETTE *and exits*)

BABETTE.   (*Speaking to* ANNA, *offstage*) Just so you'll know, Anna: you can't get off this evening—we're having company. Set places for four.

The Attic

(EISENRING *singing "Lily Marlene." There is a knock at the door*)

EISENRING.   Come in! (*He goes on singing. No one enters*) Come in! (BIEDERMANN *enters in shirtsleeves, holding his cigar*) Good day, Herr Biedermann!

BIEDERMANN.   (*Tactfully*) May I come in?

EISENRING.   I hope you slept well last night?

BIEDERMANN.   Thank you—miserably.

EISENRING.   So did I. It's this wind. (*He goes on working with the reel*)

BIEDERMANN.   If I'm not disturbing you—

EISENRING.   This is your house, Herr Biedermann.

BIEDERMANN.   If I'm not in the way—(*The cooing of doves is heard*) Where is our friend?

EISENRING.   Sepp? He went to work this morning, the lazy dog—he didn't want to go without breakfast! I sent him out for some sawdust.

BIEDERMANN.   Sawdust?

EISENRING.   It helps spread the sparks. (BIEDERMANN *laughs politely at what sounds like a poor joke*)

BIEDERMANN.   I was going to say, Herr Eisenring—

EISENRING.   That you still want to kick us out?

BIEDERMANN.   In the middle of the night—I'm out of sleeping pills—it suddenly struck me: you folks have no toilet facilities up here.

EISENRING.   We have the roof gutter.

BIEDERMANN.   Well, just as you like, of course. It merely struck me you might like to wash or take a shower—I kept thinking of that all night . . . You're very welcome to use my bathroom. I told Anna to hang up some towels for you there. (EISENRING *shakes his head*) Why do you shake your head?

EISENRING.   Where on earth did he put it?

BIEDERMANN.   What?

EISENRING.   You haven't seen a detonator cap? (*He searches around*) Don't trouble yourself, Herr Biedermann. In jail, you know, we had no bathrooms either.

BIEDERMANN.   In jail?

EISENRING.   Didn't Sepp tell you I just came out of prison?

BIEDERMANN.   No.

EISENRING.   Not a word about it?

BIEDERMANN.   No.

EISENRING.   All he likes to talk about is himself. There *are* such people!—Is it our fault, after all, if his youth was tragic? Did *you* have a tragic youth, Herr Biedermann? *I* didn't. I could have gone to college; my father wanted me to be a lawyer . . . (*He stands at the attic window murmuring to the doves*) Grrr! Grrr! Grrr! (BIEDERMANN *re-lights his cigar*)

BIEDERMANN.   Frankly, Herr Eisenring, I couldn't sleep all night. Is there really gasoline in those barrels?

EISENRING.   You don't trust us.

BIEDERMANN.   I'm merely asking.

EISENRING.   Herr Biedermann, what do you take us for? Frankly, what sort of people—

BIEDERMANN.   Herr Eisenring, you mustn't think I have no sense of humor. Only your idea of a joke—well—

EISENRING.   That's something we've learned.

BIEDERMANN.   What is?

EISENRING.   That a joke is first-class camouflage. Next comes sentiment: like when Sepp talks about a childhood in the coal mines, orphanages, circuses and so forth. But the best camouflage of all—in my opinion—is the plain and simple truth. Because nobody ever believes it.

The Living Room

(ANNA *shows in the* WIDOW KNECHTLING, *dressed in black*)

ANNA.   Take a seat, please. (*The* WIDOW *sits*) But if you are Frau Knechtling, it's no use. Herr Biedermann wants nothing to do with you, he said. (*The* WIDOW *gets up*) Take a seat, please! (*The* WIDOW *sits down again*) But don't get up any hopes. (ANNA *exits*)

The Attic

(EISENRING *is busy with one thing or another.* BIEDERMANN *is smoking*)

EISENRING.   I wonder what's keeping Sepp. Sawdust can't be so hard to find. I hope they haven't nabbed him.

BIEDERMANN.   Nabbed?

EISENRING.   Why do you smile?

BIEDERMANN.   When you use words like that, Herr Eisenring, it's as though you came from another world. Nab him! Like another world! *Our* kind of people seldom get nabbed!

EISENRING.   Because your kind of people seldom steal sawdust. That's obvious, Herr Biedermann. That's the class difference.

BIEDERMANN.   Absurd!

EISENRING.   You don't mean to say, Herr Biedermann—

BIEDERMANN.   I don't hold with class differences—you must have realized that by now, Herr Eisenring. I'm not old-fashioned— just the opposite, in fact. And I regret that the lower classes still talk about class differences. Aren't we all of us—rich or poor— the creation of one Creator? The middle class, too. Are we not—you and I—human beings, made of flesh and blood? . . . I don't know, sir, whether you smoke cigars— (*He offers one, but* EISENRING *shakes his head*) I don't mean reducing people to a common level, you understand. There will always be rich and poor, Heaven knows—but why can't we just shake hands? A little good will, for Heaven's sake, a little idealism, a little—and we'd all have peace and quiet, both the poor and the rich. Don't you agree?

EISENRING.   If I may speak frankly, Herr Biedermann—

BIEDERMANN.   Please do.

EISENRING.   You won't take it amiss?

BIEDERMANN.   The more frankly the better.

EISENRING.   Frankly speaking, you oughtn't to smoke here. (BIEDERMANN *startled, puts out his cigar*) I can't make rules for you here, Herr Biedermann. After all, it's your house. Still and all—

BIEDERMANN.   Naturally.

EISENRING.   (*Looking down*) There it is! (*He takes something off the floor and blows it clean before attaching it to the wire. He starts whistling "Lily Marlene"*)

BIEDERMANN.   Tell me, Herr Eisenring, what is that you're doing? If I may ask? What is that thing?

EISENRING.   A detonator.

BIEDERMANN.   A——?

EISENRING.   And this is a fuse.

BIEDERMANN.   A——?

EISENRING.   Sepp says they've developed better ones lately. But they don't have them yet, in the stores. Buying them's out of the question for us, of course. Anything that has to do with war is frightfully expensive. Always the best quality . . .

BIEDERMANN.   A fuse, you say?

EISENRING.   A time-fuse. (*He hands* BIEDERMANN *one end of the cord*) If you'd be kind enough, Herr Biedermann, to hold this end— (BIEDERMANN *holds it for him*)

BIEDERMANN.   All joking aside, my friend—

EISENRING.   One second—(*He whistles "Lily Marlene," measuring the fuse*) Thank you, Herr Biedermann. (BIEDERMANN *suddenly laughs*)

BIEDERMANN.   Ha, ha! You can't put a scare into me, Willi! Though I must say, you count on people's sense of humor! The way you talk, I can understand your getting arrested now and then. You know, not everybody has my sense of humor!

EISENRING.   You have to find the right man.

BIEDERMANN.   At the pub, for instance—just say you believe in the natural goodness of man, and they have you marked down.

EISENRING.   Ha!

BIEDERMANN.   And still I won't mention how much I donated to our Fire Department!

EISENRING.   Ha! (*He puts down the fuse*) Those who have no sense of humor get what's coming to them just the same when the time comes—so don't let *that* worry you. (BIEDERMANN *sits down on a barrel. He has broken into a sweat*) What's the trouble, Herr Biedermann? You've gone quite pale. (*He claps him on the shoulder*) It's the smell. I know, if you're not used to it . . . . I'll open the window for you, too. (*He opens the door*)

BIEDERMANN.   Thanks . . . (ANNA *calls up the stairs*)

ANNA.   Herr Biedermann! Herr Biedermann!

EISENRING.   The police again?

ANNA.   Herr Biedermann!

EISENRING.   It's a Police State!

ANNA.   Herr Biedermann—

BIEDERMANN.   I'm coming! (*They both whisper from here on*) Herr Eisenring, do you like goose?

EISENRING.   Goose?

BIEDERMANN.   Roast goose.

EISENRING.   Why?

BIEDERMANN.   Stuffed with chestnuts?

EISENRING.   And red cabbage?

BIEDERMANN.   Yes . . . I was going to say: my wife and I—I, especially—if we may have the pleasure . . . I don't mean to obtrude, Herr Eisenring, but if you'd care to join us at a little supper, you and Sepp—

EISENRING.   Today?

BIEDERMANN.   Or tomorrow, if you prefer—

EISENRING.   We probably won't stay until tomorrow. But today—of course, Herr Biedermann, with pleasure.

BIEDERMANN.   Shall we say seven o'clock? (ANNA *calls up the stairs*)

ANNA.   Herr Biedermann! (*They shake hands*)

BIEDERMANN.   (*At the door with a twinkle*) All set?

EISENRING.   All set! (BIEDERMANN *nods genially; then looks once more at the barrels and the fuse*) All set. (BIEDERMANN *exits.* EISENRING *goes to work again, whistling. The* CHORUS *enters below for the end of the scene. They are interrupted by the sound of a crash, as of something falling in the attic*) You can come out, Professor. (*A* PH.D., *wearing horn-rimmed glasses, crawls out of the pile of barrels*) You heard: we're invited to dinner, Sepp and me. You'll keep an eye on things. Nobody's to come in here and smoke, understand? Not before we're ready. (*The* PH.D. *polishes his glasses*) I often ask myself, Professor, why in hell you hang around with us. You don't enjoy a good, crackling fire, or flames, or sparks. Or sirens that go off too late—or dogs barking—or people shrieking—or smoke. Or ashes . . . (*The* PH.D. *solemnly adjust his glasses.* EISENRING *laughs*) Do-gooder! (*He whistles gently to himself surveying the* PROFESSOR) I don't like you eggheads—I've told you that before, Professor. You get no real fun out of anything. You're all so idealistic, so solemn . . . You can't be trusted. That's no fun, Professor. (*He goes back to his work, whistling*)

The Living Room

CHORUS.   Ready for action,
   Axes and fire-hose;
   Polished and oiled,
   Every brass fitting.
   Every man of us tested and ready.

LEADER.   We'll be facing a high wind.

CHORUS.   Every man of us tested and ready.
Our brass fire-pump
Polished and oiled,
Tested for pressure.

LEADER.   And the fire-hydrants?

CHORUS.   Everything ready.

LEADER.   Tested and ready for action.
(*Enter* BABETTE *with a goose, and the* PH.D.)

BABETTE.   Yes, Professor, I know, but my husband . . . Yes, I understand it's urgent, Professor. I'll tell him—(*She leaves the* PROFESSOR *and comes to the footlights*) My husband ordered a goose. See, this is it. And I have to roast it, so we can be friends with those people upstairs. (*Church bells ring*) It's Saturday night—you can hear the bells ringing. I have an odd feeling, somehow, that it may be the last time we'll hear them. (BIEDERMANN *calls, "Babette!"*) I don't know ladies, if Gottlieb is always right . . . You know what he says? "Certainly they're scoundrels, Babette, but if I make enemies of them, it's goodbye to our hair tonic!" (BIEDERMANN *calls. "Babette!"*) Gottlieb's like that. Good-hearted. Always too good-hearted! (*She exits with the goose*)

CHORUS.   This son of good family,
A wearer of glasses,
Pale, studious, trusting,
But trusting no longer
In power of goodness,
Will do anything now, for
Ends justify means.
(So he hopes.)
Ah, honest-dishonest!
Now wiping his glasses
To see things more clearly,
He sees no barrels—
No gasoline barrels!
It's an idea he sees—
An abstract conception—
Until it explodes!

PH.D.   Good evening . . .

LEADER.   To the pumps!
The ladders!

The engines!

(*The* FIREMEN *rush to their posts*)

LEADER. Good evening.

(*To the audience, as shouts of "Ready!" echo through the theatre*)
We're ready.

SCENE SIX

The Living Room

The WIDOW KNECHTLING *is still there, standing and waiting. Outside, the bells are ringing loudly.* ANNA *is setting the table.* BIEDERMANN *brings in two chairs.*

BIEDERMANN. You can see, can't you, Frau Knechtling? I haven't time now—no time to think about the dead . . . I told you, go see my lawyer. (*The* WIDOW KNECHTLING *leaves*) You can't hear yourself think, with that noise. Close the window. (ANNA *shuts the window. The sound of the bells is fainter*) I said a simple, informal dinner. What are those idiotic candelabra for?

ANNA. But, Herr Biedermann, we always have those!

BIEDERMANN. I said simple, informal—not show-off! Fingerbowls! Knife-rests! Nothing but crystal and silver! What does that look like? (*He picks up the knife-rests and shoves them into his pants pocket*) Can't you see I'm wearing my oldest jacket? And you . . . Leave the carving knife, Anna—we'll need it; but away with the rest of this silver! Those two gentlemen must feel at home!—Where's the corkscrew?

ANNA. Here.

BIEDERMANN. Don't we have anything simpler?

ANNA. In the kitchen. But that one is rusty.

BIEDERMANN. Bring it here. (*He takes a silver ice-bucket off the table*) What's this for?

ANNA. For the wine.

BIEDERMANN. Silver! (*He glares at the bucket, then at* ANNA) Do we always use that, too?

ANNA. We're going to need it, Herr Biedermann.

BIEDERMANN. Humanity, brotherhood—that's what we need here! Away with that thing! And what are those, will you tell me?

ANNA. Napkins.

BIEDERMANN. Damask napkins!

ANNA.   We don't have any others. (BIEDERMANN *shoves the napkins into the silver bucket*)

BIEDERMANN.   There are whole nations, Anna, that live without napkins! (BABETTE *enters with a large wreath.* BIEDERMANN, *standing in front of the table, does not see her come in*) And why a cloth on the table?

BABETTE.   Gottlieb?

BIEDERMANN.   Let's have no class distinctions! (*He sees* BABETTE) What is that wreath?

BABETTE.   It's what we ordered—Gottlieb, what do you think? They sent the wreath here by mistake! And I gave them the address myself—Knechtling's address—I wrote it down, even! And the ribbon and everything—they've got it all backward!

BIEDERMANN.   What's wrong with the ribbon?

BABETTE.   And the clerk says they sent the bill to Frau Knechtling! (*She shows him the ribbon:* "TO OUR DEAR, DEPARTED GOTTLIEB BIEDERMANN." *He considers the ribbon*)

BIEDERMANN.   We won't accept it, that's all! I should say not! They've got to exchange it! (*He goes back to the table*) Don't upset me, will you, Babette? I can't think of everything—(BABETTE *exits*) Take that tablecloth away. Help me, Anna. And remember—no serving! You come in and put the pan on the table.

ANNA.   The roast-pan? (*He takes away the tablecloth*)

BIEDERMANN.   That's better! A wooden table, that's all. Just a table for supper. (*He hands* ANNA *the tablecloth*)

ANNA.   You mean that, Herr Biedermann—just bring in the goose in the pan? (*She folds up the tablecloth*) What wine shall I bring?

BIEDERMANN.   I'll get it myself.

ANNA.   Herr Biedermann!

BIEDERMANN.   What now?

ANNA.   I don't have any sweater, sir—any old sweater, as if I belonged to the family.

BIEDERMANN.   Borrow one of my wife's.

ANNA.   The yellow or the red one?

BIEDERMANN.   Don't be so fussy! No apron or cap, understand? And get rid of these candelabra. And make sure especially, Anna, that everything's not so neat!—I'll be in the cellar. (BIEDERMANN *exits*)

ANNA.   "Make sure especially, Anna, that everything's not so neat!" (*She throws the tablecloth down on the floor and stomps on it with both feet*) How's that? (SCHMITZ *and* EISENRING *enter, each holding a rose*)

BOTH.   Good evening, Fräulein. (ANNA *exits without looking at them*)

EISENRING.   Why no sawdust?

SCHMITZ.   Confiscated. Police measure. Precaution. They're picking up anybody who sells or owns sawdust without written permission. Precautions all over the place. (*He combs his hair*)

EISENRING.   Have you got matches?

SCHMITZ.   No.

EISENRING.   Neither have I. (SCHMITZ *blows his comb clean*)

SCHMITZ.   We'll have to ask him for them.

EISENRING.   Biedermann?

SCHMITZ.   Don't forget. (*He puts away his comb and sniffs*) Mmm! That smells good!

SCENE SEVEN

BIEDERMANN *comes to the footlights with a bottle.*

BIEDERMANN.   You can think what you like about me, gentlemen. But just answer one question—(*Laughter and loud voices offstage*) I say to myself: as long as they're laughing and drinking, we're safe. The best bottles out of my cellar! I tell you, if anybody had told me a week ago . . . When did *you* guess they were arsonists, gentlemen? This sort of thing doesn't happen the way you think. It comes on you slowly—slowly, at first—then sudden suspicion! Though I was suspicious at once—one's always suspicious! But tell me the truth, sirs—what would *you* have done? If you were in my place, for God's sake? And when? *When* would you have done it? At what point? (*He waits for an answer. Silence*) I've got to go. (*He leaves the stage quickly*)

SCENE EIGHT

The Living Room

The dinner is in full swing. Laughter. BIEDERMANN, *especially, cannot contain himself at the joke he's just heard. Only* BABETTE *is not laughing.*

BIEDERMANN.   Oil waste! Did you hear that, Babette?
Oil waste, he says! Oil waste burns better!

BABETTE.   I don't see what's funny.

BIEDERMANN.   Oil waste! You know what that is?

BABETTE.   Yes.

BIEDERMANN.   You have no sense of humor, Babette. (*He puts the bottle on the table*)

BABETTE.   All right, then, explain it.

BIEDERMANN.   Okay!—This morning Willi told Sepp to go out and steal some sawdust. Sawdust—get it? And just now, when I asked Sepp if he got any, he said he couldn't find any sawdust— he found some oil waste instead. Get it? And Willi says, "Oil waste burns better!"

BABETTE.   I understood all that.

BIEDERMANN.   You did?

BABETTE.   What's funny about it? (BIEDERMANN *gives up*)

BIEDERMANN.   Let's drink, men! (BIEDERMANN *removes the cork from the bottle*)

BABETTE.   Is that the truth, Herr Schmitz? Did you bring oil waste up to our attic?

BIEDERMANN.   This will kill you, Babette! This morning we even measured the fuse together, Willi and I!

BABETTE.   The fuse?

BIEDERMANN.   The time-fuse (*He fills the glasses*)

BABETTE.   Seriously—what does that mean? (BIEDERMANN *laughs*)

BIEDERMANN.   Seriously! You hear that? Seriously! . . . Don't let them kid you, Babette. I told you—our friends have their own way of kidding! Different company, different jokes—that's what I always say . . . All we need now is to have them ask me for matches! (SCHMITZ *and* EISENRING *exchange glances*) These gentlemen took me for some Milquetoast, for some dope without humor—(*He lifts his glass*) Prosit!

EISENRING.   Prosit!

SCHMITZ.   Prosit!

BIEDERMANN.   To our friendship! (*They drink the toast standing up, then sit down again*) We're not doing serving. Just help yourself, gentlemen.

SCHMITZ.   I can't eat any more.

EISENRING.   Don't restrain yourself, Sepp, you're not at the orphanage. (*He helps himself to more goose*) Your goose is wonderful, madam.

BABETTE.   I'm glad to hear it.

EISENRING.   Roast goose and stuffing! Now all we need is a table-cloth.

BABETTE.   You hear that, Gottlieb?

EISENRING.   We don't have to have one. Not one of those table-cloths, white damask, with silverware on it—

BIEDERMANN.   (*Loudly*) Anna!

EISENRING.   Damask, with flowers all over it—a white flower pattern—we don't have to have one. We didn't have any in prison.

BABETTE.   In prison?

BIEDERMANN.   Where is that girl?

BABETTE.   Have you been in prison? (ANNA *enters. She is wearing a bright red sweater*)

BIEDERMANN.   A tablecloth here—immediately!

ANNA.   Yes sir.

BIEDERMANN.   And if you have some fingerbowls or something—

ANNA.   Yes sir.

EISENRING.   Madam, you may think it's childish, but that's how the little man is. Take Sepp, for instance—he grew up in the coal mines, but it's the dream of his miserable life, a table like this, with crystal and silver! Would you believe it? He never heard of a knife-rest!

BABETTE.   But, Gottlieb, we have all those things!

EISENRING.   Of course we don't *have* to have them here—

ANNA.   Very well.

EISENRING.   If you have any napkins, Fräulein, out with them!

ANNA.   But Herr Biedermann said—

BIEDERMANN.   Out with them!

ANNA.   Yes sir. (*She starts to bring back the table service*)

EISENRING.   I hope you won't take it amiss, madam, but when you're just out of prison—months at a time with no refinement whatever—(*He shows the tablecloth to* SCHMITZ) You know what this is? (*To* BABETTE) He never saw one before! (*He turns back to* SCHMITZ) This is damask!

SCHMITZ.   What do you want me to do with it? (EISENRING *ties the tablecloth around his neck*)

EISENRING.   There—(BIEDERMANN *tries to find this amusing. He laughs*)

BABETTE.   Where are the knife-rests, Anna?

ANNA.   Herr Biedermann—

BIEDERMANN.   Out with them!

ANNA.   But you said "Take them away!" before!

BIEDERMANN.   Bring them here, I tell you! Where are they, god-damit?

ANNA.   In your pants pocket. (BIEDERMANN *reaches in his pants pocket and finds them*)

EISENRING.   Don't get excited.

ANNA.   I can't help it!

EISENRING.   No excitement, now, Fräulein—(ANNA *bursts into sobs and runs out*)

EISENRING.   It's this wind. (*Pause*)

BIEDERMANN.   Drink up, friends! (*They drink. A silence*)

EISENRING.   I ate roast goose every day when I was a waiter. I used to flit down those corridors holding a platter like this . . . How do you suppose, madam, waiters clean off their hands? In their hair, that's how—while there's others who use crystal finger-bowls. That's something I'll never forget. (*He dips his fingers in the fingerbowl*) Have you ever heard of a trauma?

BIEDERMANN.   No.

EISENRING.   I learned all about it in jail. (*He wipes his fingers dry*)

BABETTE.   And how did you happen to be there, Herr Eisenring?

BIEDERMANN.   Babette!

EISENRING.   How did I get into jail?

BIEDERMANN.   One doesn't ask questions like that!

EISENRING.   I wonder at that myself . . . I was a waiter—a little head waiter. Suddenly they made me out a great arsonist.

BIEDERMANN.   Hm.

EISENRING.   They called for me at my own home.

BIEDERMANN.   Hm.

EISENRING.   I was so amazed, I gave in.

BIEDERMANN.   Hm.

EISENRING.   I had luck, madam—seven really charming policemen. I said, "I have no time—I have to go to work." They answered, "Your restaurant's burned to the ground."

BIEDERMANN.   Burned to the ground?

EISENRING.   Overnight, apparently.

BABETTE.   Burned to the ground?

EISENRING.   "Fine," I said, "then I *have* time . . ." Just a black, smoking hulk—that's all that was left of that place. I saw it as we drove by. Through those windows, you know, the little barred windows they have in those prison vans—(*He sips his wine delicately*)

BIEDERMANN.   And then? (EISENRING *studies the wine-label*)

EISENRING.   We used to keep this, too: '49, Cave de l'Echannon . . . And then? Let Sepp tell you the rest—As I was sitting in that police station, playing with my handcuffs, who do you think they brought in?—That one, there! (SCHMITZ *beams*) Prosit, Sepp!

SCHMITZ.   Prosit, Willi! (*They drink*)

BIEDERMANN.   And then?

SCHMITZ.   "Are you the firebug?" they asked him, and offered him cigarettes. He said, "Excuse me, I have no matches, Herr Commissioner, although you think I'm a firebug—" (*They laugh uproariously and slap each other's thighs*)

BIEDERMANN.   Hm. (ANNA *enters, in a cap and apron again. She hands* BIEDERMANN *a visiting card*)

ANNA.   It's urgent, he says.

BIEDERMANN.   When I have visitors—(SCHMITZ *and* EISENRING *clink glasses again*)

SCHMITZ.   Prosit, Willi!

EISENRING.   Prosit, Sepp! (*They drink.* BIEDERMANN *studies the visiting card*)

BABETTE.   Who is it, Gottlieb?

BIEDERMANN.   It's a professor . . . (ANNA *is busy at the sideboard*)

EISENRING.   And what are those other things, Fräulein—those silver things?

ANNA.   The candlesticks?

EISENRING.   Why do you hide them?

BIEDERMANN.   Bring them here!

ANNA.   But you said, yourself, Herr Biedermann—

BIEDERMANN.   I say bring them here! (ANNA *places the candelabra on the table*)

EISENRING.   What do you say to that, Sepp? They have candlesticks and they hide them! Real silver candlesticks—what more do you want?—Have you a match? (*He reaches into his pants pocket*)

SCHMITZ.   Me? No. (*He reaches into his pants pocket*)

EISENRING.   Sorry, no matches, Herr Biedermann.

BIEDERMANN.   I have some.

EISENRING.   Let's have them.

BIEDERMANN.   I'll light the candles. Let me—I'll do it. (*He begins lighting the candles*)

BABETTE.   (*To* ANNA) What does the visitor want?

ANNA.   I don't know, ma'am. He says he can no longer be silent. And he's waiting on the stoop.

BABETTE.   It's private, he says?

ANNA..   Yes, ma'am. He says he has a revelation to make.

BABETTE.   A revelation?

ANNA.   That's how he talks. I can't follow it, even when he repeats it. He wants to remove himself, so he says . . . (BIEDERMANN *is still lighting candles*)

EISENRING.   It creates an atmosphere, doesn't it, madam? Candlelight, I mean.

BABETTE.   Yes, it does.

EISENRING.   I'm all for atmosphere. Refined, candlelight atmosphere—

BIEDERMANN.   I'm happy to know that. (*All the candles are lit*)

EISENRING.   Schmitz, don't smack your lips when you eat! (BABETTE *takes* EISENRING *aside*)

BABETTE.   Let him alone!

EISENRING.   He has no manners, madam. Excuse me—it's awful. But where could he have picked up any manners? From the coal mines to the orphanage—

BABETTE.   I know.

EISENRING.   From the orphanage to the circus.

BABETTE.   I know.

EISENRING.   From the circus to the theatre—

BABETTE.   I didn't know.

EISENRING.   A football of fate, madam. (BABETTE *turns to* SCHMITZ)

BABETTE.   In the theatre! Were you, really? (SCHMITZ *gnaws on a drumstick and nods*) Where?

SCHMITZ.   Upstage.

EISENRING.   Really talented, too! Sepp as a ghost! Can you imagine it?

SCHMITZ.   Not any more, though.

EISENRING.   Why not?

SCHMITZ.   I was in the theatre only a week, madam, before it burned to the ground.

BABETTE.   Burned to the ground?

EISENRING.   (*To* SCHMITZ) Don't be so diffident!

BIEDERMANN.   Burned to the ground?

EISENRING.   Don't be so diffident! (*He unties the tablecloth* SCHMITZ *has been wearing and throws it over* SCHMITZ'S *head*) Come on! (SCHMITZ *gets up with the tablecloth over him*) Doesn't he look like a ghost?

ANNA.   I'm frightened!

EISENRING.   Come here, little girl! (*He pulls* ANNA *onto his lap. She hides her face in her hands*)

SCHMITZ.   "Who calleth?"

EISENRING.   That's theatre language, madam. They call that a cue. He learned it in less than a week, before the theatre burned down.

BABETTE.   Please don't keep talking of fires!

SCHMITZ.   "Who calleth?"

EISENRING.   Ready—(*Everybody waits expectantly.* EISENRING *has a tight grip on* ANNA)

SCHMITZ.   "EVERYMAN! EVERYMAN!"

BABETTE.   Gottlieb?

BIEDERMANN.   Quiet!

BABETTE.   We saw that in Salzburg![4]

SCHMITZ.   "BIEDERMANN! BIEDERMANN!"

EISENRING.   He's terrific!

SCHMITZ.   "BIEDERMANN! BIEDERMANN!"

EISENRING.   You must say, "Who are you?"

BIEDERMANN.   Me?

EISENRING.   Or he can't say his lines.

SCHMITZ.   "EVERYMAN! BIEDERMANN!"

BIEDERMANN.   All right, then—who am I?

BABETTE.   No! You must ask him who *he* is.

BIEDERMANN.   I see.

SCHMITZ.   "DOST THOU HEAR ME?"

EISENRING.   No, no, Sepp—start it again. (*They change their positions*)

SCHMITZ.   "EVERYMAN! BIEDERMANN!"

BABETTE.   Are you the Angel of Death, maybe?

BIEDERMANN.   Nonsense!

[4] The Austrian city well known for its staging of the morality play *Everyman*.

BABETTE.   What else *could* he be?

BIEDERMANN.   Ask him. He might be the ghost in "Hamlet." Or that other one—what's-his-name—in "Macbeth."

SCHMITZ.   "WHO CALLS ME?"

EISENRING.   Go on.

SCHMITZ.   "GOTTLEIB BIEDERMANN!"

BABETTE.   Go ahead, ask him. He's talking to you.

SCHMITZ.   "DOST THOU HEAR ME?"

BIEDERMANN.   Who are you?

SCHMITZ.   "I AM THE GHOST OF—KNECHTLING." (BABETTE *springs up with a scream*)

EISENRING.   Stop! (*He pulls the tablecloth off* SCHMITZ) Idiot! How could you do such a thing? Knechtling was buried today!

SCHMITZ.   That's why I thought of him. (BABETTE *hides her face in her hands*)

EISENRING.   He's not Knechtling, madam. (*He shakes his head over* SCHMITZ) What crudeness!

SCHMITZ.   He was on my mind . . .

EISENRING.   Of all things—Knechtling! Herr Biedermann's best old employee! Imagine it: buried today—cold and stiff—not yet mouldy—pale as this tablecloth—white and shiny as damask— To go and act Knechtling—(*He takes* BABETTE *by the shoulder*) Honest to God, madam, it's Sepp—it's not Knechtling at all. (SCHMITZ *wipes off his sweat*)

SCHMITZ.   I'm sorry . . .

BIEDERMANN.   Let's sit down again.

ANNA.   Is it over?

BIEDERMANN.   Would you care for cigars, sirs? (*He offers a box of cigars*)

EISENRING.   (*To* SCHMITZ) Idiot! You see how Herr Biedermann is shaking! . . . Thank you, Herr Biedermann!—You think that's funny, Sepp? When you know very well that Knechtling laid his head over a gas jet? After everything Gottlieb did for him? He gave this Knechtling fourteen years' work—and this is his thanks!

BIEDERMANN.   Let's not talk about it.

EISENRING.   (*To* SCHMITZ) And that's your thanks for the goose! (*They attend to their cigars*)

SCHMITZ.   Would you like me to sing something?

EISENRING.   What?

SCHMITZ.   "Fox, you stole that lovely goosie . . ."
(*He sings loudly*)
"Fox, you stole that lovely goosie,
Give it back again!"

EISENRING.   That's enough.

SCHMITZ.   "Give it back again!
Or they'll get you in the shnoosie—"

EISENRING.   He's drunk.

SCHMITZ.   "With their shooting-gun!"

EISENRING.   Pay no attention to him.

SCHMITZ.   "Give it back again!
Or they'll get you in the shnoosie
With their shooting-gun!"

BIEDERMANN.   "Shooting-gun!" That's good! (*The men all join in the song*)
"Fox, you stole that lovely goosie . . ."
(*They harmonize, now loudly, now softly. Laughter and loud cheer. There is a pause, and* BIEDERMANN *picks up again, leading the hilarity until they've all had it*)

BIEDERMANN.   So—Prosit! (*They raise their glasses. Fire sirens are heard near by*) What was that?

EISENRING.   Sirens.

BIEDERMANN.   Joking aside—

BABETTE.   Firebugs! Firebugs!

BIEDERMANN.   Don't yell like that! (BABETTE *runs to the window and throws it open. The sound of the sirens comes nearer, with a howl that goes to the marrow. The fire engines roar past*)

BIEDERMANN.   At least it's not here.

BABETTE.   I wonder where?

EISENRING.   From where the wind is blowing.

BIEDERMANN.   Not here, anyway.

EISENRING.   That's how we generally work it. Coax the Fire Department out to some cheap suburb or other, and then, when things really let loose, they find their way blocked.

BIEDERMANN.   No, gentlemen—all joking aside—

SCHMITZ.   That's how we do it—joking aside—

BIEDERMANN.   Please—enough of this nonsense! Don't overdo it! Look at my wife—white as chalk!

BABETTE.   And you too!

BIEDERMANN.   Besides, a fire alarm is nothing to laugh at, gentlemen. Somewhere some place is burning, or the Fire Department wouldn't be rushing there. (EISENRING *looks at his watch*)

EISENRING.   We've got to go now.

BIEDERMANN.   Now?

EISENRING.   Sorry.

SCHMITZ.   "Or they'll get you in the shnoosie . . ." (*The sirens are heard again*)

BIEDERMANN.   Bring us some coffee, Babette! (BABETTE *goes out*) And you, Anna—do you have to stand there and gape? (ANNA *goes out*) Just between us, gentlemen: enough is enough. My wife has a heart condition. Let's have no more joking about fires.

SCHMITZ.   We're not joking, Herr Biedermann.

EISENRING.   We're firebugs.

BIEDERMANN.   No, gentlemen, quite seriously—

EISENRING.   Quite seriously.

SCHMITZ.   Yeah, quite seriously. Why don't you believe us?

EISENRING.   Your house is very favorably situated, Herr Biedermann, you must admit that. Five villas like yours around the gas works . . . It's true they keep a close watch on the gas works. Still, there's a good stiff wind blowing—

BIEDERMANN.   It can't be—

SCHMITZ.   Let's have plain talk! You think we're firebugs—

BIEDERMANN.   (*Like a whipped dog*) No, no, I don't think you are! You do me an injustice, gentlemen—I don't think you're firebugs . . .

EISENRING.   You swear you don't?

BIEDERMANN.   No! No! No! I don't believe it!

SCHMITZ.   What *do* you think we are?

BIEDERMANN.   You're my friends . . . (*They clap him on the shoulder and start to leave*)

EISENRING.   It's time to leave.

BIEDERMANN.   Gentlemen, I swear to you by all that's holy—

EISENRING.   By all that's holy?

BIEDERMANN.   Yes. (*He raises his hand as though to take an oath*)

SCHMITZ.   Willi doesn't believe in anything holy, Herr Biedermann. Any more than you do. You'll waste your time swearing. (*They go to the door*)

BIEDERMANN.   What can I do to make you believe me? (*He blocks the doorway*)

EISENRING.   Give us some matches.

BIEDERMANN.   Some—

EISENRING.   We have no more matches.

BIEDERMANN.   You want me to—

EISENRING.   If you don't think we're firebugs.

BIEDERMANN.   Matches—

SCHMITZ.   To show your belief in us, he means. (BIEDERMANN *reaches in his pocket*)

EISENRING.   See how he hesitates?

BIEDERMANN.   Sh! Not in front of my wife . . . (BABETTE *returns*)

BABETTE.   Your coffee will be ready in a minute. (*Pause*) Must you go?

BIEDERMANN.   (*Formally*) At least you've felt, while here, my friends . . . I don't want to make a speech on this occasion, but may we not drink, before you go, to our eternal friendship? (*He picks up a bottle and the corkscrew*)

EISENRING.   Tell your very charming husband, madam, that he needn't open any more bottles on our account. It isn't worth the trouble any more.

BIEDERMANN.   It's no trouble, my friends, no trouble at all. If there's anything else you'd like—anything at all—(*He fills the glasses once more and hands them out*) My friends! (*They clink glasses*) Sepp—Willi—(*He kisses them each on the cheek. All drink*)

EISENRING.   Just the same, we must go now.

SCHMITZ.   Unfortunately.

EISENRING.   Madam—(*Sirens*)

BABETTE.   It's been such a nice evening. (*Alarm bells*)

EISENRING.   Just one thing, now, Gottlieb—

BIEDERMANN.   What is it?

EISENRING.   I've mentioned it to you before.

BIEDERMANN.   Anything you like. Just name it.

EISENRING.   The matches. (ANNA *has entered with coffee*)

BABETTE.   Why, what is it, Anna?

ANNA.   The coffee.

BABETTE.   You're all upset, Anna!

ANNA.   Back there—Frau Biedermann—the sky! You can see it from the kitchen—the whole sky is burning, Frau Biedermann! (*The scene is turning red as* SCHMITZ *and* EISENRING *make their bows and exit.* BIEDERMANN *is left pale and shaken*)

BIEDERMANN.   Not our house, fortunately . . . Not our house . . . Not our . . . (*The* PH.D. *enters*) Who are you, and what do you want?

PH.D.   I can no longer be silent. (*He takes out a paper and reads*) "Cognizant of the events now transpiring, whose iniquitous nature must be readily apparent, the undersigned submits to the authorities the subsequent statement . . ." (*Amid the shrieking of sirens he reads an involved statement, of which no one understands a word. Dogs howl, bells ring, there is the scream of departing sirens and the crackling of flames. The* PH.D. *hands* BIEDERMANN *the paper*) I remove myself . . .

BIEDERMANN.   But—

PH.D.   I have said my say. (*He takes off and folds up his glasses*) Sir, as a serious-minded uplifter, I knew what they were doing in your attic. I did *not* know, however, that they were doing it just for fun!

BIEDERMANN.   Professor—(*The* PH.D. *removes himself*) What will I do with this, Professor? (*The* PH.D. *climbs over the footlights and takes a seat in the audience*)

BABETTE.   Gottlieb—

BIEDERMANN.   He's gone.

BABETTE.   What did you give them? Matches? Not matches?

BIEDERMANN.   Why not?

BABETTE.   Not matches?

BIEDERMANN.   If they really were firebugs, do you think they wouldn't have matches? Don't be foolish, Babette! (*The clock strikes. Silence. The red light onstage begins deepening into blackness. Sirens. Bells ring. Dogs howl. Cars honk . . . A crash of collapsing buildings. A crackling of flames. Screams and outcries . . . fading. The* CHORUS *comes on again*)

CHORUS.   Useless, quite useless.
       And nothing more useless
       Than this useless story.
       For arson, once kindled,
       Kills many,
       Leaves few,
       And accomplishes nothing.
         (*First detonation*)

LEADER.   That was the gas works.
                   (*Second detonation*)
CHORUS.   Long foreseen, disaster
                   Has reached us at last.
                   Horrendous arson!
                   Unquenchable fire!
                   Fate—so they call it!
                   (*Third detonation*)
LEADER.   More gas tanks.
                   (*There is a series of frightful explosions*)
CHORUS.   Woe to us! Woe to us! Woe!
                   (*The house lights go up*)

SCENE NINE

Epilog

CHARACTERS OF THE EPILOG
HERR BIEDERMANN
BABETTE
ANNA
BEELZEBUB
A PERSONAGE
A POLICEMAN
A RING-TAILED MONKEY
THE WIDOW KNECHTLING
THE CHORUS

> BABETTE *and* BIEDERMANN *are revealed, standing in the same positions as at the end of the previous scene.*

BABETTE.   Gottlieb?
BIEDERMANN.   Sh!
BABETTE.   Are we dead? (*A parrot screeches*)
BIEDERMANN.   Why didn't you come down before the stairs caught fire? Why did you run to our bedroom again?
BABETTE.   I went back for my jewelry.
BIEDERMANN.   Of course we're dead. (*The parrot squawks*)
BABETTE.   Gottlieb?
BIEDERMANN.   Quiet, now.
BABETTE.   Where are we?

BIEDERMANN.   In heaven, of course. Where else? (*A baby cries*)

BABETTE.   I never imagined heaven was like this. (*The baby cries again*)

BIEDERMANN.   Don't lose your faith at a time like this!

BABETTE.   Did *you* imagine it this way? (*The parrot screeches*) Gottlieb?

BIEDERMANN.   Don't lose your faith at a time like this.

BABETTE.   We've been waiting half an eternity. (*The baby cries*) And now that baby again! (*The parrot screeches*) Gottlieb?

BIEDERMANN.   What now?

BABETTE.   How did that parrot get into heaven? (*A doorbell rings*)

BIEDERMANN.   Don't upset me, Babette. Why can't a parrot go to heaven? If he's led a good life? (*The doorbell rings again*) What was that?

BABETTE.   Our doorbell.

BIEDERMANN.   Who can *that* be? (*The baby, the bell and the parrot all sound off together*)

BABETTE.   Who needs that parrot? And that baby, too! I won't be able to take it, Gottlieb—a racket like that, forever! Why, it's just like the slums!

BIEDERMANN.   Sh!

BABETTE.   They can't expect us to—

BIEDERMANN.   Calm down.

BABETTE.   People like us are not used to it.

BIEDERMANN.   (*Considering it*) Why wouldn't we be in heaven? Everybody we know is there—even my lawyer. This *must* be heaven! We've done nothing wrong—(*The doorbell rings*)

BABETTE.   Shouldn't we answer the doorbell? (*It rings again*) How did they get hold of our bell? (*It rings again*) Maybe an angel calling . . .

BIEDERMANN.   I'm perfectly innocent. I honored my father and mother—you know that, Babette. Especially Mother—you were sore about that often enough. I never made a graven image of God—never thought of it, even. I never stole; we always had what we needed. I never killed anybody. I never worked Sundays. I never coveted my neighbor's house. Or if I did, I paid cash for it. Buying's permitted, I'm sure. And I never caught myself lying. I never committed adultery, Babette—I mean it; compared with others, at least . . . You are my witness, Ba-

bette, before the angels. I had only one earthly fault: I was too
good-hearted. (*The parrot screeches*)

BABETTE.   Can you understand what it's saying?

BIEDERMANN.   Did *you* kill anybody, Babette? I'm only asking, that's
all. Or worship other gods? Outside of a little Yoga? Did you
ever commit adultery?

BABETTE.   With whom?

BIEDERMANN.   Well, then—(*The doorbell rings*) We *must* be in heaven.
(ANNA *enters in cap and apron*)

BABETTE.   How did Anna get into heaven? (ANNA *walks past. She has
long, green hair*) I hope she didn't notice that you gave them the
matches. She might report it.

BIEDERMANN.   The matches!

BABETTE.   I warned you they were firebugs, Gottlieb. I warned you
from the beginning. (ANNA *comes back with a* POLICEMAN. *The*
POLICEMAN *has little white wings*)

ANNA.   I'll call him. (*She exits. The* POLICEMAN *waits*)

BIEDERMANN.   You see? An angel. (*The* POLICEMAN *salutes*)

BABETTE.   I thought angels looked different.

BIEDERMANN.   This isn't the Middle Ages.

BABETTE.   Didn't *you* think they looked different? (*The* POLICEMAN
turns around. Continues to wait) Should we kneel, do you think?

BIEDERMANN.   Ask him if this is heaven. (*Encouraging her with a nod*)
We've been waiting half an eternity, tell him.

BABETTE.   My husband and I—

BIEDERMANN.   Tell him we're victims.

BABETTE.   My husband and I are victims.

BIEDERMANN.   Our house is ruined.

BABETTE.   My husband and I—

BIEDERMANN.   Tell him!

BABETTE.   Ruined.

BIEDERMANN.   He simply can't imagine what we've gone through.
Tell him! We've lost everything, tell him. And it's in no way
our fault.

BABETTE.   You can't imagine—

BIEDERMANN.   What we've gone through.

BABETTE.   All my jewelry melted.

BIEDERMANN.   Tell him we're innocent.

BABETTE.   Besides, we're innocent.

BIEDERMANN.   Compared with others.

BABETTE.   Compared with others. (*The* ANGEL-POLICEMAN *takes out a cigar*)

POLICEMAN.   Have you a match? (BIEDERMANN *turns pale*)

BIEDERMANN.   I? A match? (*A tongue of flame shoots up from the ground*)

POLICEMAN.   I've got a light, thanks. Never mind. (BABETTE *and* BIEDERMANN *stare at the flame, astonished*)

BABETTE.   Gottlieb—

BIEDERMANN.   Quiet!

BABETTE.   What does all this mean? (*Enter a* RING-TAILED MONKEY)

MONKEY.   Who are these people?

POLICEMAN.   A couple of the damned. (*He hands over a report. The* MONKEY *puts on his glasses*)

BABETTE.   Gottlieb, we know him!

BIEDERMANN.   Where from?

BABETTE.   The professor. Don't you remember? (*The* MONKEY *leafs through the report*)

MONKEY.   How are things upstairs?

POLICEMAN.   No use complaining. Nobody knows where God lives, but otherwise everything's fine. No use complaining, thank you.

MONKEY.   (*Indicating the report*) Why was this bunch sent here? (*The* POLICEMAN *glances at the report*)

POLICEMAN.   Freethinkers. (*The* MONKEY *has ten rubber stamps. He chooses from them, stamping each document*)

MONKEY.   "THOU SHALT HAVE NO OTHER GODS BEFORE ME."

POLICEMAN.   A doctor who gave wrong injections.

MONKEY.   "THOU SHALT NOT KILL."

POLICEMAN.   A board chairman with seven secretaries—all blonde.

MONKEY.   "THOU SHALT NOT COMMIT ADULTERY."

POLICEMAN.   An abortionist.

MONKEY.   "THOU SHALT NOT KILL."

POLICEMAN.   A drunk driver.

MONKEY.   "THOU SHALT NOT KILL."

POLICEMAN.   Refugees.

MONKEY.   What's their sin?

POLICEMAN.   Fifty-two potatoes, one umbrella, two wool blankets.

MONKEY.   "THOU SHALT NOT STEAL."

POLICEMAN.   A tax consultant.

MONKEY. "THOU SHALT NOT BEAR FALSE WITNESS."

POLICEMAN. Another drunk driver. (*The* MONKEY *stamps the paper silently*) Another freethinker. (*Ditto*) Seven underground fighters. Sent to heaven by mistake. They were caught and shot by a firing squad; but it seems they did some so-called liberating before then.

MONKEY. Hm.

POLICEMAN. Liberating while out of uniform.

MONKEY. "THOU SHALT NOT STEAL."

POLICEMAN. Another abortionist.

MONKEY. "THOU SHALT NOT KILL."

POLICEMAN. And here's the rest.

MONKEY. "THOU SHALT NOT COMMIT ADULTERY." (*He stamps at least thirteen more reports*) Nothing but middle-class! Old Nick will be furious! And all these juvenile delinquents! I'm almost afraid of turning in this report! No general, no cabinet minister—not one celebrity in the lot!

POLICEMAN. Ts. Ts.

MONKEY. Take them down below. Beelzebub's already got the heat turned on, I think, or is about to. (THE POLICEMAN *salutes and exits*)

BABETTE. Gottlieb, we are in hell!

BIEDERMANN. Don't scream like that.

BABETTE. Gottlieb—(*She breaks into sobs*)

BIEDERMANN. There's something wrong here, Professor—it's got to be changed. How is it we're in hell, my wife and I? (*To* BABETTE) Keep calm, Babette, this *must* be a mistake. (*To the* MONKEY) Let me speak with the Devil.

BABETTE. Gottlieb—

BIEDERMANN. May I speak with the Devil, please?

MONKEY. (*With a gesture*) Sit down, please. (BIEDERMANN *and* BABETTE *see no seats to sit down on*) What do you want to see him about? (BIEDERMANN *hands him a card*) What is that?

BIEDERMANN. Driver's license—identification.

MONKEY. Not required. (*He returns it without looking at it*) You're Gottlieb Biedermann? Manufacturer? Big bank account?

BIEDERMANN. How did you know?

MONKEY. Number 33 Rosenweg? The Devil knows you well. (BABETTE *and* BIEDERMANN *look at each other*) Take seats, please. (*Two burned chairs appear onstage*)

BABETTE.   Gottlieb—our chairs!

MONKEY.   Sit down, please. (*They sit*) Do you smoke?

BIEDERMANN.   Not any more.

MONKEY.   Your own cigars, you know. (*He helps himself to a cigar*) They were burned, too. I'm sure that doesn't surprise you. (*Flames shoot up from the floor*) I have a light, thank you. (*He lights his cigar and takes a puff*) Now come to the point—what is it you want? Some bread? Some wine, maybe?

BIEDERMANN.   We have no place to sleep! (*The* MONKEY *calls*)

MONKEY.   Anna!

BABETTE.   We're not beggars, we're victims.

BIEDERMANN.   We don't want charity. We're not used to it.

BABETTE.   And we don't need it. (ANNA *appears*)

ANNA.   Yes?

MONKEY.   They don't want charity.

ANNA.   That's all right, then. (*She exits*)

BABETTE.   We had our own home.

BIEDERMANN.   We demand compensation! (*The* MONKEY *withdraws without answering, as is the way of bureaucrats*)

BABETTE.   What does he mean, "The Devil knows you"?

BIEDERMANN.   How should *I* know? (*A pendulum clock strikes*)

BABETTE.   Our grandfather clock! (*It strikes nine*)

BIEDERMANN.   I shall insist that everything be put back where it was! We were insured! (*The* MONKEY *returns from stage left*)

MONKEY.   One moment, please. (*Exits stage right*)

BIEDERMANN.   These devils put on an act!

BABETTE.   Sh!

BIEDERMANN.   Next thing you know they'll ask for our fingerprints, like the police. To try and give us a bad conscience. (BABETTE *puts her hand on his arm comfortingly*) My conscience is clear. So is yours—

BABETTE.   What if they ask about the matches?

BIEDERMANN.   I gave those boys matches, that's true. But what of it? So did everybody else. Or the whole city wouldn't have burned down the way it did. I saw the flames spring out over every roof . . . And don't forget I acted in good faith!

BABETTE.   You're too excited.

BIEDERMANN.   And even if everybody did it, you can't throw everybody into hell! What about forgiveness? (*The* MONKEY *returns*)

MONKEY.   The Lord of the Underworld isn't back yet. Would you care to speak with Beelzebub instead?

BABETTE.   Beelzebub?

MONKEY.   He's around. But I warn you he smells something awful. He's the one with the horns, the hoofs and the tail . . . But don't expect much from *him,* madam—a poor devil like Sepp!

BIEDERMANN.   Sepp? (BABETTE *jumps up in alarm*)

BABETTE.   Gottlieb, what did I tell you?

BIEDERMANN.   Babette! (*He gives her a look that sits her down again*) My wife couldn't sleep nights. That's when you toss and worry. But by day, Professor, we had no ground for suspicion—none whatever. (BABETTE *gives him a look*) At least *I* didn't.

BABETTE.   Then why were you going to throw them out of the house?

BIEDERMANN.   I didn't throw them out.

BABETTE.   That's just it.

BIEDERMANN.   Why didn't *you* throw them out? Instead of feeding them toast and marmalade and soft-boiled eggs? (*The* MONKEY *puffs at his cigar*) To be brief, Professor, we had no idea what was going on at home. No idea. (*Trumpets sound*)

MONKEY.   That's him—the Lord of the Underworld. (*Trumpets*) In a terrible temper, no doubt. He's been up to heaven; probably had another tough session.

BIEDERMANN.   On my account?

MONKEY.   On account of this last amnesty . . . (*He whispers in* BIEDERMANN's *ear*)

BIEDERMANN.   I've heard about that.

MONKEY.   And what do you say to this? (*He whispers again*)

BIEDERMANN.   You think so?

MONKEY.   If heaven thinks we're going to stand for anything and everything—(*He whispers again*)

BIEDERMANN.   You mean it? (*Trumpets*)

MONKEY.   He's coming! (*The* MONKEY *exits*)

BABETTE.   What did he say?

BIEDERMANN.   They may close the doors of hell; no more people admitted. Because hell is going on strike. (*Doorbell rings*) He says they're furious down here. They've been expecting a whole army of big shots, and it seems heaven has pardoned them all.

He says it's a hell of a crisis. (ANNA *crosses from left to right*) What's Anna doing here?

BABETTE.   I didn't tell you: she stole a pair of my new nylons. (ANNA *comes in with the* WIDOW KNECHTLING)

ANNA.   Sit down, please. But don't get up any hopes: your husband committed suicide, you know. (ANNA *exits. The* WIDOW *remains standing, there being no more seats*)

BABETTE.   It's Frau Knechtling! What does she want here? (*She gives the* WIDOW *a smile*) She's going to testify against us, Gottlieb.

BIEDERMANN.   Let her! (*The trumpets sound closer*) Why couldn't Knechtling have waited a week or two? He could have taken me aside at a favorable moment and talked it over, couldn't he? How could I know he was going to commit suicide just because I gave him his notice? (*The trumpets sound closer*) I'm not worried. (*The trumpets sound closer*) Those matches!

BABETTE.   Maybe nobody saw you.

BIEDERMANN.   There've always been disasters! Always were and always will be! . . . Besides, look at our city now—everything glass and aluminum! In fact it's a blessing, really, that the town burned down. From the standpoint of city planning . . . (*Trumpets, then organ music. Enter a* PERSONAGE, *pompous and resplendent, in a costume slightly reminiscent of a bishop.* BIEDERMANN *and* BABETTE *kneel at the footlights. The* PERSONAGE *takes center stage*)

PERSONAGE.   (*Calls*) Anna! (*He starts to take off his violet gloves*) I'm back from heaven.

BIEDERMANN.   (*To* BABETTE) You hear that?

PERSONAGE.   It's hopeless. (*He calls*) Anna! (*He goes on taking off his gloves*) I wonder if it really was heaven I saw—even though they told me it was. They had incense coming out of loudspeakers. And the medals on everybody! My old friends, the mass-murderers, with chests full of medals! And the angels hovering over them, full of smiles! Everybody chatting, strolling, drinking toasts! The saints had nothing to say; they're made of wood, on permanent loan from somewhere. As for the princes of the church—I tried to ask them where God lives, but they shut up, too, even though they're *not* made of wood . . . (*He calls*) Anna! (*He removes his hood. It is* EISENRING) I was disguised, of course. And the folks who are running things up there—and are busy blessing themselves—didn't recognize me. I added my blessing . . . (ANNA *and the* MONKEY *enter and bow*) Remove this clothing. (*The* PERSONAGE *holds out his arms to permit his four silken garments, one over the other, to be unbuttoned. These are, in order, silver, gold, violet and blood-red. The organ music ends.* BIEDERMANN *and* BABETTE *continue to kneel*) Bring my tail-coat.

ANNA.   Yes sir.

PERSONAGE.   And my head-waiter's wig. (ANNA *and the* MONKEY *remove his first garment*) I have some doubts whether it was God Himself who received me. He knew everything, and when He spoke He said exactly what the newspapers say, word for word. (*The parrot shrieks*) Where is Beelzebub?

MONKEY.   At the furnaces.

PERSONAGE.   Let him appear. (*The stage suddenly turns red*) What is this glare?

MONKEY.   He's heating the furnaces. A new batch of sinners; the usual kind. (*They remove the second garment*)

PERSONAGE.   Let him put out the furnaces.

MONKEY.   Put them out?

PERSONAGE.   Put them out! (*The parrot shrieks*) How is my parrot? (*He notices* BABETTE *and* BIEDERMANN) Ask those people why they're praying.

MONKEY.   They're not praying.

PERSONAGE.   They're kneeling.

MONKEY.   They want their home back. Compensation. (*The parrot screeches*)

PERSONAGE.   My lovely parrot! I found him in a burning house. The only creature who doesn't change his tune! He's going to ride on my shoulder when I go up to earth again. (ANNA *and the* MONKEY *remove his third garment*) Bring the bicycles, Professor. (*The* MONKEY *bows and exits*)

BIEDERMANN.   Willi, don't you know me? I'm your friend Gottlieb!

BABETTE.   We're innocent, Herr Eisenring! (ANNA *removes the* PERSONAGE's *fourth garment*) Why does he pretend not to know us?

PERSONAGE.   Bring two velvet cushions, Anna, for these people who are kneeling.

ANNA.   Yes sir. (*She exits*)

PERSONAGE.   I remember everything, Gottlieb. You went so far as to kiss the Devil. (*The parrot calls*)

BABETTE.   But, Willi, if we had known you were the Devil—if we had had the slightest inkling—(ANNA *brings the frock-coat and the cushions*)

PERSONAGE.   Thank you, Anna. They won't need those cushions now—Where's Beelzebub?

BEELZEBUB.   (*Appears*) Here. (*It is* SEPP, *wearing horns, hoofs and goat tail, and carrying a huge shovel*)

PERSONAGE.   Don't roar like that!—We're going back to earth, Sepp. (ANNA *is helping him dress*) Have you put out the ovens?

BEELZEBUB.   No. I've just shoveled more coal on. (*A reflection of flames flickers over the stage*)

PERSONAGE.   Do as I tell you. (*He calls*) Professor! (*To* SEPP) I got nowhere with heaven. They won't give up a single one of their sinners.

BEELZEBUB.   Not even one? (*The* MONKEY *enters*)

PERSONAGE.   Call the Fire Department! (*The* MONKEY *bows and exits*) Not one! They're all saved! Anybody who kills while in uniform. Or who promises to wear a uniform while killing. Or who orders killing by others in uniform—all are saved!

BEELZEBUB.   Saved?!

PERSONAGE.   Don't roar like that! (*An echo is heard from above*)

ECHO.   Saved! Saved! Saved! (BEELZEBUB *glares up at at the sound*)

PERSONAGE.   Get your earthly clothes on, Sepp; we're going back to work. (*The* CHORUS *enters*)

CHORUS.   Woe!

BABETTE.   Gottlieb, what are *they* doing here?

CHORUS.   Fellow-citizens, see
  Our pitiful helplessness!
  Tested and ready were we,
  Equipped with engines and hose;
  Now we're forever condemned
  To view the fires of hell
  As they roast our citizens well.

PERSONAGE.   Gentlemen, put out the fires of hell! (*The* CHORUS *is startled*) I don't intend to run hell for the sake of middle-of-the-roaders, lowbrows, highbrows, liberals, pickpockets, adulterers, slackers and servant girls who steal nylon stockings! (*The* CHORUS *is motionless*) What are you waiting for?

CHORUS.   Ready for action
  Axes and fire-hose;

Polished and oiled,
Every brass fitting;
Every man of us tested and ready.
Our brass fire-pump
Polished and oiled,
Tested for pressure.

LEADER.   And the fire-hydrants?

CHORUS.   Tested and ready for action.

PERSONAGE.   Then get going! (*The flickering red light, which had begun to die down, blazes up again*)

LEADER.   To the hoses!
The pumps!
The ladders!

(*The* FIREMEN *quickly take places*)

PERSONAGE.   Ready! (*The hiss of water is heard. The flames start to go out*) And now, my wig, my bicycle and my parrot!

BEELZEBUB.   What have they done to my childhood belief? "Thou shalt not kill," they said, and I believed them! (*The* PERSONAGE *polishes his fingernails*) I, Sepp Schmitz, son of a miner and a gipsy—I belong to the Devil. "Go to the devil, Sepp," they said, and I went. I told lies, because lies make things easier. I stole where I listed and whored where I lusted. The villages feared me, for I was strong with the strength of the Devil. I tripped up the villagers on their way to church. I burned down their barns on Sundays while they prayed. I laughed at their loving God, who had no love for me . . . Who closed the mineshaft that buried my father? My mother, praying for me, died of grief at my capers . . . I burned down the orphans' home—for fun! I burned down the circus—for fun! I set fire to town after town—all for fun, for fun! (*The* PERSONAGE *laughs*) There's nothing to laugh at, Willi! (ANNA *brings the wig. The* MONKEY *brings two rusty bicycles*) There's nothing to laugh at. What have they done with my childhood belief? It's enough to make one throw up! (*The* PERSONAGE *has put on his wig*)

PERSONAGE.   Make ready! (*He takes one of the rusty bicycles*) How I burn to see them again—the big boys who never get sent here . . . And a good, crackling fire—alarms that are always too late—smoke—the howling of dogs and of people—and ashes! (BEELZEBUB *takes off his hoofs and his tail*) Are we ready? (*He jumps on his bicycle and rings the bell*)

BEELZEBUB.   One moment—

LEADER.   Stop pumping!

> Down hoses
> Turn off the water!
> (*The red shimmer dies out completely*)

PERSONAGE.   Your horns, Sepp! (BEELZEBUB *removes his horns, jumps on the other bicycle and rings the bell*)

PERSONAGE.   (*To* ANNA) Thank you, my girl . . . But you're always so gloomy! I heard you laugh only once—when we were singing that song. (ANNA *laughs*) Some day we'll sing it again.

ANNA.   Oh, please do! (*The* CHORUS *comes forward*)

CHORUS.   Fellow-citizens, we—

PERSONAGE.   Make it short, please!

CHORUS.   Hell's fires are out.

PERSONAGE.   Thank you. (*He reaches in his pants pocket*) Got any matches?

BEELZEBUB.   No. Have you?

PERSONAGE.   Never mind. Somebody'll give us some. (*The* MONKEY *enters with the parrot*) My parrot! (*He perches the parrot on his right shoulder*) Before I forget, Professor: we're taking in no more souls. Tell heaven hell is on strike. And if any angel comes looking for us, tell him we're back on earth. (BEELZEBUB *rings his bicycle bell*) Let's go. (SCHMITZ *and* EISENRING *ride away, waving*)

BOTH.   Good luck, Gottlieb, good luck! (*The* CHORUS *comes forward*)

CHORUS.   O radiant sun!

> O godlike eye!
> Light up the day—

LEADER.   Above our rebuilt city.

CHORUS.   Hallelujah!

> (*The parrot squawks far off*)

BABETTE.   Gottlieb?

BIEDERMANN.   Sh!

BABETTE.   Are we saved?

BIEDERMANN.   Don't lose your faith at a time like this. (*The* WIDOW KNECHTLING *exits*)

CHORUS.   Hallelujah!

BABETTE.   Frau Knechtling is gone—

CHORUS.   Lovelier than before,

> Risen from its ruins and its ashes

Is our city.
Removed and forgotten is the rubbish;
Forgotten, too, the men and women
Whose cries rose from the flames.

BIEDERMANN.   Life goes on.

CHORUS.   Historic are they now,
Those people.
And silent.

LEADER.   Hallelujah!

CHORUS.   Lovelier than before,
And richer,
Skyscraper-modern,
All chrome and glass,
Yet ever the same
At heart.
Hallelujah!
Reborn is our city!

(*Organ music*)

BABETTE.   Gottlieb?

BIEDERMANN.   What is it?

BABETTE.   Do you think we're saved?

BIEDERMANN.   Yes, I think so . . .

(*The organ music swells.* BABETTE *and* BIEDERMANN *are on their knees*)

31
Twentieth-Century Poetry

Twentieth-century literature cannot be understood apart from the intellectual crisis of contemporary culture. Modern times have seen the alienation of human beings from their environment and from themselves, as well as the progressive fragmentation of the concepts of self and society, with all the accompanying uncertainty, anxiety, and despair. Given these circumstances, modern literature has tried to express, in the language of imagination, the intractable material of a hostile civilization. In addition, while registering the seeming futility and anarchy of contemporary life, it has endeavored to transform and triumph over the realities of the present. More than most philosophy, which has tended to become technical and irrelevant, modern literature has sought to frame the fundamental problems and dilemmas of modern society and offer some solutions to them. Writers have sought a meaningful reality on the subjective level, in the depths of consciousness. Here they hoped to recapture the simple but enduring elements of human experience that might give form and direction to the shattered surface of life. To serve these new purposes, they have had to devise new forms of expression and a new vocabulary. The results have been complex, shocking, and often obscure, with a raw or dreamlike quality that has tended to alienate a large part of the audience.

Modern poets, in trying to cope with a hostile world and their own alienation from it, have written with relentless, analytic frankness, often tinged with mockery of humanity's tragic plight. They have discarded the conventional techniques and have experimented freely, while insisting on the need for a rigorous poetic discipline. Many have used a new language that aims at both precision and allusiveness; this duality has often made their poems difficult, requiring the reader's most careful and informed attention.

The following selection includes works by Robert Frost (1874–1963), Thomas Stearns Eliot (1888–1965), and William Butler Yeats (1865–

1939), *three of the greatest English-language poets of the twentieth century. Frost's "After Apple-Picking" (1914) is a realistic account of a rural New England scene. It is written in the ordinary rhythms of speech, but its surface simplicity is deceiving. The poem skillfully suggests, through a series of contrasts, a human need to create ideals out of and beyond ordinary work and experience.*

T. S. Eliot, an American who settled in England, is considered one of the century's most influential poets and critics. In the dramatic monologue "The Love Song of J. Alfred Prufrock" (1917), he uses irregular meters, chance rhymes, strange metaphors, and obscure allusions to compel attention and stimulate imagination. The poem describes the frustrations and loneliness of a timid, neurotic, yet intelligent man, who has lost his faith and creative ability, but is still aware of a dignity he himself can never attain. Prufrock's plight symbolizes the tragedy of twentieth-century humanity.

"The Second Coming" (1921) by Yeats, the Irish poet and nationalist, expresses a grim view of the future in harsh, broken rhythms and astringent, symbolic language. Turning from the sentimental, Christian hope for a millennium, Yeats sees beyond the chaos of the present the advent of an iron age of harshness and brutality.

ROBERT FROST

After Apple-Picking

My long two-pointed ladder's sticking through a tree
Toward heaven still,
And there's a barrel that I didn't fill
Beside it, and there may be two or three
Apples I didn't pick upon some bough.
But I am done with apple-picking now.
Essence of winter sleep is on the night,
The scent of apples: I am drowsing off.
I cannot rub the strangeness from my sight
I got from looking through a pane of glass

I skimmed this morning from the drinking trough
And held against the world of hoary grass.
It melted, and I let it fall and break.
But I was well
Upon my way to sleep before it fell,
And I could tell
What form my dreaming was about to take.
Magnified apples appear and disappear,
Stem end and blossom end,
And every fleck of russet showing clear.
My instep arch not only keeps the ache,
It keeps the pressure of a ladder-round.
I feel the ladder sway as the boughs bend.
And I keep hearing from the cellar bin
The rumbling sound
Of load on load of apples coming in.
For I have had too much
Of apple-picking: I am overtired
Of the great harvest I myself desired.
There were ten thousand thousand fruit to touch,
Cherish in hand, lift down, and not let fall.
For all
That struck the earth,
No matter if not bruised or spiked with stubble,
Went surely to the cider-apple heap
As of no worth.
One can see what will trouble
This sleep of mine, whatever sleep it is.
Were he not gone,
The woodchuck could say whether it's like his
Long sleep, as I describe its coming on,
Or just some human sleep.

T. S. ELIOT

The Love Song of J. Alfred Prufrock

S'io credesse che mia risposta fosse
A persona che mai tornasse al mondo,
Questa fiamma staria senza più scosse.
Ma per ciò che giammai di questo fondo
Non tornò viva alcun, s'i'odo il vero,
Senza tema d'infamia ti rispondo. [1]

Let us go then, you and I,
When the evening is spread out against the sky
Like a patient etherized upon a table;
Let us go, through certain half-deserted streets,
The muttering retreats
Of restless nights in one-night cheap hotels
And sawdust restaurants with oyster-shells:
Streets that follow like a tedious argument
Of insidious intent
To lead you to an overwhelming question . . .
Oh, do not ask, 'What is it?'
Let us go and make our visit.

In the room the women come and go
Talking of Michelangelo.

The yellow fog that rubs its back upon the window-panes,
The yellow smoke that rubs its muzzle on the window-panes
Licked its tongue into the corners of the evening,
Lingered upon the pools that stand in drains,
Let fall upon its back the soot that falls from chimneys,
Slipped by the terrace, made a sudden leap,
And seeing that it was a soft October night,
Curled once about the house, and fell asleep.

T. S. Eliot, "The Love Song of J. Alfred Prufrock." From *Collected Poems of T. S. Eliot,* copyright, 1936, by Harcourt, Brace & World, Inc. and reprinted with their permission and the permission of Faber and Faber Ltd. [Pp. 11–16.]

[1] This epigraph is quoted from Dante's *The Divine Comedy*. One of the damned in *The Inferno* speaks as follows: "If I believed that my answer were to someone who might ever go back to the world, this flame would shake no more. But since, if I hear truth, no one ever returned alive from this pit, I respond to you without fear of infamy."

And indeed there will be time
For the yellow smoke that slides along the street
Rubbing its back upon the window-panes;
There will be time, there will be time
To prepare a face to meet the faces that you meet;
There will be time to murder and create,
And time for all the works and days of hands
That lift and drop a question on your plate;
Time for you and time for me,
And time yet for a hundred indecisions,
And for a hundred visions and revisions,
Before the taking of a toast and tea.

In the room the women come and go
Talking of Michelangelo.

And indeed there will be time
To wonder, 'Do I dare?' and, 'Do I dare?'
Time to turn back and descend the stair,
With a bald spot in the middle of my hair—
[They will say: 'How his hair is growing thin!']
My morning coat, my collar mounting firmly to the chin,
My necktie rich and modest, but asserted by a simple pin—
[They will say: 'But how his arms and legs are thin!']
Do I dare
Disturb the universe?
In a minute there is time
For decisions and revisions which a minute will reverse.

For I have known them all already, known them all—
Have known the evenings, mornings, afternoons,
I have measured out my life with coffee spoons;
I know the voices dying with a dying fall
Beneath the music from a farther room.
    So how should I presume?

And I have known the eyes already, known them all—
The eyes that fix you in a formulated phrase,
And when I am formulated, sprawling on a pin,
When I am pinned and wriggling on the wall,
Then how should I begin

To spit out all the butt-ends of my days and ways?
  And how should I presume?

  And I have known the arms already, known them all—
Arms that are braceleted and white and bare
[But in the lamplight, downed with light brown hair!]
Is it perfume from a dress
That makes me so digress?
Arms that lie along a table, or wrap about a shawl.
  And should I then presume?
  And how should I begin?

                    •   •   •

Shall I say, I have gone at dusk through narrow streets
And watched the smoke that rises from the pipes
Of lonely men in shirt-sleeves, leaning out of windows? . . .

  I should have been a pair of ragged claws
Scuttling across the floors of silent seas.

                    •   •   •

And the afternoon, the evening, sleeps so peacefully!
Smoothed by long fingers,
Asleep . . . tired . . . or it malingers,
Stretched on the floor, here beside you and me.
Should I, after tea and cakes and ices,
Have the strength to force the moment to its crisis?
But though I have wept and fasted, wept and prayed,
Though I have seen my head [grown slightly bald] brought in upon
  a platter,
I am no prophet—and here's no great matter;
I have seen the moment of my greatness flicker,
And I have seen the eternal Footman hold my coat, and snicker,
And in short, I was afraid.

  And would it have been worth it, after all,
After the cups, the marmalade, the tea,
Among the procelain, among some talk of you and me,
Would it have been worth while,
To have bitten off the matter with a smile,
To have squeezed the universe into a ball

To roll it toward some overwhelming question,
To say: 'I am Lazarus,[2] come from the dead,
Come back to tell you all, I shall tell you all'—
If one, settling a pillow by her head,
    Should say: 'That is not what I meant at all.
    That is not it, at all.'

    And would it have been worth it, after all,
Would it have been worth while,
After the sunsets and the dooryards and the sprinkled streets,
After the novels, after the teacups, after the skirts that trail along the
    floor—
And this, and so much more?—
It is impossible to say just what I mean!
But as if a magic lantern threw the nerves in patterns on a screen:
Would it have been worth while
If one, settling a pillow or throwing off a shawl,
And turning toward the window, should say:
    'That is not it at all,
    That is not what I meant, at all.'

                       • • •

No! I am not Prince Hamlet, nor was meant to be;
Am an attendant lord, one that will do
To swell a progress, start a scene or two,
Advise the prince; no doubt, an easy tool,
Deferential, glad to be of use,
Politic, cautious, and meticulous;
Full of high sentence, but a bit obtuse;
At times, indeed, almost ridiculous—
Almost, at times, the Fool.

    I grow old . . . I grow old . . .
I shall wear the bottoms of my trousers rolled.

    Shall I part my hair behind? Do I dare to eat a peach?
I shall wear white flannel trousers, and walk upon the beach.
I have heard the mermaids singing, each to each.

I do not think that they will sing to me.

---

[2] Who was raised from the dead by Jesus (John 11:1–46).

I have seen them riding seaward on the waves
Combing the white hair of the waves blown back
When the wind blows the water white and black.

We have lingered in the chambers of the sea
By sea-girls wreathed with seaweed red and brown
Till human voices wake us, and we drown.

WILLIAM BUTLER YEATS

The Second Coming [3]

Turning and turning in the widening gyre [4]
The falcon cannot hear the falconer; [5]
Things fall apart; the centre cannot hold;
Mere anarchy is loosed upon the world,
The blood-dimmed tide is loosed, and everywhere
The ceremony of innocence is drowned;
The best lack all conviction, while the worst
Are full of passionate intensity.

Surely some revelation is at hand;
Surely the Second Coming is at hand.
The Second Coming! Hardly are those words out
When a vast image out of Spiritus Mundi [6]
Troubles my sight: somewhere in sands of the desert
A shape with lion body and the head of a man,
A gaze blank and pitiless as the sun,
Is moving its slow thighs, while all about it
Reel shadows of the indignant desert birds.
The darkness drops again; but now I know

William Butler Yeats, "The Second Coming." Reprinted with permission of the publisher from *Collected Poems* by William Butler Yeats. Copyright 1924 by The Macmillan Company, Renewed 1952 by Bertha Georgie Yeats. [Pp. 346–47.]

[3] The prophecy of the Second Coming of Jesus is used as the poem's underlying theme.
[4] Circular, or spiral, motion.
[5] Christ.
[6] Latin: World Spirit.

That twenty centuries of stony sleep
Were vexed to nightmare by a rocking cradle,
And what rough beast, its hour come round at last,
Slouches towards Bethlehem to be born?

A 9
B 0
C 1
D 2
E 3
F 4
G 5
H 6
I 7
J 8